Books by Samuel R. Delany

Fiction

The Jewels of Aptor   (1962)
The Fall of the Towers:
   Out of the Dead City (Captives of the Flame)   (1963)
   The Towers of Toron   (1964)
   City of a Thousand Suns   (1965)
The Ballad of Beta-2   (1965)
Babel-17   (1966)
Empire Star   (1966)
The Einstein Intersection   (1967)
Nova   (1968)
Driftglass   (1971)
Equinox (Tides of Lust)   (1973)
Dhalgren   (1975)
Trouble on Triton   (1976)
Distant Stars   (1981)
Stars in My Pocket Like Grains of Sand   (1984)
Return to Nevèrÿon
   Tales of Nevèrÿon   (1979)
   Neveryóna   (1983)
   Flight from Nevèrÿon   (1985)
   Return to Nevèrÿon (The Bridge of Lost Desire)   (1987)
Driftglass/Starshards (collected stories)   (1993)
They Fly at Çiron   (1995)
The Mad Man   (1995, revised 1996)
Atlantis: Three Tales   (1995)
Hogg   (1995)

Comic Books

Empire   (1980; drawn by Howard Chaykin)
Bread & Wine   (1999; drawn by Mia Wolff)

Nonfiction

The Jewel-Hinged Jaw   (1977)
The American Shore   (1978)
Heavenly Breakfast   (1979)
Starboard Wine   (1984)
The Motion of Light in Water   (1987)
Wagner/Artaud   (1988)
The Straits of Messina   (1988)
Silent Interviews   (1993)
Longer Views   (1996)
Times Square Red, Times Square Blue   (1999)
Shorter Views   (2000)
1984   (2000)

1984

Samuel R. Delany

WITH AN INTRODUCTION
BY KENNETH R. JAMES

Voyant Publishing
Rutherford

Grateful acknowledgement is made for permission to reprint the following selections:

From "About Samuel Delany's Most Recent SF Novel: *Stars in My Pocket Like Grains of Sand*," by Faren Miller, originally printed in the September, 1984 issue of *Locus, the Newspaper of the Science Fiction Field*. Reprinted by permission of the author and Locus © 1984.

From "In the Once Upon a Time City," by Samuel R. Delany, originally printed in the February, 1985 issue of *Locus, the Newspaper of the Science Fiction Field*. Reprinted by permission of the author and Locus © 1985.

To new friends, old friends, and new friends becoming older: John Del Gaizo, Barbara Wise; Erin Mc Graw, Andrew Hudgins, Kate Spencer, Jeff Riggenbach; Kelly Salmon, & Justine Larbalestier.

Library of Congress Cataloging-in-Publication Data

Delany, Samuel R., 1942-

1984 / Samuel R. Delany—1st Voyant ed.

p. cm.

ISBN 0-9665998-1-0

00-131590

Contents

Epilogue: 1985

1984

An Introduction to the
Letters of Samuel R. Delany

By Kenneth R. James

I

THE CONTENTS OF THE COLLECTION to follow are easy enough to describe: 57 letters and documents written in the mid-'80s by novelist and critic Samuel R. Delany. Addressed to various friends, relatives, and colleagues, they present a vivid and exuberant mid-career portrait of a writer and thinker whose work has had an enormous influence across a startling range of literary and paraliterary genres, including science fiction, autobiography, pornography, historical fiction, comic books, literary criticism, queer theory, and more. All the trademark Delany touches can be found here—rich descriptions of urban life, incisive social observation, sensuous and sophisticated tales of a life lived on the intersections of multiple social margins (Delany is gay and black), and, especially, passionate meditations on the intersection of aesthetics, politics, and philosophy that have made Delany a figure of paramount importance both for millions of readers, and, more specifically, for a collection of writers and thinkers a mere partial list of which reads like a Who's Who of contemporary intellectual culture: Fredric Jameson, Eve Sedgwick, Um-berto Eco (a key secondary character in the pages to follow), Donna Haraway, Henry Louis Gates, Charles Johnson, William Gibson, and, we learn here—most intriguingly but perhaps least surprisingly—Thomas Pynchon.

The title of the collection, however, presents us with two problems.

The first and (seemingly) lesser problem is that while most of the letters collected here were indeed written in 1984, they are bracketed by letters from late '83 and early '85—to set the stage and provide a coda. Moreover, the collection, in spite of its heft, is not exhaustive: This is the author's selection, comprising around three-quarters of the letters written during the eponymous year. Minor elisions have been made to avoid repetition. And the conclusion of one of the letters is missing. The title of the book, then, covers both more and less historical phenomena than it proclaims. It gives us both too much and not enough. It is an approximation.

ix

The second problem, of course, is that circulating out in the world is another text with a similar (not, as we'll discuss later, identical) title, a novel, very well known to a significant percentage of the literate population. George Orwell's nightmarish tale of "common man" Winston Smith's hopeless rebellion against a gargantuan bureaucratic-totalitarian state has become unquestionably *the* great dystopian fable of the Cold War (and post-Cold War) period. The book has been translated into dozens of languages and read by millions, not least through being assigned in countless secondary school curricula. Certainly some of the most powerful and pervasive images and concepts in our mythical lexicon of anti-democratic hell come directly from Orwell's book. Room 101, the Two-Minute Hate, Doublethink, Newspeak, Thoughtcrime, and the "memory hole" — the shaft into which historical documents are flung and incinerated, to be replaced by the revised, officially sanctioned history of the Party — all of these terms leap easily to the Western mind. And, of course, the term "Orwellian" has entered the English lexicon as a signifier of anything partaking of authoritarian surveillance, suppression of thought, and the wholesale rewriting of history. Even after the collapse of the Soviet Union, these images and ideas are still habitually evoked, most often by apologists for global monopoly capitalism (and usually directed, in the name of "free trade," at the very governments the Cold War was supposedly fought to preserve). The images are pervasive, ceaselessly circulated. And so this title carries with it a heavy connotative burden. Our reception of it is bound to be influenced, inflected — as Freud would say, overdetermined — by the discursive environment. The initial comic effect of Delany's title depends on that overdetermination — on our recognition of the irony of a science-fiction novelist designating a collection of nonfiction documents from the *past* with an allusion to a dystopian novel about a hypothetical *future* — with both titles indicating, in hall-of-mirrors fashion, the "same" year.

Historical approximation.

Discursive overdetermination.

If the title poses problems, for long-time Delany readers they're familiar ones.

II

THE FACTS OF DELANY'S EARLY LIFE are perhaps most familiar to readers of his science fiction, who have been with him from the beginning. Born into a middle-class Harlem family in 1942 (his father ran a successful undertaking business), Delany enjoyed a privileged upbringing — an elite education at the Dalton school and later at the Bronx High School of Science, progressive summer camps, wide cultural exposure — within segregated America. Crossing from Harlem to Park Avenue, first by car and then by public bus, was, according to Delany, "in social terms a journey of near-ballistic violence."[1] Though seriously committed to writing at an early age, he did not publish professionally until shortly after his youthful marriage to his equally precocious high school friend Marilyn Hacker, whose

---

[1] Samuel R. Delany, *The Motion of Light in Water: Sex and Science Fiction Writing in the East Village: 1960-1965* (New York: Masquerade Books, 1993), p. 33.

poetry would eventually win her the National Book Award among many other honors. (Delany vividly documents the early years of this marriage — an open marriage, during which Delany still lived an active cruising life, with Hacker's consent — in his 1987 autobiography, *The Motion of Light in Water.*) He published his first science fiction novel in 1962 at the age of 20, and over the remainder of the '60s produced a stream of works that brought him great popular and critical acclaim within the SF genre. Delany was identified with a group of young authors, including Roger Zelazny, Joanna Russ, Thomas M. Disch, Harlan Ellison, and, later, Ursula K. Le Guin in the U.S., and J.G. Ballard and Michael Moorcock in the U.K., who were bringing a new literary and political sophistication to the genre in the '60s. Delany's work won him four Nebulas and a Hugo award, the highest honors in the genre, before he was 30.

Following the publication of *Nova* in 1968 and his short story collection *Driftglass* in 1971, Delany fell silent for the next four years, finally re-emerging in 1975 with the publication of *Dhalgren,* an enormous, phantasmagorical work that generated a good deal of debate in the SF world. Readers hoping for a more traditional science fiction read (and Delany had shown again and again that he could provide color-ful, thought-provoking space opera to beat anyone in the genre) were hugely dis-appointed, even infuriated by this long tale of a young, mentally unstable wander-er's adventures in a weirdly disrupted contemporary urban landscape. But other readers were thrilled by the novel's lucidity, passion, and uncompromising frank-ness and sophistication. By turns a frightening vision of urban apocalypse, a micro-scopically intricate comedy of manners, a sexual odyssey, and a profoundly mov-ing — even anguished — exploration of problems of individual and collective per-ception and memory, *Dhalgren* went on to sell over a million copies, reaching a readership well beyond the SF genre. A comparative study of *Dhalgren* and *Gravity's Rainbow,* that other gargantuan novel of social system-and-chaos from the early '70s, is long overdue; Delany's book has been characterized as arguably the definitive novelistic representation of the experience of the '60s counterculture.[2]

After *Dhalgren,* the overall shape and intent of Delany's work shifted deci-sively. Starting in the late-'70s, in addition to writing fiction, Delany began to publish a series of critical works concerned with articulating a theory of the SF genre. These works include *The Jewel-Hinged Jaw* ('77), *The American Shore* ('78), *Starboard Wine* ('84), *The Straits of Messina* ('89), and, more recently, sections of *Silent Interviews* ('94), *Longer Views* ('96), and *Shorter Views* ('00). In these vol-umes, Delany has explored the counterintuitive notion that SF texts are deter-mined not by generic "content" — spaceships, time travel, aliens, and the like — but rather by the set of interpretive protocols required to read these and like rhetorical figures in such a way that they make sense. For Delany, reading SF involves, among other things, a heightened attention to fictive landscape closely akin to a kind of Marxian social perspective (irrespective of the reader's or writer's specific politics). Delany calls this emphasis on critical awareness of landscape the "priority of the object," or "object critique," contrasting it with the

---

[2] See, for example, Jeff Riggenbach's synoptic account of the American literary scene, "The National Letters," from *The Libertarian Review,* March 1980, p. 28, and William Gibson's comments in the Preface to the Wesleyan edition of *Dhalgren.*

focus of mainstream literature on psychology and the self—the "priority of the subject," or "subject critique."

In his criticism Delany also explores the material/social grounding of the SF genre: its origins in American pulp magazines as middle- and working-class entertainment, the markedly different relationship that obtains between writers and readers of SF from those in other genres (recall that the 'zine originated in SF), and, most pointedly, SF's functional identity as the low-art "other" to mainstream literature. Delany has no shortage of colorful anecdotes illustrating what is really at stake in the SF/literature division:

> About a dozen years ago, in my local bookstore, I came upon a young woman in her early twenties standing next to a dolly full of books, shelving them. At the D's, she was putting away copies of Don DeLillo's *Ratner's Star*. Smiling, I said: "You know, you should shelve some copies of that with science fiction."
>
> She looked up startled, frowned at me, then smiled: "Oh, no," she said. "Really, this is a very good book."
>
> I laughed. "It's about three-quarters of a good novel. But at the ending, he just gets tired and takes refuge in a Beckettesque fable. It doesn't work."
>
> "Well, you can't make it science fiction just because of the *ending!*"
>
> I laughed again. "The ending is what makes it literature. But the rest of the book is a very believable account of a young mathematician working for the government, trying to decipher messages from a distant star. It could go upstairs in SF."
>
> Her frown now had become permanent. "No," she repeated. "It really is a good book. I've read it. It's quite wonderful."
>
> "I've read it too," I said. "I liked it very much. But that's why I'm saying it's science fiction . . ."
>
> The young woman exclaimed, not really to me but to the whole room: "That's just *crazy* . . .!" She turned sharply away and began to shelve once more.
>
> But when, after a few seconds, I glanced at her again, she was still mumbling darkly to herself—and *tears* stood in her eyes![3]

At the same time that Delany's critical work first appeared, his fiction found its subject. Gender politics, and particularly the relationship between gender and literature, had been important in Delany's early SF; certainly a sophisticated awareness of the problem of the representation of women in fiction informed all of Delany's early novels. But with *Dhalgren*, gender and sexuality moved decisively to the foreground of his work—where they have remained, tightly intertwined with explorations of literary centers and paraliterary margins, ever since. His next novel, *Triton* (reprinted recently under its original title, *Trouble on Triton*), with its tale of a sexually progressive future society viewed through the distorting lens of a misogynist bigot, remains ahead of its time nearly 25 years after its publication in 1976: a tribute to Delany's critical acumen and a sad commentary on the slow pace of change. This was followed in 1979 by *Tales of Nevèrÿon*, the first in his four-volume series collectively entitled Return to Nevèrÿon: at once an exploration of problems of historical knowledge and the ideological and discursive parameters

---

3 "The Para•doxa Interview with Samuel R. Delany," *Para•doxa* (Vol. 1, No. 3, 1995), pp. 277-8.

of contemporary narrative, as well as of the homoerotic and S/M subtext of the sword-and-sorcery subgenre. The next two installments, *Neveryóna* and *Flight from Nevèrÿon*, appeared in '83 and '85, respectively. Meanwhile, Delany also produced *Stars in My Pocket Like Grains of Sand* (1984), both an epic tale of an interstellar information war and a gay romance; and his autobiography *The Motion of Light in Water*, which won a Hugo for best nonfiction book of 1987.

In retrospect it's fairly clear that *Motion* carried forward what had already been signaled by the journal sequences in *Flight from Nevèrÿon:* a conscientious turn toward nonfiction reportage on gay life. Delany's many critical essays treating gay subjects in the '80s and '90s are heavily buttressed by autobiography. Similarly, Delany's 1995 pornographic novel *The Mad Man* contains clearly auto-biographical passages — earlier versions of which can be found in the following letters, as we'll note again later. More recently, Delany has produced a comic book with artist Mia Wolff entitled *Bread & Wine*, telling of the beginning of his relationship with his current partner, Dennis Rickett (who had been, when the two met, homeless), and *Times Square Red, Times Square Blue*, a memoir and analysis of New York public sex venues and their dismantling in the middle '90s. For the bulk of this work, from *Dhalgren* through the mid-'90s, Delany was given the 1996 William Whitehead Award for a Lifetime Achievement in Lesbian and Gay Literature; his immediate predecessors for the honor had been Audre Lorde, Adrienne Rich, Edmund White, and James Purdy. His most important essays on queer theory can be found in his collections *Longer Views* and *Shorter Views*.

In *Dhalgren*, the pivotal offstage historical events swirling around the novel's urban conflagration are the alleged rape of a white girl by a black man, the assas-sination of a liberal black activist, and a massive race riot — the uncertain chronol-ogy and reality-status of which provide key pivot-points for the story's seemingly endlessly dovetailing ambiguities. Like the politics of sexuality, the subject of race has changed its position in Delany's work over the course of his career: subtextu-ally present in his earlier SF, shifting to the center of attention in *Dhalgren* and the Return to Nevèrÿon series, and remaining strongly foregrounded ever since. Correspondingly, we see a shift in critical attention toward his work by African-American writers and critics in the late '80s. This shift clearly suggests something about the discursive limits of literary and paraliterary communities. Although the appeal to black readers of Delany's earlier SF and later gay-oriented work is clear-ly evidenced by remarks from such writers and thinkers as Charles Johnson, Robert Reid-Pharr, John Keene, and Greg Tate, it's the work which most clearly falls within the purview of a certain model of the African-American literary tradi-tion — a model that privileges works portraying the historical specificities of the black experience, and handles homosexuality somewhat gingerly — that receives the most critical attention. For instance, *The Motion of Light in Water* has been dis-cussed extensively in recent texts on African-American autobiography,[4] and a chapter of *Atlantis: Model 1924*, Delany's historical novella set during the Harlem Renaissance, has been anthologized in the prestigious *Norton Anthology of African-American Literature* — but the rest of his work has received nothing like the same

---

[4] See, for example, Ross Posnock's *Color & Culture* (Cambridge: Harvard University Press, 1998) and Hazel V. Carby's *Race Men* (Cambridge: Harvard University Press, 1998).

level of attention. Clearly, what is at stake here is not just the relative merit of a set of texts, but a certain image the African-American literary community has constructed of its own reading population and its values.

The same sort of relation between value and constituency can be found operating in the critical productions of the SF genre. For instance, in the massive and sophisticated Clute/Nicholls *Encyclopedia of Science Fiction*, Peter Nicholls' entry on Delany claims: "There is no doubt that by the 1980s his fiction (and criticism) had become less accessible."[5] Now, since the phrase "less accessible" implies "less accessible to everyone," a more accurate phrasing would be "less accessible to a particular cross-section of the SF readership." But even that posited cross-section would still exclude *this* SF reader, who finds Delany's work after *Dhalgren* to be far more readable, in the sense of deeply satisfying reading, than his earlier work, wonderful as it unquestionably is. Ultimately, it would be much more coherent and accurate to state simply that the work had begun to develop beyond the parameters of a certain populist notion of SF. Similarly, the same *Encyclopedia* entry later maintains that Delany's initially "very wide" audience became "narrower" after *Dhalgren*, and then contradicts itself a few sentences later by mentioning that the first two Nevèrÿon volumes "sold around a quarter of a million each"—well over twice the sales of Delany's earlier SF. Here again, an imaginary readership is posited and hypostatized as covering the entire reading population to reinforce an unarticulated set of assumptions about what constitutes the "center" of the SF enterprise.

But throughout Delany's career, it's precisely the notion of "center"—whether sexual, racial, political, or indeed literary—that has come under the most rigorous and exhaustive scrutiny. For Delany, whenever the notion of a center has appeared in a given sociohistorical situation to reinforce some notion of normative identity or essence, so too have the conditions for possible exclusion and oppression:

> I think that any time there was such a notion of a centered subject . . . not only
> was it an ideological mirage, it was a mirage that necessarily grew up to mask
> the psychological, economic, and material oppression of an 'other' . . . ("We
> are centered and healthy: she/he/it/they are not . . .")[6]

In a discussion of essentialist rhetoric in the works of Hegel and early Nietzsche, Delany makes as sweeping a statement as he has ever made about what has been and continues to be the experience of humanity under the thrall of the exclusionary myth of the center, of essence, of unity:

> This nineteenth-century reductionism, this plea for unity in which all that is
> anomalous can be ignored . . . is behind the whole deadly concept of race; by
> the end of that century we will see its fallout in the virulent anti-Semitism of
> the Dreyfus Affair, in what we now speak of as British imperialism, and in
> Rhodesian and South African racism. Such reductionism when essentialized
> becomes the philosophical underpinning of today's totalitarianisms, whether
> Hitler's or Stalin's . . .

[5] John Clute and Peter Nicholls (ed.), *The Encyclopedia of Science Fiction* (New York: St. Martin's Griffin, 1995), p. 317.
[6] Delany, *Stars in My Pocket like Grains of Sand* — Signature Special Edition (New York: Bantam Books, 1990), p. 384.

Our current history is the history of the abuse of such reductionism and such essentialism. It is the chronicle of their genocidal failure to support humane behavior within and between nations, within and between institutions, between individuals and institutions, and between individuals of unequal power.[7]

It's an awareness of this genocidal and totalitarian history, and the absolute necessity for the dismantling of the discourses that brought it about, that has undergirded all of Delany's creative and critical work, from the beginning of his career to the present.

III

ORWELL'S NOVEL, WE RECALL, TELLS the story of a single individual, Winston Smith, in his struggle against the repressive power of the totalitarian state, Oceania. One of the more frightening elements of that state's repressive apparatus is its ongoing revision of history through the destruction and rewriting of historical documents to suit the needs of the Party. Against this apparatus Winston Smith pits his own empirical experience—his knowledge that things have not, in fact, gone the way the now-revised official histories say they did. He secures his knowledge *materially* by keeping a personal diary: a counter-history to the State's official history. But he grounds this subversive activity *philosophically* in a faith in his own "common sense," his natural, reliable access to a transparent reality.

How does Smith confirm that he is reliable? By comparing himself to others. He knows he is more reliable than, say, his lover Julia—who, though similarly a rebel against the state, rebels only against its puritan ideology in the name of her own sexual pleasure. Her rebellion is strictly a private one; her subversiveness is depoliticized. When Smith tries to read her what he thinks is a radical political treatise, she falls asleep.[8] At one point Smith tells her she is only "a rebel from the waist downwards" (N 129). Similarly, Smith knows he is more reliable than the "proles"—the vast working class of the future state, making up more than 80% of the population. To Smith, the proles are idealized, romanticized creatures. Like Julia, they do not think. They are physical, not mental, beings. The prole women, in particular, are images of animal-like fertility. Here, Winston observes a prole washerwoman:

> As he looked at the woman in her characteristic attitude, her thick arms reaching up for the line, her powerful marelike buttocks protruded, it struck him for the first time that she was beautiful. It had never occurred to him that the body of a woman of 50, blown up to monstrous dimensions by childbearing, then hardened, roughened by work till it was coarse in the grain like an overripe turnip, could be beautiful . . .
>
> The woman down there had no mind, she had only strong arms, a warm heart, and a fertile belly. (N 181)

[7] Delany, *Longer Views* (Hanover: University Press of New England [Wesleyan University Press imprint], 1996), p. 41.
[8] George Orwell, *Nineteen Eighty-four* (New York: Harcourt, Brace, and Company, Inc. [Signet Classics edition], 1949), p. 129. Hereafter referred to as N.

"If there was an answer," thinks Smith at several points, "it lay with the proles." But Smith cannot bring himself to attribute to the proles, or to Julia, a political consciousness—or any real consciousness at all. They are, to use a term of Newspeak, unpersons. Only O'Brien, the (male) agent of the state, serves as a possible point of specifically mental identification: "Winston knew—yes, he knew!—that O'Brien was thinking the same thing as himself" (N 18). In sum, Winston Smith confirms his reliability by defining a center and placing himself in it.

(Here I am tempted to paraphrase a fictive annotation by Nabokov's mad academic, Charles Kinbote: See, *see now*, Delany's *Trouble on Triton*. Much discussed by feminist critics, *Trouble on Triton* paints a ruthless portrait of a citizen of a future society whose desire for a certain kind of centeredness—not coincidentally resembling Winston Smith's — nearly destroys him psychically, and at the very least blinds him to his society's utopian, or rather heterotopian, possibilities.)

As many critics have pointed out, Winston Smith's perceptions of the proles and of women have much in common with Orwell's portrayals of workers and women in his nonfiction work. Critic Deirdre Beddoe cites the examples of *The Road to Wigan Pier*, Orwell's book about the miners of northern England, and the diary Orwell kept during his journalistic research for the book. Both texts ignore women's labor (unless it is domestic) and their political activism—or treat them with contempt. Beddoe reminds us of the historical context:

> Lancashire women cotton operatives had been very active radical suffragists in the years before the First World War, and . . . were strong trade unionists. Lancashire women had participated in the National Hunger Marches to London organized by the NUWM [National Unemployed Workers' Movement], and Lancashire women were active members of the Women's Co-operative Guild, which in the 1930s was campaigning, amongst other things, for contraception, better health care, international peace and for full employment by the re-organization of industry on a co-operative basis.[9]

Beddoe contrasts this with the following passage from Orwell's diary:

> This evening to a social the NUWM had got up in aid of Thaelmann's defence-fund. Admission and refreshments (cup of tea and meat pie) 6d. About 200 people, preponderantly women, largely members of the Co-Op, in one of whose rooms it was held, and I suppose for the most part living directly and indirectly on the dole. Round the back a few aged miners sitting looking on benevolently, a lot of very young girls in front. Some dancing to the concertina (many of the girls confessed that they could not dance, which struck me as rather pathetic) and some excruciating singing. I suppose these people represented a fair cross-section of the more revolutionary element in Wigan. If so, God help us. Exactly the same sheeplike crowd—gaping girls and shapeless middle-aged women dozing over their knitting — that you see everywhere else.[10]

The point, of course (and I am by no means the first to make it), is that what Orwell posits as a transparent, authoritative, reliable viewpoint is hardly that: It

[9] Deirdre Beddoe, "Hindrances and Help-Meets: Women in the Writings of George Orwell," in *Inside the Myth*, ed. Christopher Norris (London: Lawrence and Wishart, 1984), p. 153.

[10] "The Road to Wigan Pier Diary," from *An Age Like This: The Collected Essays, Journalism, and Letters of George Orwell*, v. 1, ed. Sonia Orwell and Ian Angus (New York: Harcourt Brace Jovanovich, Inc., 1968), p. 181.

is in fact powerfully contoured by a set of historically specific class and gender discourses—discourses with massive censoring powers.

In light of this, upon re-reading Orwell's novel we are struck by the fact that Winston Smith's fixation on his own "common sense," beyond being epistemologically questionable, wholly fails to address the real, external, *political* problem: the socially organized, systematic destruction of historical documents. And yet the whole structure of the narrative insists on articulating the problem exclusively in Smith's terms. The entire last third of the novel focuses on O'Brien's attempts to break Winston's spirit—as if just killing him wouldn't be more efficient. When Smith himself makes this very point, O'Brien explains:

> "You are a flaw in the pattern, Winston. You are a stain that must be wiped out . . . It is intolerable to us that an erroneous thought should exist anywhere in the world, however secret and powerless it may be . . ." (N 210-11)

Isn't there some element of wish-fulfillment in a story which places the destruction of Winston's individuality—his subjecthood—on an equal footing with the systematized destruction of historical documents? Doesn't the State's fixation on Winston affirm, in a perverse way, his importance as an individual—his centrality? In sum, don't we perceive in the structure of this narrative the shaping force of a desire? But here I am simply re-stating a point Raymond Williams made back in 1958: that George Orwell's vision of "the individual" was itself inflected by a discourse, and a discourse of a very particular, and conservative, kind—a kind that saw *all* social affiliation as intrinsically oppressive to the individual.[11]

Perhaps what Orwell's novel dramatizes, then, is the paradox of trying to articulate social problems ("problems of the object," as Delany would say) in terms of the so-called "centered" individual (the "subject"). But if the problem exists in the social realm—and it does—then so must the solution. Winston Smith was on the right track when he started keeping that diary. The only coherent response to the erasure of history is to try to save the endangered documents— and to produce new counter-documents.

IV

THE LETTERS IN THE PREFACE to follow introduce us to most of the key players in the life of Samuel Ray Delany (known by his nickname, "Chip") at the time of their composition. On the home front, we meet Delany's filmmaker partner, Frank, and Iva, his ten-year-old daughter from his marriage to Marilyn Hacker (Delany and Hacker divorced in 1980). Friends and colleagues include Camilla Decarnin, a long-time member of SF fandom, writer, editor and friend; Michael Peplow and Robert Bravard, two scholars busily compiling a primary and secondary bibliography on Delany; and John Mueller, a friend from a markedly different class background, doing time in prison. Although they don't figure prominently as correspondents, Marilyn Hacker and fellow science fiction writers Joanna Russ and Thomas M. Disch have a strong presence in the following pages. And there are many additional walk-on appearances by various literary

---

[11] Raymond Williams, *Culture and Society 1780-1950* (New York: Columbia University Press, 1958), p. 291.

and paraliterary figures.

The text as a whole covers a remarkably productive period in Delany's career. As it opens, Delany has just returned from France, where a translation of *Trouble on Triton* has recently been honored. In the States, the second Nevèrÿon book, the novel *Neveryóna*, has been out for about a year, and the essay collection *Starboard Wine* stands on the verge of publication. Meanwhile, *Stars in My Pocket Like Grains of Sand* goes through final pre-publication stages at Bantam Books, while its sequel, *The Splendor and Misery of Bodies, of Cities*, creeps painfully through early draft stages (it remains uncompleted to this day) and the third Nevèrÿon book, *Flight from Nevèrÿon*, nears completion. Along the way, we are treated to a wonderfully candid portrayal of the splendors and miseries of the freelance writer's life, from battles with recalcitrant publishers over cover art and contractual agreements to SF conventions and publication parties.

More than anything, we are treated to a rich vision of New York City, refracted through an admirably refined critical sensibility. For Delany, who navigates cultural and class spaces with a confidence that has become legendary, New York is an endlessly inviting heterotopia, a social space under perpetual construction, collapse, and provisional reconstitution. Tracing a trajectory that continues the ballistic one of his childhood, Delany finds his way up to Harlem to visit his old home, down to 42nd Street and the gay cruising areas of the porn theaters (a social arena he documents extensively in *Times Square Red, Times Square Blue*), and across town to upscale publication parties. Armed with the critical tools of modernist *flâneurs* (Baudelaire, Benjamin) and more contemporary theorists (Foucault, Derrida), Delany traverses a landscape shot through with popular signs of the times (Michael Jackson, Boy George).

But it's not all postmodern fun. Beyond ever-present domestic difficulties — Delany's perpetual battle with severe dyslexia, wranglings with Marilyn over the care of Iva, and ongoing problems with Frank's chronic anxiety — over the course of the year the Delany household slides into an ever-deepening financial crisis that eventually finds Chip and Frank scouring the streets for change, and reaches its emotional nadir with Delany's desperate letter of September 1 to Camilla Decarnin.

But beyond the precincts of this private crisis there is a much larger crisis developing, a political crisis involving ideology, propaganda, censorship, and repression of a sort that we might well call Orwellian, in both its popular and — in light of the re-readings of Orwell mentioned above — critically redoubled sense.

New York City in 1984 . . .?

Of course I am speaking of AIDS.

V

IN RETROSPECT IT SEEMS CLEAR that the transition from 1983 to 1984 was a pivotal one for Delany. After '84, as I've said, autobiography moves decisively to the forefront of Delany's work, variously refracted through memoir, cultural criticism, or overtly autobiographical fiction. But all of it, with varying degrees of explicitness, arises specifically as a response to AIDS. Even the 1987 autobiography *The Motion of Light in Water*, which covers pre-AIDS New York, can be read as an extended essay on the necessity of understanding the mutual imbrication of discourse and memory in order to construct an accurate picture of AIDS as a sociocultural phenomenon. (And, of course, *Motion* contains explicit discussions of AIDS.)

But it seems equally clear that Delany's earlier work of the '70s carved out a huge analytical space for his later disquisitions on AIDS. *Dhalgren*, with its meticulous tracking of the creation, diffusion, and confusion of urban rumor, myth, and history as they cross and re-cross class borders, scrambled along the way by pre-existing discursive pressures and a capricious, conservative media; *Trouble on Triton*, with its dissection of the perverse logic of patriarchy as it weaves its cloddish way, in the person of the unsympathetic protagonist Bron Helstrom, through an urban space that wholly confounds its reductions and certainties; and the first two Nevèrÿon books, with their intricate disquisitions on the intersections of sex, power, knowledge, and history, and in which the gay content takes center stage — these works now read like preliminary critical sketches for Delany's subsequent statements about AIDS.

Delany readers will recognize in the pages to follow numerous passages dealing with AIDS that find their way into Delany's later fantasy fiction. Here, for example, we find much of the raw material for Delany's *Tale of Plagues and Carnivals*—the longest story in *Flight from Nevèrÿon*—which cuts back and forth between the ancient fantasy-city of Kolhari, where an AIDS-like illness has struck, and contemporary Manhattan, where Chip Delany works steadily on the story of the disease. Delany's ongoing correspondence here with his bibliographers, Peplow and Bravard, adds a new layer of historical specificity to the allegorical tale embedded within *Plagues* of the aristocratic young Master's misconceived quest for exhaustive biographical knowledge of one of Nevèrÿon's "great men," the inventor Belham. Other stories recounted in the following pages—of one-legged Arly, Jeff the junky, a mysterious serial murderer—and of the ways in which people on the street, in the face of massive media distortion and blackout, cobble together a reassuring semblance of knowledge about AIDS from the very slimmest of evidence—all this and more can be found in *Plagues* in transmuted form.

We also find here an account of the experiences which provided the template for the story of Gorgik's encounter with the nameless young thief in the framing-narrative for the later Nevèrÿon tale, "The Game of Time and Pain." And one of Delany's key correspondents, the incarcerated John Mueller, is the real-life model for the young smuggler in "The Tale of Fog and Granite" and "The Mummer's Tale" in *Flight*. (Mueller is also the dedicatee of *Return to Nevèrÿon* [1987].)

Here, too, we find the early working-through of critical positions which would eventually culminate in a series of what this reader, at any rate, believes will ultimately stand as classic statements about the social discourses surrounding AIDS.

"Street Talk / Straight Talk," which first appeared in the feminist journal *differences* in 1992, covers much of the same critical ground first dramatized in *The Tale of Plagues and Carnivals*, with the added advantage of historical hindsight. It analyzes the ideologically loaded conflations and confusions between "straight" and "street" discourses on AIDS transmissions vectors—that is, between officially sanctioned scientific accounts (with supposedly rigorous criteria for the acceptance of evidence) and rumor, hearsay, and hunches—the informal realm where, in Delany's words, "all is evidence."[12] (Example from Orwell: "Thoughtcrime" is a term of straight talk, while "memory hole" is a term of street talk.) Similarly, "The Rhetoric of Sex / the Discourse of Desire," first presented as a lecture at MIT in 1993, gives a popularizing account of the concept of discourse itself, culminating in an exploration of the ways in which clinical studies, for all their rigor, tend to slide evidence about AIDS transmission vectors into prior discursive grooves —with lethal results. As Delany indicates in "Street Talk / Straight Talk," the only solution to such confusions is the ongoing production of new and more accurate documentation of sexual behavior:

> What I am asking is that all of us begin to put forward the monumental analytical effort, in whichever rhetorical mode we choose, needed not to interpret what we say, but to say what we *do*. That requires first and foremost speaking to others *about* what we do. That is the only way that we can destroy the discursive disarticulation that muffles and muddles all, that drags all into and within it, that represses and suppresses and lies and distorts and rereads and rewrites any and every rhetorical moment within its field.[13]

Finally, in Delany's letter of November 28, 1984, readers will find the source-material for an extended sequence from the second chapter of Delany's 1995 novel *The Mad Man*; here, it serves as something of a climax to the whole book. Commencing with a brilliant series of portraits of urban marginals at a local porn theater, the sequence culminates with an intense insight about the provisional nature of all knowledge about the disease. But recall the words of Reverend Amy, the street preacher of *Dhalgren*, considering the wrecked American city of Bellona:

> "Where is this city? Struck out of time! Where is it builded? On the brink of truths and lies. Not truth and falsity—Oh, no. No. Nothing so grand. Here we are sunk on the abyss of discrete fibs, innocent misobservations, brilliant speculations that turn out wrong and kill . . ."[14]

Recall, too, the thoughts of Kid, experiencing his own quasi-mystical insight into the limits of his own knowledge near the novel's climax:

> I got chills. I was being nudged, pushed, about to be reminded of . . . what? Anything more than the vast abysms of all our ignorances? Whatever, it was vastly sinister and breathlessly freeing. But I did *not* know; and that mystic ignorance wrung me out with gooseflesh.[15]

(Recall as well that in *Dhalgren*, it's precisely the *unreliability* of Kid's perceptions [his amnesic episodes, his uncertainty about chronology — i.e., his tenuous hold on history] that define, clearly and unmistakably, who his *political* enemy is: Roger Calkins, Bellona's self-appointed newspaper editor — the controller of the city's media and scrambler of its history.) Reading all this against the text of the letter of November 28, consider just how much that text shares with the spirit of *Dhalgren*, completed ten years before.

---

[12] Delany, "Street Talk / Straight Talk," in *differences*, vol. 3, no. 2, 1991, p. 33.
[13] Ibid., p. 38.
[14] Delany, *Dhalgren* (Hanover: University Press of New England [Wesleyan University Press imprint], 1996), pp. 469-70.
[15] Ibid., p. 775.

VI

GEORGE ORWELL'S LITERARY LEGACY has been arguably the most contested of the second half of the twentieth century, as John Rodden extensively documents in his book on the Orwell phenomenon, *The Politics of Literary Reputation*.[16] In the '50s, after Orwell's death, conservatives seized on Orwell's last novel as a definitive statement against any and all socialism, notwithstanding Orwell's blunt statements to the contrary prior to his death. Responses on the left were more complex, ranging from flat-out rejection of what was interpreted as Orwell's pernicious conservatism, to acknowledgment and affirmation of Orwell's exemplary moral commitment to social change, if not of his critical acumen. This rhetoric died down in the '60s and '70s, only to reach a new pitch as the fateful year approached. Over the course of this long debate, the entire productive apparatus of the culture industry was deployed, with the publication of countless articles, editorials, essays, anthologies, and monographs on Orwell, to say nothing of television and screen adaptations of his work.

Contrast this with the observation of Delany's bibliographers, Peplow and Bravard (in the *Black American Literature Forum* [Summer 1984]) that many, if not most, of the extant secondary sources on Delany (literary and paraliterary) up until 1979 fail even to spell his name correctly.[17] This, like the book clerk shelving DeLillo we encountered earlier, is another mark of paraliterature: Literary institutions, predicated on the disposability of paraliterature, see no need to document it rigorously, and paraliterary institutions don't have the necessary documentary apparatus. Thus the risk of flat-out loss of information is much higher in the paraliterary realm. But as the reception histories of both Delany and Orwell indicate, the literary and paraliterary realms are each subject to contestation and the possibility of change—change in value, in function, even (and especially) in the relation between them. Because the literary and paraliterary canons are, as Delany has indicated, social objects,[18] change can be effected by the production of new social markers—new texts:

> ...the canon 'believes in' the society that produces it. Thus the canon can only be the canon *of* that society. If we want to displace [extant] social markers promoting canonical (or pre-canonical) literary (or paraliterary) consideration, we must start producing our own. We must produce social and critical markers that put in circulation values *we* think are important—and we must do that with works (literary or paraliterary) that *we* think are worthy of critical attention. However contestatorily, we must join in our society. We must become (to borrow a term from Bloom) *strong readers* of the paraliterary.[19]

Having noted this, let us do a brief reading of a genre that Delany has also identified as paraliterary: criticism itself.

Even the most cursory review of critical essays written about Orwell shortly

---

[16] John Rodden, *The Politics of Literary Reputation* (New York: Oxford University Press, 1989).

[17] Robert S. Bravard and Michael Peplow, "Through a Glass Darkly: Bibliographing Samuel R. Delany," in *The Black American Literature Forum*, vol. 8, no. 2, Summer 1984, p. 70.

[18] "The Para•doxa Interview with Samuel R. Delany," p. 259.

[19] Ibid., p. 285.

before and shortly after the year 1984 reveals certain rhetorical patterns, patterns which suggest the kinds of values that have actually governed critical discourse until recently, how those values have begun to change, and what those changes have to do with class, gender, and the literary/paraliterary split. Broadly, whenever these essays suggest a connection between Orwell's novel and SF (or what was then the rough U.K. equivalent to the SF genre), they either immediately downplay the connection or make the connection specifically to highlight the superiority of Orwell's novel to these "lesser" works.

To cite just one example: Jonathan Rose, in a review of the pop-cultural predecessors to, and possible inspirations for, Orwell's book, makes a series of comparisons between it and Olaf Stapledon's 1942 novel of futuristic totalitarianism, *Darkness and the Light*. Noting that Orwell and Stapledon had moved in the same political circles and even worked together at one point, Rose goes on to show that Stapledon's book anticipated Orwell's in a number of significant respects.[20] But Stapledon is much more closely associated with genre science fiction than Orwell: Though he himself did not write for the pulp magazines, his influence on them was very great. *The Encyclopedia of Science Fiction* speculates that "the acclamation he received as an sf writer may partially account for his total neglect by historians of modern literature"[21] — a notion that is certainly borne out by Rose's subsequent comments. First Rose compares Orwell's concept of the two-way "telescreen" (through which the citizens of Oceania both receive propaganda and are monitored by the State) with Stapledon's notion of a skull implant through which propaganda can be transmitted directly, and thoughts be read, by the police (the Thought Police?). But then Rose calls Stapledon's concept "cheap Buck Rogers stuff, too incredible to be really frightening" (IS 134). Now this reader, at any rate, doesn't see that much of a difference. Readers will recall that Kurt Vonnegut's much-anthologized story "Harrison Bergeron" takes precisely this kind of skull implant as its primary premise. (But Vonnegut, of course, is packaged as a mainstream writer.)[22]

Rose goes on to defend Orwell's possible appropriations from Stapledon on the grounds that Stapledon's is "a remarkably incompetent book . . . characterless in every sense of the term — devoid of artistry, description, color, or individualized portraits" (IS 135). Beyond the fact that exactly the same criticisms have been leveled at Orwell's book, we simply have no way of knowing whether Rose's evaluation is accurate: No actual examples of Stapledon's supposed incompetence are given. And as Rose continues his argument in this vein, it begins to have

[20] Jonathan Rose, "The Invisible Sources of *Nineteen Eighty-four*," in *The Revised Orwell*, ed. Rose (East Lansing: Michigan State University Press, 1992), p. 134. Hereafter referred to as IS.
[21] Clute/Nicholls, p. 1153.
[22] Contradictory positions of this sort abound. Anthony Easthope, in an otherwise sophisticated reading of Orwell from a poststructuralist angle, praises Patrick Parrinder's argument that *Nineteen Eighty-four* ought to be considered part of the science fiction genre. He adds in passing: "Classic science fiction . . . presupposes the realist mode" of nineteenth-century fiction. But then, in the very next sentence, he says: "But *Nineteen Eighty-four* is not classic science fiction. Relatively low on fantasy situations and high on psychological complexity, it is much closer to the traditional realism of the nineteenth-century novel." ("Fact and Fantasy in *Nineteen Eighty-four*," in *Inside the Myth*, pp. 270-71) Beneath the blatant surface contradiction lies the much larger contradiction that the one thing virtually all critics agree Orwell's novel conspicuously lacks is psychological complexity.

precisely the opposite effect from the one the author intended. Rose mentions, for example, a whole series of earlier British dystopian novels with eerily similar elements to Orwell's, and sporting titles like *1920, 1925, 1938, 1944, The 1946 Ms., 1957,* and *2010* (IS 141-44). Although Rose assures us that they are all "rubbishy" (again giving no illustrative examples), by the end of the discussion one cannot help wondering about all these other now-forgotten novels. Most telling in Rose's argument, of course, is the use of loaded words like "rubbishy" and especially "cheap" as terms of disparagement. "Cheap," in this context, connotes "vulgar," or more specifically, "pulp" — which in turn denotes, among other things, "intended for a working-class readership."

But other essays written during the same period suggest a very different structure of attitudes towards literary history, a structure suggestive of a new set of values in ascendancy in early-'80s literary studies. In an essay covering much the same kind of material as Rose's — a survey of popular antecedents to Orwell's novel — Andy Croft takes a diametrically opposed approach. Rather than try to reinforce Orwell's canonical position, Croft instead reviews the literature on its own merits. What he discovers is that Orwell's book "was only the tail-end of a more original and important literary and political development in this country in the late 1930s and 1940s."[23] Presenting a list of utopian/dystopian works much longer than Rose's and encompassing a far wider ideological range, Croft notes that the most sizable portion of them were written specifically as responses to the rise of fascism in Europe and the threat of fascism in England (WWE 190).

In Croft's view, "the most sophisticated and original" of these futuristic antifascist books was Katherine Burdekin's feminist critique of Nazism from 1937, *Swastika Night* (WWE 209). Preceding Orwell's novel by over a decade, the book contains any number of similarities to it, including the rewriting of history, the "official enemies" of the state, the perpetually deadlocked war, and so on. But the book also makes a pointed critique of the cult of masculinity underlying fascist ideology, arguing that fascism "was originally misogynist and ultimately self-destructive, and that its racial theories had roots in sexual hysteria" (WWE 209). As critic Daphne Patai notes in another study, what is metaphorical in Orwell becomes literal in Burdekin: Women "have been driven to an animal-like state of ignorance and are now kept purely for breeding purposes."[24] Patai points out that analyzing fascism down into its masculinist components gives us far more to work with than Orwell's hand-waving explanation of totalitarianism as a generalized power-seeking tendency in "human nature": "[T]o refuse to address the issue of gender roles is to circle fruitlessly around the problem, viewing it as an 'essence' rather than as a particular social configuration" (OM 259).

Patai also makes the point that, in contrast with Orwell's obsessively revisionist Party,

> Burdekin's solution [to the problem of information control] is much simpler: Restrict literacy, promote ignorance, issue no books or papers at all. Thus there

---

[23] Andy Croft, "Worlds Without End Foisted Upon the Future: Some Antecedents of *Nineteen Eighty-four*," in *Inside the Myth*, p. 186. Hereafter referred to as WWE.

[24] Daphne Patai, *The Orwell Mystique* (Amherst: The University of Massachusetts Press, 1984), p. 255. Hereafter referred to as OM.

is nothing to revise, nothing to censor beyond the initial acts of destruction of the past (which, she says, took about 50 years). (OM 260)

As Croft notes, we find an ironic affirmation of Burdekin's model in the subsequent reception history of the whole U.K. dystopian genre:

> There is no evidence that Orwell ever read *Swastika Night*, or indeed that he read any of the anti-fascist novels mentioned above. Whether or not he was influenced, either in general or specific ways, by this body of writing is not important. What is important is that . . . these anti-fascist novelists have been disregarded by literary history, and their novels are long out of print. (WWE 210)

For all its sophistication, Croft says, *Swastika Night* "is wholly forgotten today" (WWE 209).

Croft was writing in 1984. I note, as a marker of historical change — change brought about by concerted social effort like the writings of Croft, Patai, and the entire movement of feminist literary criticism, only relatively recently off the ground in the mid-'80s — that as of this writing, *Swastika Night* is back in print.

VII

RE-READING THE TITLE OF THE PRESENT collection, I am reminded not so much of Orwell's title as I am of the act of appropriation itself, the social context that makes such appropriation necessary, and what it might mean to readers today, now, as the real 1984 recedes into history.

I am reminded of the political act of seizing back control of oppressive names —names like "queer," for example.

More specifically, I am reminded of the appropriation of canonical titles by feminist authors — authors like the late Kathy Acker. Here is the opening paragraph of Part Two of Acker's novel *Don Quixote*, taking place just after the "death" of its eponymous female protagonist:

> Being dead, Don Quixote could no longer speak. Being born into and part of a male world, she had no speech of her own. All she could do was read male texts which weren't hers.[25]

Acker, incidentally, wrote the Preface to the recent Wesleyan reprint of *Trouble on Triton* — the Delany novel with, as we've noted, the closest thematic links to Orwell's dystopia. And like Delany, Acker has not been untouched by the exclusionary rhetoric of "literature," as indicated by the following anecdote from Acker's friend Lynne Tillman:

> Kathy writes a quote for my novel *Haunted Houses*. I receive a phone call from a copy editor and fact checker at Simon & Schuster (my imprint's "parent") who says, adamantly, "Kathy Acker is not the author of *Don Quixote*." I respond, with assurance, "Yes she is and so is Cervantes." There's a long pause. The woman asks, "Well, what else has she written?" "*Great Expectations*," I say.[26]

[25] Kathy Acker, *Don Quixote* (New York: Grove Press, 1986), p. 39.
[26] Lynne Tillman, "Selective Memory," from *The Review of Contemporary Fiction* (Vol. 9, No. 3, Fall 1989), p. 70.

Finally, I am reminded of a fact that no "common sense" could ever discover without access to the historical record: The proper title of Orwell's novel is *Nineteen Eighty-four*. As Rodden has observed, its numerical variant is actually the popular name by which it quickly came to be known—a process aided and abetted by countless publishers, who have indiscriminately used the numerical title on the covers of various editions.[27] The current text, then, appropriates and indicates not simply the title of Orwell's book, but its subsequent reduction, distortion, and mythicization in time.

Certainly the author of the text you are about to read has his own idiosyncrasies, his own blindnesses. (We are all inside discourse.) But in his passionate ethical commitment to critical rigor, as opposed to an uncritical trust in some hypostatized, transparent, transcendent (extra-discursive, extra-social, centered) common sense, Delany seems the more reliable guide to today's systematic oppressions, exclusions, and historical erasures.

VIII

ONE LAST QUESTION: WHERE, precisely, do these letters fall in the history of AIDS?

The arrival of AIDS in the mainstream media—with the death of Rock Hudson and the stigmatizing of the young hemophiliac AIDS patient, Ryan White—will not happen until later in 1985; the virus will not actually be named HIV until 1986; the formation of ACT UP, the first appearance of the AIDS Memorial Quilt, and FDA approval of the experimental use of zidovudine (the first HIV reverse transcriptase-inhibiting drug) will not happen until 1987; and the beginning of a decline in AIDS cases within the gay community (brought about primarily by conscientious action within the community itself) will not be seen until 1988—by which point the death toll will have passed 60,000.[28]

Today, with new drug therapies, increased media coverage, continued grassroots education efforts, and belated action by the Clinton administration, both new AIDS cases and AIDS-related deaths have begun to drop in the United States. Nevertheless, the death toll in this country long ago passed 385,000.

Meanwhile, the pandemic continues to explode across the world. As of this writing, estimated worldwide infection stands at over 33 million, with infection rates skyrocketing in Southeast Asia, India, the former Soviet Union, and Africa. In parts of sub-Saharan Africa, estimated infections have reached the stupefying ratio of one person in four. The global death toll has passed 16 million.

But the first letter in the collection to follow was written only two years after the first reported deaths of gay males due to opportunistic diseases arising from

---

[27] Rodden, p. 24.

[28] Chronological information and statistics are taken from *Acquired Immune Deficiency Syndrome: Biological, Medical, Social, and Legal Issues* (3rd ed.) by Gerald J. Stine (Upper Saddle River: Prentice Hall, 1998), *AIDS and HIV in Perspective* (2nd ed.) by Barry D. Schoub (Cambridge: Cambridge University Press, 1999), and *The Gay Almanac* (New York: Berkeley Books, 1996). U.S. statistics are from the U.S. Department of Health and Human Services (Fact Sheet, Oct. 28, 1998). Global infection and mortality estimates are taken from the report issued on November 23, 1999, by the Joint United Nations Program on HIV/AIDS (UNAIDS) and the World Health Organization (WHO) just prior to World AIDS Day (December 1): AIDS Epidemic Update—December 1999.

immune system suppression by an unknown agent; one year after the worldwide acceptance of the acronym AIDS (earlier, one acronym used had been the stigmatizing GRID — Gay-Related Immune Deficiency); six months after the formation of Gay Men's Health Crisis, in response to massive inertia on the part of the government and the media; and just one month after the announcement by Luc Montaigner and the Pasteur Institute team (echoed by Robert Gallo in April 1984) of the discovery of the virus that causes AIDS.

Elsewhere in the world, the totalitarian bureaucracy of the Soviet Union is still intact. The Berlin Wall is still up.

In the free nation of South Africa, Nelson Mandela is still in prison.

And Samuel R. Delany, not yet the university professor some of us have known for the past dozen years, is a 41-, then 42-year-old freelance novelist and critic struggling to make ends meet in New York City.

IX

Documents retrieved from the memory hole: Delany's *1984*.

1984

A Note on the Correspondents

Here are some brief identifications of people to whom Samuel R. Delany (SRD) wrote between 1983 and 1985.

In 1984, Robert S. Bravard was director of library services at the Stevenson Library at Lock Haven University, Lock Haven, PA. He was co-author, with Michael W. Peplow, of *Samuel R. Delany, A Primary and Secondary Bibliography, 1962–1979* (Boston: G.K. Hall, 1980), and (again with Peplow) a major bibliographical article extending that work through 1983 in *The Black American Literature Forum* (Summer, 1984; Terra Haute, editor Joe Wexelman; see p. 125).

Camilla Decarnin, who went by the nickname "Mog," was a San Francisco writer. She co-edited the anthology *Worlds Apart: An Anthology of Lesbian and Gay Science Fiction and Fantasy* (San Francisco: Alyson, 1986) with Eric Garbert and Lynn Paleo. She first became friends with SRD through a letter she wrote him about his 1975 novel *Dhalgren*. She later published *Marjoon*, a fanzine of sexual politics, out of Minneapolis.

Born in 1974, Iva Hacker Delany was SRD's daughter with Marilyn Hacker. SRD and Hacker had divorced in 1980. At the time of Delany's letter to her, she was a ten-year-old camper spending July and August at Camp Thoreau-in-Vermont.

Ron Drummond was a Seattle-based writer and science fiction enthusiast who befriended SRD during a visit to New York City. He helped correct galleys for SRD on several occasions and eventually founded Incunabula, a small press that published works by SRD and John Crowley.

Gerald Jonas was a writer and the regular reviewer of science fiction for *The New York Times Book Review*. In 1983 he interviewed SRD for a longer piece he was planning to write on science fiction.

Victor Gonzales was a teen-aged Seattle-based fan who planned to publish an essay by SRD in his fanzine. Although the fanzine reached the galley stage, it never actually appeared.

Marilyn Holt and J.T. Stewart took over the directorship of for the west coast chapter of the Clarion Science Fiction Writers' Workshop, which, from 1984 on, was held for six weeks each summer at Seattle Central Community College.

Tom LeClair was a professor of English at the University of Cincinnati and co-editor with Larry McCaffery of the interview collection *Anything Can Happen*. More recently, he is the author of *The Art of Excess* and *Passing Off*.

John P. Mueller was a New York street person and hustler in his mid-20s. In 1984 he was serving a two-year term in jail.

Mrs. Joseph P. Marshall was Admissions Director of the Brearly School for Girls in New York City.

Michael W. Peplow was co-author, with Robert S. Bravard, of *Samuel R. Delany, A Primary and Secondary Bibliography, 1962-1979* (Boston: G.K. Hall, 1980). In addition, he was the author of a biography of the black social critic George Schuyler. He also edited an anthology of Harlem Renaissance writings.

Joanna Russ was a science fiction writer and professor of English at the University of Washington, Seattle. She is the author of *Picnic on Paradise* (1968), *And Chaos Died* (1970), *The Female Man* (1975), *We Who Are About To...* (1977), *On Strike Against God* (1980) and *The Two of Them* (1984), as well as, among her non-fiction, *How to Suppress Women's Writing* (1983) and *What Are We Fighting For?* (1998).

David N. Samuelson was a professor of English and critic of science fiction who taught in California.

Greg Tate was a writer who interviewed SRD for a combination profile and review of *Stars in My Pocket Like Grains of Sand*, which appeared that year in the *Village Voice*.

Bill Thompson was a speakers' agent working at the time for Lordley and Dame. Subsequently he left to found his own agency, Briarwood Writers' Alliance.

Tom Zummer was a young scholar who was also a friend and occasional student of Michel Foucault. In 1984, Zummer worked at the St. Mark's Bookshop, where he and SRD became friends.

The letters are dated in the order they were begun; they are published, however (and numbered), in the order in which they were completed and sent. This explains how a letter (e.g., #27) begun on July 27 may preceed a letter (e.g., #28) begun on July 23, which in turn precedes one (e.g., #30) begun on July 19. The one begun July 19 took perhaps ten to twelve days to finish, whereas the ones begun later were completed in notably less time and so were sent to their recipients earlier.

Prologue
1983

suck your dick.' I said, 'Fuck, yeah!' And his partner, right next to us, arrests me."
Another case of entrapment. "I wished the fuck he'd sucked on it!" Jeff laughed.
"I can't get a hard-on no more anyway, you know? I even come soft—when I can
come at all. It's the fuckin' dope, man. Anyway, I thought: Imagine this fuckin'
cop's gonna suck on a soft dick for 20 bucks? He really should have. Served him
right!" He scratched his head as we walked up the sweltering sidewalk. (This was
while I was taking him to a Chinese dinner, after I'd run into him on the street
when I was between Empiricon and Forbidden Planet Con. Just as he was coming
up to say hello, some kids from the Con came up to ask me for my autograph. Jeff,
after they went: "Hey, you really are famous, huh? Mike Elkins, he told me you
were famous. But I didn't believe him. But I guess you are. At least a little?" He
laughed again.) "I knew he wasn't no cocksucker when he asked me, you know?
I knew it. He didn't look like no cocksucker. Shit! He looked like a fuckin' *cop* is
what he *looked* like!" But, since recounting that story (over which he spent a month
in jail), he's gone back to his "ain't been arrested since I was thirteen" line on several occasions. He deserves it back: which is my appraisal of victimless crimes.

One of the most pathetic images I retain from our year-and-a-half friendship:

In just a pair of dark blue dress slacks, worn for a week of sleeping in the park
(a beige t-shirt with iridescent and metallic letters across the front proclaiming,
"How can you be Humble when you're as Great as I am?" stripped off his bare
chest now hung from the back corner), Jeff sat in a red, wooden kitchen chair.
With toes reddened from a summer of ill-fitting shoes given him by somebody,
his small feet, peppered with needle marks, were bare on the maroon linoleum.
Earlier that day, sick on some park bench, he'd shit in the pants, but, being the
only ones he had, he still wore them. He rolled up one pants leg to the thigh, bent
way over, so that his brass-colored hair, a little matted, fell forward in dull hanks;
and I watched him stick what looked like a child's tiny toy hypodermic from a
Let's Play Doctor Kit again and again into his knee cap, his shin, his thigh, trying
to find a hit, where black red blood would gush into the already pale pink solute
at the hypodermic's bottom, indicating a functioning vein. Blood drooled his
arms in half a dozen places from more than half a dozen attempts in the few minutes before, now in his forearm, now between his knuckles, now on the inside of
his biceps, three or four obliquely-angled stabs apiece, with a little joggling of the
needle to try and break into his body's more and more well-guarded circulatory
system. One dribble over his elbow was thick and long as an earthworm; the others strung like yarn down his forearms, over his wrists and infection-swollen
hand. (Among the beer bottle caps and folded bits of wax paper on the kitchen
table were two crumpled yellow paper towels, blotched with blood from where
he'd already twice wiped away the red drool from his mutilations.) Now, here
and there, more blood ran down his leg. He went on prodding his pale inner
thigh with his thick thumb, then sliding the inch-long needle in to its hilt, out, and
in again, lifting white tents of skin.

But most of his accessible veins have collapsed.

From under his hair, strained with the bent position, he mutters: "Damned if
I'm gonna blow this hit. . .!" Blowing a hit means inadvertently injecting the drug
under the skin, so that it simply blows up into a dime-sized bubble of liquid,
which is absorbed into the body too slowly for the user to feel any effects.

Later, he stood up, wiping his arms off with another towel, his pant leg still up over his thigh. "I look like a fuckin' dartboard, don't I?" Forehead sweating with the first rush, he grinned—long under-teeth and naked upper gum. "I'm in the hospital a couple of months ago, and they're trying to do a blood test. And I tell 'em, please, please! Lemme do it! Please! You gonna be pokin' around in my arm for an hour and you ain't gonna get no blood."

What does Jeff look like?

Standing together against the wall of McHale's next to la Fiesta, we were talking together, when a heavy black woman came past with her six- or seven-year-old daughter, rough pigtails beribboned all over her head. The little girl pointed at Jeff and looked at her mother: "Momma, that's Jesus Christ . . . ?"

Jeff turned to me and gave me a big, distorted and disgusted grin. "Man, that happens to me a *lot!* They all think Jesus Christ looked like some fuckin' toothless junky!" (Later he volunteered to put a roof on a small church nearby, that paid him in food and a place to sleep. He spent the rest of the year complaining about how much money he could have made if he'd done the work at standard carpenter's wages. "That was a $2,000 roofing job. Two thousand dollars I could've got. But not me, man! Not fuckin' Jesus Christ! I'm a fuckin' asshole!") Another time he told me: "This guy takes me home with him—he's 41. He takes me in the bathroom with him, and we look in the mirror together. 'Look at yourself,' he says. 'You're 30, and you look older than I do. You look 60.' I don't look like no fuckin' 60, do I?"

Jeff was 30 on July 27th. (And *I'm* 41!) Whether he looks older than I do has never really struck me before. But there is certainly an ageless quality to his bony face that just doesn't fix itself to any year at all.

Fragments of a remembered bedtime conversation with Jeff, our faces inches apart in half-dark: "Jeff, how about if I put a dog collar on you and chained you up in my back room? I'd give you 25 bucks a day, let you out for six hours to get your bag—you'd still wear the dog collar, while you were out—and then you'd come back to your room, and I'd chain you up again while you got high. I'd put food in there for you. You could stay as high as you want. I'd leave you a pot to shit and piss in. From time to time, I'll come in and fuck you—bring my friends in and you can suck them off. How would you like that?"

Without any irony, he says: "I'd love it. Maybe you wanna try it for three or four days? You might even get to like it . . . ?"

I laugh. "That's what I'm afraid of. Naw, I'm just talking through my hat."

"Yeah, a fantasy," Jeff says, understandingly. "But I'd like to do that. Especially with you, man. I'd probably end up falling in love with you and never wanna leave you."

"Yeah," I say. "I'm afraid of that, too."

We laugh again.

Still, fifteen minutes later, while sweat dripped from my face, my shoulders, ran from my hips onto his, the "fantasy" got me off somewhat to my surprise. That particular kind of S/M power trip is not what usually turns me on.

Later Jeff said, "If you wanna do that thing with the collar and the chains, could I have a TV set in the room with me? Otherwise, I'd get kind of bored."

"Jeff," I said, "really, I was only fantasizing." Still, with that maniac hacking his way through Jeff's summer nights, and the police sweeping up the Avenue by day, I can understand why it doesn't seem like such a bad one.

Still later, we compared pocket photos of our daughters. Jeff has an eleven-year-old daughter in Boston, born when he was nineteen. (Twice since I've known him, he's actually gotten it together enough to go up to Boston and visit her.) Iva and Cindy (?), with their blonde hair and round faces, look uncannily like sisters. Cindy has a birthday, he tells me, on September 29th.

Interestingly, none of this has made its way into *Nevèrÿon* — the collars and chains, I mean. (Perhaps *Nevèrÿon* is where they came from . . . ?) Well, I'll save it for *Plagues and Carnivals*. Ah, the self-critical construct . . .

The thing I've noticed about hustling, starting with my couple of dozen experiences doing it in the vicinity of the Folsom period, which jibes pretty well with what I've noticed from what's only, when all is said and done, less than a couple of dozen times on the purchasing end: As a profession it appeals basically to an extremely lazy personality. The percentage of fundamentally pleasant, goodhearted people you run into as a hustler is certainly not substantially lower than in any other profession. The only thing is: A successful hustler has to spend 60–80% of his (or her — this much I know is identical for women) time doing nothing. And an unsuccessful hustler (among whom, finally, I'd have to class Jeff), spends 95% percent of his or her time at it — nothing, that is. As an 18-to-23-year-old, I certainly felt being a hustler was equally as romantic as being an artist. If it hadn't been so overwhelmingly boring, thanks to the time one must spend waiting for something to happen, I probably would have done a lot more of it than I did.

Another Bobby is a 55-year-old john, balding and with pale framed glasses, whom I've talked to at la Fiesta from time to time. He was one of Mike Elkin's steady customers. Last summer, I recall, he got into some ridiculous, drunken, and ugly argument with Jeff at one point, where I was pretty sure Bobby was in the wrong and Jeff was in the right. Last night, I dropped into la Fiesta. Bobby, surprise of surprises, was working as a substitute bartender for the evening. Jeff was at the bar, sick and/or half asleep, as though whatever differences Bobby and he had had the summer before were long since resolved. Bobby, behind the bar tonight, sounded positively avuncular towards Jeff, half dozing with his head down on the counter on the customer's side. There was practically no one there and, while I had a beer beside Jeff, the few that were left emptied out, and Bobby came over to ponder with me what a bartender has to do in a gay bar to keep the place full. One can't help thinking: Besides the obvious (letting the working men hang out without buying *too* many drinks on their own), I suspect the answer is to be 25 rather than 55. Or know a lot of johns.

Finally Jeff woke up, saw me, and said, "An angel! Hey, an angel's come to say hello to me." He gave me a hug and told me about the five new hacking victims that I mentioned above. Also told me some story about Bobby Russo, who, according to Jeff, has now become a rip-off artist and should be avoided. He and Jeff are no longer partners. I note that Bobby behind the bar says no word to confirm this. And all it takes is a suggestion of such a complaint from one of the johns, and the hustler is eighty-sixed from the bar for a month. More than one such complaint and it's permanent. (That's why John Mueller was always afraid to go into the Fiesta and would hang out instead on the corner in front of

McHale's.) Then Jeff had to run off for a while to "take care of business," leaving a white and black–checkered wool hunting shirt over the counter. Bobby Russo came in only minutes later, and we had a beer together. (I'd seen him on the street earlier with an older man in glasses and a pale beige suit, and Russo'd waved: "You lookin' for Jeff . . .?") And we made those noises that everybody knows, in such situations, are just noises, about maybe getting together some other time. Russo, who seems a lot more together than Jeff, despite Jeff's stories, strikes me as pretty much his old self, and I suspect some of Jeff's warnings may just be inter-hustler paranoia—if not jealousy. "I bring him johns, man," Russo tells me. "He tells 'em to get lost 'cause he can't get it up no more. They know that before I bring 'em. That's not what they're into. I'm tryin' to get Jeff to stay with me. I got this place for $40 a week. It's got an icebox, a hot plate where you can cook. Look at 'im, he needs food. But he don't get any, most of the time. I hope he don't get that AIDS shit!"

Earlier, Jeff told me another story of a street hustler who suddenly started losing weight. Everyone thought it was AIDS. The man finally went to the hospital emergency room. Turned out to be lung cancer. "But do you think they'd take him into the hospital? No, they gave him some medicine and told him, 'Go die someplace else.' You see, if you walk into the hospital and you ain't got no money, they won't take you in. If you need a bed or something, you gotta come in with an ambulance. So we all got together and called the ambulance for him, you know? I mean, the fucker'd lost 70 pounds and could hardly walk. And you know what? Two days later, I saw him again on the street. I say to him, 'What is it, they put you out?' He says, 'Naw, I just didn't wanna be there. They don't want me. I don't want them.' I tell, him, 'Man, you should be in the hospital. I mean, they feed you there. In two days, you already look better than you did.' And he really did. I mean, he was still clean. But he just didn't want that. Hey, why don't you come on down and talk to me sometimes? You don't have to pick me up. Just come down and talk. I ain't hard to find."

But the truth is, half a dozen times now I *have* come down to look for Jeff and talk, and he *is* hard to find. Only 23 and far more energetic, Bobby Russo isn't. Last night Bobby and I talked about Jeff. "I'm worried about him. You see how thin he is? He didn't used to be that thin. And he was sick for about a month. You get sick on the street, and that's hard on you. I wanna be his partner again. We'll go up to Boston together. He wants to go up to Boston and see his family. That'd be good, you know? I wish he'd come stay with me." Talking to Russo, I recalled Jeff's warning. ("You know," Jeff told me, "once he even said we'd should get together and rip *you* off? How you like shit like that? I ain't into that shit." Anything is possible in this world. And though I doubt it, I wasn't doing more than talking last night anyway.) When I first met Russo, he was hanging around Jeff, and I gave him some fried whiting over in the Barking Fish. For a while they were close, but now Jeff isn't interested, and Russo seems to be pushing for it. Maybe I'm romanticizing things, but I think Russo feels something between love for, and identification with, Jeff. After all, Jeff *is* lovable; if he wasn't, he'd be dead. And in seven years, Russo will *be* Jeff. And a half-Puerto Rican Jeff at that. The result in Jeff, however, is the standard one in such cases: Get away from me. I don't want to know about it. The two of them have never had sex together, they both tell me. Russo says he wouldn't mind it. Jeff says he'd be embarrassed. Interestingly enough they share a quality in bed — one that's rare in this world, where most hustlers still lie naked on hotel room beds, like embalmed dreams, with only a hard-on and, at last, a load to signal life at all. They are both astonishingly affectionate men. In Jeff's case, because he can no longer get an erection, I suspect it comes from his definite sense of himself as being of limited sexual use — indeed, not only is he affectionate but energetically so: There must be something more to it than that, but though I have my suspicions (his boyhood lover, perhaps), I can't know. In Russo's case, I don't know at all. He has a certain bantam quality — maybe it's just a youngster's desire to please. (One of the more pathetic images I have of him: Walking up Eighth Avenue once, as I neared the gray, painted-over cement steps beside the comic book store, I saw Jeff and Russo sitting together on the stoop. Neither wore shirts. Russo was in shorts and sneakers. Jeff, his forearms over his knees, gazed up at the hot sky, eyes unmoving. Russo's head was slumped between his wide, jack-knifed legs, his hands on the step's edge, one with the fingers curled down, loosely holding the cement, one with palm up, clawing air. [Russo is a nail-biter, incidentally, unlike Jeff.] As I got nearer, Jeff saw me, smiled and came over. He looked back at Russo. "Ain't that a shame?" He shook his head. "A kid all that fucked up, out in the middle of the street in the daytime." But that was back from when they were "partners.") Married at eighteen somewhere in Brooklyn to a woman a year or two his senior, Russo split with his wife a couple of years back because of his drug involvement. After the first time we made it, he told me: "Look, please! Please, don't tell anybody on the street that I suck dick, huh? That's not part of my street image. You know, I'm out there on 42nd Street, sellin' valiums and pills and shit. The other guys know I hustle. But they don't wanna know about no cocksucker out here, okay?" Once, though, I took him into the Cameo, and although he recognized a few people from the street in the balcony, he shrugged and went down on me with a vengeance anyway. "Do *you* think of yourself as gay?" I once asked him. He shrugged: "I don't think I used to be. But I'll tell you, I ain't been with any women in a long time. And the truth is, I don't miss it." His standard greeting to me is, "Hi, you lookin' for Jeff?" And immediately afterwards, he flips out his upper plate with his tongue, winks at me, grins and says, "You wanna take me to the movies . . . ?"

Now Russo looks at me over his Budweiser that I've bought him. Jeff's wool shirt still lies on the counter beside us. Bartender-Bobby is getting the Puerto Rican porter at the counter end (a tall kid with tattoos from wrists to sleeveless shoulder, who's been winking at me all evening), to get some ice for him. In the orange light, Russo says, "I worry about Jeff . . ."

And I try not to worry about either one of them. The fact is, as a convergence of social needs, both are bottomless. They need: identification (to get into a drug program. Jeff: "Hitler invented methadone, didn't he . . . ?"), clothes, work, food, help for their families, a place to stay, someone to talk to, a dick to suck, someone to hold onto and a $25 bag of dope a day. . . .

Oh, well. But one of the things that's occasioned all this is that the *New York Post* yesterday carried a headline:

ANTI-SEMITIC SNIPER SLAYS ONE–hurts four!

It seems some nut up in Washington Heights has been gunning from a passing car for students coming out of some Yeshiva. To date, he's wounded four — and in an attempt to get another, he missed and killed some Puerto Rican woman driving by in her car! A $10,000 reward for information leading to his capture has just been upped to $15,000. Nuts are nuts and must be stopped. Still, I can't help noting that the maniac this summer we have down in the 40s, who's already killed one, possibly two, women and seven men (which puts him ahead of Jack the Ripper — so maybe he hasn't roasted anyone's kidney yet and eaten part of it . . .), with his "Death to the Street People" note, which makes the murders just as classist in structure as the Yeshiva attempts (but a long time ago, I realized that *all* "gratuitous" murders of both men and women were essentially racist/classist in form), doesn't seem to warrant any headlines. Yes, I know, the headlines encourage other such nuts. But no private individual is going to offer thousands of dollars' reward for someone who's going around into dark doorways to cut out the odd junky's heart. . . .

Perhaps another impetus to record all this sordidness is that this past Saturday's *Times* had a fine front-page article on William Kennedy and his Albany novels. I think I told you, I spent part of a drunken St. Pat's evening with Kennedy at a party when I was teaching up at SUNY-Albany, while he was friendly and signed numerous copies of *Ironweed*, which was still in piles in the B. Daltons' windows of Manhattan. I've only read *Legs*. But his small chapters come at you like handfuls of hard-boiled dime-store jewelry. It's as if, in a way, he's really writing the novels that everybody ascribed to Raymond Chandler. The article in the *Times*, with four fine pictures, basically takes a walk with Kennedy through the ruins of the city, while he reminisces about politics, crime, and history. The writer, Susan Chira, managed to get a sense both of the city and Kennedy in it. I cut it out and rubber-cemented it into the scrap book I made of my three weeks in Albany. Alas, I still haven't written the commentary notes to paste in with the "exhibits."

Earlier in August, I was interviewed by Larry McCaffery and his wife, Sinda Gregory. They had just come back from trying to interview Kennedy, but he'd been too busy, working on the run, on set at the new Coppola film, *The Cotton Club*, which, it turns out, my cousin, Norma Jean *(Spoonbread and Strawberry Wine)* Darden, is also working on as a researcher.

Last thought about your and Pep's article before I sign off. At one point, toward the bottom of your p. 6, you quote "Fictional Architecture" as saying, "Damn Ace Book covers." I defy you to find that line in the text. What you will find is "Damn Ace Books proofreading." The caption to the accompanying illustration (and both illustration and caption are by Gaughan) reads: "Damning an Ace cover." I leave you to make appropriate changes.

At the last minute, I called up and canceled my German trip. I just had too much work to do. I really want to make this Wagner/Artaud lecture something special. And there's just no way to do that over five days while you're listing with jet-lag. And this of course is not counting the proofs of *Starboard Wine* and the copy-editing of *Stars/Sand* to go over. And "Fog and Granite" is within sight of its end, and will be short *(Einstein Intersection)* novel-length. Frank will be unhappy (if not furious), but we were only going to have a couple of days together, anyway.

So we'll just have to miss them. But after last month's jaunt to France and with what remained to do this month, I just couldn't hack it.

Oh, yes, and one final request—if it's possible? If not, I'll fake it. I told you I was trying to put something coherent together from all this epistolary rambling. But I didn't begin it all keeping meticulous copies of everything. (Really, I'm still not.) But do you have:

From a letter dated "Labor Day, 1982," pp. 2 & 3?

And from a letter dated October 9th, 1982, do you have p. 39?

Somehow these pages managed to slip out of my own copies. If I had them, I could finish the mosaic presentation from them that I'm trying to put together about life on Eighth Ave.

Some pleasant times with Iva since she came back from camp, now observing the giant blue whale that leaps beneath the ceiling of the Marine Biology Hall at the Museum of Natural History, now at brunch together at Marvin Gardens, now visiting a street fair down on Columbus Avenue, where she became enamored of a feather boa . . . But she's back at her mother's now. And I'm hard at work. And I plan to be sending you the first 75 pages of "Fog and Granite" in about a week.

See you at my Bucknell lecture!

All my love,

• 4 •

TO JOANNA RUSS

October 17th, 1983

Dear Joanna,

This is not the long-promised letter, rambling easily over K/S,[1] your essays and stories on same, your new books, and a more than interesting volume I would recommend to you, *Powers of Desire: the Politics of Sexuality*, edited by Ann Snitow, Christine Stansell, and Sharon Thompson (New Feminist Library, Monthly Review Press: New York, 1983). Rather it's just the briefest of notes to acknowledge receipt of your Guggenheim "recommendation," which I shall dutifully transcribe and sign when the application arrives, and also your most kind invitation of Sept 8th, reiterated formally on October 15th—for which many thanks.

The long and short of it, alas, runs rather like this: For the last year and a half, my speaking/reading fees have been $1,600 plus expenses (or $2,300 without). The main reason they're set so high is—bluntly—to keep the number of requests down. And, believe it or not, it doesn't work all that well! But it's a price I'm kind of locked into at this point.

I would love to come down and see you, and will happily come and talk to your (and, indeed, any one else's) class(es) for nothing. But for any kind of lecture, I more or less have to ask what I've been asking. Lay it on your committee, and if they look at you like you're nuts, just tell me and I shall come informally and we shall carouse together and solve all the problems of the world just the two of us.

---

[1] A genre of fan-written pornography, usually authored by women, about Captain Kirk and Mr. Spock from *Star Trek*. In later years, it was referred to as "slash fiction."

Do I feel silly taking that kind of money for a lecture where, due to zero-publicity and badly handled timing, 75 people show up—which has happened on a couple of occasions now? Yes, I do. But then, with proper publicity (generated no doubt because everyone suddenly realizes how much they're paying me and suddenly decides they have to get their money's worth!), I can fill up a 500-seat auditorium with 50 standees crowding in the back—which happens more and more these days. So, as I said, I have to go with it.

At any rate, I shall plan on coming to see you the day after V-con. (I probably have a speaking engagement down in L.A. a day or two later, so I will, as 'twere, be barn-storming the West Coast right about then.) Working very hard on a new Nevèrÿon story ("The Tale of Fog and Granite") which will probably end up short (*TEI*) novel-length. And two more short stories are in the note stage—at which point I think I will be finished once and for all with the Nevèrÿon construct.

I notice, by the by, looking over the typescript of *Stars/Sand*, there are so many typos in the he/she business that I wouldn't be surprised if much of it were simply incomprehensible! The copy-edited version is sitting on my desk right now, waiting for me to re-insert some sense into it. At any rate,

All my love,

• 5 •

To Gerald Jonas

October 29ᵗʰ, 1983

Dear Gerald Jonas,

Night before last I got back from something called The Fiction Festival, a near-annual event (four times in five years now) put on by the University of Cincinnati. My fellow festees this years were Margaret Atwood, Ross Feld, Edward Doctorow and Jayne Ann Phillips. Feld and Atwood were the only ones I actually overlapped *in vivo*. Apparently the administration wants the students to fest for at least two weeks. This means withholding the later guests until the earlier ones go home. At any rate, while my right sinus drained away through it all, I festered and made merry.

Many thanks for the return of the *Michigan Quarterly* (and the copy of the article!). Last night I went to bed early (that sinus . . .) and re-read the Ashbery interview.

You'd asked if some of the things Ashbery was saying in his interview were an example of "what I meant" when we were talking together. But since I didn't remember A's interview very well, and, also, in the course of our own discussion I had "meant" so many things, I wasn't too sure of your question. As soon as I looked at the Michigan piece, however, it all cleared up.

I had said, back when we were talking in my living room, that I believed that, for the last hundred years or so, the so-called literary genres, considered as a set of codes by which we make certain texts called "literary" make sense, may be characterized—the lot of them—as overwhelmingly determined by "the priority of the subject."

Certainly Ashbery's early statements in the interview about the way to understand his poem, "Leaving the Atocha Station"[1] are a textbook example of what I meant:

> That poem was written after my first trip to Spain. The Atocha Station is a railway station in Madrid . . . I was in a strange city going somewhere . . . [I]t strikes me that the dislocated, incoherent fragments of images which make up the movement of the poem are probably like the experience you get from a train pulling out of a station of no particular significance. The dirt, the noises, the sliding away seem to be a movement in the poem. The poem was trying to express that, not for itself but as an epitome of something experienced; I think that is what my poems are about . . . [T]he movement of experience is what I'm trying to get down . . . [M]ost of my poems are about the experience of experience . . . I'm trying to set down a generalized transcript of what's really going on in our minds all day long. First of all, I'm in a strange place with lots of lights whose meaning I don't quite understand, and I'm talking about a poem I wrote years ago and which no longer means very much to me. I have a feeling that everything is slipping away from me as I'm trying to talk about it—a feeling I have most of the time, in fact, and I think I was probably trying to call attention to this same feeling in "Leaving the Atocha Station" and in other poems as well.

I'm certainly willing to accept this as an example of what I mean by poetry's (as a concept, as a literary genre) being largely controlled in the post-modern mind by "the priority of the subject." By the same token if you go through the same passage and pull out the phrases and sentences that, in the above reduction, are represented by ellipses, you get the following:

> My poems aren't usually about experiences, because I don't find my experiences very interesting as a rule . . . When they are about them, they are about them in a very oblique, marginal way. It was really nothing for me to be leaving this particular railway station. It meant nothing to me at the time . . . It doesn't particularly matter about the experience . . . [T]he particular occasion is of lesser interest to me than the way a happening or experience filters through me. I believe this is the way in which it happens with most people . . .

If we agree that "experience" in this text is synonymous with "external situation" (while, in the former, it tends to mean "internal happenings"), I think it's valid to read this as subject-dominated literature's traditional concomitant dismissal of the object. And yet by still the same token, I think we can read the last sentences of the section ("Maybe once it [the subjective state in which everything is seen to be slipping away] is called attention to, we can think about something else, which is what I'd like to do.") as expressing a dissatisfaction with this subject priority and object dismissal. As a marxist (of, alas, the most Champagnoise persuasion), I am pretty sure that different external situations cause experience to "filter through" people in different ways. I'm just as sure of that as I am sure that "the modes of production influence the economic, religious, and social aspects of a social life."

Indeed, I think the last two sentences refer pretty much to the same processes-in-the-world.

But at this point (and I suspect Ashbery would agree that different external situations modulate internal happenings differently), we have (by the literary code) only two alternatives: Art very quickly becomes one with politics and thus should

---

[1] In *The Tennis Court Oath,* by John Ashbery (Wesleyan University Press: Middletown, 1962).

become one version or the other of something resembling socialist realism; or art must become completely divorced from politics and eschew representation even more strongly — which works only up till the time that the next most ingenious critic manages to show that even so, the art text still is managing to reify the status quo: Its turning away from reference is, itself, an allegory of one or another political oppressor's refusing to "see" the effects of oppression. And we're right back where we started.

Today what I see as happening is this: With the above argument taken not as a conclusion, but rather as a kind of circular dialectic, various literary artists simply find themselves stalled at one point or another in the process — or, indeed, sometimes they move on, their current position in the cycle more or less pretty clearly signed by the critical vocabulary they consciously or unconsciously fall into.

My basic feeling is that this itself represents the tyranny of a critical tradition at work. Ashbery is a highly literary fellow, and his is a language very similar to the one Kafka uses in his diaries when he wrote of *The Metamorphosis* that he was trying to "express his inner world" and was "not concerned with reality."

(One would start a formal deconstruction of my argument here with the ambiguity implicit in "experience" [inner/outer], world, and reality.)

For an example of how the same subjective phenomenon that Ashbery claims to be dealing with in his poem might be handled in science fiction, with its paraliterary "priority of the object" organizing the readerly response, you might take a look at *Dhalgren*, i.e., the marginal rubric, p. 806. There are a handful of references to Ashbery's poems scattered throughout *Dhalgren*, the most important of which are probably the references to "The Instruction Manual" and to "These Lacustrine Cities." But the section on p. 806[2] was written in response to the very poem Ashbery is discussing with Poulin — or, more accurately, it was written after I spent some months thinking about the Paul Carroll essay, "If Only He Had Left from the Finland Station," which was the initial occasion for the Ashbery/Poulin discussion.

My early readings of both the Ashbery poem and the Carroll essay are, of course, ten years or more in the past, and I don't have the text of the Carroll essay to hand, but as I recall it, after actually identifying Atocha as a station in Madrid, Carroll asks in his essay if, indeed, the interpretation that Ashbery later gave in this November 1972 interview was the right one. And he is unhappy with the poem because he is not sure if it is. There is not enough evidence in the poem to be certain that this is what the poem is about.

At any rate, the poem and Carroll's discussion inspired the p. 806 section in *Dhalgren*, in the form of one of Kid's own writerly experiments. ("92nd Street" refers to the closed-down subway station on the westside IRT; "St. Croix" is a similarly closed-down station on one of the lines of the Paris Metro. You see them, dark, ruined, graffiti-wracked and impregnable, out the windows of the subway as you speed by.) But in an SF novel, the thrust is not toward the subject — the SF text simply can't stop with (or, indeed, start by) merely reproducing/documenting/critiquing a subjective state (either with or without the objective experience that is one of the factors in generating it) without a frame. In the SF novel, the sub-

---

[2] P. 731 in the 1996 Wesleyan edition.

jective state becomes a framed and delineated object of examination, if only framed by the notion of "SF." The object is, in Kid's own words, "Not thinking but the way thinking feels. Not knowledge but knowledge's form." Or, in Ashbery's words: ". . . the experience of experience."

Ashbery's poem presents its topic wholly as a subject state. What renders this same state an object for critique in *Dhalgren* are many: The particular bit of text is framed at both ends by more "communicative" modes; and, which I think is the most important, in SF things simply are looked at as objects of exploration. Even the fact that it is, in the text, an allusion (I assumed that a few readers would probably realize that, at one point or another, Kid had read the Ashbery poem) helps objectify it. I'd even hazard that there's a crispness, an artifactoriness in the *Dhalgren* text that is not there in the Ashbery poem, which, in *Dhalgren,* contributes to the object quality. But I'm sure you could find a dozen or more rhetorical figures in the text itself that support the interpretation of an object critique. And I suspect it's SF's paraliterary position and its concomitant object tradition that urges you/me/one (?), more than anything, toward this reading.

The problem, of course, is that where, in SF, there is a tradition of reader response, there is no very old tradition of formal critical response. Thus when one brings the rhetoric of literary criticism to SF, it becomes very hard to discuss this aspect of the SF text simply, without sounding simple-minded.

As they say in the fanzines, this letter is DNQ[2] —not for public quotation. I deplore writers quoted in print authenticating their own allusions within authoritative quotes and explaining (away) their intentions—especially ten years after the fact. It spoils the fun for other readers. Still, I feel two people can talk about these things as much as they want and don't stop being human beings just because one or both of them happen to write.

Once again, it was much fun talking with you.

Best of luck,

• 6 •

Breaking the Realist Teacup

—a fable for critics

I took out my post-structuralist elephant gun, gave it a shot, and damned if the delicate blue and white Wedgwood didn't blow up big as an Olympic-sized pool. So, turning to look out the window of the airplane smoothing me back from Cincinnati to New York, I scooped up the night-lights of Dayton, down like a doily on the dark, and stuffed that big cup full. "There," I said, "that ought to make it glimmer with unholy radiance." It just vanished! Then, last night, when I thought it was gone for good, suddenly I saw the ceramic run, the glaze glisten, and wouldn't you know: It reappeared, a small juice glass full of milk on my butcher-block desk—just as I turned and knocked it over. Shattered on the office

---

[2] DNQ stands for "Do Not Quote" and means the letter (or section of it so marked) is not to appear in a fanzine or magazine.

floor, too. "Lord," I thought. "Now I've got to clean this up before Frank gets home." But it was no more gone than when Neret Oppenheim lined it with fur way back in the '20s. So, I thought, with milky fragments gentle in one hand and the wet paper napkins not too tight in the other, now we'll chuck it into the Glad Bag and be done with it. But soon as I tinkled them in, the pieces sailed out, become a whole set of fucking cups, ringing in the air, clear and limpid as sixteen identical words. Tiny teacups swarmed after me like fat gnats for the day, until, one theoretical letter later, I found a seat in the Penn Central railway waiting room between a mumbling black man in a foul coat and a serious white woman in jeans and a London Fog: They'd melted together and formed into one ivory styrofoam container—which got knocked off the seat by a bag lady, also mumbling: As its invitreation the night before had splashed white fingers, now it splattered beige dregs. And I thought: You know, Tom, as long as that there cup can fragment, multiply, and metamorph, it's just a subset of meaning; not to worry. When it's on paper, reference is just not that privileged. And for a teacup, really, big guns aside, the unreal changes I can put it through, however insistently it persists, must mean it's just not very realistic.

• 7 •

To Tom LeClair

October 29th, 1983

Dear Tom LeClair,

As you can see, I have been giving your exhortation to shatter Ms. Atwood's teacup some thought. By temperament and theoretical upbringing, as 'twere, and certainly by the light of the fiction and criticism I like to read (and write), I'm on what I take to be your side. Nevertheless, I think a firm philosophical understanding of the relation between meaning and reference renders the reference problem, as the "realists" propound it and most "metafictionists" conceive of it, a non-problem. The "realists" simply use fuzzy terminology for what they talk about; but what they are talking about can always be translated into a harder terminology that should be acceptable to the rest of us—if not to them.

Reference is a particular type of meaning—or, more accurately, it is meaning in a particular situation, i.e., when there is something for the signifier not only to signify but to refer to. The bottom line is that any word in the language can be referential: It can always be used to refer to what one means in the usual situations in which one uses it (i.e., "the usual meaning of Y . . ."). But this bottom line case (which we'll call case X) has some unusual aspects to it. To make those aspects clear, however, we have to say a few more things about the relation of meaning to reference. And when we do, I think we'll soon see that this bottom line case X *is* the condition of *all* fiction in the Barthesian sense, i.e., fiction as any systematic enterprise.

Any word can be referential. Any word can also be simply meaningful without having a referent.

George

Set right there in the middle of the line, it has no referent, though it is a locus of possibility for many meanings, meanings that range from the meaning of "George" in the '20s slang phrase "It's real George" [It's real fine], to the first name of the Father of Our Country.

"The white horse with the spiral horn growing from her forehead's rough hide and the silver hooves showing below the matted hairs around her feet was certainly a unicorn," is a perfectly a-referential sentence. Neither unicorns nor silver-hooved horses with spiral horns exist. But just as certainly, "white horse with . . . spiral horn growing from . . . her forehead . . . and . . . silver hooves" *refers* to "unicorn," as "unicorn" *refers* to "white horse with . . . spiral horn."

Reference is a subset of meaning, i.e., it is a limited kind of meaning. Language to be useful must be able both to refer and to mean-in-non-referential-ways. If it could only refer, then it would strongly suggest that the universe is total and complete and there will be nothing new in it ever. The bottom line use of a-referential meanings such as "unicorn" has is simply that, if a unicorn ever shows up, we'll be able to talk about it. I have a book of essays coming out in a few months (called *Starboard Wine*) all about some far more interesting uses of a-referential statements, but mayhap you will see it some day.

At any rate, the problem as it plagues the metafictionist is that, in general usage, "meaning" includes "referring," while referring in no way includes all the types of meaning. Okay: To clear things up, then, let us make up a new verb: Call it "to mean[/]" and it specifically refers only to those meanings which are not referential.

So now, we will either "mean[/]" or we will "refer," but we will always distinguish between them. No more fuzzy terminology that refers to both.

With me? All right:

Language, in order to be fully and richly complete as a system, then, should be able to refer to reference; it should be able to refer to meaning[/]; it should be able to mean[/] meaning[/]; and it should be able to mean[/] reference.

Looking closely at some of these, one begins to wonder of course if some of them actually exist. Is there any referent for "to mean[/] a meaning[/]"? My suspicion is that there isn't, i.e., that it is just a meaning[/], the way "The color of the smell D-flat" has only a meaning[/]. In which case, "to mean[/] a meaning[/]" means[/] a meaning[/], though it refers to nothing. So we're okay, at least on that one, which is certainly the hardest. To mean[/] a reference is what, I assume, one is doing when one uses a metaphor that has a literal meaning[/], which, only through understanding it, indicates a metaphorical referent, so that what it was doing was meaning[/], even though reference enters into it at the other end, so to speak.

Yet the most interesting one, to my mind, rather than all these problematic cases, is the one we've called: "referring to reference." The reason why it is interesting is that the only way to refer to a particular reference (a particular process of referring), rather than to refer to a particular referent (a particular thing referred to), is if the total complex statement is a-referential, that is, if the total complex is restricted to meaning[/].

Let's go back to our a-referential "George." Suppose, strictly by language, we want to refer to a specific referential potential "George" might demonstrate. We don't just turn to someone named George and say, "George is sitting in the chair there." Some way or other, either by statement or by implication, we must say:

"Consider the situation in which one says, 'George is sitting in the chair there.'" Only now are we referring to (one of) the word's reference(s). In short, to refer to its reference ability/potential, we cannot just use the statement referentially; we must tell a story about its referring. Since the *considered* situation is not the *real* situation (even if a real situation inspired it), and the statement, thus framed, is no longer a statement referring to anything (even if what inspired it was the fact that, in the room you are lecturing about all this, there really is someone named George sitting in the chair there), apparently the only way to refer to reference is to create a non-referential complex statement—which is, of course, what fictions do.

Pretty much the same argument goes for referring to meaning[/]. I can mean[/] something—a unicorn, say. But to refer to that meaning, I must imbed/express the a-referential term or terms in language, specifically a language frame that states or implies, "consider the meaning[/]," such as this letter—or a story. Once again, to refer to meaning[/] or reference I must enclose that meaning[/] or reference in an explicit or implied a-referential language frame.

In short, to refer to either reference or meaning[/] while staying solely within the bounds of language, one must use a meaningful[/] complex of statements, and one cannot become mired in a referential complex. (When you become so mired, you are only referring to the world; you are not referring to meanings[/] or references.) Since meaning[/] and reference make up, together, the ordinary term "meaning," what we are left with then, in ordinary language, is: To refer to meaning, one must avoid reference. Or, in our specially constructed language: To refer to meaning (i.e., meaning[/] and/or reference) is necessarily, itself, an act of meaning[/].

It doesn't matter, for instance, that in the "fable" I began all this with, the lights of Dayton, the broken glass of milk, the styrofoam cup, the seat in the Penn Central waiting room (where I drafted the fable this afternoon in my notebook), the black man, the bag lady, the white woman, the theoretical letter (sent to an acquaintance this morning about something in an Ashbery poem), Neret Oppenheim, or pretty much everything else that wasn't overtly surreal by syntax happens to be, as a matter of fact, as "referential" as the "teacup" of the title (which refers to your use of a word/idea mentioned by Atwood). Until this addition to the story, however, to you they (or most of them) were only meanings[/]. And even *with* this addition, their fabular reference *in* the fable (to the extent the fable recognizably refers to the problem of reference in fiction) hasn't changed. But the point of all this is simply that there's no way to refer even to their worldly referentiality without adding another frame, i.e., this one. You see, I can only refer to that particular aspect of their reference by telling you yet another story— this story *about* their reference. And, of course, if we *stay* within the bounds of language, you have no way to confirm the truth of this part of the story for sure— without your own referral to things outside the text, like your appraisal of my character from our brief meeting, etc. And even to refer to that referral, you see I have to tell you this further little story, here, about it.

For me, this necessary structure of reference takes care of the realists who want their teacups to refer to teacups. The point is: In order to refer to any kind of meaning (referential or meaningful[/]) the word "teacup" may have, if they want to do it using only language, they are stuck with doing it via acts of meaning[/].

Not acts of reference.

And they are constrained to it in the same way that I am constrained to refer to their references by telling the above fictions about them, George, expanding, fragmenting, and multiplying teacups, and about language.

If you believe teacups on a table are meaningful, you cannot just mention that "Teacups are on the table" in a room where a table happens to be set for tea. You have to say: "Consider the situation in which there are teacups on the table." Even if you have the teacups on hand as an aid, you still have to say it in a tone of voice that implies, consider it as situation: "Consider, my friends, the teacups sitting just over there." And that framing, of course, is what fiction does. And *that*, as we have seen, is to render the statement meaningful[/] and to divorce it from direct referentiality.

So, as the fable says: Not to worry about realists. Like the expanding, contracting, and fragmenting teacup (which, one assumes, frustrates their realistic referential pretensions), they, too — when it comes to any understanding of how language works — are just not very realistic.

All best wishes,

• 8 •

To Thomas Zummer

October 30th, 1983

Dear Tom,

Many thanks for the xerox of the Foucault interview.

Can't think how our lunch got bollixed up. I was here the whole morning of the 16th with a spread of Zabar's best smoked salmon and a bottle of champagne —and, if I recall, fresh strawberries and various other nosherie. Besides going out to the store some time in the morning to get it, I was in all day — till at least four o'clock. The only thing I can think of is that, somehow, I managed to give you an improper phone number. If that's what I did, once more my dyslexia has turned to plague me!

In any case, my apologies for any inconvenience I may have caused you! And there certainly were no hard feelings here. At the time, I just assumed you hadn't gotten back from San Francisco yet and that you hadn't been able to get in touch.

I've only read the Foucault piece, which you just sent me, cursorily, but it intrigues me to note that he is beginning to sound more and more like the Ancient Writers he's been studying. This piece, for example, could be a bit of medieval scholasticism itself!

Has Paul Rabinow become Foucault's agent? A young friend of mine (well, not so young: he's 25, but I've known him since he was sixteen), Robert Morales, who writes for the *Village Voice* and, nevertheless, is a very smart young man (at one time he was a student at Clarion) called Rabinow in California (as per instructions from Atheneum) in order to arrange an interview with Foucualt for (yes, it's a little odd, I know) *Omni*, and Rabinow had the temerity to ask over the phone, "Well, how much do you intend to pay him?" and apparently declined even to suggest a place to write M. Foucault until this information was forthcoming.

Given the fact that, short of celebrity interviews in *Playboy*, most people are not paid for such pieces, unless Rabinow has taken over as Foucault's business manager, that really should be between Foucault and *Omni* anyway. In Robert's words it sounded both unprofessional and pushy. But perhaps I'm just telling tales out of school about folks whom you like—and whom I, after all, have never met.

In which case, rack it up to a novelist's sense of gossip.

At any rate, I look forward to seeing you around Christmas. Once again, many thanks for the material.

Oh, yes. One other question: What in the world is the current publication status of *L'Usage des plaisirs, Les Avoux de chair,* and *Le Souci de soi*—both in France and as far as any English translation is concerned? If you get a chance, drop me a postcard with at least the answer to that one...?

With great gratitude, I send you,

All best wishes,

1984

• 9 •

To Robert S. Bravard

January 20th, 1984

Dear Bob,

By my own estimates, I haven't written you a real letter since I saw you at Bucknell, back on October 8th, '83!

Just received yours of Jan 17th yesterday.

Am awash in guilt and chagrin!

First off, however, accept my condolences on your mother-in-law's death. Mrs. Buttolph's name appeared from time to time in various of your letters, and so I felt I had something of a picture of her. Please convey my sympathies to Cynthia.

The death of relatives — even when it's an expected death — is a taxing time. And the living can react rather oddly, accepting it or not accepting it according to their wants and abilities—which the rest of us then have to deal with on top of the realities of grief. It sounds like you had more than your share with R——. What does one say?

I'm glad you both got a chance to see Tom.[1] I only wish that it had been under more cheerful circumstances.

And I'm glad things are moving back to normal.

I'm debating whether to try to give you the intervening *histoire de ma vie* in terms of what's most important coming first—or what's earliest chronologically.

To start with, when I returned from Bucknell, there was a note from Mr. Greenberg of the IRS waiting for me, stuck in the mailbox door. And to condense the next very fraught two weeks: At the end of fifteen or so days, a lien was put on my personal account! Chip Writings, Inc., was stripped of all its very meager moneys, and Frank and I, once again, found ourselves facing November, December, and the New Year without, for all practical purposes, a penny.

This, you'll recall, makes the third year in a row that some catastrophe or the other has landed just about this time to blight the coldest stretch of the year.

After many consultations with each other, my accountant, Henry, *et alia*, my part of the job of survival was assessed to be: Write your ass off.

So on January 15th I finished "The Tale of Fog and Granite," which weighs in at about 50,000 words, making it short-novel length. I'm taking this day off (a week after the fact, Iva is having a birthday party today: I.e., three of her friends are over for a slumber party, two of whom, along with Iva, are more or less amusing each other in the living room right now) to write a letter or two; tomorrow I launch into two more short Nevèrÿon stories, which will bring the series to a close for a while and which will round out the final volume of a trilogy, *Flight from Nevèrÿon.*

Well, that has somewhat jumped the chronological gun. So let me fill in the between times.

By the bye, I have the ending to my "Jack the Ripper" account for you. Around the end of October, while walking up 8th Ave., I ran into Jeff of the missing teeth. He was wearing a new set of clothes, including a new "leather" (most probably plastic) jacket, and clearly feeling very chipper. He grinned and greeted me hap-

---

[1] Bravard's son.

pily. Obviously, at least for a couple of days, things had been going well for him. "Did they ever catch that guy who was going around killing people?" I asked.

"Oh, yeah. Caught him two weeks ago." In the midst of his good humor, however, my question seemed to bother him.

"Tell me about it," I urged.

"He killed five people," Jeff said. "And they caught him. That's all."

"I thought you said he killed nine . . . ?"

"Naw, somebody else killed the other four," and he quickly changed the subject again. In short, there are still homicidal nuts loose on the street—and the street people, in all their powerlessness, really would rather just not think about it.

In the last six weeks, I haven't seen Jeff at all. I suspect he's no longer in New York.

One of the things I did shortly after the IRS landed was something I've wanted to do for years. And suddenly, under the pressure of catastrophe, I realized that, since there would never be any "time" to do it, I might as well do it anyway.

I joined the staff of *The Little Magazine*, the poetry magazine David Hartwell has been editing for the last eighteen years. David has repeatedly invited me to become an editor. For about a year Marilyn was on the staff, which pretty much kept me away. But there was another opening, so—every Thursday night, since about mid-October, I have been busy at editorial staff meetings on the 46th Floor of Manhattan Plaza, at 43rd and 9th Ave., where the magazine has been having its meetings of late, at the apartment of my fellow editor, Dennis Cooney. There are six people currently on the staff and one, Ginger Buchanan, is just out of the hospital. She's the wife of SF editor John Douglas, who used to be David's assistant at Pocket Books.

The editorial meetings, from 6:30 to midnight on Thursday evenings, usually start with a session of paperwork, filing, mailing, and what-have-you, followed by reading of submissions and, after a couple of hours of silent absorption, some discussion during which the six of us consume about $12 on the average of cheese, crackers, cold-cuts, soda, and coffee.

So that when I finally slog home over chill 43rd St. to the bus or subway, usually with Joel (another editor, she) or David, I go home tired—but feeling like a civilized human being.

Somewhere in the midst of all this, the page proofs for *Starboard Wine* finally showed up. The mistakes are minuscule; and the volume is actually being printed, now even now, out in Ann Arbor. Copies are to be shipped east on February 28th. At last night's meeting, David had "silverprints" of the first signature that the printers had sent him.

So the book is a breath away from becoming real. I made Xeroxes of the page-proofs, and on the 25th, when Henry M. returns from St. Thomas, all three of my non-fiction critical books go to Vintage, where they're to be considered for Vintage Paperback Reprints: That's *The Jewel-Hinged Jaw: Notes on the Language of Science Fiction, The American Shore: Meditations on a Tale of Science Fiction, "Angouleme," by Thomas M. Disch*, and *Starboard Wine: More Notes on the Language of Science Fiction*.

The other thing I've been doing, for much the same reasons as I took on the *Little Magazine* job, is recording Howard Wise's reminiscences. Howard Wise is, of course, Barbara Wise's husband. (Barbara produced my 1971 film, *The Orchid*.) Howard is 82, and has (thankfully dormant right through here) prostate cancer. So Wednesday mornings I go down and record him. So far we've only had two sessions, but it's fascinating.

December and January have been particularly hectic. Iva was ostensibly to spend this Christmas with Marilyn — indeed, it was Marilyn's idea, which she had insisted on sometime back in the summer. So Frank and I decided not to get a tree this year and to let M. do Christmas for Iva.

We decided, however, to have Iva for a day about a week before Christmas, for a kind of pre-mini-Christmas. But, of course, as it drew closer and closer, we schemed and planned and scrimped and saved and borrowed to make it — well, you know: just a little nicer. And, indeed, a rather nice mini-Christmas it was. True, there was no tree — but we more than made up for it with tinsel and lights and Christmas bulbs and decorations hung around every door frame and over every wall — really, I don't think the house has ever looked as Christmassy!

Then, three days before Christmas proper, we found out, rather indirectly, that Marilyn, for odd and incomprehensible reasons, had decided to send Iva to my mother's for Christmas day! This, of course, when all is said and done, meant real Christmas for Iva fell on Frank and me again. So now we found ourselves having the prepare a second Christmas! Was there a bit of ire? Yes. But we did it, and I think it worked out well. And whatever was going through M.'s head, we just decided not to question.

For what I assumed was going to be a quiet New Year's Eve with Frank, I bought a bottle of champagne and we settled in to feeling smug about all the places we weren't going that night, talking between ourselves and feeling rather good. An old friend of Frank's, Francy, and her New Boy Friend, dropped by: He was a photographer, and they were going down to photograph the hordes at Times Square. They left, and we had another glass of champagne. At about eleven o'clock, the doorbell rang, and it was our country-singer friend, Lavada, looking like a million dollars in mink over leather. We must go out — to Larry Goucheman's, who lives a few blocks away and who, indeed, had invited us over.

Well, all right . . .

So we barreled out into the snow, and by twenty-to-twelve had joined Larry's party. At midnight, Larry's TV blared "1984!" (which still feels a little weird to me, though I have now written the date about half a dozen or more times) over pictures of the fallen ball; and fireworks went off, booming, over Central Park. We drank more champagne, and went home.

I went up to my mother's for her traditional New Year's Day dinner: pigs-feet, chitlings, barbecue, black-eyed peas, and rice. And of course egg-nog. Mom's single (I think) superstition that she indulges flagrantly is that no woman can enter her house on New Year's Day until after a man has crossed the threshold, even if it's just the newspaper delivery boy. This was our first New Year's without Grandma, and in the past, of course, it was indulged for her sake. I think this year Mom was indulging it more in memory of Grandma than anything else, but several times, Aunt Eva (who lives up on the 20th floor) and Mrs. Jackson, who lives on the floor below my mother, lending a hand with this or that, had to do it by passing things back and forth over the threshold without actually stepping into the house.

Frank had come to my mother's for Christmas dinner, but the traditional New Year's Eve menu, which I love, simply holds no delight for his upstate New York/Italian palate. So he went out somewhere else.

Getting on the bus up at Broadway that night, I noticed the cardboard sign hanging from the rail in front of the bus-driver reminding us all that on midnight, January 2nd, bus and subway fares would go up from 75 cents to 90 cents. (Which, indeed, they have.) And as I sat in the fluorescent-lit bus, joggling home down upper B'way, I kept looking at the advertising placard on the back of the driver's seat, over which someone had scrawled with a black marker: "WHAT, 1984 ALREADY!"

Shakespeare and Company has done a "1984" display window, featuring Orwell and Orwelliana in the middle, with other SF dystopias ranged around it, including *Dhalgren.*

On the 12th, I took what I thought was the last draft of "Fog and Granite" out of the typewriter, and handed it in. And the next day decided to re-write the last 100 pages. And did over the next two days (only possible with the word processor here); and have handed that in. (On the 15th, as mentioned.)

The 14th of January was actually Iva's birthday. My big girl will never be able to write her age with a single figure anymore. Gar (Garland Hartsoe) came over for that. For various reasons (basically a futile attempt to catch the Icecapades, which were supposed to be at Madison Square Garden by now, but weren't), Iva decided to have her party a week later, i.e., today.

But what all this means is that, without a penny to our names for all practical purposes, Frank and I have had non-stop holiday/birthday since a week before Christmas. And it won't really be over until the kids go home tomorrow afternoon.

Frank and I are both a bit frazzled. Though I must say, the girls have amused themselves very well this afternoon. Frank cleaned and scrubbed and got things ready for the party from one end of the apartment to the other — then quit the premises in terror and despair (I don't blame him), leaving the supervising of the actual event to me; but so far, they have allowed me to write this much of this letter since I ferried them here in a cab after school at 3:30. We're only awaiting Iva's friend Chlöe, who is coming late, before we go out to dinner (what would the penniless do without American Express?) — whoops! She just rang the bell.

* * *

Well, here we are, back from dinner. After playing "Theater" for an hour or so, the girls are in their night gowns. One amusing anecdote from the evening. At Teachers, the girls were given a booth. (Various customers and waitresses who know me commented that I deserved a medal for parent of the year for this enterprise, which is hyperbole, but which nevertheless made me feel good.) The girls got themselves seated and I retired to the bar with my notebook, a vodka gibson, and wrote the opening of the new Nevèrÿon story, "The Mummer's Tale" (that will precede *Plagues and Carnivals*). They behaved admirably, through $28-odd dollars worth of hamburgers, cokes, quiche, et cetera, until finally the waitresses all convened on their table with a piece of cake, sporting a small pink candle, to sing "Happy Birthday." Somewhere in the midst of all this, little Danielle decided she must have chocolate brownies. All the girls concurred.

I had to pick up some dinner for myself anyway.

56

Okay, come with me to the Red Apple Super Market. Now, you wait inside here, kids. And I'll run get the brownies and be right back. Passing by the meat counter, I snag up a piece of steak for my dinner and, holding the plastic-wrapped package in my hand, I go up to a squat, elderly Puerto Rican stock-clerk in a blue smock and a knitted cap and ask him where the brownie mix is. He tells me an aisle number; I go get it.

Looking at the instructions on the back of the brownie mix box, however, I find that it requires half a cup of oil as well as eggs. We don't have any oil at home, and I don't really want to buy it. These kids, I think, will be perfectly happy with chocolate chip cookies. So I put the brownie mix back on the shelf, and take my piece of steak over to the refrigerated pre-packaged sticks of chocolate-chip cookie dough. But, I think, I better tell them what I'm doing. The chocolate chip dough is way in the corner, so I leave the steak in with the chocolate chips, and turn around and start to the front of the store to tell the kids a white lie: "They're out of brownie mix. Will chocolate chip cookies do?"—planning, after their approval, to return and pick up both from where I left them.

Halfway there, the same squat stock clerk suddenly accosts me. "Hey! Hey . . .!" he says.

"Oh, that's all right," I say, thinking he still wants to show me where the brownies are.

His English, beyond grunts, however, is incomprehensible. I'm trying to explain, "No, I don't want the brownies. And I have to go tell my kids something . . ." He's tugging on my arm. I'm kind of drifting with him.

Finally he gets out, "The meat. Where is the meat?" and starts pawing around in my large, down coat, now and again turning to point to one of the store's TV cameras peeking down from the ceiling.

Though I have indeed been rushing around the store at double speed, at no point, you understand, has anything been in my coat pocket, or even under my arm!

But here I notice the 23-year-old security guard, lurking shyly behind him in his black leather cap and nervously fingering his billy-club. And it finally dawns on me that the stock clerk thinks I've taken something! "Aw, come on!" I tell him. "The meat's over there in the cookie dough. I have to go tell my kids I'm not getting them the brownies."

This guy does not speak that much English. I look at the security guard for help. He's just bewildered. And young. Finally, I decide that logic won't do. I take the stock clerk bodily by the arm, as, moments before, he'd taken me, and drag him across the store to the refrigerated dough bin. I point out the meat. "There's the meat," I say. "I put it here so that I could go tell my kids I'm getting them cookies, not brownies. Then I was going to come back and get it." (The guard is still following, somewhat at a distance) Still dragging this stock clerk, who is still going on about the TV cameras ("They see! They see! You put it back. It'll all be okay. Come on. Put it back," half in English, half in Spanish), I then march to the front of the store where Iva and her three friends are chattering away about nothing in particular and trying to pull each other's caps down over each other's eyes.

"They're out of brownies," I say. "How about chocolate chip cookies?"

There is a chorus of, "*Yes!*"

At this point the security guard finally twigs as to what's happening and bursts out laughing. "You see," he says to me, "he's always jumping to conclusions." I go back, get my steak, cookies, and a package of frozen broccoli, go up to the cashier and, after a five-minute wait in line to pay, return to the manager's tower, under which the kids are still chattering—they all immediately want to know what that was about. "I'll tell you in a minute," I explain. I call up to the manager, in his green army jacket: "You know, you have a real nutcase back there!"

"I'm sorry, sir," he says. "The guard just explained what happened. I was just about to come down and apologize to you."

"No hard feelings," I say. "But if the guy can't understand English, you can't have him running around grabbing people in the store."

During the course of it, three or four other customers, more or less realizing what was going on, had been adding their typically New York comments: "Sue 'em. Go ahead, let 'em arrest you. Then sue 'em."

Explaining the details to the clamorously curious kids, we left by the wrong door (at the manager's gracious invitation), out into Broadway's slushy night and snow-banked sidewalks—whereupon, as we were waiting to cross at 82nd Street, Catherine said, "Did you drop this?" bent down, and handed me up a folded $20 bill that someone had dropped in the street!

Thus the patient are rewarded.

After the ice-cream and cake at home (the cake was supposed to be all-chocolate, but turned out to have been misordered: vanilla cake with chocolate filling) the girls put on a show, using the double-doors between the living room and the dining room as a stage, with dad as the light-man. Now they're all in their nightgowns, having settled into a quiet and civilized round of Barbie dolls.

But back to What's Been Happening:

* * *

Let me see: Toward the end of October, Mog Decarnin returned from Denmark and spent a few days in New York, en route to San Francisco, during which we went to the Met and bought standing room for a really tepid production of *Tristan und Isolde*. Good singing. Appalling conducting from James Levine. (You just can't conduct Wagner as if it were Debussy. Though Mr. Levine tried.)

While Mog was here, I went to see an all day showing of Syberberg's *Our Hitler: a film from Germany*, at the Metro (neé the Midtown), up at 100th St. Well, it was long. Seven and a half hours. After five and a half hours of standing through *Tristan*, however, Mog excused herself from sitting through Syberberg. So I didn't see her that day. But I don't really blame her.

It was very similar to his *Parsifal* in many ways. And, naturally, very different in many others. (You may have read Sontag's discussion of the movie in her collection, *Under the Sign of Saturn*—the essay's also contained in the *Sontag Reader*.) It was impressive.

Over the New Year's weekend, the Paula Webster Gallery down in Soho arranged a marathon reading of Gertrude Stein's *The Making of Americans*, as, indeed, they have been doing every year for a decade now. Barbara Wise and I came for the opening of the 24-hour-a-day recitation; then we returned to read for an hour or so with each other toward the end. Other readers included Susan Sontag, Richard Kostelanetz, Virgil Thomson, Charles Ludlum, and John Cage, among some 75 or 80 other volunteers over the three-odd days. . . . We were really among some rather auspicious company.

Oh yes, in the midst of things my computer broke down once and had to go into the shop—just to complicate matters. But it's out now and functioning beautifully. And that really just about brings me up to date on what's been happening.

Oh, yes—

Lunch a couple of days ago with Lou Aronica at Bantam. When I followed Ian Ballantine (of the gnome-like demeanor and prehensile eyebrows) and Fred Pohl into the office and met Lou, Lou was in the midst of writing an irate letter (on his word-processor) to P—— Y——.

Seems that Y—— has gotten into a rather silly project with the irrepressible K—— L——, who, at some con, bombarded Lou with an idea for a book he want-ed to do in collaboration with Y——, and took Lou's polite show of interest ("Yes, I'll look at the proposal.") as an assured sale and represented it as such to Y——.

Upon the subsequent rejection, Y—— had shot off an irate letter, accusing Lou of non-professionalism and threatening SFWA[2] action, etc., etc. Lou was explain-ing back that L—— had simply misrepresented the situation to Y——; that, indeed, L—— has done this several times before with several other editors in the past few months, in the course of which he is making a very bad professional name for him-self; and that the only thing Lou had "promised" to do was look at the proposal—and he had done it—before rejecting it. As I pointed out to Lou, when profession-al writers write letters like that, usually it simply means their lives are going badly. And L—— is just an over-enthusiastic not-so-young-anymore man, who's been trying to make the transition from "fan" to "pro" for years.

We ended up having lunch at the Top of the Sixes, the restaurant on the top floor of the Tishman building that houses Bantam itself: Usually a beautiful view of the roofs of mid-town Manhattan and profoundly ordinary, when not terrible, food—though for that afternoon the snow swirled around the glass picture win-dows, removing us from the city and putting us off in some cloudy dimension-X. Most of our talk was about what awful shape book publishing is in, in general—which, I'm afraid, kind of undercut Lou's constant reassurances that, despite it all, I'm somehow in a good position.

(Tell it to the IRS, I kept thinking, quietly.)

Well, it is now almost ten o'clock, and I have to bulldoze my little harridans into bed shortly.

Myself, I'm exhausted, as I haven't been asleep later than five thirty in the morning for the last two and a half months.

The one other moment of relaxation during the month was when Frank and I stayed up to watch the American Music Awards, where Michael Jackson swept away the field. Since I saw him in that ridiculous movie, *The Wiz*, I've felt he was a truly astonishing performer — kind of a male Barbara Streisand, only maybe more so. And the video of "Thriller" is a stunning homage to all sorts of my favorite people and things, from George Romero to EC comics. I was enchanted by its marvelously tongue-in-cheek ghoulishness.

Long may he sing and dance.

Frank, who was planning to return tonight at about 11:00, when, hopefully, the

---

[2] Science Fiction Writers of America, an organization founded in 1965, under the presidency of Damon Knight.

girls would all be in bed, just called to say he was spending the night at Gar's and will return in the morning. I just put the beds out (mattresses all over the living room floor, the sofa pulled out, sheets, quilts and pillows strewn about and flecked with Barbie clothes). The girls just had a final glass of soda, and it sounds like one of them has the hiccups—though no one has yet run to me to complain . . .

This letter is just to let you know I'm alive and thinking of you—indeed, I have been thinking of you lots and lots! But between the IRS, *Nevèrÿon,* and attendant hassles, I'm afraid I got a little down for a while; and since work only got heavier, correspondence suffered.

All my love to Cynthia, Jonathon, and of course yourself.

All best and better,

• 10 •

To Michael W. Peplow

January 23rd, 1984

Dear Pep,

Hello from ice-bound Manhattan!

Belated seasons greetings, to you and Judy and Davone!

I've been meaning to write you for months. But, as I wrote Bob a day or so back, since October I haven't written anyone. But he'll bring you up to date, I'm sure, on my IRS hassles and what have you.

One of the things I've been meaning to write you about is, of course, your "Delany" paper of last autumn. Usually with you guys, I've found myself in the famous Pascal situation. You remember — "Not having had time to write you a short letter, I'm afraid I have written you a very long one . . ."

But one of the things I hope I've been able to do in the intervening months is to condense into a fairly brief space some of what, indeed, I've been trying to say to you since, at least, my letter to Bob of January 9th, 1980 (q.v.). And whether I make my point or not, this time, I promise: These will be my last words on the topic, and I will then leave you to get on as best you can, without my carping.

Consider, then, a brief parable:

Passing through the student lounge one morning, an English professor overheard an undergraduate from one of his literature classes saying to another: "Joyce Kilmer? Yes, she was that famous American writer who wrote *Ulysses* . . ."

Smiling, the professor called the undergraduate to him and suggested the young man pay a visit to his office later that afternoon. And when the student duly arrived and was seated beside the professor's desk, the kindly gentleman explained to the youth that Kilmer was a man and the writer of a famous poem, "Trees," and that Joyce was the name of an Irish writer who wrote in Europe during the teens and twenties. "Now," said the professor, "if you haven't done last week's paper yet" — which the student assured him he hadn't — "I want you to look up Joyce and Kilmer in the library and write me just the briefest, 150-word paragraph on them. Just slip it in my office mailbox. You may do that instead of the paper."

And a day or two later, the professor found a page in his mailbox that began:

"Joyce Kilmer was an American woman writer who wrote a famous novel, *Ulysses*. For a while she lived in Ireland, where, like George Eliot and George Sand before her, she took a man's pen-name, 'James,' and wrote a poem, 'Trees,' which many people think is even better than her novel . . ."

I'm sure I don't have dwell at too great a length on what's happened here: The student has a model of the situation that is simply wrong. Further, he's tried to fit all the professor's (not to mention the library's) new information into his model as revision and elaboration, without changing his basic model at all. As long as he has that model, he will not be able to write an accurate sentence about either Kilmer or Joyce. And until he throws out that model and substitutes an accurate one—one acknowledging that there are two individual writers, both male, one of whom is a minor American poet and one of whom is a major novelist in English —he will not be able to write an accurate sentence about either. Against this over-all situation, single "mistakes" (such as the notion that "Trees" was written in Ireland) are trivial, and correcting them alone doesn't really improve matters any.

Now you guys are much more sophisticated than our undergraduate. And your model of the publication of *TEI*[1] and the events that lead from it to the publication of *Nova* is more complex (and consequently more tenacious) than his. But it's just as wrong-headed and your attempts to revise it in light of further information produce the same sort of compounded chaos. Until you throw it out and replace it with an accurate one, you'll continue to produce chaos—among which the specific—factual errors (". . . *Nova* was published by Nelson Doubleday . . ." [!]) are quite secondary.

As it stands now, the two paragraphs in your paper *anent* the publication of *Nova* simply refer to nothing in the real world. (You juxtapose a sentence from Terry[2] and a sentence from me as though they express conflicting accounts about a single situation when, actually, they are, both of them, perfectly accurate statements about *two* events eighteen months apart!)

Really, I'm not trying to lambaste your admirable effort. I'm only trying to elucidate a principle which keeps your efforts from coming to very much, at least as far as this particular bit of history is concerned.

The basic model you seemed to have gotten locked into is that of the young, ambitious writer (24-year-old Delany), turning his back on shoddy publishers to seek out more prestigious and better paying markets. Specifically, in terms of events, you have constructed a story that seems to run as follows: "Tensions developing between Delany and Ace over the cover of *TEI* caused Delany to take his next novel, *Nova*, to Doubleday, a more prestigious and better paying publisher, leaving some ire behind him at Ace. . . ."

You have to throw out the whole model. None of it is correct. You can't revise it into the truth. And as long as you take my protests that the Doubleday contract for *Nova* was signed well before I became aware of any problems with the *TEI* cover; or that what tension there was with the cover was between Gaughan (the cover artist) and Ace, not me and Ace, and was, indeed, of the most ordinary and workaday sort; or that there is no economic conflict between a hardcover pub-

---

[1] *The Einstein Intersection,* Ace Books, 1967.
[2] Terry Carr (1937-1987), science fiction editor for Ace Books.

lisher and a paperback reprint house such as Ace to produce "ire" if a writer publishes with both; or that the economic gain from the Doubleday sale was minimal;
or that, finally, in the summer of '68, when Bantam bought the paperback rights
to *Nova* for a record price from Doubleday (and thus aced out Ace), I was as surprised as anybody — as long as you take these facts, or, indeed, any of the facts
from Terry's letter, as revisions of your model, you will go on producing recompounded chaos of the same sort as our befuddled undergraduate above.

What all these "revisions" do, of course, is to define an entirely different situation from the one you have assumed—a situation wholly incommensurate with
yours. You can't adjust your model; you have to replace it.

I suggest that the situation was more complicated than you see it, yes; but more
to the point, it was simply other. In place of your ambitious young writer trying to
direct a career, you must think of me as a very young man (24), living a chaotic and
highly marginal life (evicted from one apartment [739 East 5th Street] and negotiating a precarious relation back and forth between my gay lover on St. Marks Place
and my somewhat estranged wife [embroiled in her own, equally complex affairs],
first on Henry Street and then on 11th Street), a young man who wasn't even sure
if he would continue writing SF or would become a professional pop musician, a
young man whose ambition seldom went beyond what he was putting on the
page in front of him. (In such a life situation, who would have time to "direct" a
career?! Had you spent any 24-hour period with me back then, going with me to
our intense six-hour music rehearsals [this was before the Heavenly Breakfast
commune], stopping with me at some coffee shop to write in my notebook for an
hour or two, now typing in the evening at St. Marks Place, or carousing at the Old
Reliable bar for an evening, or listening for hours to Marilyn detail her hassles
with the St. Mark's poets and/or her sometime lover, Link, you'd realize that there
simply was no *time* for the tale you're so anxious to tell to have taken place!) What
was happening as far as my career went is wholly covered by the following:

On the early 1966 publication of *Empire Star* and *Babel-17* while I was still in
Europe, a certain interest began to grow in the SF community of writers and editors, an interest I was more or less oblivious to, at least till the Nebula Award for
Babel-17—though indeed it had been enough to get *The Ballad of Beta-2* nominated
for a Nebula Award (unknown to me at the time) the previous year. In real terms,
that interest was not enough, after my April return, to affect the sale of *TEI* to Ace
in August (?) '66, but after I'd put in a personal appearance at the Worldcon in
Cleveland and, a week later, another at the Milford SF Writers' Conference (where
I wrote "Aye, and Gomorrah . . ." and sold it to Harlan Ellison[3] for his forthcoming *Dangerous Visions* anthology), the interest began to snowball.

Sometime around the end of October '66, I received a call (at St. Marks Place,
I believe) from Doubleday's Larry Ashmead, and with the call an invitation to
come to lunch. Ashmead was an astute and urbane man, who, though he knew
zilch about science fiction (he had never heard of the Hugo Award), at least knew
that SF was selling. A month or so before, he'd managed to convince Doubleday
to up its SF from two books a year to 24 books a year, and he was now out looking for new writers to fill up his expanded list.

---

[3] Harlan Ellison, a west-cost writer of wonderfully imaginative fiction, famous for his personal energy
and often combative opinions.

Are you working on anything? he wanted to know, over martinis and Dover sole.
I mentioned I was working on *Nova*.

I'd like to see some of it, he said.

A week or so later, I brought him in the first three chapters. Three weeks or five weeks later at another lunch, he told me he'd accepted it; and, on February 10th, '67, a couple of weeks after I'd gotten back from a second, rather impulsive, trip to London, contracts were signed.

But here I am waxing anecdotal again, which I promised myself I would not do. In brief, the Doubleday sale of *Nova*, the Nebula Award for *Babel-17* (on March 25th), the sale of *Nova* to Bantam (in the summer of '68), and the Nebulas for "Aye, and Gomorrah . . ." and *TEI* (in April '68) were all fallout from that initial spurt of snow-balling interest and excitement. Neither I nor Henry (!) "directed" a thing. I wrote the books, and people's responses, usually to the previous book, took the next on and me with it to wherever it was we ended up.

As far as the specific events that have occupied so much of our correspondence, here is the account you must substitute for the one you have been using:

In autumn '66, while *TEI* was in production at Ace, I submitted the opening of my new novel, *Nova*, to Doubleday, who contracted for it in February '67.

Completely unconnected with this in any causal manner: In March of '67, at the Nebula Awards banquet, I became aware of some tension between Gaughan and Ace Books over the cover-painting of my new book, *TEI*, copies of which had just appeared that day. As it was my book, I was an interested party, yes. But that's all.

Again, without any causal connection with either of the above incidents, in the summer of '68, after Doubleday had published the hardcover edition of *Nova* and everyone — Henry, myself, and probably Don and Terry at Ace — was expecting Ace Books to purchase the paperback rights and reprint it, and thus continue as my paperback publisher, a much larger paperback house, heretofore all but uninterested in science fiction (outside of Ray Bradbury and Walter Miller), Bantam Books, astonished everyone by arriving out of a clear blue sky to offer a record price to Doubleday for *Nova's* paperback rights, thus "acing out" Ace Books, who, on hearing of Bantam's bid, did not even make a counter-bid, as they were financially unprepared to out-bid them.

If you take the above account as your basic model and firmly banish the first from your mind, then, when you reread my various letters on the subject, when you look over Terry's letter, details will fall into place and things will become clearer and clearer.

If, however, you stay with the first model, trying to fit the facts, dates, and details that, here and there, research turns up to that model, you will slide into more (and more preposterous) misconceptions about the period, about science fiction, and about my very modest place in it.

I don't mean to sound like Wagner in *Mein Leben*,[4] denying his part in some scandal about which a later Newman will discover him to have been a debtor of many thousands on thousands of Thalers. Nevertheless, it was only that growing

---

[4] *Mein Leben*, the autobiography of Richard Wagner, was begun in 1865. A private edition was published in an unspecified year during his lifetime, but was recalled by Wagner's wife, Cosima. The first edition in German was published in 1911.

interest which made me a good person for Terry, Jack, or others to cite as they looked about for examples to bolster their own positions, as in the initial Carr quote that has occasioned so many pages of explication, or in the situation with the *TEI* cover. Situations occurred. I had feelings about them, and about how science fiction should and should not be published (I still do, and they haven't changed much). I expressed those opinions to Terry, to Jack, and to others. They agreed with me about some of them. They disagreed with me about others. But because I was becoming something of a name, these opinions were sometimes quoted—and sometimes, even, misquoted. All I'm saying is that while these feelings may well have been reasons for me to be sad or happy or annoyed about various things that happened to me along the way, they were not causes for any of those things as you read them in the progress of my doings during those days— at least outside of what I put on the pages of my SF novels and stories.

May I suggest that if you have further need of confirmation, you send this letter to Terry and ask him for comment. If he takes exception to anything I've said here, then you can honestly write that Terry and I have different interpretations or memories of the events and happenings in which we were both involved. And, no doubt, I will find those differences as illuminating as you will. But till that happens, I haven't seen any contradictions between Terry's and my accounts of things so far, where you apparently have. And, I submit, the contradictions you see are only because you are using new facts to recomplicate errors that originate in an already faulty model.

Needless to say, the above only applies to the two paragraphs in the paper in which you detail the publication of *Nova*. The rest of the paper's points, *anent* the misspellings of my name, etc., are very well taken. And perhaps it is only my bias that makes me see those two paragraphs as the center of what you have to say.

As concise as I am trying to be, this may still be an overlong exegesis — for which, sincerely, I apologize.

And now, I promise you, I leave the subject forever. You may write anything you wish in the future, and I will protest it no more.

Well, it seems I haven't been as brief as all that. My "Formatter" tells me I've run on already to ten pages. But it's not 40. So you have something to be thankful for.

Something I didn't write Bob about was a distressing mix-up back in October *anent* the copy-editing of *Stars/Sand*. Basically, it was done so badly that, after struggling over it for a couple of days, I called up Lou Aronica, read him a handful of examples from the first half dozen pages, whereupon, in a most gentlemanly fashion, he volunteered to take the MS back and have it redone. (When I say it was bad, I really mean bad!) As I told him, if I were 20 I would have bulled through the whole thing, but I am now 41, going on 42: In the state it was in, checking it over would be a good two/three weeks' work (for a job that, had it been done properly, should have only taken me a couple of days); and I was in the middle of another writing project anyway—for Bantam!

I'm still waiting for the re-copy-edited MS promised by mid-January, to arrive for checking.

Ah, Pep; this was to be brief — and, indeed you'll admit, I'm sure, that it's briefer than some . . .

Mark Gawron just turned up in New York from Edinburgh, where, after getting his doctorate in linguistics from Berkeley, he's been working on Artificial Intelligence.

He came over about 10:45, I fixed him some brunch, and we had pleasant conversation, croissants, and wine until he had to take off around 1:00 to go, of all places, to a State Senate Investigation on the status of high school drop-outs. What this has to do with either linguistics or artificial intelligence, I'm not quite sure. . . .

He's staying with his girlfriend, Jenny Walter, in Brooklyn—she turns out to be the niece of an old elementary school-friend of mine from Dalton, Wendy Osserman, with whom I was passionately in love with from about the ages of six to seven-and-a-half. She's Wendy's older sister's daughter—a very odd situation it is too, to find such a person the live-in girlfriend of someone you consider practically a contemporary, the way I do Mark!

Oh, by-the-bye: Seth McEvoy's book will be out from Ungar in mid-February. I'll see that you guys get a (couple of) copy(s).

All my best wishes to you and Judy.

Love and stuff,

• 11 •

To Robert S. Bravard

March 5ᵗʰ, 1984

Dear Bob,

You're probably wondering whether I'm alive or dead. I'm alive. And working pretty non-stop—more or less ten to fifteen hours a day.

On January 15ᵗʰ, I finished "The Tale of Fog and Granite" at 48,000 words. A month later, I finished "The Mummer's Tale," at c. 17,000. I'm now well beyond the halfway point on another novella, *The Tale of Plagues and Carnivals*, which I project at c. 30,000. I have about 80 pages written, about 50 of which I am truly satisfied with at this point.

The first two of those have already been submitted to Bantam. The three will complete the third and final volume of the Nevèrÿon series, *Flight from Nevèrÿon*.

I don't know how much of this I've told you before. Really I'm rather punchy over it all at this point. Between last October and now, "Fog and Granite," for example, went through eleven drafts! And "The Mummer's Tale" went through at least six or seven. Even with a word processor, that's a lot!

I have a carton full of drafts that—if you're interested—I'll send to the Mugar in Boston via you folks down there.

The money situation has been truly surreal. One of the reasons I haven't sent you guys copies of F&G and MT is simply that I haven't been able to afford the Xerox copies, and it takes about five-and-a-half to six-and-a-half hours to print up a copy on my single-sheet, hand-fed printer.

And it's been so long since I've seen six-and-a-half free hours in a row, I doubt I'd recognize them if they came along!

I hope my last letter to Mike wasn't too rough. I intended it to be *un peu amusant*, but it was written in the midst of all sorts of *Sturm und Drang*, and I might have gone a bit over the mark. I know he's busy and that you both have worked terribly hard at all this. But I couldn't see how else at the time to cover what strikes me as a fundamental problem. But, as I said in it, I am going to drop any more detailed attempts to correct things *anent* that particular period/situation, because you (plural) really do have all the information to correct it several times over by now. In *P&C*[1] there're a couple of (light, light!) suggestions of the same sort of thing that I hope will make you smile.

February was a pretty rough month all around—the only thing that made it bearable was the fact that the weather was astonishingly mild for what is traditionally the bitterest month in New York.

Inscribe my briefest accounts of the following on a field of No Money at All (and the general scufflings and hand-to-mouth strategies such a condition puts on general survival matters) and you'll have some notion of what Life in These Here Climes has been like of late.

Enclosed is a newspaper article that began the month for us: I think I've told you, since October I've been giving my Thursday evenings to *The Little Magazine*. We meet on the 46th floor of the building in Manhattan Plaza where the murder recounted in the article occurred, a handful of floors below. The only thing that the building gossip added that isn't in the article is that both Ms. Jones and her murderer were deeply involved with Amway—you may have seen the exposé of that particular scam on *60 Minutes* some months back . . .?

M. has been talking for some time rather vaguely about taking Iva to France for a school year, and I have been talking rather explicitly about not liking the idea at all. But this month it came up as a Thing to Be Finally Decided. Iva is ten. She's already changed schools once. She has some troubles getting along with her mother—nothing terribly serious—which she doesn't have with Frank and me, and when it was brought up with Iva, her rather straight forward, ten-year-old response to the notion of going off was:

"You mean live with my mother for nine months? No way!"

M. has received a $15,000 dollar Ingram Merril followship for next year; a Parisian professor who is coming to this country to teach in New York has volunteered to swap apartments with her; and M. loves France. I can understand the urge and ease with which it might be done. But she says she won't go without Iva—she would miss Iva too much. And, in a word, that's exactly the way Frank and I feel. Ten strikes me simply as too young for that kind of separation from a primary parent who takes care of her 50% of the time—not to mention for a primary parent.

At any rate, we had a two-and-a-half-hour discussion between M., Frank, and myself over the whole matter. M. has found what sounds like a very good bilingual school for Iva in Paris and is anxious to send Iva back to us for vacations. Indeed, as everyone has tried to explain to her, it's not the quality of her plans that's in question. We just don't want Iva to go; and in a joint custody situation, this kind of veto power must be respected, however unpleasant or inconvenient. It went fairly calmly as such things go, and Frank and I both thought by the end of it that it had been decided and understood. But a week later M. called up wanting to know if we could all meet with a therapist (a woman psychiatrist who does family counseling), who would presumably tell me and Frank that it was okay for

---

[1] *The Tales of Plagues and Carnivals*, which ended up at more than 60,000 words (i.e., novel length), in *Flight from Nevèrÿon* (Bantam, 1985).

suck your dick.' I said, 'Fuck, yeah!' And his partner, right next to us, arrests me."
Another case of entrapment. "I wished the fuck he'd sucked on it!" Jeff laughed.
"I can't get a hard-on no more anyway, you know? I even come soft—when I can
come at all. It's the fuckin' dope, man. Anyway, I thought: Imagine this fuckin'
cop's gonna suck on a soft dick for 20 bucks? He really should have. Served him
right!" He scratched his head as we walked up the sweltering sidewalk. (This was
while I was taking him to a Chinese dinner, after I'd run into him on the street
when I was between Empiricon and Forbidden Planet Con. Just as he was coming
up to say hello, some kids from the Con came up to ask me for my autograph. Jeff,
after they went: "Hey, you really are famous, huh? Mike Elkins, he told me you
were famous. But I didn't believe him. But I guess you are. At least a little?" He
laughed again.) "I knew he wasn't no cocksucker when he asked me, you know?
I knew it. He didn't look like no cocksucker. Shit! He looked like a fuckin' *cop* is
what he *looked* like!" But, since recounting that story (over which he spent a month
in jail), he's gone back to his "ain't been arrested since I was thirteen" line on several occasions. He deserves it back: which is my appraisal of victimless crimes.

One of the most pathetic images I retain from our year-and-a-half friendship:

In just a pair of dark blue dress slacks, worn for a week of sleeping in the park
(a beige t-shirt with iridescent and metallic letters across the front proclaiming,
"How can you be Humble when you're as Great as I am?" stripped off his bare
chest now hung from the back corner), Jeff sat in a red, wooden kitchen chair.
With toes reddened from a summer of ill-fitting shoes given him by somebody,
his small feet, peppered with needle marks, were bare on the maroon linoleum.
Earlier that day, sick on some park bench, he'd shit in the pants, but, being the
only ones he had, he still wore them. He rolled up one pants leg to the thigh, bent
way over, so that his brass-colored hair, a little matted, fell forward in dull hanks;
and I watched him stick what looked like a child's tiny toy hypodermic from a
Let's Play Doctor Kit again and again into his knee cap, his shin, his thigh, trying
to find a hit, where black red blood would gush into the already pale pink solute
at the hypodermic's bottom, indicating a functioning vein. Blood drooled his
arms in half a dozen places from more than half a dozen attempts in the few minutes before, now in his forearm, now between his knuckles, now on the inside of
his biceps, three or four obliquely-angled stabs apiece, with a little joggling of the
needle to try and break into his body's more and more well-guarded circulatory
system. One dribble over his elbow was thick and long as an earthworm; the others strung like yarn down his forearms, over his wrists and infection-swollen
hand. (Among the beer bottle caps and folded bits of wax paper on the kitchen
table were two crumpled yellow paper towels, blotched with blood from where
he'd already twice wiped away the red drool from his mutilations.) Now, here
and there, more blood ran down his leg. He went on prodding his pale inner
thigh with his thick thumb, then sliding the inch-long needle in to its hilt, out, and
in again, lifting white tents of skin.

But most of his accessible veins have collapsed.

From under his hair, strained with the bent position, he mutters: "Damned if
I'm gonna blow this hit...!" Blowing a hit means inadvertently injecting the drug
under the skin, so that it simply blows up into a dime-sized bubble of liquid,
which is absorbed into the body too slowly for the user to feel any effects.

Later, he stood up, wiping his arms off with another towel, his pant leg still up over his thigh. "I look like a fuckin' dartboard, don't I?" Forehead sweating with the first rush, he grinned — long under-teeth and naked upper gum. "I'm in the hospital a couple of months ago, and they're trying to do a blood test. And I tell 'em, please, please! Lemme do it! Please! You gonna be pokin' around in my arm for an hour and you ain't gonna get no blood."

What does Jeff look like?

Standing together against the wall of McHale's next to la Fiesta, we were talking together, when a heavy black woman came past with her six- or seven-year-old daughter, rough pigtails beribboned all over her head. The little girl pointed at Jeff and looked at her mother: "Momma, that's Jesus Christ . . .?"

Jeff turned to me and gave me a big, distorted and disgusted grin. "Man, that happens to me a *lot!* They all think Jesus Christ looked like some fuckin' toothless junky!" (Later he volunteered to put a roof on a small church nearby, that paid him in food and a place to sleep. He spent the rest of the year complaining about how much money he could have made if he'd done the work at standard carpenter's wages. "That was a $2,000 roofing job. Two thousand dollars I could've got. But not me, man! Not fuckin' Jesus Christ! I'm a fuckin' asshole!") Another time he told me: "This guy takes me home with him—he's 41. He takes me in the bathroom with him, and we look in the mirror together. 'Look at yourself,' he says. 'You're 30, and you look older than I do. You look 60.' I don't look like no fuckin' 60, do I?"

Jeff was 30 on July 27th. (And *I'm* 41!) Whether he looks older than I do has never really struck me before. But there is certainly an ageless quality to his bony face that just doesn't fix itself to any year at all.

Fragments of a remembered bedtime conversation with Jeff, our faces inches apart in half-dark: "Jeff, how about if I put a dog collar on you and chained you up in my back room? I'd give you 25 bucks a day, let you out for six hours to get your bag—you'd still wear the dog collar, while you were out—and then you'd come back to your room, and I'd chain you up again while you got high. I'd put food in there for you. You could stay as high as you want. I'd leave you a pot to shit and piss in. From time to time, I'll come in and fuck you—bring my friends in and you can suck them off. How would you like that?"

Without any irony, he says: "I'd love it. Maybe you wanna try it for three or four days? You might even get to like it . . .?"

I laugh. "That's what I'm afraid of. Naw, I'm just talking through my hat."

"Yeah, a fantasy," Jeff says, understandingly. "But I'd like to do that. Especially with you, man. I'd probably end up falling in love with you and never wanna leave you."

"Yeah," I say. "I'm afraid of that, too."

We laugh again.

Still, fifteen minutes later, while sweat dripped from my face, my shoulders, ran from my hips onto his, the "fantasy" got me off somewhat to my surprise. That particular kind of S/M power trip is not what usually turns me on.

Later Jeff said, "If you wanna do that thing with the collar and the chains, could I have a TV set in the room with me? Otherwise, I'd get kind of bored."

"Jeff," I said, "really, I was only fantasizing." Still, with that maniac hacking his way through Jeff's summer nights, and the police sweeping up the Avenue by day, I can understand why it doesn't seem like such a bad one.

Still later, we compared pocket photos of our daughters. Jeff has an eleven-year-old daughter in Boston, born when he was nineteen. (Twice since I've known him, he's actually gotten it together enough to go up to Boston and visit her.) Iva and Cindy (?), with their blonde hair and round faces, look uncannily like sisters. Cindy has a birthday, he tells me, on September 29th.

Interestingly, none of this has made its way into *Nevèrÿon* — the collars and chains, I mean. (Perhaps *Nevèrÿon* is where they came from . . .?) Well, I'll save it for *Plagues and Carnivals.* Ah, the self-critical construct . . .

The thing I've noticed about hustling, starting with my couple of dozen experiences doing it in the vicinity of the Folsom period, which jibes pretty well with what I've noticed from what's only, when all is said and done, less than a couple of dozen times on the purchasing end: As a profession it appeals basically to an extremely lazy personality. The percentage of fundamentally pleasant, goodhearted people you run into as a hustler is certainly not substantially lower than in any other profession. The only thing is: A successful hustler has to spend 60–80% of his (or her — this much I know is identical for women) time doing nothing. And an unsuccessful hustler (among whom, finally, I'd have to class Jeff), spends 95% percent of his or her time at it — nothing, that is. As an 18-to-23-year-old, I certainly felt being a hustler was equally as romantic as being an artist. If it hadn't been so overwhelmingly boring, thanks to the time one must spend waiting for something to happen, I probably would have done a lot more of it than I did.

Another Bobby is a 55-year-old john, balding and with pale framed glasses, whom I've talked to at la Fiesta from time to time. He was one of Mike Elkin's steady customers. Last summer, I recall, he got into some ridiculous, drunken, and ugly argument with Jeff at one point, where I was pretty sure Bobby was in the wrong and Jeff was in the right. Last night, I dropped into la Fiesta. Bobby, surprise of surprises, was working as a substitute bartender for the evening. Jeff was at the bar, sick and/or half asleep, as though whatever differences Bobby and he had had the summer before were long since resolved. Bobby, behind the bar tonight, sounded positively avuncular towards Jeff, half dozing with his head down on the counter on the customer's side. There was practically no one there and, while I had a beer beside Jeff, the few that were left emptied out, and Bobby came over to ponder with me what a bartender has to do in a gay bar to keep the place full. One can't help thinking: Besides the obvious (letting the working men hang out without buying *too* many drinks on their own), I suspect the answer is to be 25 rather than 55. Or know a lot of johns.

Finally Jeff woke up, saw me, and said, "An angel! Hey, an angel's come to say hello to me." He gave me a hug and told me about the five new hacking victims that I mentioned above. Also told me some story about Bobby Russo, who, according to Jeff, has now become a rip-off artist and should be avoided. He and Jeff are no longer partners. I note that Bobby behind the bar says no word to confirm this. And all it takes is a suggestion of such a complaint from one of the johns, and the hustler is eighty-sixed from the bar for a month. More than one such complaint and it's permanent. (That's why John Mueller was always afraid to go into the Fiesta and would hang out instead on the corner in front of

McHale's.) Then Jeff had to run off for a while to "take care of business," leaving a white and black–checkered wool hunting shirt over the counter. Bobby Russo came in only minutes later, and we had a beer together. (I'd seen him on the street earlier with an older man in glasses and a pale beige suit, and Russo'd waved: "You lookin' for Jeff. . .?") And we made those noises that everybody knows, in such situations, are just noises, about maybe getting together some other time. Russo, who seems a lot more together than Jeff, despite Jeff's stories, strikes me as pretty much his old self, and I suspect some of Jeff's warnings may just be inter-hustler paranoia—if not jealousy. "I bring him johns, man," Russo tells me. "He tells 'em to get lost 'cause he can't get it up no more. They know that before I bring 'em. That's not what they're into. I'm tryin' to get Jeff to stay with me. I got this place for $40 a week. It's got an icebox, a hot plate where you can cook. Look at 'im, he needs food. But he don't get any, most of the time. I hope he don't get that AIDS shit!"

Earlier, Jeff told me another story of a street hustler who suddenly started losing weight. Everyone thought it was AIDS. The man finally went to the hospital emergency room. Turned out to be lung cancer. "But do you think they'd take him into the hospital? No, they gave him some medicine and told him, 'Go die someplace else.' You see, if you walk into the hospital and you ain't got no money, they won't take you in. If you need a bed or something, you gotta come in with an ambulance. So we all got together and called the ambulance for him, you know? I mean, the fucker'd lost 70 pounds and could hardly walk. And you know what? Two days later, I saw him again on the street. I say to him, 'What is it, they put you out?' He says, 'Naw, I just didn't wanna be there. They don't want me. I don't want them.' I tell, him, 'Man, you should be in the hospital. I mean, they feed you there. In two days, you already look better than you did.' And he really did. I mean, he was still clean. But he just didn't want that. Hey, why don't you come on down and talk to me sometimes? You don't have to pick me up. Just come down and talk. I ain't hard to find."

But the truth is, half a dozen times now I *have* come down to look for Jeff and talk, and he *is* hard to find. Only 23 and far more energetic, Bobby Russo isn't. Last night Bobby and I talked about Jeff. "I'm worried about him. You see how thin he is? He didn't used to be that thin. And he was sick for about a month. You get sick on the street, and that's hard on you. I wanna be his partner again. We'll go up to Boston together. He wants to go up to Boston and see his family. That'd be good, you know? I wish he'd come stay with me." Talking to Russo, I recalled Jeff's warning. ("You know," Jeff told me, "once he even said we'd should get together and rip *you* off? How you like shit like that? I ain't into that shit." Anything is possible in this world. And though I doubt it, I wasn't doing more than talking last night anyway.) When I first met Russo, he was hanging around Jeff, and I gave him some fried whiting over in the Barking Fish. For a while they were close, but now Jeff isn't interested, and Russo seems to be pushing for it. Maybe I'm romanticizing things, but I think Russo feels something between love for, and identification with, Jeff. After all, Jeff *is* lovable; if he wasn't, he'd be dead. And in seven years, Russo will *be* Jeff. And a half-Puerto Rican Jeff at that. The result in Jeff, however, is the standard one in such cases: Get away from me. I don't want to know about it. The two of them have never had sex together, they both tell me. Russo says he wouldn't mind it. Jeff says he'd be embarrassed. Interestingly enough they share a quality in bed — one that's rare in this world, where most hustlers still lie naked on hotel room beds, like embalmed dreams, with only a hard-on and, at last, a load to signal life at all. They are both astonishingly affectionate men. In Jeff's case, because he can no longer get an erection, I suspect it comes from his definite sense of himself as being of limited sexual use — indeed, not only is he affectionate but energetically so: There must be something more to it than that, but though I have my suspicions (his boyhood lover, perhaps), I can't know. In Russo's case, I don't know at all. He has a certain bantam quality — maybe it's just a youngster's desire to please. (One of the more pathetic images I have of him: Walking up Eighth Avenue once, as I neared the gray, painted-over cement steps beside the comic book store, I saw Jeff and Russo sitting together on the stoop. Neither wore shirts. Russo was in shorts and sneakers. Jeff, his forearms over his knees, gazed up at the hot sky, eyes unmoving. Russo's head was slumped between his wide, jack-knifed legs, his hands on the step's edge, one with the fingers curled down, loosely holding the cement, one with palm up, clawing air. [Russo is a nail-biter, incidentally, unlike Jeff.] As I got nearer, Jeff saw me, smiled and came over. He looked back at Russo. "Ain't that a shame?" He shook his head. "A kid all that fucked up, out in the middle of the street in the daytime." But that was back from when they were "partners.") Married at eighteen somewhere in Brooklyn to a woman a year or two his senior, Russo split with his wife a couple of years back because of his drug involvement. After the first time we made it, he told me: "Look, please! Please, don't tell anybody on the street that I suck dick, huh? That's not part of my street image. You know, I'm out there on 42nd Street, sellin' valiums and pills and shit. The other guys know I hustle. But they don't wanna know about no cocksucker out here, okay?" Once, though, I took him into the Cameo, and although he recognized a few people from the street in the balcony, he shrugged and went down on me with a vengeance anyway. "Do *you* think of yourself as gay?" I once asked him. He shrugged: "I don't think I used to be. But I'll tell you, I ain't been with any women in a long time. And the truth is, I don't miss it." His standard greeting to me is, "Hi, you lookin' for Jeff?" And immediately afterwards, he flips out his upper plate with his tongue, winks at me, grins and says, "You wanna take me to the movies . . . ?"

Now Russo looks at me over his Budweiser that I've bought him. Jeff's wool shirt still lies on the counter beside us. Bartender-Bobby is getting the Puerto Rican porter at the counter end (a tall kid with tattoos from wrists to sleeveless shoulder, who's been winking at me all evening), to get some ice for him. In the orange light, Russo says, "I worry about Jeff . . ."

And I try not to worry about either one of them. The fact is, as a convergence of social needs, both are bottomless. They need: identification (to get into a drug program. Jeff: "Hitler invented methadone, didn't he . . . ?"), clothes, work, food, help for their families, a place to stay, someone to talk to, a dick to suck, someone to hold onto and a $25 bag of dope a day. . . .

Oh, well. But one of the things that's occasioned all this is that the *New York Post* yesterday carried a headline:

ANTI-SEMITIC SNIPER SLAYS ONE–hurts four!

It seems some nut up in Washington Heights has been gunning from a passing car for students coming out of some Yeshiva. To date, he's wounded four — and in an attempt to get another, he missed and killed some Puerto Rican woman driving by in her car! A $10,000 reward for information leading to his capture has just been upped to $15,000. Nuts are nuts and must be stopped. Still, I can't help noting that the maniac this summer we have down in the 40s, who's already killed one, possibly two, women and seven men (which puts him ahead of Jack the Ripper—so maybe he hasn't roasted anyone's kidney yet and eaten part of it . . .), with his "Death to the Street People" note, which makes the murders just as classist in structure as the Yeshiva attempts (but a long time ago, I realized that *all* "gratuitous" murders of both men and women were essentially racist/classist in form), doesn't seem to warrant any headlines. Yes, I know, the headlines encourage other such nuts. But no private individual is going to offer thousands of dollars' reward for someone who's going around into dark doorways to cut out the odd junky's heart. . . .

Perhaps another impetus to record all this sordidness is that this past Saturday's *Times* had a fine front-page article on William Kennedy and his Albany novels. I think I told you, I spent part of a drunken St. Pat's evening with Kennedy at a party when I was teaching up at SUNY-Albany, while he was friendly and signed numerous copies of *Ironweed,* which was still in piles in the B. Daltons' windows of Manhattan. I've only read *Legs.* But his small chapters come at you like handfuls of hard-boiled dime-store jewelry. It's as if, in a way, he's really writing the novels that everybody ascribed to Raymond Chandler. The article in the *Times,* with four fine pictures, basically takes a walk with Kennedy through the ruins of the city, while he reminisces about politics, crime, and history. The writer, Susan Chira, managed to get a sense both of the city and Kennedy in it. I cut it out and rubber-cemented it into the scrap book I made of my three weeks in Albany. Alas, I still haven't written the commentary notes to paste in with the "exhibits."

Earlier in August, I was interviewed by Larry McCaffery and his wife, Sinda Gregory. They had just come back from trying to interview Kennedy, but he'd been too busy, working on the run, on set at the new Coppola film, *The Cotton Club,* which, it turns out, my cousin, Norma Jean *(Spoonbread and Strawberry Wine)* Darden, is also working on as a researcher.

Last thought about your and Pep's article before I sign off. At one point, toward the bottom of your p. 6, you quote "Fictional Architecture" as saying, "Damn Ace Book covers." I defy you to find that line in the text. What you will find is "Damn Ace Books proofreading." The caption to the accompanying illustration (and both illustration and caption are by Gaughan) reads: "Damning an Ace cover." I leave you to make appropriate changes.

At the last minute, I called up and canceled my German trip. I just had too much work to do. I really want to make this Wagner/Artaud lecture something special. And there's just no way to do that over five days while you're listing with jet-lag. And this of course is not counting the proofs of *Starboard Wine* and the copy-editing of *Stars/Sand* to go over. And "Fog and Granite" is within sight of its end, and will be short *(Einstein Intersection)* novel-length. Frank will be unhappy (if not furious), but we were only going to have a couple of days together, anyway.

So we'll just have to miss them. But after last month's jaunt to France and with what remained to do this month, I just couldn't hack it.

Oh, yes, and one final request—if it's possible? If not, I'll fake it. I told you I was trying to put something coherent together from all this epistolary rambling. But I didn't begin it all keeping meticulous copies of everything. (Really, I'm still not.) But do you have:

From a letter dated "Labor Day, 1982," pp. 2 & 3?

And from a letter dated October 9th, 1982, do you have p. 39?

Somehow these pages managed to slip out of my own copies. If I had them, I could finish the mosaic presentation from them that I'm trying to put together about life on Eighth Ave.

Some pleasant times with Iva since she came back from camp, now observing the giant blue whale that leaps beneath the ceiling of the Marine Biology Hall at the Museum of Natural History, now at brunch together at Marvin Gardens, now visiting a street fair down on Columbus Avenue, where she became enamored of a feather boa . . . But she's back at her mother's now. And I'm hard at work. And I plan to be sending you the first 75 pages of "Fog and Granite" in about a week.

See you at my Bucknell lecture!

All my love,

• 4 •

TO JOANNA RUSS

October 17th, 1983

Dear Joanna,

This is not the long-promised letter, rambling easily over K/S,[1] your essays and stories on same, your new books, and a more than interesting volume I would recommend to you, *Powers of Desire: the Politics of Sexuality,* edited by Ann Snitow, Christine Stansell, and Sharon Thompson (New Feminist Library, Monthly Review Press: New York, 1983). Rather it's just the briefest of notes to acknowledge receipt of your Guggenheim "recommendation," which I shall dutifully transcribe and sign when the application arrives, and also your most kind invitation of Sept 8th, reiterated formally on October 15th—for which many thanks.

The long and short of it, alas, runs rather like this: For the last year and a half, my speaking/reading fees have been $1,600 plus expenses (or $2,300 without). The main reason they're set so high is—bluntly—to keep the number of requests down. And, believe it or not, it doesn't work all that well! But it's a price I'm kind of locked into at this point.

I would love to come down and see you, and will happily come and talk to your (and, indeed, any one else's) class(es) for nothing. But for any kind of lecture, I more or less have to ask what I've been asking. Lay it on your committee, and if they look at you like you're nuts, just tell me and I shall come informally and we shall carouse together and solve all the problems of the world just the two of us.

[1] A genre of fan-written pornography, usually authored by women, about Captain Kirk and Mr. Spock from *Star Trek.* In later years, it was referred to as "slash fiction."

Do I feel silly taking that kind of money for a lecture where, due to zero-publicity and badly handled timing, 75 people show up—which has happened on a couple of occasions now? Yes, I do. But then, with proper publicity (generated no doubt because everyone suddenly realizes how much they're paying me and suddenly decides they have to get their money's worth!), I can fill up a 500-seat auditorium with 50 standees crowding in the back—which happens more and more these days. So, as I said, I have to go with it.

At any rate, I shall plan on coming to see you the day after V-con. (I probably have a speaking engagement down in L.A. a day or two later, so I will, as 'twere, be barn-storming the West Coast right about then.) Working very hard on a new Nevèrÿon story ("The Tale of Fog and Granite") which will probably end up short (*TEI*) novel-length. And two more short stories are in the note stage—at which point I think I will be finished once and for all with the Nevèrÿon construct.

I notice, by the by, looking over the typescript of *Stars/Sand*, there are so many typos in the he/she business that I wouldn't be surprised if much of it were simply incomprehensible! The copy-edited version is sitting on my desk right now, waiting for me to re-insert some sense into it. At any rate,

All my love,

• 5 •

To Gerald Jonas

October 29th, 1983

Dear Gerald Jonas,

Night before last I got back from something called The Fiction Festival, a near-annual event (four times in five years now) put on by the University of Cincinnati. My fellow festees this years were Margaret Atwood, Ross Feld, Edward Doctorow and Jayne Ann Phillips. Feld and Atwood were the only ones I actually overlapped *in vivo*. Apparently the administration wants the students to fest for at least two weeks. This means withholding the later guests until the earlier ones go home. At any rate, while my right sinus drained away through it all, I festered and made merry.

Many thanks for the return of the *Michigan Quarterly* (and the copy of the article!). Last night I went to bed early (that sinus . . .) and re-read the Ashbery interview.

You'd asked if some of the things Ashbery was saying in his interview were an example of "what I meant" when we were talking together. But since I didn't remember A's interview very well, and, also, in the course of our own discussion I had "meant" so many things, I wasn't too sure of your question. As soon as I looked at the Michigan piece, however, it all cleared up.

I had said, back when we were talking in my living room, that I believed that, for the last hundred years or so, the so-called literary genres, considered as a set of codes by which we make certain texts called "literary" make sense, may be characterized—the lot of them—as overwhelmingly determined by "the priority of the subject."

Certainly Ashbery's early statements in the interview about the way to understand his poem, "Leaving the Atocha Station"[1] are a textbook example of what I meant:

> That poem was written after my first trip to Spain. The Atocha Station is a railway station in Madrid . . . I was in a strange city going somewhere . . . [I]t strikes me that the dislocated, incoherent fragments of images which make up the movement of the poem are probably like the experience you get from a train pulling out of a station of no particular significance. The dirt, the noises, the sliding away seem to be a movement in the poem. The poem was trying to express that, not for itself but as an epitome of something experienced; I think that is what my poems are about . . . [T]he movement of experience is what I'm trying to get down . . . [M]ost of my poems are about the experience of experience . . . I'm trying to set down a generalized transcript of what's really going on in our minds all day long. First of all, I'm in a strange place with lots of lights whose meaning I don't quite understand, and I'm talking about a poem I wrote years ago and which no longer means very much to me. I have a feeling that everything is slipping away from me as I'm trying to talk about it — a feeling I have most of the time, in fact, and I think I was probably trying to call attention to this same feeling in "Leaving the Atocha Station" and in other poems as well.

I'm certainly willing to accept this as an example of what I mean by poetry's (as a concept, as a literary genre) being largely controlled in the post-modern mind by "the priority of the subject." By the same token if you go through the same passage and pull out the phrases and sentences that, in the above reduction, are represented by ellipses, you get the following:

> My poems aren't usually about experiences, because I don't find my experiences very interesting as a rule . . . When they are about them, they are about them in a very oblique, marginal way. It was really nothing for me to be leaving this particular railway station. It meant nothing to me at the time . . . It doesn't particularly matter about the experience . . . [T]he particular occasion is of lesser interest to me than the way a happening or experience filters through me. I believe this is the way in which it happens with most people . . .

If we agree that "experience" in this text is synonymous with "external situation" (while, in the former, it tends to mean "internal happenings"), I think it's valid to read this as subject-dominated literature's traditional concomitant dismissal of the object. And yet by still the same token, I think we can read the last sentences of the section ("Maybe once it [the subjective state in which everything is seen to be slipping away] is called attention to, we can think about something else, which is what I'd like to do.") as expressing a dissatisfaction with this subject priority and object dismissal. As a marxist (of, alas, the most Champagnoise persuasion), I am pretty sure that different external situations cause experience to "filter through" people in different ways. I'm just as sure of that as I am sure that "the modes of production influence the economic, religious, and social aspects of a social life."

Indeed, I think the last two sentences refer pretty much to the same processes-in-the-world.

But at this point (and I suspect Ashbery would agree that different external situations modulate internal happenings differently), we have (by the literary code) only two alternatives: Art very quickly becomes one with politics and thus should

---

[1] In *The Tennis Court Oath,* by John Ashbery (Wesleyan University Press: Middletown, 1962).

become one version or the other of something resembling socialist realism; or art must become completely divorced from politics and eschew representation even more strongly — which works only up till the time that the next most ingenious critic manages to show that even so, the art text still is managing to reify the status quo: Its turning away from reference is, itself, an allegory of one or another political oppressor's refusing to "see" the effects of oppression. And we're right back where we started.

Today what I see as happening is this: With the above argument taken not as a conclusion, but rather as a kind of circular dialectic, various literary artists simply find themselves stalled at one point or another in the process — or, indeed, sometimes they move on, their current position in the cycle more or less pretty clearly signed by the critical vocabulary they consciously or unconsciously fall into.

My basic feeling is that this itself represents the tyranny of a critical tradition at work. Ashbery is a highly literary fellow, and his is a language very similar to the one Kafka uses in his diaries when he wrote of *The Metamorphosis* that he was trying to "express his inner world" and was "not concerned with reality."

(One would start a formal deconstruction of my argument here with the ambiguity implicit in "experience" [inner/outer], world, and reality.)

For an example of how the same subjective phenomenon that Ashbery claims to be dealing with in his poem might be handled in science fiction, with its paraliterary "priority of the object" organizing the readerly response, you might take a look at *Dhalgren,* i.e., the marginal rubric, p. 806. There are a handful of references to Ashbery's poems scattered throughout *Dhalgren,* the most important of which are probably the references to "The Instruction Manual" and to "These Lacustrine Cities." But the section on p. 806[2] was written in response to the very poem Ashbery is discussing with Poulin — or, more accurately, it was written after I spent some months thinking about the Paul Carroll essay, "If Only He Had Left from the Finland Station," which was the initial occasion for the Ashbery/Poulin discussion.

My early readings of both the Ashbery poem and the Carroll essay are, of course, ten years or more in the past, and I don't have the text of the Carroll essay to hand, but as I recall it, after actually identifying Atocha as a station in Madrid, Carroll asks in his essay if, indeed, the interpretation that Ashbery later gave in this November 1972 interview was the right one. And he is unhappy with the poem because he is not sure if it is. There is not enough evidence in the poem to be certain that this is what the poem is about.

At any rate, the poem and Carroll's discussion inspired the p. 806 section in *Dhalgren,* in the form of one of Kid's own writerly experiments. ("92nd Street" refers to the closed-down subway station on the westside IRT; "St. Croix" is a similarly closed-down station on one of the lines of the Paris Metro. You see them, dark, ruined, graffiti-wracked and impregnable, out the windows of the subway as you speed by.) But in an SF novel, the thrust is not toward the subject — the SF text simply can't stop with (or, indeed, start by) merely reproducing/documenting/critiquing a subjective state (either with or without the objective experience that is one of the factors in generating it) without a frame. In the SF novel, the sub-

---

[2] P. 731 in the 1996 Wesleyan edition.

jective state becomes a framed and delineated object of examination, if only framed by the notion of "SF." The object is, in Kid's own words, "Not thinking but the way thinking feels. Not knowledge but knowledge's form." Or, in Ashbery's words: ". . . the experience of experience."

Ashbery's poem presents its topic wholly as a subject state. What renders this same state an object for critique in *Dhalgren* are many: The particular bit of text is framed at both ends by more "communicative" modes; and, which I think is the most important, in SF things simply are looked at as objects of exploration. Even the fact that it is, in the text, an allusion (I assumed that a few readers would probably realize that, at one point or another, Kid had read the Ashbery poem) helps objectify it. I'd even hazard that there's a crispness, an artifactoriness in the *Dhalgren* text that is not there in the Ashbery poem, which, in *Dhalgren*, contributes to the object quality. But I'm sure you could find a dozen or more rhetorical figures in the text itself that support the interpretation of an object critique. And I suspect it's SF's paraliterary position and its concomitant object tradition that urges you/me/one (?), more than anything, toward this reading.

The problem, of course, is that where, in SF, there is a tradition of reader response, there is no very old tradition of formal critical response. Thus when one brings the rhetoric of literary criticism to SF, it becomes very hard to discuss this aspect of the SF text simply, without sounding simple-minded.

As they say in the fanzines, this letter is DNQ[2] —not for public quotation. I deplore writers quoted in print authenticating their own allusions within authoritative quotes and explaining (away) their intentions—especially ten years after the fact. It spoils the fun for other readers. Still, I feel two people can talk about these things as much as they want and don't stop being human beings just because one or both of them happen to write.

Once again, it was much fun talking with you.

Best of luck,

• 6 •

Breaking the Realist Teacup

—a fable for critics

I took out my post-structuralist elephant gun, gave it a shot, and damned if the delicate blue and white Wedgwood didn't blow up big as an Olympic-sized pool. So, turning to look out the window of the airplane smoothing me back from Cincinnati to New York, I scooped up the night-lights of Dayton, down like a doily on the dark, and stuffed that big cup full. "There," I said, "that ought to make it glimmer with unholy radiance." It just vanished! Then, last night, when I thought it was gone for good, suddenly I saw the ceramic run, the glaze glisten, and wouldn't you know: It reappeared, a small juice glass full of milk on my butcher-block desk—just as I turned and knocked it over. Shattered on the office

---

[2] DNQ stands for "Do Not Quote" and means the letter (or section of it so marked) is not to appear in a fanzine or magazine.

floor, too. "Lord," I thought. "Now I've got to clean this up before Frank gets home." But it was no more gone than when Neret Oppenheim lined it with fur way back in the '20s. So, I thought, with milky fragments gentle in one hand and the wet paper napkins not too tight in the other, now we'll chuck it into the Glad Bag and be done with it. But soon as I tinkled them in, the pieces sailed out, become a whole set of fucking cups, ringing in the air, clear and limpid as sixteen identical words. Tiny teacups swarmed after me like fat gnats for the day, until, one theoretical letter later, I found a seat in the Penn Central railway waiting room between a mumbling black man in a foul coat and a serious white woman in jeans and a London Fog: They'd melted together and formed into one ivory styrofoam container—which got knocked off the seat by a bag lady, also mumbling: As its invitreation the night before had splashed white fingers, now it splattered beige dregs. And I thought: You know, Tom, as long as that there cup can fragment, multiply, and metamorph, it's just a subset of meaning; not to worry. When it's on paper, reference is just not that privileged. And for a teacup, really, big guns aside, the unreal changes I can put it through, however insistently it persists, must mean it's just not very realistic.

• 7 •

TO TOM LECLAIR

October 29th, 1983

Dear Tom LeClair,

As you can see, I have been giving your exhortation to shatter Ms. Atwood's teacup some thought. By temperament and theoretical upbringing, as 'twere, and certainly by the light of the fiction and criticism I like to read (and write), I'm on what I take to be your side. Nevertheless, I think a firm philosophical understanding of the relation between meaning and reference renders the reference problem, as the "realists" propound it and most "metafictionists" conceive of it, a non-problem. The "realists" simply use fuzzy terminology for what they talk about; but what they are talking about can always be translated into a harder terminology that should be acceptable to the rest of us—if not to them.

Reference is a particular type of meaning—or, more accurately, it is meaning in a particular situation, i.e., when there is something for the signifier not only to signify but to refer to. The bottom line is that any word in the language can be referential: It can always be used to refer to what one means in the usual situations in which one uses it (i.e., "the usual meaning of Y . . ."). But this bottom line case (which we'll call case X) has some unusual aspects to it. To make those aspects clear, however, we have to say a few more things about the relation of meaning to reference. And when we do, I think we'll soon see that this bottom line case X *is* the condition of *all* fiction in the Barthesian sense, i.e., fiction as any systematic enterprise.

Any word can be referential. Any word can also be simply meaningful without having a referent.

George

Set right there in the middle of the line, it has no referent, though it is a locus of possibility for many meanings, meanings that range from the meaning of "George" in the '20s slang phrase "It's real George" [It's real fine], to the first name of the Father of Our Country.

"The white horse with the spiral horn growing from her forehead's rough hide and the silver hooves showing below the matted hairs around her feet was certainly a unicorn," is a perfectly a-referential sentence. Neither unicorns nor silver-hooved horses with spiral horns exist. But just as certainly, "white horse with . . . spiral horn growing from . . . her forehead . . . and . . . silver hooves" *refers* to "unicorn," as "unicorn" *refers* to "white horse with . . . spiral horn."

Reference is a subset of meaning, i.e., it is a limited kind of meaning. Language to be useful must be able both to refer and to mean-in-non-referential-ways. If it could only refer, then it would strongly suggest that the universe is total and complete and there will be nothing new in it ever. The bottom line use of a-referential meanings such as "unicorn" has is simply that, if a unicorn ever shows up, we'll be able to talk about it. I have a book of essays coming out in a few months (called *Starboard Wine*) all about some far more interesting uses of a-referential statements, but mayhap you will see it some day.

At any rate, the problem as it plagues the metafictionist is that, in general usage, "meaning" includes "referring," while referring in no way includes all the types of meaning. Okay: To clear things up, then, let us make up a new verb: Call it "to mean[/]" and it specifically refers only to those meanings which are not referential.

So now, we will either "mean[/]" or we will "refer," but we will always distinguish between them. No more fuzzy terminology that refers to both.

With me? All right:

Language, in order to be fully and richly complete as a system, then, should be able to refer to reference; it should be able to refer to meaning[/]; it should be able to mean[/] meaning[/]; and it should be able to mean[/] reference.

Looking closely at some of these, one begins to wonder of course if some of them actually exist. Is there any referent for "to mean[/] a meaning[/]"? My suspicion is that there isn't, i.e., that it is just a meaning[/], the way "The color of the smell D-flat" has only a meaning[/]. In which case, "to mean[/] a meaning[/]" means[/] a meaning[/], though it refers to nothing. So we're okay, at least on that one, which is certainly the hardest. To mean[/] a reference is what, I assume, one is doing when one uses a metaphor that has a literal meaning[/], which, only through understanding it, indicates a metaphorical referent, so that what it was doing was meaning[/], even though reference enters into it at the other end, so to speak.

Yet the most interesting one, to my mind, rather than all these problematic cases, is the one we've called: "referring to reference." The reason why it is interesting is that the only way to refer to a particular reference (a particular process of referring), rather than to refer to a particular referent (a particular thing referred to), is if the total complex statement is a-referential, that is, if the total complex is restricted to meaning[/].

Let's go back to our a-referential "George." Suppose, strictly by language, we want to refer to a specific referential potential "George" might demonstrate. We don't just turn to someone named George and say, "George is sitting in the chair there." Some way or other, either by statement or by implication, we must say:

"Consider the situation in which one says, 'George is sitting in the chair there.'" Only now are we referring to (one of) the word's reference(s). In short, to refer to its reference ability/potential, we cannot just use the statement referentially; we must tell a story about its referring. Since the *considered* situation is not the *real* situation (even if a real situation inspired it), and the statement, thus framed, is no longer a statement referring to anything (even if what inspired it was the fact that, in the room you are lecturing about all this, there really is someone named George sitting in the chair there), apparently the only way to refer to reference is to create a non-referential complex statement—which is, of course, what fictions do.

Pretty much the same argument goes for referring to meaning[/]. I can mean[/] something—a unicorn, say. But to refer to that meaning, I must imbed/express the a-referential term or terms in language, specifically a language frame that states or implies, "consider the meaning[/]," such as this letter—or a story. Once again, to refer to meaning[/] or reference I must enclose that meaning[/] or reference in an explicit or implied a-referential language frame.

In short, to refer to either reference or meaning[/] while staying solely within the bounds of language, one must use a meaningful[/] complex of statements, and one cannot become mired in a referential complex. (When you become so mired, you are only referring to the world; you are not referring to meanings[/] or references.) Since meaning[/] and reference make up, together, the ordinary term "meaning," what we are left with then, in ordinary language, is: To refer to meaning, one must avoid reference. Or, in our specially constructed language: To refer to meaning (i.e., meaning[/] and/or reference) is necessarily, itself, an act of meaning[/].

It doesn't matter, for instance, that in the "fable" I began all this with, the lights of Dayton, the broken glass of milk, the styrofoam cup, the seat in the Penn Central waiting room (where I drafted the fable this afternoon in my notebook), the black man, the bag lady, the white woman, the theoretical letter (sent to an acquaintance this morning about something in an Ashbery poem), Neret Oppenheim, or pretty much everything else that wasn't overtly surreal by syntax happens to be, as a matter of fact, as "referential" as the "teacup" of the title (which refers to your use of a word/idea mentioned by Atwood). Until this addition to the story, however, to you they (or most of them) were only meanings[/]. And even *with* this addition, their fabular reference *in* the fable (to the extent the fable recognizably refers to the problem of reference in fiction) hasn't changed. But the point of all this is simply that there's no way to refer even to their worldly referentiality without adding another frame, i.e., this one. You see, I can only refer to that particular aspect of their reference by telling you yet another story— this story *about* their reference. And, of course, if we *stay* within the bounds of language, you have no way to confirm the truth of this part of the story for sure— without your own referral to things outside the text, like your appraisal of my character from our brief meeting, etc. And even to refer to that referral, you see I have to tell you this further little story, here, about it.

For me, this necessary structure of reference takes care of the realists who want their teacups to refer to teacups. The point is: In order to refer to any kind of meaning (referential or meaningful[/]) the word "teacup" may have, if they want to do it using only language, they are stuck with doing it via acts of meaning[/].

Not acts of reference.

And they are constrained to it in the same way that I am constrained to refer to their references by telling the above fictions about them, George, expanding, fragmenting, and multiplying teacups, and about language.

If you believe teacups on a table are meaningful, you cannot just mention that "Teacups are on the table" in a room where a table happens to be set for tea. You have to say: "Consider the situation in which there are teacups on the table." Even if you have the teacups on hand as an aid, you still have to say it in a tone of voice that implies, consider it as situation: "Consider, my friends, the teacups sitting just over there." And that framing, of course, is what fiction does. And *that*, as we have seen, is to render the statement meaningful[/] and to divorce it from direct referentiality.

So, as the fable says: Not to worry about realists. Like the expanding, contracting, and fragmenting teacup (which, one assumes, frustrates their realistic referential pretensions), they, too — when it comes to any understanding of how language works — are just not very realistic.

All best wishes,

• 8 •

To Thomas Zummer

October 30th, 1983

Dear Tom,

Many thanks for the xerox of the Foucault interview.

Can't think how our lunch got bollixed up. I was here the whole morning of the 16th with a spread of Zabar's best smoked salmon and a bottle of champagne —and, if I recall, fresh strawberries and various other nosherie. Besides going out to the store some time in the morning to get it, I was in all day—till at least four o'clock. The only thing I can think of is that, somehow, I managed to give you an improper phone number. If that's what I did, once more my dyslexia has turned to plague me!

In any case, my apologies for any inconvenience I may have caused you! And there certainly were no hard feelings here. At the time, I just assumed you hadn't gotten back from San Francisco yet and that you hadn't been able to get in touch.

I've only read the Foucault piece, which you just sent me, cursorily, but it intrigues me to note that he is beginning to sound more and more like the Ancient Writers he's been studying. This piece, for example, could be a bit of medieval scholasticism itself!

Has Paul Rabinow become Foucault's agent? A young friend of mine (well, not so young: he's 25, but I've known him since he was sixteen), Robert Morales, who writes for the *Village Voice* and, nevertheless, is a very smart young man (at one time he was a student at Clarion) called Rabinow in California (as per instructions from Atheneum) in order to arrange an interview with Foucualt for (yes, it's a little odd, I know) *Omni*, and Rabinow had the temerity to ask over the phone, "Well, how much do you intend to pay him?" and apparently declined even to suggest a place to write M. Foucault until this information was forthcoming.

Given the fact that, short of celebrity interviews in *Playboy,* most people are not paid for such pieces, unless Rabinow has taken over as Foucault's business manager, that really should be between Foucault and *Omni* anyway. In Robert's words it sounded both unprofessional and pushy. But perhaps I'm just telling tales out of school about folks whom you like—and whom I, after all, have never met.

In which case, rack it up to a novelist's sense of gossip.

At any rate, I look forward to seeing you around Christmas. Once again, many thanks for the material.

Oh, yes. One other question: What in the world is the current publication status of *L'Usage des plaisirs, Les Avoux de chair,* and *Le Souci de soi*—both in France and as far as any English translation is concerned? If you get a chance, drop me a postcard with at least the answer to that one . . . ?

With great gratitude, I send you,

All best wishes,

1984

• 9 •

To Robert S. Bravard

January 20th, 1984

Dear Bob,

By my own estimates, I haven't written you a real letter since I saw you at Bucknell, back on October 8th, '83!

Just received yours of Jan 17th yesterday.

Am awash in guilt and chagrin!

First off, however, accept my condolences on your mother-in-law's death. Mrs. Buttolph's name appeared from time to time in various of your letters, and so I felt I had something of a picture of her. Please convey my sympathies to Cynthia.

The death of relatives — even when it's an expected death — is a taxing time. And the living can react rather oddly, accepting it or not accepting it according to their wants and abilities—which the rest of us then have to deal with on top of the realities of grief. It sounds like you had more than your share with R——. What does one say?

I'm glad you both got a chance to see Tom.[1] I only wish that it had been under more cheerful circumstances.

And I'm glad things are moving back to normal.

I'm debating whether to try to give you the intervening *histoire de ma vie* in terms of what's most important coming first—or what's earliest chronologically.

To start with, when I returned from Bucknell, there was a note from Mr. Greenberg of the IRS waiting for me, stuck in the mailbox door. And to condense the next very fraught two weeks: At the end of fifteen or so days, a lien was put on my personal account! Chip Writings, Inc., was stripped of all its very meager moneys, and Frank and I, once again, found ourselves facing November, December, and the New Year without, for all practical purposes, a penny.

This, you'll recall, makes the third year in a row that some catastrophe or the other has landed just about this time to blight the coldest stretch of the year.

After many consultations with each other, my accountant, Henry, *et alia*, my part of the job of survival was assessed to be: Write your ass off.

So on January 15th I finished "The Tale of Fog and Granite," which weighs in at about 50,000 words, making it short-novel length. I'm taking this day off (a week after the fact, Iva is having a birthday party today: I.e., three of her friends are over for a slumber party, two of whom, along with Iva, are more or less amusing each other in the living room right now) to write a letter or two; tomorrow I launch into two more short Nevèrÿon stories, which will bring the series to a close for a while and which will round out the final volume of a trilogy, *Flight from Nevèrÿon*.

Well, that has somewhat jumped the chronological gun. So let me fill in the between times.

By the bye, I have the ending to my "Jack the Ripper" account for you. Around the end of October, while walking up 8th Ave., I ran into Jeff of the missing teeth. He was wearing a new set of clothes, including a new "leather" (most probably plastic) jacket, and clearly feeling very chipper. He grinned and greeted me hap-

---

[1] Bravard's son.

pily. Obviously, at least for a couple of days, things had been going well for him. "Did they ever catch that guy who was going around killing people?" I asked.

"Oh, yeah. Caught him two weeks ago." In the midst of his good humor, however, my question seemed to bother him.

"Tell me about it," I urged.

"He killed five people," Jeff said. "And they caught him. That's all."

"I thought you said he killed nine . . . ?"

"Naw, somebody else killed the other four," and he quickly changed the subject again. In short, there are still homicidal nuts loose on the street—and the street people, in all their powerlessness, really would rather just not think about it.

In the last six weeks, I haven't seen Jeff at all. I suspect he's no longer in New York.

One of the things I did shortly after the IRS landed was something I've wanted to do for years. And suddenly, under the pressure of catastrophe, I realized that, since there would never be any "time" to do it, I might as well do it anyway.

I joined the staff of *The Little Magazine,* the poetry magazine David Hartwell has been editing for the last eighteen years. David has repeatedly invited me to become an editor. For about a year Marilyn was on the staff, which pretty much kept me away. But there was another opening, so — every Thursday night, since about mid-October, I have been busy at editorial staff meetings on the 46th Floor of Manhattan Plaza, at 43rd and 9th Ave., where the magazine has been having its meetings of late, at the apartment of my fellow editor, Dennis Cooney. There are six people currently on the staff and one, Ginger Buchanan, is just out of the hospital. She's the wife of SF editor John Douglas, who used to be David's assistant at Pocket Books.

The editorial meetings, from 6:30 to midnight on Thursday evenings, usually start with a session of paperwork, filing, mailing, and what-have-you, followed by reading of submissions and, after a couple of hours of silent absorption, some discussion during which the six of us consume about $12 on the average of cheese, crackers, cold-cuts, soda, and coffee.

So that when I finally slog home over chill 43rd St. to the bus or subway, usually with Joel (another editor, she) or David, I go home tired—but feeling like a civilized human being.

Somewhere in the midst of all this, the page proofs for *Starboard Wine* finally showed up. The mistakes are minuscule; and the volume is actually being printed, now even now, out in Ann Arbor. Copies are to be shipped east on February 28th. At last night's meeting, David had "silverprints" of the first signature that the printers had sent him.

So the book is a breath away from becoming real. I made Xeroxes of the page-proofs, and on the 25th, when Henry M. returns from St. Thomas, all three of my non-fiction critical books go to Vintage, where they're to be considered for Vintage Paperback Reprints: That's *The Jewel-Hinged Jaw: Notes on the Language of Science Fiction, The American Shore: Meditations on a Tale of Science Fiction, "Angouleme," by Thomas M. Disch,* and *Starboard Wine: More Notes on the Language of Science Fiction.*

The other thing I've been doing, for much the same reasons as I took on the *Little Magazine* job, is recording Howard Wise's reminiscences. Howard Wise is, of course, Barbara Wise's husband. (Barbara produced my 1971 film, *The Orchid*.) Howard is 82, and has (thankfully dormant right through here) prostate cancer. So Wednesday mornings I go down and record him. So far we've only had two sessions, but it's fascinating.

December and January have been particularly hectic. Iva was ostensibly to spend this Christmas with Marilyn — indeed, it was Marilyn's idea, which she had insisted on sometime back in the summer. So Frank and I decided not to get a tree this year and to let M. do Christmas for Iva.

We decided, however, to have Iva for a day about a week before Christmas, for a kind of pre-mini-Christmas. But, of course, as it drew closer and closer, we schemed and planned and scrimped and saved and borrowed to make it—well, you know: just a little nicer. And, indeed, a rather nice mini-Christmas it was. True, there was no tree—but we more than made up for it with tinsel and lights and Christmas bulbs and decorations hung around every door frame and over every wall—really, I don't think the house has ever looked as Christmassy!

Then, three days before Christmas proper, we found out, rather indirectly, that Marilyn, for odd and incomprehensible reasons, had decided to send Iva to my mother's for Christmas day! This, of course, when all is said and done, meant real Christmas for Iva fell on Frank and me again. So now we found ourselves having the prepare a second Christmas! Was there a bit of ire? Yes. But we did it, and I think it worked out well. And whatever was going through M.'s head, we just decided not to question.

For what I assumed was going to be a quiet New Year's Eve with Frank, I bought a bottle of champagne and we settled in to feeling smug about all the places we weren't going that night, talking between ourselves and feeling rather good. An old friend of Frank's, Francy, and her New Boy Friend, dropped by: He was a photographer, and they were going down to photograph the hordes at Times Square. They left, and we had another glass of champagne. At about eleven o'clock, the doorbell rang, and it was our country-singer friend, Lavada, looking like a million dollars in mink over leather. We must go out — to Larry Gouche-man's, who lives a few blocks away and who, indeed, had invited us over.

Well, all right . . .

So we barreled out into the snow, and by twenty-to-twelve had joined Larry's party. At midnight, Larry's TV blared "1984!" (which still feels a little weird to me, though I have now written the date about half a dozen or more times) over pictures of the fallen ball; and fireworks went off, booming, over Central Park. We drank more champagne, and went home.

I went up to my mother's for her traditional New Year's Day dinner: pigs-feet, chitlings, barbecue, black-eyed peas, and rice. And of course egg-nog. Mom's single (I think) superstition that she indulges flagrantly is that no woman can enter her house on New Year's Day until after a man has crossed the threshold, even if it's just the newspaper delivery boy. This was our first New Year's without Grandma, and in the past, of course, it was indulged for her sake. I think this year Mom was indulging it more in memory of Grandma than anything else, but several times, Aunt Eva (who lives up on the 20th floor) and Mrs. Jackson, who lives on the floor below my mother, lending a hand with this or that, had to do it by passing things back and forth over the threshold without actually stepping into the house.

Frank had come to my mother's for Christmas dinner, but the traditional New Year's Eve menu, which I love, simply holds no delight for his upstate New York/Italian palette. So he went out somewhere else.

Getting on the bus up at Broadway that night, I noticed the cardboard sign hanging from the rail in front of the bus-driver reminding us all that on midnight, January 2nd, bus and subway fares would go up from 75 cents to 90 cents. (Which, indeed, they have.) And as I sat in the fluorescent-lit bus, joggling home down upper B'way, I kept looking at the advertising placard on the back of the driver's seat, over which someone had scrawled with a black marker: "WHAT, 1984 ALREADY!"

Shakespeare and Company has done a "1984" display window, featuring Orwell and Orwelliana in the middle, with other SF dystopias ranged around it, including *Dhalgren*.

On the 12th, I took what I thought was the last draft of "Fog and Granite" out of the typewriter, and handed it in. And the next day decided to re-write the last 100 pages. And did over the next two days (only possible with the word processor here); and have handed that in. (On the 15th, as mentioned.)

The 14th of January was actually Iva's birthday. My big girl will never be able to write her age with a single figure anymore. Gar (Garland Hartsoe) came over for that. For various reasons (basically a futile attempt to catch the Icecapades, which were supposed to be at Madison Square Garden by now, but weren't), Iva decided to have her party a week later, i.e., today.

But what all this means is that, without a penny to our names for all practical purposes, Frank and I have had non-stop holiday/birthday since a week before Christmas. And it won't really be over until the kids go home tomorrow afternoon.

Frank and I are both a bit frazzled. Though I must say, the girls have amused themselves very well this afternoon. Frank cleaned and scrubbed and got things ready for the party from one end of the apartment to the other — then quit the premises in terror and despair (I don't blame him), leaving the supervising of the actual event to me; but so far, they have allowed me to write this much of this letter since I ferried them here in a cab after school at 3:30. We're only awaiting Iva's friend Chlöe, who is coming late, before we go out to dinner (what would the penniless do without American Express?) — whoops! She just rang the bell.

* * *

Well, here we are, back from dinner. After playing "Theater" for an hour or so, the girls are in their night gowns. One amusing anecdote from the evening. At Teachers, the girls were given a booth. (Various customers and waitresses who know me commented that I deserved a medal for parent of the year for this enterprise, which is hyperbole, but which nevertheless made me feel good.) The girls got themselves seated and I retired to the bar with my notebook, a vodka gibson, and wrote the opening of the new Nevèrÿon story, "The Mummer's Tale" (that will precede *Plagues and Carnivals*). They behaved admirably, through $28-odd dollars worth of hamburgers, cokes, quiche, et cetera, until finally the waitresses all convened on their table with a piece of cake, sporting a small pink candle, to sing "Happy Birthday." Somewhere in the midst of all this, little Danielle decided she must have chocolate brownies. All the girls concurred.

I had to pick up some dinner for myself anyway.

Okay, come with me to the Red Apple Super Market. Now, you wait inside here, kids. And I'll run get the brownies and be right back. Passing by the meat counter, I snag up a piece of steak for my dinner and, holding the plastic-wrapped package in my hand, I go up to a squat, elderly Puerto Rican stock-clerk in a blue smock and a knitted cap and ask him where the brownie mix is. He tells me an aisle number; I go get it.

Looking at the instructions on the back of the brownie mix box, however, I find that it requires half a cup of oil as well as eggs. We don't have any oil at home, and I don't really want to buy it. These kids, I think, will be perfectly happy with chocolate chip cookies. So I put the brownie mix back on the shelf, and take my piece of steak over to the refrigerated pre-packaged sticks of chocolate-chip cookie dough. But, I think, I better tell them what I'm doing. The chocolate chip dough is way in the corner, so I leave the steak in with the chocolate chips, and turn around and start to the front of the store to tell the kids a white lie: "They're out of brownie mix. Will chocolate chip cookies do?"—planning, after their approval, to return and pick up both from where I left them.

Halfway there, the same squat stock clerk suddenly accosts me. "Hey! Hey . . . !" he says.

"Oh, that's all right," I say, thinking he still wants to show me where the brownies are.

His English, beyond grunts, however, is incomprehensible. I'm trying to explain, "No, I don't want the brownies. And I have to go tell my kids something . . ." He's tugging on my arm. I'm kind of drifting with him.

Finally he gets out, "The meat. Where is the meat?" and starts pawing around in my large, down coat, now and again turning to point to one of the store's TV cameras peeking down from the ceiling.

Though I have indeed been rushing around the store at double speed, at no point, you understand, has anything been in my coat pocket, or even under my arm!

But here I notice the 23-year-old security guard, lurking shyly behind him in his black leather cap and nervously fingering his billy-club. And it finally dawns on me that the stock clerk thinks I've taken something! "Aw, come on!" I tell him. "The meat's over there in the cookie dough. I have to go tell my kids I'm not getting them the brownies."

This guy does not speak that much English. I look at the security guard for help. He's just bewildered. And young. Finally, I decide that logic won't do. I take the stock clerk bodily by the arm, as, moments before, he'd taken me, and drag him across the store to the refrigerated dough bin. I point out the meat. "There's the meat," I say. "I put it here so that I could go tell my kids I'm getting them cookies, not brownies. Then I was going to come back and get it." (The guard is still following, somewhat at a distance) Still dragging this stock clerk, who is still going on about the TV cameras ("They see! They see! You put it back. It'll all be okay. Come on. Put it back," half in English, half in Spanish), I then march to the front of the store where Iva and her three friends are chattering away about nothing in particular and trying to pull each other's caps down over each other's eyes.

"They're out of brownies," I say. "How about chocolate chip cookies?"

There is a chorus of, *"Yes!"*

At this point the security guard finally twigs as to what's happening and bursts out laughing. "You see," he says to me, "he's always jumping to conclusions." I go back, get my steak, cookies, and a package of frozen broccoli, go up to the cashier and, after a five-minute wait in line to pay, return to the manager's tower, under which the kids are still chattering—they all immediately want to know what that was about. "I'll tell you in a minute," I explain. I call up to the manager, in his green army jacket: "You know, you have a real nutcase back there!"

"I'm sorry, sir," he says. "The guard just explained what happened. I was just about to come down and apologize to you."

"No hard feelings," I say. "But if the guy can't understand English, you can't have him running around grabbing people in the store."

During the course of it, three or four other customers, more or less realizing what was going on, had been adding their typically New York comments: "Sue 'em. Go ahead, let 'em arrest you. Then sue 'em."

Explaining the details to the clamorously curious kids, we left by the wrong door (at the manager's gracious invitation), out into Broadway's slushy night and snow-banked sidewalks—whereupon, as we were waiting to cross at 82nd Street, Catherine said, "Did you drop this?" bent down, and handed me up a folded $20 bill that someone had dropped in the street!

Thus the patient are rewarded.

After the ice-cream and cake at home (the cake was supposed to be all-chocolate, but turned out to have been misordered: vanilla cake with chocolate filling) the girls put on a show, using the double-doors between the living room and the dining room as a stage, with dad as the light-man. Now they're all in their night-gowns, having settled into a quiet and civilized round of Barbie dolls.

But back to What's Been Happening:

* * *

Let me see: Toward the end of October, Mog Decarnin returned from Denmark and spent a few days in New York, en route to San Francisco, during which we went to the Met and bought standing room for a really tepid production of *Tristan und Isolde*. Good singing. Appalling conducting from James Levine. (You just can't conduct Wagner as if it were Debussy. Though Mr. Levine tried.)

While Mog was here, I went to see an all day showing of Syberberg's *Our Hitler: a film from Germany*, at the Metro (neé the Midtown), up at 100th St. Well, it was long. Seven and a half hours. After five and a half hours of standing through *Tristan*, however, Mog excused herself from sitting through Syberberg. So I didn't see her that day. But I don't really blame her.

It was very similar to his *Parsifal* in many ways. And, naturally, very different in many others. (You may have read Sontag's discussion of the movie in her collection, *Under the Sign of Saturn*—the essay's also contained in the *Sontag Reader.*) It was impressive.

Over the New Year's weekend, the Paula Webster Gallery down in Soho arranged a marathon reading of Gertrude Stein's *The Making of Americans*, as, indeed, they have been doing every year for a decade now. Barbara Wise and I came for the opening of the 24-hour-a-day recitation; then we returned to read for an hour or so with each other toward the end. Other readers included Susan Sontag, Richard Kostelanetz, Virgil Thomson, Charles Ludlum, and John Cage, among some 75 or 80 other volunteers over the three-odd days. . . . We were really among some rather auspicious company.

Oh yes, in the midst of things my computer broke down once and had to go into the shop—just to complicate matters. But it's out now and functioning beautifully. And that really just about brings me up to date on what's been happening.

Oh, yes—

Lunch a couple of days ago with Lou Aronica at Bantam. When I followed Ian Ballantine (of the gnome-like demeanor and prehensile eyebrows) and Fred Pohl into the office and met Lou, Lou was in the midst of writing an irate letter (on his word-processor) to P—— Y——.

Seems that Y—— has gotten into a rather silly project with the irrepressible K—— L——, who, at some con, bombarded Lou with an idea for a book he wanted to do in collaboration with Y——, and took Lou's polite show of interest ("Yes, I'll look at the proposal.") as an assured sale and represented it as such to Y——.

Upon the subsequent rejection, Y—— had shot off an irate letter, accusing Lou of non-professionalism and threatening SFWA[2] action, etc., etc. Lou was explaining back that L—— had simply misrepresented the situation to Y——; that, indeed, L—— has done this several times before with several other editors in the past few months, in the course of which he is making a very bad professional name for himself; and that the only thing Lou had "promised" to do was look at the proposal— and he had done it—before rejecting it. As I pointed out to Lou, when professional writers write letters like that, usually it simply means their lives are going badly. And L—— is just an over-enthusiastic not-so-young-anymore man, who's been trying to make the transition from "fan" to "pro" for years.

We ended up having lunch at the Top of the Sixes, the restaurant on the top floor of the Tishman building that houses Bantam itself: Usually a beautiful view of the roofs of mid-town Manhattan and profoundly ordinary, when not terrible, food—though for that afternoon the snow swirled around the glass picture windows, removing us from the city and putting us off in some cloudy dimension-X. Most of our talk was about what awful shape book publishing is in, in general— which, I'm afraid, kind of undercut Lou's constant reassurances that, despite it all, I'm somehow in a good position.

(Tell it to the IRS, I kept thinking, quietly.)

Well, it is now almost ten o'clock, and I have to bulldoze my little harridans into bed shortly.

Myself, I'm exhausted, as I haven't been asleep later than five thirty in the morning for the last two and a half months.

The one other moment of relaxation during the month was when Frank and I stayed up to watch the American Music Awards, where Michael Jackson swept away the field. Since I saw him in that ridiculous movie, *The Wiz*, I've felt he was a truly astonishing performer — kind of a male Barbara Streisand, only maybe more so. And the video of "Thriller" is a stunning homage to all sorts of my favorite people and things, from George Romero to EC comics. I was enchanted by its marvelously tongue-in-cheek ghoulishness.

Long may he sing and dance.

Frank, who was planning to return tonight at about 11:00, when, hopefully, the

---

[2] Science Fiction Writers of America, an organization founded in 1965, under the presidency of Damon Knight.

girls would all be in bed, just called to say he was spending the night at Gar's and will return in the morning. I just put the beds out (mattresses all over the living room floor, the sofa pulled out, sheets, quilts and pillows strewn about and flecked with Barbie clothes). The girls just had a final glass of soda, and it sounds like one of them has the hiccups—though no one has yet run to me to complain . . .

This letter is just to let you know I'm alive and thinking of you—indeed, I have been thinking of you lots and lots! But between the IRS, *Nevèrÿon*, and attendant hassles, I'm afraid I got a little down for a while; and since work only got heavier, correspondence suffered.

All my love to Cynthia, Jonathon, and of course yourself.

All best and better,

• 10 •

To Michael W. Peplow

January 23rd, 1984

Dear Pep,

Hello from ice-bound Manhattan!

Belated seasons greetings, to you and Judy and Davone!

I've been meaning to write you for months. But, as I wrote Bob a day or so back, since October I haven't written anyone. But he'll bring you up to date, I'm sure, on my IRS hassles and what have you.

One of the things I've been meaning to write you about is, of course, your "Delany" paper of last autumn. Usually with you guys, I've found myself in the famous Pascal situation. You remember — "Not having had time to write you a short letter, I'm afraid I have written you a very long one . . ."

But one of the things I hope I've been able to do in the intervening months is to condense into a fairly brief space some of what, indeed, I've been trying to say to you since, at least, my letter to Bob of January 9th, 1980 (q.v.). And whether I make my point or not, this time, I promise: These will be my last words on the topic, and I will then leave you to get on as best you can, without my carping.

Consider, then, a brief parable:

Passing through the student lounge one morning, an English professor overheard an undergraduate from one of his literature classes saying to another: "Joyce Kilmer? Yes, she was that famous American writer who wrote *Ulysses* . . ."

Smiling, the professor called the undergraduate to him and suggested the young man pay a visit to his office later that afternoon. And when the student duly arrived and was seated beside the professor's desk, the kindly gentleman explained to the youth that Kilmer was a man and the writer of a famous poem, "Trees," and that Joyce was the name of an Irish writer who wrote in Europe during the teens and twenties. "Now," said the professor, "if you haven't done last week's paper yet" — which the student assured him he hadn't — "I want you to look up Joyce and Kilmer in the library and write me just the briefest, 150-word paragraph on them. Just slip it in my office mailbox. You may do that instead of the paper."

And a day or two later, the professor found a page in his mailbox that began:

"Joyce Kilmer was an American woman writer who wrote a famous novel, *Ulysses*. For a while she lived in Ireland, where, like George Eliot and George Sand before her, she took a man's pen-name, 'James,' and wrote a poem, 'Trees,' which many people think is even better than her novel . . ."

I'm sure I don't have dwell at too great a length on what's happened here: The student has a model of the situation that is simply wrong. Further, he's tried to fit all the professor's (not to mention the library's) new information into his model as revision and elaboration, without changing his basic model at all. As long as he has that model, he will not be able to write an accurate sentence about either Kilmer or Joyce. And until he throws out that model and substitutes an accurate one—one acknowledging that there are two individual writers, both male, one of whom is a minor American poet and one of whom is a major novelist in English —he will not be able to write an accurate sentence about either. Against this over-all situation, single "mistakes" (such as the notion that "Trees" was written in Ireland) are trivial, and correcting them alone doesn't really improve matters any.

Now you guys are much more sophisticated than our undergraduate. And your model of the publication of *TEI*[1] and the events that lead from it to the publication of *Nova* is more complex (and consequently more tenacious) than his. But it's just as wrong-headed and your attempts to revise it in light of further information produce the same sort of compounded chaos. Until you throw it out and replace it with an accurate one, you'll continue to produce chaos—among which the specific—factual errors (". . . *Nova* was published by Nelson Doubleday . . ." [!]) are quite secondary.

As it stands now, the two paragraphs in your paper *anent* the publication of *Nova* simply refer to nothing in the real world. (You juxtapose a sentence from Terry[2] and a sentence from me as though they express conflicting accounts about a single situation when, actually, they are, both of them, perfectly accurate statements about *two* events eighteen months apart!)

Really, I'm not trying to lambaste your admirable effort. I'm only trying to elucidate a principle which keeps your efforts from coming to very much, at least as far as this particular bit of history is concerned.

The basic model you seemed to have gotten locked into is that of the young, ambitious writer (24-year-old Delany), turning his back on shoddy publishers to seek out more prestigious and better paying markets. Specifically, in terms of events, you have constructed a story that seems to run as follows: "Tensions developing between Delany and Ace over the cover of *TEI* caused Delany to take his next novel, *Nova*, to Doubleday, a more prestigious and better paying publisher, leaving some ire behind him at Ace . . ."

You have to throw out the whole model. None of it is correct. You can't revise it into the truth. And as long as you take my protests that the Doubleday contract for *Nova* was signed well before I became aware of any problems with the *TEI* cover; or that what tension there was with the cover was between Gaughan (the cover artist) and Ace, not me and Ace, and was, indeed, of the most ordinary and workaday sort; or that there is no economic conflict between a hardcover pub-

---

[1] *The Einstein Intersection*, Ace Books, 1967.
[2] Terry Carr (1937-1987), science fiction editor for Ace Books.

lisher and a paperback reprint house such as Ace to produce "ire" if a writer publishes with both; or that the economic gain from the Doubleday sale was minimal; or that, finally, in the summer of '68, when Bantam bought the paperback rights to *Nova* for a record price from Doubleday (and thus aced out Ace), I was as surprised as anybody — as long as you take these facts, or, indeed, any of the facts from Terry's letter, as revisions of your model, you will go on producing recompounded chaos of the same sort as our befuddled undergraduate above.

What all these "revisions" do, of course, is to define an entirely different situation from the one you have assumed — a situation wholly incommensurate with yours. You can't adjust your model; you have to replace it.

I suggest that the situation was more complicated than you see it, yes; but more to the point, it was simply other. In place of your ambitious young writer trying to direct a career, you must think of me as a very young man (24), living a chaotic and highly marginal life (evicted from one apartment [739 East 5th Street] and negotiating a precarious relation back and forth between my gay lover on St. Marks Place and my somewhat estranged wife [embroiled in her own, equally complex affairs], first on Henry Street and then on 11th Street), a young man who wasn't even sure if he would continue writing SF or would become a professional pop musician, a young man whose ambition seldom went beyond what he was putting on the page in front of him. (In such a life situation, who would have time to "direct" a career?! Had you spent any 24-hour period with me back then, going with me to our intense six-hour music rehearsals [this was before the Heavenly Breakfast commune], stopping with me at some coffee shop to write in my notebook for an hour or two, now typing in the evening at St. Marks Place, or carousing at the Old Reliable bar for an evening, or listening for hours to Marilyn detail her hassles with the St. Mark's poets and/or her sometime lover, Link, you'd realize that there simply was no *time* for the tale you're so anxious to tell to have taken place!) What was happening as far as my career went is wholly covered by the following:

On the early 1966 publication of *Empire Star* and *Babel-17* while I was still in Europe, a certain interest began to grow in the SF community of writers and editors, an interest I was more or less oblivious to, at least till the Nebula Award for *Babel-17* — though indeed it had been enough to get *The Ballad of Beta-2* nominated for a Nebula Award (unknown to me at the time) the previous year. In real terms, that interest was not enough, after my April return, to affect the sale of *TEI* to Ace in August (?) '66, but after I'd put in a personal appearance at the Worldcon in Cleveland and, a week later, another at the Milford SF Writers' Conference (where I wrote "Aye, and Gomorrah . . ." and sold it to Harlan Ellison[3] for his forthcoming *Dangerous Visions* anthology), the interest began to snowball.

Sometime around the end of October '66, I received a call (at St. Marks Place, I believe) from Doubleday's Larry Ashmead, and with the call an invitation to come to lunch. Ashmead was an astute and urbane man, who, though he knew zilch about science fiction (he had never heard of the Hugo Award), at least knew that SF was selling. A month or so before, he'd managed to convince Doubleday to up its SF from two books a year to 24 books a year, and he was now out looking for new writers to fill up his expanded list.

---

[3] Harlan Ellison, a west-cost writer of wonderfully imaginative fiction, famous for his personal energy and often combative opinions.

Are you working on anything? he wanted to know, over martinis and Dover sole.
I mentioned I was working on *Nova.*
I'd like to see some of it, he said.

A week or so later, I brought him in the first three chapters. Three weeks or five weeks later at another lunch, he told me he'd accepted it; and, on February 10th, '67, a couple of weeks after I'd gotten back from a second, rather impulsive, trip to London, contracts were signed.

But here I am waxing anecdotal again, which I promised myself I would not do. In brief, the Doubleday sale of *Nova*, the Nebula Award for *Babel-17* (on March 25th), the sale of *Nova* to Bantam (in the summer of '68), and the Nebulas for "Aye, and Gomorrah . . ." and *TEI* (in April '68) were all fallout from that initial spurt of snow-balling interest and excitement. Neither I nor Henry (!) "directed" a thing. I wrote the books, and people's responses, usually to the previous book, took the next on and me with it to wherever it was we ended up.

As far as the specific events that have occupied so much of our correspondence, here is the account you must substitute for the one you have been using:

In autumn '66, while *TEI* was in production at Ace, I submitted the opening of my new novel, *Nova,* to Doubleday, who contracted for it in February '67.

Completely unconnected with this in any causal manner: In March of '67, at the Nebula Awards banquet, I became aware of some tension between Gaughan and Ace Books over the cover-painting of my new book, *TEI,* copies of which had just appeared that day. As it was my book, I was an interested party, yes. But that's all.

Again, without any causal connection with either of the above incidents, in the summer of '68, after Doubleday had published the hardcover edition of *Nova* and everyone—Henry, myself, and probably Don and Terry at Ace—was expecting Ace Books to purchase the paperback rights and reprint it, and thus continue as my paperback publisher, a much larger paperback house, heretofore all but uninterested in science fiction (outside of Ray Bradbury and Walter Miller), Bantam Books, astonished everyone by arriving out of a clear blue sky to offer a record price to Doubleday for *Nova's* paperback rights, thus "acing out" Ace Books, who, on hearing of Bantam's bid, did not even make a counter-bid, as they were financially unprepared to out-bid them.

If you take the above account as your basic model and firmly banish the first from your mind, then, when you reread my various letters on the subject, when you look over Terry's letter, details will fall into place and things will become clearer and clearer.

If, however, you stay with the first model, trying to fit the facts, dates, and details that, here and there, research turns up to that model, you will slide into more (and more preposterous) misconceptions about the period, about science fiction, and about my very modest place in it.

I don't mean to sound like Wagner in *Mein Leben,*[4] denying his part in some scandal about which a later Newman will discover him to have been a debtor of many thousands on thousands of Thalers. Nevertheless, it was only that growing

---

[4] *Mein Leben,* the autobiography of Richard Wagner, was begun in 1865. A private edition was published in an unspecified year during his lifetime, but was recalled by Wagner's wife, Cosima. The first edition in German was published in 1911.

interest which made me a good person for Terry, Jack, or others to cite as they looked about for examples to bolster their own positions, as in the initial Carr quote that has occasioned so many pages of explication, or in the situation with the *TEI* cover. Situations occurred. I had feelings about them, and about how science fiction should and should not be published (I still do, and they haven't changed much). I expressed those opinions to Terry, to Jack, and to others. They agreed with me about some of them. They disagreed with me about others. But because I was becoming something of a name, these opinions were sometimes quoted—and sometimes, even, misquoted. All I'm saying is that while these feelings may well have been reasons for me to be sad or happy or annoyed about various things that happened to me along the way, they were not causes for any of those things as you read them in the progress of my doings during those days— at least outside of what I put on the pages of my SF novels and stories.

May I suggest that if you have further need of confirmation, you send this letter to Terry and ask him for comment. If he takes exception to anything I've said here, then you can honestly write that Terry and I have different interpretations or memories of the events and happenings in which we were both involved. And, no doubt, I will find those differences as illuminating as you will. But till that happens, I haven't seen any contradictions between Terry's and my accounts of things so far, where you apparently have. And, I submit, the contradictions you see are only because you are using new facts to recomplicate errors that originate in an already faulty model.

Needless to say, the above only applies to the two paragraphs in the paper in which you detail the publication of *Nova*. The rest of the paper's points, *anent* the misspellings of my name, etc., are very well taken. And perhaps it is only my bias that makes me see those two paragraphs as the center of what you have to say.

As concise as I am trying to be, this may still be an overlong exegesis — for which, sincerely, I apologize.

And now, I promise you, I leave the subject forever. You may write anything you wish in the future, and I will protest it no more.

Well, it seems I haven't been as brief as all that. My "Formatter" tells me I've run on already to ten pages. But it's not 40. So you have something to be thankful for.

Something I didn't write Bob about was a distressing mix-up back in October *anent* the copy-editing of *Stars/Sand*. Basically, it was done so badly that, after struggling over it for a couple of days, I called up Lou Aronica, read him a handful of examples from the first half dozen pages, whereupon, in a most gentlemanly fashion, he volunteered to take the MS back and have it redone. (When I say it was bad, I really mean bad!) As I told him, if I were 20 I would have bulled through the whole thing, but I am now 41, going on 42: In the state it was in, checking it over would be a good two/three weeks' work (for a job that, had it been done properly, should have only taken me a couple of days); and I was in the middle of another writing project anyway—for Bantam!

I'm still waiting for the re-copy-edited MS promised by mid-January, to arrive for checking.

Ah, Pep; this was to be brief — and, indeed you'll admit, I'm sure, that it's briefer than some . . .

Mark Gawron just turned up in New York from Edinburgh, where, after getting his doctorate in linguistics from Berkeley, he's been working on Artificial Intelligence.

He came over about 10:45, I fixed him some brunch, and we had pleasant conversation, croissants, and wine until he had to take off around 1:00 to go, of all places, to a State Senate Investigation on the status of high school drop-outs. What this has to do with either linguistics or artificial intelligence, I'm not quite sure. . . .

He's staying with his girlfriend, Jenny Walter, in Brooklyn — she turns out to be the niece of an old elementary school-friend of mine from Dalton, Wendy Osserman, with whom I was passionately in love from about the ages of six to seven-and-a-half. She's Wendy's older sister's daughter — a very odd situation it is too, to find such a person the live-in girlfriend of someone you consider practically a contemporary, the way I do Mark!

Oh, by-the-bye: Seth McEvoy's book will be out from Ungar in mid-February. I'll see that you guys get a (couple of) copy(s).

All my best wishes to you and Judy.

Love and stuff,

• 11 •

To Robert S. Bravard

March 5th, 1984

Dear Bob,

You're probably wondering whether I'm alive or dead. I'm alive. And working pretty non-stop — more or less ten to fifteen hours a day.

On January 15th, I finished "The Tale of Fog and Granite" at 48,000 words. A month later, I finished "The Mummer's Tale," at c. 17,000. I'm now well beyond the halfway point on another novella, *The Tale of Plagues and Carnivals,* which I project at c. 30,000. I have about 80 pages written, about 50 of which I am truly satisfied with at this point.

The first two of those have already been submitted to Bantam. The three will complete the third and final volume of the Nevèrÿon series, *Flight from Nevèrÿon.*

I don't know how much of this I've told you before. Really I'm rather punchy over it all at this point. Between last October and now, "Fog and Granite," for example, went through eleven drafts! And "The Mummer's Tale" went through at least six or seven. Even with a word processor, that's a lot!

I have a carton full of drafts that — if you're interested — I'll send to the Mugar in Boston via you folks down there.

The money situation has been truly surreal. One of the reasons I haven't sent you guys copies of F&G and MT is simply that I haven't been able to afford the Xerox copies, and it takes about five-and-a-half to six-and-a-half hours to print up a copy on my single-sheet, hand-fed printer.

And it's been so long since I've seen six-and-a-half free hours in a row, I doubt I'd recognize them if they came along!

I hope my last letter to Mike wasn't too rough. I intended it to be *un peu amusant,* but it was written in the midst of all sorts of *Sturm und Drang,* and I might have gone a bit over the mark. I know he's busy and that you both have worked terribly hard at all this. But I couldn't see how else at the time to cover what strikes me as a fundamental problem. But, as I said in it, I am going to drop any more detailed attempts to correct things *anent* that particular period/situation, because you (plural) really do have all the information to correct it several times over by now. In *P&C*[1] there're a couple of (light, light!) suggestions of the same sort of thing that I hope will make you smile.

February was a pretty rough month all around—the only thing that made it bearable was the fact that the weather was astonishingly mild for what is traditionally the bitterest month in New York.

Inscribe my briefest accounts of the following on a field of No Money at All (and the general scufflings and hand-to-mouth strategies such a condition puts on general survival matters) and you'll have some notion of what Life in These Here Climes has been like of late.

Enclosed is a newspaper article that began the month for us: I think I've told you, since October I've been giving my Thursday evenings to *The Little Magazine*. We meet on the 46th floor of the building in Manhattan Plaza where the murder recounted in the article occurred, a handful of floors below. The only thing that the building gossip added that isn't in the article is that both Ms. Jones and her murderer were deeply involved with Amway—you may have seen the exposé of that particular scam on *60 Minutes* some months back . . .?

M. has been talking for some time rather vaguely about taking Iva to France for a school year, and I have been talking rather explicitly about not liking the idea at all. But this month it came up as a Thing to Be Finally Decided. Iva is ten. She's already changed schools once. She has some troubles getting along with her mother—nothing terribly serious—which she doesn't have with Frank and me, and when it was brought up with Iva, her rather straight forward, ten-year-old response to the notion of going off was:

"You mean live with my mother for nine months? No way!"

M. has received a $15,000 dollar Ingram Merril fellowship for next year; a Parisian professor who is coming to this country to teach in New York has volunteered to swap apartments with her; and M. loves France. I can understand the urge and ease with which it might be done. But she says she won't go without Iva—she would miss Iva too much. And, in a word, that's exactly the way Frank and I feel. Ten strikes me simply as too young for that kind of separation from a primary parent who takes care of her 50% of the time—not to mention for a primary parent.

At any rate, we had a two-and-a-half-hour discussion between M., Frank, and myself over the whole matter. M. has found what sounds like a very good bilingual school for Iva in Paris and is anxious to send Iva back to us for vacations. Indeed, as everyone has tried to explain to her, it's not the quality of her plans that's in question. We just don't want Iva to go; and in a joint custody situation, this kind of veto power must be respected, however unpleasant or inconvenient. It went fairly calmly as such things go, and Frank and I both thought by the end of it that it had been decided and understood. But a week later M. called up wanting to know if we could all meet with a therapist (a woman psychiatrist who does family counseling), who would presumably tell me and Frank that it was okay for

---

[1] *The Tales of Plagues and Carnivals,* which ended up at more than 60,000 words (i.e., novel length), in *Flight from Nevèrÿon* (Bantam, 1985).

Iva to go to school in France for a year.

Frank was kind of miffed. He'd been bothered by the whole thing more than I had — and he too had thought it was finished. But here it was being opened up all over again. M. wanted all three of us to come. But Frank and I decided between us that the best thing was for myself and M. to see the therapist togeth-er. If the therapist wanted him there and felt a second session was necessary — or that, indeed, a session with Iva, M., myself, and Frank was called for — he would be more than willing to come then.

I must say I thought the session was very good; so was the therapist. M. pretty much went through her entire emotional repertoire in the course of it. The therapist was about as non-judgmental as it's possible to be. But one thing that she said made me want to applaud: "You seem to feel," she told me, "that Iva is very fragile. More fragile than a child is. Children are very resilient and can deal with almost anything. But you," she said, turning to Marilyn, "seem to feel that Iva is more autonomous, more independent, and more mature than any child could possibly be. The kind of judgements and independence you're expressing for Iva is the kind no fourteen-, fifteen-, or sixteen-year-old could have—much less a ten-year-old." M. argued with her. But the therapist stuck to her guns. And I really think M. finally began to hear her. But if I could sum up in a sentence what Frank, my mother, my sister, and, indeed, I have been saying about M. and Iva for years, that's it.

Treating a kid like a human being is fine. I try to. Almost everybody I know does. But treating a child like an adult (and often doing it so that you can be the emotional child, which, if you'll forgive the armchair psychology, frequently seems to be M.) is not. At any rate, at the end of another two and a half hours, M. had accepted that Iva could not be taken away to France, and the two of us were actually getting along pretty well.

I give Dr. Margaret Neuman all kudos.

Frank has been under a great deal of pressure through all this. The last time he's worked was a part-time job he had at the *NY Times* back when I was in Milwaukee, just after we met. And he hasn't worked full-time in over ten years. He's felt very bad about the money situation and really wants to do something about it. But he also has many deep and severe anxieties involving self-worth and competency (which, years before we met, got him hospitalized several times). In this last month, he's made several serious stabs at getting a job, which haven't worked out. This has been very hard on him, and his tensions about these efforts — before, during, and after — permeate the house; and if anything, that has been the most difficult thing for me to deal with in the past months, money, M., and work notwithstanding.

Iva was back on Saturday (the week before at her riding academy's horse show, Frank and I went up and watched her take two second-place ribbons!), and Frank seems to be relaxing somewhat under her terribly beneficent ten-year-old vibes.

But there have been moments, trying to finish up this book, when I've had a kind of: "Stiff upper lip, eyes straight ahead, nose to the grindstone, shoulder to the wheel—now try to work in that position," feeling about life in general.

Nevertheless, the work is getting done.

There's something about a word processor—or at least the Perfect Writer pro-gram—that discourages letter writing. Or, after all of the above, is that superfluous? Anyway, I've certainly planned out half a dozen letters to you in the interim. But this is the first I've actually gotten on paper; and I haven't even checked my various notes for this one.

Oh, yes!

Starboard Wine finally exists in volume form. I have a copy; I should be getting more tomorrow when I go up to David Hartwell's to sign 500 of them . . .! Will send you one along soon as I can.

Let me just say thanks very much for your last letter.

Much love to you, Cynthia, Jonathon, et al.,

• 12 •

To Robert S. Bravard

March 13th, 1984

Dear Bob,

Well, here it is, 4:54 in the morning, and I am pulling into the end of my first cup of coffee. I've been up for about half an hour, enjoying the silence, the darkness.

It's been snowing on and off. They've promised up to eight inches.

Iva won't be up till seven, and Frank not till a little later—when we'll have a cup of coffee together and an hour or so of conversation, once Iva's off to school at seven-forty.

. . . my day.

Yesterday and today have been mostly writerly "housekeeping." That's a handful of unavoidable letters—I'm GOH[1] at V-Con 12 in May, and while I'm out there, I'll be lecturing/reading at the U. of Washington at Seattle, thanks to the good offices of Joanna. So I had to write both the con committee in Vancouver and Joanna in Seattle. Also a letter to Mog. I finally delivered the checked-over manuscript of *Stars in My Pocket like Grains of Sand* to F. X. Flyn at Bantam yesterday morning at eleven twenty (surprise, surprise: Francis Xavier has gone and shaved off his black and curly beard!), but more about that, anon—though, briefly, I ended up having an hour conference with Lou Aronica (more about that, too), who also gave me a color proof of the mass-market cover for *Neveryóna* (out in July). Then down to Henry's to get Danny—Henry's son-in-law and office manager—to cash a much circulated and exchanged half of a royalty check for me, as I have been living without the benefit of a checking account since last October, thanks to Uncle Sam. Eight hundred dollars' worth of royalties from Doubleday on *Nova*. That, incidentally, is my first actual "income from writing" since last year. Sigh.

Somewhere in the midst of all this I helped Iva build a "Science Fair" project on series and parallel circuits, which turns out not to work . . .

I must trouble-shoot that by Fair time, two weekends hence.

Your letter of February 15th/March 7th has been received, read, and reread with much affection.

And after I get this letter off to you, I shall plunge into the conclusion of *Plagues and Carnivals*.

[1] Guest of Honor

Flashdance!

Last summer was our *Flashdance* summer, here in New York, and my response was pretty much the same as yours, i.e., I loved it, despite its endless illogicalities. Frank saw it first and decided that Jennifer Beal was the most beautiful human being he'd ever seen.

She looks very much like a woman friend of ours named M——, a stunning Puerto Rican woman (who, it turns out, lived with writer John Crowley for several years and is reputedly the model for one of the characters in *Little, Big,* though I don't see it myself). Sadly, M—— doesn't do too much right through here except sell pot, and we haven't seen her for a couple of years with any frequency.

At any rate, I saw it a few days after Frank.

And a couple of months later, Frank decided that Iva would love it. So, indeed, we took her to see it. Turns out Frank had forgotten some of the more explicit scenes in the movie, and had just remembered the basic conflict over her dancing career— and although Iva was not bothered at all by such things (what nine-year-old would be? Bored? Perhaps. Bothered, no), he squirmed a bit during some of those scenes.

But Iva liked it—and, of course, fell totally in love with the music, which, even until last night just before she went to bed, she was playing on her Christmas tape-player-radio. (Indeed, she hasn't played it for a couple of weeks, but she decided to put it on last night for a while, just before she turned in.)

It's odd. You took from it more the "escape from this place" theme, while both Frank and I took from it more the "will you have the nerve to try what you may fail at?" theme. But you're absolutely right about the two foils, the cook/comedian who comes back from L.A. and the young skater-turned-stripper. They are what allow us to put such a rich interpretation on Jennifer's conflict—which is basically just a problem of self-confidence.

I remember Bernie[2] saying to me, perhaps six months before his death (when we were talking about Frank, I believe), that in all his experience as a therapist, he'd really found only one problem: whether a person thought he or she could do it or not.

He said it clearly had nothing to do with intelligence or education or even a good home-life vs. a bad home-life; still, there were some people who pretty much thought of themselves as able to do pretty much whatever it is that they wanted to do, while there were others who basically thought they couldn't. The first group, even if they're completely schizophrenic, are more or less happy people with greater or smaller problems. The others, even if they're Phi Beta Kappa graduates who've gone on to become General Motors executives, are miserable.

How one gets to be that first type, I'll never know . . . although it's what my whole goal with loving, supporting, and guiding Iva is all about.

Fleshdance, huh? You mean there's one I *haven't* seen? I'll keep an eye out for it.

---

[2] Bernard K. Kay (1910–1983) lived with his wife Ivanetta (after whom SRD and Marilyn Hacker's daughter Iva was named) at 845 West End Avenue at 103rd St., in a roomy second-floor apartment. Psychologist, musician, actor, writer and translator, Kay became SRD's mentor, when they met during SRD's seventeenth autumn. SRD was first introduced to Kay by a young sculptor, David Logan, then living in the older couple's back room. Their close friendship continued through Kay's death from lung cancer in October, 1983, an incident elided from these pages by the selection of letters in the Prologue.

"...Will Marilyn think through her relationship with your child...?" you write. Well, as I was going down to the corner postbox to mail my last letter to you, I looked in our own mailbox in the vestibule. There was a letter from Marilyn, asking basically that I reconsider yet again her taking Iva to France — just as though the entire therapy session hadn't happened. It concluded with a paragraph about how much Iva wants to go, and she actually had Iva sign the letter jointly with her!

I don't know whether I mentioned it; but after M. had been going on for ten minutes about how the entire idea had been Iva's in the first place (Iva had said how nice it would be to live in France one day last June when the two of them had been walking along some street in Paris), how it was only because Iva wanted to go, etc., etc., another of the therapist's major points to M. was: "In a decision like this, really, the child can have no input at all. A child just doesn't have that kind of judgment. If you had to go to France because of a job, say, and your child didn't want to go; would you say, 'Well, you can stay home'? Or, 'I'll give up my job because you don't want to go'? No, you wouldn't. Well, by the same token, to talk about such a decision stemming from a child—or that it's because the child wants it—is very unrealistic."

That was another place when I wanted to applaud.

But, I'm afraid, that one really didn't sink in.

After Iva had been here for a few days, I asked her about it one afternoon when we were going to see *The Right Stuff* together. (Good movie!) To which Iva explained, as only a ten-year-old can: "Well, she [Iva's mother] said she didn't think there was much chance of your changing your mind, but she thought she'd try it."

I've written an answer to the letter, calm and firm: No. I still haven't sent it, though. I want to look it over once more to extract all traces of ire that may remain.

I could go into more detail.

But I won't.

The much-worried-over article . . .? Ah, my friend, my friend. Let me begin (and, I'm sure, I should end as well) by saying that my memory certainly is not of the best. And if the mumbled truth be known, I have been sweating over two pages in one of my letters of last August because I really think I goofed up, even there, as to the actual publication dates of *Nova:* They may be off, in that letter, by as much as six months.

Let me elucidate briefly: At this point, I'm pretty sure that Bernie's diary entry for April 6th, 1968, refers not to the galleys of the Book Club edition, but to the Doubleday galleys, which would mean that the citations on the copyright page of the first Bantam edition are more or less correct (August '68 for the Doubleday edition; May '69 for the Book Club edition—which would mean that I didn't give Terry a copy of the Book Club edition in the summer of '68, as I claimed, but rather a hand-corrected copy of the Doubleday edition—which, really, is kind of more "me" anyway). Those dates [Aug '68/May '69] are, of course, publication dates and do not take into account the three to six weeks between "copies available" and "publication"—which means in both cases possibly copies were available a month (maybe two months) before the date stated. *Mea culpa, mea culpa.* This probably has thrown things off for you by as much as six months, if you're really trying to keep an accurate, month-by-month chronology.

But six months from eighteen months still leaves twelve; this means even if you've been going by the resultant mistaken chronology, you're still confounding things a year apart — which, if you accept the documentary evidence, are more like a year and a half apart; which, at this point, I'm more inclined to accept myself. But as I've said, details aren't relevant until the basic model is straightened out.

"Your version has some of the events occurring in 1967 and Terry Carr's version put them later towards 1969," you write me with what I assume is a straight face.

Bob!

You are writing about TWO events!

First is *Nova's* submission to and acceptance by Doubleday, which occurred between October 1966 (approximately) and February 10th, 1967, which is the date of the signing of the Doubleday contract, all of which: one, jibes with my memory and, two, after all, is written down — unless you want to assume that the contract was misdated by a couple of years, seventeen years ago . . .? By and large, this has nothing to do with Ace Books. This is a situation which Ace could not have had any real objections to, because, as a paperback reprint house, there was just no economic conflict between Ace and Doubleday to support such objections.

Apparently Doubleday scheduled the book to appear some sixteen months after contracting for it — which, you should certainly realize by now, is common enough, considering that the book was not yet finished when the contract was signed. If Bernie's diary is to be trusted, galleys were not ready till c. the beginning of April, 1968. And if the first printing of the Bantam paperback edition's copyright pages is to be trusted, the book's official Doubleday publication date was August, 1968, which means copies could have been available from the end of June, '68 on.

The second event is *Nova's* paperback sale, in late summer of 1968, after the Doubleday edition had appeared. *This* is the time that Ace could reasonably have been interested in the book. *This* is the time I gave Terry a hardcover copy of the book. *This* is the time I urged/begged Terry to purchase the book.

This is also the time that Bantam put in a $10,000 bid to Doubleday.

And this is the time that Terry (or, more accurately, Terry's boss, Don) didn't buy the book. Needless to say, this is the situation that Terry is giving you factual and non-suppositional information about in his letter. The rest of his letter is clearly speculation — from page two of his letter on — based on his assumption that you guys know what you're talking about at places where, clearly, you're just wrong, i.e., his speculations on Bantam's being the prime licensee of the novel, which might then have been farmed out to Doubleday, which, as I said, he obviously has picked up from a mistake in *your* communication to him!

He was "nobody" in 1967, Terry says. (This is somewhat over-modest. Had he been "nobody," he never would have been invited to be an editor at Ace on the strength of his fanzine work in '65/'66. But let it stand.) Clearly by mid-'68, which is the time we are talking of, the article had appeared — both Terry and I concur — as well as the first eight/nine Ace specials, which, with the very first (Lafferty's *Past Master*, January, 1968) attracted considerable attention.

This is the time when there could have been, indeed, some tensions between

Ace and Bantam, as these two companies are both paperback reprint houses and are indeed in economic conflict with one another.

Clearly from Terry's letter — and, indeed, from common sense — there was minimal conflict there: Bantam had more money and used it. That's all. But given the minimal nature of the Ace/Bantam "conflict," common sense should leave it indisputable that any Ace/Doubleday conflict, if it existed at all, could only have been a fraction of that—and equally clearly it wasn't even fractional. Find any reference to it in Terry's letter!

Let me say, just as gently as you have reminded me about my faulty memory (to which I freely, even gladly admit!): I talked to Terry personally about all this (at Phoenix, c. 1980). I read his letter more than half a dozen times (before I misplaced it).

Terry doesn't see any conflict with my version. I don't see any conflict with Terry's version. If I recall, Terry said in the first page of his letter that my version is essentially correct. The only thing he takes me (via you) to task about is the intensity of his own "dissatisfaction" with Ace Books—a correction I absolutely accede to.

Now if Terry and I have seen each other's versions and agree that in all particulars they are both correct and do not contradict each other — while you still see some discrepancies between them (i.e., the two quotes you juxtapose, which, as I say, simply refer to two different incidents), then I most gently suggest this may be because you are working from an essentially incorrect model:

If you see some conflict between my statement to the effect that "I begged Terry to take the book" (in the late summer of 1968, when the book was up for paperback sale) and Terry's statement that "the manuscript was never submitted to me" (in autumn of 1966 when, indeed, the MS was submitted to Doubleday), then, yet again, I submit you are working from a faulty model that simply confounds the two occurrences.

Your tale about your graduate school friend at the library who tells the party story about the attempted seduction and the spiked orange juice is, indeed, exactly what we have here. If you look back over my letter of January 9th, 1980, you'll find I initiated this whole discussion with an anecdote quite similar to yours. And the only distinction, if I may belabor the obvious, is that you are not telling a party story (in which case I too would keep silent, believe me), you're writing a scholarly paper—and what's more, a scholarly paper whose specific topic is accuracy!

But here I am, violating my own decision to say no more. So I return to it. ("I shall say no more . . .!") But believe me, all of the above was written with a large smile on my face . . .!

I'll send the drafts of "Fog and Granite" and "The Mummer's Tale" up to the Mugar directly. Having seen all the detritus to *Neveryóna*, you can't really want to see more dead leaves . . . And as soon as I can (probably when I finish *Plagues & Carnivals* and I can send the whole thing), I'll get you a draft of *Nevèrÿon*, Vol III.

Let me see: What else did I want to mention to you? Oh, yes. A left-over notion from *Flashdance*. Back in December (the 18th?), Barbara Wise threw a Christmas party that I went to—as I was coming up their front steps that evening, at about six thirty, there was John Hanhardt, on the steps just ahead of me — John is video/film curator of the Whitney Museum, and, on and off throughout the party, we had a pleasant talk. (Indeed, I ran into him twice, I think, in the next couple of days, once at the Museum and once outside his bank in the village while he was standing in line at the automatic teller window.) But for entertainment at the party that evening, Barbara had hired a pair of fifteen- or sixteen-year-old break-dancers—whom, she said, she'd seen performing in the street one day when she'd happened to be passing through the South Bronx.

They arrived about nine-thirty at night and performed on the sprawling red tiles of the Wises' floor-through kitchen, while the 50/60 guests stood around in awe at the whole thing. The dancers were really quite spectacular—most of the time they were upside down and/or invisible, they were spinning so fast!

Once, when one of the kids was doing some unbelievable shoulder spin, his blue running shoe hit one of the guests (a tall man with a gray beard and wearing a beige hunting jacket) in the arm, but it wasn't serious; hands were shaken all around. And that was as close as we came to a casualty. (Outside, sitting on a car fender, the kid said about it later: "Man, I'm down there spinnin', and suddenly I felt *bone!*")

Barbara's nineteen-year-old daughter, Julie, is rather punk and I just assumed that she must have had something to do with this—there was also a young black pop group there that night who did some really fine rap-songs with Pointed Social Messages.

While the dancers were performing, Barbara in dazzling red was standing just in front of me, and I leaned over my vodka and tonic to whisper: "Where did you find these kids? Was this Julie's idea? They're great!"

Barbara glanced back over her shoulder at me, smiled wryly, and said: "Julie's idea? Are you kidding! South Bronx, just below East Tremont."

After they finished, I went outside to talk with the dancers (where they'd gone to sit on that car fender to cool off); the rap group went with them, congratulating them on their performance. The two boys were about the most ordinary sixteen-year-old Puerto Ricans you could imagine: pleasant, outgoing, friendly, pleased with themselves, and something of a pair of operators, if you know what I mean — only countered, I suspect, because I doubt they were really bright enough to bring off the kind of operations they were envisaging.

(Today the Wises; tomorrow, the World . . . !)

At any rate, your talk about *Flashdance* reminded me of them, and actually I'd been meaning to tell you about them since December, when I wasn't writing anyone. . . .

December, did I say?

Stars in My Pocket is currently scheduled for December, '84. (Thus the train of associations runs on.) The story of its copy-editing involves as beleaguered a bunch of fuck-ups as any since the *Neveryóna* cover story—and I'm wondering if I'm really up to recounting it.

Briefly, however, the MS came to me back toward the end of October, supposedly copy-edited. When I finally got around to looking at it, I found that (one) the gentleman who had done it was next to illiterate (at least in the fine points of narrative punctuation); he had also (two) engaged shamelessly in "creative re-writing" all through the manuscript; and (three) he had copy-edited it in some sort of indelible red pencil that simply would not erase. (Bantam's "Copy-editors' Guide

Sheet" instructs the copy editor to do the work in a No. 3 medium point lead pencil, and for a very good reason: Any and every correction must be easily erasable — because invariably some of them are going to *be* erased, if only because the writer may want to correct the problem in a way other than the way the copy editor has suggested. If the corrections aren't easily erasable, the job is practically useless.)

Well, back in October, I'd called up Lou, and read him half a dozen examples from the first three pages over the phone. "Is it like this all through the manuscript?" he wanted to know.

As far as I could tell, the copy editor had worked on the MS over about six sittings. For the first four/six pages of each sitting, he had gone crazy — then he'd probably gotten tired and fallen back into marking/making just your ordinary bloopers and mistakes.

It seems that the copy editor was a personal friend of F. X. Flyn's, indeed, a struggling writer himself who needed a job and who was apparently a great enthusiast of my work and "very familiar" with "my style." He had been anxious to work on one of my manuscripts, and everyone at Bantam had expected a particularly pristine and sensitive job from him.

What they'd gotten, alas, was one of the two or three worst jobs of professional copy-editing I've seen in 23 years of professional writing — and, believe me, I've seen some dillies!

"Lou," I said, "this should be a three- or four-day job. The state it's in, it'll take me two or three weeks solid to correct. If I were 20 years old, I'd probably just sit down and do it. But I'm 41, tired, and am trying very hard to finish another book..."

Gentleman that he is, Lou volunteered to take it back and have it redone.

So, indeed, the job went back to Bantam.

But in order to avoid paying someone else to re-do the job from scratch (I had suggested to Flyn over the phone by now that he just have someone in the production department take on the tedious task of erasing and/or whiting out the indelible red pencil marks, and I would take it from there), Flyn felt he had to give it back to the same guy to "correct."

The manuscript came back in January. Of course the guy had as much trouble erasing his red pencil marks as I had, and had finally more or less given up, and gone about "stetting" over his re-writings with what I can only assume was a black, felt-tip pen!

At any rate, his new corrections were in some black ink that wasn't just hard to erase: It was simply un-erasable — period.

Instead of calling Bantam and raising hell, I got my white-out and an eraser (and a number-three lead pencil) and went about carefully correcting this guys debacle of sloppiness, ignorance, and pretension. Working at it over a full morning, trying to correct his mess, as well as make what final corrections I wanted to add of my own, etc., I could do about 40 pages a day (i.e., working from about 5:30 in the morning, with an hour's break to get Iva off to school, till noon). At this point, of course, I was also working my hardest on "Fog and Granite" and "The Mummer's Tale," so I ended up only putting in a couple or three mornings a week on it—sometimes a couple of mornings more, and, sometimes, a couple of mornings less.

No, the nearly-600 pages didn't go very fast.

Last Wednesday, F. X. called to say that they really needed the MS by Monday (yesterday) in order to keep to the production schedule. And so *Plagues & Carnivals* was put aside, and over Thursday, Friday, Saturday, and a few hours on Sunday morning, I finished up the remaining couple of hundred pages of the manuscript.

And, to come full circle to the first pages of this letter, I delivered the MS yesterday morning at 11:20. F. X. came out to meet me in the Bantam lobby (on the 25th floor of 666 Fifth Ave—I mentioned his new, beardless demeanor . . .?) and we went back to his small, cluttered office. (At least it *is* an office. Most of the people there are stuck merely with cubicles.) I pointed out that the guy had done his re-corrections in ink, not pencil, to which F. X.'s response was: "Oh, Jesus Christ . . .!"

I also had brought in one last correction that had slipped through my fingers for the re-release of *Tales of Nevèrÿon* that will accompany the rack-size edition of *Neveryóna*, out this July—F. X. Xeroxed it up and swore he'd take care of getting it in personally.

Oh, yes. And Lou wanted to see me.

So F. X. took me down the long, long, pale gray halls of Bantam, till we found Lou's cubicle — empty. As we were standing about looking confused, Lou, in a blue pinstriped shirt and a battleship gray tie walked up—and F. X. bid me *adieu.*

We sat down together in the cubicle, and Lou leaned back in his lean-back chair beside his word processor screen. "Chip," he said, "we have a problem."

"Henry suggested to me that you might," I said, smiling; for, indeed, Henry had:

In brief, Lou had read "Fog and Granite" and "The Mummer's Tale," both of which he likes very much as stories. He thought the "characterization" in both was "wonderful." And ". . . 'Fog & Granite' gives me more of a sense of Nevèrÿon as a place than anything in either of the other two volumes . . ." But ". . . the fantasy element . . ." in "Fog and Granite" is minuscule and in "The Mummer's Tale" it's "nil."

Which is quite true. And I allowed as how it was so.

And if the third story is along the same lines, he explained, "I don't see how we're going to be able to market it as a fantasy. Or even how we can reasonably contract for it as such."

I figure in this kind of case, I'd best do some of his work for him: "Well," I explained, "the third story in the volume—which should be finished in a couple of weeks, incidentally—actually has a rather large fantasy payoff: It climaxes with a kind of underground dionysiac magic ceremony, where the magic really works. On the other hand, the story deals directly with AIDS, switches back and forth from our present to the past, is dotted with newspaper clippings and the like, and in general is highly experimental—dealing as it does with the way[s] fantasy can relate to the realest of real life; it's more than just a fantastic story. I suspect it won't really resolve anything so much as it will be the most problematic thing in the book," I said, more or less.

Lou's comment: "It sounds both fascinating and ambitious . . ." and he's anxious to see it. "Now Henry says you are in need of money . . .?"

"Rather . . ." I said, and gave him a few chilling examples.

He seemed sufficiently chilled. "Still, you owe Bantam two books, at $150,000 apiece. We—the powers that be, that is—are just not going to be all that anxious to negotiate a new contract with you in that situation, over a book that has such limited commercial possibilities; or, at least, such marketing difficulties—"

"The bottom line," I said, calmly, smiling, but not really liking such fiddle faddle, "is whether you want to give up the third volume of a trilogy, the first volume of which has sold very well, the second volume of which has gone into two printings in trade paperback and sold respectably and is about to come out in mass market with a stunningly commercial cover. Well, that's what you have to decide."

At which point, Lou came forward in his chair. "No no no no no, Chip," he declared, smiling. "We want to be your publisher. *I* want to be your publisher. Certainly there'll be some way we can publish it. I'm just saying that I'll have to fight for it, and that it will take time. Now here's another possibility. Think about this one. Instead of making a new contract, we might be able to renegotiate the existing contract to include three books—of which *Flight from Nevèrÿon* would be the first. And the remaining two books would be books two and three of this new contract. That way we can get you some money immediately, and Bantam will feel like it's getting a book for nothing." (*Feel* like . . . ? I couldn't help thinking.) "The truth is," Lou went on, "yours are the only $150,000 books Bantam has out today." ["Out" is publisher's slang for "outstanding"] "Five years ago, we were making deals like that. But you know what bad shape publishing has been in for the last couple of years. Today, we just can't do that any more. We have a few $100,000 books out. But $150,000 originals are a thing of the past, now. Mention it to Henry, and see what he says. How does it sound to you . . . ?"

I smiled. Because I smile. "Lou," I said. "It sounds wonderful. If we could work that out, I would be so grateful. Of course you know I can't commit myself to anything in this kind of informal way, but I will speak to Henry and see what he says."

"Okay," Lou said, smiling.

We stood up, shook—he remembered he had a cover proof for the mass-market edition of *Neveryóna*, which he gave me along with some new Silver-Bob[2] reprints.

And with warm good-byes, I left this 26-year-old apprentice Mafioso twerp!

[Note that I call him a "gentleman" earlier in this same letter. The truth is, personally I like him. I know it's just a game one must play. But my dinner seems to be the pawn . . .]

Need I pull out what lodges between the lines? What he is saying of course is: Since you are in immediate need of funds, if you will give us the new book for nothing, we will take a few thousand dollars away from what we have agreed to pay you for your next two books and let you have it now. If, however, you want to be paid at all for this new book, we will hold up negotiations on this new book for three or four months or longer before we get around to paying you anything.

I wonder if he thinks I've forgotten that two years ago, when Bantam was negotiating for *Neveryóna*, they went so far as to hold up my October royalties for three months on the excuse that because I was negotiating a new book with them, they didn't know what my "status" was. But then, of course, that was under Karen, not Lou.

---

[2] Occasional nickname for science fiction writer Robert Silverberg.

The logic is simple: If you know somebody is in need, if you hold up paying them as long as possible, you can force them to take less and less.

Frank's response when I got home and told him about it (trying, I confess, to milk some good out of it): "Chip, that's just shabby. In fact, it's more than shabby. It's slimy."

The one thing that would make it psychologically worth it for me (and, of course, nothing could make it financially worthwhile) is if they gave me enough right away so that I could get out from under this tax nonsense, or at least could reasonably see the light ahead—then I'd probably give them the book. The honest truth is that I don't think books are *worth* $150,000 dollars. I don't really think they're worth $100,000. But I didn't ask for this three-book contract. In fact I did everything I could to make it a single book contract. But they literally insisted on a multiple book deal—to insure their "investment in my future," they said.

I suppose if they would give me enough up front to get, say, $35,000 to the government with $12 or $15,000 left over to live on for the rest of the year, I'd do it.

But $40,000 is the most Henry can get for it, if he fights, and Lou has practically said that will be, minimum, a three-month-plus negotiation (because the book—sequel to two begrudged high sellers—is difficult to "categorize"). And, truthfully, I don't know whether I can last that long.

I still haven't talked to Henry, who is too tied up in his coming office move to talk to anyone for a few days; and Lou is off to California today till the middle of next week. But the kind of grandstands this is going to require from Henry doesn't make the best atmosphere for me to work in.

Oh, yes. While I was on the subway, I took out the cover proof that Lou had given me for the mass-market paperback of *Neveryóna*. Pictorially, it's really quite something. If anything, Rowena's cover-painting looks even better in rack size that it did in trade-size.

But then I turned to look at the back cover and read over the copy, which begins (and I quote):

"In the ancient, fabled land of Nevèrÿon, they tell of a gleaming golden city, sunken beneath the waves of history . . .

NEVERYÓNA . . ."

Now, when cover copy was being written for the trade edition, the first back cover-copy I was shown was very like this; and I pointed out to Lou that, in Chapter One, the sunken city is nameless. By the end of Chapter Two, "Neveryóna" has been clearly established as the old name for Kolhari, though it is now only the name of one neighborhood within Kolhari where the hereditary nobility lives. Neveryóna is what Madame Kayne aspires to. It is where Gorgik has ended up by mistake. Its fancied intrigues are what Pryn is fleeing (symbolically), when she leaves the city.

Only in the penultimate chapter of the novel do we indeed learn that Neveryóna is *also* the name for the sunken city—which explains why the neighborhood in Kolhari is named Neveryóna and why it was once the name of all Kolhari. Thus, to say on the cover that "Neveryóna" is the name of the sunken city is tantamount to saying on the cover of a mystery that, indeed, the butler done it.

I called Lou 40 minutes after I left the Bantam office, to tell him. But he'd already gone for the day—and, as I said, won't be back from California till next week, at least so said the receptionist. So I left a detailed message with Lou's assistant, David Stern, who told me that, actually, Lou was supposed to drop by the office again at five for a few minutes, just before he left. At quarter past five I called again, just to see if he was there. David said that Lou hadn't arrived yet, but that he and Tappan both were waiting for him to get there momentarily.

"Did you tell Tappan?" I asked.

"Eh . . . no," said David.

"Well, do," I said. "Please."

But that is the kind of morass of non-communication that characterizes publishing on almost all levels today.

Well, they corrected it on the trade paperback. I wonder if they'll get round to fixing it here . . .?

A couple of weeks ago our downstairs neighbor-across-the-hall had a small stroke—at 86 or so! He's a strong old man, who walks five miles every day. The effects of it were that he lost his speech, and, apparently his ability to respond to other people at all. But all his habits were the same. At about one o'clock in the afternoon, I was coming home from somewhere or other, and there was old Mr. Neilson, literally dragging his niece Margaret (with whom he lives) down the stoop and toward the corner.

"Help me!" she all but whispered, in a high, frightened little voice, hanging onto his arm. "I can't stop him. Please, help me! He wants to go out in the street! Help!"

I and Señor Bertrand (another neighbor) came over to lend assistance. It took the three of us adults to hold that 86-year-old man back from wandering out in the street and into Amsterdam Avenue's fast and copious commercial traffic! Finally we had to walk him across the street and down to Broadway, then swing him around and march him back home. And of course it began to rain in the middle of it, and both Mr. Neilson and Margaret were without coats. Through it all, he simply did not seem to realize any of us were there—even as I talked to him loudly and constantly, trying to calm him down and reassure him. He was only striving to walk forward. We finally got him upstairs. Margaret called the doctor (while grumpy old Señor Bertrand, I discovered as we stood outside in the hall together waiting for Margaret to phone [first the church, then the police], speaks quite passable French! Till now, I'd thought he was limited to Spanish; we have been chatting away amiably when we pass on the stairs ever since), and Mr. N. went into the hospital that evening. I've seen his niece a few times since. (Only a year or so older than I, Margaret is nevertheless already an old woman in ways that my mother, at 70, isn't: Margaret is almost pathologically shy, if not terrified, of the whole functioning world, shrill, excitable and—finally—not very smart.) She says Mr. N.'s regained his speech and is coming along. . . .

Still it was quite an adventure for us all.

> All my love to you, Cynthia, and the boys,
> and all good things and thoughts,

• 13 •

To Robert S. Bravard

April 22nd, 1984

Dear Bob,

Alas, this is not the long letter "full of gossip" and the like I promised. I have "misplaced" its first ten pages on some disk or other, and will no doubt eventually find it. Briefly, however, the problem is this: One of the instructions in the vast tome/pamphlet that accompanies the Perfect Writer program reads more or less *in toto*: "Name your files creatively, so that you will remember what they are when you need them."

I now have about seven disks full of letters, and—*mea culpa*—I have not been creative.

I hang my head in shame. Lack of creativity in the computer world is a crime clearly as heinous as failing to make back-up files. ("You'll rue it! You'll rue it!") But I have been naming my individual letters perfectly prosaic things like "Bob1," "Bob2," "Bob3," and "Bob4." And I have even, now and again, been so pedestrian as to call some "Let1," "Let2," "Let3," and so forth. Well, now I find that while I thought every letter to the same person had at least a different number, it seems I have overlaps on several disks. I can't remember whether your letter fragment was a "Bob" or a "Let" and I'm lost in a sea of overlapping 6s, 7s, and 8s—seven overlapping seas, actually. At some point I've got to go through all the letter files and check out which is which and then do some "creative" renaming.

Clearly my correspondents should each have a different number (or letter) that I keep on a major list somewhere; then the central part of the file name should be a date, followed by a number. You could be number one, two, or three, say; so that the file name for a letter to you might be something like: "1A22847.mss," which would translate, Bob, April 22, '84, letter-seven (manuscript source). Certainly *that's* creative, no? (I mean, anybody could look at a file directory and tell that "W5836.mss" was a far more creative name than "Joanna6.mss," *n'est-ce pas?*) And of course I must make sure there are no overlappings. . . .

"Change is neither merciful nor just . . ." Ms. Hacker wrote in a poem somewhere back in our childhood. Last night, as I went downstairs to pick up a quart of milk, coffee filters for the automatic GE coffee maker (you use the last one and it's always such a surprise), a piece of fried chicken from the little "Cheun Shing" Chinese take-out store across the Avenue, a can of beer for me and some ice-cream and cookies for Frank, I ran into Robin, the little partridge of a book-clerk who used to work at Shakespeare & Co., and who lives with the owner, Bill, and his brother in the house next to mine. The file of five apartment [read "tenement"] buildings is all owned by the same landlord, one P—— M——, and their third-floor apartment is pretty much the same as ours. Three of them share it as roommates, and the landlord is getting $1,500 a month from them! (I pay $461 a month for ours, and I think *that's* high.) Actually, Robin's just left the bookstore to start working for Crown Publishers. At any rate, she had a bunch of letters in her hand, and as we stepped to the corner, she suddenly frowned: "Chip," she said, "wasn't there a mailbox here . . . ?"

And, indeed, only the previous morning I had sent off some pub-pictures and stuff for Joanna (I'll be lecturing in Seattle late in May, after I'm guest of honor at

Vancouver Con IV, on the weekend of May 25th) there the previous morning; more than half my letters to you have been dropped through that same, now-vanished slot. But there were only four little stains on the concrete paving stone where the blue-painted metal legs have stood all these years.

And across the Avenue, the diminutive Beacon Paint Store (Est. 1904) and Mrs. Ucker's Hand Laundry (which always looked to me as if it had been established a good deal earlier) have in the last month given place to a diminutive restaurant, specializing in chicken and ribs ("The Yellow Rose of Texas") and an equally diminutive shop specializing in fancy lamps.

Looking down from my fifth floor window this morning, I can see the smart and awkward front of "Pizzas of the World," a "chic" pizza parlor, if you can imagine such a thing, which everybody in the neighborhood has pronounced a failure—though it still dotters on. It's only been open six months, and although I saw what used to be there everyday of my life for nearly seven years, I can't even remember what it was—oh, yes. It was a tiny, dusty, *"botanica de fe,"* which sold religious statues and candles and where, no doubt, you went in order to make contact with the local *"bruja"* (or *"brujo"*), a Puerto Rican medicine-woman-*cum*-warlock, if you needed anything from a midwife for an apartment-bound birth to someone to put a curse on your malicious, gossipy neighbor (Bernie Kay was a great enthusiast over Puerto Rican folk-superstitions, as they survived transplantation from the island to New York), as well as herb teas and dream books.

Frank and Tony, the two antique dealers downstairs (who turn up in *Plagues and Carnivals* as "Richard" and "Billy"), say that all the old little shops are being driven out. Some ex-Dalton girl (a white lady of great taste, with a black jazz-musician husband, whose children went to Manhattan Country with Iva, back in those palmy days) opened up something called the Cafe Burgendy, just up the street, about a year back. A set of international newspapers in several languages (*La Figaro, Der Speigel...*) on old-fashioned bamboo-splinted poles, like they once used to have in (New York) libraries, await you at the door. The service is all glass. I tried it for lunch, once, and had a very good one (as well as a nostalgic conversation with the owner: Her name escapes me but, like so many people once you become a parent, she's always been for me, "Marika's Mother," as I, to her, no doubt, am "Iva's Father")—but also got a $27 bill for it, so I haven't been back. Though it's crowded every night when I wander past.

Oh, well. I believe it's called gentrification.

I will miss the mail-box, though.

Many thanks for yours of March 21st, 30th, and April 5th-and-on, all of which sit on my little black metal text stand, waiting to be answered! I haven't gotten around to Fussel's *Class* yet, though I hope to. I've liked just about everything else of his I've read—I believe we were enthusing to one another a couple of years back over *The Road to Oxiana*, that marvelous Byron travel book he unearthed.

The only Academy Award-nominated films I've seen were *Terms of Endearment*, which is certainly a Nice Movie, if not a great one. And *The Right Stuff*, which is kind of fascinating—I mean seeing historical reconstructions of all this stuff that was once so insistently The Future...! I took Iva to see it, actually, and the stream of questions she barraged me with all through it were absolutely fascinating—ten-year-olds having the kind of non-historical sense that they do.

I have heard only good things about *Tender Mercies* and will try to catch it.

And, oh yes, Iva and I also saw *Splash* and liked it. In fact, we went to see it twice. But on the first day it opened, the lines were so long up at the Olympia, the dingy little neighborhood theater on 106th Street, that we were turned away (four people ahead of us were too, and about 50 behind), so contented ourselves more or less with a feature-length Smurf cartoon. Both of us found it a bit dull.

But the next Saturday we got there a little earlier, were appropriately *Splash*ed, and quite pleased about it. Although both Iva and I independently arrived at the conclusion that the hero should have grown a tail at the end. I mean, after all, if she grows legs when she gets dry, don't you think that he should grow a fish-tail when he gets wet? And if, under the final credits, during their swimming time together, if finally he'd shed his pants and shoes and socks and ended with a perfectly nice fish-tail, I think everyone in the audience—who cheered their way all through the film when we saw it—would have been pleased.

My Germanic carpenter's-assistant-*cum*-hustler, John Mueller (whom you may remember from a year or so ago), writes me that he's in jail again, in Florida. He spent his 22nd birthday in jail, as I recall, and, after a year or two of—more or less—freedom, has just spent his 24th birthday behind bars as well; I realize I've known him for almost three years, now! He'll apparently be there for a while. (He says it was assault while drunk — well, several assaults while drunk, which brought him back to the same judge several times.) He was wondering if I would write him some pornography, as, he says, what's available in the jail is pretty nil. (His particular "thing" is lesbians making it together.) If I have time, I'll probably give it a try. But how can one resist such a commission?

Let me see:

The address of the Mugar, that you asked for in your letter of the 30th March:

> The Samuel R. Delany Collection,
> c/o Dr. Howard Gotlieb,
> Director of Special Collections,
> Mugar Memorial Library

I don't remember if I ever described my (first and only) trip up there back in October ('83), when Frank and I drove up to see the collection. It was a very moving afternoon. I brought back a catalogue of their special collections for you, but misplaced it until a couple of weeks ago. So I am definitely sending it on to you in this letter. (I mean, there I am, right up there with Samuel Beckett, Martin Luther King, and Bette Davis . . . !)

How do I feel about your writing *Inscape*? Please do, if you have anything to tell them.

Do I know anything about K. W. Jeter's *Dr. Adder*? Only the following rumor, via David Hartwell: In the mid-to-late-'70s, SF publishing became very conservative, thanks to economic pressures. But there were a number of SF novels, mostly written by younger writers, which, while they were rejected by publisher after publisher, nevertheless gained something of a reputation as "controversial." "In less economically-oppressed times," became the general editorial consensus, "this would be a very interesting book to publish." Such a book was *Dr. Adder*. Indeed, there were about three of four of these novels whose reputations survived their repeated rejections. Jim Frenkel, one-time fan at Stony Brook, late SF editor of Dell Books, the husband of Hugo-winner (and #1 *New York Times* Best Seller-list writer, *The Return of the Jedi* picture book) Joan Vinge, and now the publisher/editor of Bluejay Books, suddenly decided, "This is silly. People have been talking about these books for half a dozen years. I'm going to buy them all up and publish them."

This is what he's done.

And *Dr. Adder* is the first. Which is to say, the book was actually written at least five years ago, if not longer.

Interestingly enough, this is a somewhat repeated pattern in SF publishing. The same logic was basically what prompted Fred Pohl, back when he was at Bantam, to take my *Dhalgren* and Joanna's *The Female Man*, which—Joanna's book —had been finished by '72 and had been seeking a home for the two years before Fred bought it. And *Dhalgren*, in a somewhat earlier draft, had been accepted by Doubleday in '72 (?), and then, less than a week later, rejected again with much embarrassment, starting its own reputation in the small and talkative SF world, so that Fred had heard quite a bit about it by '74, when he bought both books for Bantam.

Dear me! It dawns on me, I have managed not to tell you the major news:

The day after I put my last letter to you — the one about the Bibliographical Article—in the mail to you, Bantam bought *Flight from Nevèrÿon* for $40,000. (The same price as they paid for *Neveryóna*.) The contract has not actually materialized. And when the money shows up, I could give every penny of it to the government, still leaving me about $20,000 in debt. But the feds have consented to take only half, with the state taking another third, leaving me with about $15,000 to live on for the year.

April 16th I had lunch with Lou again; gave him absolutely final drafts of "Fog and Granite" and "The Mummer's Tale," and a near-complete draft of *Plagues and Carnivals* and an "Appendix." I say they bought the book for $40,000 but, as I mentioned in an earlier letter, basically what they did is offer $15,000 new money and scrape off $25,000 from future books owed for this one. Still, I eat—if not very royally.

Indeed, *The Tale of Plagues and Carnivals* has about 20 pages to go, which, with the various fiddlings I have to do to the rest of the MS, should take me about another two weeks. Really, since October, when I went into high gear on "Fog and Granite," I've been nothing if not productive. In another epoch, I'd have counted both "Fog and Granite" and *Plagues and Carnivals* as complete novels, for both are marginally longer than *The Einstein Intersection*.

The whole *Flight from Nevèrÿon* volume will weigh in at about a 110,000 words. (*Neveryóna* was c. 168,000. *Tales of Nevèrÿon* was about 85,000.) Which means the whole series ends up at somewhat over 360,000 words — a bit longer than *Dhalgren* (c. 280,000). Not bad for ten years' work.

At any rate, it's five after eight in the morning. I just heard Frank get up. And I must go make morning coffee — using the lovingly secured coffee filters from last night's trip to the store. My love to Cynthia, and to you

All my love,

• 14 •

To Robert S. Bravard

April 25th, 1984

Dear Bob,

A grim day in New York. The sky outside my office window is the color of a scorched aluminum pot bottom. It's 20 degrees colder than normal for the time of year. And there is no heat at all. I'm sitting here, typing this letter to you, in my sweater, autumn jacket (zipped), and wearing a knitted cap.

And my fingers are cold.

The money situation is still surreally bad. Though I should be signing the contract for *Flight from Nevèrÿon* any day now, it will still be a few weeks after that before a cheque arrives. The Friday before Easter, I borrowed a thousand dollars from John Hancock against my insurance policy, but as of Monday the cheque for it had not come either—and, when it does, hopefully this afternoon or tomorrow, I begin the arduous three-day process of getting it cashed through my mother, which is where I am without a bank account of my own.

(Thank you, Uncle Sam.)

As of now, there are a five dollar bill, a few ones, and not a *lot* of change on the pale ivory-painted top of the bedroom bureau, and that's it—until some more materializes.

About a month ago I spoke to a class at NYU for—supposedly—$300. (It's down to the point where I take anything that comes in the line of speaking engagements, as long as it pays.) But do you think *that* cheque has arrived in the mail? No way.

And during all this, of course, I've been working away like the proverbial beaver to finish up *Plagues and Carnivals*. Today, I was up before five, and only gave up a little while ago to have a cup of coffee with Frank, at about 9:00. Coffee is over with. But I've done almost three hours' work on the new scene (the Master's attempted flight from Nevèrÿon), and it's just too fucking *cold* to go back to it.

So I am taking time off for a letter, which is easier and more fun. Forgive me for using you to bitch at and complain to. My only excuse is that it makes me feel better.

The bare facts are, of course, that, with here and there a week's respite, it hasn't been too much different since last October. But at least during the cold months before, we had heat. Living in the house in your overcoat, however, just adds the turn of the screw that breaks what's left of the camel's spirit—if I may mix homilies.

Fortunately Iva is at her mother's this month. Frankly I don't know what we would have done with her in the midst of these last three weeks—something, no doubt.

Speaking of Iva, I went to my mother's for Easter. Marilyn sent Iva up, and Frank prepared his traditional Easter Basket and, though he didn't go himself, I took it up. Iva looked wonderful and happy, and after my mother's knock-out dinner of roast lamb and fresh asparagus, Iva dragged me off into the den and initiated a conversation with me in French (!) about a movie (in French) she'd just seen with her mother about Martinique. I was impressed and rose to the occasion, to question her (in French) about it further, as best I could.

My cousin Dorothy was there—who, at this point, speaks French better than

Marilyn—so a couple of times when Iva was stuck for words, she ran out into the living room, asked Dorothy how to say this or that, and came barreling back in, threw herself down in the armchair, and went on with her Gaullic explanation of life in the jungle.

I took her back to her mother's that evening. She comes to us for our month on the 1st of May.

Monday, of course, we were all cautiously excited about the AIDS "breakthrough." It's found its way into *Plagues and Carnivals*,[1] where, indeed, I'd been kind of hoping for it to go. I worked on new material for the novel for about three hours this morning, but as of now, I just *can't* anymore for a while.

Ah, yes! The crowning insult from nature: As you know, Frank and I live on the fifth (top) floor of a moderately grungy New York walk-up tenement—so you would think our windows were pretty safe from splattered mud and the like...?

Well, apparently some passing condor (I refuse to think it was a pigeon) had an accident during the night, while the wind was blowing against our kitchen window. (Possibly it was a whole flight of albatrosses, all sick at the same time . . . ?) At any rate, when I inched, shivering, into the kitchen this morning to make my first cup of coffee as the 4:30 sunrise did not quite break through the overcast, the outside of the kitchen window was splattered with birdshit. Nor do I mean a couple of dime-sized starbursts, with a single inch of dribble. There are, by count, a good 27 blotches, from the size of silver-dollars on up to hand-size, and all, of course, at this altitude, absolutely unreachable by anyone save a professional window washer.

Clearly, from their oblique slants, they were blown against the pane by some rather violent gustings.

It never rains, but it . . . what?

Really, I'm going back to bed!

By the bye, one reason I thought you might be interested in that reconstructed transcript of the "Paperback Packaging" talk is because it gives primary evidence for what I was saying in early '68 about paperback book covers—just about a year after the Gaughan cover for *TEI* and the sale of *Nova* to Doubleday, but at least four months before the actual publication of *Nova* in hardcover and six months before resale of *Nova* to Bantam. Both Terry Carr and Don and Elsie Wolheim were in the audience, by the bye, when I delivered that talk. Notice also that I was still referring to myself as "writing for Ace Books" at that time, which was, indeed, how I still thought of myself—to the extent that I was writing at all.

Did I say last letter? I'm pretty sure Terry had suggested the topic to me, since it was a subject I'd often expressed opinions to him about.

Bundled up under the covers last night, I was rereading at the first volume of the Leon Edel *James* biography. Is it just me, or is that a rather silly book?

There is something about the Jamesian notion of the artist, saturated with life, feelings, and sensations, in every cell of his body — who is nevertheless too refined to shake his pecker free of the extra drop of pee — which strikes me as somehow contradictory—or, at any rate, as something of a pose. Nor do I think it's just my own 20th century perspective on a basically 19th century stance. I

---

[1] *Flight from Nevèrÿon, The Tale of Plagues and Carnivals* (Wesleyan University Press), p. 345.

mean, I don't have any such problems concerning the Major Romantic Poets, if you know what I mean. Well, possibly in 1953, when the first volume was published, people were just a little more gullible. Or at least Leon Edel was—still is, if that piece of nonsensical fluff that I read of his last year, *Stuff of Sleep and Dreams*, is any indication.

Also started the Andrew Hodge biography of Alan Turing—supplemented by the article on Turing Machines in this month's (May's) *Scientific American*. While the article leaves something to be desired, the biography strikes me—at least after the first hundred odd pages—as quite a piece of work. All of which brings me back to that Ronald Taylor biography of Wagner I mentioned a couple of letters ago.

Current in modern biography, there really do seem to be two basic models of human life, and they depend not on the biographical subject but on the biographer. One is the model which presents the biographical subject as one who "does," "shapes," and "makes." And the other model presents the biographical subject as one who "perceives," "is affected," "is changed." Although I haven't really read it, it's been quoted enough by the other biographers—usually to argue with—so that I have at least a sense of it: The initial Glassenape biography of Wagner, following the model of Wagner's own *Mein Leben,* showed Wagner basically as an energetic perceiver — the whole point about "Wagner's enemies," about which Wagner himself was so vociferous, was that things only seemed to happen to him. And I suspect, simply from having lived 42 years of what some people might call a rather active life, nevertheless, the facts are that most of life *is*, indeed, involved in things happening *to* you—and very little of the most active person's time, *especially* the artist's, involves actually *doing*—at least outside the imaginary precincts of the artist's art.

Newman's vast uncovering of all Wagner's exorbitant debts, love affairs, *et alia*, when you read it closely, is basically all placed in the service of turning Wagner from the magnificent absorber, mirror and transformer of the values and experiences of a century, which the official biographers tried to make him out as, to the maliciously active agent of his own fate. Though Newman (and, after him, Westerhagen, Gutman, Watson, and Gregor-Dellin) are busy tearing down the passive monument to reveal the active scoundrel, the real battle is not between monument and scoundrel but between passive and active—and, as I said, I'm afraid I'm on the passives' side.

The Taylor book, as it goes back a lot to *Mein Leben,* is the first Wagner biography in a long time to present Wagner as basically passive. This doesn't mean that Wagner wasn't incredibly energetic. But it means that the energy doesn't do too much to change the world that is the case. To live energetically as an artist means to observe energetically.

There's the examined life that's worth living; and there's the unexamined life that may, indeed, not be. But neither one of you is going to be that much more efficient at the shaping of life.

That can only be done by social *groups*.

The Heavenly Breakfast—or Bantam Books—changed the lives in recognizable ways of everyone who passed through them. But Chip Delany — or Lou Aronica—did not "change themselves" simply by joining those respective social organizations at whatever times they did.

Rather, we *were* changed.

At the Fiesta, there is a school teacher named Allan, whom, it seems, I first met when I was 20 or 21. I have only the vaguest memory of the encounter. Apparently I ran into him, while cruising on Central Park West, late one afternoon, 20- or 21-odd years ago.

As Allan tells the story—and, I gather, has been telling it for some time—he, at about the same age, got picked up by this young SF writer. They didn't do anything sexually, but said SF writer sat around with him on the benches of Central Park West and talked with him for several hours, during the course of which said SF writer told him he mustn't be guilty about being gay, and that he should go out and do what he wanted and enjoy it. And, said Allan, this encounter changed his life. (And, from then on, he started looking up and reading this particular SF writers' books, when he could find them.)

We never saw each other again until about two/three years ago, when, through Mike Elkins, we re-met in the Fiesta. Oddly, we recognized each other's faces. But Allan had to recount the incident of our meeting—it would never have surfaced in any autobiographical reminiscence I wrote on my own. (Though, indeed, a couple of others like it might.) The point, however, is: It was the *encounter* that changed Allan's life . . . to whatever extent it was changed.

And it was the *encounter* that didn't make too much of an impression on me.

And the encounter entailed a social group of two.

But as far as individuals changing things? Well: master of your soul? Maybe. Captain of your fate? Never.

Lévi-Strauss's statement of some years ago is not a bad one to remember: "I am merely the accidental convergence of a number of events."

But, whether consciously or unconsciously, I still think that's at the basis of your/Pep's problems with the publication of *TEI/Nova* and the "change of publisher." Or, at any rate, it's interesting to speculate that it might be.

Incidentally: The biographers who follow the Man-as-Active model are usually the politically conservative ones . . .

Have also been reading at Walter Benjamin. *One Way Street* was fey, but fun. (Could one possibly imagine a more passive *auto*biography than that?) Liked some of *Understanding Brecht*, especially "The Artist as Producer."

One place where I think Benjamin was almost totally wrong was in "The Work of Art in the Age of Mechanical Reproduction." By and large, it's a brilliant essay that again and again brings points to our attention that must be part of any civilized worldview . . . I guess. But: Benjamin's notion that what was lost in mechanical reproduction was the aesthetic "aura" (which he rightly analyzed as a purely socially grounded phenomenon) is absolutely ass-backwards. *As* a purely socially grounded phenomenon, the *only* thing that endures in mechanical reproduction *is* the aura. What is lost in reproduction is, of course, the material specificity of the work of art, which, in the case of painting and sculpture, very often constitutes its true richness as an aesthetic form. To know, or even to suspect, that something is a "Work of Art," however, immediately makes us pore over the worst reproduction, trying to see beyond its distortions to guess at *just* that material specificity the reproduction denies us. We struggle to compensate for the blurry focus and the badly justified color plates to intuit whatever makes the purely symbolic "original" great — almost the way we read for greatness in the translation of a foreign classic, while we create an "original of the mind" in some language we ourselves cannot speak.

Reproduction — or translation — mires us in a double work, one of which is a shimmering and ideal ghost, which (ontologically speaking) is never more than a socially constructed phantasm — while the other is the dim print or the awkward translation under hand. Together they glimmer, creating the stereoptical effect we, today, call "Art." Indeed, I suspect, we could not have what *we* know as "Art" today *without* mechanical reproduction.

Or have the Art Aura that survives that reproduction.

Our heightened attention *is*, of course, the aura — whether it is heightened because we have actually entered the King's palace (or the Frick or the Barnes museum) in order to see the "original," or because we simply know that, at one time, in the King's palace was, in fact, where the "original" hung. (That is, to generalize on Benjamin's terms, we know that some Authority adjudged it "great.") But it is the aura that survives, even when the specific details are blurred, because the aura was never *in* the work itself. It was always the web of signs in which the work was embedded—and that comes to us, not *in* the work, but *with* it. I think this is the same paradoxical process one finds in linguistics by which the connotations of a word will survive intact far longer than the denotations, which sometimes shift over a century or so: e.g., "proof," "literature," "shambles," "camp," "waste," "spirit," "expense," etc. But I've written on that before in the essay on "Gay Slang."

The Arcades Project (*Passagen-werk*) is a fascinating fragment—or, better, collection of fragments. Apparently Benjamin intended it to be his masterpiece and worked on it "with increasing intensity" in the last ten years of his life, before his suicide in '40. What we have of it is the *"Methodological Prolegomenon,"* a collection of some 40 pages of notes and quotations,[2] recently translated and published in Vol. XV, Nos. 1-2, Fall-Winter 1983-84 of *The Philosophical Forum*, and 170-odd pages of essay and essay starts on Baudelaire. (*Charles Baudelaire, A Lyric Poet in the Era of High Capitalism*, Walter Benjamin, translated by Harry Zhon, Verso: London, 1973). The Baudelaire material was originally conceived as the central section of the three-part work—from time to time he considered taking it out and making a separate book of it.

Which is what its most recent publishers have, in a sense, done.

The arcades, the intended subject for the first third of the book, were basically indoor shopping malls. They were constructed of iron trellises covered with glass panes, and along their aisles were shops and counters full of marvelous goods. Initially a 19th century Parisian response to the textile explosion, they were the forerunners of the modern department store and were great tourist attractions in France; indeed, if France has the reputation as a center of fashion, the 19th century Paris Arcades were as much responsible for it as anything.

What survives of Benjamin's *"werk,"* beyond the Baudelaire material, is a handful of brief essays — colorful and intelligent *feuilletons*, really — on the arcades themselves and their architecture, another on Dauguerre and early 19th

---

[2] SRD is greatly in error here about the extent of *The Arcades Project*. Indeed, translated into English and published in 1999 by Harvard University Press, it amounts to more than eight hundred pages.

century photography, one on the famous Paris Exhibition, and two or three others equally intriguing and equally brief on 19th century topics, handled with brio and insight (. . . in the 19th century, iron and glass were used in the construction of the arcades, train-stations and public buildings in general—but never in homes . . . the train rail was the prototype of the building girder . . .), and that quirky intelligence that characterizes Benjamin at his best is energetically in evidence throughout.

It's interesting to me that Benjamin has been taken up so enthusiastically of late, because he is such a nostalgic writer in so many ways, who, for all his rampant Marxism, as well as his very intelligent championship of Brecht and epic theater, in so many other aesthetic matters borders on the reactionary again and again. Though, alas, that just may *be* what his fashionable appeal is right now.

Also got in a couple of Baudrillard essays, published in two intriguing little pamphlets by Semiotext(e): *In the Shadow of the Silent Majority* and *Simulations*. He was apparently at the Center for 20th Century Studies last year, along with Jane (*The Daughter's Seduction*) Gallop. (*The Daughter's Seduction* is actually a very stimulating book, though I still think in the long run she's wrong—or, rather, not right enough.) Wish I could have gotten out there for a while.[3] There's something in Baudrillard's Marxist revisionism that I like very much — while there is something else in it that, as much as I like it, also feels *dead* off. And so far I haven't got the time or the energy to sit down and tease out what exactly it is, though I honestly suspect if I did, not only would *I* be a better person, but the *world* would be a better place.

Ran into Tom Zummer down at the St. Mark's Bookstore a few days back, who's promised to send me (in French) the MSS of the next two volumes of Foucault's *History of Sexuality*. I'm going to pass them on to my friend James Harkness,[4] up at Albany. I'm sure he thinks I've forgotten him by now. But as the books haven't even come out even in France yet, Jim might get a foot in the door toward translating them—I think he did a very good job with *Ceci n'est pas une pipe*. And Tom says there's been no talk of translation yet, except that Foucault is pretty unhappy with all the ones that have been done of his books so far *except* Jim's.

* * *

Well, I have paused for a couple of hours of penny-rolling. Frank has carried our handiwork to the bank, and we are each $15 richer. And not only that, but there are two more coffee cans full of pennies, to get us through tomorrow—that is, if one or another of the expected cheques doesn't arrive.

I think I'm going to mail this and go out to a dirty movie—just to watch, of course. The temperature has warmed up a little bit—I've taken my hat off—but, having made one trip out myself already today, I really feel that if I'm going to be chilly, I might as well do it outdoors and be going somewhere.

My love to you, Cynthia, and all children and animals,

---

[3] Six years earlier, in the spring term of 1978, SRD had been a Senior Fellow at the Center for 20th Century Studies at the University of Wisconsin.

[4] James Harkness was the American translator of Foucault's study of Margritte, *Ceci n'est pas une pipe* (Montpellier: Fata Morgana Press, 1973)

PS—[April 26:] Well, I didn't go to a dirty movie after all.

I went out for a while to browse over the green carpets and mahogany shelves of the Endicott Booksellers, where, as I was leaving, I noticed a tallish, gaunt, blond figure in a nondescript gray coat looking over the polished wooden rack where once were kept the scholarly journals but which, only since last week, has given way to small-sized coffee-table books.

At some point or other, I may have talked to you about the demise of the B——, the rather fine little 72nd St. bookstore, whose owner, Y——, snorted away all her profits? Also recall I said something about misplacing my favorite book-clerk from that ill-fated store, Bob.

Well, there he was, unshaven, grubby as ever, thin and in his glasses. "Well, Mr. Delany, and how are you!" Bob's about 30 or 32. I have just careened through my 42nd birthday, and his "Mr. Delany" is always full of subtle ironies; he calls me "Mr. Delany" the way I sometimes call you, "Mr. Bravard," when I see you— the way, I always fancied, my grandfather called my grandmother throughout their marriage, "Miss Nan," and she called him, "Mr. Beard." Which is very different, say, from the way Tom or Jonathon called me Mr. Delany when I was down visiting you folks at Lock Haven, lo, these many years back. At any rate, Bob informed me (faded red turtleneck with a snag in it up about his gaunt, grayish neck) he was still collecting unemployment and looking for good books to read. We discussed the James biography: He didn't much like it either, but for diametric reasons. He said he found it just a list of dinner parties with not much else to it—but then, he'd started with a later volume. We traded information on the whereabouts of various other book-clerks from Y——'s—there's a new Village bookstore I must check out down on Spring Street (which will widen my biweekly bibliotechnic peripatesis by a bit), where some of them have ended up—and finally parted.

From there I crossed 82nd Street to go shopping at the local Associated Foods, just up Columbus Avenue, bought a two-quart container of Queensboro Milk, a can of Campbell's Oyster Stew, and a loose onion bagel ("Please Use Tongs" hand lettered on the lid of the clear lucite case, up near the cash register), and a ninety-nine cent box of Breaktime Coconut Cookies, and went home, prepared to have the stew for a late lunch. (It was about 3:30 by then.)

Lugged my white plastic shopping bag up five, leg-breaking flights.

Frank was in the kitchen with the door closed, and didn't answer when I called hello, so I figured he might be doing something he didn't want to be disturbed at; put my purchases out on the living room window sill, in lieu of the refrigerator, and, a minute later, climbed into bed (!), just to keep warm, with a plan to read a little before I got up again to heat up my stew.

The next thing I knew it was dark.

I'd gone to sleep and slept through till 8:13! I got up, still very sleepy. Frank said I'd been out like a light all afternoon—that, indeed, the only reason why the kitchen door had been closed is because he'd had the stove on for heat and the reason he hadn't answered when I'd called hello was because he was in the midst of counting more pennies.

I made my stew, went back to bed at about 9:20, read a little more of the James biography. (It still seems very silly: All the things in James's fiction that are historical sedimentations—the fear of intimacy, the endless love relations that lead to the death of one or more of the characters—instead of dealing with these as fictional conventions of the times and discussing the social causes behind them in social terms, Edel tries to "armchair psychoanalyze" away in terms of James' early family life. At the same time, he rather ignores, at least he has so far, the idiosyncratic excellences James was able to inscribe on this perfectly mindless, received material. But, indeed, isn't this always the failure of thematic criticism? Of course, as I think I hinted yesterday, in 1953 what else *was* there?) And went to sleep.

About two months ago, when I wasn't writing (letters), I was reading lots of Dante, both in the Mandelbaum and the Ciardi translations, comparing long stretches of each. (The Ciardi is infinitely superior, as translations go.) I was even translating little snippets myself, here and there:

> At the median of our life's road
> I came to myself in a dark wood,
> for the direct way had strayed.
> Ah, it takes so much to say how hard
> that savage wood, harsh and dense,
> so that even in thinking of it, fear renews.
> It was so bitter, death is only a little more so!
> But to treat of the good I found there,
> I'll tell of the other things I saw. . .

If it wasn't a bit mawkish, I'd make that the epigraph to *Plagues and Carnivals.*

In the course of it, also managed to read most of the old C. Day Lewis *Aeneid*, which is, I think, also better than the Mandlebaum. Well, at least Mandelbaum's Dante has the Italian *en face*. (The Dante followed naturally upon the Russians; you can't read Mandelstam without knowing your Dante pretty well. So Mandelbaum's Virgil has, at least, the virtue of being clean. Can only wonder what happened when he got to the Italian, which falls into the pompously periphrastic, again and again. At any rate, it was all very good for *Plagues and Carnivals*. Which, I hope, I will soon be able to send you a copy of.)

So here it is this morning: first cup of coffee and yesterday's bagel (the worse for a night in its little paper bag, sitting in the empty terra cotta planter atop the refrigerator) down; and another scene of *Plagues and Carnivals* to go. I must say, I feel a lot better this morning. It's still cold. But not *as* cold. A mere sweater is doing nicely now, where yesterday I needed coat and hat besides. I can hear the super's West Indian accent echoing alley upward (though, thankfully, *not* through dim snow). Someone has already got their radio on too loud—at *this* hour of the morning! (Diana Ross, singing about *something* or other . . .) It's not 6:00 yet! And all sorts of aches and stiffnesses that were making the cold *particularly* miserable yesterday seem miraculously to have gone away.

Which—the day-long sleep, the general grumpiness of yesterday—makes me suspect I'd come down with some little something that needed a good twelve hours' rest to get rid of.

Royalty statement arrived from NAL on *Driftglass* yesterday: They're claiming that, after five printings and a bookclub sale, the thing *still* hasn't earned out its initial $6,000 advance in thirteen years now. $415.25 to go, they say. This is croggling, but we've already written them about it once; and they stick to their story.

Frank should be up and about in an hour and a half or so. A bit after that, I have to go down and record some more of Howard Wise. (This is our second from the last session.) Then there's a *Little Magazine* meeting tonight. I'm supposed to have written the front matter for this issue. Should probably go on to that next. Will probably get my dirty movie in today, sometime between finishing Howard and the editorial meeting.

[April 27, 6:40 am:] Well, yesterday at least *one* of the cheques arrived — the thousand, from Hancock. Frank phoned to tell me while I was down at Howard's, finishing up the taping. (We have one more session, next Thursday.) Afterwards, I got the cheque and took it up to mother's. She, alas, like half of New York, is down with flu. But in good spirits. And the day was wondrously warm. (Only stayed at the *Little Magazine* meeting long enough to read three new batches of poetry and to deliver my "front matter" to them; only one other editor, Joel Heatherington, showed up, and I was just exhausted.) As is this morning (not even a sweater, now!), with a blue sky and wisps of white and silvery clouds and sunlight dribbling down through all the fire escapes out my office window over the still skeletal branches of the few trees (some brown leaves hang straight down, the tenacious dead from *last* summer) and the concrete yards they grow in. And even, if I crane, one or two with new green! But at this point, I can't remember what of this letter I've sent you . . .! I know I put at least half of it in the mail, but not *which* half! So I'll send the whole thing.

All my love again,

• 15 •

To John P. Mueller

April 25th, 1984

Dear John,

Two letters from you—and I'm just getting around to writing you for the first time since you left!

Basically, I've been feeling pretty shitty. There've been problems with my publishers. Problems with money. But I'm in one of those moods where even to explain just what the problems are seems like too much trouble. At one point in your letter you asked about my sex life. Well, it's been hectic, even a little frantic —though, at least in terms of the energy I've been putting out, not much fun. If anything, I've been on a kind of binge since you left: I don't mean drugs or drink. But, I've been running after dick like it was going out of style, all day every day. At least that's what it seems like.

One funny story: Once, while I was walking through the Grand Central Station waiting room, I saw a guy sleeping on one of the benches. He was kind of hefty, in his late thirties, I figured. He had a couple of days' beard, and wore a soiled blue down jacket. His knees were drawn up, and his hands were shoved down between his legs, so that when you walked around him, you could see the ends of his fingers sticking out between the thighs of his jeans.

His fingers, which were nice and thick, were — how shall I say? — much like yours.

I sat down beside him and watched him sleeping for about ten minutes. I thought about waking him up. But finally I decided that the poor guy needed his rest, so I got up and left him sleeping there.

The next part you'll probably have some trouble believing, John. But I swear, what I tell you happened next is the God's-honest truth:

The following afternoon I happened to be walking up Eighth Avenue. As I came under the row of movie marquees just before 46th Street, I looked across at McHale's. (They've changed the name, since the fire, to "The Gaiety." Though the big McHale's sign is still hanging up, the new name has already been stenciled in gold on the doors.) A guy was leaning against the ledge in Your Spot. As I crossed the street, I saw he had a bottle of beer in a paper bag under one arm; as I reached the corner, he was just asking some young secretary on her way past for spare change, only she wasn't having any. That's when I recognized him as the guy I'd seen the day before sleeping over in Grand Central. (I had figured him for a probable drunk when I'd first seen him.) The secretary went on by, and he swung that big hand with all those beautifully bitten nails around to me. "Hey, you got any change?"

So of course I stopped, dug in my pocket, and came up with a half a dozen quarters., which I handed him.

He was really surprised: "Hey, gee! Thanks!" — and I stayed to talk to him a bit. I told him I'd seen him the day before, sleeping in Grand Central.

"Yeah?"

And he admitted he'd been there. (He said I should have woken him up.) He must have figured I was gay pretty quick, because about the third thing he said was that he'd been staying with a gay friend until about a week ago, who gave really good blow jobs and sucked on his dick three or four times a day; but he'd finally been put out, he said, the week before. He didn't understand why. Maybe his friend was just too cheap, and had got tired of keepin' him drunk. I asked him his name; he said it was Bobby S——. He was 37 years old, alcoholic, and on the bum. He was very pleasant, and seemed to enjoy talking and laughing. You know: telling lies and swapping bullshit.

I kept wondering if I should tell him about his hands and about you and yours, and meeting you in the same identical spot (with a beer bottle in a bag) four-and-a-half years ago.

Finally, I told him I wanted to suck his dick. (I bet him I'd give him a better blowjob than his friend who'd put him out.) He said that would be fine, but where? So I took him across the street to the Capri.

That turned out pretty funny too. He said he wasn't used to doing stuff in the movies, and at first he kept wanting to find a darker place to sit, before he would do anything. So we moved about three times. Then, he wanted to move again — only this time, suddenly, he went for the brightest spot in the orchestra, sat down right under one of the lights, and dropped his pants down to his ankles. What would I say to doing it here? he wanted to know.

I said: I thought you didn't want people to see.

Naw, he said. Let's do it here.

Well, it seems that he was really something of an exhibitionist. After a while, he explained that it really got him off doing "weird shit" when people were standing around watching. He just hadn't want me to think *he* was weird at first. (This, it turned out, was what had gotten him kicked out of his gay friend's house the previous week. He'd been waving his dick at the woman who lived across the hall and she'd complained!) Well, I can get into just about anybody's thing, at least for an afternoon—so with a pretty large audience from time to time standing around or sitting around gawking at us, we carried on in the movies for about five hours!

When this guy said it got him off to have people watch, he really meant it: He was jumping up and down, and moaning, buck naked pretty soon, and shouting stuff out in the theater and generally enjoying the shit out of himself. I guess just because he seemed to be having so much fun, I kind of enjoyed it too. There were about five or six old guys who just sat around us, grinning, and occasionally grabbing a feel or a suck when I got tired—which he seemed to like. And there was one black prostitute (transsexual, probably) he kept shaking his dick at (didn't have much to shake, I confess) every time she'd walk by. Then he'd tell everybody standing around, "Man, if she'd just fuckin' *look* at it, man, I'd shoot so high I'd hit the fuckin' ceilin'! But she just wants to break my balls!"—him, sitting on the arm of the aisle seat naked as a jaybird, beating off for all he was worth, his clothes all under the seat and on the floor. Then he'd turn around to me and say, "Hey, suck on this some more for me." Then he'd rough up my head and say to the guys watching me blow him, "This cocksucker here's my buddy! He likes to suck my fuckin' fingers, too!" Then he'd stick a couple of them in my mouth. "He's fuckin' *weird*!" he'd say (meaning me!), then get up and walk up and down the aisles a while in just his very dirty (and smelly) socks, still beating off, stopping to look at somebody else getting a blow job, or asking somebody for a cigarette. He had just about everybody in the theater laughing — even the macho lunch-time beat-off Puerto Ricans who don't want to smile at anything even vaguely "queer" for fear their asses'll drop off. I know pretty much everything goes on there, but I'm really surprised we didn't get kicked out. But nobody bothered us.

Well, once actually somebody told him to shut up, so he put (most of) his clothes back on and we went upstairs. And pretty much started all over.

I had to go at about 4:00, so I gave him my phone number. He stuffed it into his wallet that had come out of his jeans pocket under his chair. I told him that, if he wanted to get together again, he should call me on Monday, and I would at least keep him drunk and fed for the day. (He was pretty soused when I left. And that, he claimed, was all he was interested in.) I was kind of wondering what would happen if I took him in for a session at Beefsteak Charlie's. But I figured if I did, he'd want to stand there and do it right in my glass at the table (if not in my face), and I don't think I'm *quite* ready for *that* one yet.

He'd told me some story about waiting for some money to be sent to him; he had a friend, who was going blind, out in Elizabeth Port, NJ, who, he said, had a lot of money and liked to stay drunk—so he was going out to help him out, sponge off him and lay around on the beach. I figured there was about a one out of five chance of the story being half-true—and one out of a hundred of it being wholly true; but he said he'd call me Monday, whether he was in New York or New Jersey.

Figuring I'd probably never hear from him again, I left him still sitting in the movies with all his clothes off.

I didn't hear from him on Monday, of course. And I confess, I went out that afternoon and spent an hour or so kind of looking for him around on the strip, and in Grand Central and Penn Station—more from curiosity than anything else. I mean, this guy was a real character; as well as being a kick.

But I didn't find him. So I put him out of my mind.

About a week later, when I was sitting in my office, trying to work and not being able to, the phone rang. I recognized the voice as soon as he said hello. It seems, indeed, he was in Elizabeth Port, NJ, stranded. His friend who had had lots

[Remainder of letter missing]

• 16 •

To Robert S. Bravard

May 1st, 1984

Dear Bob,

It's a beautiful day. I'm only slightly sweaty—for some reason I keep fearing it's going to turn cold after I go out, so I've started off each day for the last week in a long-sleeve flannel shirt, which, from time to time, leaves me too hot. But I'll give up and change to something lighter soon.

Just returned from Henry's office, downtown, where I signed the "contract" (actually it was three copies of an addendum letter to the previous contract) for *Flight from Nevèrÿon*. That means some real money—$10,000 or so—by the end of the month. (Enough to pay off the debts of the last six moneyless months. . .) Going over it all and getting it straight occasioned a couple of calls to Nancy Kenny, of the Bantam Accounting Department, to check over a couple of figures, here and there (in the end, they, of course, were right), but I now know that since 1978, Bantam has paid me a total of $220,000 plus $70,000 for reprinting the Ace Books, totaling $290,000. The last of those payments was a $15,000 payment in August '83 for the synopsis of *The Splendor and Misery of Bodies, of Cities*. Forty-three thousand of that was Henry's commission. And the first year's payment was roughly $100,000 (i.e., $85,000) so you can figure out more or less how I've been living these past six years.

That's $246,000 for me since '78, or six years. With $85,000 off for the first year, that's $161,500 for the remaining five years, or $40,375 per year on the average. Basically, with a $40,000 income, one cannot *pay* the taxes on an $85,000 year. Last year, $18,000 of my income went for back taxes, and that's only to the feds, not the state—which means in effect we lived on $22,000, which, today, in New York City, puts one at the most median of median income levels; and I've got a kid in private school—as well as a word-processor to feed! So you can guess at the general state we've been living in here.

Ah, well.

This past St. Patrick's Day, I walked with Iva up messy, quiet (it was a Saturday morning), garbage-strewn Amsterdam Avenue to the Claremont Riding Academy — read "stables" — for her riding lesson. We talked, about the usual things a ten-year-old daughter and her 41-year-old father talk about . . . whatever they are. I confess, at this six-weeks-plus remove, I remember none of them.

What I recall is that the stables send an annual contingent of their better riders to the St. Patrick's Day parade on Fifth Avenue; and when we reached the red-walled building, the riders, men and women, in their beige jodhpurs, black boots, black top hats and blazers, with their green-and-white, over-the-shoulder-and-around-the-body, six-inch-wide ribbons, were filling up the crowded office, happy, animated, and waiting for their horses to be called up from the basement and down from the loft. And while Iva, in her own black-flocked helmet with her brazen hair hanging down from under it (and her crop and brown leather windbreaker) waited to join her class to ride off to their lesson in the park, I found myself remembering that a year before to the day, I was up at Albany—and, indeed, the night of St. Pat's I spent at a boisterous party with a slightly inebriated William Kennedy, who was signing copies of the then-just-published *Ironweed* for various friends who'd brought them along to the boisterous gathering and making-merry.

* * *

A week or so later, on my birthday, Iva presented me with a wonderful present: a red notebook (in which I've drafted many of the long-hand notes for this letter) whose first pages she decorated with her own, home-made birthday card, complete with a mystery message. You lift up the secret flap to find out what it says: "Guess who sent this?" Open the flap: "Iva!"

That same day, as a "birthday-present in return," I took her out to see *Greystoke,* which we both enjoyed. We went to see it down at Broadway and 45th Street; the sprawling mid-town theater was very crowded. As we were coming down the wide and orange carpeted steps afterwards, amidst the hundreds of viewers, I slipped and sat down, hard, on the stairs—catching myself on my arm on the step behind me. Half a dozen people paused to help me up. Iva was most solicitous, and when we got home, she rushed in ahead of me to confront Frank: "Okay, now, Frank, *don't* get upset! There's *nothing* to worry about! But my father fell when we were coming out the theater. He's all right now."

Frank said he almost had a heart attack from her announcement.

Well, although I walked out of the theater all in one piece despite my mishap, my arm was still sore for the next ten days and my hip, a month later, still aches in certain positions—the one I usually sleep in, wouldn't you know.

On April 2, Iva went back to her mother for the month. She's due back with us for May tomorrow. And I really feel like I'm kind of getting ready to wake up and smile, when she comes.

* * *

A recent note from my journal:

"To sit for two hours and simply *think* about what you're writing, what you're doing, how they relate to the world, history, and your own deeply cherished theoretical perceptions, in an attempt to wrest some small, hard conclusions from the whole diffuse enterprise — what word or sentence do I write next; how do I organize the next scene in my book—is to end in a state of physical pain: The stomach sours, the lower back aches, the mouth films over and becomes distasteful, and the shoulders grow sore.

"Indeed, I would rather do it walking than sitting, simply because it is less hard on the digestion."

Well, it occurs to me that there have been an awful lot of such two-hour sessions during the composition of *The Tale of Plagues and Carnivals,* some sitting, some walking, and not a few in the bathtub. Thinking about the meaning of what you write may or may not be necessary to great writing, but it's sure a way to insure that you remain a terribly unhappy person—starting with the wear and tear on the body. At any rate, such considerations may or may not be why, a few days ago, I decided to take a couple of days off from the work.

What I've been doing for the past three—well, almost five days now—is *reveling* in Walter Benjamin, particularly the Baudelaire book, which I mentioned last letter.

I really think that, on this most recent reading, it's joined my minuscule shelf of very most favorite books ever: Barnes' *Nightwood,* Van Puersen's *Understanding Wittgenstein,* Nabokov's *Gogol,* Quine's *The Philosophy of Logic,* Reynold's/ McClure's *Freewheelin' Frank,* Brown's *Laws of Form,* Dinesen's *Ehrengard,* Dickey's *Deliverance* (Well, I could explain . . .), Mereshkovsky's *Leonardo da Vinci,* Davenport's *Tatlin!* . . .

Part of the charm of the Benjamin book is, no doubt, that it cries out to be re-edited: The book begins to involve the imaginative reader from the very outset.

Apparently during the last decade of his life, Benjamin planned out and researched obsessively a book on *Paris, the Capital of the 19th Century,* or, as it is often referred to, the *Passagen-werk (the Arcades Project).* But I talked a bit about the Paris Arcades—indoor shopping malls-under-glass—in my last letter. Benjamin's "research" consisted of endless notes[1] and quotes from a variety of 19th century memoirists, which he mined for telling observations on mid-19th century life in France. One gets the impression that, after a while, the research began to swamp the realization of the project itself. But at some point he decided to put some of it together, and actually wrote out a hundred-page essay, "The Paris of the Second Empire in Baudelaire." He submitted this to the Frankfurt School's journal, the *Zeitschrift fur Sozialforschung;* and Adorno rejected it.

After the rejection Benjamin rewrote the piece, in a much briefer version of some 40 pages: "Some Motifs in Baudelaire." (The shorter version is included in this book after the longer; but I first read it in the Benjamin collection *Illuminations,* with Hannah Arendt's stimulating and sensitive introduction.) Not only did Benjamin cut it by more than half, but, here and there, he expanded on the material that remained. The new parts in the shorter piece are certainly the strongest. They cry to be integrated into the longer version. (It could probably be done with scissors and paste.) Nevertheless, compared to the longer, earlier piece, the shorter one seems dead, lacking in energy, vividness and imagination. For, apart from the new material, what remains of the old is the theoretical underpinnings without the sparkling and astutely observed examples that make the longer one a scintillating read.

From two notes that remained in with the extant mss, we learn that even of the hundred pages we have, the first sixteen pages of "Paris of the Second Empire in Baudelaire" are missing: The first nine concerned (say the notes) the standardiza-

---

[1] Here, SRD seems to have grasped a better sense of Benjamin's project—possibly through more reading since his last letter to Bravard (April 25th).

tion of Paris architecture under Baron Haussman's influence, and the next six gave a history of the *boheme*. A consideration of the mid-19th century version of that romantic character, and his relations with anarchists and conspirators (and one particular conspirator, the people's general, Blanqui), opens the extant part of the essay. At the essay's end (after Blanqui's brief, suggestive return to round things out) there is a short, two-part addendum, the first part—little more than a page— on the problems of the historical materialist critic, who turns to his object and finds not the pure and historically understood object waiting for a new interpretation but rather "the object riddled with error." The particular problem with Baudelaire is mentioned (with the implied extension that it pertains to all historical literary texts): The tradition that the commentator has absorbed becomes part of the critical object—whether erroneous or not—and must presumably be worried out.

Granted that the intended sixteen-page introduction was lost, this little addendum squib (p. 103) would make a wonderful introductory note to what remains. I'd advise anyone who can to go right to it and read it first.

The second part of the addendum is a brilliant two-and-a-quarter page divagation on the way, economically, "taste" came to replace "real knowledge of objects" (their durability, their long-term use) in the consumer commodity market during the 19th century. It is a ready-made epilogue for the *Second Empire* essay. Read it as such if possible.

The topic of the 100-page essay is how the mid-19th century (Parisian style) saw itself, and why; Baudelaire is used merely as *one* of its most astute observers, in the poems of *Les Fleurs du Mal* and, here and there, a few miscellaneous fragments and prose pieces. One place where the essay cries out for re-editing is in the notes to the numerous Baudelaire quotes bespangling it. Benjamin worked from a two-volume critical edition of Baudelaire: *Oeuvres*, edited by Yves-Gerard Le Dantec: Paris, 1931-32. Any time a quote from Baudelaire appears, Benjamin's footnote cites only the volume and page number from Dantec, e.g., a complete note will read "23. II, 408." or "125. I, 119." The English translator, Harry Zohn, has gone to the trouble of providing standard English translations of all the poetic fragments quoted, from the New Directions edition of Baudelaire, done by various hands from George Dillon and Edna St. Vincent Millay to Roy Campbell and James Elroy Flecker, so that at the end of each translation (which, in parentheses, follows the French text), we are given the name of a translator. Yet he still does not provide us with the names of the individual poems—neither in English nor in French. And frequently, when the quote is small and the point made refers to it only in passing, Benjamin does not mention the title either.

This means that those of us with our Penguin *Baudelaire* (the French texts with serviceable prose translations beneath), or even those of us with the Godine edition of *Les Fleurs du Mal* (preceded by Richard Howard's energetic, when not downright luminous, translations), we're just up Shit's Creek. Presumably Benjamin wanted his readers to read through his essay taking the Baudleiare quotes as part of the fabric he himself was weaving, rather than as *bijoux choisis*, displaced from an extant canon of Great Poems (though if the essay had indeed been accepted for publication, it's arguable he might have elaborated his notes a bit further). Nevertheless, if the English editor was willing to "interrupt the flow" with a bunch of translator's names, why not at least provide compensatory foot-notes that will allow English readers to do what Benjamin's readers could have done with an edition not available to us, i.e. locate the poems by title?

There is an index, made *by* the German editor (not Benjamin), which, under "Baudelaire," lists all the French titles of the poems referred to or quoted in the text, so that if, indeed, you want to find out if a *particular* poem is mentioned, you can look it up in the index and turn right to it (if it occurs to you to do so under "Baudelaire," and not under the title itself; for the poems are *not* listed in the index as such). But it still remains dauntingly difficult to find out, just by reading the essay, the names of the poems from which a goodly number of the quotes come. This seems the utmost pedantic scholarly willfulness.

Sometimes, of course, Benjamin does give us the title in his own text, when he is quoting more than a quatrain or two. Thus, in the first half-dozen pages, he gives us Baudelaire's poem (#107 in *Les Fleurs du Mal*), "*Le Vin des chiffoniers,*" ("Ragpickers' Wine,") in which a drunken ragpicker staggers through the muddy streets, bumping into walls, babbling boasts and proclamations to the police-spies and all the rest of the passers-by, and wagging his head. Benjamin follows the poem with a fascinating account of the recent change in wine taxes, around the time the poem was written, that forced the drinking establishments to move from central Paris to the outskirts, and we read other accounts of, indeed, the droves of drunkards, some of them actually ragpickers, and most of them laborers, who paraded from the city to these establishments daily.[2] We learn what the police were doing there in the first place. (People became quite frightened of this army of alcoholics.) We also learn just *how* poor the average rag-picker was: Benjamin quotes a page detailing the living expenses of a typical 19th century French rag-picker, from Frederic le Play's *Les Ovriers Europeen* (1855). Benjamin then goes over the various revisions Baudelaire made in the poem's closing stanza, the ear-liest versions of which has God giving wine to man as an afterthought to the gift of sleep (a rather trifling notion, and a cliché since Anacreon); and the final ver-sion, which has man necessarily making wine to extend the inadequate benefits of sleep—with the strong implication that it may not have been such a great idea after all: Certainly each subsequent version subsumes a greater and greater awareness of public drunkenness as both a human and social problem.

The effect is illuminating—and, yes, also somewhat silly, in that it says little about the poem as poetry. Indeed, if criticism today were dominated by this sort of thing, I can easily see such a passage as Benjamin's considered a real critical hor-ror. One can just hear Adorno's complaint: "Benjamin, this is vulgar Marxism at its worst! No matter how interesting this 'materialist insight,' the poetry is clearly in excess of it; and it's even more clear from the poem that Baudelaire himself was spectacularly unconcerned with such things in his impressionistic rendering of his pathetic, excitable drunk. Really, your exegesis trivializes a fine poem beyond bearing. Unless you can definitely say that the tax came between the first version and the last and that Baudelaire knew about it, this is really just social speculation and not a scholarly find in any way."

Well, myself, I don't care. It may not be scholarly; it may be 'vulgar Marxism,'

---

[2] Karl Marx mentions the same situation in *The 18th Brumaire of Louis Bonaparte* (1852), possibly the source of Benjamin's more elaborate discussion.

but it's fun. What it does, of course, is create endless and interesting suggestions about 19th century life. But suggestion is not fact.

And the section is gone from the second version, revised in the light of Adorno's criticism.

One of the pivotal pieces in the essay is Baudelaire's famous sonnet, poem #95, *"A une passante."* ("To a Passing Woman.") Stephan McIntyre is probably my least favorite translator of French and German poetry forever and for all time—as an adolescent, I suffered for years with his Verlaine, his Mallarmé, his Rilke, when they were all that were widely available. His, alas, is the translation Harry Zohn chooses for the English text. And here, I confess, looking up Howard's version, I find it not up to many of his others; so I offer my own:

> *The street resounded round me, screaming.*
> *Tall, thin, in deep mourning and high sorrow,*
> *a woman passed, her gloved and ringed hand*
> *lifting, balancing her gown's black flounce:*
> *So agile, so noble her sculpted leg!*
> *Me, I drank—shivering like a madman—*
> *from her eye (a livid heaven where storms begin)*
> *the sweetness that fascinates, the pleasure that kills.*
> *Lightning!—then night. Fugitive beauty,*
> *in whose glance I was suddenly reborn,*
> *will I see you again before eternity?*
> *Possibly very far from here! Too late! Never, perhaps!*
> *For I don't know where you went; you don't know where I go . . .*
> *you, whom I might have loved (you, who know).*

Benjamin makes the point that this universal urban experience (Auden talks of its gay equivalent somewhere as: "Those beautiful men on the up escalator when I am riding down.") is a particular manifestation of the crowd as one finds it in a city, after it reached its 19th century size. Indeed, the book abounds with urban insights:

One of my favorite anecdotes — possibly apocryphal — is that only ten *days* after the date in 1839 on which Louis Jacques-Mandé Daguerre applied for a French patent to his famous invention,[3] the first man was arrested on the steps of the Louvre for selling obscene photographic postcards, in which naked women were posed in positions recalling some of the famous nudes on the walls within. Thus photography and photographic pornography begin their histories almost simultaneously, both intimately and ambiguously related to High Art. (Again, it doesn't *say* anything; but it suggests much.) Benjamin does not mention this little anecdote, but he has a quote from a letter written by a woman sometime within a year or so of Daguerre's invention that certainly expands its suggestiveness: "At present much attention is being paid to Mr. Daguerre's invention, and nothing is more comical than the serious elucidations which our salon scholars are giving of it. Mr. Daguerre need not worry; no one is going to steal his secret from him . . . Truly, his invention is wonderful; but people do not understand it, there have been too many explanations of it," (p. 28). Which is to say that considerations such as those that make up Sontag's *On Photography* or Barthes's *Camera Lucida*

---

[3] The Daguerrotype camera: the start of photography.

are not new, but merely the most recent additions to a verbal commentary on the photographic image that commences with photography itself.

(How many young students of film are surprised to learn that some of the best and most intelligent commentary on it was *written* in the '20s, '30s, and '40s . . . ?)

Another insight: The advent of public transportation in cities—trolleys, buses, ferry boats (up and down and across the Seine)—suddenly meant that, daily, people had to spend long periods of time *looking* at each other without actually speaking. Benjamin sees this as the origin of a whole raft of literary endeavors and observations.

Or we find him simply commenting: "A criminal career is a career like any other." Could anyone notice that *outside* a city?

But all this leads to a wonderful discussion of the urban crowd, with much attention paid to Poe's intriguing description of a London crowd-of-the-mind (Poe was only in London from ages six to eleven) in his story, translated by Baudelaire: "The Man in the Crowd." The Poe/Baudelaire crowd is contrasted with the Victor Hugo crowd of *Les Misérables*. Hugo's crowd was made up of citizens—or people who *should* have been citizens — of which Hugo was one. The Baudelaire/Poe crowd was made up of impressions and sensations and types that never quite fit into their molds, who hid mysteries, murder, and sex—who embodied all the various forms of desire and desire run rampant. (Some of Benjamin's most interesting quotes come from a now extinct species of 19th century genre writing called *Physiologies*, which were little books of amusing descriptions of social types,[4] especially as might have been seen on a Paris street — or strolling through a Paris Arcade.) The *flâneur*, or idle stroller, becomes the prototype of the poet and, eventually, the modern hero. Benjamin's examples and exegeses make some of the best parts of the essay. Indeed, this is one of the sections [concerning the crowd — the material for the *flâneur's* observation] that gets expanded in the shorter version, leading to a whole meditation on Proust and Proust's own pedestrian vision as it is reflected as his Bergsonian concept/critique of time.

Chronologically, of course, Proust is much too late for what Benjamin is writing about—save as what these mid-19th century concepts became or gave way to. I *still* say it goes right *here*, in the longer version, along with the new Poe material.

In general, Benjamin combs through a daunting range of 19th century commentators for apt descriptions of 19th century city life — bourgeois street life in particular — to embed them in his own commentary. Here and there he makes some startlingly luminous juxtapositions. For instance, here is a description from Baudelaire's sonnet, "The Albatross," (certainly, here, a metaphor for the socially reviled poet, via Coleridge):

> *Torn from his native space, this captive king*
> *Founders upon the deck in stricken pride,*
> *And pitiably lets his great white wing*
> *Drag like a heavy paddle at his side.*
>
> *This rider of winds, how awkward he is, and weak!*
>   *(Trans. Richard Wilber)*

---

[4] Gustave Flaubert's young nobleman de Cisy is intrigued with them in *Sentimental Education* (1869), his novel of the 1840s and '50s.

Right after it, Benjamin places an 1861 quote from a German, Fredric Theodore Vischer, writing of the wide sleeves of fashionable men's jackets in France: "Those are not arms any more, but rudiments of a wing, stumps of penguins' wings and fins of fishes; and the motions of the shapeless appendages when a man walks, look like foolish, silly gesticulating, shoving, rowing."

Again, one can hear Adorno's objection: "Benjamin, just *what* are you trying to say here? Do you mean that Baudelaire actually had *these* jackets in mind when, around the same year, he wrote his description of the socially beleaguered poet-as-an-albatross? If so, *say* so. If not, why do you have it here at all . . . ?"

And how does a scholar defend such a juxtaposition?

"Well, I didn't mean *exactly* . . . I just thought it was . . . well, suggestive."

It is. Infinitely suggestive, infinitely pleasurable — and omitted from the revised version.

Indeed, I suppose Benjamin's essay is a classic example of what people used to joke about, speaking in the voice of an older scholar commenting on the energetic work of a younger: "Brilliant—but, I'm afraid, unsound."

And although the *Zeitschrift* no doubt needed sound scholarship, it's too bad they could not have made an exception for what is, after all, basically a piece of sociological poetry.

It is certainly a wonderful piece of *sensuous thought*—Nabokov's characterization of art in his *Don Quixote* lectures (p. 13). And in the end, for all its want of a final, integrated version, the brilliance triumphs.

No doubt both a weakness and at once a point of charm in the piece is that Baudelaire is not really used as a "poet," but only as one of the most important observers of the 19th century—important, certainly, because he *was* a poet; yet the "transcendence" of his verbal creations is seldom what's discussed. And still yet, because they're good poems (and this edition has the good sense to quote them in French as well as give the English renderings), this only makes them register as that much *more* poetical.

The various superlative claims that have been made for Benjamin I find a little difficult to follow.

The greatest 20th century critic?

Or even "the last European"—an odd misreading of a rather grim joke he once made himself about the possibility of emigrating to America, where, he said, they would have no use for someone like him at all. ("All they will do there is exhibit me up and down the country as the last European.")

I gather that he was a sparkling German stylist — and German just doesn't seem to translate all that well at the best of times. Still, I've read most of the three collections that are available, as well as the Brecht book and the Baudelaire book, and have read *at* the *Trauerspeil* book. Unless the untranslated volumes of letters contain his greatest work, I think one can say: He's no Erich Auerbach. He's no M. M. Bakhtin—to take two truly great critics writing from about the same time. Indeed, he's not an Adorno.

Nevertheless, his own somewhat skew version of "historical materialism" as well as his willingness to look with sympathy on the "bad new things" (Brecht advised him: "Don't start from the good old things. Start from the bad new ones," and he took the advice) gives him a distinctively modern air that seems more like someone who lived through the '60s than someone who destroyed himself in despair 20 years before they arrived.

Personally, I found all sorts of fascinating material in the essay that expands on stuff that came to me during the time I was writing my Wagner piece. Baudelaire championed Wagner's *Tannhauser* in Paris, of course. But personally they had little or nothing to do with each other. How odd, then, to see them spouting many of the same extra-aesthetic opinions, on everything from a shared vision of an active, secular Christ (Wagner's outlined but never written play on Christ as a human revolutionary; Baudelaire's sonnet on the crucified Christ with lines to the effect, ". . . Hanging there, don't you miss the time when you were driving the money changers from the temple, whirling the flail about your head—in short, when you were a true leader?"), similar outbursts of anti-Semitism from both, and a revolutionary fervor that was for destruction first and foremost, no matter what did or didn't come out of it. And both had an equally ambiguous attitude about pure art, or *"l'art pour l'art,"* championing it one minute and crying for social consciousness in art the next. Indeed, it confirms my sense that these are probably best considered as social givens of the period rather than as meticulous and uniquely individual ideas from either Wagner or Baudelaire.

Knowing of Benjamin's suicide in 1940, the sudden eruption toward the essay's end of a two-page meditation on suicide as the logical reaction of the true hero to modernism is both disturbing and intense.

It too vanishes from the shorter version.

No, it was not particularly well anchored to the rest of the argument by logic — only, sadly, by what we know of its writer's history. So one misses it — or, indeed, in this book, one retains it as a troubling memory.

At any rate, along with the brief essays in the back on Daguerre *et alia*, the fragments collected in the book (*Charles Baudelaire, A Lyric Poet in the Era of High Capitalism*) make the 19th century and its burgeoning urban problematics come alive in vivid, tumbling images. I wouldn't dare assume Benjamin's theory exhausted them. Nor can I be so generous as to suggest that Benjamin didn't *think* his theory was the last word: Clearly he writes with the commitment of the committed. But if he didn't, I doubt he'd write as well. It's understandable—with all his suggestiveness instead of facts — why he was a problematic writer for the German Marxist scholars of his day. And it finally speaks well of those same scholars that they—particularly Adorno, and later Hannah Arendt—after rejecting at least this one, rather eccentric essay (however much they admired Benjamin himself), started the movement to retrieve his work for posterity.

But it's sad that it took his 1940 suicide, at the Franco-Spanish border (when he thought he would not be allowed to leave for America, as Adorno and others had done, but would be shipped back to Germany and the concentration camps), to commence the retrieval.

* * *

A couple of nights back I had a fascinating dinner with two friends from my past, Ivan Burger and Sue Schweers. Ivan used to be Ana Perez's boyfriend, and lived downstairs from her on 2nd Avenue at 12th Street. Something I'd completely forgotten: Ivan knew me, Marilyn and Bob back in the days when Folsom was living with us. During one of our pornographic photography endeavors, Ivan even wrote a script for a never-filmed pornographic movie the three of us were thinking of making, called "Shoes." Actually, I don't think he ever got around to showing us the scenario, once he wrote it (or wrote out however much of it), but he reminded me of all this that night.

Sue, of course, was "Lee" in *Heavenly Breakfast* and, as much as there was a model for "Lanya" in *Dhalgren* (not, alas, all *that* much), she was, indeed, it.

Of the minuscule number (eight?) women I've been to bed with in my life, Sue is the one I remember as by far the most uncomplicated fun. And our affair (June '67 into April '68), if you can call it that, lasted most of a year. She was—and is— a bright, affectionate and very natural woman. You once asked me, in a letter, if I would ever consider going to bed with a woman again? Well, though it was only the vaguest of stirrings, two nights ago at the Thai-Song-Restaurant on Broadway, for the first time in a long time, some heterosexual feelings stirred in me, just as natural and pleasant, in all their manifestations, as I could perceive them, as you please. Really, I was quite charmed with myself and I wish all heterosexuals could from time to time have similar gay stirrings as untroubled and as pleasing.

(Actually, I suspect most—however rarely—do.)

At any rate, Sue (who now goes by the name of Rachel) has a fourteen-year-old son by Richard Vriali, long since vanished into the sunset (I believe he's seen somewhere in passing, soldering a couple of wires together in *Heavenly Breakfast* — for a while he was ostensibly our "Sound Man"), named Morgan (after a strange kid named, yes, "Morgan," who came to the Breakfast after I left it). At any rate, Sue/Rachel and I made noises about getting him and Iva together, since both of them are interested in computers. I hope to follow it through.

All sorts of things occur to me that have been out of mind for nearly a decade now. I haven't seen Sue since Morgan was about a year old, and she and Richard were living in San Fransisco on the ground floor of a house on Bryant Street, across from the park, with a sweet, lanky, carrot-haired and copper bearded postman and comic book collector, named Mike. Mike lived out on the roomy porch of the Bryant Street house with a mattress, a sink, and his comics in piles against the wall. (You can live on the porch for most of the year in San Francisco with just a sweater.)

Richard and Sue's previous (pre-Morgan) house on —— Street[5] was the model for the house in which the Scorpions have their nest in *Dhalgren* — the one they leave, looking for another nest, and *seem* to come back to all over again. Indeed, the porch on *that* house in the novel is just Mike's porch from Bryant Street moved back over to —— Street. My first November in San Francisco, with Sue highly pregnant, we (Marilyn, myself, Ana Perez, Steve Guilden, Paul Caruso, Steve Greenbaum, Janet, Linda, Joe Cox, Bill Brodecky and surely a few others) all had Thanksgiving dinner there at the first house together: Everyone brought something, I recall — Marilyn and I brought the sausage- and nut-stuffed, 28-pound turkey, cooked at our house on Natoma (along with a pot of cream-and-brandy gravy) and carted it through the streets, somewhere up into the Haight. I remember Richard was sulking through much of it because he really disliked Ana (she

---

[5] The dash is in the original letter text. Apparently, in 1984 SRD ocould not remember the name of the street where his friends had lived fifteen years before.

had a personality too much like his own, I'm afraid) and hadn't realized she was coming. But it all worked out.

Marilyn and my and Paul's own sprawling flat at 1067 Natoma Street (where Paul still lives today, by the bye) was the model for Madame Brown's house, where Lanya lives toward the novel's end, and where Kid, Denny and the Scorpions pick her up from to go up to Calkin's party . . . the preparations for which were inspired by the Great Costume Party on my second New Year's Eve in the city, given at the old Sally Stamford Mansion where Steve Guilden ("Little Dave" of *Heavenly Breakfast*) was then living with a bunch of other odd and eccentric late-'69 vintage hippies.

Ah, memories . . . !

The fourth person at dinner with us that night was a slight, blonde creature, about 28, with great energy, a wraparound denim skirt and no breasts. Ivan had brought her along, and, though I can't remember her name (Carol . . .? Carolyn . . .?) she had just sold her first SF novel. Her editor is Kathy Malley, who, years ago, was Marilyn's and my editor at Paperback Library for the *Quark* anthologies. At any rate, she was terribly lively, terribly friendly, and terribly embarrassed, but she'd begged Ivan to be allowed to come along as she wanted to know if she could have her publisher send me galleys of her novel, and could I *possibly* read them and say something that they could put on the book as a quote, and wasn't it awful of her to use a social occasion like this for this kind of thing, but still, everything was going wrong with her book, because the buyer for Daltons, for God's sake, had made them change the title (from what to what I don't remember, but either the old version or the new had something to do with DNA), *and* the cover, so what could you do, and she just *loved* all of my books, and . . .

I think I handled it lightly, pleasantly, and without committing myself to anything I'd regret later. ("By all means, send along the galleys. But just understand that I can't promise you anything until I see it. And if I *don't* come up with a quote, you mustn't take it personally. Chances are, it only means that I simply couldn't find time to read it. You really have no idea how busy I am, and will be, for—really—the next three years. And do give my love to Kathy.") But fortunately I have been through that one so many times I can field it in my sleep.

What was oddest about the whole dinner (the little SF writer got the hottest chicken they could make: "Now, you never make it spicy enough for me here. When I say spicy, I mean *really* spicy. You *can't* make it too hot for me, even if you try!" We all tasted it; and it *was* hot) was that 90% of the evening's conversation was about computers! Can you imagine a quartet of perfectly normal adults (Rachel is 40, I'm 42, and Ivan is about 46) spending a whole evening talking about l-*dos*es and creative file names and the like? The little blond one, when she isn't writing SF, teaches word-processing. And young Morgan (not with us) is a computer maniac, already writing programs in assembly language at fourteen. And Ivan currently writes a computer column, so what could we do . . .?

Well, at this point my vacation has been spent. Got in an odd, English-dubbed Italian movie—soft-porn-*cum*-sword-and-sorcery—called *Conquest*. There's some thought in it, yes, but it's not put to much use. And the whole thing seems to take place in the fog, or be slightly over-exposed. Which doesn't work. I don't recommend it much. The only interesting thing in it really is that much of the logic is old-fashioned silent-film logic, which, here and there, for a few minutes, works. And as interesting as I can find hard-core, the particular kinds of sadisms that are always creeping (slithering?) into soft-core come about as close to offensive as I can find in an art-work. Later this evening (or, more likely, tomorrow morning) I'm going to plunge back into *Plagues and Carnivals*. (And think some more; and feel pain.) The addendum letter I signed at Henry's earlier had a paragraph stating that the finished manuscript for *Flight* would be in "no later than May 1st."

"Oh, don't worry about that," said Henry, confirming what I know myself from 20 years in this unbusiness-like business. They'll get it by May 15th, I'm sure. But it gave me a little nudge, nevertheless.

So I'll use it.

While writing this, I just heard (on my Aiwa-walkman earphones for early morning listening) two bang-up and unlikely pop-record duos: Donna Summers and Barbara Streisand doing a song called "Enough is Enough" and Willie Nelson and Julio Iglesias (now *that's* a combination of voices!) doing something called "To All the Girls I Loved." Maybe I'm just hyper-receptive right through here, with dawn breaking blue out over the white beacon light on the tower of the Beresford Apartments off toward the park (yes, this letter has, once again, lapped over into the next morning), but they both sounded great!

Or perhaps it was just the supremely healthy emanations from Boy George and Culture Club in which they were embedded. (He is/they are a kind of Herman's Hermits in drag for the '80s. Well, I liked Herman too.)

My love to Cynthia and the boys.

All best and stuff,

PS—From Sontag *(Under the Sign of Saturn)* to Terry Eagleton (*Walter Benjamin, or Toward a Revolutionary Criticism*), Benjamin's commentators have run up against the fact that much of his most interesting work is simply impossible to synopsize. The "Paris of the Second Empire in Baudelaire" essay is a case in point.

How would you make a précis of it?

"In the mid-19th century many different kinds of people were walking around the streets of Paris. There were more of them than before, and there were more different kinds of places for them to walk than there had been. All this, in conjunction with changing commodity relations, affected the way people looked at each other and their attitudes to each another. Some of this is reflected in Baudelaire; some of it isn't."

That's really the best you can do—not much of a synopsis for a 100-page essay. Yet that's about all the "Paris" essay, when construed as an argument, "says."

Where is Benjamin's *position* in it all? What's he saying is the main factor in all these interrelations and attitudes? What causes is he pointing out that are different from what others have said about the same things?

Well, despite the essays that fill up last quarter's *Philosophical Forum*, I don't think there are systematic answers to those questions. Indeed, Benjamin seems to be suggesting—*not* saying—that any causal relation breaks apart into infinitely many causes; far be it from him, then, no matter how clever the particular argument he privileges in any one case, to say that *that* is *it*.

One could write that Benjamin was out to recreate the *experience* of life in the Paris streets for his modern readers. Well, yes. But to most people that suggests a descriptive, largely sensory approach, which the text just doesn't live up to. Benjamin's method was sensory only in passing, and then usually sideways through the offices of the exemplary writers he quoted. One comes back to Nabokov's "sensuous thought" as a characterization not only of art in general, but of Benjamin's method in particular—for dealing with just about anything. "What might one think about it if one experienced it just a little more fully, had a little more information on it?" is the unstated question he always seems to be in the process of trying to answer. On finishing the "Paris" essay, one is likely drawn to the statement: "Benjamin wanted to recreate how and why the 19th century *thought* itself the way it did." Again right —except that makes him sound like a kind of 1930s Foucault, involved in some kind of "intellectual archaeological" enterprise. But the fact that there are, indeed, little resonances here and there with Foucault that one can spot, only emphasizes the difference between the two as thinkers, as methodologists, and as writers.

Sontag and Arendt get around the problem of synopsis in their different ways by basically concentrating on the personality retrievable from the essays (and, in Sontag's case, from the photographs), supplemented, even swamped, by the anecdotal and emotional material of the letters and, finally, by the fairly full accounts of him by Benjamin's surviving contemporaries: T. W. Adorno, Sigfreid Kracauer, Gershom Scholem. . . . Eagleton uses Benjamin simply as the take-off point for his own rather Derridean flights into his own ideological concerns (interesting enough on their own, certainly), pausing every few pages to touch base in case we forget completely that his book is called *Walter Benjamin*—interesting, but still an avoidance tactic.

For all of them are, finally, defeated by the simplest task of paraphrase.

I certainly can't do much better. But to point out to a reader who is actually going to tackle Benjamin's text just how hard the job is, it would not be amiss to read "Some Motifs in Baudelaire"—the new material excepted—as Benjamin's own attempt to write a synopsis of "The Paris of the Second Empire." The pages covering the material in the former essay number about 20: they fall very flat.

If Benjamin had that much trouble synopsizing his own "argument"—or, perhaps better, his own enterprise—it's no wonder the *rest* of us have the problems with it we do.

Benjamin will probably remain, then, one of the harder writers to write about. I recall Frank Kermode struggling in the *New York Times Book Review* a few years back to say something intelligent about Benjamin's then newly translated *The Origin of the German Tragic Drama* (the book on the *Trauerspeil*, or "German baroque period mourning-play")—Benjamin's proposed university thesis, which was rejected for much the same reasons as Adorno rejected "The Paris of the Second Empire": it suggested lots, but said little . . . at least little that could be repeated in précis.

Yet pieces like *"The Work of Art in the Age of Mechanical Reproduction," "The Arcades Project"* the pieces on Baudelaire, the Brecht commentaries (*Understanding Brecht*), and even the more recondite *Trauerspeil* book—as well as the more accessible memoirs and autobiographical reminiscences, *One Way Street* and *A Berlin Chronicle*—can make extraordinarily pleasurable reading if, indeed, the reader can catch them at the right angle as they flex and glimmer past.

Oh, yeah. In my translation of *"A une passante,"* in line thirteen, "where were" should, of course, be "where you."[6]

Lots of love, and thanks for putting up with my ramblings.

---

[6] Already corrected in this edition.

• 17 •

To Robert S. Bravard

May 15th, 1984

Dear Bob,

And suddenly you are two up on me!

I have your letter of April 27 (a gem! "I find life weird enough and am unable to subscribe to conspiracy theories . . . stupidity is sufficient." I shall be quoting *that* one for a long time; it joins your already much-quoted—by me—remark of some years ago: "I am a First Amendment fundamentalist.") and yours of May 10th, both. For which much thanks. Both read—and reread. And read yet again.

Thoroughly enjoyed your descriptions of B—— A——, though I'm sure you're aware of all the myriad ways academia passively encourages hysterical women— especially if they truly are intelligent—and actively discourages level-headed ones, the latter usually by simply saying, truthfully, there are a whole lot of situations other than this one where you'd probably be happier. Underneath the ire that such odd and odious behavior as Ms. A——'s produces in her colleagues, some- how men—and the overwhelming majority of her colleagues are, certainly, men —find themselves being protective of this sort of twit. I've had more than one aca- demic woman tell me, with some indignation, that if she tries to play the game by male rules, going entirely on good fellowship and intellectual competence, she's totally ignored — until one day she decides to get hysterical in a departmental meeting and flees the room in tears from a too-intense reaction to the wallpaper texture or something; whereupon she suddenly finds herself co-chairman of some juicy interinstitutional symposium.

Somehow university women seldom reap the fruit of prestige and advance- ment unless the men of these same institutions can feel that they are giving it, gra- ciously, to bright but fragile emotional paraplegics — otherwise, zilch. The psy- chological projection is pretty clear: I think a lot of academic males feel that they are always on the verge of being rendered emotional cripples themselves by their institutions, and the women around become, by a kind of evolutionary process, a strangely masculinist projection of the men's own fears and failings. (You can bet that Mr. A—— (?) justifies to himself Ms. A——'s dissertation in terms of: "She's doing it the way I should have done it, back when I was in graduate school. I'm going to help her get it right, this time." Well, however interested she may truly be in the topic, however validly helpful he is with her work, this is still projec- tion.) But, psychological mechanics aside, the socioeconomic matrix this stabilizes is as oppressive to academic women on the whole—first by keeping their num- bers down, and second by driving out all who do not fit the emotional require- ments of the men, i.e., objects to be chivalrously protected and at the same time to be disliked and feared—as any woman who ever launched a sexual discrimi- nation suit has ever claimed.

I recently saw a T-shirt that declared, sensibly enough: "If Reason and Understanding Fail, Bitch!" Well, social evolution being what it is, if you have a situation where reason and understanding aren't given much of a listen, eventu- ally you end up with a small but unprecedented number of bitches.

Found your comments on *A Woman of Destiny* interesting. Orson Scott Card (called Scott by his friends) is an awfully interesting (and good!) man. I over-lapped with him by a day or two at the last Clarion I taught. I saw *A Woman of Destiny*—a whole lot of copies of it—in a large dump at the front of Shakespeare & Co. some months back, and felt happy for him and for the distribution; read a page, and thought, well, maybe, someday, if I have time...

But time is what I haven't had at all.

Where are we work-wise?

Well, *The Tale of Plagues and Carnivals* now stands at a bit more than 250 pp., and has about 20 pp. to go (they need be inserted here and there: This book is a Benjaminesque montage/mosaic if there ever was one), making it a bit above 65,000 words.

In short, what Bantam is getting for their $15,000 (and my $25,000!) is a 48,000-word novel, a 17,000-word novelette and another 68,000-word novel—with a few thousand words of appendix (already written) thrown in.

That's approximately 140,000 words, or 10,000 words longer than *Stars*. But as we know, the *Nevèrÿon* series, into which I have put ten years of my life and thought, is just a minor *jeux d'esprit*, only tolerated by my high-minded publish-er, whose basic concern is with the more serious side of my output, like *Stars/Sand*, which, while it is certainly a good book, was still written over one six-month break from *Nevèrÿon* and rewritten over another, and is, says Bantam, ". . . Major Delany . . ." Oh, well, let me not get started.

The first copy or two of the rack-sized edition of *Neveryóna* has materialized. It looks pretty good. They used the frontmatter I suggested. It works.

I'd given them a list of some 44 corrections which, indeed, they made. Checking the text over, I discovered—somewhat frustratingly, however—that I'd failed to include one that I'd marked in my own file copy: on p. 18 (of the rack-size) there is a "pediment" that should have been, of course, a "pedestal." Somehow, though I'd marked it for change, I'd accidentally left it off my list. On the very next page, however, all by themselves they managed to drop a word ("made her way by" becomes "made her by"), and in "Appendix A," someone inserted an "a" in "sci-entifiction" — making it "scientification." That last one just infuriates me, and I actually stood up and threw books on the carpet and punched walls. The book was set by computer, you understand and, to reprint it, even with new type and new pagination, the tape is simply run through the machine again. This means that someone—probably whoever put in the other corrections—in flipping through the book must have *looked* at the "scientifiction," decided it was wrong, and insert-ed that "a." Since there was no reason to do anything with the tape except insert the corrections I'd given them, and since this particular error I've had "corrected" for me twice before in the same way by well-intentioned (or illiterate, however you want to read it) printers (in *The American Shore*, of all places!), I was particularly furious—for five minutes. I mean, I make enough mistakes all by myself without needing *their* well-intentioned assholes inserting their own!

But you can check. It's correct in the trade and wrong in the rack-size. And with computer typesetting, that's the only explanation.

Fortunately, nobody was home when I threw my little tantrum. And I haven't mentioned it to Bantam yet. And until another printing comes up, I may not.

Well, one good thing: Bantam is so anxious to prove me an ass over the

Nevèrÿon series, that while, true, they are more or less dawdling in anything and everything connected with it, they're really going to push with *Stars/Sand*. ("We'll show Delany what *Major* Delany is . . ." they chortle.) They've managed to secure a quote from Ursula (!), though, when you see it, you too, I'm sure, will suspect as did I that she didn't read it. (*Must* write her a little thank-you . . .) They also got a rather bombastic paragraph from Michael Bishop, which, frankly, goes a *bit* over the mark. But it's well meant.

What is it George Eliot said about *Ramola*: "I began this book a young woman and finished it an old one." That's kind of how I feel about the Nevèrÿon books. And who knows? Perhaps my Nevèrÿon series is my *Ramola*, my *Temptation of St. Anthony*, my *Eureka*, my own version of the indubitably central, though finally unreadable, text.

Anyway, when Nevèrÿon (the series) is finally done (in a week? two weeks? three?), I refuse to take more than six months to write the second volume of *Stars (Bodies/Cities)* — at least the first draft.

My Uncle Lenny died last Friday; he was somewhere in his mid-80s. He was a dentist, one of the three I had among my uncles and aunts. (My Uncle Hap and my Aunt Bessie, my father's brother and sister, were the other two.) Along with my Uncle Hap, he did a lot of my childhood dental work for me. His wife, my mother's sister, Virginia, was killed in a car accident sometime while I was in England. Recently, my cousins Dorothy and Boyd were having much trouble with him, much like the trouble I reported to you my mother was having with my grandmother in her last year.

I saw Uncle Lenny just at Easter, when he came over to my mother's with Dorothy. He was his usual sweet and gentle self, though he couldn't remember who Iva was, or even that I *had* a daughter, and kept thinking she was someone else's little girl.

Ah, age!

Dorothy had to fly to London the next weekend — something to do with a job possibility. She was only going to be gone four days and had been planning the trip for several months. The day she was going to leave, Dorothy called my mother to say that that morning her father had thrown up a couple of times. Should she go?

Mother said, of course she must. It was probably just the flu everybody has had right through here.

Dorothy's eighteen-year-old son, Geoffrey, was staying home with him; and, indeed, Dorothy took off. The next day, I guess, uncle Lenny was still not feeling so well. Geoffrey decided to call the doctor, and that night Uncle Lenny went in the hospital where, they decided, he'd had a minor heart attack. Dorothy got back. And over the next thirteen days he had another minor attack (while still in the hospital), then a massive one — this last coming as something of a surprise.

Altogether, the three attacks came within thirteen days.

By this time, however, Lenny's son, my cousin Boyd (a dermatologist in Detroit), had flown in to see his father. On Friday, my mother called me, in tears, to say that Lenny was dying. (I really think he was her favorite brother-in-law.) After the last attack they couldn't stabilize him. And that night she called to tell me that, indeed, he'd died at around four that afternoon.

My favorite Uncle Lenny story was one he told me when I was a child. Back home, in whatever small southern town he grew up, he had two older (?) brothers, one of whom was nicknamed Pepper. Some aunt or friend apparently baked Pepper his very own sweet potato pie one day, and Pepper, so as not to have to share it with his brothers, wrote a sign and stuck it on the pie before he put it up on the kitchen shelf:

"I spit on this pie,
— Pepper"

So young Lenny wrote a note under Pepper's:

"I spit on it too,
— Lenny"

Of course eight- or nine-year-old me had to know: "But, Uncle Lenny! Who finally ate the pie?"

As the sheer white curtains of my aunt's and uncle's Montclair living room silvered the light over the dark, paneled walls, Uncle Lenny smiled: "I don't think anybody did." And I went upstairs to lie on the shaggy, pink rug in Dorothy's room and look through the *Heap* comic (ancestor of Berni [Wrightson]'s *Swamp Thing*) I'd bought earlier that morning.

Sigh.

No, I doubt my version of *"A une passante"* will ever see print. Every once and a while, I dash off one of these little things. Usually they just stay in my notebook. Whoever (if anyone) edits my journal can cull some of them out, perhaps, in ages to come. Back in San Francisco, while I was working on *Dhalgren*, in one of my breaks I did a complete *"Cimitière marin,"* and up at Buffalo, with my all-but-nonexistent German, I did my own "translation" of Rilke's *"Die Erste Elegie"* and Xeroxed it up for my class — because I needed an example of the Heideggerian notion of *"Dasein"* ("being there") for them, and Rilke uses the word (in his own manner) in the first few lines of the first *Duineser*, and pretty much goes on to give one example of it after another throughout the rest of the poem. But, save the hand-written version up in some moisture-proof box in Boston, I don't know anyone with a copy. I certainly don't have one.

But that is the way of writerly ephemera.

That indeed, I suppose, is why I'm always sending such odd little collections of it to you.

Frank says to me, at least once a month, "Chip, don't you *ever* think about *anything* except writing?" Well the truth is, since I was a teenager, I haven't. Most of what I think about, I certainly think of in *terms* of writing, either directly or indirectly. Just to walk down the street means to me a series of visual, olfactory, and auditory experiences, some of which I know I can write about with a fair degree of accuracy and immediacy, and some of which I realize as I encounter them I'd have difficulty articulating. And the upsetting experiences, the ones I dwell on, the ones that obsess me, are not the dramatic ones in any sense, but simply the latter.

During Frank's and my morning coffee hour, I usually try to keep writing out of the conversation. But just a couple of days ago, we both found ourselves embroiled in a discussion — I'd been having a problem earlier that morning — about how to render a particular, ironic, wordless grunt from a laboring man talking to an upper-middle-class acquaintance. The semantic message of the particular grunt was, "Yeah, sure, *I* know..." but it was done with the chin suddenly raised, and a wordless sound like a wavery, "Uhhhhh . . ." I needed it for a scene in *Plagues and Carnivals;* it had to be rendered with brio and precision, preferably in a phrase—the scene didn't allow me to dwell on it for a sentence or two. And after an hour's discussion, I more or less figured out what I wanted and went to put it in my text where, eventually, you'll read it.

But an encounter in life with these hard-to-write experiences are my real emotional dramas. And when they're solved in the text, they no longer *look* like dramas. On the other hand, often things that might look to most people far more dramatic and intense (after a futile attempt to cash my NYU lecture cheque [which arrived the day before yesterday] at the cheque-cashing place across the street, this morning Frank smashed his keys down on the floor of the hall, and shouted: "I can't *stand* this any more! I can't take it, being this poor!" The ring shattered. Brass keys spun over the tile, hit the wall, or clinked against the radiator cover. Startled, I turned on the stair to look back at him, where he stood before the vestibule door's sunlit curtains. He looked almost as surprised at his own outburst as I was. Upstairs in the apartment, he went into his room and closed the door for an hour. Later he came into my office where I was working, looking much better, to search through my top desk drawer to see if there was another key ring there; we laughed some, hugged. There was) are finally less emotionally important in their lasting effects, simply because they lend themselves to language more easily.

The above is all pretty much psychological. I'd certainly hate to see it become anyone's notion of the aesthetic center of my work. It suggests that writing is somehow exhausted by mimesis, and there's *much* more to it than that! Nevertheless, that's more or less who I am on a stroll through the city, or even a trip to a university to give a lecture. And it's pretty much been me—with time out for music—since I was fifteen or sixteen.

Speaking (however parenthetically) of poverty, all we've had since I last wrote, in the line of money, is the $1,000 borrowed on the insurance policy from Hancock. And that, as of this morning, is down to two-hundred-and-the-change-in-our-various-pockets. (About twelve dollars in mine; about the same, I'd guess, in Frank's.) The NYU $300 finally arrived, but is (as mentioned) still uncashed.

But Danny (Henry's son-in-law and office manager) just called to say that Nancy Kenny (chief of accounting up at the Rooster[1]) phoned him that the first $13,000 cheque will be in Henry's office by messenger at two o'clock this afternoon.

Though that still means no cash in hand for at least a few more days, it nevertheless lightened the general mood. And Frank, who was laid-up all last week with a tooth-ache that turned into a painful and recalcitrant root canal job (only happens when you haven't got the faintest idea what you're going to do with a few brand new hundred dollars' worth of dental bills) was beginning to wonder about my coming trip to Vancouver on the 24th. He'll be here with Iva, and he was afraid I was going to leave him with no money at all—"Not," as he said, "because you wanted to, but just because I didn't know where you were going to *get* it!"

Indeed, if this last six months has been hard on me, it's been brutal on him. I've already suggested that Iva visit with my mother for the five days I'm away in Vancouver and Seattle. I really think he could use a few day's vacation from me, Iva,

---

[1] Bantam Books' logo was a rooster in silhouette.

and all this general pressure, which, if it isn't over, is at least on the upswing.

There're two things I began this letter really wanting to write you about. First there's an incident that's lingered in mind since last summer. It happened on the night of Ted Berrigan's funeral. I wrote you out a pretty full account of that, I know, but that evening, which was far stranger, I was too tired to detail. So I didn't mention it at all.

What happened was as follows:

Back at last summer's Empiricon, I'd ended up on a panel with Eugene Gold, son of the late Horace Gold, the famed editor of *Galaxy*. Afterwards, he invited me to dinner — told me he'd call to confirm sometime later.

A couple of weeks laters, I got a call from one Morgan Fairchild (certainly *not* the actress of the same name), a girlfriend who had been with him that day at the Con: Could I come to dinner? It was to be at the Riverside Church (really a large, interdenominational cathedral overlooking the Hudson near Columbia University, right by Grant's Tomb): I should come to the 11th (?) floor, where they would be. It so happened that the dinner turned out to be on the same Friday (?) as Ted's memorial service down at St. Mark's-in-the-Bowery. When I got home from the service, after I talked some to Frank about it (for the same reasons he hadn't felt like going to the memorial, he didn't want to go to the dinner, though he'd been invited), I took off on the B'way bus up to Riverside Church.

The 11th floor of Riverside Church is about halfway up its 25-story pseudo-gothic tower. You come out of the elevator, go across a somewhat dingy gray rug, push through some double doors, to find yourself in a medieval hall!

There's a raised dais along the back with carved and canopied seats—and a fireplace almost as high as a man. Wooden beams cross the high ceiling. Vaulted windows at either side lead out to stone balconies, looking down over Riverside Drive and Morningside Heights.

To one side a door leads to an institutional kitchen; through a door on the other was a little library with all sorts of old and interesting books, locked, alas, in glassed-in shelves. From the titles and the bindings I suspect they'd been there since the '30s or '40s.

Gene has apparently become the guru of a bizarre kind of self-realization group — incorporated, yes, as a religion. I'd thought I was just going to meet him there and, with his girlfriend, we would take in some Chinese or Italian restaurant. But this "dinner" to which I had been invited was for some 50 or 60 of his "people," and the guests of honor turned out to be me, Lin (*"Thongor of Lemuria"*) Carter, and Michael Itkin — this last a diminutive little man whom, while I did not at first recognize him, I suddenly realized that I'd once screwed back in San Francisco at the Club Baths. Under the name of "Father Mike," he had once been a good friend of Link's.[2] (Later, when we had a couple of minutes to talk I learned he hadn't known Link was dead.) The purpose of the dinner was a fairly unsubtle pitch for converts and money. Many of Gene's regular "people" were entertainers, musicians, mimes, acrobats, and dancers who, indeed, performed for us after the food. Now and

---

[2] Link (a.k.a. Thomas Luther Cupp: 1947–1974) was a half American-Indian writer and poet who was born in San Francisco and died in Cambodia; he was a member of the Spicer Circle and wrote for and performed with the Cockettes Theater Troupe.

again, during the course of a long and somewhat vegetarian dinner, Gene would suddenly hand the microphone to me, Lin, or Itkin and ask us to make some little homiletic address about life and its purposes: "Tell us, in a few words, *your* philosophy of success, Chip. How have *you* become so successful in your field?"

Torn between curiosity and a kind of vague horror, I'd manage to get out something I thought was non-committal enough—which Gene would comment on, turning it into an endorsement for his group, his seminars, *his* philosophy . . .!

Itkin used his time at the mike to tell some interesting anecdotes about a childhood meeting with Gurdjieff—his uncle (?) once took him to visit the aging sage in a hotel room in New York. One interesting thing is that little Itkin's anecdotes were, on their own, fascinating and also absolutely un-coöptable by Gene (so much for the non-committal!): All he could do was repeat them!

For a picture of Gene as a child, take down your treasured copy of *The Jewel-Hinged Jaw* (Windhover edition), turn to p. 107, and read on for a page or so . . . Last summer he was an oversmiling, balding, hefty and nasal-voiced 41. Perhaps it was my own childhood experience with him, but I kept thinking he had the kind of smile which could become furious anger any moment. Size-wise and body-type, actually, he's not far from me.

Some of his "people" were quite interesting — specifically one 25-year-old biologist I got to talking with. (He later called me up about some article we'd been discussing, but the number he left on my phone machine turned out not to be the right one.) During the course of the dinner, I actually wondered whether Gene had, indeed, read the piece I'd written about him in "Shadows" and he was trying, in some subtle way, to get back at me for it! But after talking to him on and off through the evening, I decided that he was just too volatile, too ebullient, and (in a word) too unsubtle for that sort of conniving. If he'd thought I'd once said something unpleasant about him, he'd be far more likely not to want to have anything to do with me at all.

Also one gets the feeling there isn't much overlap today between Gene and books—at least not a book of criticism.

He inhabits a complete fantasy world. And he's got a number of folks in there with him: "All you have to do," he told the people at the dinner, over the microphone sitting on the tablecloth before his plate, sometime between dinner and desert, "to be any kind of success you want is to take my courses of spiritual instruction, and you can *be* anything! You can *do* anything! Anything at *all*! You can go out to Las Vegas, walk into a gambling casino, and win $100,000 if you want to! And on your first time up at the roulette wheel. It's easy. There're people right in this room, right at this table with you, tonight, who've done it. I've done it. I took a group out to Las Vegas three years ago. We gambled for a week and won so much money we got bored. I had $600,000 in my pockets, probably the pockets of these same khaki slacks I'm wearing tonight. Some of it was in cash, and some of it was in certified checks from the casinos. Right while I was there walking down the main street of Las Vegas, I gave about $1,000 of it away, just to people in the street. Hey, John"— Gene called out to one of the people down the table—"you were with me on that Las Vegas trip, back three years ago. Tell them what we did, after we won all that money!"

And John (who turns out to be a rather accomplished acrobat), chuckling like some young, midwestern businessman, called back: "We opened our own casino!"

"That's right!" Gene banged the table with his fist. "And we took in more money there! Till we got bored with that. But now we're back here; and I want to share with you some of the things I've learned in my spiritual exercises. I want to give them away to you, just the way I gave away money to the poor people on the Las Vegas streets. I want to teach them to you, if you want to learn them. You can go win a lot of money too—if you want to waste your time with something so silly. Or you can learn how to provide yourself with real spiritual happiness. Now this weekend, I'm running a spiritual growth workshop. We're going to use puppets and masks. It will be quite wonderful. It's $35 a head, not counting art materials. And it'll *probably* change your life — believe me. I'm only doing this workshop once. If you don't get these spiritual lessons, you'll never be able to get them from me again. And there are things that you can learn about yourself, about the universe, and about the world, using puppets and masks, that you can't learn any other way. Believe me. I know what I'm talking about. Any of those among you who've taken any of my other workshops can tell you. These are quite wonderful experiences that I can give you. There's nothing like them anywhere else. That's $35 for a whole weekend of spiritual instruction!" and so on, like that, through the evening—while we ate a kind of macrobiotic vegetarian stew, salad, with a very little bit of roast lamb on the side. (Most of the attendees, not guests like myself, Lyn, and Mike, had paid ten bucks apiece for this dinner. Wine extra, of course.)

Then something Oriental with nuts in it (*not* baklava) for dessert.

Wine. Coffee. Entertainment—some of which was pretty good.

I have no idea how much of his spiel Gene believes and how much of it is conscious hokum. I really suspect he's pretty unsure himself at this point. I have no idea what he does in his workshops. The I.Q. of some of the people there who've taken them is high enough that he probably has to give them *something* to think about. And he's not a stupid person, though I suspect just from talking with him a few times, he's not a terribly deep one either—or, rather, what depths he has at this point are pretty well protected by the public persona. But I couldn't help notice that there was an extraordinary number of young, attractive mothers (eighteen to twenty-five) in the group, mostly without men in evidence, usually with a couple of one-, two-, or three-year-olds in tow. But if one wanted to pick the group that had the greatest psychological need for this kind of dominating father, promising spiritual happiness via Las Vegas and puppets, this would be it.

(Same group, one notes, that Charles Manson appealed to.)

I'm really surprised he hasn't changed his name. But Gene is still just Gene Gold; or, sometimes, jokingly, "Brother Gene."

At any rate, that warm summer night as I walked down Broadway among the crowds of Columbia students after it was all over, heading back to 82nd Street, I felt I'd just been through one of the weirder evenings of my life. Now graft *that* onto the end of the account of Ted's memorial service, and you have the complete story of that particular summer day. . . .

I've gotten a couple of mailings from Gene's group since then, but I still don't know its name. It doesn't seem to have one. But I'm sure it will, if it endures at all.

Well, that's *one* of the things I've been meaning to write you about all these months.

The other thing I wanted to tell you about was our recent Mother's Day.

It was quite as pleasant and wholesome and enjoyable as that evening with Gene's group was displaced, uncomfortable, and weird. It was the pleasantest day I've spent in months, actually, if not in years!

I think I wrote you some time back that my sister recently broke up with her boyfriend of some 25 years, E—— H——. Since then, things have become "hot and heavy" between her and her former driving instructor, a pleasant, gentle, little Puerto Rican guy of about 42 or 43, named Ray G——.

Ray comes from a large, sprawling Puerto Rican family; he's the single boy among six sisters, all of whom have two-to-five sons (and one niece among the lot of his nephews, a seven-year-old named Jennifer). Divorced for some years, Ray has a fourteen-year-old son (named, of course, "Little Ray"—as, indeed, I was called "Little Sam" when my father was alive); the family is all quite close.

Well, just last month Peggy and Ray set up house in an apartment in a housing complex in Bull's Head, a neighborhood of Staten Island. And for Mother's Day, Peggy, invited me and Frank and Mom and Iva and Ray's parents and Ray's sisters and bothers-in-law and nephews—and niece—all to come visit for that Sunday.

Iva, alas, had already made plans to go up the country with her friend Chlöe Sladden, and Frank just doesn't like large, close families: He has one of his own, which today he avoids at every opportunity.

I was up at 4:30 that morning working. At 9:00, I fell into the bathtub. And at 9:30, Mom got me, still dripping, on the phone, to say she'd called a car-service to come take her down to South Ferry—be downstairs in fifteen minutes. She'd pick me up.

We went into the Ferry Terminal, nostalging together about when the ride was a nickel (until about 1968, when it went up to a quarter—which it remains today). I called Ray and Peggy a couple of times, because they'd said call them from the Manhattan side, so that he could come and pick us up on the Staten Island side. But they were out at the store.

We took a sunny, breezy trip across upper New York Bay and I called again from the Staten Island Terminal—and got them.

Twenty-five minutes later, as we came wandering out the terminal's open bus area, Ray drove by in Peggy's new, sea-green Datsun and chauffeured us out to the house.

It's one of those housing developments that have sprung up by the hundreds across the country (the kind the Hooper/Spielberg *Poltergeist* was basically about), with three or four dozen more or less look-alike houses arranged in streets and alleys and T-roads, with a couple of swimming pools lost among them. Once you move beyond the development's landscaping, however, there is just turned-up dirt and desolation. It is now inconceivable what scrubby bit of humanity was replaced or displaced to put this artificial citylet of brown and white buildings here. The only other structures standing within sight were a church and, in the distance, a bile-green A-frame house, propped up on rollers, in the process of being moved off somewhere else.

Peggy and Ray are on the second floor.

When we arrived at the light six-room apartment, with its wooden floors and arched interior window spaces between roomy kitchen and dining area, from front hall to living room, Peggy was working over a veritable tub of lasagna and about a bushel of fresh asparagus.

Ray handed me a beer (at one point we went out to get another case, he and I; and also another jar of Ragu for Peggy—the party had "grown a little," she told us) and over the next hour, sisters and brothers-in-law and nephews and grandparents began to arrive in droves from New Jersey, Connecticut, Brooklyn.

What can I say?

I've known my share of big families—and I certainly had enough Puerto Rican friends as an adolescent (Mike, Jesus, Chu . . .), whose houses I was in and out of all through high school. But this has got to be the warmest, liveliest, and at once *gentlest* bunch of people, from the adults to the kids, I've ever met!

The boys are all into break-dancing. Jimmy (fourteen, in first-year vocational school up at New London) is the best at "breakin'" (that's the floor-work) and Anthony—fifteen and the only one with any air of street-hip about him—comes next. Little Ray is a really skilled at "poppin'" (that's the sharp-edged mime-style stuff they do, including the "moon-walk," where you look like you're walking forwards but you move backwards, and the "king-tut" and the other various "moves"). Only the day before, I'd seen the film *Breakin'* on 42nd Street, which is mindless as far as story goes, but which is visually informative about the dancing in a way that I would recommend. So, thanks to the movie, which the boys hadn't yet seen (it's only been out two or three days), at least I had a vocabulary to talk to them with about it. And at one point they had me down on the floor, teaching me the elemental break: arm over, leg under, turn, leg under, arm over, turn . . . which is enough to get you airsick in about twelve seconds!

Fortunately, Bob, I am *not* a pederast —

These boys are unbelievably affectionate, always all over you, and—physically—they've got to be the most stunning collection of pubescent male flesh this side of Menudo . . . possible exception, Little Ray, who is all upper teeth and no chin.

Big Ray took home-video tapes of them/us dancing in the back room, and played them on the living room TV to much applause.

Interestingly, the fathers are endlessly physically affectionate to their sons and nephews. I am sure that one of the boys is gay. I have no idea if his parents (or, indeed, he) knows it yet. But he indulges the same physicality as the others with his father (standing for minutes with their arms around each other, suddenly kissing each other almost exactly as I occasionally sometimes kiss Iva) and with his cousins. And he seems perfectly sure of himself within this family group. No particular shyness, and no apartness. When Little Ray came in, late, from visiting his mother, he was in a hurry to get his thermal vest off and put his stuff in his room; Jimmy called to him, indignantly: "Hey, Little Ray, I haven't seen you all month! I need a kiss!"—not a "hug," mind you, but "a kiss." So Little Ray stopped and, one after another, gave each of his half-dozen cousins a hug and kiss, before he went off to put his stuff in his room. There was no irony—or macho-style camping—in this, either. (Nor is it particularly Puerto Rican.) It's just this particular family's greeting style.

The kids incidentally are bright — Jimmy's attendance at vocational high school not withstanding. The only kids near that age in our family are Dorothy's two boys, Geoffrey and Christopher, certainly nice enough boys and whom I certainly love. Nevertheless, at Christmas and other family gatherings, they are, by comparison, zombies. These kids have things to say, opinions about politics and current events! With Ralph, Jr. (sixteen), for example, I sat around for a while and we discussed a couple of newspaper articles in some detail. Little Ray (fourteen) is quite proficient on a TR-600, which is set up in the corner of his room, complete with peripherals. Also, he'd read *Babel-17* before he knew I was Peggy's brother.

The grandparents have heavy Hispanic accents. The children (my generation) have none—sisters Carmen, Linda, Betsy. . . A couple of the in-laws, however, like brother-in-law Ralph (senior), my age, who has freckles and wears designer jeans, have a "Nuyorican" slur and lilt.

The kids are accent-free. (Little Ray did not speak any Spanish at all till his father took him to Puerto Rico for a year and put him in a school there specifically to learn.) Grandpa is a retired electrician—waiting, he claims with a laugh and a beer, for his second retirement, when he can stop doing free work for all his children. He's already been over to rewire the place. And Grandma G——tells my mother that Peggy is her "new daughter" and she is very proud.

They are all a little awed at mom's age and spryness. She's 71, after all, and looks about 50. But then, you know how long-lived both the Boyd and the Delany women tend to be. And they seem to age proportionally.

There's much talk of property — the really successful ones own a house or houses from which they receive income.

Time and again, someone takes me off to tell me how wonderful my sister is, how good she's been for Ray, for Little Ray, and what a special person she is. (They are, incidentally, right. But it's terribly warming to find people who see it and say it.) At the end of the day, Betsy (Jennifer and Jimmy's mother) drove me and Mom back to Manhattan on the car-ferry. I got out of the car on 86th St. and walked home down Amsterdam Avenue in the light, night sprinkle.

On the phone the next day, I talked to mom. Both of us have fallen in love with Peggy's new family. I'm really anxious for Iva to spend some time with them. It's a wholly pleasant, if not downright therapeutic, experience. And what they have and give in such generous abundance in precisely what Iva, thanks to my age as a father, lacks.

And there, *now* I've told you just about everything.

Iva's finished her homework. (Our friend Lavada just called to say that she's making plans to adopt her great niece, a six-year-old girl, off in Atocha, Oklahoma, in a truly appalling family situation. But that's another story . . .)

Did you catch, by any chance, the PBS series on Alger Hiss? It was interesting (and sympathetic), but so simplified! I'll be having Tony (Alger's son and my old Dalton friend) and Lois (my ex-student from Buffalo) over for dinner in week or so. Thought the Jane Fonda version of Hariet Arnow's *The Doll Maker* was superb. I wonder if it will get into theaters. The only thing is, staying up to see such late TV fare, I was bushed the next day . . . !

Well, like it says on the TV, I'm going to go make sure I've hugged my child today. Then back to work.

My love to you, Cynthia, and all little ones,

P.S. — Ah, yes! One last note, hopefully of interest. At any rate it's a bit of a gig-gle. A letter or so ago I told you about Allan, the guy I once picked up as a kid and re-met 20 years later through Mike Elkins at the Fiesta . . . ?

Well, the day before Mother's Day, Saturday (the day after Uncle Lenny died), I worked as usual from about five in the morning till about two in the afternoon. Iva had gone off to the country with Chlöe after her riding lesson and would not be back till the next night. So when I got finished for the day at the word proces-sor, I went downtown on the subway, took in *Breakin'* at the Harris (?) on 42nd (as I said), then walked on to Eighth Avenue and up to 46th (with the coming attrac-tions for both *Breakin'-Part II* [*Electric Bugaloo*] and still another break-dancing film, *Street Beat*, glimmering in my eyes. Is this a new genre? I kind of hope so) to drop into the Fiesta for a couple of beers. I guess it was around five.

The sometime bouncer (or "doorman," as they call themselves) is a 30-year-old, friendly little gorilla of an Irishman, named Mike (who, from time to time, it's just nice to sit around and look at . . .). At any rate, while I was sitting along the back "shelf" — I guess you'd call it — drinking a can of Schmidts, Allan came in and we started talking.

I told him I had written a friend something about his account of our initial meeting, 20 years ago, back on Central Park West. At which point he frowned: "But I didn't meet you on Central Park West, Chip."

So I frowned.

"But you said . . ." I explained.

"You know," he explained back, "I just got out of five months in an alcoholic detoxification halfway house — about six weeks ago."

"Uhh . . . yes," I said. "I think Mike Elkins mentioned that to me a week or so ago on the phone."

"How long ago did I tell you this?" Allan is small and red-headed, teaches somewhere in Brooklyn, and has somewhat bad breath and a consuming interest in biology. "Was I drunk?"

"It was about six months or a year ago, and it was in here. So I'm sure you'd been drinking. But I'm sure we actually met. You told Mike that before I even came in."

"Oh, yeah," Allan said. "You picked me up, cruising. But it was in the Village. The East Village, I think. We walked around for a while, talking, then you took me back to your apartment, and just . . . went on talking! Finally I went home. All you did was preach at me, about everything and anything. God, you could go on!"

"Mmmm," I said. "I suppose I could. I wonder why you said Central Park West?"

"*You* probably asked me, 'Was it on Central Park West?' and I just took off from there."

"Ah-ha!" I said. "So it didn't *really* change your life."

Allan looked at me with a sort of Oh-dear-did-I-say-that? expression. "I was dazzled," he finally admitted, with a kind childish nod. "You did talk very well. But I was also pissed that we couldn't get around to doing anything. I was a horny little son of a bitch back then." (It occurs to me, so was I. But no matter.) Allan took anoth-er swallow of his Bud, then said: "You know, I've never *really* read a single book you wrote. You tell me which one you think is the best. I'll buy it and go read it."

At which point Mike came in, his plaid shirt open to the waist over a veritable rug of amber hair and a tattooed knife spearing through the jungle of his forearm from under one of his rolled-up cuffs. Allan called him over and introduced me (I had mentioned to him that our young bouncer was the reason I'd come in, and Allan really *is* a good sort), and we talked for a few minutes, the three of us, about the tactics Mike's landlord was using to get him out of his $400 a month apartment so that he could up the rent.

But so much for barroom stories of long ago chance encounters. The point I was making in my other letter about the social being the agent of change in the individual still remains, I suppose. But Allan's "recantation" on my life-changing effect on him, in person and in my work, is kind of amusing in a *Rashomon*-sort of way, even if it makes me look a little more . . . uh, human.

After Mike went off to talk to someone else, Allan told me about the time he'd met Tennessee Williams in a bar and gone dancing with him. "He had a friend with him, who was *very* protective. He kept on trying to get Williams and me apart. It was about the same time I met you—" but he was rather unsure, indeed, of the bar, of the neighborhood, or even, it turns out, of the city.

They were both, he explained, *very* drunk . . .

• 18 •

To Robert S. Bravard

June 9th, 1984

Dear Bob,

Where to begin? Where to begin? Certainly, with a great and heartfelt "Thank You!" for the wonderful copy of *Mein Leben!*[1] It was waiting for me when I got back from Seattle. I completely rearranged (and organized!) my whole two-and-a-half shelves of Wagneriana to accommodate it. I've been browsing in it, here and there. And hopefully by the next time or two I write you, I'll have really read it.

About eight o'clock, the morning of your Wednesday phone call to alert me that your "surprise" was coming, I'd finished *The Tale of Plagues and Carnivals*. And a couple of hours after I hung up, at about three, I brought it in to Lou Aronica—who'd shaved his beard.

Lou took the manuscript and handed me the galleys for *Stars in my Pocket Like Grains of Sand*; whereupon I made a long and sincere pitch to the effect that they should hire and pay Mog Decarnin to proofread them. She's done a fantastic and intelligent job so many times before (for free! though I didn't mention that), and they have fucked up so spectacularly on their last few tries, I felt at least they owed me that. Lou looked doubtful, and placed a call to F. X., who wasn't in. Apparently, Lou went on to inform me, Bantam is no longer *using* outside proofreaders. For the last few months, thanks to the famous economic crunch, it's all been being done "in-house" by their endless supply of Smith, Wellesley, and Radcliffe graduate secretaries-who-hope-to-get-ahead-in-publishing. I said I *still*

---

[1] Peplow and Bravard had sent Wagner's autobiography to SRD as a present that June.

thought it would be a good idea to hire Mog. And took home said galleys.

I left Lou your and Mog's addresses, and asked him when they made their copies of the MS, would they send you a copy and Mog a copy. And Lou said sure.

After glancing through the *Stars/Sand* galleys at home (actually they're in pretty fair shape), I decided I'd best put them out of mind till I got home from Vancouver/Seattle a week later.

The next morning I was up at five, out of the house at six, to lug my suitcase up 82nd St. to Broadway, where I caught a cab to 42nd and 6th, to catch the train-to-the-plane, and off to JFK, to take a nine o'clock plane to Vancouver by way of Seattle. (Thanks to a quick — i.e., two-minute — change of planes there in Washington, my luggage went hopelessly astray and didn't catch up to me in Vancouver till sometime that night. But no matter . . .)

Needless to say, in flight I made many notes on revisions to be inserted in the Nevèrÿon book as soon as I got back. Also read most of Teresa de Lauretis's *Alice Doesn't: Feminism, Cinema, Semiotics*, a remarkably good introduction, by the bye, to the semiotics of cinema and the various political controversies currently embroiled in that young, vigorous discipline. Somehow the semiotics of film has been the one area of the post-structuralist dialogue that, till now, I've just found deadly dull. But Teresa's presentation has some real intellectual life in it.

The Vancouver Con itself (see enclosed program book — if you read the Donald Keller essay/sketch of me, you can have a good time playing "What's wrong with this picture?" Myself, I find minimum eight misstatements of fact. But, by this time, you may even find more!) was the warmest and friendliest such group I think I have ever been in. Ted Sturgeon and Jayne Tannehill were there. I got a chance to have a couple of long conversations with Frank Robinson (*The Power* (1956), *The Glass Inferno* (1974), *The Prometheus Project* (1975) . . .). He was partway through a nonfiction book on AIDS and had just decided to shelve it. Part of the reason was a lack of publisher interest. The other part, he said, was that he kept on finding himself having to represent the gay community in a very bad light (Frank himself is gay), and that just wasn't what he felt, right through here, he wanted to do. At any rate, I told him I'd just finished a novel with AIDS as a theme *(The Tale of Plagues and Carnivals)*, and we had a good long conversation (three hours) in which he gave me all the results of his research which, indeed, effected a few notes I'd made to incorporate into *P&C* when I got back.

I got picked up at the airport by a heavy young woman and a gaunt young man, JoAnne and David — charming and nervous, the two of them. From what I could gather, they more or less *were* the con committee. Indeed, it was a rather small con, with not more than 450 people in attendance. The first day of the actual con, there was some mixup regarding the dealers' room. It had been scheduled to open at eight o'clock in the morning, but it turned out not to be available till 1:30 in the afternoon and a couple of dealers, who'd stayed over at the hotel the night before so they could set up early, were a little miffed. For them, of course, this is first and foremost a paying job. And an extra night's hotel charges, with no compensating income, really hurts some of the smaller ones. One of them started distributing buttons that said, "Where's the Con . . .?"[2] That gesture seemed to mollify them, and by the afternoon

---

[2] This parodied a then-popular television commercial for Wendy's Hamburgers, whose famous tag line was: "Where's the beef . . .?"

things were going along smoothly.

One reason the con was so small is because there had been a three-month newspaper strike in Vancouver, which ended the Friday the con opened: so much for publicity. And Saturday, there was a citywide bus strike — and the con was somewhat on the outskirts, at the University of British Columbia: so much for public transportation.

Saturday night—or rather Sunday morning—at around four o'clock there was a disturbance involving some local kids, about twelve years old on the average, who started off by stealing name badges, then trying to sell drugs, and eventually trying (rather futilely) to start a fight. One of them kicked in a glass door. They were eventually ousted by the campus police. But I was asleep through that and only got a somewhat mangled report of it at Sunday brunch.

Also got some time to speak with (or rather listen to) Lauren McGregor. Which was lots of fun. Also I was interviewed by a local gay newspaper, by two guys, the larger of whom ("Spence") I found rather cute. Sitting in the convention center lobby, I got a chance to talk at some length with him the next day. Indeed, there was some very interesting gay programming at the con (though, intriguingly, it doesn't "show" in the program), that got an absolutely crowded attendance (I'm sure the audience was overwhelmingly straight, and just interested in what we were going to talk about), as well as a gay reception, that was just marvelous fun —and which, after about 20 minutes, had brought in about a third straight attendees who simply decided they didn't want to miss out.

(My people *do* know how to have a good time!)

The first night of the con there was a wonderful "moose meat" dinner at Joanne's house—the con-committee chairman, she. Her mother, Donna, cooked, and there (really) was roasted moose as well as baked salmon, along with mashed potatoes, salad, and many fresh vegetables. There were a dozen or more people, including Frank Robinson. And Judy Merril arrived late and gave everybody hugs. Jayne and Ted Sturgeon arrived just as everyone was finishing up, but joined in the eating anyway.

On Sunday night, at another part of Vancouver entirely (Kitsillano), a video artist named Michael MacDonald held a showing of Russell FitzGerald's paintings at his house. Dora (Russell's widow), and her new young man, a very pleasant American Indian, with tattoos, of about 23 (he said I was fatter than he had imagined me), had taken the paintings out of storage and hung them, and there was a party at Michael's, where people's reactions to — and, among those of us who had known Russell, our reminiscences about— the paintings were recorded and videotaped.

It was a truly moving experience to see those paintings again. And a series of some 30-odd, eighteen-inch square paintings [along with some half-dozen bronze castings of the same subjects] called *The Sleepers*, which Russell had done in Vancouver in the years before he died, I got a chance to see for the first time. Dora also gave me a copy of Russell's illustrations for her translations of Rilke's *The Life of the Virgin Mary*, which were his last work and which had been printed (alas, badly) in *The Capilano Review*. Most of the paintings I was, of course, familiar with. Russell was not very well for the six(?)-odd years he was in Vancouver, and also he was away from his inspiration: His true subject was the encounter between black and white culture, and Vancouver just doesn't have any black culture to speak of. So that, other than *The Sleepers*, he had not done very much while in Canada. (Apparently he'd been working on a novel—but Dora said that, about three months before he died, he destroyed it one day.) I had not seen most of the pictures since '67 or '68. And at least one of them, *Prometheus*—one of a set of four seven-foot-high allegorical panels — had been intimately involved with *Nova*. Indeed, I would love to see it used someday as a cover for a reprint of the book! Along with the Tarot deck Russell made at about the same time I was writing the book, anyone would find the painting illuminative of the novel and, indeed, vice versa. And pages of *Nova* were written out in my notebook as I sat in the corner of the "black studio" down on Second Street, while Russell, with a glass of white wine on the table beside him, stood working on the endless eagle feathers which gave him such difficulty (and which are, today, so luminously and sumptuously beautiful) on Prometheus's towering enamel-black ground, while Harold, the sometimes drug addict who was Russell's main model for the series, was in and out with Roosevelt, another young black man who was also part of the Russell/Dora *menage* back then.

The only thing I have really written about Russell is the description of "Proctor's Studio" in *Equinox*. Visually, that was about as accurate a description of "the black studio" as I could write. The painting described there, as I recall, was one of those four panels, the "*Götterdämerrung*" painting, which shows Siegfried and Brunhilde cowering in the split and fiery carcass of Grane, in flames on the funeral pyre, which is a pile of flaming money (*pace*, George Bernard Shaw), while the feet of the dead heroes dangle down into the fires along the top of the picture. Though the painting still exists and was hung there, that night, with the three others, Dora tells me that many of the objects in that studio, as I described it back then, have been lost.

Jayne Tannehill (Lady Sturgeon) drove me and Jerry Kaufman over to see the exhibition Sunday evening. Jayne was very impressed. And Jerry was simply "blown away," as they say.

There were a couple of pleasant dinners that weekend: a marvelous Japanese meal with Judy Merril and a psychiatrist friend, along with John Singer and a few others; and the next night I went out with Debby Knotkin, again John Singer, Jerry Kaufman, Ctein, and a few more: Tom, Allen, Janet. . . It was equally pleasant.

On Monday, the con was over, and I drove down to Seattle in a pleasant enough van. Thin brown Ctein, with lots of long black hair, did the driving. I sat beside him. And Jerry stretched out in the back on the van's traveling bed. In Seattle we stopped briefly to let Jerry off and to say hello to Suzle Tompkins, Jerry's housemate and sometimes girlfriend. They have a truly lovely house though it's haunted by the ghosts of dozens of dead mimeograph machines, entombed behind a wooden door in the cellar. Then Ctein delivered me to Joanna's. He had to come back forty minutes later, though, because I'd managed to leave my brown leather jacket in the van—which had my passport and my airline ticket home in it. But the weather was uncharacteristically bright and sunny for Seattle. Other than that, the transfer was made without pain.

At one point, while I was in Joanna's bare little upstairs guest room, lying on my bed and reading at a copy of Brecht's *Die Hauspostille*, which I'd found in Joanna's downstairs bookshelf (Joanna herself was in her room taking a nap at that point), I suddenly picked up my notebook and wrote, almost straight out:

ABOUT THE DROWNED GIRL
     —after Brecht

When she was drowned,
her body was washed down
among the streams and rivers.
Winding weeds looped and bound

her. Under her feet
dim fishes still
flick silver, meet,
and swim around.

As night awoke,
the sky grew dark as smoke,
and the stars chuckled
at the brilliant joke.

When they were done,
they watched to see
where she would come.
At last, when her pale body

began to rot, it happened,
very slowly, God forgot her there:
first face, then hands,
at last her hair,

at last her liquid flesh:
scum on the river's scum.

I first did this translation—Lowell's term, 'imitation,' would be more accurate, because it isn't very literal, especially in the middle part—sometime toward the autumn of 1960; indeed, it was just before I did the *Bateaux Ivre* translation. You may recognize a few lines of it from that surviving fragment of *Voyage, Orestes* I sent you. I think in another letter I told you about the German woman, Mrs. Bernheimer, whom I (and the other waiters) liked so much up at Breadloaf.[3] She spent part of an evening, when we'd all come down to have wine and pastry at her house in the town, discoursing on Brecht's poetry in general, and on that poem in particular.

Once I got home, using the Stanley Bernshaw volume *The Poem Itself* as a crib, I worked out the above version, which eventually became a part of *V/O*.

For years, however, I had not been able to remember the opening lines. But there, in Joanna's guest room, looking at the original German, suddenly my eighteen-year-old version came rushing back to me, word for word; so I jotted it down.

Joanna herself seems in fine fettle — though the truth is, we are all getting older. After a comparatively long silence, she has had three books out this year. While I was there, I read through a sheaf of many, many reviews of all of them. And the attention seems to be doubling back and creating more attention. Most

---

[3] The Breadloaf Writers' Conference that SRD attended, working as a waiter, in the summer of 1960.

of the reviews were good—but how, with such a superb writer, could they *not* be! I couldn't be happier for her. Her eating habits, always strange, are getting stranger, however. For "two weeks' shopping" one day, I went with her while she bought *eleven* (!) cartons of "Eggs Beaters" (imitation eggs), three quarts of plain yogurt, and three packages of tofu. And that's really *all* she'll eat for those two weeks! Her tendency to monologue rather than converse is getting stronger. She seems to be constitutionally incapable of listening to another person for more than ten seconds, without launching in to a (cheerful, witty, and intelligent, to be sure) five- or ten-minute monologue of her own. I noticed this not only with me, but when we went to dinner at Don and Tatiana Keller's our first evening. They are two infinitely sweet people, and obviously cherish her deeply—as, indeed, do I. And, when all is said and done, I only had to put up with the former for two days, and the latter has never bothered me at all.

She certainly seemed up and well; and during the discussion period after my lecture, she was full of brilliant and insightful comments and questions.

The second morning I was there, I took a phone call from a young woman at her agent's office in New York, who needed some information in relation to the foreign sale of some short stories. At the time, Joanna was closeted up stairs, doing her morning exercises. When she was finished, I gave her the message. Almost immediately she began to pooh-pooh their need for this information, but she was obviously delighted that they were asking. And five minutes later, she was on the phone to give them said data.

My Tuesday night lecture at the University, indeed, went well. There were a good hundred attendees — which about filled up the room. And there was a pleasant reception afterwards.

Joanna and I (yet *again* with John Singer, who showed up that afternoon) had lunch at Ivar's "Salmon House." And my last evening in Seattle, I went out to dinner with Pat Muir and his wife, Sharon. Pat was kind of my love-object for summer '71 (?), when I was teaching at Clarion West. At the time, he was the speed connection for the University of Washington, and traveled around in black leather pants with a knife strapped to his right boot. After Clarion, he and I took a motorcycle trip up to Vancouver together, stopping off at various communes on the way, and stayed with Russell and Dora for about three days—then drove back, whereupon Pat put me on the bus to San Francisco. I think I did more acid in those two weeks—we're talkin' twice daily, two, three days in a row, with a day off, and then start all over—than I had or have had all together before or since. But the Spike chronicles it all somewhere in *Triton*, while she and Bron are at dinner, I believe. When I was in Vancouver at the retrospective of Russell's work, Dora showed me some pictures, including some Polaroid snapshots of these two veritable children on a motorcycle—Pat and me!

And do you know, back then, I was actually thinner than Pat. Today, I am substantially the heavier. And he is a graying, 40-year-old, electronics repairman . . . During that first trip, Robin Blazer said something to me that I've always remembered. At one point, while we were all having brunch with Russell and Dora, Robin took me aside and said: "You know, you're going to be very important to that young man. The simple fact is, Chip, nobody as intelligent as you has ever thought he was as important as you do. And he's always going to value that."

And almost fifteen years later, I realize Robin was right. Always a sculptor of small and lovely objects, starting from the time I was last in Seattle and had spent an afternoon with him, Pat had made me a marvelous little sculpture, of a kind of gargoyle, mounted on a piece of quartz crystal, the whole under a glass bell and set on an onyx-like slab.

It's really lovely, and graces the top of the hi-fi cabinet even now.

After dinner, we dropped Sharon off at home (their house, in the city but backed by an overgrown drop of 50 feet to a rushing stream, is quite an object of lower working-class confusion, and someday I want to use it in a novel), and Pat drove me to the airport; his step-kids, who range in age now from eighteen to twenty, are a real problem. Of the two boys, the older is a high-grade juvenile delinquent and the younger is a low-grade one; and eighteen-year-old Collin is on her way. Pat copes. But he's just too sweet a guy to have to put up with some of the stuff he and Sharon have been having to deal with.

Ah, well.

After a night-long flight, I arrived in New York, found the galleys of *Stars/Sand* —and your wonderful gift! (Please convey my thanks to Michael. I shall try and write him too. Really!)

And also, almost equally warming, *The Black American Literature Forum.*

Once again, thanks.

I spent the first week back putting in my last-minute corrections on *The Tale of Plagues and Carnivals,* working morning and night, then running into Bantam in the afternoon with 50 replacement pages one day, 20 the next, and 35 the day after that.

What, I wanted to know, had been the decision on Mog's doing the proofing of *Stars/Sand*? Well, said Lou, F. X. has had them done "in-house"—twice over. And he handed me the proofed galleys. Why don't you take a look at these?

So I took them home.

Oh, yes. Lou explained that the Copy House, which does Bantam's copying, had had some sort of catastrophe the day they sent the MS of *Flight from Nevèrÿon* over: Half the pages came out illegible. So they *hadn't* sent you and Mog copies yet. They would do that after copy-editing.

The new *Nevèrÿon* book—scheduled for February '85—is going into production practically immediately. At the same time, the galleys for *Stars/Sand* were due in today (Tuesday the 15th of June), but the heat, up till this morning, has been paralyzing, and at lunch this afternoon (I am writing this paragraph a few hours after your phone call) I got Lou to give me till Friday at 11:00. I'd indeed asked for next Monday. But, said Lou, no. So Friday it will be. I'll manage, but I'm really working off a kind of crazed overdrive. Indeed, I have been since before I flew off. And it hasn't stopped yet.

That, indeed, has been the main reason I haven't sent a letter till now. There just hasn't been time.

Flight from Nevèrÿon was written in a kind of committed joy. And aside from all the Machiavellian machinations on the business side, Lou has been highly complementary. It's just a bit of publisher's hyperbole, I know, but he said it sincerely enough: On the day I brought in the second batch of replacement pages, while we were standing in the Bantam lobby he told me: "You know, Chip, I read most of the book the night you gave it to me. And I finished it at home the next day. As soon as I put the last page down, I walked in a kind of daze out of my door, wandered up the street and turned into my best friend's house. He looked up and said: 'What's the matter, Lou?' And I said: 'I think I may just have read the most brilliant book I've ever read in my life!' Really," he went on, "that's how it affected me." Hyperbole it may be, but it still gave me a little lift.

On the other hand, the galleys for *Stars/Sand* have been fighting me all the way —as did, indeed, the MS while I was checking the copy-editing. The only time I can ever remember a book's being this much hell—at every reading and rereading of every paragraph—is the second volume of *The Fall of the Towers.* I've been claiming heat and work as my excuse for not having the galleys done, but the truth is I simply can't read it for more than 20 minutes at a stretch without having to get up and take a good hour break. I even think it's a good book—that's not the problem. But every paragraph seems *just* beyond my ambition to achieve with the precision and panache I would have liked for it. The organization of *Triton,* say, or "The Tale of Fog and Granite," is something that I can recognize as art. But this wild and woolly writing by the seat of one's pants, however well— here and there — it succeeds, is still vaguely distasteful to me. It's literature as rhapsody—which, when you're 42, just doesn't stay with you very long. Or perhaps it's simply that the book was finished, for all practical purposes, by 1980— so that to work creatively on it today, adjusting sentences, reorganizing scenes, and the like, is simply very hard to do with two novels, now, in-between.

I've had an endless spate of letters from John Mueller, my nail-biting, beer-swilling, 23-year-old German carpenter's assistant-*cum*-hustler friend, who will be languishing in jail in Florida till September 16th. I've only written him twice, and also sent him, at his request, a package of my books. But I must have gotten ten letters from him! One of them—just after he finished *Dhalgren*—was really quite insightful. He said, quite accurately, that knowing what our sex was like, he could spot many things that were, indeed, sexual that probably most readers wouldn't notice—then went on to catalogue them, rather accurately.

Basically John's problem is that he's a low-grade anxiety neurotic. He drinks only to keep that under control. And until he does something about that, he's not going to make too much progress. (He's in an alcoholic program in the jail.) What he needs is a general, low-grade tranquilizer program; he's quite intelligent, and if he gets that basic anxiety taken care of, he'll probably be able to function. But until he gets on such a program, I don't think he really will. It's something to talk to him about when I get round to writing him again.

I believe I wrote you about my one-legged friend Arly. I've run into him a few times since then, now at the movies, now on the street. A few times I've left notes on his rather spectacularly squalid apartment door in the abandoned building where he lives. A couple of months back, Iva and I were walking down from my mother's, on a sunny Broadway Sunday. Somehow the subject of physical disabilities came up and I explained to Iva that I had a friend named Arly who only had one leg and how very well he got around. Thirty seconds after we'd gone on to talk about something else, I looked up to see Arly, on his crutch, coming up the street.

I said hello. I introduced Iva to him. They shook hands. He seemed quite taken with her. He, indeed, was on his way to see his own mother. And a minute later

when we were walking on, Iva said: "He's *very* nice, daddy! He must be a very kind person."

"I suspect he is," I told her.

And the couple of times I've ran into him since, he always asks me: "How's your daughter? She's so *beautiful*, man! She's a really beautiful little girl!" And indeed, she is.

Ah, well. I suppose I'm thinking of him because there is an Arly-based character who figures prominently in *P&C*. But I must really wind this up and get back to those accursed galleys. It was very good to speak to you on the phone.

A dream a few nights back stays with me. It was one of those sweltering evenings, and I'd turned in early. You couldn't use either covers or pajamas. Somewhere about three or four in the morning, I *dreamed* that I was lying in bed, half-asleep, but it was on some sort of screened-in country-house porch, in the dark. Somewhere outside, among the trees, a dog was barking. Lying on my back, I wondered sleepily (in the dream) what could be bothering it. As I lay there, the barking began to move, now and again interrupted by some kind of scuffling. Suddenly I realized that the dog was barking *at* someone, who was moving around outside along the porch.

At the same time I realized I couldn't move, where I lay, more or less on my back.

The intruder began to make his way along the outside of the porch, while I thought, no, certainly he couldn't be coming in here; but then I heard the porch door open on my right. I tried to turn or get up, but of course I was still paralyzed. Then, suddenly, a face bent down above mine, only inches away, to stare at me. I could make out very little of it with only the dim light behind—indeed, it was too dark to see the actual features. As much as I could tell, it was a youngish man in his early thirties, with long hair, but starting to go bald on top. I tried to cry out, but I could only make some painful, inarticulate grunts. I tried to twist away, and finally I was able to tear (I originally wrote "dare") free from the paralysis and roll to the left, where, from a bookshelf, I seized up a copy of the trade paperback of *Gravity's Rainbow*, which lay on top of some other books shelved there, rolled back, and struck at him. I missed, and the man stood up—I was still unable to see his face, though he seemed extraordinarily real. (Jeans. A short-sleeved shirt or tank top, just visible in the vague back-light.) He began to fade, and my real bedroom formed around me as I woke, on my back, in bed—my body was encased in chills, which went and returned over the next five minutes, while I sat up on the edge of the bed, got up to go to bathroom, and lay back down to go to sleep again.

In our living room bookshelf, right behind the couch, on top of some other books, there *is* a copy of the Viking Compass edition of *Gravity's Rainbow* . . .

Your letter of the 30th was *another* gem!

Little Magazine meetings have been going well, but as you may imagine amidst all this, they haven't been getting my first energies. And on the 23rd, I have to moderate a debate between Harlan Ellison and Stan Lee at something called "Dimension Convention" here in New York. I really should do at least an afternoon's homework on that one, but it will probably wait till a day or two before the event itself. And Iva is due back from England on the 29th.

Somewhere in the midst of all of this, while Frank was up at his mother's, I had dinner with Greg Frux at an interesting local restaurant called Bazzini's. Then we went to see *The Search for Spock*—at the same theater I fell in, when I took Iva to see *Greystoke*. It was a colorful, adventurous bit of ho-hum. Then, a few days later, when I was seeing spots in front of my eyes from a full morning with the galleys, I staggered from the house, went down to 42nd Street, and took in *Beat Street*. The production values are higher than *Breakin'*, but it was still not as good — though do you recall the break dancers I described in one letter who entertained at Barbara Wise's Christmas party? Well, one of those kids (he's in the first dance contest in one of the red gym suits, and then again in the subway-station sequence — again in a red jumpsuit — when the kids are arrested for dancing because the police assume they're fighting) was in the film and did some very nice work. What *Beat Street* doesn't quite seem to be aware of as a film, however, is that the kids' dances are, indeed, artistic compositions, however demotic and dionysiac, and must be filmed as such, coherently and intelligently. This film, unlike *Breakin'*, handles the moves as endless background filler or transition material, without any sense of break-dancing *as* dance—they try to make of it a kind of abstract film-painting. And that just doesn't work.

And its story is as dumb as *Breakin'*'s, or even dumber—though there's another mindless attempt to get something on the Subway Writers into the *Beat Street* film. Well, at least you can learn some of the terminology, if you didn't know it before. Catch 'em if you can. But Twyla Tharp still uses them—both breakin' *and* writin', really—better.

I look forward to hearing from you—and also to seeing the MS of your coming chapbook.

And now back to those galleys.

My love to Cynthia, Jonathon (and Robert and Tom, when next you speak or write to them).

And all my love to you,

• 19 •

To John P. Mueller

June 22nd, 1984

Dear John,

Where to begin? Where to begin? Certainly, with a heartfelt "Thank You!" for all your letters. I'm pretty sure at this point I have them all.

But since I wrote you last, I have been starting work between 4:30 and 5:30 in the morning and knocking off at about seven at night—at which point I just fall out. Yesterday, I delivered a new novel to Bantam Books, my publisher, and this is truly the first day I've had to do just about anything that wasn't work.

Oh, yes. There was a week-long trip to do some lectures out on the West Coast, first in Vancouver, then in Seattle. But that only took up more time, when I couldn't write you.

I'll try to give you a bit more detail about what's been going on:

About eight o'clock, the morning of Wednesday May 20th, I finished a book that I've been working on for close to a year now, called *Flight from Nevèrÿon*. It's the third volume in a series of three. The first is called *Tales of Nevèrÿon* and the second is called *Neveryóna*. They were published, respectively, in 1979 and 1983. Bantam tells me that the third volume will appear in February, 1985.

My editor, a 26-year-old kid named Lou, took the manuscript from me and handed me the galleys for another book of mine, called *Stars in my Pocket Like Grains of Sand*, which is scheduled to come out this Christmas ('84). Galleys, which I'm sure you probably know, are long sheets of paper with the first version of the type for the book. They're usually filled with lots of mistakes. You proof-read these and correct all the mistakes in the margin, whereupon the type-setter takes this all back and puts in the corrections.

After glancing through the *Stars/Sand* galleys at home (actually they're in pretty fair shape), I decided I'd best put them out of mind till I got home from Vancouver/Seattle a week later.

[After recounting how his 1960 translation of Brecht's "About the Drowned Girl" returned to him while visiting with Russ (letter 18, pp. bottom 120-122, all but verbatim), SRD continues:]

It's strange how, for years, you can't remember something, and then it comes back.

When I was 23, I lived in Greece for about six months, back in 1965/'66. I had a room with two other guys in a big, cold, drafty house run by an energetic little old woman who rode all over Athens on a motorcycle (it belonged to her 30-year-old son, but he never used it, and his mom, in her old black dress, and usually with a black head rag around her stringy white hair, rode it all the time). She and her family lived on the ground floor, and she rented rooms on the second and third out to students and young workers. For a while we had a room inside the house; then, when we couldn't find all the rent one week, she moved us up into a cheaper room on the roof—it was kind of like a maintenance shack built on the roof, divided in two. You didn't even go into the house to get to it. Around the back, there was a spiral black metal staircase that went up by the wall, at the top of which you climbed over the retaining wall. (The house was three stories high.) The kid in the other half of the shack, next door, was about 20 years old and a house painter, I remember, named Costas. But he, at least, could afford to have his whole half of the roof shack (each half had a separate door) to himself.

He thought the three of us (by that time, two Americans—myself and a guy named Ron, whom I'd worked with in Texas, and a tall, skinny Englishman named John Witton-Doris, whom we'd met on an island called Mykonos; we'd just lost a bumptious Canadian named Bill who'd been part of our group till then), crammed into a space that really wasn't too much larger than my bathroom today, were very funny. And I guess we were.

I lived there for maybe three months.

To get to the house, you went up a moderately large street called Hippocratou Street, which ran up a steep hill. Eventually, after about a 20-minute walk, you turned onto the small side street where the house itself was. But about six months after I got back from Greece, one day I realized I just couldn't remember the address to save myself — though I remembered just about everything else about the house, from the little two-burner "petrogaz" stove and the shallow gray marble sink in the bare second floor kitchen, to the high ceilinged rooms, with their peeling plaster walls.

But even though I went looking through some old letters people had sent me while I was there (I'd always picked up my mail from the American Express office, down on Constitution Square), none had ever come to the house. So that didn't help me much.

In 1978, Frank and I went to Europe, and in the course of the trip we visited Athens. It wasn't very hard to find Hippocratou Street. It crosses Stadiou Street (which is like Athens's Fifth Avenue) right near the university. I started up the hill —and the first thing I noticed, right off, was that there were a lot more new buildings than there had been twelve years before. I recognized a good number of the cross-street names, too—even ones I hadn't thought of since I left Athens. I was sure as soon as I saw the street I'd lived on, I'd recognize it.

There'd been a medium-sized *"taverna"* on the corner, where Ron, John and I usually ate lunch or dinner (often *"aginares kai kremedi"* [artichoke and onion stew] or *"kalimaria,"*— which, as in Italian, is squid, and, as I recall, was usually poached, pale pink, and swimming in olive oil), where they served resonated white wine in quarter-liter and half-liter cylindrical copper carafes. In order to get the waiters' attention (all of whom were very fond of us, by the end of our stay), you were supposed to clap loudly. And if you did just raise your hand and signal with your finger (in the French [which is also the American] manner), the white-smocked waiter (another Costas!), leaning against the red-painted column in the middle of the restaurant, reading his paper, would look up, smile, wave back, then go on reading—thinking you were just being friendly, and with no notion in the world that you wanted him to get you something!

The houses on the street itself were big, wet-sand-colored things, little square blue number plates nailed to their sides with white numbers enameled on them. Along the tops ran ornate cornices, and high, shuttered windows, whose lower sills hit you about shoulder level, along the walls.

At the crest of the hill is a famous monastery called Lykabetis. (Indeed, the whole hill is called Lykabetis Hill, after the monastery at the top.) After about 40 minutes of climbing, I could see the monastery ahead — and I knew the house wasn't that far up! But I hadn't passed any little street with such houses on it as I remembered. There were just a lot of newish, condominium style houses with little poured concrete balconies. After walking around for an hour or so, I finally figured out what must have happened:

My old house—as well as the *taverna*—had been pulled down and replaced with new buildings. The street itself had only been a couple of (short) blocks long. By '78, the whole street had been built over and no longer existed.

And I still couldn't remember the name.

So Frank and I came home. A few years passed. Maybe once every couple of weeks, or couple of months, I'd try to remember: *What* was the name of that no-longer-existing little street in Athens a dozen years ago?

And couldn't.

Until one summer night in 1982.

It was about three o'clock in the morning, and I was in bed, in the midst of some fuzzy and unclear dream about riding in a taxi cab at night in some foreign city. Suddenly I woke up and said, out loud, *". . . Hodos Voltetsiou, deka-'efta . . ."*

"Deka-'efta" is Greek for "seventeen." And *"Hodos Voltetsiou"* means "Voltet-siou Street." And, indeed, my address in those months had been: 17 Voltetsiou Street.

A couple of times, back in Athens, I'd come home late at night by cab (much cheaper in Athens in 1966 than it is in New York today!), and *"Hodos Voltetsiou, deka-'efta . . ."* was what I said to the Greek cabdriver in order to get home!

In my bedroom, I turned on the light, jotted it down in my notebook, and haven't forgotten it since.

But memory is a very funny thing!

Anyway: back to Seattle . . .

[Here SRD retells all-but-verbatim his trip to Seattle as on pages 124 and 125 of letter 18]

I spent the first week back putting in my last-minute corrections on my book, working morning and night, then running into Bantam in the afternoon with 50 replacement pages one day, 20 the next, and 35 the day after that.

I'd been trying to get a friend of mine a free-lance job doing some proofreading for my publisher, but—unfortunately—that didn't work out. I felt kind of bad about it, because she really needed the work.

That, indeed, has been the main reason I haven't sent a letter till now. There just hasn't been time!

I've had four letters from you (since) I sent off the books. I've only written you twice (not counting the books), but I hope this makes up for a little, and gives you some idea how busy I've been.

I was very touched by both your letter in which you talked about *Dhalgren* and the letter where you told me about how embarrassed you could sometimes feel over your nail-biting. You, of course, were very right when you said that you could understand things about *Dhalgren*, from knowing me, that probably (some of) my other readers could not.

Embarrassment is, of course, a funny thing. My best friend in elementary school was a kid named Robert, who bit his nails as severely as you do. And I always used to think his hands were beautiful. I never had any kind of sex with him, but we were in school together from the time we were five till the time we were thirteen. And by the third or fourth grade I knew he wished he didn't bite them and thought people didn't like it.

Whereas I, of course, wished I did!

Once or twice a year I would suddenly decide that I was going to have nails as nice and short as Robert's (or Johnny Kronenberger's, another school friend of mine, who was a nail biter), and I'd cut my nails as short as I possibly could. A couple of times, I even took a needle and worked it under the rim of the nail to pry more loose from the quick, so I could cut more away and expose more of the crown. But I could never get them as short as either Robert's or Johnny's. (And, of course, using the needle on them, or sometimes a razor blade to pry them loose, *hurt!*) But for a few days or so, I'd go around thinking my hands looked pretty good. But a week or two later, the nails would have grown back. And I couldn't establish the habit of just biting them to save myself. So pretty soon my hands would look like everybody else's—which they pretty much still do.

And that's when I'd wish they didn't.

It probably doesn't do you any good, because your embarrassment comes from your family's constantly harping on you about it. But the next time you feel embarrassed about your nails, try to remember that some people think they're beautiful and almost unbearably sexy. Believe me, if it happens to be your judge, I can assure you, you *will* do better. If a waiter who bites his nails serves me food in a restaurant, almost always he gets a bigger tip. When I've had a store job, I'm always friendlier to customers who come in with bitten nails. You just can't help it, if that's the way you happen to be set up.

By the way, I'm not the only person I know like that, either.

Years ago I knew a woman, once, who felt the same way. She was about 23 back then, and her boyfriend was a red-headed guy about 25 who worked as a leather craftsman, and had hands much like yours. We were all sitting around together once — maybe we were drinking. At one point her boyfriend looked at his hands and said, in passing, "You know, I really have to stop biting my nails. I been doing it since I was a kid . . ."

His girlfriend took his hand, grinned, and said: "You probably will, too — and then I'll leave you forever."

I don't think it even registered to most of the people sitting around. But I immediately picked up on it. And sometime later, when I got her alone, I asked her about it.

So she told me:

Basically, it seems, she felt pretty much about hands the way I did. As with me, it had started for her when she was a very little girl, and all through school she remembers being attracted to the little boys in her class who were nail-biters.

She wasn't a nail-biter herself. But she was a very pretty, rather petite little blond.

Odd. But at this point, I can't remember either her or her boyfriend's name. What I can remember is, of course, his hands. . . .

I pause here with a bit of news. Frank just called to tell me that a very great man has just died. He was a French philosopher, named Michel Foucault. He was only 57. He died in a hospital in France, yesterday, though the newspaper article did not say of what.[1] I've been reading his books since 1968, or so; and his work was very important to me. (Some of the ideas about madness lurking in the depths of *Dhalgren* came from him.) I know a few people who knew him, though I never met him myself. I once wrote an article about his most recent book. In fact, part of my lecture in Seattle was about him. Ah, well. It's a real loss to the world.

But we go on, anyway.

I'm glad to hear you're in an alcoholic program. Has anybody ever used the term "anxiety neurosis" or "low-grade anxiety neurosis" with you about yourself? As somebody who's brought you more than one six-pack before ten o'clock in the morning, and has known you on and off now for over two years, I've noticed various things about you. I mention them, not at all to criticize you, but rather to tell you some things that you yourself may be able to use for your own good.

An "anxiety neurosis" can be a very mild situation and still make you very

---

[1] Michel Foucault died of AIDS-related complications in Paris on June 25th, 1984, though the confirmation that it was AIDS was more than five years away.

unhappy. People with anxiety neurosis show two basic characteristics.

First, is a vague but constant feeling of restlessness—that something is always going wrong, or is about to go wrong. They always want to move on, get out of the situation where they are, and move into another; even when it looks to everyone else as if things are going pretty well. People who suffer from this are worriers. They tend to be people who arrive for appointments fifteen minutes early—or else don't show up at all, because the whole thing is just too difficult.

Second, is a general intermittent (but sometimes persistent) lack of self-confidence: the constant and nagging feeling, whenever you're under any kind of pressure, that you're not good enough, or that other people will suddenly turn and stare and wonder: "What's *he* doing here? Who does he think *he* is?" Anxiety neurotics are constantly apologizing for themselves — even when they do things that anybody else would think are good. They always need someone to reassure them that "It's okay." And it doesn't make much difference whether what they're actually doing is or isn't okay. (Often it is; often it isn't. But the point is the anxiety neurotic often can't really feel the difference. It *all* feels *not* okay, no matter what it is.)

I've seen you demonstrate and heard you talk about both these feelings, many times.

Often anxiety neurotics drink to suppress the vague and gnawing feeling that "something is wrong" or that "something is going to go wrong at any moment." And they also drink to forget those periods of lack of self-confidence.

The only problem is that, at hangover time, all those feelings come back in spades, as well as the physical sickness to boot. And the drink can pretty well do your body in in not too much time, too.

What frequently helps people who drink for this particular set of reasons is a mild tranquilizer, taken steadily, every day, over a period of six to eighteen months, reduced at the end of that time simply to the occasional periods when you're under particular stress. You might ask about this.

I'm no doctor. But to me, John, you have always seemed like a text-book anxiety neurotic. Write me and tell me what you think, and what your program leader has to say about it, if anything . . . ?

Well, I have gone on. I'll really try to write more frequently. My letters may not be as long, but I'll try to keep more of them coming.

You asked about the addresses last time. Lemme see if I can run this all down for you:

The stamp that gave Henry Morrison, Inc.'s zip code as "10010" is just a mistake. It should have been "10011," and that's why I usually don't use it.

Yes, it's better if you write me at the "Henry Morrison, Inc., 58 West 10th Street, New York, NY 10011" address than it is if you write me here at 82nd Street. I certainly get the letters when you send them here; but I get them there, just as fast. And when they come here, they do bother Frank. He certainly knows I have a friend, named John Mueller, who's in jail in Florida. But we do have a personal agreement that we don't mix what goes on at 42nd Street (for either one of us) with what goes on here at the house. And Frank is the kind of person who, if he doesn't see something, doesn't worry about it. (Where do you think I learned all about "anxiety neurosis" from?) And since it *is* part of our agreement, and since he keeps to his half pretty well, I like to keep to my part. And, yes, you would help me do that by writing in care of "Henry Morrison." That's the reason I've always asked you to write me at Henry's.

No offense is intended. But that's really the way I prefer it. And if I don't write back for a while, it's not because *I've* taken offense, or because I'm angry. It's only because I'm busy. When I'm angry at you, believe me: I'll *tell* you I'm angry at you —and why. And if I get angry enough that I don't want to see you any more or have anything else to do with you, I'll tell you that too, straight out. So, until I do, you can just assume I'm not. That's one of the ways you can trust me: You won't have to waste any time at all worrying about it.

You say you would like to be friends. Well, so would I. You know perfectly well that I like you and think you're a pretty good guy. And, after two-and-a-half years, that goes beyond either your hands or your dick—to call a spade a spade. But it's easier to be friends with someone you can trust to do what you ask him to do in little matters like that, that certainly don't harm anyone, than it is to be friends with someone who can't quite bring himself to do what you ask in such matters. But, so far, that's a matter of whether you want to be an easy friend to have or a difficult friend.

But, no matter, friendship it still is.

I look forward to hearing from you again, whatever address you write to. But I've told you the one I prefer. And I'll try to write back soon.

Good luck with your program.

• 20 •

To Michael W. Peplow

June 26th, 1984

Dear Pep,

This is, of course, first to thank you for my wonderful present! *My Life* was waiting for me on my return from Vancouver and Seattle. I have gone through the first section, on Wagner's childhood. It's fascinating and illuminating both. For all the famous inaccuracies that subsequent biographers are always going on about, it's really enough to make you feel as if you've known nothing of Wagner at all till now.

I wonder if anyone will ever isolate an "ecological" school of biography/autobiography? I mean, the reason I was so taken with Amy Lowell's two-volume *Keats* in the days of my ephebehood was because it began with a description of the *weather* on the day of Keats's birth! And after that, I was ready to forgive the doyenne of Brookline, Mass., practically *anything*. (As one, indeed, *had* to, to finish it. But it's still a charmer.) Weather and atmosphere aren't so important for birthdays and death days, I suppose. But consider: When Wordsworth went wandering lonely as a cloud out over the field of golden daffodils, we have a pretty clear picture of the morning of the experience. But an hour or a day or three days later, when Bill sat down at his desk to write the actual sonnet, was the weather outside the same, balmy, cumulously-fleeced blue? If so, it suggests one relation between poem and man. But were it pouring rain since dawn with lightning flickering at the lake-side cottage's windows when he took up his pen to tell us about a flowery stroll in earlier good weather, it suggests a wholly different one.

And the poem would not have had to be a word different for either case.

But these are the relations biography — or, even more frequently, autobiography — gives you. At any rate, Wagner is quite weather-conscious enough for me.

Thank you, once again.

Much saddened by Michel Foucault's death in France yesterday. He was only 57. But I shall probably be going on at some length to Bob about that, sometime soon . . .

I've been maddeningly busy. And it doesn't look like it wants to let up much. But we struggle on. (Sound of writers struggling in the background, please . . .)

Bob tells me you're physically well. For which I am grateful.

Has your local computer bookstore gotten in a book called *Perfect Writer Made Perfectly Clear* by Elyse Sommer, Chilton Book Company: Radnor, Pennsylvania, 1984? I just got it about two weeks ago. Even after nearly a year on the machine, I've found it very helpful in only a couple of days. And for clarity, it beats the manual all hollow.

And are you mastering CP/M yet?

Try at least to get a handle on STAT and PIP. Those two can really make your word-processing life much easier.

My main problem is that I've been so busy, I still can't add two and two on the thing. (Truly, that's no exaggeration.) All I can do is process words . . . !

I hope you are having a wonderful summer. So far, in the city, the weather seems much more human this year than last. I hope it's the same for you folks.

My love to Judy, Davone, and to you,
and to all others with you and around you,

• 21 •

To Joanna Russ

June 27th, 1984

Dear Joanna,

This is just a belated thank you note to say how much I enjoyed seeing you again and what a pleasant stay I had. Everything from the weather to the reception was lovely!

I've been so busy I haven't had time to turn around! Since I've been back I've been through the galleys of one book (*Stars/Sand*) and the copy-edited manuscript of a second (*Flight from Nevèrÿon*). And just this past weekend I did a huge and unpleasantly commercial convention here in New York City, called Dimension Convention, in which I was on three odd panels, and then moderated a "debate" between Harlan Ellison and Stan Lee, in front of just shy of a thousand twelve- to twenty-year-olds, who applauded when *anybody's* name was mentioned, from Plato to Spider-Man to Judith Krantz!

The next thing is to get busily to work on the next volume of my double-decker novel. Part of me keeps saying that it shouldn't be too hard, and another part of me keeps saying, "Why don't you go and do something really interesting, like write a non-fiction book on the concept of art in America, and say everything you really want to about Wagner and Guy Davenport and Joanna and . . . ?"

But common sense will prevail.

I just sent your colleague, Charles Johnson, a copy of "The Mummer's Tale" for a black literature thing he phoned me about. Hope he likes it. Outside, they're repaving my block of Amsterdam Avenue, which, with the cement mixers and the jackhammers and the beeping trucks, has been loud enough to drive Frank from the city to visit his mother in Troy. But I endure here — with ear plugs. Thanks once again for a wonderful visit.

• 22 •

TO CAMILLA DECARNIN

June 28th, 1984

Dear Mog,

The ghosts of all sorts of things I've been meaning to tell you flicker about this evening, as the first raindrops hit my office window pane and, now and again, lightning flickers in the yellowish evening air outside. There, a trundle of thunder . . . David Hartwell called minutes ago to remind me of the *Little Magazine* meeting this evening. I've got to be there just after 7:00, and it's 5:30 now. I'd just gotten started cooking some black beans and chorizos, after spending most of the day correcting and printing out a copy of "The Mummer's Tale" for a West Coast magazine called *Callaloo*, which will be running a joint interview with me and Joanna this autumn (it was done while I was out in Seattle by a young black writer named Charles Johnson). They called yesterday to beg me for a piece of fiction to print along with it.

Of late, the two Major Events in My Life have been (1) the city's decision to repave a seventeen-block stretch of Amsterdam Avenue, the middle of which runs five stories below our half-dozen avenue-facing windows. This means that, for the last four days, from maybe seven in the morning until five in the evening, we live with the roar of cement mixers, beeping trucks, racketing jack-hammers, shouting workmen, etc. Also, outside, it is all but impossible to walk up the street. It's really quite a project. Do you remember the mailbox I told you they'd taken away a couple of months back? Well, two weeks later it showed up again, bolted neatly in place to the pavement. But, of course, in the midst of this operation, it's vanished once more.

Event (2), I suppose, was last weekend's "Dimension Convention," here in the city. It was a large (c. 3,000 attendees) combination comic book and SF convention, with a truly unpleasant commercial atmosphere to it all. I moderated two panels, which went very well. I sat on a third with two NASA guys, which didn't. (Go terribly well, that is — largely because I *wasn't* moderating.) And then, on Sunday at 5:00, I hosted the convention's main program: a "debate" (if you could call it that) between Stan Lee and Harlan Ellison, in front of *many* hundreds of youngsters.

This last was, to put it mildly, A Smashing Success . . . at least in theatrical terms.

But these two occurrences, I suspect, lurk mistily under the various musings to follow.

I guess it was sometime around last May or June. Just about that time Henry had switched all his accounts up to a Chemical Bank on 41st Street and Park Avenue South, just below Grand Central Station, and it had seemed convenient for many of his clients to go along with him; so instead of a weekly trip down to the Village, as in the half-dozen years before, I was now taking the subway down and across to Grand Central and then walking down to the much busier, but finally much more efficient, branch on 41st.

The trade paperback of *Neveryóna* appeared a couple of weeks before my birthday, and a month or so later, the *New York Times Book Review* had run the very complimentary Jonas review.

At any rate, I was walking back through the Grand Central Station waiting room, through the large, mottled, tan marble vestibule in front of the steps down to the men's room, and out and down into the corridor to the subway. As I walked, I suddenly realized I was *reciting* the Jonas review to myself — with a great and pleasurable grin on my face!

And suddenly I had an insight that stopped me where I stood, one foot on one step and one on the step below. The content was not terribly profound. The intensity with which I felt it is a little hard to convey. But I was suddenly aware of the psychological mechanism by which a writer or an actor or a performer becomes addicted to this kind of public feedback. Such public attention is terribly pleasurable. The pleasure lasts for a few days, or even weeks. And under the pressure of such pleasure, even the most dedicated and conscientious artist can have his or her mind move into the configuration—without even realizing it—that connects writing (or anything else) in his or her mind *with* this kind of pleasure. And that's a very different kind of pleasure from that which you get in front of the page when you put words on it to organize an intense picture of the universe around you and a self within it, from which, for moments here and there, if you're doing it right, you can vanish as a pained personality into some universal cascade of order and accuracy. That pleasure you turn to the page again and again for, hoping to find it — and sometimes you do. But it is a rational pleasure, finally. This publicly mediated pleasure, however, you can become truly addicted to: It would be very easy to get yourself in a mental state where you honestly felt you couldn't write without it. In fact, what I realized is that if you don't put some conscious energy into fighting it—because finally, in psychological terms, it's just a matter of following the path of least resistance—you *will* become addicted to it.

So many writers, on whatever level, already have. How many writers have I talked to over the years who've told me: "I can't work without a contract"? Most of them are particularly high production writers, too: Brunner, Moorcock, Malzberg come to mind. I could probably name more if I thought about it. But this is just the poor man's version of this addiction. They truly need that "shot" that comes from getting an idea, and having some editor say: "Hey, that's a great one! I'll buy it from you! Here's a contract and a check! Go home and write it!" In fact, one of the weirdest things in the world to me has always been to sit around in some professional party and listen to these guys talk seriously and intently about how much this editor or that editor is crazy about some book or other—of which not a page has actually yet been written!

By the same token, editors learn very quickly that they *have* to supply this sort of enthusiasm. Lou Aronica, for example, if you went by what he says at lunch, is just as enthusiastic over the unwritten *Splendor and Misery of Bodies, of Cities* as he is over *Stars in My Pocket*, which he's actually read three times now! It makes you kind of wonder.

But how often does a Malzberg or a Brunner or a Moorcock *get* a Sunday *Times* review? Once, twice, three times out of a lifetime production of 50 or 150 books or so. It's not much. And so they become hooked on the editorial substitute. In a way, I'm lucky that I've had as much of the strong stuff as I have, if only to see how it works.

And the other source of feedback is, of course, the conventions. In a sense, the conventions are a lot more realistic: For one thing, there the feedback is for work written and published, not an editorial substitute for an addictive craving. And it's not the inflated sort that comes with mechanical reproduction, i.e., knowing that a few hundred thousand readers, who, indeed, *haven't* read your book, are sharing in the praise being heaped on you by the reviewer. The only place where, you realize, there is still a lot of room for misconstruing what is going on around you is an incident of the sort that happened to me at least once at last weekend's convention: I had been chairing a panel on Visual Interpretation and the Written Word. The participants were (from right to left) Howard Chaykin, Kelly Freas, me in the middle, Walt Simonson, Harlan Ellison, and Richard (*The Shattered Stars*) McEnroe.

Richard was filling in for Alfred Bester, who hadn't shown up. He's young (29?), stocky, serious, and I don't think he's done very much of this sort of thing before. The rest of us are all old convention panel hacks, and Harlan is irrepressible and brilliant, and can make just about any audience glitter. And Howie is *almost* as good. Now we're all smart. All of as have things to say on just about any topic. Really, our only difference is how much experience we've had with (and our personal style in) saying them.

I felt the topic itself was a loser. But somehow everyone rose to the occasion, and the whole thing—as a performance—was among the better such I've been on . . . not a little because, as moderator, I'd done about fifteen minutes' thinking before it got started, kept notes while it went along, and I simply *wouldn't* let it die.

At any rate, afterwards, while Harlan fled somewhere else as fast as he could run, and the various other panel members dispersed (as friendly as we all are on the dais, a kind of immediate exhaustion sets in the moment the terminal applause is over, and rarely do even good friends speak to each other afterwards, as this one heads off to the bar, or another is beset by a dozen kids wanting autographs, or that one hurries off to take part in another program starting five minutes later, or this one wanders away toward the hucksters' room, just to walk around in circles for fifteen minutes, to give himself or herself a chance to come down from the buzz of attention, applause, and even that much thinking and feeling in public, if it's been a Good Show), as I was leaving the curtained-off area of Exhibition B (where we'd been exhibited), some guy about 25, blond, and wearing some light beige sports jacket, stopped me to say: "You know, Mr. Delany, I really enjoyed that panel. I thought you did a very good job moderating, and you really had a couple of very intelligent things to say yourself that I'd never thought about before. Tell me, what do you do? Do you ever write anything? Or do you just go around to the conventions and moderate these panels?" Clearly he only knew my name from the panel itself and, presumably, the "pocket program" where it was listed among those of the other participants.

The feeling was moderately like being kicked in the nuts. I don't think my public smile wavered, and I probably said something like, "Yes, I write science fiction. Thank you for the comment. It was nice of you to take the time to tell me you enjoyed it." (That's my standard response to post-panel praise.) "You'll have to excuse me, though. I have to get upstairs to another program...?"

And smiled.

And left.

But one really negotiates these entire affairs with the feeling that one is a known—even a well-known—personage. And somehow, all compliments, even all attention, are saturated with the fact (at least in your own head) that you are somehow being paid back, socially, for having sweated your ass off for 23 years, making, as best you can, in isolation, fine books; so that to receive a perfectly honest and sincere compliment for something perfectly real that you just actually *did*, followed by your praiser going on to say, in effect, "And what's more, I don't know you from Adam," somehow leeches the entire narcotic charge; and your gut reaction, no matter how well you maintain your cool, is pretty much the same as an addict's, who just pushed the plunger on the hypodermic, only to realize ten seconds later that what he'd thought was heroin was only a glassine envelope full of milk sugar.

Burned again.

And it is precisely that aspect of it that, I feel, is ultimately unhealthy—for me, as a writer.

The young man putting on this convention was John Estrin. Six years ago, he was a nineteen-year-old fan running the New York "Empiricons" that were sponsored by Columbia University's fan group. Today he's a 25-year-old junior executive at some public relations firm, which was the sponsor for *this* particular convention. Last summer, John ran "Empiricon" down at the Milford Plaza, on 8th Avenue (where I chaired at least one panel); and simultaneously there was the Forbidden Planet comics/SF con, where I interviewed Van Vogt and did a couple of programs as well.

A few months back I did a convention called "I-con" out on Long Island, at Stony Brook, where I moderated still another panel, also with Harlan Ellison. Harlan is certainly one of the SF community's best public performers. And though, here and there, I have some minor disagreements with him, I deeply respect the man. Also, I'm just personally very fond of him. Harlan, on a panel, *does* require a bit of moderating. When you're dancing that fast and furiously, it helps to have somebody who'll remind you where the edge of the stage is, so that you don't fall off into the lap of someone in the front row.

On that same panel, I had one complete public-presentation disaster case, Raymond Z. Gallun,[1] who is in his late seventies or early eighties, is a terribly nice old man, but tends to mumble on unstoppably, for 40 minutes if you'll let him, about, "How I wrote this, in 1933. And how I wrote that, in 1934. And how I wrote the other, in 1935." Nor does it matter, particularly, what question you've hap-

[1] Raymond Z. Gallun (1911-1994) was a science fiction writer whose best-known work appeared in the 1930s.

pened to put to him. The answer is the same monologue. (I'm sure you've seen the odd aging professor caught up in the same syndrome.) Well, Ray needs another kind of guidance, i.e., every 20 minutes by the clock, you ask him a question to which some portion of his monologue is applicable, let him run on for 50 seconds by your watch (a minute thirty, if he's actually being coherent), at which point you cut him off at the next comma. (Don't try to wait for a full period. He doesn't use them. And even with the microphone, beyond the third row, no one can hear him anyway.)

At any rate, Estrin was in the audience. And, as he called up to say, a few weeks later: "I figured, Chip, if you could keep Ray from looking like a total fool, could keep things from turning into Harlan's one-man comedy show, and at the same time could keep the subject going and the energy up—well, I figured you could moderate *anything*! Would you like to moderate a Sunday afternoon debate for us, between Stan Lee and Harlan?"

"Okay," I said.

On the first day of the convention I arrived at twelve. Stan Lee was doing a solo bit at that time in the Sheraton Center's Imperial Ballroom, and though I'd had a pleasant talk with him on the phone, long distance, while he was in L.A., about possible topics for the coming debate between him and Harlan, I'd never met him in person, and I had no idea what kind of public self-presentation he had, though I'd heard from a few people that he was very good at it, spent a lot of time going around to colleges and speaking in public, and—from what he said on the phone—he was willing to field just about any kind of question.

The program was late getting started, so I walked into the *vast* Hucksters' Room—acres of comic books, many less SF novels, and various SF-related toys and gizmos—which was kind of the social center of the convention. Saw Barry Malzberg for a few minutes. Then, I practically tripped over Ike (Asimov), with his fly-away mutton chops and western string-tie, the actual Guest of Honor, and we stood around and made "great-to-see-you" noises, while fans came up and thrust books between us for him, for me, to sign.

A moment later Harlan came up to me. "Hey, Chip," he said. "You were supposed to call me, about this debate. Everybody said: 'Chip's going to call you!'"

So I cupped my hands to my mouth and called: "*Har*lan . . .!"

That got him to laugh. There was some odd encounter with a young, black fan whom Harlan managed to mistake for Marvel's single black comic artist. "I know, I know," said Harlan with his hand over his face in mock embarrassment, "all you black guys look alike." People began to thrust books between us. Harlan said: "I'm sorry, but we are in the midst of a conversation, now." Fans scurried away. And I took a couple of notes in my omniscient notebook (The Notebook That Knows More Than I) on the proposed debate. Then Harlan went off to hug a bunch of young women who seemed to be waiting for him, all in matching beige T-shirts.

When the Stan Lee program was announced over the loudspeaker, I escalatored upstairs again to the Imperial. The organizers were hanging about, clearly worried because only about 500 people had come upstairs for Stan's "talk," when they had been expecting a turn-out of close to a thousand. (There must have been another clear thousand down in the hucksters' area. But inertia seemed to be keeping them below, and they weren't surging up for the second floor programs as expected.) On my way in, I passed a tall, slender late-middle-aged man who, later, I realized *was* Stan (I'd never actually seen him before), lingering outside with a couple of people I recognized as among the con organizers. Back-reading a little, I'm pretty sure what they were talking about was some version of the following: Stan was politely suggesting that they let him go on now, since this was the time they'd announced him for; and they were saying, well, gee, no, maybe if they waited another ten minutes, another fifty or a hundred people might wander in.

I took a seat toward the back, and, indeed, in another ten minutes (after a wholly inept young man took the mike and tried, nervously, to keep the audience entertained and expectant, while they waited), Mr. Lee loped onto the stage, took the microphone, and began to present himself in a most personable and relaxed manner. Clearly what he was there for was to plug "Marvel Productions," of which he is now the "Creative Vice President," out on the coast. And with a host of funny stories and the dropped names of movie stars and comic book characters, that's what he did. He was clearly as self-confident as Harlan. Very entertaining. And he obviously knew what he was doing.

No, I didn't think there would be any problems with him and Harlan the next day.

I stayed for about 25 minutes of it.

Then, suddenly, I was hit by an overwhelming desire to be out of there. No fear or anxiety, mind you. Just a kind of: "What am I listening to this idiocy for . . .? I want a drink and some lunch!" What I'd come to see Stan for was to find out how well he did what he did, how comfortable he was doing it, what his style was, so that I would know how to integrate it with Harlan's. I hadn't come to learn anything having to do with the content of what he might have to say. And, really, after ten minutes I had what I needed. So fifteen minutes after that, I left in the middle, quit the hotel, wandered down and across town to 46th Street and Eighth Avenue, and went into Joe Allen's, where I had a Tequila-Wallbanger and some sautéed chicken with capers, while I worked diligently in my notebook on the long prologue of *Splendor and Misery*.

Spilled some chocolate syrup from desert (a hot fudge eclair, filled with ice-cream) on my white shirt — which, as I quipped to the actor-*cum*-waiter who brought me some club soda to scrub it out — "This only happens when you have to perform in front of 300 people in an hour." Then I wandered back to the Sheraton, in time for my four o'clock panel: the one I told you about, with McInroe, Harlan, Chaykin, Freas, and Simonson. And went home.

The next morning, Sunday, the second day of the convention, I woke up with knotted guts and watery shit. Somehow I'd come down with stomach flu. And there was yet another infirmity, which had plagued me the day before and was to produce unexpected agonies all that day as well — though, frankly, I'm almost embarrassed to mention it. Nevertheless: I'd had a hangnail on my right forefinger the previous day (fortunately I'm left-handed); while trying to bite it off, I'd pulled a sliver of nail loose from the quick. It had bled. It was now swollen and under the tiniest of scabs. And anything that touched it, from another finger to a piece of paper, to a comic book picked up at the wrong angle, sent a shooting pain through my hand and into my forearm. You may assume that, on top of all else I say, such shooting pains indeed shot, quite at random, about every 20 minutes all through the weekend, whether I was wandering by myself in the hucksters' room, moderating a panel, signing a book, or talking to friend or fan. And I don't think I acknowledged it once.

A hang-nail . . . ?

Well, that's the kind of pain, as we know, Real Men ignore (while not eating quiche)—especially if they have to run through another day of SF convention.

Frank wasn't up, yet.

I wondered out to the Associated Supermaket over on Columbus Avenue to pick up a bagel and some yogurt. While I was at the back of the check-out line, a vaguely familiar voice passing by behind me said: "Chip . . . ?" And I looked up to see a hefty, white-haired male in a pale blue shirt and silver sunglasses. How I recognized him, I'll never know, because he'd lost at least 80 pounds since I'd last seen him, and *that* had been in East Lansing, Michigan, three or so years back at a Clarion. "A.-J. . . . .?" I said.

"Yeah. It's me." He smiled behind his shopping cart. (It was A.-J. Budrys!) "How're you doing, Chip?"

"Fine!" I said, grinning in spite of my stomach; and my hand—which *touched* something just then. "What on earth are you doing here? Are you here for the convention? That's where I'm going, as soon as I go home and eat a bagel."

"Nope," he said. "I didn't even know there *was* a convention in New York this weekend. I'm visiting my mother. I'm just doing some shopping for her — she lives right around the corner from you," which, by now, I'd actually remembered his telling me once, years ago. At one time, this area of New York was a Ukrainian/Lithuanian neighborhood; there's an old Ukrainian Church, a few buildings away from me on 82nd Street that I'd just walked past this morning on my way to the store. A.-J., who's Lithuanian by nationality, had grown up here— though he'd lived in Chicago most of his adult life. "I'm leaving this evening," he told me, "to go and see my wife's family in Connecticut. So I won't have time to drop down there."

We enthused a bit more about the chances of just running into each other in the supermarket like this, hundreds of miles away from our last meeting, or indeed, any other of our ten or so meetings in the last twenty years. Then I walked out onto sunny Sunday Columbus Avenue.

I almost lost my *very* light breakfast three times on the way to the con.

Just before my first panel, I sat around in the art show area with Bob Whitticker and Jonni Seri, two of the more civilized long-time fans, who seem to have been on the verge of getting married now for going on six years. Jonni gave me a backrub, which I truly appreciated. Between two panels, I had lunch with Denny O'Neil[2] (across from the hotel at the Stage Deli, of all places) and his girl-friend whom I hadn't met before, a red-headed dance therapist named Maggie. At the same lunch I learned that Larry O'Neil, Denny's son by Anne, whom I remember as a perpetual six-year-old on East Sixth Street, was now eighteen, a senior at the High School of Music and Art, was *still* a vegetarian (twelve years ago I'd just assumed it was a passing phase), and was apparently determined to become a comic book artist, somewhat to his father's chagrin!

[2] Long-time friend of SRD's and editor and writer for D.C. Comics.

Then we went up to the con's hospitality suite, where the pros could, presumably, escape the fans. The clutch of rooms was dominated by Marvel Comics' resident "Spider-Man," a very nice, 26-year-old actor-*cum*-body-builder, a Peter Parker look-alike whom Marvel retains at such functions to zip around in blue long-johns with a red head-mask over his face, throwing nets and climbing things. He's really quite bright, knows the character well, and sometimes even leads tours through the Marvel offices, here in the city. He's personable, and good at answering questions. Most of the afternoon, however, he was bouncing about the Sheraton's pale egg-shell 29th-floor suite, three-quarters naked (between costumes), combing his hair a lot, while his petite blonde girlfriend in designer jeans hung on his impressive biceps, and generally being friendly and decorative.

I can't remember his name.

Denny, Maggie, and I were talking in the corner. I sipped a bit of ginger ale to settle my still-queasy stomach and ate a totally uncalled for chocolate cookie. Ray Gallun sat down to join us — and created that crashing lull that sometimes happens among even the most lively and witty conversationalists when someone interrupts the flow of repartee with an intensely mumbled account of something terribly important that occurred in (as best I could make out) 1932.

Quarter to five, and I took off downstairs for the Georgian Ballroom, with Ray still tagging along. In the ballroom (Imperial: read "modern." Georgian: very "traditional," with red drapes along the walls, much copper, hanging "crystal," and gold) there were about 800 kids and lots of confusion. George (Mr. Sulu) Takei was just finishing up his program, plugging *Star Trek III*. (I'd ridden out with him to I-con a couple of months back. He's a truly nice guy and as big-hearted as they come, if just a bit hyper in a perfectly understandable, actorly sort of way.) Harlan was swamped with fans at the front. No one quite knew where Stan was.

No one was announcing anything, so I went up on the stage, took up the microphone, and, well, created order.

Stan was just waiting out of sight, of course, for something to happen. There he came, loping up.

There was Harlan.

And we launched in.

I introduced them with cute anecdotes, to loud cheers. And we were off and flying. Both were in fine form. About a third of it was serious (a debate about gun advertising in comic books, which really got the audience hopping) and about two-thirds of it was tap-dancing (what's wrong with movies; are comic books good for you)—which, it was clear, was just about the proper proportions such an audience could handle. And when it was over, just to be different, I managed not to go running off, but broke through the ring of autograph seekers to say thanks to both of them, while the applause was still going on: Harlan was fighting his way downstairs to get to the limo that was to take him to the airport. Stan was signing veritable mountains of comic books but, over the hubbub, shouted me a smiling invitation to visit him, next time I was in L.A.

A minute or so later, as I made my way up the side of the ballroom, a hand fell on my shoulder. I looked aside into Len Wein's[3] curly hair and brown beard.

---

[3] Long-time comics writer.

"That was great, Chip!" He shook my shoulder. "I know *I* wouldn't have wanted to be up there with those two! Talk about being between a rock and a hard
place . . . !"

"Thanks!" I grinned.

A second later, there was Marv Wolfman and Denny and Maggie, seconding
him.

I grinned again; said thanks again.

And made my way out.

I walked up to 57th Street and across, then up Broadway. And the feeling, Mog,
was . . . very much a downer.

I'm sure in the course of the weekend, I'd signed my 75 or 100 books. (If,
indeed, not more.) I'd had the obligatory half-hour conversation with the 22-year-
old, recent Stony Brook graduate (in accounting) who'd read *Dhalgren* three times
and given it to all his friends, and who said, a lot: "Damn, I just can't believe it!
That I'm sitting here, talking to you, like this! I just never thought something like
that would happen! I mean, to me!" (I believe this one's name was Gregg.) Then,
there was the time when, wandering through the hucksters' room, somebody
brushed against me, and I looked up to see this kind of hulking, 30-year-old,
beardless Puerto Rican bear in a yellow T-shirt (he was probably some kind of
mechanic), holding a bunch of comics in a *huge* hand, with nails bitten breath-
stoppingly back — yes, for a moment I really stopped breathing! I kind of followed this guy around for, maybe, ten minutes, wondering if one could start a
conversation. And didn't, of course; and finally said to myself (as I have said so
many times before), "Really, this is a little silly. That's *not* what you're here for."
Still, though he may not be the direct subject of them (and certainly does not even
know, as the song says, I exist), I am sure he will contour my masturbation fantasies for the next six months or so. (If you've ever been at some particularly
crowded social gathering and have suddenly been brushed past by some particularly attractive boy with particularly handsome buns, or what-grabs-you, you
know both how important *and* how irrelevant such an occurrence is: a gift that
means everything and nothing.) And I've told you about the guy who'd never
heard of me, but—really—that stands out *because* it was the exception. I suppose
the point is simply the two-fold one: On every level one could get something out
of such a convention experience, I'd really gotten all that was there to get. And,
also, I had and still have the basically good feeling that what I do at these things,
I do well. And I do it with life, energy, and a big smile.

Unlike a lot of the writers, I think fandom is a wholly good thing—at least for
the fans.

Maybe it was the end of the stomach virus. Or, more likely, it was what doing
such an event with a stomach virus meant: As much as I had gotten from it, this
was all show business; and if you're a performer and you're able to go on, you go
on. And though from time to time writing was discussed, and even discussed
intelligently, what we were doing had nothing to do *with* writing. (That had been
confined to an hour after lunch in three-quarters-deserted Joe Allen's, while the
waiters began to take off their white aprons and relax at the waiters' table.) And I
really found myself asking: Then *what* were you doing it for?

Yes, I've always had a performerly streak in me. That, no doubt, set me up for it. But the real answer seems to be: Because that's what people in my field do. That's what's done. But, still, it makes you an addict to a kind of attention that, in the end, is neither good for you nor very satisfying.

Which is how this all relates to that little revelation I had passing through Grand Central Station last spring.

At the small con I did in Vancouver, somehow the addictive mechanism was not so much in evidence. There was a lot of real, human contact going on there that absorbed it. But in the commercial atmosphere in which a large con like Dimension Convention takes place, that mechanism seems to be highlighted in a terrible glare; the size and intensity of *what* occurs tends to strip all *that* occurs in it to nothing *but* that mechanism.

I wish I could say this has all resulted in my decision not to do any more of it. But over the July 4th weekend, I'll probably do a couple of panels, as usual, at Empiricon. In October I'm going to Contradiction in Buffalo and then to some NASA related to-do called Star-Con (?) in Washington D.C. I've been committed for these last two for almost six months now. And Empiricon is kind of a regular thing. And, of course, these will probably be much more like Vancouver Con than they are like Dimension Convention — with the possible exception of Star-Con, which I just don't know anything about.

But the point is, the addiction mechanism is still the same, no matter how tasty the social mixer with which the addictive substance is served up. Here, and in like conventions, we're just getting it straight, with nothing else added to disguise the basically unpalatable taste of the stuff, when taken neat.

Ah, well.

And a week before, I'd sat on the steps by the comic book store on Eighth Avenue (which, last weekend, sent over three quarters of its stock to the Dimension Convention Hucksters' Room; and probably sold half of it there, too) for an hour or so with Jeff, while we yakked about nothing in particular and various other street people bopped by, stopped, yakked a while too, and drifted away. And in the middle of it, Jeff pulled up the sleeve of his filthy shirt to show me a plum-sized abscess on his arm, that was leaking pus into his sleeve, the cloth, I could see now, crusty yellow under the dirt.

"Jesus," I said. "How did you get that?"

"Missin'," he said.

"'Missin''?" I repeated. "What do you mean?"

"You know," he told me. "When the needle misses the vein, and then, later, it gets all infected."

"Oh," I said. And took him down to Robin's discount house on 38th Street, brought him a new $3 shirt and a bandage for his arm.

And went home.

I guess we addicts have to stick together.

* * *

And what has happened since I began this letter? Well, I went to the *Little Magazine* meeting. Then, the next day Frank and I drove out to Kennedy Airport —this time I wrote down the directions in my notebook, so that we *didn't* get lost coming back—and we picked up Iva and her friend Chlöe, who were flying back

145

as "unaccompanied minors" together from England. They got through customs by about two, gave us hugs, surrendered up their passports, and chattered on after as we hiked back to the car. After delivering Chlöe to her baby-sitter over on West End Avenue, Iva and I went for some Häagen-Dazs "cookies and cream ice cream," which seems to have become a coming-home ritual over her last half-dozen jaunts. And a pleasant one it is, I must say.

The beans (bet you've forgotten the first paragraph of this letter by now) were quite good.

I had a real lesson on inflation at the *Little Magazine* meeting, Thursday night. David went over the history of our production costs. And in 1971—not '61, mind you, but '71—it cost between $200 and $275 dollars to print 1000 copies of the *Little Magazine*, which then sold for $1.50 apiece. Today, the same 1000 copies costs us approximately $1,500 to print. When overhead, envelopes, and postage are figured in, each copy of the magazine actually costs us $2! And the cover price on newsstands is only $5. To make the same profit percentage we were making in 1971—and believe me, even in 1971 that was no profit—we'd have to charge an $8 cover price for a 64-page issue! And that, of course, for a poetry magazine, is impossible.

Today Iva and I have to visit grandma; and tomorrow, Sunday morning, one week after the Dimension Convention described above, she's off to Summer Camp, a truly interesting place called Thoreau-in-Vermont. Chlöe is also going, as are several other of her friends. (Iva has really been proselytizing for the place quite vigorously over the winter.) She must have recruited them a good half-dozen campers. But, then, it really is an exceptional camp.

Well, *must* wind this up. Once again I have asked Bantam to send you copies of *Flight from Nevèrÿon* and bound galleys of *Stars/Sand*. There is a very small surprise for you on the dedication page of *Flight*. . . . But let us hope, once more, that *this* time they actually *get* it to you.

Read two interesting books in a single day a few weeks back—an unusual occurrence for me: *Assault on Truth,* by Jeffrey Moussaieff-Masson, and *In the Freud Archives,* by Janet Malcolm. Hugger-mugger in Freudian scholarship. Readable, fun, but not profound—though, here and there in them were some truly interesting points.

* * *

Reading all this over, it seems rather down—like someone trying to pull out fine points of sensibility from a narrative that is simply too gross to dramatize them. Oh, well. You win some and you lose some. One of the things that, I suppose, added a lot of not-so-pretty highlights to the Dimension Convention for me, after the fact: When I got home Sunday, I found out from Frank that it was Gay Pride Day. He'd gone to the parade, while I had been messing about at the Sheraton. The new New York Archbishop has been doing a real number on us— saying that Catholic day-care centers will *not* hire homosexuals, no matter *what* the city's anti-discrimination laws say. And Frank, who is not really religious, but from time to time has acknowledged the Church as a possible Good Thing, simply exploded at this one and has Severed All Connections. And this year, the Gay Pride Day March decided to go right past St. Patrick's Cathedral on Fifth Avenue.

And Frank was there, to see.

The Gay Men's Choir, who, though shamefully I've never been to one of their concerts, I've heard are a truly spectacular choral group, stopped across from St. Pat's and sang the Gunoud *Ave Maria*—at which point everybody released *hundreds* of purple and lavender balloons, which swirled up around the cathedral. (An overheard line, from one very working-class woman to her friend, while the two of them watched the parade: "Oh, Mildred, I think something really *pretty* is comin' up next!") Frank said it was impressive and, at that point, he joined the parade himself.

And then they all marched on.

Monday after Sunday, we planned to meet over at the Museum of Natural History to see the "Ancestors" exhibit, in which all the various fossil humans, from "Lucy" through Neanderthals and Cro-Magnon, have been assembled. I was still here at the house, working, when Frank called to tell me that he'd just read in the *Times* of Foucault's death the day before — while Frank had been marching for Gay Pride . . . and I'd been moderating a debate about comic book ads and getting my shot of ego-boost.

No doubt that colored my feelings about the con still further. The news of the death was truly shocking. We still went to the exhibit, later that morning, but it was all pretty cerebral and I really couldn't get into it too much. Sometime later I spoke to Robert Morales on the phone—he's a Puerto Rican journalist, about 26, whom I've known since he was sixteen. He was once a student at Clarion, and now writes occasionally for the *Voice, Heavy Metal,* and the like. And he's really been quite generous to me over the past few years with general time, attention, and friendship. He'd been supposed to go to France at the end of the summer and interview Foucault for *Omni,* of all magazines—for a couple of thousand; and I had been kind of coaching him, lending him material and talking with him about Foucault's work as I understood it—although he really had been doing a lot of good, solid thinking on his own.

He was just a bit down, now that his French trip, an interesting assignment, and a decent bit of money had vanished out from under him, just like that. Robert's 23-year-old sister has breast cancer (she's already had a double mastectomy), and for the last six months he's been virtually her in-house caregiver, while she has kind of bounced in and out of the hospital. She's a pretty lively young woman in her own right, but it's been a terrible year for him—indeed for them both. And the French trip had been a kind of looked-for vacation from what, as we all know, is a grueling task.

Ah, well.

* * *

Well, it's July 1st, pouring rain, and I've just came back from putting Iva on the bus to Summer Camp. Michael, Chlöe's father, drove us down, with Ellen, Chlöe's Filipino baby sitter, and Tugger, Chlöe's dog (who is small, sat in Chlöe's lap, and looked lonesome). The run from the station wagon to the camp buses, waiting beside Bryant Park behind the New York Public Library, was like a dash through Niagara Falls—and the paper bag holding Iva's lunch decomposed in her hand in nine seconds flat, and her tuna-fish sandwich fell out onto a puddle on 43rd Street.

But her Twix Bar, apple, and can of Sprite were saved, and there were going to be sandwiches for the kids on the bus, anyway.

She took it all very well.

Though she's only been away a month (two weeks in London, two weeks in Paris), she really seems to have grown up a lot. (Frank spends a lot of time slapping his forehead and being amazed — at least when she's not there — over the fact that she has definite breasts, even if she's still at size triple a-cup.) Yesterday we went to see Grandma, and then, at Iva's suggestion (!), went to see *Gremlins*. As such things go, I thought it was a good picture. And so did she. We've had a running thing for three or four years, now. I've always told Iva I'm waiting for her to learn to like scary pictures so I can have somebody to go with when I watch grade-c horror movies. And she has firmly insisted that she doesn't want to see *any* picture with *any* bad guys in it at *all*. Needless to say, this has tended to limit her movie fare quite a bit. At the same time, on TV she'll watch vampire pictures without an eye-blink. But she has been unable to watch a movie if, say, it concerns a twelve-year-old boy (or girl) who gets caught for doing Something Bad — both *Little House on the Prairie* and *The Brady Bunch* contain endless moments of such moral horror at which, as recently as six months ago, Iva had to get up and turn the TV off. (The point, of course, is that the fear is basically moral. But blood, guts, and your usual Saturday Morning cartoon violence — even when done realistically and with high production values — didn't phase her a bit.) Well, apparently one of her peers had told her that *Gremlins* was a must-see. And even I was impressed at how well she maneuvered some of the more shocking scenes: the odd squeal, followed by a giggle, but not a single clutch at daddy's arm — unlike the response to *Mary Poppins* which was (I kid you not), four years ago, almost traumatic: Both the dancing chimney sweeps and the chorus of bankers had to be viewed from my lap, her head most of the time in my arm-pit. Though, afterwards, she demanded to see it three more times within the next two days. This morning she was up at five-thirty. I dawdled in bed till six. And we had breakfast together and then found ourselves in a detailed conversation about the film that lasted practically an hour. That kid is sharp!

Did I say? Her report card came in from Fleming while she was in England. Straight A's! (Her lowest marks were two A-minuses, which were neatly balanced by two A-plusses. The rest of her marks were snugly in between.)

This year Frank did the entire camp preparation by himself, including the sewing of name-tags (for the last seven years all sewing in the house has been my job). It was really enough to make my feel quite guilty. But, as I said, it's all done, and she's off. She was only here half a day, a full day, and a morning. Really, it makes me miss her much more than if she hadn't been back at all! But I'm glad we got in a movie, a meal or two, and a talk. But with all this international traveling, there are moments when I feel Iva is my favorite house guest, rather than my daughter!

* * *

A few hours later, I learn that the torrential rains that beleaguered the city starting on the Sunday Iva left for camp were severe enough to close Kennedy Airport for three days. If she'd returned from London two days later, she would have been detoured up through Boston or down through Washington D. C.!

Recent reading, starting before Iva's return: I did a fairly careful going over of Davenport's "On Some Lines of Virgil." It's the short novel that concludes his book of stories, *Eclogues*. The writing is sumptuous, of course. And for the first time, he deals with homosexuality directly. Which is a plus. But for the first time I find the sexist elements strong enough to look askance at. It's at about *Babel-17* level — which means it could be a lot worse. The single young woman, whom I assume is about fifteen, is simply a kind of unbelievable supergirl. Reads Proust. Loves sex. And is so witty and self-assured that, after a while, you kind of suck your teeth and resist the urge to skip, every time she comes on.

The story is a pedophile's dream.

You probably would like most of it.

In a sentence, it's about three boys and a girl (ten to fifteen), living in southern France, who spend their summer reading books far beyond their years and, for the rest of it, masturbating themselves and each other into insensibility — when they are not appeasing eccentric relatives or exploring prehistoric caves.

Needless to say, the girl does not get to explore the cave. (Be warned.) But it's still worth a look. I have very little of the pederast about me, but he makes the boys (ten, fourteen and fifteen) almost unbearably delicious.

Structurally it's intriguing.

Looking at it on the page, your first thought is to wonder if Davenport isn't presenting it as some sort of prose poem. Each of its 125 chapters is five paragraphs long. Each of the paragraphs is between 42 and 52 words, with the vast majority clocking in at about 44, 45, or 46. One would think with such a precise structuring, the piece would be unbearably cold and stilted. To the contrary, however: It's among the most luminous and liquid cascades of narrative I've ever read in English.

In his first story collection, *Tatlin!*, Davenport has a tale called "Robot," another pedophile's daydream, in which a bunch of French boys, around World War I, following their dog across a farmer's field, discover the prehistoric caves, with their incredible paintings, at Lescaux. (They pause, every so often, to compare the size of their penises . . .) It's (peter comparisons aside) a truly marvelous story. And Robot is the name of the scruffy little spaniel who first digs into the cave opening. "On Some Lines of Virgil" is a kind of sequel, I suppose, set 60-odd years later.

It does not develop the same intensity as "Robot." But then, I don't think he was trying to. And it's two or three times as long, anyway, and much more panoramic — at least psychologically.

At any rate, with both stories, I thought of you a lot. Take a look, if you can find them. I could easily see some of Davenport's tales becoming as much of a favorite with you as *You are Not Alone* . . .

Then, from the sun-drenched precision of Davenport, last night I turned to Part One of *Crime and Punishment*. It's a marvelously lively mess. And you really get a sense that, whatever was wrong with him, Dostoevsky was a novelist down to his left little toe-nail.

In the introduction to her translation of M. M. Bakhtin's *Problems of Dostoevsky's Poetics*, Caryl Emerson writes of "the great, baggy, 19th century novels that Bakhtin loved." Well, baggy it certainly is!

But a bag filled with what marvels!

Raskolnikov's eccentric Zimmerman hat, which sets up the never-to-be-purchased workman's cap as part of his disguise, is beautifully, psychologically accurate. The way the drunken peasant shouting at him from the cart in the street sets up the nightmare of the murdered sorrel mare (actually it's the cart and the dray horses—and the drunken peasant, of course—that connects them) is masterful. The way the set piece of Marmeladev's monologue balances the equally impressive set piece of Raskolnikov's mother's letter is sensually gorgeous.

And the incessant inability to leave Aliona Ivanovna's apartment, through Lizaveta's return and the eventual arrival of the other clients, is handled invisibly and superbly, so that you almost don't recognize what's happening.

At the same time, making the overheard scene of the student and the soldier a *flashback* right after the dream is pure sloppiness. It should have been the opening scene of the novel, or, even better, sandwiched between *two* visits to Aliona (which would have allowed us to see him visit her in *two* states: the first time *before* he conceives of murdering her, the second time *after* he conceives of it); and then he kills her on the third visit. This is, of course, just what happens as far as "plot" goes, but visit #1 is elided from the direct narrative thanks to the flashback.

Another sloppiness is the second dream fragment; you can almost see him starting it, then remembering: "Oh, wait; I just *did* that, didn't I . . .?"

Still, the overwhelming psychological rightness of tone to each section is impressive. And you don't have a true intrusion of *purely* "objective" narrative voice until p. 61, i.e., the paragraph that introduces the nightmare, so that it's really startling when it comes, and launches you into what is certainly the most realistic *feeling* scene in Part One: the dream in which drunken Mikolka murders the mare. Surrounding this, the rest of reality—including the double murder of the two sisters—is a kind of frenzied day-dream of a terribly alienated young man.

What could be novelistically more correct for such a tale?

I suspect, however, he could never have written his novels if the Russian temperament were not so volatile. That rather Southern European-style passion, placed there in the Steppes, meant that the drama of day-to-day life was high enough to sustain a flow of novelistic material that comparatively cool New York, say, just does not offer up so easily, save in *some* of its ethnic neighborhoods. Also, I find myself wondering: Just who *are* all these people in 1864 Petersburg? By and large, they're poverty-stricken. They are *not* peasants or descended from peasants. They seem to be, indeed, all petty state officials or the poor relations of same; yet they live like sub-welfare cases, most of them, the drunkards, prostitutes, and madfolk among them. It's just *not* the same social—and more familiar—stratum you find in, say, Dickens' picture of London poverty at all, though at first glance we Westerners tend to read it as such, struck by little exoticisms at every page that suggest *something* is off . . .

Really, it occurs to me: The books that have probably most illuminated Dostoevsky for me are Nadezhda Mandelstam's two memoirs about herself and her husband, *Hope Against Hope* and *Hope Abandoned*. By the end of them, you really have a much better picture of who and how the impoverished urban dwellers in a Russian city are. And suddenly Dostoevsky seems *far* more socially coherent, even though the urban life of Petersburg that Mrs. Mandelstam writes of is 50 to 70 years and a revolution or so after the Petersburg Dostoevsky paints with such rich impastos.

Have also been working through some of the new Derrida essays, e.g., *Signsponge* (on the French poet Francis [author of *Things* and *Soap*, both of which are charming] Ponge) and the new bit on literature and psychoanalysis, *My Chances*, which is the centerpiece in an overpriced volume of the same name, surrounded by commentary from some good people, including Samuel Weber, which is why I shelled out 20 bucks for it. But this seems to be the way Derrida has been getting published/translated of late.

Also saw *Ghostbusters* and, when Iva was here, *Gremlins* . . . But then, I'm beginning to repeat myself. So it *must* be time to close this letter.

Then there was the Joseph Campbell lecture at the Endicott Bookstore, the night of July 2nd (I finish this on the afternoon of an overcast July 4th). A charming old man who writes charming old books — if you can squint at the neo-fascism always lurking under such historicist reductionism. He told us, in passing, that of course *nothing* could be done about the poverty and misery in India. (He'd been there, and he knew.) That's why Buddhism was such a wonderful religion: It made you so accepting of misery. I wonder if he's ever had a chance to listen to a virulent, young, intelligent *anti*-Buddhist explain that that's precisely what's *wrong* with it *as* a religion. . . .

Hope those MSS get to you soon. Just read them—and send any comments you want. But don't worry about corrections. With all my complaining, we finally *have* gotten a decent job done on both of them at this end. Yes, I'm still going to push for them to hire you on whatever comes next. But until they do, I really can't let you do that kind of work for nothing.

I think about you lots, hope you're well, and send you

All my love,

• 23 •

To Robert S. Bravard

June 28th, 1984

[Within days of sending letter 22 to Mog Decarnin, SRD sent largely the same letter to Robert S. Bravard, minus the discussion of Davenport's story. The following are some paragraphs not included in Decarnin's version.]

And your letter of June 25th arrived. With the Joyce clippings. Indeed, I'd already seen the longer one from the *Times*. Though the shorter one was new. And just a bit over four years ago *you'd* commended to me Hugh Kenner's article on *The Computerized 'Ulysses'* in *Harpers*, where this new edition was first talked about in some detail. (My copy of the April, 1980 *Harpers*, which you sent me, I believe, is sticking out of my bookshelf among the eighteen-odd inches of Joyciana there.) Although I note that between Kenner's article and actual publication, the mistakes seem to have fallen from 6,000 to 5,000. It rather reminds me of the three-volume "revised" Proust translation. But that was only $85 in hardcover, as I recall. Not $200.

[. . .]

I loved your description of the animals behaving like . . . well, animals.

I'm glad Christopher is back and doing well.

I'd be delighted if you — or *The Lock Haven Review* — wanted to consider my translations. (I'll enclose clean copies, with final thoughts, in this letter.)

[. . .]

• 24 •

TO JOHN P. MUELLER

July 5th, 1984

Dear John,

Yours of June 24th arrived a few days ago; has been read; and reread. Just got my daughter off to summer camp Sunday morning, July 2nd — in the pouring rain.

Frank and I are both well.

I could complain about money, but nobody likes to hear that — especially your friends. Suffice it to say I've been having much trouble with the IRS; I owe them a lot. And every time I get a little bit ahead, they show up and take it all, while I argue with them: If they'd let me keep enough to live on, I could do the work that would allow me to really make enough to pay them off. But if they keep stripping me to nothing, then I have to scuffle just to stay alive; and if I'm scuffling, then I can't write the books that will make the kind of money that would let me get out from under the debt.

The last year and a few months, since they first showed up, have really been hell.

Ah, well.

One thing I meant to say in my last letter (it just got lost among all those pages I suppose) was how happy I was for you about your father's saying you could work with him again. I think it's a really important for you to have as good a relationship as possible with your family.

Your brother's always going to be a problem.

But if you can work it out so that you can get along with your old man, I think you'll feel better about yourself; and that will probably allow you to *do* a lot better *for* yourself.

Glad you liked *Heavenly Breakfast*. Yeah, I used to be a musician — in fact, up through my first eight books, I really thought of myself as a musician first; writing was just kind of a hobby I did on the side.

Then I took a year off writing and tried to devote all my energies to music — (the year before and including the *Heavenly Breakfast* period) — and discovered, not that I was a better writer than I was a musician, but just that I seemed to be able to get further with the writing than with the music.

So I turned around and decided to commit myself to writing. By that time, I was 26 going on 27. But as you can see, it took me a little while to make up my mind just what I was going to do. Besides, at the same time I was messing around with writing and music, I was just as serious about acting and directing!

But at a certain point, you decide on one thing and more or less stick to it, if for no other reason than, by the time you're 30, you really just don't have as much energy as you did when you were 20 . . . and you can't do as much as you could before!

(And we won't talk about 40 . . .)

In your letter, you wrote some very interesting things about hustling. Let me quote them back to you:

"When I was hustling, Chip, in some ways I would enjoy it, and in other ways I would hate it. Of course if I made money it was good, if I didn't, it was lousy. But I have to also look at it sexually. I don't think I'm gay. I'm pretty sure I'm bisexual. I like getting a blow-job — from anyone. But I worry about when I'm with a guy, what it will do to me psychologically when I'm with a chick. Maybe I worry too much. It's kind of hard to explain. What I'm really trying to say is I don't want to have to hustle anymore. But if I really look back in my mind, maybe the reason I do it is because I want to be with a guy. I'm not being honest with myself. I rationalize it by saying I need money, so that's why I hustle. But I know I could get money working on a day job of some sort where I get paid by the day. I guess what I'm saying is that all this time I've been here I've finally realized the real reason why I hustle. This is a little jumble[d], but write me back and tell me what you think."

Well, first, it isn't all *that* jumbled. But I *will* take your invitation to tease it apart some, and give you my thoughts.

Your basic insight — that you get *something* out of it besides money — is unquestionably right.

You've been doing it, you told me, since you were fifteen. And given the fact that, when I first met you, three years ago this November, you were standing on the corner of 46th Street with a beer bottle in a paper bag, asking guys for $3 — well, I guess it's a fair bet that money couldn't be the *only* reason, since the Fiesta was around the corner, where, as you well know, the bidding starts off these days at $35, at which point we johns try to argue you working men down to $15. (With me, if I can't, I go beat off by myself — that is, when I was in the mood to pay, which, truthfully, I don't do that often).

The question, however, is what do you get out of it?

You write: "I don't think I'm gay."

Well, I agree with you. I don't think you're gay, either.

If you need a label for yourself (and, really, most of us do) I think a pretty good test is what you think about when you jerk off.

I think about men.

So I am pretty sure I *am* gay.

You've said on several occasions that you think about women. So I suspect you're straight.

(If you'd rather think about a man *and* a woman, rather than *just* a man, or *just* a woman, chances are you're bisexual. But you've never said anything about that.)

The complexities that follow — that the men I think about tend to have big hands and bite their nails and are frequently taking a leak, or that the women you think about often come in pairs and are giving each other head — well, those are fine points that you can worry over if you want to; but, if you do choose to worry about them, it probably means you don't have enough *real* problems to occupy yourself with.

As far as worrying about what going with one will do to you psychologically when you go with another, well . . . I wouldn't, if I were you. I was married for thirteen years. The eight of it I lived with my wife (starting when I was nineteen), we went to bed pretty much on the average of twice a week, no matter what, year in, year out. And that *certainly* didn't do anything to hurt my going to bed with men.

I suspect it works the other way around as well.

You've said, several times, that you'd rather eat pussy than fuck it, any day. And I know that Chinese women turn you on particularly.

Well, what you ought to do, then, the next time you're in New York with free time is, instead of hanging out on 46th Street, get your ass down to Chinatown, spend a few days hanging out *there*, and try and make some friends and see what happens.

You could probably find yourself a Chinese woman who likes to eat a little pussy herself—and, who knows, she might turn out to be someone who thinks that you, with your hands (and, after all, you really *are* a pretty nice person; let's *not* forget that), are the hottest thing since sliced bread.

The question isn't why we make do with what we're used to. (The answer there, I guess, is: We make do with it *because* we're used to it.) The question is: Why do we so seldom put out any energy toward really getting what we want?

If that, indeed, is what you *do* want.

Then, again, maybe you'd *rather* watch the ladies lap each other up on a movie screen while some cocksucker nurses on your pecker. (In which case, call me! Lord knows, I've met several others who want *just* that. And I don't think there's anything wrong with that either.) But if you *really* don't want to hustle any more, that means you're going to have to start doing that for free.

You know, you really do (and I think you've already had a hint of this, if you don't already simply *know* it) meet nicer people when you stay away from business transactions in matters of sex, however you like it.

I started hustling when I was about eighteen. On and off I did it till I was almost 25. (Most of it was concentrated into the year when I was 23.) And if you discount the time, about six years ago, some 60-year-old guy blew me in a movie theater, then shoved $5 into my shirt pocket before I really knew what he was doing, and fled, I haven't done it since.

Now that's not counting the times before and after that I survived for a few days—or a few weeks—by being willing to go to bed with a series of guys, who, in the course of it, were willing to give me a meal or a place to sleep in exchange. I've done that both in Europe and here.

But the thing *I* hated about real, set-a-price, do-it-and-take-your-money hustling was that the johns I ran into always seemed such *scared* men; and not only scared; it was as if their fear had reduced them to being only half-people. Very seldom did anybody ever smile; or make a joke. Or, when they did, it was usually at my expense. There was a kind of coldness to it all that, after a while, made me wonder: Why bother?

Faces of these guys come back to me, as I write about this: There was an opera singer, I remember, and an English professor at NYU, and an electrician who had an electronics repair shop on St. Marks Place, and some rather fat (and rude!) character who lived on Park Avenue in a vast apartment full of deco glass, and another who lived in a ratty rented room on 24th Street, and another really low-life theatrical agent who handled a few male nightclub singers (and who gave me my first popper), and some rather Casper Milquetoast-like fellow on West End Avenue who always wanted to pay me by check (!), and some guy I had to take a train up to see in Westchester, and . . .

But you have your own string of faces.

Yes, a *few* of them were very nice.

But *not* most of them.

Myself, I thought of it as a job.

But, finally, I found myself also thinking: If this *was* an ordinary job, and I had to work with people who were as generally cold, unpleasant, and basically out-of-it as these johns are, I'd find another one.

So I did.

Now, that was 1960 to '65. There was no gay liberation in those days; there was no Phil Donahue Show. Maybe the personality of your average john has changed since then for the better. But even today, among the guys I've met who buy regularly at the Fiesta, I still see an awful lot of that coldness and fear.

These guys really leave you — or at least they left me — with the feeling that nobody was really home. You know what I mean?

And the hustlers who can be happy in that kind of situation have to be pretty thick-skinned, if not blatantly insensitive. And being downright (in a word) stupid doesn't hurt, either. Because you really *don't* want to think too much when you're selling like that.

Well, you're *not* stupid, John. And you are a pretty sensitive guy. But, straight, gay, or whatever, you don't have the personality for being a serious hustler any more than I did. And I will be very surprised if you carry it on too much after 25, 26, or 27.

By the same token, I don't think I have the personality to be a serious john. When I got to be 38 or 39 and found myself 50 pounds heavier than I'd been at 30, I thought: "Well, the scene is there; let's check it out. Maybe I can buy myself some fun." So, for maybe three years I did. But, frankly, the same things that were wrong with it on the selling end when I was 20 were still wrong with it on the buying end when I was 40. I haven't paid anyone for sex in about eight months (with my IRS troubles, I couldn't afford it if I wanted to); frankly I don't intend to start again. I'd rather hunt a little harder on the free-cruising grounds. It may not work as frequently as it did when I was 25. But *when* it works, it's *always* better.

What you do get, hustling, I think, is a kind of half-way friendship, from time to time, that isn't as demanding as the real thing.

(We're not talking about "lovers" at all.)

The hustler's always holding things back.

The john's always holding things back.

I suspect that margin makes *some* kinds of communication *feel* a little safer, at least for a while.

I remember once, when I was about 22, going to turn some trick—this 50-year-old guy who lived somewhere in the city with his mother. She was off for the weekend visiting her sister, so he had the house free. I was coming on as dumb as I could—it always seemed to work more easily if you did. But I must have said something that made him wonder about me a moment, because he laughed and said something like: "I don't think you're as dumb as you look." And afterwards, when I was leaving, I thought: "Here I am: I've published four novels; I can play hell out of the guitar; and I'm probably the smartest guy this man has talked to in six months, if not six years. And yet all he sees is a friendly, half-breed nigger with a big dick and cute buns.

"And, right now, that's *all* I want to be.

"Why . . .?"

Well, 20 years later I *still* don't have an answer. And I'd be lying if I told you I did.

But I do know that that *is* what I wanted to be, right then; and it wasn't sex *or* money.

I knew where to get better in both departments.

Now, whatever the reason, I don't think it did me much harm. And I certainly learned one hell of a lot about a lot of strange people.

But I suspect that you'll come up with lots of reasons, from time to time, why you hustle. And you'll discard most of them. And then, a year or so after you've stopped doing it, you'll realize it hasn't bothered you at all—one way or the other.

You wrote: "Maybe I worry too much." I'd say: Think about it all you want. It's an interesting subject. But if you *worry* about it for even five minutes, yes, you're worrying too much. It's not to worry at *all*, believe me.

At any rate, that's the way it worked with me.

But often you really *do* want to be just a moderately friendly piece of meat. And if you can do that, and make $5, $10, or $15 while you're at it, then you do it.

I mean, look at it this way: There're an awful lot of people who want to and can't.

It's an education.

And nobody says you *have* to.

By the way, the weather in the city is miserable. It's gray, hot, and the air is so sticky you can roll it up between your fingers in little black balls and throw it on the floor.

I've got to go out and buy myself something for lunch from the supermarket. It's the kind of day where I'd like to spend the whole thing drinking beer and reading.

But, unfortunately, I have to do some writing too — other than just letters to friends.

I look forward to hearing from you soon.

Best wishes from

• 25 •

To Robert S. Bravard

July 5th, 1984

Dear Bob,

All morning the day has been gray, muggy, and hot. At about four, the sun broke through: Now it's sunny, muggy, and hot. I'm cooking a late lunch/early supper, and getting ready to scoot off to yet another *Little Magazine* meeting.

Have been reading more Derrida, *Crime and Punishment*, Guy Davenport,

Bakhtin on Dostoevsky, and, of course, *My Life:* Indeed, I've peppered the margins of the first hundred pages with notes toward a kind of Davenportesque short story about Wagner as a child, centering on a group of acrobats seen in one city, and then a visit to his uncle Adolf a few months later in another, where the old man, in his cluttered study, is wearing the same felt hat that the clown in the city square wore, months before.

(Wagner was an excitable child who woke up nightly screaming from bad dreams all through his childhood, till his seven brothers and sister refused to sleep near him.)

Probably the most famous incident from Goethe's *Dichtung and Warheit* is the tale of the puppet theater given him by his grandmother. (Wagner's Uncle Adolph had been praised by Schiller and owned a goblet sent to him as a present by Goethe.) How many readers never get beyond it? Well, Wagner also has an incident with a puppet theater, built by his stepfather, Guyer — which I'm sure is perfectly true (my father once built me a puppet theater, and added some store-bought puppets to it as a Christmas present, when I was about eight; one, I'll always remember, was called Kilroy the Cop; he had a record that went along with him, which you played while you made him bob up, down, and about; and I have been threatening to build Iva such a theater for years), but I am also equally sure that Wagner wrote the incident with tongue in cheek:

Wagner's puppet theater — like mine [*Ahem* . . .!] — never quite worked the way it was supposed to and finally died in a tangle of string and wood, while his older sister teased him for years about the inanity of the lines he'd contrived for his never-completed puppet pageant. I'm convinced the tale is presented as just the gentlest jibe in the direction of Goethe, who, according to his own account, presented one marvelous fantasy play to his family after the other (at age seven or so) with his puppets. At any rate, I'd like to get all this into the story.

But should work on *Splendor and Misery* instead.

Enclosed is the most recent leg of the Delany/Mueller correspondence.

Spoke with Lou A. on the phone today: He was just back from Westercon. There's a cover for *Stars/Sand,* and I'll see it when I pop in with some stuff for him on Monday.

• 26 •

To Robert S. Bravard

July 18th, 1984

Dear Bob,

When this reaches you, you'll probably just be getting back from vacation — I hope you had a wonderful, relaxing, fun, and therapeutic time!

I've been working hard on *Splendor & Misery* and watching the Democratic Convention. (Like everyone else, I was impressed with Cuomo. A bit ho-hum on the others.) "Did Joanna say anything about being photographed for a big spread on Women in SF in *Life*?" you asked, last letter. Yes, indeed she did. It was actually the subject of a rather funny and particularly Joannaesque anecdote: Basically, it had to do with all her various aches and pains (endless as those of someone with terminal arthritis)—all very real, but she can laugh about them at times (which is probably the only relief she gets)—and the attendant difficulty in getting to and from the various photographic sessions in the Seattle Rose Garden, in the rain, where her picture was taken. Apparently that day there were only about ten minutes (divided into two minutes here, three minutes there . . .) when it wasn't pouring cats and dogs—not that unusual in Seattle for that time of year. The photographer, indeed, caught her in a moment of foggy sunlight. But it took them two long sessions to get the picture—both of which were at about six in the morning. So when the photographer called for a third session, Joanna groaned and said: "I'm terribly sorry, but I just *can't* go through another one!"

So they used what they had.

And it *was* rather nice, wasn't it?

What? Never eaten a *chorizo*, you write? Well, if the mumbled truth be known, I don't think *any*body save the most die-hard lover of things Hispanic actually eats *chorizos* by themselves—although I note on the package in which mine came that the instructions suggests pan-frying them with eggs! To me, that sounds ghastly! (All that orange lard!—*manteca*, in Spanish) But they do make marvelous flavoring when their skins are split and the sausage meat is cooked till it is dispersed throughout the . . . well, black beans, red beans, stews, even Spanish style spaghetti sauce. But don't, in an experimental fervor, go out, buy some, cook them, and *eat* them by themselves. (Alone, they taste like *very* greasy wads of salted and peppered newspaper.) If you do, you may never eat a *chorizo* again!

The "Marvel Glut," you ask about? That, indeed, was a secondary topic on the list of possibles in the Lee/Ellison debate I moderated—a topic which, in point of fact, we never got 'round to. A good number of the people I talked to in the course of doing my homework seemed to feel, however, that the "Glut"—or at least the supposed bad effects of the Glut on the comic stores and independent companies —is something of an invention of the occasionally over-zealous *Comics Journal*. And my informants included a couple of comic store people as well as people who worked for Marvel and the Independents also. And the simple fact is: Stan has not had anything to do with Marvel Comics directly for almost half a dozen years. He has no real input into business policy anymore—nor does he have time to. Harlan had some feelings about it all (naturally); but, as I said, we're talking "show business," not "Great Truths." And Stan (who doesn't read the *Journal*) wasn't even sure what the "Glut" was. And the idea wasn't to make anyone look like a fool. If I'd been moderating a debate between, say, Jim Shooter[1] and Gary Groth,[2] that would have probably been the first thing I'd have asked. But I wasn't.

John Brunner was in town a few days back, so I had him and Tom Disch for brunch; broiled scrod, with paprika and butter, homemade spoonbread (with yellow cornmeal, instead of white), and a hefty avocado salad with hydroponically grown tomatoes—as I told them: "We've all been writing about them for 20 years; I couldn't resist buying some when I saw them down at Fairway. Though you wouldn't believe what they cost." And plenty of white wine; and good conversation, with Frank (who'd been off apartment-sitting for Lavada June) joining us

[1] Jim Shooter at the time was editor-in-chief of Marvel Comics.
[2] Gary Groth is the publisher and former editor of the *Comics Journal*.

later that afternoon.

Then up to my mother's for Cornish game-hen and tales of her recent teas at the Hemsley Palace with Ruth (Mrs. Ralph) Bunche.[3]

And a day or so back, Judy Ratner, my old friend and downstairs neighbor, took me for a sea-food lunch at Broadway Bay. Lobster for Judy — a sea-food-based chef's salad for me. Quite nice!

The only "news," though, is another "funny" cover story for you:

Last week, Thursday or Friday (July 5th or 6th), Lou Aronica called me up to say he had some cover art for *Stars/Sand.* Why didn't I drop in to see it on Monday?

"How do you like it?" I asked. There'd been much talk about a new advertising artist, named Royo, whose first cover for Bantam this would be. And Lou had told me, some months before, that he had been very excited by the man's portfolio.

"Well," said Lou. "I have some problems with the central figure. So you come in and see what you think."

You understand, I do *not* have "cover-control" on this particular book. But from our various conversations, Lou has decided that I have some good ideas, as well as some critical understanding *anent* the subject, and he's been inviting my input.

So Monday, at about ten-thirty, I soared up 25 flights in the 666 Fifth Avenue elevator, and stepped out into the Bantam offices. Lou met me in the lobby and walked me back to his office, there among the white partitions, gray rugs, and glass windows. "I don't have the color proof here, yet," he apologized as we turned into his door. "I've only got a black and white photostat. I thought the color proof was going to be in by now; that's why I asked you here on Friday. But it isn't . . . And you can't tell very much from what I've got. But take a look anyway." And he pulled out an eighteen inch by nine inch black and white pho-tostat of a starscape, with a couple of planets hanging in it, toward the front of which floated a small, agonized figure in a ribbon of light. The figure—the shirt-less man wore futuristic fatigue-style pants, one work glove, and was (presum-ably) Rat Korga—was amateurishly drawn, but it had the virtue of being minus-cule against the starscape.

In black and white, it didn't look *too* awful though: "Well, it's not that bad," I said.

"I still don't like the figure."

"You could really paint it out entirely, and the painting would probably be just as good, if not better," I said.

"That was my thought," Lou said. "We're actually going to try that."

"The type will make all the difference," I said. "If you paint out the figure, come up with some good type, and drop it right in the middle, where the figure is now, with the planets above and below, it could work. Though at this point, the figure doesn't look *that* awful."

"Agreed," said Lou, reaching into a carton under his desk. "Oh, a couple of other things. Bound galleys came in for *Stars.* You want a few?"

"Sure," I said. "In fact, why don't you give me half a dozen? Henry will want

---

[3] Ralph Bunche (1904–1971), in 1950, was the first African-American to win the Nobel Peace Prize—for negotiating an Israeli-Arab peace in 1949. Ruth Bunche (his wife), Gladys Smiley, and Margaret Delany were close friends who saw each other weekly for a number of years.

some to send out for foreign sales."

So I took a half-dozen of the pale blue semi-books (that look like European editions in their plain paper covers) and arranged them against my notebook.

"Oh, yes. One more thing," Lou said. "We all want Rowena to do the cover for *Flight from Nevèrÿon*. But the art department called her agent, who told us she was absolutely swamped with work and wouldn't be able to get to it—at least not in time for us to do the book in February. So, we're wondering about holding the book back a few months, till she can do it. Otherwise, we'll have to change artists."

"Well, you really don't want to change cover artists in the middle of a trilogy," I said. "Do you?"

"Absolutely not. Actually," Lou went on, "I was wondering; you know her, don't you?"

"Yes," I said. "We get along pretty well."

"Perhaps if you spoke to her directly—not through her agent—and asked her, she might be able to juggle things; or do something about . . . or, well, you know. That way we might have a chance to keep the book on schedule . . ."

"Well, I can certainly call her and ask," I said.

About an hour after I left the office, I called Lou back to say that, after 40 minutes on the subway, I really had come to the conclusion that the central figure on the *Stars/Sand* cover just wasn't acceptable. Before, I'd been looking at it, I told him, in "rack-sized" terms. But when I tried to consider it specifically in hard-cover terms, it fell apart completely. "Good," Lou said. "We feel the same way." And later that night I placed the first of about six phone calls to Rowena—and got her answering machine, where I left a message. Indeed, I got her answering machine and left messages all week long.

Which brings us to yesterday morning—

—when, at about ten-thirty, Lou called me to say: "We got the color proof in, Chip. I just don't like it. So we're not going to use it at all."

"Would it be okay to drop in," I asked, "and take a look at what you're not using?"

"Sure," he said. "Come in around three this afternoon."

As soon as I put the phone down with Lou, I thought: Why not give Rowena one more call, just in case I catch her? And called; and instead of the phone machine's familiar tape-hiss, Rowena's eternally teenage voice answered: "Hello—Rowena Morrell . . ."

Seems that just about an hour before, she'd walked in from a two-week vacation with her boyfriend in the country, and had only minutes ago finished going over her phone messages. She'd been going to call me later that day.

"I've got a favor to ask you," I told her, "that you very possibly won't be able to say 'yes' to. So I'm ready for a 'no.' But I thought I'd try, anyway. You know how much we all loved the two covers you did for the first two volumes of the *Nevèrÿon* books. Well, I've just finished the third volume. Bantam is very anxious for you to do the third cover—but your agent says you're swamped. I was just wondering if there was any way you might juggle things to fit us in over the next month or so."

Rowena laughed. "That's very funny," she said. "I'd be delighted to do the third cover. I'm not swamped at all. And I don't *have* an agent. Nobody from

Bantam has talked to me about it. I've been away for two weeks, as I said; but there isn't any message from Bantam on my machine here."

"How interesting," I said. "I will convey this to Lou. I'm seeing him this afternoon. Is there any time I can tell them to have somebody call you?"

"Well," she said. "I'll be out later today. But I'll be in between ten and eleven tomorrow morning."

And so at 3:10 I came into the Bantam office. Lou met me in the lobby; walked me back to his office . . .

The color proof of the *Stars/Sand* cover—which Lou had wrapped around a copy of Harry Harrison's *West of Eden*—is probably the worst cover on a science fiction book I've *ever* seen in my life! First of all, they'd blown up the unacceptable central figure till it dominated the entire front, leaving out most of the starfield entirely. What I hadn't been able to see in the black and white stat at all were the colors: they were red, white, blue, pink, yellow, orange, and purple . . .

It looked like an oil cloth for the sweet-sixteen picnic table of some high-school freshman summer weenie-roast, thrown by the daughter of a chamber of commerce member of Little West Peoria. ("Somethin' real cheery an' colorful, that the kids'll like. Know what I mean?") As Lou said: "Well, it's just not 'upscale' enough . . ." which is jargon for saying that it's cheap, gaudy, and just does not look like a novel someone paid $150,000 for. Indeed, it looks rather like the chintziest in a line of "SF for fourteen-year-old boys" as it might have been packaged in 1957.

I began to list what was wrong (the yellow type over the flare of light, on the bottom of what was left of a back-lit planet, was unreadable—as yellow on white often is; and . . . and . . . and . . .), in the midst of which Lou stopped me: "We've already decided we're throwing it out and starting again, Chip. I've already told them, they've got to go *way* upscale on this."

Just at that point, Ian Ballantine, who'd been standing outside, leaned in the door, shook his head over the cover, and laughed. "Well, Chip," he said. "The best thing, of course, would be if you just rewrote the book in the style of L. Ron Hubbard. You know, that would really be easier than changing the cover."

"It's true," I said. "I could just take out the disks, put them in my word processor, and every place there were no adjectives at all, I could stick in three."

Ian laughed and wondered off.

Really, the cover looked as if an amateur fifteen-year-old aspiring comic artist had tried to do a spin-off of the (paperback) cover for *Battlefield Earth*—and had failed disastrously.

But quietly I felt glad that this book had *not* been done on disk; it was all too easy to see somebody taking my and Ian's joke seriously!

"Oh, by the way," I said to Lou. "I spoke to Rowena this morning on the phone, just after you called. She's been away for the past two weeks on vacation. She says she'd be happy to do the new Nevèrÿon cover. I told her what you told me—that her agent told your art department that she was swamped. She said that was odd, because she didn't have an agent. And nobody from Bantam has spoken to her—at least not yet. She's got some time. She said she'll be home tomorrow morning between ten and eleven. Why don't you have somebody call her between those hours—especially if, as you say, you're pressed for time—so she can get started. Would you like her number, just in case someone in your art department was calling the wrong one . . .?"

"Would I ever," Lou said, making a note of her number and the hours.

He let me take home a copy of the rejected cover to show Frank; and also gave me the page-proofs for *Stars/Sand* that had just come in that morning.

As Lou walked me out to the lobby, I said: "You know, I hope this Rowena business turns out to be just a funny story, Lou. Maybe the art department just couldn't get her because she wasn't home. Then, when they were passing the message on, someone just assumed she had an agent, and it crept into the story by the time it got to you."

"I hope so too," he said. Then he gave me a really sour look as we went passed the water cooler. "But the truth is, Chip, it isn't very funny at all."

That was all yesterday — the rest of which I spent with the *Stars/Sand* page-proofs. They're pretty good, but they *still* haven't got the double-tongue stuff right, though Flyn and I marked it together in his office and I didn't think there was any way it could go wrong, now.

Which merely goes to show you.

And this morning, at five after eleven, I called Rowena again: No, no one from Bantam had, as yet, called her. Called Lou at Bantam — he was in a meeting. So I got David Stern, his assistant, to slip him a note:

"Five past eleven. No one has called Rowena yet.
—Chip."

Yes, Lou told him, someone (in the art department, named Laura) had been delegated to do it.

So we shall see.

Rowena, bless her, has a sense of humor about it all. And she's not hurting for work. (She told me, in fact, that this is the second time she's heard about this mythical "agent" of hers, saying she was too busy to work. The last time it involved the cover for a romance someone wanted her to do at Pocket Books.) But if they don't get to her in the next 48 hours, she *will* have another job and *won't* be able to do it for them in time.

Isn't it a strange world we live in . . .?

Well, last night I cooked black beans (and *chorizos*) *again*. They made a very good lunch this afternoon!

Once again, hope you and Cynthia had a wonderful vacation. Best to you both. Good wishes to the boys, cats, raccoons . . .

All my love to you and to all around you,

• 27 •

To Robert S. Bravard

July 27th, 1984

Dear Bob,

Tomorrow Frank and I are driving up to Vermont to see Iva on her camp visiting day. We're taking my mother this year. I wish I could say I'm looking forward to it, but I'm just exhausted. In fact I'm too exhausted to figure how to convey with any incision just how exhausted I am. Still, I wanted to get some stuff out of the way. Basically I'm sending you a bunch of letters; they form a kind of addendum to my last letter to you (July 18th); reading over them will at least keep you abreast of what's been going on in the complex plot of my life.

I won't repeat anything here you'll find there.

Several times now, John Mueller has asked me to supply him with some pornography. So I have tried to oblige my unlucky friend. Knowing your interest in same, I'm including a copy for you.

Although I think pornography certainly *can* be art (and I even feel that I have written some that is), I also feel that, in this case, whatever "A John's Story . . ." is, it's just not real writing. It came out over a four-hour session, with a break for lunch, followed by a three-hour session — both in a single day. I tidied up some of the more unspeakable sentences before I sent it off to him two days later — the ones I couldn't bear to live in the same universe with. But that really doesn't improve the piece's basic vacuousness.

The tale was tailored to John's sexual fantasies as I've been able to understand them over three years, in which we've had *maybe* a baker's dozen sexual encounters. Basically, lesbians turn him on. His fantasies are almost completely oral. Actual penetration with women is "problematic" for him. Though he's talked about it with me a *lot*, I'm still unclear at this point whether he's actually been able to do it yet or not. The male cum shots in porn movies make him feel queasy — or, sometimes, if he's not expecting one, can even make him lose his hard-on. (Another reason why I don't think he is in the least gay, whatever sexual performance problems he might have with women.) His favorite way to masturbate is to use a clean T-shirt and, on finishing, immediately throw it away, so that he doesn't even have to see his own ejaculate. Oriental women are his favorite. Black women he finds a sexual turn-off. Yet a surprising amount of his johns are black men — although *he* doesn't think that means anything in particular.

There was an interesting psychological side to the writing. While I was actually putting it down, I realized that I felt exactly the same way I used to feel when I would write a story at sixteen or seventeen — you know, pouring it all out in a single sitting, without regard for anything save the shape of the silence the next sentence would fill. Oddly, though I associate that time with writing far faster than I do today, at the same time I was far *less* engaged with the writing than today, when I'm really working at full capacity.

Over the last couple of years, I believe I've pretty much sent you copies of just about every letter I've written to John, during what is now his two stretches in jail. (The first was up in Monticello, New York, this second down in Miami, Florida.) I've never shown you his to me, because he certainly hasn't given me permission to.

But his letters have not — most of them — been terribly interesting for anyone who didn't know him personally, anyway. They tend to be abstract, complaining, and repetitious. Though he writes and writes copiously, he doesn't usually write in specifics as to people, the situations around him, or "through the senses" (as they say in the creative writing classes). The exception has been his last three letters.

The first two of these included sudden rather surprisingly specific sections, as he ruminated on his life. And the third seems to be, almost from beginning to end, informative about specifics in a way that — while I already knew lots of it from

just talking with him over the years in personal conversations when I could ask
—has been unusual for him up till now.

I'm going to transcribe for you his last letter. I don't know if it's an anomaly or
if it means he really is growing into a new phase, where he can think more specifically about the elements in his life.

I think I've told you, though: During this stretch in jail, he's read both *Dhalgren*
and *Heavenly Breakfast,* cover to cover, and has had some intelligent comments to
make about them.

John is currently within weeks of his 24th birthday. He comes from a German
working-class family. His father is a carpenter. John himself a big, friendly, basically good-natured guy—but he usually has to drink to stay relaxed. (When I first
met him in November of '81 ('80?), when he woke up in the morning he usually
needed a beer to get out of bed.) When he doesn't drink, he becomes edgy and
nervous. He's been in and out of trouble since his teens. This is basically his
answer to the letter where I wrote him about my own hustling experiences. My
notes appear in square brackets. The parentheses are all his. The punctuation and
spelling are John's.

* * *

July 9th, 1984
Dear Chip,

Just got your letter this evening. Thank you for writing so quick. I hope writing that letter didn't screw up your schedule too much. I always enjoy getting a
letter from you. Please write whenever you have a chance.

Well, your letter gave me some food for thought. I'll try and make myself clear
on some of the things I tried to get across to you in my previous letter.

I'll try and start this way. When I first started hustling, it was like this. I was at
Under-21 when I first started out. [Under-21 is a shelter for runaway youths in New
York City; it takes in destitute teenagers and is on Eighth Avenue between 43rd and
44th. It has been there for more than ten years now and is run by a priest.] One of
the guys (kids) told me of a way to make money. That was to hang out either at the
Bus Station or up on 8th Avenue and wait till some guy approaches you to talk or
ask you for a drink or something. He told me it most likely would be a fag. He said
go along with the guy and when he asked if you wanted to do something go with
him. Then when you go to wherever you were going, to rip him off.

I'm sure I told you this before. Anyway that's how I started out. Then I got
involved with it for real. That's why I never went into the Fiesta or Haymarket. I
was always afraid I would run into someone I ripped off. It didn't make no sense
to hang around right outside, but I didn't think they would do anything in the
open. Being closed up in a dark, gay bar and meeting one of these guys I ripped
off, who might happen to have some friends, kind of scared me. So that's the reason I hung out on 46th Street.

I hustled because I needed the money. I was afraid I would hurt someone if
I kept on ripping off. So one day I really went along with the guy. All he wanted
to do was suck me off and feel my muscles. It was easy. $10 for a hard-on eight
years ago was like $20-30 now. So I did that for a while. Then I went home to
stay with my folks again. Got myself a girlfriend. Then the problems started. The

first time I tried to screw her I couldn't get a hard-on. She tried and tried. I just couldn't. I told her not to worry, it wasn't her fault. It was all the beer I drank. So O.K. Then it happened a second time and a third time and a fourth time. I couldn't keep on blaming it on the beer. To this day I don't know if it was because of my hustling. I think it, but I just don't know. So that's why I worry about it psychologically.

The reason I hustled was because of the money. I really don't like guys. When I jerk off I think about chicks. But I like a blow job. It feels better than my callused palm. I'm not a Casanova-type guy. I'm nervous around chicks. If I could get laid every night, I'd never even think about hustling. But because of my nervousness, I had a problem about sex. So I'd go out and get paid for something I liked. It was also a way to con myself. I'd say to myself, well I'm only into sex with guys because I had to hustle to get money. But like I said I could have done anything else. All it was was a mind game.

Now that I've had time to really think about it, I can see all the flaws of my logic. If I really want to be honest with myself I hustled because it was easy money. That's all. There were very few guys I enjoyed being with. You are one of the few guys I really like. I guess you can say I like a cocksucker on my dick when I'm seeing a movie. And like you say, I'm going to have to do it for free.

Let me tell about my exploits since I came down here last July up till November, when I got busted.

I hustled a little here and there. When I needed a few bucks I did it. It's different down here. There's an avenue named Biscayne Boulevard, and the guys would cruise up and down, pick someone up and barter about the price. I do a lot better down here money-wise. I usually asked between $15 and $30. I don't know if I told you this before, but guys nowadays don't want me to just lie there while I get sucked off. They want me to participate. I just can't. Most of the time I can't even get a hard-on unless they have a magazine or something. [For sexual stimulation, John usually requires a straight porn magazine, preferably with pictures of lesbian activity, or a pornographic film.] That's why I like being with you.

Anyway, I was just getting done with work at a labor pool (a day-labor place that pays at the end of the day). I made $20. You know how I like to drink, so that wouldn't last me too long. I was walking out of a deli with a hero and six pack. I sat outside and ate and drank. This guy walks by a few times. I'm not naive. I know he's gay and think I can pick up a few bucks. So I start a conversation, etc. He says he was waiting for someone. The guy didn't show up. He asks me if I'd like another six. The deli closed so I said yes. I go off with him. He buys it and invites me for something to eat at his place. He sees I just ate a hero, thinks that maybe I'd like a real meal. So I said sure. We go to his place. On the way nothin' was said about money. He asks me if I'd like to take a shower. I do. He makes a nice steak dinner with baked potato. We eat. Then he asks if I'd like to see an X-rated flick. I say sure. Still no money conversation. He undresses, I undress. We watched it. I came three times watching it while he sucked me off. Then I went to sleep. He took me to the labor pool the next morning. I didn't ask and he didn't give me any money. I seen him three more times after that and only asked for five bucks once because I didn't get out to work.

So what I'm trying to say is I enjoyed that. I wasn't hustling, but I enjoyed what we did. He had a VCR and plenty of movies which you know I like. He didn't put any demands on me to suck him, play with him. Only what I wanted to do. I like it that way. So if I come back to N.Y. I hope you'll want to see me.

Give me your thoughts about all this. Did I explain it any better?

Like you said in your letter, the guys do seem afraid. I was always wondering if they were afraid of me or what they were doing. And faces do come back to me every once in a while. Some good, some bad.

I'm not sorry that I ever hustled. I'm kind of glad I started. I never would have met you if I didn't. Most of the "johns" were nice guys. Then some weren't. I was just a piece of meat for them to use. Very impersonal. Most of them would never talk too much. Others thak [ask?] what do you like, how big are you, etc. So I know what you were saying.

Well enough of all that. I'm glad things are going pretty good with you. I'm sorry about your problems with the IRS. I hope you clear them up soon so you can go back to living a normal everyday life again. Keep writing and do your best.

I guess I'll stop now, I wish you well in all. Take care and stay healthy.

Your friend
John

P.S.—I'm sorry about writing on the back of this paper. I don't like to, but this is all the paper I have. I have no money in my account. [This refers to the prison accounts where inmates are allowed to keep money for cigarettes, stationery, and toilet articles. Two months ago John was transferred from a jail where he'd been allowed to work, making $10 a week, which could go for cigarettes and so forth. The jail he's in now apparently does not have such a program.] I'm hunting in ashtrays for butts to unroll so I can smoke a cigarette. It's pretty bad. Where I used to be they would give you welfare commissary [Issues of cigarettes and soap.], here they don't give you anything. If you can see your way clear to sending a couple of dollars down, it would really help me out a lot. If not, just write me back. Your letters are a real pleasure. Oh, yeah, you still haven't said anything about 42nd Street. Is it still there and still the same? I'll be coming back soon, I have 67 days left. September 16 come quickly please! Take it easy.

John

* * *

Well, now that you've had some of it from John's side, I'll ask you (using John's words) to "give me your thoughts about all this"—at least if you have the time and/or inclination.

To the bathroom for a bath, then—after a few more pages of *Winter's Tale*[1]—it will be bed; and up to Vermont tomorrow, leaving before dawn. (We pick up Mom at five-thirty in the lobby of her apartment building on LaSalle Street.) Today has been spent getting all of Iva's visiting day requests: a new flashlight (the one she took arrived broken), stationery (hers got wet and all the envelopes stuck together), and her knapsack (that inadvertently got left out of the duffel bag at the last minute), and a jack-knife, and a deck of cards . . . and . . . and . . .

[1] *Winter's Tale*, by Mark Helprin (New York: Harcourt Brace Jovanovich, 1983).

But I actually think we've got it all.
Again, I hope you and Cynthia had a wonderful vacation.
Give her my best.

My love to you and all around you,

• 28 •

To John P. Mueller

July 23rd, 1984

Dear John,

Your letter of July 9th just reached me, and here it is July 23rd. Indeed, I'd meant to write you before now, anyway. (I'd thought of dropping you at least a letter a week; but I haven't been able to keep that up even with my daughter in summer camp.) But as soon as I finished my last letter, I plunged into a period of much work and turmoil—indeed, it's still going on.

I was up at five-forty-five this morning, at work by six, to keep at it till ten (correcting page-proofs on my Christmas novel), then into my publisher's office, where I worked till almost four-thirty. I thought I was going to finish them in one of the empty offices there (which was the point of my coming in), but all that happened was that the hardcover editor dumped another six-page list of corrections on me that had to be correlated with one set of galleys and then transferred to the page-proofs, which took an extra two-and-a-half hours, so that by the end I had to take it home, where I'll have to work on it tomorrow. I should be working on it now, instead of writing you, but at this point I'm actually kind of punchy. (Little letters flicker in front of my eyes every time I blink.) That's why I took a break, when I realized I was missing mistakes in the text.

That's why you're getting a letter.

I'm afraid this is all still left-over energies from a pretty exhausting day. It's not much. But it's well meant.

I very much liked your last couple of letters. When you want to write about something directly and specifically, you make it very clear. I know you were at Queens (?) College for a year. I don't know how it was for you, but have you thought of continuing your education? Although you really do learn things at college, more than anything else going to college changes the kinds of people you're comfortable hanging out with. That doesn't mean you become uncomfortable hanging out with the kinds of people you're comfortable with today. But it means that, over a period of four years, you learn to be comfortable in lots of other social groups as well.

Recidivism—going back to jail—is nine-tenths a social matter. If you come out and go back to hanging around the same kinds of people (exclusively) you were hanging out with before, if only by following the path of least resistance you'll end up in the same sorts of situations, with the same sorts of pressures and the same sorts of licenses (lack of pressures); and when that happens, believe me: You'll end up back in the clink.

I've had an awful lot of friends over the years who've spent much of their lives in jail. I've been very close to some of them. Some I've just known in passing. (Some have managed to keep themselves out of trouble. And a couple of them are

167

still there—after many, many years.) But it's always seemed to me that the hardest thing for most of you guys to see is that:

You didn't put yourselves there.

The situations you were in put you there.

And if, when you get out, you go back to the same situations (or same kinds of situation) you were in before, sure as God made little green apples, *they'll* put you back in the clink.

So, in a funny way, when you get out, it's kind of a waste of effort to put your energy directly into "staying out of jail." Your energy has to go into putting yourself in different kinds of situations from the ones you were in before: But if you get yourself in a good situation, staying out of jail will more or less take care of itself.

This is a hard thing to hear, much less fully understand, when everyone around you is saying you've got to take responsibility for yourself. The hard thing to understand is that you *can't* change yourself directly. All you can do is work to make sure you're in another situation, which will *make* you act differently—and *that's* what you have to take responsibility for.

Well, grandpa will stop preaching how. I'm sure you get enough of that where you are.

You asked me how was 42nd Street? In fact, you've asked about it three times in the last three letters. So let me see what I can tell you . . .

• 29 •

A JOHN'S STORY

Lately I haven't spent that much time down on that strange fold in the city that seems to collect so many crumbs and so much lint: 42nd Street itself? Well, there's pretty much the same collection of Puerto Rican loose-joint dealers and pill hawkers, in their tank tops or with their shirts off for the July afternoon, with their homemade tattoos and their endless deals and arguments, laughing in little bunches, now one running out after this score or that one, or half a dozen of them standing around, squinting in the sun, while the white or black policemen amble by, with pretty much the same dazed look as the dealers. Now and then, in jeans and a too-tight top, or in some theatrically short skirt high over heavy, grayish thighs, one of the white or Puerto Rican prostitutes strolls through with a friend or stops to laugh or argue with this or that dealer.

Like a streaming veil, across it all rush the hot, sweating, ordinary people, the guys in shorts, the guys in gym suits, the office women in loose, dark dresses and the waitresses in tight, light ones, the black couples on their way to the movies, the five eleven-year-old Puerto Rican boys feeling grown-up and expansive because they're disobeying parental orders ("Don't you go down to that place, today! Hear me?"), the younger cousins from some Hispanic family with a kiddie stroller and a blue canvas bag for the baby bottle, the fried chicken, and the pasteles, him in a white T-shirt and gray-brimmed hat, her in a red striped top and orange pants, them and the four kids going to *Conan the Destroyer* at Brandt's Lyric, or the three fourteen-year-old white girls, coming out of the subway by the newsstand, vigorously chewing their gum and wandering through it all, wide-eyed, in from Brook-lyn, on their way to one of the (slightly) better movie-houses up on Broadway.

Around the corner, the Puerto Ricans still give way to the black grifters. About half the time, the middle-aged black shoe-shine guy is there by the phone booths, in his baseball cap and glasses, with his portable stand, still with his gaffes and goofs on all the passing women, white, brown, yellow, and black: "Oh, darling, you are *so* beautiful I don't think I can *stand* it!" Immediately, he tips his cap to her boyfriend, who's looked back, surprised: "Take care of that lady, sir. She's a truly good woman . . . ! Want a shine?" The Beer & Burger on the corner right now is in the process of being changed into a fried-chicken joint; its glass windows are covered with plywood; the construction involves some digging in the sidewalk on the Eighth Avenue side; for the last two months, the plywood partition — on that busiest corner of the city — has taken up half the sidewalk, so that the pedestrians must veer out, around the wire trash baskets, over the clotted gutter, breaking at the phone booths, some squeezing in front, some striding behind and into the street, before swinging back onto the sidewalk to continue up by the gay burlesque house ("Hot! Gay! Kinky! Bizarre!"), the peep-show, the green front of the Irish hot-plate bar and toward the blue awning of the Barking Fish, the Greek pizza and souvlaki joints, and the corner liquor store and tobacco shops with their glassed-in inner walls, the little overpriced delis.

At 46th, beyond the porno movies, out in front of the blue wall and wrap-around glass window of McHales [I still think of it as Your Spot], it's a lot calmer than it used to be. Further up the Avenue, the Haymarket has been closed for getting on a year now, if not two; that's what used to bring in the serious hustlers, with the Fiesta, on 46th, and O'Neal's, on 48th, taking up the overflow spilling in either direction. But since then, O'Neal's has become the bar for the hard-core working men — myself, I never did like the atmosphere; and if, in the last year, I've walked in and out of there three times, just to see what's going on, I'm surprised. And the Fiesta, which used to be able to offer at least three or four 20-year-old junkies for the johns to choose from on a good day, doesn't even attract that much trade any more. The men who want a couple of beers' worth of relief from the high pressure of O'Neal's just come to sit and relax, with or without a trick. I've only had half a dozen beers there in twice that many months.

Still, it's the strip in the city where, for years, it's always seemed to be happening — and yet, if we're honest, it never happens *enough* at any particular hour, day, or season . . .

I'd gone into that Eighth Avenue porn theater, the Cameo. In the lobby, in his blue uniform, cap and a brown sweater, the bored security guard sat on his stool, his billyclub over his lap, and didn't look up, even when I went over beside him to look at the poster in the glass case above his shoulder: Seka and Mai-Lyn were sharing some new Oriental sex-opera. Coiling over the four-color poster, a scaly dragon spread huge wings from one side of the glass case to the other, flicking a forked tongue above the two stylized bare-breasted skin stars.

"Hello, honey . . . want a blow job?"

The security man still didn't look up. I did, though: Wearing a gray, sequined blouse with the shoulder torn, and torn-off jeans, a very tall, very black queen—

at least a head-and-a-half taller than I am — nodded at me from the door to the orchestra.

"No," I said.

He flashed me a wicked look. "Don't know what you're missing, honey." His lips were maroon. His eyes were touched with gold glitter about the lids. "I give a truly beautiful blow job. Five dollars. Complete with kleenex, wipe-up service, and a cigarette afterwards — if you smoke menthol . . .?" He held up a pack of something I sure wouldn't smoke.

Whenever one of these characters comes on to me, I'm always torn between saying, "Take a walk," and laughing.

He said: "You ain't gonna do to much better than that in here. We're under new management, you know."

"I don't have any money." And I laughed.

He raised his chin as if to say, "*Ahhh . . .!*", put away the pack, and moved to the steps that lead up to the Cameo's balcony, where the serious hustling goes on, anyway. As he walked up beside the pay telephone, grinding his buttocks at me dismissively in his frayed cut-offs, I shook my head — for the benefit of the security guard. Who still didn't look. So I went into the door to the orchestra.

In darkness I walked to the side aisle and gazed down over the scattered and flickering heads of the all-male audience.

The dozen committed jack-off artists were seated widely down toward the front. Most, however, were divided between the bored and the business-like, each of whom ignored the other, and none of whom would make use of what he'd watched till back in the privacy of his own bedroom or bathroom.

On screen, blonde Seka closed her china blue eyes and caught her breath as Mai-Lyn dropped her face into the bulge of a shaved cunt, black hair falling forward over high cheek bones touched with Revlon blush, so that you could just see her tongue, through the dark strands, trolling like a red-mouse between the folds of plump pussy flesh as Seka moved her thighs.

An occasional young black queen or aging white faggot drifted listlessly in the aisles, while, big as Thanksgiving Day balloons, the two women's hands, their thin fingers and long red nails brushing, joining, entwining, suggested something between lust, friendship, and a film editor's whim. Then, from another angle, Mai-Lyn pushed her other hand down between her legs, as, from behind, the camera caught the melons of her buttocks. She spread her cunt lips, and — once — quivered as though she'd hit something inside her moist envelope, igniting a pleasure momentarily beyond that called for by her $300 per day contract.

Out of the light I found a seat toward the side of the theater, put my hand between my legs, moved my knees up against the back of the wooden seat ahead of me, and looked at the screen . . .

The thin kid who slipped in to sit two seats away wore gray sweatpants and a gray sweatshirt with the hood up — which the Cameo's air conditioning, always on minimal, just doesn't warrant in mid-July. I glanced over and thought: Now here's some seventeen-year-old Chinese queen, going to try and hustle me.

I was wondering how long I was going to go on being polite to the guys who kept bothering me.

In return for my very uninterested glance, I got a dazzling friendly smile. Well,

I thought, at least he's not wearing makeup.

The kid immediately moved over, with a movement that was mostly hips, into the seat next to mine, shoulder against my shoulder, legs (with knees together) leaning against my legs; he touched my thigh with a hand as feminine as any I've ever seen, the nails long and neat under clear polish. "Do you want to have some fun?" he said in a surprisingly girl-like voice, with just the faintest accent—not foreign so much as simply from some other part of the country, or even of the city. Then, almost as if the question was a joke, he leaned toward my ear to hide his dark, Oriental eyes from me and laughed in a way that, I'm not kidding, made me think of small bells.

"Look, sweetheart," I said, "you're working. I'm just here to pull on my own prick a little, all by myself. Why don't you go find somebody else to hit on?" I like to be polite to any working man or woman, but I also know that, sometimes, with the desperate, you have to be firm. "I don't bring any money with me when I come into these places," I said. "So even if I fall asleep after I cum and you or one of your friends slips back and slits my pockets, all you'll find is my subway token home. Believe me."

I felt his lips brush my ear: "Not for money!" came the intense whisper, still on the edge of laughing. "Just to have a good time! You know . . . you and me!"

The Oriental kid sat back now and took a finger and drew it diagonally across the sweatshirt's chest—"Cross my heart"—and then diagonally the other way— "and hope to die! I just want to have a little . . ." He shrugged. ". . . fun!"

As the gray cloth gave under that slender hand, I realized there was something under that sweatshirt. The breasts there were about as large as tea-cups stood upside down. And the first thing I thought was: On a guy as slender as that, they're just too big for even the most intensive hormone treatments. While, at the same time, I also figured any transsexual who'd actually saved the $6,000 I'd heard the operation costs these days would have *certainly* gotten them bigger.

I frowned. "*Are* you a girl . . ." I asked, disbelieving, looking closely at the young, Oriental face with the straight black bangs inside the gray hood.

For answer, the lower lip pulled in between the teeth in an effort of concentration and decision. Quick glances left and right; then the delicate hands hooked into the waist of the sweat pants while he (or she; at this point I was really befuddled) lifted hips a little from the theater chair and slid the elastic waist down the substantially full hips (no panties) until the black bush of pubic hair pushed over the rim. "Touch me there! Go on! I like it! Touch me . . .!"

I touched . . . well, yes, *her.* In the hot closure between her legs, soft with dark hair, my fingers bunched up in the crevice, opened up when she moved her legs apart some, and my middle finger found the warm lips and slipped through them to find that always surprising inner heat.

Now I *know* what a pussy put in by a plumber feels like. (The working girls call it a "roll and tuck job." And *that's* $20,000 or up.) I've had my hands *and* my dick in more than one. Scar tissue is scar tissue; and it feels like a scar. Also, neither KY nor Vaseline—there since leaving the house that morning—has the same texture as a lady's natural moisture.

Her hands came together to press mine further in, and the elastic of her sweatpants pulled over my wrist.

"Hey, look . . ." I whispered. "If you got some pimp waiting in the back of the theater to beat the shit out of me when I don't come up with any bread . . . I mean, I'm not kidding you: I'm broke! You can go score with somebody else—"

She moved her thighs on both sides of my hand. "I know. But I don't *want* any money! I already crossed my heart, didn't I?"

"Well, look . . ." I took a breath; and, yeah, moved a finger.

"Please," she whispered. She put her mouth up against my ear again. "I gotta get somebody to eat my pussy for me!" Her thighs kept moving around my hand, and the lips of her cunt rubbed, with them, on the sides of my two middle fingers, which, without even trying, I was working deeper into the tight, the narrow, the wet, the hot. "I really want it . . . I'm so hot! You like to eat pussy?" she asked me, breathlessly—with, between 'to' and 'eat,' a catch in her voice as if one or another of my knuckles had brushed the same spot that, minutes before, had made Mai-Lyn twitch.

I took a deep breath myself. "Fine wines," I said. "French food . . .? There's nothing I like better! Hey, who are you? What's your name?"

Her voice caught again, only this time there weren't any words around it. She pressed my hand still harder, and whispered, her lips still tickling my earlobe: "My sister just bought this theater. You want to meet her?"

"Huh?" I said, turning to look at her. (Really, I've always been kind of curious who owned some of these scum-bag houses, but I've just assumed it was organized crime; certainly not the sister of some seventeen-year-old Oriental nymphomaniac.) "Your sister? What do you—?"

What she did to stop my question was, with her diagonally lidded eyes wide, stick her tongue in my mouth. Then her eyes closed. And maybe, for a moment, I closed mine too. Cool lips moved on mine. Her hot tongue moved over and under my own, while moments of air came between our mouths, which we both kept pushing closer, in order to drive the cool spots from between them. I got my other arm around her. Moments later, when our mouths dragged apart and my face was in her neck (the hood of her sweatshirt had fallen back, and I could hear her breathing in time to the work I was doing between her legs with my hand), I growled into her collar: "Oh, honey, I'm gonna eat your pussy till you shiver like the San Francisco earthquake! I'm gonna tongue your clit till you're crazy enough to run all the kooks out of Bellevue! I'm gonna eat your cunt till you can't even fucking *walk*! I'm gonna suck your goddam pussy till — " but didn't finish, because suddenly we were both going after each other's tonsils again.

When one or the other of us stopped to breathe, she whispered: "All right. You come meet my sister, then . . ." and pulled back, both her small hands flat against my chest. Her straight hair was long, I saw, now that her hood had fallen; it was held on one side by the kind of long, white barrette little girls wear. On the other side, it hung down by her face before it went back in her collar.

On screen, panting Mai-Lyn pulled at her cunt lips, while Seka's paler, pinker tongue caressed and caressed the wet snatch Mai-Lyn held further and further open.

"Come on," she said. "Let's go. Now. Please . . .!" She glanced around again. "We can't do it here!"

Which was kind of a surprise, because God knows enough of these crazy queens do a lot worse. But then, this was a real girl.

I looked around too, for the first time since she'd sat there.

Two black guys in the row behind us, a Puerto Rican in the row in front wearing just his undershirt, and a red-headed white guy, narrowed-shouldered, about nineteen, and with glasses, who'd slid into our row two seats away, all had their scrawny little peckers out, beating off for all they were worth, getting off on me making out with this crazy Oriental chick. (Actually, one of the black flashers wasn't so little, either. But never mind.) "Ah, shit!" I said, loudly. "Yeah, come on. Let's go!"

While the red-headed kid tried not to catch the head of his dick in his zipper, I pushed in front of him, holding her by her arm.

As soon as we hit the aisle, she was a step, three steps, five steps ahead. Hurrying behind her, I watched her hips working as she half walked, half ran toward the back of the theater: Her sweatshirt was no longer tucked into her pants, and bare flesh showed across the top of her buttocks, so that, even in the dim light, I could see two inches of the crack in her ass. Her black hair had come out of her collar and swung against her shoulders. I wondered how I could have thought she was a boy or even a transsexual. Though, Lord knows, enough of both work that place!

At the back of the Cameo, the men's room is left of the entrance: The door is always open, and the pale yellow light falls out from the steps leading down to the very busy, very smelly urinals.

Right of the entrance is the soft-drink machine; next to that stands the water-cooler, and beside that is a door that's almost always locked. It says:

LADIES

In most porno theaters, ladies' rooms are pretty superfluous; though, if a couple does come in and the woman really wants to use it, she can sometimes get the key from the cashier or the manager—unless they decide she's a pro.

About a year ago I was in the theater when the men's room broke down and got locked up for the day; so, with a hand-written sign on a paper towel scotch-taped to the door jamb, they opened up the ladies' room for male use: a set of steps down a narrow, paint-peeling stairwell to a cubicle one-quarter the size of the men's, with a sink and single stall at the bottom.

The pipes over the ceiling had dripped a lot. And it stank.

The girl went right to that locked door and from the front pocket of her sweatshirt got out a key. As she was fooling around with it in the old lock, I went up behind her, slid my hands under the back of her pants to hold both of her buttocks and, while I kneaded them, began licking her neck. She laughed and turned the door-knob.

The door opened, and the first thing I saw was that the light inside was very red. She moved into it, and practically pulled me, stumbling, in behind her—till my hands came loose from the elastic.

She reached past me and yanked the door closed sharply, while I blinked, surprised, looking up and down. Somebody had done a hell of a lot of work on this place since the men's room broke.

We were at the top of a stair, yes. But it was three times as wide as I remembered. The walls were covered with that red-flocked wallpaper like they have in

Tad's Steak Houses, only the design was more complicated and, as I looked around, I was pretty sure it was also a lot more expensive. Brass banister rails were fixed to the walls. And the only smell in the place was as if somebody two or three days ago might have burned a little incense there. The stairs themselves ran down beyond a kind of beaded curtain made with lots of transparent glass globes on gold chains, so you could just see beyond it. The scarlet carpet here on the upper landing, which ran off under those hanging baubles to cascade down the steps, had a nap long enough to attack with a weed-whacker.

"What the *fuck* . . .?" Not very original. Still, it's what I said.

She stepped away from the door, looked around, turned to me, smiling, and began to push her sweatpants down over her hips, wiggling them, with her beautiful Oriental pussy coming into view over the waistband that slanted left, slanted right, till at last the pants fell around her ankles. She stepped free, first with one bare foot (leaving her sandals somewhere in folded material), then with the other. Arms crossed over her stomach, she pulled up the sweatshirt from beautiful tits that were bigger than I'd thought, under that loose gray.

Smiling, she shook out her dark hair and slipped, naked, between the beaded curtain, starting down.

I didn't slip. "Hey—!" I crashed through clattering globes.

Five steps below, she'd stopped, turned back, and, with one hand on the polished banister, watched me. She moved a finger from her tit up toward her neck and back, breathing hard.

There was a some kind of light right beside her—more brass, with all sorts of crystal hanging around it; but though she was clearly lit, I couldn't see much beyond her.

As I started down, she leaned forward, reaching out with both hands and just . . . well, caught my crotch. So I stopped. "I want to suck you . . ." she whispered. "I wanna suck your beautiful penis . . .!" (Only girls say "penis" with that uncertain excess enthusiasm compensating for a conditioned embarrassment, which, for the duration of the word, leaves them a-quiver someplace where they cannot know the judgement upon them.) She got my belt open, pulled apart the top button on my jeans, and slid my zipper down. "I want to suck you and make you feel so good . . .!"

"Eh . . . sure," I said, wondering if I should help with the undressing; but she slid my pants down my hips and pulled my underpants down. The next thing, she was on my cock like a covey of hot, frenzied oysters. I let her suck; and she sucked *very* well. I caressed her black hair, rubbed her neck, then reached down to play with her tits. A breast in each hand, I rolled her nipples between the sides of my fingers. Now some women, when you play with their tits, it doesn't do shit. Others, well—she was one of the others.

Kneeling on the steps at my feet, her body began to quiver, then get real still (just her tongue going inside her mouth over my dick), then she'd quiver all over again, moving her head forward and back. She sucked and shivered at the same time—while I kneaded her breasts I could feel her tongue vibrating at the base of my balls. I mean, while she sucked me her *shoulders* blushed!

I could've come any time. But after about a minute, I said: "Oh, baby, let me get my face in that pretty pussy." I pulled my cock from somewhere deep inside her head. (Really, that's what it felt like.) As I stood up, her breasts slipped out of my hands.

My pants down around my thighs, I kind of hobbled around her, running my hands over her sides, her tits, her ass; then kissing them, then licking them, while she stretched out along the banister, one arm above her head, one hand back to follow me around; she kept trying to touch my ear.

Behind her, I turned, sat on the carpeted stair, and wedged my head up between her legs. She lifted the outside one to the step above, and I ate pussy like crazy. There was the faint smell of soap, the faintest taste of salt, and a faint odor of some toilet water or perfume she must have dabbed earlier that day on some other part of her body. With my nose full of soft cunt hair and her thigh hot against my left ear, she started to flex pussy muscles around my tongue; I licked, now deep inside her, now lifting the little knob of flesh at the folded roof of her cunt, now trolling through the sparse forest of her pussy, and digging deeply, then lightly, then doing it all over again, while she breathed, then moaned, then grunted; the muscles of the one leg against my ear actually shook, as though some musician had plucked the nerve that ran the length of her thigh like a harp string, while she whispered: "My . . . sister! Oh, yes, my . . . sister! You come back here, a lot! Yes. We'll do this lots and lots. My sister, she'll *love* you . . ."

Now a funny thing happens to your cock when you take it out of a hot mouth: it feels a little cold. Now and then I kind of played with it, which felt good, but what I really wanted was to make her freak out, and mostly I held on to her legs and licked.

She was pretty nearly over her hump.

Me too.

But suddenly, something hot and soft was on my dick, and a hand was leaning against my leg. Someone from down below had crawled up the stairs to suck me!

Given we were in the hall to a porno theater ladies' room, I thought some queen who'd been downstairs had come up to lend a mouth. Not that I mind who sucks on my crank as long as I'm getting mine, but I kind of wanted to know who it was and say, "Hey, motherfucker, I *see* you . . ."

I pulled my head out and looked down.

Another oriental face looked up, eyes smiling, with my dick a couple of inches in her face. This woman was about 35. Her lips around my cock were red as the skin of polished delicious apples. Her eyelids were blue with make-up, her cheeks colored with rose blush, and I could see that she wore black stockings, and black, high, high heels. Her nylons were held on by a black garter belt. She kneeled on the step below me, the stiletto of one heel pointing back into shadow. Her heavy breasts were full and naked.

With red nails long as those of Seka or Mai-Lyn, she took my dick softly and lovingly in her hand and licked it, now and again gazing up at me with eyes lidded by that Oriental fold pulled down over her eyes' inner corners—or perhaps she gazed, I realized a moment later, at that other pussy still hanging inches over my head.

The first girl came down a step to stand beside me, her hand on my shoulder, her leg against my arm. "My sister!" she panted. "See! She likes you!" Then she said something in chink. And between licks, her sister said something in chink back. (I bet it was something like: *See, he likes you too,* with the answer: *Far fucking out!*) "I told you she would . . ." came down to me in English.

I thought about saying, "Eh . . . glad to meet you. Real nice porno theater you got here," but it didn't seem appropriate. I said instead: "Suck on daddy's *dick,* mama!" and reached down for her fuller, swaying tits. "Suck on it and make it dribble!" At the same time I nuzzled over toward the crotch of the younger one, leading with my tongue.

The older one did (suck my dick, that is), and I got my face back home into pussy-land, feeling the nails on the older one's hand flex against my belly like a kitten's claws, while, with those on the other, first she tickled the delicate place behind the sack of my nuts, then must have reached back between her own legs to do a Mai-Lyn.

Her mouth's engine seemed to roar around my cock. And the pussy over my face worked my jaw till the base of my tongue was sore.

The three of us kept getting closer, till they were embracing above me. I ducked my head, took a breath, slid down a step, and stood up. Touching a shoulder of each with each of my hands, I moved around to look at them from the side, close enough to see the faint down on the younger one's cheek and the grain in the rouge on the older one's; my breath shifted gears in their ears' cartilages. Turning, brushing, pressing, one pair scarlet, the other pink-white, their lips moved centimeters apart. Their tongues traveled over and around each other, more than crossing the distance between.

They pulled their mouths apart, leaned back in one another's arms, their flattened breasts rounding. Swaying, those seventeen-year-old tits and 35-year-old jugs brushed nipples. The stockinged legs of the older one bent, rubbing my knee, as, panting, she lowered her face across her sister's belly.

I sat down on the other side of the steps, leaned against the brass banister, my cock in my hand, and watched. (Yes, I'd come once; and I was pretty near it again.) In their very different ways, they were very beautiful women. The older licked out that cunt I'd been so happy in, her tongue spreading, thinning, now going straight up into the red gorge separating the black hair, now dipping forward, now sliding back, while, with her red claws, she massaged her own pink clit at the vault of the raw declivity falling through the hair between the black bands of her stocking tops. The younger one's head was back against the wall. She smiled at me once, then closed her eyes, her lips touching and parting, now wetting under a sweep of her tongue, now drying with her loud breath, to stick and pull open as if she whispered dirty words in a language I didn't know and couldn't quite hear. Articulating them, her tongue made little twitches in her mouth.

When I came the third time, the older sister was standing against the wall, her hands high and wide on flocked crimson and her head down, while, squatting behind her, her little sister ate out her asshole with such avidity that, as I watched black hair shake down on those naked shoulders, as I heard the standing one cry out while the one on her knees grunted like some mad and famished gorilla, I was sure would leave one or the other of them sobbing on the steps in a minute, just from sheer excitement.

I say I'd come three times, now; and they'd each gone panting and quivering around the bend seven, ten, or more, in quivering, jaw-clenched (the younger one) or keening (the older) orgasmic cascades. And I *still* wanted another shot.

I thought about saying something like, "Hey, make room for me, ladies," but I just got up, stepped over, while they pulled apart a little, breathing heavily, both of them blinking at me with faint perspiration under their dark hairlines. Then the older one smiled as if I was the greatest thing since disposable chopsticks. Somehow we were all holding each other, and I felt their different-sized breasts against my naked chest; then all three of us spent a lot of time with our tongues in the other two mouths. Without stopping, we were all three going down the steps together in a way that could have been real clumsy, but, because nobody tripped, I hardly noticed.

For a while, I know, I sat on a step again, with two sets of thighs hot on each ear, while they rubbed cunts and kissed, and I ate double pussy that, I'm not kidding, made me shoot a forth wad off through my fist and into the dark. (We're talking an hour-and-a-half, two hours, here.) Then I was up, holding the older one around her shoulders, while she ran her nails over my back, and I kissed her, rubbing my cock (*still* hard!) from her pussy hair up over the edge of her garter belt, while the younger one, crouched down where I had been, between our legs, rubbed my thighs with her small hands and flicked her tongue back and forth between the base of my dick and her sister's snatch. I began to quiver in a combination of heat and indecision on which hole, mouth or cunt, I should put it in first. I think it went in one, then the other, then back, then back again. But it all felt so good, I couldn't tell you which was which.

Down there, my balls kept dragging over her face. So she licked them too.

When I shoot a few times, close together like that (and, no, it doesn't happen *that* often), finally I loose the edge between coming and not-coming. My hard-on gets permanent, and my whole body becomes sensitive. Orgasm at that point is beyond what most of us think of as pleasure. It becomes more like a burning that spreads through the whole body, at many times the intensity of your ordinary, satisfying cum. The fire runs from the back of my throat and deep in my ears down to the place below my kneecaps, to my insteps and the skin behind my ankles. Really, it's like my whole body becomes pure dick. (During one of those, sometimes juice comes out, and sometimes it doesn't—but there were already four wet spots on the carpeted steps around us.) And I was on my way to one of them, nearing it, falling away, and nearing it again; I kept on having the fantasy that the whole red stairwell was one raw, pulsing cunt while I was a man-sized cock, fucking it.

They were embracing, were kissing, and I was behind the younger one, with her hair damp in my face, and the underside of my prick running up and down her ass's scalding crevice, while over her shoulder, in much less light, I watched her and her sister's lips close and open around their tongues. (We were much further down the stairs now; it was much dimmer.) I tried to make my movements especially gentle, almost slow-motion, because I knew I was on some edge that, if I let myself go over, I'd be on them both like a fucking animal — as slow as I moved, I was close to the kind of frenzy where I could have bitten a tit or an ear or sunk my teeth to the blood in a cunt-lip without even meaning to. As I moved to their side, one of them held my dick and one of them held my balls; and they *still* kissed and rubbed snatches; I leaned to get my own face in-between them —

When their mouths came apart, and I slid my tongue out against theirs, the tongue of the elder seemed, for a moment, *terribly* long; and, in that half-dark, I could have sworn its end, six inches from her small, white teeth, was thin and forked. The back of the younger one felt so smooth and warm. But my hand, moving on the older one's shoulder, felt cool and, as it moved, encountered something like cloth — rough cloth; or even leather. I moved my hand down, away from the roughness, while she took some great breath that thickened her waist, and the garter belt that, fifty times now, I'd run my tongue or my fingers or the head of my dick under, front and back, suddenly went limp, raddling against my palm.

The thing had snapped!

Again, I wondered whether I should say anything, but I didn't even know if the older sister spoke English.

My hand went down to her buttocks; and something seemed *very* wrong—as if one of her legs was bent much too far back, or, as I ran my hand around it, as if she had a third leg, or something, there. I moved my hand up again, and the small of her back was not only cool, but cold; the roughness I'd felt, here and there, before, actually changed under my hand to a hardness like plastic, like metal.

I opened my eyes and pulled back.

Then I staggered back.

Because her face turned to me—and it was as long as an iguana's; the eyes in it had reversed their slant till they were almost vertical, big as the bottoms of beer bottles, and yellow as urine. Her face was that of some beast and covered with black scales; and the breath, which, between us, had been a three-way thunder, was suddenly cut by her liquid *Hissss* . . .

Glimmering, her tongue snaked out a foot, flickered, and forked. What I'd felt at her haunches was not a leg, but a thick, saurian tale that swept the stairs first to pound my wall, then to crash the far one. Great wings rose behind her, their talons high as the ceiling, their tremendous folds fluttering hugely, looking for space to expand.

Her stockings ripped from her expanding thighs.

Beneath black hair, made little blades by the sweat, the younger turned her boyish smile to me. "You like my sister . . . ? This is her place now!" No longer red except for the highlight from the lights further up, a claw moved black talons tenderly from the younger one's breast to her belly. I slipped down a step, grabbing for the banister behind me, started to run up. But one wing swung out to block the stairs — and the light. In sudden dark I could no longer see the younger one at all. So, turning, I barreled down into black. Slipping on the carpet, I only kept from going head over heels because I was still holding the rail.

I ran down, kept running, and underfoot I could tell there that was no more rug.

Then I saw a light, like day, below. I ran for it, came down to the end of the stairs, and sprinted out into it, only stopping halfway across the theater lobby.

From his stool, the security guard looked up.

I took a breath and turned, almost falling, to stare back up past the pay phone to the balcony steps.

Then I looked at the guard again. Under the poster of Seka and Mai-Lyn, he frowned, dropping his hand from his billy-club. I tried to say something, but found myself looking back at the stairs I'd half-tumbled from because . . . something was coming down:

The black queen who'd tried to hit on me when I first came in stepped into the light. When he saw me, he frowned too; he adjusted the shoulder of his sequined blouse, letting his head fall to the side. "You look like you been busy, honey . . . You comin' up for air before getting yourself into another session? . . . Too bad it wasn't with me!"

I looked down at myself.

My shirt was open and hanging off one arm. My jeans were apart and pushed so far down my hips you could see pubic hair and the top of my dick.

Behind me, the guard finally said: "Look, fella! We let a *lot* of things go on in this place. Upstairs, you can take your pants off and get fucked in the aisle if you want. I'm just here to see nobody picks your pocket while you do. But you *still* gotta put your clothes on before you come out. Otherwise I ain't gonna let you in here no more. Comin' down here like that, I don't care *what* you're on, it just don't look right. And the new owners don't want you to go quite *that* far, know what I mean?"

I turned again, started to speak.

Then I pulled my pants up, trying to tug my shirt together with one hand, buckle my belt with the other, and shove my shirt-tails down inside at the same time, while I shouldered out the glass doors into the July evening. I went down Eighth Avenue, squinting to get the goddam buttons into their goddam holes, while I passed half a dozen guys who weren't wearing any shirts at all in the muggy heat.

In his cap and glasses, the shoe-shine guy was pulling the dirty canvas cover down his stand.

My entire body tingling, I swung around the plywood partition, onto crowded 42nd, making for the subway.

—*New York City*
July, 1984

* * *

[*Conclusion to July 23rd letter to Mueller:*]
We've just gone through a really hot, muggy, end of July day. It's dark now — almost ten o'clock. Gotta be up at four tomorrow to do all the corrections I didn't do while I was writing out my adventure at the Cameo for you. Then, at eleven, it's back into the publisher's office, for another day's work.

Well, John, that should keep your right hand busy for a half-day or two. And that's what's been (or may have been) happening downtown around 42nd Street. Better try and keep my account out of anybody else's hands except yours, though. Believe me, I know whereof I speak. Got to wind this up — really, I've worked too long on it already, considering what I have to do by tomorrow.

You know, there's a very funny thing about "desire" (in the sense of "lust"). A famous French psychiatrist, named Jacques Lacan, said it: "Everyone desires the desire of the other." That is, what turns everyone on is the fact that some other person is turned on. Most (supposedly) normal people presumably want the desire to go in a circular path with only two stop-off points: A is turned on by B. B is turned on by A. And everybody else is supposedly excluded from the sex act. But a surprising number of us aren't like that. We want A (whether a man or a woman) to be turned on, but we really don't give a flying fuck who or what A is turned on by, as long as we can get our own in there somewhere. That's why I can get off on your watching the movies. And that's why you can get off on what you like in the movies themselves. Indeed, anybody who gets off on pornography at all has, by definition, broken that simple circular path of desire and stretched it into a more complex pattern, since the person appreciating the pornography is never one of the people taking part, except in imagination—and even there, most people only imagine that they're watching, not doing.

At any rate, I hope you enjoy this letter and can get some use out of it. (Let me know how long—that is, how many times—it works for you.) Do yourself a favor and don't show "A John's Story" to any of your friends in there. If you do, I promise you, you'll get yourself in trouble—if not me. In fact, if I were you, I'd use it till it didn't get you off any more—then tear it up into *very* small pieces and throw it away. Anyway. If, when you get a chance to write back, you might drop me a couple of pages or so about how much you enjoyed pissing in some cocksucker's mouth (and maybe finger-fucking him there like it was a pussy), and I'll more than consider us even. Feel free to be as imaginative as I was. (The truth I have to live with every day. But other things besides the truth can be a turn-on, right . . .?) It's an interesting thing, trying on somebody else's fantasy, even when it isn't yours.

If nothing else, it's something to talk about when we see each other after you're out and settled in a job with your father in September.

Well, Frank just came in, laughing, to show me a personal ad he just ran across in the *New York Native:* Some guy wants to find somebody to give him "exotic enemas: coffee, oil, vanilla pudding, yogurt, tapioca . . ." I tell you, there are times, even sitting with you over a pitcher of what-have-you at Beefsteak Charlie's, when I feel like the most normal cocksucker in the world!

Then, five minutes later, out back of my office window, above the buildings that run along Central Park, we had ten minutes of beautiful and unexpected fireworks, busting higher and higher (followed by the ten-second delayed booms!), silver, gold, purple, green, red, and multi-colored, like fast-action flowers blooming. When they were over, I heard people in the windows all over the back alley cheering and applauding. And a few minutes later, out the front windows, I could see more than the usual number of people swarming across Amsterdam Avenue toward Broadway—so there must have been a concert or something in the park tonight; now the folks were returning to the Broadway subway.

It'll be another couple of weeks before I get around to writing again. But it's only my crazed schedule. (I have to go to Vermont for a long weekend.) Still, I send you all my good wishes. Hope September doesn't take too long to get here for you.

• 30 •

To Camilla Decarnin

July 19th, 1984

Dear Mog,

To say that I have been busy, does not (as they used to say in Victorian times) even comprehend the situation. *Splendor and Misery* goes with excruciating slowness and infinite pain[s]. I'm hoping that I will eventually break through and be able to pull out the working text a little faster. Two to five hours a day at the machine here — and all my waking hours spent thinking about it is producing between a shy page and a small paragraph per day.

I showed someone the fifteen pages that the last three weeks have garnered. The response? "Well, it seems lively, colorful . . .and interesting." What more, of course, could fifteen pages of an SF novel seem like? But I reeled a moment, astonished that the ceiling hadn't fallen in and angels hadn't erupted through the clouds to play on hautboys and omphaclides — till I remembered that words on paper are comparatively limited in their effect, no matter how good they are or how much work you've put into them. ". . . lively, colorful [and] interesting . . ." probably means they're okay. Still, the soul boggles . . .

A few days back Lou Aronica at Bantam showed me a jacket for the hardcover edition of *Stars/Sand* that has got to be the worst cover on an SF novel I've *ever* seen. But, apparently, Bantam thinks so too. They're throwing it out and starting over. (Nightmare: "Well, yes, Chip. I know we *said* we were going to do another one. But you see, it turned out we didn't have time and there was nothing we could do in the end, so finally we just decided to go with it . . .")

Its basic colors are red and white and blue and purple and pink and orange and yellow . . .

At that same meeting, Lou told me, guardedly (as one desperately trying to remember if he indeed spoke the truth), that he had sent you the manuscripts or galleys (manuscripts *or* galleys . . .?). Do let me know if you got them — especially the MS to *Flight from Nevèrÿon*. If you have time to read it, tell me what you think.

I now have page proofs of *Stars/Sand*. That's the galleys with all the first set of corrections (mine and the initial proof-reader's) incorporated and the whole cut up with real page numbers and headings and stuff. They look very good. There's still the odd mistake, but they're fixable. The "multiple tongue" stuff, of which they made total oatmeal in the long galleys (and which I went over, practically word by word with F. X., and watched him mark it properly himself), while it is now in the ballpark of the comprehensible, is still in left field. Spent yesterday trying to get F. X. on the phone to make a date to get together with him to go over them. Yes, he was in the office. But no, he was not at his desk.

Apparently he wasn't at his desk from nine o'clock in the morning till five in the evening, when the office shut down for the day. So I have to start over again this morning.

I am debating whether to tell you a perfectly preposterous story which just got to me in yesterday's mail—and which could conceivably make you rather pissed. (It did me.) But it's just another case of Bantam's ability to fuck up. Oh, I suppose I might as well:

Sometime in June Lou went out on a two-week trip to the coast that ended with his dropping in for a day or two on Westercon. The day before he took off is the day I begged him, pleaded with him, did all but order him to send you the galleys and hire you as proof-reader — the day he hemmed and hawed and left. Two weeks later, at Westercon, he apparently ran into one Ron Drummond, a (currently) Seattle-based fan, whom you might know; a very large, very bright, very good-natured young man. (For some years he's been working on a surreal

novel about the life of John Lennon . . .) At some point while they were both at
Westercon, Ron approached Lou about the "Lennon" book, and in the course of
it, mentioned he was one of the people that Jeff (the Seattle printer) had gotten to
proof-read *Starboard Wine*. From here on, it is all surmise on my part and will
remain so until my next lunch with Lou when I can ask him about it, but I just
assume that Lou (who, we must remember, is personally responsible for about 50
books a year at Bantam, 30-odd of which are SF and only two of which, this year,
are mine) probably thought: "Oh, yeah. That's right. There was somebody out
here Chip wanted me to send galleys to." Drummond no doubt asked for them,
said he would love to proof-read them; so Lou, in one of his daily phone calls
back to the Bantam office, had David Stern, his assistant, send Mr. Drummond a
set of long galleys.

Lou never mentioned this to me; I don't know if, when he got back, he realized
he had sent them to the wrong person. Or if he remembered he'd sent them to
anyone. Anything is possible.

At any rate, what lets me surmise all this is that, in yesterday's mail, I received
six pages of meticulously-typed pages of errata for the *Stars/Sand* galleys, from
Ron Drummond, with a note explaining that this is a Xerox of the errata already
sent to Bantam, by Express ($16 a throw) Delivery Mail, as Lou had told him time
was of the essence, etc., etc.

What makes this story terribly sad is that, first of all, I know Ron is not in any
better financial shape than you are. (No, he wasn't paid for the work.) His corrections are geared to the first set of long galleys by galley number, paragraph,
and line. Since we are at page proof stage, however, there is absolutely no way for
anyone to figure out where his corrections go, since the page numbering has been
radically changed *twice* now since the first galley stage, and is currently entirely
different.

(The original galleys have—randomly—between three and four final pages to
a sheet. The bound galleys have—also randomly—more or less one and a half
final pages to a sheet. [The random amount of lines on the first two sets means
you can't even do it by mathematics, figuring out where the corrections would
fall in each new generation.] And the page proofs have—exactly—one final page
to a sheet . . .)

I actually took Drummond's corrections and at least tried to go through the
"Prologue" and fit them in. It took me 40 minutes to find the first six—at which
point I gave up.

Just so Drummond's sheer *work* doesn't go to waste, when I get Flyn to make
my page proof date, I'm going to ask if there is still a set of original galleys in the
office. (I haven't had those for five weeks.) That way I *may* be able to correlate
them, using my privileged knowledge of the text as writer. But I'm perfectly
ready to be told that they were all thrown out a month ago . . .

At any rate, I had *no* idea about *any* of this until I opened my mail yesterday.

I suppose I'm telling you about it because, should the story or part of it get
back to you, I'd hate for you to feel that somebody — me, for instance — was
machinating *against* your doing the proof-reading and trying to get someone else!
Lou didn't know Ron from hunger, at least until they met at Westercon. I've met
him twice and exchanged half a dozen letters with him over three-odd years—

indeed, unbidden he sent me some errata on *Neveryóna* when it appeared in trade paperback last April, for which I wrote to thank him. But the fact is, nobody — you, him, or anyone else — should be doing that kind of $6-$10 an hour work without pay. I've always been very grateful to you for doing so much work for me. And on Dragon Press Books *(The American Shore)*, or even the Gregg *(Dhalgren)* Press, I've felt comfortable accepting it, because they were not a money-making proposition for anyone, me or the publisher. But Bantam is a big company that makes lots of money. And for you to do that kind of work for *them* without pay has a very different flavor to it, at least in my mouth.

Yes, I also know you have to make your own decisions about such things. Still, if I were in a position to pay you myself right now, I would. But, alas, I'm not. And they haven't even obliged me by sending you stuff in time to correct it and get it back.

* * *

Just spoke to F. X. *Flinn* (whose name I learned how to spell in the course of the conversation: the Gaellic diphthong "oi" in the midst of the usual "O'Flynn" spelling was traditionally transliterated as "y" — except in the odd boat-load of immigrants who were told, "Get rid of the 'o'" and who, therefore, dropped both the initial "child of" particle as well as the first part of the diphthong) who said: "Oh, yes. Of course, I should have a file copy of the long galleys. Just a second."

Seems he couldn't find them, but will look further.

And there is another Bantam story which I *won't* bore you with *anent* Rowena and the new *Nevèrijon* cover . . .

My first *Little Magazine* is out. (Vol. 14, No 3.) That is, the first on which I have been on the staff from first selection to publication. I must say, I'm *very* proud. I'll try and send you a copy, though David is making "only one copy to an editor" noises: Our standard print-run is 1,000 copies, and usually we get 20 or 30 extras. But this time the printer seems to have short-changed us by c. 150 copies. But there's probably (hopefully) another carton somewhere en route to us. Maybe you'll at least see it on a newsstand somewhere; maybe at City Lights (does it still exist?). I know it gets distributed at Cody's in Berkeley.

Really, this is just a note to let you know your last letter was received, read, and felt. And that I'm thinking of you.

All my love,

• 31 •

To Iva Hacker Delany

July 20th, 1984

Dear Iva,

Hello!

You must have thought we'd forgotten you, since nobody wrote. But we didn't. We were all just *very* busy!

I'm working hard on my new book, and I've had to do a lot of running around because of the covers on the two that will be published this winter.

Yesterday, Ashley came up, changed the gas-pipe on the stove (it had sprung a leak) and Frank and I spent the evening talking and cleaning the thing, inside and out.

To clean it, you get this spray-can full of lye (which is like a very powerful acid) and spray it all over the parts with burned-on grease and stuff, which all turns into brown, runny gook that drips and dribbles over everything—and you get a sponge and wipe it off.

You have to wear rubber gloves, or you can burn your hands with the lye. And it takes two or three sponges, actually, because even with rinsing them and wringing them out, pretty soon they just about fall apart—at least if you start out with a stove as dirty as ours was!

It was really *yucky*—but also kind of fun. And it was very interesting suddenly to see the real color of the inside of the stove: dark, dark gray with little white speckles.

But there must be things like that (both yucky and fun) at camp, too!

A few days back I had lunch with Judy Ratner, from downstairs. We went to Broadway Bay, the restaurant you used to like so much. Judy had lobster and I had a chef's salad. But while we were eating and talking, I told her how much you had liked the movie *Gremlins,* and she asked me if I thought Maya would like it too.

I said, "I don't see why not."

Judy said: "Well, I've got money today. I think I'll take Maya later on this afternoon, when she gets back from day camp."

Later on that evening, when I was at the dining-room table, working on my galleys, the phone rang, and when I sat down in the red chair and picked up the receiver, I heard a little girl say: "Hello . . . Chip?"

"Maya?" I asked. "Is that you?"

"Yes," she said. "I wanted to thank you for telling my mother to let me see *Gremlins!*"

"Oh, did you like it?" I asked.

"Yes!" she declared. Then she laughed.

We talked about it a little more. I asked her what parts she liked the best, and what parts she thought were the scariest. She wasn't too sure, because basically she had liked it all.

Then we hung up.

But I thought you might enjoy hearing about it.

We're all going to see you this weekend: me, Frank, and . . . guess who else? A surprise. No . . . I couldn't keep this kind of a secret. Grandma Margaret is going to come up with me and Frank this year!

Me and Grandma (probably) will be spending more time at the camp this year that we have in the past. This year I've asked Frank to let you and me stay on the camp grounds and take part in the programs there more than we have before. Frank will go off when he feels like it. But we'll have you out at least for overnight and breakfast.

Even though I've been *very* bad about writing, I love you lots and lots; and I've *thought* about you every day.

You say camp is not as good as last year. But that it's okay. Maybe you could talk with some of the campers and get together and make some suggestions to Gregg about what might make it better. I bet he'd really appreciate it that you and the other kids were concerned.

Or maybe it was just because you were feeling bad that day you wrote me, because I hadn't written you. I hope that was what it was—and believe me, from now on I'll be much better.

I promise.

(I hope you're not "almost crying" now!)

Glad you like riding and tennis. I'll bring you a flashlight and your knapsack, and some paper, pencils and envelopes. I love you lots and lots, and I'm really looking forward to seeing you on visiting day.

Love,

• 32 •

To Camilla Decarnin

July 27th, 1984

Dear Mog,

One beat SF writer here. This last month has been exhausting, and I truly understand what's meant by the cliché "bone-tired." July has been dominated— a much better and more accurate word, now that I think of it, would be "oppressed"—by the production on *Stars/Sand*.

I told you about the Drummond list of errata in my last letter. I enclose a copy of a letter I just finished to Ron this morning, just to bring you up to date on the events surrounding that, if nothing else.

But, indeed, the depths of the exhaustion have probably been hollowed out by all the auxiliary goings on. Toward the beginning of the month, I was in the crowded 42nd Street men's room on the IRT subway, zipping up my trousers and about to leave, when Officer Pennell (Badge #4610) came in with his partner and pointed, as far as I can tell at random, to, "You . . . and you!" The first 'you' was me, and I was issued a ticket for "loitering" (read "cruising") with orders to appear in court to pay an unspecified fine on August 7th.

The second "you" was a large, muscular young man about 33, in glasses and a lavender sweat-shirt with the sleeves torn off, named Brad G——, who turned out to be from Colorado and who has some job that takes him back and forth from there to New York. While his ticket was being issued, he did a whole lot of indignant protesting, and I would bet dollars to doughnuts that he's actually straight— probably liberal, more or less sympathetic with gays. I suspect he was quite well aware of what was going on in the men's room, didn't really care, and had—like myself—just come in to pee. But I also suspect that, because of all of that, straight as he might be and for all his protests, having been arrested for being one, he actually felt somehow that he had become guilty.

Later, I stopped him over by the line of pay phones on the wall, where he'd gone to put in a frustrated call to his answering service, and told him if he wanted to, I was willing to fight it with him. The sad truth is, no-one who has ever fought such a charge in New York has ever lost—but by the same token, though probably, around the city, 600 or 800 people are issued tickets on such charges per month, only about 500 people have ever chosen to fight it in the last ten or fifteen years. And in the course of a five-minute conversation with Mr. G——, after the officers had wandered off, I listened to him go from absolute certainty that he would fight it with me to, well, maybe it would just be easier not to be in New York at all around the first weeks of August . . .

Do I have the time, energy, or what have you to go through a full jury court trial over this kind of thing? Not this summer. But I just may, anyway. The police action is harassment, and currently the only answer is to harass the system back—which is what bringing a $75 victimless "misdemeanor" to a full court trial means.

Well, this is the third time it's happened to me. The first time was in England —and the experience, which ended up with my spending a day in a London jail cell, was the basis for the scene where Bron is arrested on Earth in *Triton*. Wonder if I'll get anything out of this one . . .?

Then, while all that was going on, there were various numbing (when not chilling) meetings with Ed, my accountant, and the IRS-people. (At the last of these, I discovered—somewhat to my surprise—that Ed is 64 years old, and will probably retire out from under me even before all this is cleared up in a couple of years!) Indeed, we had just managed to get the Feds to agree to stay off my back till the first of the year and allow me to work . . . when the news came in that the State, to which of course I also owe money, had just slapped a levy directly on Bantam Book's accounting department to hold-up all moneys due me, which, in this case, meant the delivery payment for *Flight from Nevèrÿon*, on which I had been planning to live till the first of the year.

Phone calls, meetings, and letters later, and they let me off with an up-front payment of $1,000 (which I didn't have and had to borrow from Henry, putting me even deeper in the hole to him than I already am) and the promise of $300 a month, which I may or may not be able to pay. How did the State get to Bantam Books, you of course want to know? (Ordinarily, given that I'm down professionally as a "freelance writer," all they would be able to do in my case is attack my bank account, which, since last October, I haven't had.) Apparently I have a fan in the State Tax Department. Thanks to various meetings with Ed, *et alia*, I even know that her name is "Louise." Apparently when my case came across her desk, she recognized my name, remembered that I published with Bantam, and took it from there.

What price fame . . . !

Then there were the cover hassles that I told you about last letter. And then . . .

And after that . . .

One oddly good thing amidst all of this—probably it's because the membrane to my brain has simply been worn away, and I am so vulnerable to the entire world right through here—is that *Stars/Sand*, in the last two weeks or so, has finally come alive for me again and, with it, possibilities for going on with *The Splendor and Misery of Bodies, of Cities* have also begun to sprout, bud, and even bloom. At this point, as I struggle on, I'm convinced that *Splendor and Misery* will certainly be no worse a book than *Stars/Sand*, which, as I told you, I never thought was bad (just, occasionally, uninteresting and dull) and conceivably quite a bit better.

What I need is three solid days' sleep, if I'm to feel anything less than dead.

But tomorrow, at four in the morning, Frank and I (with my mother) take off in the VW rabbit up to Vermont to visit Iva at summer camp. I'm afraid I won't be much of a parent, but I'll do my best.

And seeing Iva is always therapeutic for me. So maybe I'll come back feeling a little better.

Have been reading Mark Helprin's stories in *Ellis Island* and his novel, *Winter's Tale*. That this last got reviewed on the front page of the *New York Times Book Review* kind of boggles me. He writes with energy, yes. But not with *that* much energy. He doesn't know what prepositions do to the English language; and, as a result, sometimes his prose is downright thin—if not threadbare. The stories are much better than the novel; and I don't love them a lot. Indeed, the novel takes what is weakest in the stories—a faint sense of whimsy—and tries to turn it into a swash-buckling virtue. (I suspect he thinks of it as "manly" fantasy. But any *Unknown* writer could give him a lesson on what must go into "urban fantasy," which is really what it is.) Both as simple narrative (entertaining action), and as political construct (the political implications of choosing these actions and not others), *Winter's Tale* is truly, even inspirationally, bad. His main character, for a hundred pages now, does not *want* a thing—not because Helprin is writing about a man who doesn't want, but because he has simply forgotten or overlooked the fact that desire (and I don't mean fucking; Peter Lake, from age ten, does enough of that) is what makes novels novel (that last "novel" is a verb, not an adjective). And the fantasy element keeps veering it away from the truly interesting material and into the hopelessly safe.

And if some graduate student tells me that that was the whole point, I will know that said graduate student simply doesn't know how to read a book. . . .

I hope your silence means you are involved in all sorts of good things that simply don't leave you time to write. But if not, I don't mind listening to any and all complaints. (Even about me, if you must.) At any rate, I send

all my good wishes, love, and affection to you,

• 33 •

To Ron Drummond

July 27th, 1984

Dear Ron,

Thanks for your two sets of errata for *Stars/Sand*. When the first six pages arrived, I realized they were keyed to the long galleys. We were then just into the page-proof stage, where the numbering is completely different. I called Bantam up to see if I could get a set of long galleys, only to find that nobody seemed to be able to put their hands on the file copy.

That meant it looked like your work was all going to go to waste.

Four days later, when I went into the office, F. X. Flinn (the managing editor of the hardcover/trade paperback line) told me that a copy had, indeed, turned up. So I moved into an empty cubicle and spent some three hours looking up your corrections on the long galleys, then finding them on the page proofs and correcting them.

Then, a couple of days later your second batch arrived, and I went in for another two-and-a-half hour session.

Out of your nine pages of corrections, there were exactly seventeen mistakes which you caught that neither I nor the Bantam proof-readers found. There were about six things you thought were mistakes that either weren't, or which had already been corrected differently from the way you did. And I was just a little surprised at a couple you failed to get: at the beginning of the last chapter of the novel proper, "Formalities," the second and third page of the typescript had been set in the wrong order—rendering the section, as far as event sequence and dialogue went, oatmeal.

But all that has been taken care of.

Again, I want to thank you—most deeply—for your time and your work. You and some others (notably my good friend Camilla Decarnin in San Francisco) have been insistently generous with your energies in a way any dyslexic writer *must* be grateful for! Still, I can't help reflecting: Professional proofreaders get paid between $6.50 and $10 an hour for the kind of work you were doing. It just doesn't seem right for you to do it for nothing. For the combination of your who-knows-how-many hours and my five-and-a-half hours of work, there will be, indeed, seventeen less errors in the published version of *Stars/Sand* than there would have been without it. I'm a perfectionist, and I would have been willing to work twice that long, on my end, to correct half that number of mistakes.

But I couldn't feel right *asking* somebody to do what, on your end, was certainly much *more* than five-and-a-half hours of work!

Jeff's requisitioning you, Debbie Notkin, and the Neilson Heydens to proof-read *Starboard Wine* is another matter; I'm not making any money on that, and neither is Dragon Press. (In fact it already seems to have stalled somewhere in the red. And my personal errata sheet for that still comes in at over 50 errors already in the published version.) But Bantam is a large company that makes lots of money. I've tried to get them to hire Camilla—but it hasn't worked out, thanks to their general sluggishness, uncomfortableness with doing anything new, and simple size. (You know: The length of time it takes a nerve impulse to get from the dinosaur's brain to her hind legs, so she can go running off after the mouse—which has been out of sight at least two minutes before the brontosaurus can move . . .) If, when a book of mine is published and the urge strikes you, you make a list of errors and send them to me at your leisure, so that I can insert them into the next edition (the next paperback printing, for example), as you did last year with *Neveryóna,* I will always be grateful.

As, indeed, I'm truly grateful for what you've done here.

But I'd like to suggest that you not put yourself out in this way anymore—certainly not for free, for a publisher the size of Bantam Books. With the combination of work, rush, and even mailing expense to you, there just seems something terribly disproportionate about it.

I hope this letter doesn't seem presumptuous. It's meant for your peace of mind as much as mine. I look forward to reading the "triple-review" of *Stars/Sand* you promise in *Inscape-3.* My best to Don Keller and Tatiana, when you see them. Good luck with your novel; I hope it's coming well.

All best wishes,

• 34 •

To John P. Mueller

August 21st, 1984

Dear John,

Once again, I haven't kept up my end of the correspondence as frequently as I'd hoped. But I've got books coming out this winter and this spring, and as soon as the production work ended on the first (a book called *Stars in My Pocket Like Grains of Sand*), I was slapped with galleys and stuff on the second (a book called *Flight from Nevèrÿon*).

Yesterday I delivered off the most recent set of galleys to be copied, with all the corrections. They should come back to me today or tomorrow for a final going over. I'll turn them in on Friday or Monday. In the little breather while they're away, I'm writing.

I'd meant to write you just after I got your letter with "Chip's Story."[1] Thank you very much. I was kind of touched that you'd taken the time to do it—and, of course, I enjoyed it. A lot. I was still running my answer through my head and wondering when I'd get time to sit down and write it to you, when your next letter arrived.

Also, many thanks for that. I'll get back to that one in a moment.

As I said, yesterday I went off to deliver galleys to the copier along with doing various other bits of running around, quite sure I'd get to writing you last night or this morning (which is when I'm doing this), only to find your letter with "A Hustler's Story" waiting for me when I got home.

Yes, it was a lot better than the first one! Really, I got quite a charge out of it. It was quite something. As I said, when you put your mind to it, you write clearly and well. Thank you very much, too!

* * *

To the middle letter, however, before I go on:

As I think I wrote you in other letters, I've had friends before in jail, so I'm very aware of how much you really and honestly do need money; I know how useful some extra bread would be to you, both now and for when you get out. I don't think you're bullshitting me about the situation at all, when you say you need it.

But the fact is, I don't have it. To go up and see my kid at her summer camp on their parents' visiting day three weeks ago, in Vermont, we had to hunt for cans in the street to get the toll money. Gas went on a Mobil credit card, and the bill for that (and we're talkin' $24) is now sitting on the kitchen table, looking very unpaid. And I still have a pile of notices from the IRS. Not to mention the State Tax Board. Right now, my friends know I'm broke and invite me to their houses for dinner a lot. And I've lost twelve pounds in the last six weeks or so—given where I started, not the worse thing in the world I could do. But still.

Do I mind your asking?

No. That's what friends are for.

But I hope you don't mind my saying, "No." Friends also have to understand that, too.

---

[1] Mueller's pornographic response to "A John's Story."

My kid gets home on Saturday, and right now I'm scuffling to set up a week-end up at her grandmother's, some afternoons at her friends', and the like, in the week she's with me, before she goes back to her mom in September. Basically, so she can eat. Dig? Right now, John, I couldn't send my mother ten bucks if she were the one in jail. I'm just not the right person to ask it, right through here; nor will I be for a goodly while.

And that's not bullshit either.

Our friendship is going to have to consist of other things — talk, letters, good feelings, and the like. Not much when you're hungry. But that's what's there.

* * *

I understand why you're so excited about getting out. It's an exciting time for you, and the possibilities must look large as freedom itself. Does the prison have any program to help get you back into the real world? I know programs like that don't do all that much, but it may be something for you to get started with.

It was interesting to see the pictures of your family. And I really enjoyed looking at them. They look like good people — though I think I see a small, cold streak in your brother's eyes . . .? Well, he sent them to you. So he can't be all bad.

Do I go through times when I can't read? Ah, John . . . there are months when I think I've forgotten how to read fiction at all! The problem with being a professional writer is that you seldom read for pleasure. Also, the truth is, as you get older, no matter who you are, less and less fiction seems pleasurable at all—even things that you know are good. More than once I've asked myself in the last ten years, "What the hell are you writing it for if you can't stand reading it?" Though the truth is, I do pretty much enjoy reading my own.

Sometimes.

Yesterday, I got hold of a book of short stories by Raymond Carver, *What We Talk about When We Talk about Love*. They're very nice, very short, and Carver has a very precise eye for the way people in a state of despair try to pretend they're feeling something else entirely. And he lets the language flop about and clunk a bit, not just in the way that real people talk (which clever writers have been doing since back in Rome with Patronius Arbiter), but in the way real people might even, now and again, write about their own situations if someone asked them to put down what happened. And that's kind of interesting. But even so, you'd really have to work to write a duller bunch of tales.

Like I say, it's the problem of being a professional. You end up reading lots of stuff that you respect, but very little you honestly enjoy.

This has been a very hot and muggy summer, although over the last couple of days the weather in the city has taken a turn for the better. Last night I actually slept under a blanket for the first time since the end of June. Summer is always a slow-down in writing for me. Often, it's just too hot to work. And everyone has been complaining this year about what a muggy and depressing time we've had of it. There was even an article in some magazine recently about what a down summer it's been for so many people in the city.

Oddly, though, it hasn't been so bad for me. I think that's because last summer I broke out with these really awful sores under both my arms. I had them for about ten weeks; they hurt a lot, and just did me in.

This summer, wet as it's been, I haven't had them; and, by comparison, that's just been pure heaven.

One nice thing happened recently:

About a year ago, I did a little piece that just turned up in a magazine published in California, called *Fiction International*. My piece was in a collection of a lot of little pieces by lots of writers on *"Writing and Politics."* My contribution wasn't very interesting, I'm afraid; but one of the other writers in the issue turned out to be a guy named Harrison Fischer, who was a student of mine in a course I did last March up at SUNY Albany, where I taught a month-long workshop. He was one of my two favorite students in the class, too. It's always fun to see one of your ex-students get a piece published somewhere. It's happened to me about a dozen times, now—one of the little joys of life.

Well, it's about seven twenty-four in the morning. And I have to get on with the day.

Once again, thanks for all your letters. And your *two* stories. I've *really* enjoyed them!

I'll try to get at least one more letter to you by Sept. 6th. Let me know where you are and what you're doing when you get out. At this point (after all my huffing and puffing, too!), maybe it *would* be a good idea to write directly to the house for your next few letters. When I was going down to my agent's office twice a week, I could just pick up your letters there a day, or two at most, after they arrived. But for a while I'll only be seeing him, maybe, once a month or so. So write your next letter to my home address above.

Sorry this is so short, and not more . . . imaginative (if you know what I mean). But next time.

Good luck and good things!

Your friend,

• 35 •

To Camilla Decarnin

August 21st, 1984

Dear Mog,

I guess this is the long-promised letter — though Lord knows I don't feel like writing it; just physically. At 7:24 this morning, while I was at the word processor, writing a letter to a hustler friend, John (who's in jail in Florida), suddenly and unaccountably both sides of my back seized up, just about at the area of my kidneys. It hurts excruciatingly for fifteen minutes, then the major pain goes away, and it just aches for an hour or two. Then, suddenly, it happens again.

It's not quite 2:45 in the afternoon, and I've been through the whole process maybe three times today (not counting the minor twinges): And — you understand — this was a day where I worked all morning (four-thirty on), went to deliver a copy of *"We in Some Strange Power's Employ"* to D. C. Comics' Julie Schwarz (turns out, which I didn't know, they're on the 8th floor of the same office building [666 Fifth Avenue] that Bantam occupies the 24th, 25th, and 29th floors of), who wants to turn it into a comic book, then up to Bantam for an interview with Peter Heck of *Newsday* and *Xignals* at eleven, then down to see Henry, in the Village, who, out of the goodness of his heart, volunteered to front the moneys for some copies of the *Flight from Nevèrÿon* galleys, so I could finally send you same.

Only Henry's son-in-law and office manager, Danny (who is sweet and aspires to run a machine shop in Israel somewhere), took it on himself (1) to give me only two copies instead of the three I'd asked for and (2) to have them reduced by half! Yes, it's cheaper. But it means what I'm sending you is practically micro-type. And I was *un peu* pissed.

And this evening, I'm going to my first dinner engagement of the year, at Greg Frux's — and I just *refuse* to miss it. Besides, today I can't really afford to eat unless someone *does* feed me, and I would like to have *something* today; so I'm going.

But this seems to be how my life has been going of late.

The Rowena story, you ask?

July 10ᵗʰ, 1984 (same day as Lou assured me galleys and manuscripts were being sent to you):

While I was leaving his office, Lou said: "Oh, incidentally, Chip. We want to get Rowena to do the cover for the new *Nevèrÿon* book. Everyone here loved her cover-paintings for the first two volumes. But her agent told our art department that she was completely booked up, and there was no way she could have a cover painting done in time for us to do the book in February, when we have it scheduled for. Tell me; I know you know her. Do you think maybe you might give her a call and ask her if maybe she can adjust her schedule a little? Perhaps if it doesn't come through her agent...?"

"Sure," I said. "I can try."

And for the next five days I left messages on Rowena's phone machine. On July 15ᵗʰ, I was going in again to see Lou at three about something or other, and I thought: well, let me give Rowena one more call, and see if I can get her.

And lo and behold, when the ringing stopped, instead of the hiss of the prerecorded tape, there was Rowena's own permanently adolescent voice, piping: "Hello. Rowena Morell...?"

"Hi!" I said. "This is Chip Delany."

"Oh," she said. "I just got back from the country about an hour ago. I'd just finished going over my messages and was going to call you."

"Well," I said. "I'd actually called to ask you a favor. If you can't do it, please just say no and I'll understand. But me and everyone else at Bantam absolutely love the two covers you did for the first two *Nevèrÿon* books. I just finished the third volume, and we all wanted you to do the third cover. But your agent told Bantam that you were all booked up — and I was kind of wondering if there was *any* way you might be able to juggle your schedule around and fit us in. Otherwise, they'll have to delay the book from February, which is when they wanted to do it."

Rowena gave her silvery (and it really is) laugh, and said: "That's very funny, Chip. I'd be delighted to do the cover. Though I've got plenty of work, I'm not tied up all *that* solid. I've been away for the last five days, out in the country with my boyfriend," and Rowena is the only 30-year-old woman I know who talks seriously about a "boy"friend, totally without irony; perhaps it goes with looking permanently sixteen. She *is* lovely. "But there're no messages from Bantam on my machine here. And I don't *use* an agent. I work entirely by myself."

At which point *I* felt a little strange.

We talked a bit more, and laughed a bit over the confusion, and it ended with my saying:

"Well, they're pressed for time, I know. What would be a good time for somebody from Bantam to call you? I'm going in to see Lou at three this afternoon, and I can tell him."

"Well," said Rowena, "I'll be out this afternoon. But I'll be in tomorrow morning between ten and eleven."

And at three I went in to see Lou.

I gave him the discussion from my phone call with Rowena pretty much as I've given it to you. He was both surprised and not happy. (I don't think he was purposely lying to me; I think somebody else in the company had been giving him the run-around.) I gave him Rowena's phone number, just in case the art department had it wrong. While he was walking me back to the lobby (I think that's the day he gave me the first cover-proof — the one they're not using — for *Stars in My Pocket*), I said: "You know, it's probably just that they called her when she was off in the country. For some reason they didn't leave a message. And in the course of the story working its way back to you, somehow the agent and the rest crept into it, and it'll all turn out to be a funny misunderstanding."

"I hope so," said Lou. "Only the truth is, I don't think it's funny at all."

"Well, I said," I said, "you've got her proper phone number. And if someone calls her tomorrow between ten and eleven, you'll get her. She says she'd love to do it, and has the time."

At about eleven the next day — in fact it was ten after eleven, as I recall — I called Rowena. "Did anyone from Bantam call you yet?"

No, they hadn't.

"Just a second," I said. "Let me call Bantam, and I'll call you right back. "

So I did. Lou's assistant, David Stern, told me Lou was in conference with someone right then. Well, I said, could you possibly just slip in and say I'd mentioned that no one had gotten to Rowena yet . . . ?

I'll slip him a note, David said.

And a minute later, he was back. Lou had said that, yesterday, it had been delegated to Linda Gray in the Art Department. She would be taking care of it.

I called Rowena. "Look," I told her. "You know how slow these big companies are. Someone will be calling you from Bantam in the next few days." (I thought that was giving them enough margin.) And we hung up.

I believe I saw Lou once after that about a week later, and asked quite casually if they'd gotten to Rowena, really expecting him to say that it was all taken care of. He was sure they had. I said, as lightly as I could, well, you know you said you were pressed for time. Maybe you should check and make sure Linda got to it. Yes, he said, he really must do that. And by then I thought I'd pretty much done what I could. Lou has other writers to take care of besides me. There just didn't seem to be any reason to harp on it.

Cut to Thursday, August 3rd:

Shortly after five o'clock I got a call from Rowena. She just thought she ought to let me know that no one from Bantam had yet called her. No, she didn't hold it against me. She understood how these things worked. She was by no means begging for the job, but since I'd called her about it, she was just returning the favor.

I was surprised. After I talked to her, I called Henry.

"I don't want to sound paranoid," I said. "But . . ." and I told him what had happened.

"I'll call Lou," Henry said. "And I'll let you know what's going on."

Friday, Henry called me. "We've got an explanation," he explained. It seems that three days before (c. the 1st/2nd of August), the Bantam Art Director of more than 30 years, Len Leone, had officially announced his resignation. Apparently within the company, this had been known about for some two or three weeks. Directives had been issued that no one in the company was to mention this to anyone outside till it became official. But the result had been that the art department had been thrown into complete chaos. Things were in a state of total paralysis. It was fair to say that nothing had gotten done in the entire company as far as artwork went for nearly a month.

But now that the resignation had been officially announced, we could expect things to move a bit back to normal as soon as the new Art Director was announced. No, everybody *really* wanted Rowena to do the cover. But nobody had any authority to commission anything until there was someone in the driver's seat to approve it.

Lou phoned me himself, minutes later, apologized. Yes, now things would be going on more like normal.

It made sense to me. I called Rowena. It made sense to her. "So," I concluded, "somebody will be getting to you, if not in a couple of days, then in a week or so."

"Okay," and Rowena laughed.

Cut to Monday, August 20th:

On Saturday, I'd spent the day with Robert Morales, comparing galleys/manuscript for "The Mummer's Tale." I'd done enough re-writing on it since it went to the printer so that I really needed help to insert all the micro-changes. Friday and Sunday I went over "Fog/Granite" and *"Plagues/Carnivals."* Basically, as galleys go, they seemed in pretty good shape.

When the galleys had first arrived, however (and I only found out that they were in the office because I happened to call Mary Lucas, the mass-market managing editor, and asked; and she told me, yes, I sent them to Lou yesterday), I noticed right away that they had been set in ten-on-eleven, a typeface one point smaller than the type used in *Triton, Tales of Nevèrÿon,* and *Neveryóna.* (Indeed, it's the type size that was used in *Dhalgren.*) It's a type size reserved for either very long books (as in the case of the big *D*) or books the company deems "unimportant": the smaller type means they can save the odd signature's worth of pages.

Well, they couldn't very well have made the decision on the type size on the basis of length (as Mary agreed, when I asked her if there was any way to run the tape through again at the larger type size), since *Neveryóna,* which was published in rack-size only three months ago at the larger point, is approximately 30,000 words *longer* than *Flight* . . .

Monday was also exactly one week *beyond* the date Henry had given Lou to get the cover mess cleared up, one way or another. Henry called me to say that he'd called Lou. Lou was not in. Would I mind calling Rowena just to *see* if they'd gotten hold of her yet . . .?

She wasn't in at four. But around six, I got her. No. No one from Bantam had yet called. And Tuesday morning — yesterday when I began this letter — I left a message at Henry's (when I went to pick up the *Nevèrÿon* galley copies) that, indeed, they hadn't.

Well, as I was rising from an hour's nap, just before I went off to dinner at Greg's last evening (see paragraph 3), Henry called to say that he hadn't gotten Lou, and he would, in the next day or two, be on his way up the corporate ladder, trying to get them to straighten things out.

I mentioned the type-size — and also reminded him of the rather controversial nature of the book (a gay Sword & Sorcery collection, whose last 68,000-word novella deals with AIDS); and one in which, from the beginning, Lou's complaint was that there would be marketing difficulties because there wasn't enough fantasy in it.

"Is this just a case of your basic black paranoid gay SF writer?" I asked Henry. "Or could it be that this is their way, not exactly of sabotaging the book, but of consigning it to the realm of those projects of no importance and no priority, the ones they try to skim over as though they don't really exist, and which — without really mounting a full-scale conspiracy — they hope will sink without a trace and be, they pray, totally ignored?"

"That," said Henry, "is very possible. It's happened before at Bantam. It will no doubt happen again. I'll see what we can do to make sure it isn't happening to you."

And that's the tale up until yesterday, when I went out to dinner, where, of course, I talked of none of this.

The evening itself was fun. Greg's lover, Gill, had me down, along with Greg and some others, with the promise of a lamb dinner, cooked by a cooking friend of his, Hank. But apparently the painters had been working in the apartment (on Greenwich Street, in the same building where Baird Searles and Martin Last used to live) all weekend and had *not* finished Monday night as promised, and were indeed still doing final trim when I walked in.

So Gill took all six of us out to the Peking Duck Palace in Chinatown, which was truly a treat.

Beforehand, there was a wait in a flooded subway station, with water pouring from the ceiling and people standing back against the wall, trying to avoid a soaking from the internal rain. And afterwards, coming home at about eleven, I watched the workmen, under the street light, across from Central Park, laboring on into the night, over the torn-up pavement, with their pumps and sluices, getting at the water main that had broken earlier and flooded the station when I'd first gone down.

Thanks for your consolations on the fleetingness of Gloria Monday (Mundi — believe me, that was an unintentional typo. Otherwise, I'd never let it stand!). They gave me a chuckle.

Iva gets back from camp on Saturday. Although I'm looking forward to it, the money situation is going to be a little grim. But not to worry. Somehow one manages.

Re your comment about writing turning into "ought to" work, I *certainly* know the feeling.

What was it Isak Dinesen said? "I try to write a little every day without either hope or despair." Well, as you get older, that's the way you do it. More and more. And I really don't think you have a choice. The point is, the hope goes. But the despair will hang around no matter what. So you put your intellectual effort into banishing the despair; if you do that and don't waste thought yearning after the vanished hope, you may be able to break even on the pain/pleasure meter — if not come out the tiniest bit ahead.

But any other strategy is simply going to mean misery, and that probably holds true even if you've just received that telegram from the Swedish Academy about this big prize they want to give to you this October up in Oslo...

I went to show the "disclaimer" (for want of a better word) that you'll find at the end of *Plagues and Carnivals* to some folks at the Gay Men's Health Crisis. They were very supportive and told me to include the hotline number. I may, indeed, even do a recreational writing workshop for people with AIDS under their auspices, though where I'll find the time, the dear only knows. But some things you make time for.

I really would like any of your thoughts about *Flight*, no matter how brutal. At this point, the only people who have read it are me, Lou, the Bantam secretary who proof-read it, and Frank. I don't even think Henry has had time to read the first or the third story, yet. (He said he liked the middle one, which he looked over when he was sending it to various places that didn't want it.)

Well.

Along with the galleys, I'm enclosing a manuscript mailer and six bucks towards first class postage. *If* you feel like it, and *if* you have the time, you might, while reading it, make corrections on these micro-galleys [?] in red ballpoint or red pencil and return them to me; I'll be able to incorporate the corrections at page proof stage if they arrive here in New York by September 20th. It's not a lot of time, but it's not two/three days either; and at least, if you decide to, you won't be out the postage and wrapping costs!

If you don't have the time, or the energy, or it's in the least difficult for *any* reason, please don't do it!

Couple of recent thoughts (or, really, not so recent) on AIDS:

On the one hand, it's just not the kind of thing you can ask anybody to stake his (or her) life on, but more and more the statistics of AIDS suggests a two-population spread for the disease, much like hepatitis-B. Both Harvy Marks ["Peter"] and myself are immune to hepatitis-B, at this point; we've both been tested, and our bodies are swarming with antibodies to the disease. But eight or nine years ago, Harvy was sick with it for nearly a year, in bed for three months, and on a restricted diet for months more and unable to work, while I never even knew I had it and didn't lose even the unexplained pound.[1] And today, of course, it's known that the majority of promiscuous gay men went through it in the way I did, not in the way Harvy did — though no one knows what separates the two populations, yet. (The suspicion, however, is that it's the body's general level of resistance.) What the two-population spread (for AIDS, hepatitis, or anything else for that matter) means is that, on the one hand, you have a small population who, for any reasons ranging from genetic to dietetic to god-only-knows, are suscepti-

---

[1] At the time, one of the symptoms of AIDS most widely talked about was "an unexplained loss of weight."

ble to a dangerous and symptomatic case of the disease and, when they're infected (with the HTLV-3 virus, say), they come down with a fatal form of AIDS. On
the other hand, you have a much larger population that (for whatever complementary reasons), when they catch the virus, develop antibodies, kill the virus off,
and come down with something no more serious that the common cold, if even
that. Given the amount and prevalence of gay sex, this is the *only* way to account
for the *phenomenally slow* spread of the disease.

As the American Secretary General announced on TV more than a year ago,
AIDS has got to be one of the *least* contagious diseases we've ever had to fight.

Yes, the two population-spread will have to be proved. But, really, if it were
anything else, you would just have a run-away logarithmic growth, among both
gays and straights. And you don't. Even with the damper on the curve that (as
some have suggested) AIDS doesn't transmit orally but only anally (or transmits
much more easily anally than orally), you'd still have some sort of clear geometric progression. And though it's rising, it's flattened out to an almost pure, if
erratic, arithmetic increase at this point.

No, I'm not living my life as though this were the case (assuming that I must,
therefore, be among the immune). But I'd be willing to bet that, within five years,
this is what we'll be hearing — or, indeed, as soon as the HTLV-3 antibody test
becomes widespread enough.[2]

The one little statistical check Harvy himself did using the GMHC's figures:
There was clearly no one-to-one correlation between people who came down
with symptomatic hepatitis-B and people who came down with AIDS, nor was
there any one-to-one correlation between people who (like me) got asymptomatic
hepatitis-B (the majority) and people who came down with AIDS. So (although
it's still only anecdotal evidence until it's checked on a larger scale) we can make
a pretty good (unofficial) guess that it's not the same two-population spread for
both AIDS and hepatitis-B.

All my love,

• 36 •

TO JOHN P. MUELLER

September 1st, 1984

Dear John,

I'm going to drop this in the mailbox at the general Post office at 34th Street this
afternoon, in hopes that it reaches you before the 6th of September. Once again, up
until late yesterday afternoon I've been buried in a swamp of work: more galleys,
which I just handed in yesterday afternoon.

Also, because my daughter, Iva, is with us and home, things have been going
a bit more slowly than usual. Well, those are my excuses for not getting around to

---

[2] This perfectly erroneous theory is a good indication of how little information was available on transmission vectors of the disease, even three months after the American announcement by Secretary of
Health Margaret Heckler of Gallo's work on the virus (April 24th, 1984). (Montaigner's work, which preceded Gallo's in France, was all-but-unknown in this country until several years later.) The real explanation for the 'two populations' among gay men is simply preferences for oral or anal sex among men. The
virus is not spread by 'gay' sex. The virus *is* spread by anal sex — to both men and women.

writing you until this morning.

Got your last letter. I'm glad you understand about the money.

Don't feel bad about asking — as long as you don't feel bad about the answer.

What about your immediate plans after you get out? You probably won't have time to write me about them before you actually leave the jailhouse. And I know once you *do* get out, you won't have so much time for writing letters.

Still, I've very much enjoyed hearing from you. A couple of times now I've read over all your letters in a bunch (there're fourteen of them!) — not just the last three! — and it's been almost like sitting down and talking to you. Like you say, friends are good things to have, even if just for knowing that someone likes you and wants good things to happen to you.

If you have time to drop me another line, tell me if you'll be coming straight back north. Or if you'll be staying in Florida for a while. (It's already getting a little chilly up here — a little *too* chilly for living on the street, that is.) I know you said your father wants you to work for him again. That sounds really good.

I wish I had time to write another story for you! In fact, I've got one in my head, very much with you in mind, and given the one you wrote about your own fantasies and what I know about you, you just might find it fun. If you do stay down in Florida for at least a month or so (somehow that seems most likely, yes?), once you get an address, let me know what it is, and in a couple of weeks I'll have time to knock it out for you and send it on.

You've sent me three to my one! Somehow, kid, I think I'm coming out the winner, here!

But send me your outside address, and I'll catch up to you!

Oh, yeah. One kind of funny thing. I'd said something about "finger fucking" in my letter to you . . .? (You know, of course, my thing about hands and fingers like yours.) And, in your *very* fine "literary" efforts, you were very obliging. The only thing is, I meant in the mouth! Not that I'm complaining about what you wrote — all three of them were really great — but I more or less feel about *anything* going up my ass pretty much the same way as you do! At any rate, when I realized I hadn't been clear, it just kind of made me laugh, is all.

Leaving jail is going to be a big change — in many ways, of course, for the better. But in some ways it gives you some of the same problems as leaving the army. For better or worse, someone's been seeing that you were fed and that you had a place to sleep. And now all that stops.

As I've told you, I've had a couple of friends who've spent their whole lives bouncing in and out of jail. In a couple of cases, I really think the reason they kept on getting into trouble and going back was, frankly, because when they got into trouble was the only time *anyone* ever paid any attention to them — even if the attention was just some cops yelling at them and beating them up and hauling them in, and then having to go to court and be tried and sentenced. For weeks at a time, when they *weren't* in trouble, nobody ever even *spoke* to them!

So if you ever find that you're feeling that nobody gives a shit and you're thinking why don't you go out and get drunk and do something dumb, write me a letter. And (eventually!) I'll write back.

The other thing that you've got going for you is that you read books. It's a funny thing, but it's true. The guys I've known who have been able to come out and make it on the outside have all been readers. It's like developing a whole host of different kinds of friends, from all times and places. A good thing to do is to try reading not only the kinds of books you know you're going to like. From time to time, try to pick up a book outside the sort that you usually can trust yourself to enjoy and just make yourself go through it. You'll be surprised at the kind of pay-off that starts to bring you in very little time.

A couple of thoughts about the alcoholism. I'd imagine in jail you don't get much — if anything — to drink. When you get out, probably the first beer you'll have will taste like hell and make you feel pretty bad to boot. So why don't you just go with it, as it were, and try not even to get started on it?

You remember I put away my share of beer (not to mention whatever) too. Well, for the last six months or more, I haven't been able to afford to drink. And somehow, I didn't drink anything for three months at all. I wasn't trying to do it — between work and poverty, it just came out that way. Well, about a month back, I dropped over to a friend's house, and he offered me a can of beer.

I drank it, and it tasted like shit and half an hour later, I had a headache.

So I said to myself, why not take this as a blessing? John, I haven't had another one since. (And the only difference is, now I don't feel like I want one which had not been the case up till then.) And although for a person in my financial condition, boasting about not drinking is kind of like a one-legged man boasting about never kicking his dog, I'm still sort of proud of myself.

So, if it gives you any moral support, know that your friend Chip, here, is off the suds as well.

Oh, well, enough of this preaching. I know you get more than your share where you are. (I can see you reading some of the sections of some of my letters, and saying to yourself: "Hey, I wish this cocksucker would just shut up!" Well, think of it as noise to pass the time. [And remember what a halfway decent cocksucker I am! Side thought: You know, another fantasy of mine was to have a friend who'll called me "Cocksucker" just as a kind of friendly nickname. Some day I'm going to get a letter from somebody that starts, "Dear cocksucker," and I'll probably cum in my pants! I tell you, it's great to be appreciated for what you do (or try to do) well! Isn't it strange? Nowadays, everybody — especially blacks — just calls every body else "sucker." But somehow plain "sucker" just doesn't do it for me, you know? Maybe I've lived into an age not mine. Anyway. Maybe someday when it'll be useful, some of what I've said will come back to you. Not as a warning. Just as a help. That's what I hope, anyway.] I can just bet this is one hell of an exciting week for you. You must be bouncing off the walls with anticipation!

Well. A slew of cousins have come into town from various other cities, some of whom have never met my daughter. So we'll be going up to see them later today.

Right now it's about two minutes to seven in the morning. I've been up since about quarter past five, puttering at this and that.

And after this letter, I go back to it.

Good luck on everything. Enjoy your freedom. And use it to do fine and wonderful things for yourself and others that'll make you feel great about yourself and the world!

• 37 •

September 2nd, 1984

Dear Victor Gonzales,

Thanks for your letter of July 31st. I'm sorry that it's taken me a month or more to get back to you, but things have been a mite hectic. The final production work on *Stars in My Pocket like Grains of Sand* segued directly into the production work on *Flight from Nevèrÿon,* the galleys for which were just turned in this past Friday, and it's Monday.

All three errors that you sighted in *Stars/Sand* have already been caught. But thanks for pointing them out. Concomitantly, Bantam is bringing out a new printing of *Dhalgren* this Christmas. In the sixteenth printing, they finally got 'round (after ten years!) to correcting about 150-odd errors — in the course of which they introduced half a dozen new ones! And through the offices of myself and various friends, another dozen-plus have come to light. As far as I know, these more or less complete all corrections that I would want to make in the text. And Bantam has promised me to insert them in the seventeenth printing, forthcoming.

Your correction on p. 250 is, I hope, the last to go onto the list! (The list will only work for the sixteenth printing, as half a dozen of the corrections on it remedy errors made in correcting other typos in the sixth through fifteenth printings!) It's kind of an interesting one and is the trace of a former layer of re-writing.

In an earlier draft of *Dhalgren,* the Richards family was indeed moving from seventeen-A to nineteen-B. In my mother's co-op building, on which the Labrys Apartments are loosely modeled, apartments A and B are directly across the hall from one another, and are mirror images (as, indeed, are apartments F and E). But as I read over the text, I realized that, for most people, apartments A and B suggest apartments contiguous on the same side of the hallway. So, somewhere about the seventh or eighth draft, I decided to separate the apartment letters by a bit, and the current letters were decided on. (In Morningside Gardens, these would be apartments diagonally across from one another at opposite ends of the hall, which indeed would *also* be [double] mirror images of one another; this way the internal veracity seems higher [it strengthens the feel of truth]; as well, the modular veracity with the real is also preserved, if anyone thought it important enough to check . . .

Apparently, when I was making the change, I missed one mention (now on p. 250), and in the course of all the various corrections (first in the sixth printing, then again in the sixteenth), nobody caught it until you did.

Well, as you can see in the list I'm including with this letter, it's now on the correction sheet that goes in to Bantam tomorrow morning. (And which they may — honoring their promise — make use of, or, indeed, as they have done for fourteen out of the book's sixteen printings, they may ignore.) The corrections there added to the corrections made in the sixteenth printing should yield an all-but-perfect text.

Many thanks!

There's a similar instance of over-rewriting in *Madame Bovary,* which has become something of an emblem for all us compulsive revisers, where Flaubert has one of his characters counting out 51 francs in two franc pieces — again, a trace of a former draft where the character was counting out fifty-*six* francs instead of fifty-one.

It's probably somewhat ingenuous of me to feel like I'm in good company.

I'm also enclosing a draft of an article very similar to the one I delivered as my talk in Seattle. Alas, there is no completely written-out version of the talk as I delivered it. But you are welcome to the paper that formed the basis of it. It was originally published (in French) in a journal called *Cahier Confrontation* out of Paris, about two years back. Although I have used it for the basis of several talks, it's never appeared in English before.

If you publish it, do let me know when it may appear and send me a file copy.

Hoping that we see each other soon and have some more good conversation, I send you

All best wishes,

• 38 •

To Camilla Decarnin

September 1st, 1984

Dear Mog,

"Well," Frank said, folding the blue fitted sheet (the white elastic in the corner slipped from the Formica counter to the 82nd Street Laundromat's floor, behind rippling Prussian), "it *doesn't* tell you how they did their laundry."

I nodded, getting another T-shirt out of the yellow plastic basket on its aluminum casters, turning it deftly right-side out, folding in the arms, folding up the bottom, then adding it to the pile of T-shirts on the table corner.

That's Frank's comment (and my agreement) on Dorothy Farnan's *Auden in Love*, a new book that details the 30-odd year relation between W. H. Auden and Chester Kallman.

I confess that, though Frank devoured it, I've only dipped in, here and there. Still, my criticism of what I've read so far is that Farnan (older than Chester by a year and married to his father, Dr. Edward Kallman) seems to have no idea of the range of "normal" homosexual coupling habits, so that she's always comparing the Auden/Kallman *menage* (either directly or by implication) to a traditional middle-class heterosexual marriage. Against that model, *all* her judgments are untrustworthy, and finally you find yourself — at least if you're gay — questioning any and all information she presents in whatever form, unless it's a quote or a name and address.

On the other hand, you also find yourself reading *through* the book and constructing a revised picture of your own. But then, this has been the experience of gay readers (and I suspect, by this time, a good many who are not gay but nevertheless know something about the topic) with "official reports" of anything having to do with homosexuality for years. Even as a child I did it almost automatically. I remember one of the first times I became aware that that *was* what I was doing — and to what extent I was doing it; and how untrustworthy this revisionary process had to be since it was a personal, reactionary fiction imposed on what was already a conservative lie — was when I read Enid Starkie's Rimbaud biography, stretched out in the loft bed at 110 East 13th Street, back c. 1971. When you're gay, it's comforting to think that you have a ready algorithm that can take the official misreport and translate it into "truth." But, sadly, it's *just* comfort you're getting. Not history. That's why we need our Jonathan Katzes and our John Boswells.

Most intriguing, of course, was the way all Bob Bravard's and my huggermugger of '82 over the misplaced Auden letters has contributed to Ms. Farnan's efforts.

We have been referred to in the acknowledgements by the most indirect citation I think I've *ever* seen: "I am also grateful to Professor Mendelson for his permission to publish Auden's poems and letters, particularly the new letters he himself discovered," she writes. From the text, I can *only* assume that these "new letters he himself discovered" are the letters that Bob Bravard and I started the ball rolling for the return of back then. . .? Or did I tell you about that? Oh, well . . .

The book was just reviewed in this Sunday's *New York Times Book Review* by John Fuller. His article suffers from the same uncritical hypostasis of heterosexual norms as the book itself. The model that sees Chester as some sort of ungrateful monster endlessly torturing the Great Man by his unfaithfulness is nonsense. No doubt they had their problems. Who doesn't? But they were the problems of an "open" relationship, not a "closed" one. My first social reports of Auden and Kallman were from an elementary school friend, Johnny Kronenberger, the son of Louis and Emmy Kronenberger. (Auden collaborated with Louis on a number of occasions, most notably on *The Viking Book of Aphorisms*.) Johnny remained a friend up through the first years of my marriage. Auden and Kallman were regular attendees at the Kronenbergers' annual Christmas party; and besides being the first one to give me their 77 St. Marks Place address and urge us to go see them, Johnny would also regale me with accounts of Chester's impersonations of Diana Trilling (which apparently put everyone on the floor with laughter) and like outrageousnesses at these winter fêtes on 96th Street and Lexington Avenue, where Johnny's family lived in a narrow three-story private house with deep green walls and darkly varnished wooden paneling and an entire room called "the library," where, here and there, besides the open shelves, were rows of leather-bound books behind glass. (The Trillings, Lionel and Diana, were also friends of the Kronenbergers.) People tended to like both of them, including Mr. and Mrs. K—and Johnny had been fond of both since his childhood. (I believe he once told me that either Wystan or Chester had baby-sat for him and his sister Liza on a couple of occasions, but I may be misremembering that.) But what became perfectly clear, after even five minutes, on the night in '62 when Auden and Kallman came to dinner with Marilyn and me on East 5th Street, was simply that Chester was far more socially at ease than Wystan. And I'm sure that, in the day-to-day dealings with store owners, taxi-drivers, landlords, drop-in acquaintances, and the like, Chester had a far easier time in the world. The general biographical consensus seems to be that, after three years, "all sex went out of their relationship." Nevertheless, well after that three years they were sharing lovers, both established ones and casually picked up ones. (This sort of thing is absolutely beyond Ms. Farnan—and, I suspect, Mr. Fuller too—either to comprehend or even to mention. Quite possibly she just didn't know.) But if both of you are picking up men, say, bringing them home, and one of you has sex while the other waits in the kitchen, then you switch off, I'm afraid that gives an entirely different context to a statement like: "There's no sex between *us* anymore."

The book's general style—only a step or two above that of a '50s true confessions magazine, however amusing parts of it are—does not militate for a memorable volume.

At any rate, I may give you more thoughts on it when I've read more of it. Or then, again, I may not . . .

Iva has been back from summer camp for ten days now. She goes to her mother's this morning (September 4th) at eleven. (It's not quite 5:30 now, while I'm writing. I've been up for about an hour and a half. Outside it's black and rainy.) Marilyn—just back, as of a phone call yesterday, from Yaddo, up at Saratoga—had enrolled Iva in a riding program for the week, between her return from Vermont and the beginning of school, up at the Claremont stables, where Iva's been taking riding lessons lo these four/five years now.

Right after she got back, we had two days of preadolescent kvetching: soul-piercing arguments of the sort one can *only* get into with a ten-year-old, where, beyond the tears, one glimpses all of moral life and psychological autonomy strewn in compromised ruins: Does or does *not* the weather warrant an undershirt this morning? ("But I don't *want* to wear one, daddy! I don't care *how* cold it is!") It was enough to make Frank say, while we were waiting for her to get home at one on the third day of her riding program, "I hope she's in a better mood than she was yesterday!"

"Well," I said, "don't *expect* her to be in a bad one. It'll only reinforce it if she is."

"I'll try," Frank said.

Twenty minutes later, she rang the bell. I opened the door, and called hello to her down the stairwell. She came tramping up in her riding boots and declared: "I just had the best day of my life! Absolutely the best!" *Every*thing had gone well, she explained, from the time I'd walked her up to the stables till now. Her horse had behaved superbly. Both her teacher and her fellow riders had complimented her. And on her way home, she'd looked into an open cellar door in time to see a gray mother cat having her fifth (!) kitten, last in a litter of five, there in the cement's protected shadow. After a quick tuna-fish sandwich, she went into her room and (an absolute first!) cleaned it up from the top of her upper bunk bed to underneath her work table, complete with final vacuuming, all without a word from either Frank or me!

The next day began cheerfully enough. That morning Iva's group was scheduled to have its end-of-season "show" — a mini-event; not like the big ones, in which she's done so well, these last three Februaries. Parents could come—and I'd planned to go up and see her. One reason I'd walked her up to the stables that morning was to find out what time the indoor events were scheduled.

Some kids in black velvet helmets, jodhpurs and rat-catchers or polo shirts were milling before the Claremont's big red-paneled door, chattering around Matthew (a rather solid, black-haired young man in riding boots and a ratty green T-shirt); 11:30 was the time I should come, he told me. I said good-bye, went back to the house, bought a bagel (my breakfast), did some work, and at 11:15 took off to the stable again.

Under the dark and broad-beamed ceiling, standing on the mixed loam and dried horse-shit covering the ramp up into the rink (it smells like a warm, sweaty, friendly drunk standing much too close), along with three or four other parents I watched the kids pace their ponies for the red-headed woman judge; with their intense young riders, the horses walked, cantered, posted and reversed direction to the caller's echoing, "Trot on, now! Trot on! . . . Seated trot, now! Seated trot!" by the peeling walls.

Most of the kids had been there for the whole summer, while Iva was off camping in Vermont. Since Iva was the last to join the group, she'd been given a horse that was very much what was left of the leavings. She'd complained of having had trouble with him several times, but the day before, as I said, she'd told us she'd gotten him to behave perfectly. Hanging from the wooden board that serves as a window guard behind the top bunk in her room, she has a string of second- and third-place ribbons from the much larger and more competitive shows she's been in both at Claremont and at other places. But that morning her rather big-bellied gray nag did everything a horse can do not to cooperate; it kept wanting to swing over and look at something by the wall; it kept trying to break from a canter into a forbidden gallop; and though, that day, no ribbons were awarded (the non-spoils of a "mini-event"), Iva was judged fourth in the group of four. The girl two years older and a head shorter than she, who has taken the blue ribbon in Iva's class for the last three Claremont horse shows—nudging Iva down to second place—again came in first. And two nondescript boys took nondescript second and third. Iva had been trying hard, and she *is* a good rider. But when she came into the office, her jaw was set against tears.

Holding in that bit of pity and terror your child's tragedies settle so sharply in your abdomen, somewhere below your navel (eat your solar plexus out, Aristotle!), I gave her a hug—which she shrugged off—and told her that I thought the horse's difficulties were very real, that she'd clearly tried hard, and that she shouldn't feel bad. "Well, I do," was all she said, and threw herself down in the ratty old armchair, staring out from under her black flocked visor.

I gave her another hug and left her to finish up the day.

When she got home, she was still glum.

A little later, though, the sound of the broom on the floor came from her room. And minutes after that, she walked into my office and asked: "Daddy, do we have an old sheet?" I got her one. And over the next two hours she turned her room into an Arabian harem, with curtains about her bunk bed, the whole draped with various boas, lamé scarves, and gypsy shawls from among her "dress-up" clothes. She seemed to be in a fine mood by the time hamburgers and corn-on-the-cob came round for dinner.

I was talkative and relieved.

Well, September's weather has plunged into the premature chill that, no doubt, will be with us till our (as they use to call it in your city) "annual unseasonable October hot spell" comes along—Indian summer.

Last night I read Mandelstam's glittering 1925 autobiographical memoir, *The Noise of Time*. If you could combine, in some formal mosaic (and not in some emulsified porridge!) the impressionistic flights of Mandelstam with, say, the analytic acuity you find in Barthes (but not, oddly, in *Roland Barthes by Roland Barthes*), I think you'd really solve the problem of post-modern autobiography. It's interesting that, Goethe's *Dichtung und Warheit*, George Sand's *My Convent Life*, and Wagner's *Mein Leben* aside, the best *modern* autobiographies (unlike my favorite biographies) are short: Nabokov's *Speak, Memory*, Louise Bogan's *Journey Around My Room*, Pasternak's *Safe Conduct* — though *Bound for Glory* (Woody Guthrie), always one of my prizes, is certainly a decent-sized book.

Mandelstam writes, in a much quoted passage that opens Chapter XIII of *Shum vremeni* (*The Noise of Time*—though note: Nabokov usually translated *shum* as "hubbub"): "My desire is to speak not about myself but to track down the age, the noise and the germination of time. My memory is inimical to all that is personal. If it depended on me, I should only make a wry face in remembering the past. I was never able to understand the Tolstoys and Aksakovs, all those grandson Bagrovs, enamoured of family archives with their epic domestic memoirs — my memory is not loving but inimical. A *raznochinets* [an intellectual disaffected from any particular class interests] needs no memory—it is enough for him to tell of the books he has read, and his biography is done."

I think if Professor Brown had taken the daring leap of translating the word now rendered "personal" as "interpersonal," the passage would make more sense in light of the recollections around it. For these impressions of the Summer Garden in old Petersburg, of the Jewish quarter in Riga, of the concerts at Nobility Hall, and of the high and vaulted halls of the Tenishev school (which, a decade later, Nabokov was to attend as a student) could not be *more* idiosyncratic, *more* personal. Brown himself writes in his introduction: "And yet what are we to do with the plain fact of the matter: that all of Mandelstam's prose is intensely and immediately personal when it is not openly autobiographical?" What is missing in the memoir is the novelistic priority of personal *relationships*. Even the portraits of his fellow students ("Barats. His family intimate with Stasjulevich (*Messenger of Europe*). A passionate mineralogist, mute as a fish, talks only of quartz and mica." Or: "Leonid Zarubin. Large coal-mining industry in the Dan Basin. To begin with, dynamos and batteries; later on, nothing but Wagner.") are tiles in a dim, glimmering and gold mosaic. Even Mandelstam's Jewish grandparents in Riga, or, later, his contemporary friends Boris Sanani or Sergej Ivanych, or the comic portraits of the old Julij Matveich or the theater manager, Komizarzevkaja ("Vera Fedrovna Komizarzevska [1864-1910]," reads the bland note at the back of the book), each of whom receives a whole chapter, are given as glittering constellations of single and successive impressions, not as continuous and coherent fictive subjects, interrelating now with the young poet, now with the others around them.

But if we take Mandelstam at his word, biography can't have been what he was after, anyway—since books as reading experiences are not part of the "hubbub" any more than are relationships: They appear mostly as dusty heaps at the bottom of some bookshelf, as whatever text waits inside the much stained cover of his mother's Pushkin; the closest we get to texts *per se* are his impressions of the various recitation styles of the participants reading bits of Natikin, Gogol, or Nekrasov at a school literary program.

In the early pages, Nadson emerges as a kind of auctorial presence, loved and revered by the young, the focus of an almost Byronic cult: But even he is not rendered as the writer of specific books, poems, essays, letters, and journals (all of which were widely available and widely read at the time), absorbed, felt, responded to, and reported on, however impressionistically. In Mandelstam's evocation he is, rather, the coloring atmosphere in which the Russian young of a certain intellectual bent tended to move before the Revolution of 1905.

Yet I feel wholly in sympathy with what I take to be Mandelstam's project: "My desire is . . . to track down the age, the noise and germination of time." In a sense, I suppose, that's what the best biographical attempts should do, whether or not they indulge—as do the rest of us—in the fictions of love, friendship, influence, approval, disapproval, envy or enmity.

But I suspect we are to take the noise, the hubbub, the hum of time as the sensory and ephemeral specificity of life that, for all it makes up of our lives while they are happening to us, is nevertheless precisely in excess of the Prose of the World — the logic, the arguments, the structures, the subjective relations and objective patterns that most fiction and non-fiction texts strive to pull out of the world; and which, certainly in terms of literature, Mandelstam himself dealt with adequately enough in his essays on Villon and Chenier and Pushkin, in the dozens of reviews and letters written throughout his life that today make up the daunting volume from the émigré publishers, Ardis (725 pages of it, including the index), *Mandelstam: The Complete Critical Prose and Letters.*

There are odd sections in *Shum vremeni* that strike false notes to the American reader: Chapter XI, "The Erfurt Program," gives the poet's impressions of the political youth group he belonged to as a boy; it rings somewhat shrilly, not because of the politics expressed: "Yes, I heard with the sharpness of ears caught by the sound of a distant threshing machine in the field the burgeoning and increase, not of the barley in its ear, not of the northern apple, but of the world, the capitalist world, that was ripening in order to fall!" Since we haven't fallen yet, and since the most virulent Marxist critics are beginning to admit that, *vis-a-vis* the Gulag, *something* positive must be going on in the U. S. A., one shrugs at this and reads on. Nevertheless, while reading, one notes that the text has shifted its rhetoric profoundly: "Early, O Erfurt Program, you Marxist propeylaea, too early did you train our spirits to a sense of harmoniousness, but to me and to many others you gave a sense of life in those prehistoric years when thought hungered after unity and harmoniousness, when the backbone of the age was coming erect, when the heart needed more than anything the red blood of the aorta!" The final clauses bring us back to a specificity more characteristic of Mandelstam's other prose than that opening bombast—though I doubt "blood" and "backbone" are very far from political clichés in Russia either. As to the opening apostrophe, I don't know if it seems more skillful and sincere in Russian than in English; but as it's the only apostrophe in the book, there's no context against which I can read it more generously.

We know Mandelstam's tragic history — his death in a forced labor camp, on the far side of the uneasy border between sanity and insanity, slowly freezing to death, emaciated, trying to live off the camp's garbage heap or stealing food from the other prisoners, terrified of being poisoned. Stalin, in his horrendous and paranoid attempt to obliterate all dissent throughout Asia, had heard of a single poem that Mandelstam read to five "friends" one evening in Boris Pasternak's apartment, in November, 1933, containing references to "The Kremlin Mountaineer," his fingers "fat as grubs," "The murderer and peasant slayer." One "friend" had reported it to the secret police. (The name of the betrayer, who died even before Mandelstam, is seldom mentioned.) It's known Stalin himself knew of it; he short-ly phoned Pasternak about Mandelstam personally. Still, to think that this pro-party passage in the memoir published eight years earlier is parody or conscious deception is naive: Were it intentional, it would have been more skillfully done. But, once it is left behind, Mandelstam's finale to the book is as wonderful as any I know of in any *biographia literaria*:

Reviewing what the greater period that little space of his memoir (c. 1894-1906 or '07) completed, he wrote:

> "Looking back at the entire nineteenth century of Russian culture — shat-tered, finished, unrepeatable, which no one must repeat, which no one dares repeat—I wish to hail the century, as one would hail settled weather, and I see in it the unity lent it by the measureless cold which welded decades together in one day, one night, one profound winter, within which the terrible State glowed, like a stove, with ice.
>
> "And in this wintry period of Russian history, literature, taken at large, strikes me as something patrician, which puts me out of countenance: with trembling I lift the film of waxed paper above the winter cap of the writer. No one is to blame in this and there is nothing to be ashamed of. A beast must not be ashamed of its furry hide. Night furred him. Winter clothed him. Literature is a beast. The furriers — night and winter — "

This is beautiful; it is also indeseverable from a Marxist outlook, whether pre-sented by a later victim of Stalinist Marxism or not. And, I suspect, it is right.

And then, Mog, your package arrived today (Friday the 7th), with letter(s), cor-rections, galleys, and *Riverside Quarterly*...!

The letter has just been read several times; and on the most recent go-through, I put little stars in the margin for those things I wanted to talk about.

But let me start with a warm thanks for the time, effort, thought, and feeling behind them all.

I read your *Riverside Quarterly* article last night (it's now Saturday, the 8th), yes, for the first time.

I'd been afraid that, when I saw it, I'd realize that it *had* been sent me, and that it would turn out I'd simply not said anything about it through sheer thoughtless forgetfulness. But, no, I really hadn't seen it.

It's so complimentary that, frankly, I hesitate to compliment you back on it, because it would seem immodest. What I'm compelled to say, quite bluntly and immodestly, is that it's one of the three really intelligent things I've seen written about *Dhalgren*. It's a truly fine piece of work.

By the bye, the other two are, first, Marc Gawron's "Introduction" to the li-brary edition, and, second, an essay by Mary Kay Bray, in *The Black American Literature Forum*, "Rites of Reversal: Double Consciousness in Delany's *Dhalgren*."

Just so I don't fall all over myself with praise, let me say I question the point of the comparison of *Dhalgren* and *Triton* as you've spelled it out—if you were anoth-er kind of critic, I'd say, "I fail to understand the ontological status you're giving the connection between the books. It seems vaguely psychoanalytical, but it's psy-choanalysis of the most 'vulgar' sort." If you read your comparisons carefully (perhaps more carefully than you wrote what is, after all, only two or three sentences in the piece which actually "compare and contrast," as they used to say, the books), it seems you are (inadvertently?) making the psychoanalytic point that the Kid and Bron are conscious/unconscious projections of the writer, to which, alas, my response is "ho-hum." Both the Kid and Bron are constructs, some of the material for which comes from conscious and some from unconscious recollections of incidents in my own life but the vast majority of which, in both cases, is from elsewhere. And construction is just not the same thing as projection. Still, I'm willing to accept this hypostasized "projection" as the metaphorical fiction (in this case the similarity between the situations of the two characters, mediated by the author, as a metaphor for the similarity-revalued-by-much difference between the two works) the critic always has to tell herself/himself to write anything at all. *Every* piece of criticism hinges on one such fiction or another. And if the criticism is worth reading (and yours most certainly is), usually that fiction can be ignored.

But let me end with more praise:

What I can say and get away with, I guess, is: Your piece is one of the few things on *Dhalgren* (and, sigh, I have read ever so many) where I can recognize the thought processes the critic is going through as being largely congruent with some of my own thinking at one stage or another during my work on the book.

It was very warming to read; and when somebody *does* understand some of what you're trying to do, it makes the various claims by all those crying out that it's incomprehensible self-indulgence seem a little less daunting, or even threatening, to your own sanity.

Thanks for writing it. Thanks for (finally!) showing it to me.

As to the piece in *Inscape*, I'm certainly and highly complimented by all its astute and intelligent attention. A couple of places you were really *too* kind! In terms of its ideological reduction, much of *Tides/Equinox* is simply god-awful! You suggest that, of course; but by not coming out and saying precisely how and why, you leave the suspicion that it's godawful in other ways than it is. Given the political reduction, you the critic are left with the problem: *Is* a piece of writing worth anything more than its political reduction; and if so, what? And how? And how does the critic tell people about it? (I don't think it's by soft-pedaling the ideological atrocities. But this, by the way, is the problem those writers who give me so much pleasure and that make you so angry and outraged seem to me to be finding valid answers for.) I think that, faced with the problem, which is, after all, a daunting one for the critic, while Mog-the-writer remained her usual lucid and witty self, Mog-the-critic became tired or timid, and the result was that, quite apart from the personal and informal organization of the random ideas gathered in no hard and fast formal order (that aspect, as pure writing, was charming), the piece nevertheless lacked a certain energy.

Yet for all that, I still thought it was very good and, really, I'm *not* being disingenuous. (Nor am I trying to be ingenuous, either!)

Incidentally, I began *Equinox* right after I left the Breakfast[1] in April '68, and finished it, for all practical purposes, in early October/late September 1968. Bits

---

[1] SRD refers to the months between November '67 and the first days of April '68 that he lived at and worked with the Heavenly Breakfast rock group and commune, as chronicled in his extended "essay on the winter of love," *Heavenly Breakfast,* first printed by Bantam Books in 1979 and more recently reprinted by Bamberger Books, 1997.

were added and parts were polished in San Francisco, early in '69, but the book was more or less what it is now by the time I left New York on New Year's Eve, '68, even though it wasn't published till '73, while I was off in London. This is in answer to some developmental point you made in one sentence or another (one phrase?) which placed *Equinox* in the wrong compositional time with one or another of my books. (And I may even be misremembering that.)

"Another little mag person wants a story of mine . . ." Congratulations! I hope you send me a copy when (or before!) it appears. In practical terms, of course, her "world rights for a year" will probably never mean anything—though you really should explain to her, politely as possible, that she's simply talking nonsense. What she wants is "Exclusive first English language serial rights (and/or, possibly [depending on her publication schedule: If it's a "one-shot," even an inadvertent one-shot, it may be an anthology], non-exclusive anthology rights) for one year." But "all world rights" means that if, somewhere off in the southern Crimea, a Russian film company sees your story and decides to pay millions of rubles to film it, your magazine's publisher gets all the moneys, while you get zilch. If, when you explain this to her, she tells you something like: "Well, I feel that because I'm publishing it, *any* income the story makes in the first year *should* all go to me, even if it's a million for a film," then simply smile and tell her:

"All right. But if the story *should* make any extra income in the first year, I'll take you to court for it—and win. Because that's simply an illegal contract by the copyright laws of the U. S. of A. And illegal contracts aren't binding."

Then give her the story and forget it—because, one, you *would* win, if it ever came to that, even in small claims court without a lawyer, and, two, the chances of its being filmed in the Crimea (or even being republished in an American anthology that pays $75 dollars, i.e., your chance of having to go to court over any extra income) inside the first year is *very* slim. And we're talking airline-catastrophe slim. Winning the lottery slim. Stuff like that.

You might also explain to her that it's illegal for *writers* to sell "all world rights." If a publisher wants all world rights, s/he must make a "work for hire" contract with the writer. (That is, the publisher must say: "I want you to write this particular piece of work for me, to my specifications, for which I will pay you so much, and which, from then on, I will be the sole owner of." And what is usually thought of as "creative writing" is well outside these bounds.) The publisher, by law, must specify what rights are bought; and the legal convention is, one, that "all world rights" is just illegal wording, and that, two, all rights not specified remain with the writer.

Point out to her that the little rider you see on all writing contracts today, "All rights not herein specified remain with the author," is a way of protecting the *publisher*. It's a way of saying to the court, should it ever come to litigation: "See, we're not crooks; we know the proper way to do things; and clearly we're not trying to cheat anyone." A contract (or a letter of agreement) for "all world rights" with no rider simply says to a judge that the publisher is both ignorant and malicious; and, in court, she would be treated as such.

See what she says.

If, after that, she persists in her folly, I'd still give her the story; it's not a very big gamble. But I'd also avoid her in the future, the way one avoids certain nincompoops—because, really, she's just off in Cloud-cuckoo-land somewhere.

Worry thee not about the copies of *Starboard Wine* or *The Little Magazine*. I simply stole both of them. (David and I sat down and carefully worked out what the finances of the book[s] had to be, how many we could give away, how much they had to be sold at, what discounts we could give, etc., in order to break even, to pay for the printing, etc., etc. It was all figured clearly and accurately, to the penny. Then he promptly stole a few copies and I promptly stole a few — both within each other's sight. But that's what [or one of the things that] makes it a non-profit venture.)

"I didn't realize it *[Stars/Sand]* was going to be a tall book." It's not. I assume you were looking at the bound galleys when you wrote that. (And I assume what you actually read — please, please, please, God! — were the Xeroxed page-proofs I sent you. (They're the ones with the line across the bottom.) You recall in one letter or other (*anent* Ron Drummond), I went on about the different amounts of type on the long galleys, the bound galleys, and the page proofs . . .

Well, now you've got sets of them all. But imagine if somebody sent you a nine-page list of corrections (as Ron did) keyed to the long galleys, with things like:

galley sheet 102, paragraph 19, line 8:
"about" misspelled

—when all you've got is bound galleys or page proofs, and the long galleys have long since vanished into the shredding machine or your publisher's hopeless cellar storage spaces.

Most of the poems you picked out of the *Little Magazine* are ones I really liked myself—and fought for. So for all your kvetching about how much you hate "pretty good writing," I still feel mildly vindicated. A poem I liked *very* much, which you didn't mention (and which I think is both "about something" and "pretty" in the way I think you to mean), is Lee Maurey's "Flood Plains on the Coast Facing Asia." He's an Australian poet, with, I learned only after we accepted the poem, a very substantial reputation down under, though I'd never heard of him until he submitted his batch of poems. (The people that the other editor became very excited over were Edward Kleinschmidt and Geoffrey Movious, who, while I think they're good, are just too fashionable [*à la* Ashbery] for me to get all *that* excited over.) My criticism of the magazine (too?) is that it's much too conservative.

But the only people really interested in having things swing on out to catch more exciting material are myself and Lilia. And as it *was* my first issue, I just didn't wield that much clout. Still, the others are beginning to listen to me when I discuss the poems at the meetings, and are beginning to realize I have *some* critical sense. So we're getting there.

And the other problem is, of course, submissions. We *do* take the best of what we get. And if you could see *most* of what we get . . .

Incidentally, there are *no* academics on the staff of the magazine. Other than me, they're all nine-to-five office workers and regular poetry readers. And Lilia and Kate Jennings are the only two who are also poets themselves. The rest of us are just readers. All of which I think is *very* healthy.

We discuss and vote on all submissions that don't simply get three out-and-out rejections from the first three readers on grounds of total amateurishness (and, when they do, I often try to read them anyway [if one of the rejectors wasn't me—and, indeed, so do the others]); and we need a majority for an acceptance. I've seriously questioned this as a strategy. Both Lilia and I have suggested that, while we might continue this way for the bulk of the magazine, we try giving each editor three pages per issue, say, to put in anything s/he really likes. That would certainly give us more range—and on several occasions there's been the odd poem that one or another of us loved a lot to which the rest were indifferent. Almost invariably this would be a poem with a truly unusual topic or in a truly unusual style, which only one or so of us could "hear." I just don't think it's ever good for the arts to get *too* democratic.

After Lilia's and my having made the suggestion, and our discussions about it (though it hasn't been accepted), five or ten times now the other editors (and us) are beginning to accommodate to something like our suggestions in the actual voting. If somebody is really hot on a poem, and your objections are merely lukewarm, the other five editors now and then will support (or abstain) in favor of local enthusiasm. That's how Dennis and I got the Patrick Leary piece in. The four others didn't see the point. And that's how Dennis, all alone, got the Michael Casey poem in. The rest of us thought it was both sexist and uninteresting—though Casey, as you probably know, was a Yale Younger Poet a few years back, and when his first book of poems was actually reprinted by Avon (!), it looked for a while as if he were on his way to becoming a working-class Rod Mackuen. Only it didn't happen. (He was too good . . . ?) You can get the idea of the importance of local enthusiasm across in an affable and intelligent group of six. Still, the committee nature of the construct (as Cassirer said of mythology) militates for the conservative, nevertheless. Never-the-never, most of the poems you've chosen to like were either pushed in by me, or were gotten in by other people relying on methods I've been trying to instigate at the magazine. So I can feel only so bad about your complaints.

" . . . tight little safe things in it, and you think . . . shit, won't anyone print anything else?" Honey, "Won't anyone *write* anything else?" is the question. Or, at any rate, won't anyone submit it to *us*?

Having said that, having politely listened to all you think is dreadful about it (more important, having shown you at least a little of what we can do, or want to do in the future), may I officially invite you to submit? I very much agreed with the *Village Voice* critic who praised your poems in *Coming to Power*. An invitation is not, alas, a guarantee of acceptance, because the committee still, in the long run, reigns. But I'd certainly like to see some (a sheaf of two to five is the preferred submission form—with three the ideal number), if you'd care to send them to the Pleasantville P.O. Box number (*The Little Magazine*, Box 78, Pleasantville, NY 10570) with a self addressed stamped envelope—or, if that's hard for you, send them to me and I'll stick in a SASE for you.

Hope you take me up on my invitation!

Sometimes, Mog, I just think the problem may be that most people really *don't* like to read contemporary poetry. As more than one person has noted, there are probably more people *writing* contemporary poetry today than there are people who read it with any regularity. And I mean people writing it at that level of minimal competence you decry.

For better or worse, poetry is as much a genre as SF or mysteries or westerns or

gothics. That means that the people who *do* get something out of reading the com-
petent/mediocre are eventually going to be the arbiters of "the great."

There are SF novels (as you know!) that people who don't like and never read
SF are quite likely to get enthusiastic about. Sometimes these are novels that the
cognoscenti will also endorse. And sometimes not.

And it's the same with poems.

I remember I was seventeen when a very intelligent poet, Marie Ponsot, who
spoke very fine French and read poetry constantly, said to me: "The truth is, I just
don't really like what Rimbaud *does* with language. And I get tired of it awfully
quickly. I'd really rather read Françis Ponge." I still like Rimbaud. But I don't read
French that well. It may just be an adolescent taste. But then, often, what seems
poetic in the Romance languages becomes adolescent in the Germanic ones; while
what seems poetic in the Germanic languages becomes dead, dense, and prosaic
in the Romance tongues. (With American English as a halfway ground . . .?)

Walter Benjamin, in an ass-backwards way, had the problem of "greatness"
well down in matters artistic. "Greatness"—as opposed to simple enjoyment—is
a socially manufactured aura that accrues to certain privileged works of art. He
was afraid that, in our "Age of Mechanical Reproduction," this aura would vanish, since so much of it ["Greatness"] up till the end of the 19th century, actually *had*
been a response to the king's court in which the "great" painting had hung, or the
expensive edition in which the "great" poem was printed, or the royal box from
which the "great" play or opera had been applauded. But "greatness" turns out to
be a much finer social construct than that. Now, an awareness of a work's previ-
ously judged "greatness" is—and has always been—the best frame of mind for
the reader to be in when encountering what is (for that reader) a new work, especially a work posing (first) historical difficulties of understanding and (second)
conceptual difficulties of sophistication. When it's doing its job, "greatness" stabilizes both tolerance and attention, which all art requires, more or less. Still, it's the
general reader of whatever genre who is, first, most immune to "greatness" in that
genre—and whose responses comprise the most sophisticated enjoyment.

Unfortunately, "greatness" is composed of a great deal more than the sum of
sophisticated responses. Like the selection of our poems in the magazine, it too is
a committee affair, so tends toward the ideologically conservative — which is
what's wrong with an uncritical acceptance of the "greatness" approach to art in
general.

Myself, I don't have any "great works." I get larger or smaller enjoyment, more
or less sophisticated, out of a more or less broad and idiosyncratic range of texts
—which includes about a third of the poems in *The Little Magazine.* And I'd like
to push that up to about two-thirds. But that's why (I guess) I'm good to have on
the magazine staff. And that's why I hope you'll submit.

On to *Stars/Sand:*

"I would have advised against certain things—not that it would have meant
you would change them, of course, any more than you changed the line about
nonconsensual S/M (and I still fail to see how you can read the words 'especially consensual' or whatever as anything but the assumption that the other kind is
nonconsensual); it's an on/off system, with 'nonconsensual S/M' merely standing for rape, murder, torture, child abuse, etc."

Dear God, woman, is *that* what you meant all this time? There is no line, or even mention, of "non-consensual S/M" in the book—which was more than a little confusing. But finally, nerd that I am, I twig to what you mean. Yes, I will *change* it in the paperback edition! I'll make it something on the order of: "especially those cases where the consensual aspect had been put in words or writing," which *really is* what I meant!

Alas, those straights who read it (and think about it) will probably misunderstand—and, yes, that's my fault. Probably most promiscuous gay men who read it will get it as I intended *unless* they stop to think about it. Then they'll either misunderstand, or understand and realize I've written clumsily.

Let me try to explain what really *was* a sad misunderstanding—and which, come paperback time, I'll try to remedy. Put the following in the context of the fact that, yes, of *course* I know perfectly well what "consensual S/M" means:

Out of the ten to fifteen thousand sexual encounters I've had since I was seventeen, I'd characterize between 40 and 55 of them as S/M; perhaps six of those have been since I was 30. I don't include my fabled "rape" by the two Greek sailors back when I was 23—nor did I at the time. I'm sure the fact that they had me by force gave them no extra pleasure. Believe me, they'd have preferred me to go along with it. And that, at the level of ordinary gay male parlance, takes it out of the realm of sadism. Since reading Sade at sixteen, I've never felt sadism was one with "unthinking cruelty," not that there isn't a *lot* of that in Sade. Still, on that purely subjective level, where you talk to yourself without regard for politics, simply using the language as you learned it ("at the level of the signified," another rhetorical tradition might put it, a little more coldly, a little more economically), the *enjoyment* of aggression and of various social acts and postures that, in another context, might be deemed cruel, seemed (and seems) to me to be the criteria for sadism. At some point, my inner dictionary tells me, the sadist has got to feel: "I'd *rather* do it this way than some other." More context: At times, in a couple of orgy-like situations, I've pressed my attention to the point of orgasm on guys who, I suspect, would rather I hadn't—but were not so put out by these attentions that they got up and left. A *couple* of times guys have pressed their attentions to the point of orgasm on me, when I would have preferred they didn't—but also not to the point where I left. (And at other times, I did leave; and at other times, guys have left me.) But I and they would have been much happier if the partners (me and them) had gone along happily, rather than unhappily, with it. Thus I don't consider these experiences either sadism *or* rape. Nor do I think most promiscuous gay men over 35 would either. (I don't know about those under 35.) What we're talking about here is sexual impoliteness. Again, to give a sense of the proportions of what I'm talking about: In a field of ten to fifteen thousand encounters, I've probably been the perpetrator of such impoliteness perhaps five times; I've met with it as the unwilling object maybe 25 times. So we're still talking about something that occurs well under one percent of the time and (to repeat) that I and most promiscuous gay men would consider neither sadism nor rape.

Back to my 40 to 55 S/M encounters. Maybe ten to fifteen of them I can say I honestly enjoyed. The rest, just as honestly, I found dull and particularly low in erotic content for me (though not necessarily for my partner); and that's probably the simplest reason why I am not "into" S/M today. Of these 40 to 55 experiences, maybe six were what, up till now, I would have characterized as "consensual" to myself—that is, both of us sat down and talked about beforehand what we were going to do and what we weren't; then, in the session, we more or less played by these rules. Of these six, five most certainly were in the group of experiences I did *not* enjoy. They were not ego-scarring, physically dangerous, or particularly harmful, emotionally or any other way. The rules were followed. And I had agreed to them, or even specified them. They just "weren't me." And though I went through them, sometimes to orgasm, sometimes not, mostly I was bored.

The one of those which I did enjoy, the "consent" was more or less on the order of: "You know this is going to be S/M, 'cause that's what I'm into," from my partner, who started talking to me in a beer bar on Folsom Street, back in San Francisco, when I was about 27. And, "Okay," from me; which, in that case, basically meant, "Yeah, I'd realized that already from the leather strap around your wrist, even though, true, you aren't out in full leather." That incident was, incidentally, the basic referent for the encounter on the bridge in "Fog and Granite." My response (to this guy, who went by the nickname "Dynamite") was pretty much that of the young smuggler's to the one-eyed man, i.e., it was the most intense physical pleasure I've *ever* had, by an amazing margin, and I now saw *why* people enjoyed it; I was really glad I'd had it—but it *still* didn't interest me as something to pursue.

[Diverting side note: As a fallout to Foucault's *History of Sexuality*, Foucault and Richard Sennett co-authored an article with some daunting documentation which maintained that the Victorian taboo on masturbation began with the open admission by early Victorian doctors that masturbation (and, indeed, the other "perversions") inarguably produced greater physical pleasures than ordinary heterosexual penetration, especially heterosexuality after a year or two within the confines of (Victorian) marriage; ergo, people should neither be allowed to indulge them nor, indeed, allowed even to know of their existence, because without question the good-old pleasure principle would ensure that everyone would seek them out and, as a result, bourgeois society would come to an end. Though they clearly underestimated the forces that held "bourgeois society" together, and as well misunderstood the emotional calculus in which sexuality was imbedded, wouldn't it be great if these early Victorian conservatives turned out to be right?! But what that early Victorian program actually tells us is just how isolated certain intellectual groups, like doctors, could be in a largely illiterate (80% or more) society.[2]]

But back to contemporary S/M: The ten or fifteen S/M experiences, out of the 40 to 55, I'd enjoyed up till the Dynamite encounter (with a few of them coming since) were ordinary enough encounters that began in an ordinary enough, vanilla-type manner (or with only the faintest lacing of leather flavoring, as it were, visible on the ice cream's surface), in the course of which, after a bit, very carefully, my partner decided to be a little rougher, and I'd responded if I was willing to go on in that direction all non-verbally. (In all of these, my partner was the initiator; in about two-thirds of these it was finally decided [again, completely non-verbally], that I would be the top; and in the other third, I was the bottom.) These

[2] SRD is probably mistaken. The only Foucault-Sennett article in the bibliography ("Sexuality and Solitude") does not fit this description.

are the experiences which, till now, in my own private speech, I've characterized as "S/M" without the word "consensual" attached to it. And within a certain area of the promiscuous gay community, I really believe this is the way it works.

And I believe promiscuous gay male readers of *Stars/Sand* will read the line as it stands, now, and understand it.

Certainly I know this goes against the dictionary meaning of the word; but I still think I can explain why I used the word as I did, nevertheless and why others, in my language community (promiscuous gay males), do too.

From time to time I discussed the phenomenon of preferring non-verbally specified S/M to verbally specified S/M, as I've outlined it to you above, with other gay men during the '60s and '70s when most of these experiences occurred; some of them were heavily into S/M, some of them (possibly most) were not. And the explanations were interesting, complex, and often insightful. But the basic thing I learned is, whatever the reason for it, many other gay men found themselves with the same reaction I'd had. And the cliché response, once the public discourse started about "consensual S/M," was frequently: "If it's consensual, then it's no fun!"—especially among these vanilla types who had about the same amount of interest or range of experience as I did.

The reason for the phenomenon?

Possibly it's that, when you're paying enough attention to another person's body signals to change the course of the sex in such a direction through (largely) kinesthetic signals alone, chances are you're just relating to the other person more sensitively on all counts.

The reason for the cliché?

I don't think at basis it was political. (Though everything has its political side, of course. And certainly the cliché expresses a certain political fear of too much public articulation about a socially castigated activity.) Rather I suspect it was linguistic.

There's a language phenomenon called "semantic exclusion" that I may have commented on before. Pairs of perfect synonyms seldom *stay* synonyms—at least not if both are in constant use. Frequently people will pose a formal word or a phrase as an exact synonym for some informal word or phrase (possibly because the informal term is considered inexact or vulgar—or simply because, with use, it has recently changed its own meaning), but pretty soon, with more usage, the terms divide the semantic area between them, often with the formal phrase or term referring to the more formal aspects of the referent and the informal phrase or term referring to the informal aspect of the same referent.

Seldom, in real speech, do such divisions form equal and opposite semantic fields: Linguistically, "white/black" divisions are both rare and unstable. They almost always have to be maintained artificially, with the help of writing; and even with writing's help, at the level of the signified they still flop over into the much more usual division of "milk/skim milk"—general category, specific subset. ("White/black," as soon as it becomes vaguely social, or becomes the basis for any metaphor, loses all equality: white=self, black=other; white is the acceptable and good; black is the anomalous and bad, etc., etc.) As soon as they have flopped (at the level of the signified), almost any attempt to use them as equal opposites begins to hide, mystify, and exploit the hierarchical relation.

(And, just as a note, roughly the first ten years of "deconstruction" [1967-1977] was largely devoted to unmasking such hidden hierarchical exploitations in allegedly objective language — which made a lot of people confuse "deconstruction" with "demystification," since that was what it was [largely] being used for.)

During the '50s and '60s, "S&M" (as it was called back then), in the social field of promiscuous gay sexual activity, was a branch of cruising that — whatever the straight world said — was *perceived* by those in the promiscuous gay community to be just as consensual as any other kind of widespread sex. The guys in the leather jackets had been there since the '50s — doing pretty much what everyone else was. So when the term "consensual S/M" became common in the mid-'70s, among that same community, of which for better or worse I'm a member, semantic exclusion quickly skewed the meaning of the new term (which, if it hadn't changed, would have just been redundant to the general perception of S&M, since the leather jacket crowd certainly wasn't running up and jumping on anybody) to mean these S&M encounters in which the consent and range of the experience was *verbally* articulated.

At the level of the signified for most promiscuous gay men, there is the larger category of S/M, which has always been perceived inside that community — even by these who really didn't generally enjoy it — as consensual. Then there was the sub-category of "consensual S/M," which was the S/M encounter in which the rules were verbalized.

Thus, within the linguistic community I belong to, there isn't a conceptual opposition between "consensual S/M" and "non-consensual S/M." That's an artificial and purely journalistic distinction — and a rather unstable one (that has already flopped into a hierarchical relation, which is [rightly] why you're so up in arms about it). Thanks to semantic exclusion, there is a statistical hierarchy between "S/M" (the widespread general category) and "consensual S/M" (the subset of S/M encounters in which the rules are clearly verbalized before play begins). Needless to say, for people whose sexual encounters are largely within the S/M community itself, the statistical hierarchy of encounters with articulated rules vs. encounters with non-articulated rules (still having little to do with consent) may be very different from the statistical hierarchy at the interface of the S/M community and the non-S/M community of promiscuous gay males. But that interface, at least from first-hand experience, is all I know about.

And that, as the children used to say, is where I was coming from.

But, as Roman Jacobson pointed out so astutely, we are all members of many linguistic communities. *Stars/Sand* is writing. And thus it has to be comprehensible to readers.

And although more and more I'm coming to see my audience as gay and male (after all, we got problems too; and it is, for better or worse, my group), still, one has got to hold the language steadier than that if communication is to endure.

As I said, by paperback time I'll do something about it. (Though, lord, for an often powerful and eloquent writer, sometimes — informally — you can express yourself rather unclearly!) Still, unless you've been able to figure out what someone was *trying* to say, often it's impossible to correct him/her. And unless you were just being stubbornly disingenuous, I guess you really didn't understand my intentions in the phrase, which haven't changed. (And I did change the passage, twice (!), to make clearer what I *thought* you were objecting to — which was, alas, something else again.) Oh, well. Once again, thanks for making me aware of it. Though it never occurred to me till now we were simply wrangling over the definition of the word "consensual"—a word I was taking to mean "verbally articulated consent," and which you were (very rightly!) just giving its dictionary meaning.

Another way to look at it, now that I've dragged you through all this, is simply that I got caught in a local, transitory, demotic usage that the term "consensual S/M" passed through about 1973 (just before I went to England); and because I was out of the country for two years (and was in another one with almost no gay lib at all), I wasn't subjected to the media pressure to shift the meaning to the one it's settled at for you and (certainly) many, if not most, other Americans.

Sigh . . .

And I'll keep on the lookout for "about."

"The last parts (you knew it) I didn't like nearly so well. To the point that I began to feel very wretched about your dedication, which I already felt a bit stung about sharing with all these men. (Iva, with her attitude about women, is hardly a solace!) I wanted to ask you to take it out. All my reactions this past week or so have been very much on the negative side—you're not the only beneficiary . . ."

Oh, dear!

Of course, *naïf* that I am, I *didn't* know it!

Something about the dedication, Mog, though it'll take me a bit to say it:

The last four years have been unquestionably the worst years of my life—with number four sinking to true depths of awfulness. (The years in which I was writing *Dhalgren*, from San Francisco to London, were probably the next worst low period.) I'm not the suicidal type, but involved and overwhelming tax problems are something that more than one person has killed him- or herself over. And certainly since the whole situation escalated last October into its current realm of surreal nightmare, a dozen times or more I've sat, numb, on the edge of my bed for an hour or so and thought: "Well, I know *why* people kill themselves over all this."

After your first early morning two-and-a-half-hour session at the IRS office with your IRS agent and your accountant (three days after you've discovered that, without warning, they've taken all your money from your bank account because you went to draw your weekly check and the teller told you you can't, and, when you went to see a bank officer, after half an hour's protesting about mistakes and people running around trying to check them down, you finally discover the government has gone in and taken it), a meeting during which your whole life has been laid out to the penny, and argued over and questioned and criticized and juggled up and down and laid out again, as you get ready to leave, your IRS agent, Mr. Greenberg, who's about ten years younger than you, asks: "Oh, by the way. How much money do you have in your pocket, Mr. Delany?"

Now you borrowed $20 the night before from your downstairs neighbor so you'd be able to get to the meeting that morning and afterward pick up some groceries to feed your kid. So you think, I've spent $1.80 of that for two subway tokens. And then I got a can of tuna-fish for her lunch out of it last night. And you say, "I don't know. Maybe . . . fifteen dollars."

Mr. Greenberg says, over his joined fingers, looking up through his round lenses: "Why don't you leave it with us?"

"No," you say. "No . . .! I'm sorry! I can't . . .! I don't have any money!"

But Mr. Greenberg has already closed his folder and is getting up from the gray aluminum desk to walk out of his cubicle, leaving you blinking at your accountant, who, embarrassed, looks down to close his attaché case in which are the scraps of paper and forms and lists and notes that are the traces of your entire material life.

And you go through not one but a dozen of these meetings.

And at the end of each, you and your accountant and Mr. Greenberg (and his supervisor) agree to a strategy which, while it is neither logical nor livable, at least means their harassment will stop; only within two days to two weeks, again you learn it has begun (they do not call you to tell you; simply the next bit of money you are expecting from here, there, or wherever does not reach you, and when you inquire after it you learn there is another lien, hold, or levy) because, as you find out when you call them, there is something *they* had not taken into account.

Not anything you had kept from them or failed to tell them.

And so it begins again.

At other times, again without warning, Mr. Greenberg will ring your doorbell, unexpectedly, around four o'clock.

You ring him in, thinking it's Judy downstairs who's left her key home again, and when you open the door to the knock, you see him standing on the landing, in his gray raincoat with a worn attaché ease in one hand and a clipboard in the other.

"Oh, hello," you say. "Mr. Greenberg. What did you want?"

"To ask you some questions."

"Sure. Come on in. What are they?"

"I want to know what you're living on."

You laugh. "Not much. Come on inside. Actually, I'm kind of glad you came." You step back from the door for him. "When you left that note in my door last month and I wasn't in, really, I got to thinking, if you came here and could see the ordinary level I live at, maybe some of what I was saying to you at our last meeting with Ed would make some sense."

"Tell me what you're living on."

You take a breath. "Personal loans. From friends. Some from my family."

Clutching up his attaché case awkwardly, he makes a mark on his clipboard, mutters, "Thanks," and starts back downstairs.

"Aren't you coming in . . .?"

"No," he calls up, and disappears down, leaving you in the open doorway, invaded, bewildered, and, at last, rejected. "Good-bye," you hear, vaguely, from the landing below. Then you close the door and go back to the office where you try, very hard, once again to get your young smuggler to the other side of the bridge (it was "Fog & Granite" I was working on), which had been going slow as hell anyway.

Or, at another eight-thirty in the morning meeting, when, at your respective sides of that scarred metal desk, both you and Mr. Greenberg, after an hour and a half, are exhausted and frazzled but somehow, without either of you trying, as it occasionally happens in the conversation of two very tired people who've been working very hard, a moment of human exchange has broken through and he's sitting there in his shirtsleeves, smiling and saying: "You know, my fourteen-year-old son is a nut about science fiction. He'd probably like your stuff. I never read it, but he loves it."

So you sigh and say: "Really? I've got a whole stack of cartons of my out-of-print books standing outside the apartment door. I'll bring him a few copies next time I come in."

And he reaches up to adjust his wire frame glasses and, with no smile at all now, looks down at his folder, and says: "I can't accept them. That's a bribe."

And so, with all the guilt of a man who's just been caught offering to bribe an Internal Revenue agent, you go back to the draining and exhausting figures and forms.

But, as Ed, my accountant says: "This Greenberg is a pretty nice guy, Chip. Besides, he likes you. Some of these guys I've worked with can be *real* bastards."

Indeed, if you didn't spend the months of this in a state of emotional and physical exhaustion, wondering how you can work, wondering if you should go on working, having conferences with your agent where you go over your carefully worked out plans about how you won't write any more for at least six months while you get a steady job, and then you can't *get* a steady job, and then three weeks later it looks like, maybe, it may, just barely, be financially feasible to go on writing after all—well, if that weren't your state, maybe you'd find these small, cruel epiphanies funny or informative or mildly annoying. But while they are not the specific things that make it bad (what makes it bad are all the things sketched so briefly in *this* paragraph) these are the things that focus your feelings of guilt, of despair and the sheer human impossibility of it all, that hound you to the verge of tears and into the two-, or three-, or ten-hour depressions from which, each time, you emerge, true, but from which, each time, by a minuscule amount, you emerge less and less fully.

Because of it all, Mog, I've simply not had the energy to reach out to very many people—especially since last October. The people in the dedication are those who have been kind and caring enough, over that time, to reach out to me—to occasionally write me a letter, or give me a phone call, and, when they hear about the problems, to say: "Hey, that's too bad. I'm sorry." And go on being friends. When you're reduced to very small psychological margins, often that seems to make the difference between going on and not going on.

The dedication was a way of saying thank you. You'll note that they're not *that* many of you and, alas, it really covers the list. And, yeah, it would be nice if there were more women on it. (Joanna isn't on it only because she was included in the first volume.) But there ain't.

Now, of course I understand: *The Tale of Plagues and Carnivals* makes *Flight from Nevèrÿon* a highly political book; and who would want to have a dedication read as an endorsement—especially to something you didn't endorse at all!?

Well, there were people who asked to be disassociated from *Dhalgren* too, because they Didn't Approve. While I was working on the middle drafts in the Albert Hotel, I had one friend whom I saw almost every other day for nearly a year. He kept insisting—often when I would urge him not to, because I thought he was forgetting his own concerns for the sake of my book—on reading all my new pages, and discussing them, and being very supportive and offering many helpful criticisms. (I was using his last name as the book's title, back then, though there was nothing of his character in the book, save an exchange he'd once told me about between him and his therapist, which I'd changed some and transferred to Lanya.) One night, as I frequently did back then, I took him out to dinner at a little Greek restaurant above 14th Street. I thought we'd had a perfectly pleasant time. But the next morning, I found a letter waiting for me at the hotel desk. He wanted to break off all relations with me, disassociate himself from the book, and wanted me not to use his name as the title. He felt that I was sapping all his energies from his own life and his own work. Though I wrote a letter back, bowing to his wishes, I was very hurt. As I had often told him, I would have been quite willing to do without his reading and criticism, but the withdrawal of his friendship was wounding. For the next three-and-a-half years, he refused to see me again or speak to me—though several times, I later learned, when he found himself outside a mutual friend's loft apartment door and he heard my voice inside (and several other times when he only thought he heard it), he turned around and left. The only thing that mitigated my hurt was that over the years I had known him (and we'd been friends for a decade), I'd seen him go through such separations with at least three other people (a woman painter and a couple of male poets), complete with hiding in doorways and running off in the street when they passed and cowering behind windows when they went by outside, with whom, for a year or so before, he'd been intimately close — though I'd actually *thought* I'd been protecting him from some of the things that had caused this kind of break with other friends.

It's interesting that all of the people he broke with, including me, had basically the same reaction: "I'm certainly not mad at him, and would like to be friends again, or at least talk to him and find out what my crime really was. But, I guess that's just Q——." Because we *were* close, I harbored hurt, but not resentment.

I suspect the others did too.

Later, in England, when *Dhalgren* was finished, only with great trepidation did I include him in the dedication—and out of alphabetical order. And when, later, after the book was published and we ran into each other on the street while I was walking with another friend of his, we did speak again; and became, after a fashion, friends once more. Then he told me that when he'd first learned I'd disregarded his wishes and included him in the dedication anyway, it made him feel good and paved the way to re-opening our friendship. I was glad. But when I decided to put his name down on the dedication page, it was really quite a gamble.

Believe it or not, I had friends who were highly disapproving of *Babel-17* in the manuscript stage because I was, in their opinion, turning from the meaningful social portraiture of *The Fall of the Towers* and the social relevance of *The Ballad of Beta-2* to indulge myself in pretty language about language—which, for them, was a case of a talented young writer's fall into aesthetic masturbation. And a couple of those who'd kept up an uneasy friendship with me anyway simply stopped all relations at *Nova*, because they felt I'd gone entirely into fascistic navel-gazing. (I mean, novels about writing novels with an industrial scion for a protagonist!)

But back at Ace, even Don Wolheim made it perfectly clear that *Out of the Dead City* was a big comedown in energy, excitement, and readability from *The Jewels of Aptor*. And we spent what was, for me at any rate, a *terribly* uncomfortable lunch at the old Blue Ribbon restaurant on 48th Street, while I squirmed and sweated and grew sticky in my suit pants, and Don went on explaining to me in a fatherly manner how usual it was for a writer's second or third novel to lose all the energy and focus of their first work; and how I really shouldn't feel too bad about it; after all, lots of writers, especially young ones, only wrote one book worth reading . . . "After all," he said, "you've written one good work, and at nineteen no less; think how many people will go to their graves never even able to say that?" It was kindly, well-meant, and devastating. And for a week I seriously wondered if he'd go on to publish *Out of the Dead City* at all. But when he did, Don made it clear this was only out of the goodness of his fatherly heart.

What I can see from this distance that I couldn't see then was that this was a guy who, when he'd accepted *Jewels*, was under the impression it had come in through the slush pile.

This was a guy who'd walked around the Ace Books office showing sections of the MS to people and comparing it to the *Odyssey*.

This was a guy who'd decided that it must have been written by an established writer who was using a pseudonym for an eccentric foray into science fantasy.

And this was the guy who was quite surprised to learn that it had actually been written by this 20-year-old black kid, who'd finished it just before his birthday and was living on the Lower East Side and married to Ace's nineteen-year-old Jewish editorial assistant who'd lied about her age to get the job.

It's all very silly now, but the fact is, Don really felt *Jewels* represented something important, if only here and there, in its language.

So when, ten months later, the same kid showed up with the first volume of a grandiose trilogy, wholly different in style, and, after all, marred with blatant awkwardnesses and odd confusions here and there, Don felt—and felt personally—that this talented kid was going off into a half-baked and over-extended project that utilized none of his writing strengths to the full. Even in 1968, for the uncut reprint of *Jewels*, Don was to characterize it as "the first and perhaps the greatest" of my books, in the back cover copy he wrote for it—copy which, I suspect, allowing for advertiser's hyperbole, gave his honest appraisal of it.

On its first publication *The Jewels of Aptor* had got a single review (in *Analog*). But it was a good one. And as I've told many young SF writers since (and this is where learned it): In SF you are never selling the book you're currently submitting (whether complete or in portion-and-outline), no matter what your editor tells you. What you are selling is the reviews on your last book. And I'm as sure as I'm sure of the slant in the September shadows below the fire-escape on the brick wall across from my office window now, that P. Schuyler Miller's review of *Jewels* is the reason Don first published *Out of the Dead City*.[3] (I remember how strongly he advised against announcing it as the opening book in a trilogy: He simply doubted I'd ever write the rest.) But *The Fall of the Towers*, as its volumes appeared, got me more and better reviews. So Don continued to publish me.

Well, what can I say?

The reviews on *Neveryóna* were better than the reviews on *Tales*. And I hope the reviews on *Flight* are better than the reviews on *Neveryóna*. I certainly feel it's

---

[3] The joint title of the trilogy comprised of *Out of the Dead City* (1963), *The Towers of Toron* (1964) and *City of a Thousand Suns* (1965) is *The Fall of the Towers*, the one-volume edition first published in 1970.

a satisfying conclusion to the series.

Tom Disch loved *Dhalgren* and saw it through a couple of its middle drafts, and offered advice, and was endlessly encouraging and supportive about it. But when he read *Triton* in manuscript he told me: "Chip, I've read the book — and pretty carefully, I think; and I have no idea *what* it's about, or any concept of *why* you would want to write it." To him, after *Dhalgren*, it seemed like a return to SF at its silliest and most trivial; and he's been unable to read anything I've written since (unless it's about him). And when Bantam sent him (not at my suggestion, either) one of the *Nevèrÿon* manuscripts, he told me in effect that if we were to remain any kind of friends, I must not give him any more of my stuff to read. He just couldn't read my work anymore and being asked to upset him too much.

Of course the *Nevèrÿon* manuscript was a few years after another incident.

This was in the first two years Frank and I were together. I was writing *Tales of Nevèrÿon*, trying to decide whether I could still write fiction at all or not, after the two-year halt that followed *Triton*. Tom and Charles invited me to their house for dinner to meet a friend, a black, gay nuclear physicist at Columbia University named Tony, who was a great fan of mine, they said, and very anxious to meet me. When Tom extended the invitation, I told him, "He sounds very nice, Tom. But, really, right through here, it would probably be a very uncomfortable dinner, just for me. I'm just not up to meeting an admirer right now." To which Tom replied, rather shamefacedly, "Well, I'm afraid, Chip, that I went out on a limb and already promised you to him. I wish you'd come just as a personal favor." Tony indeed proved to be very nice, but all through the evening Charles kept making the oddest and most discomforting innuendoes and, when I finally asked him what was going on, turned on me directly and attacked me for two hours straight — while Tom and Tony defended me.

Synopsized from the two hours, Charles's three criticisms were, one: By mentioning Marilyn's NBA[4] in the brief author's biographies at the end of my books, I was trading off of her reputation — especially since I was now living with Frank. (Though we'd separated in January '75, M. and I were not officially divorced until '79 or '80.) Two, by mentioning wife and daughter in the same bios, I was fooling readers into thinking I was straight. And, third, I did not like him and had no respect for him as a writer.

The first two were unintentional, and I'd already tried to do something about them, and would continue to, I told him. The third, as I explained in a phone call the next day, was just patently untrue. I'd always considered him a friend and had great respect for his writing talents. He told me: "I don't like any of your work, Chip, except *The Einstein Intersection*. You know it. It's perfectly understandable. That's probably why you don't like me. I think you think Tom is a good writer, but you just think I'm a silly little proofreader." (Proofreading was how Charles earned most of his living.)

"Charles," I said, "the truth is, I've always thought that, sentence for sentence, you were a more skillful writer than Tom. And I've always been confused, and sometimes worried, that you weren't writing more. You get very uncomfortable when someone asks you about your writing. So I've learned, in twelve years, not

---

[4] Marilyn Hacker, SRD's ex-wife, had won the National Book Award for Poetry in 1975.

to do it. But I've always asked Tom about your work, because I was sincerely interested. And no six months has gone by when I haven't urged Tom to make it easier for you to write — and I'm sure he's told you that — simply because the things you've written have given me great pleasure."

"He has," he said. "But I think you were lying." He said a great many other very ugly things that, while they didn't particularly bother me (they were so off-the-wall), I'm sure an hour later made him feel dreadfully uncomfortable, even if he believed them, because he's a sensitive man.

Well, on the receipt of a letter I sent him the next day, saying I did consider him a friend, and I was open to friendly relations whenever he felt he could have them, he decided to sever all relations with me. And although my friendship goes on with Tom, I haven't seen Charles since, save at Joan Thurston's funeral, where, even to my hello, he refused to speak and simply walked away. Tom has told me since that he thought, with my letter, I was trying to bully him (!) into liking me. But he also refuses to come to any social function where I'm going to be. And before and after, over the last half dozen years, he's accused Charles Platt, and David Hartwell, and Gregory Sandow, and Jerry Mundus, and Barbara Wise of similar lying—and will see *none* of us anymore!

Though Tom continues to be friendly with us all.

Yet for all its neurotic aspect, I did (and still do) take Charles' criticisms seriously.

I know I've told you Damon Knight's first words to me, just before he rejected "Time Considered as a Helix of Semi-Precious Stones": "Chip, *what* is this story about?" And you might take a look at "note 1" on page 243 of *Starboard Wine*, *anent* the response of Moorcock, who first published the story.

I don't wonder if — I *know* that — rehearsing all this, here, now, is a self-protective strategy on my part. But to write *about* anything at all, Mog, is to risk losing people who are close to you — because you're not writing the right *things* about it; while the new audience you get comes to you precisely *because* you're writing about that and not something else, regardless of what specifically you're saying about it. Indeed, the new audience is as happy to disagree as to agree; that's what makes you a rich writer for them.

I care, deeply, about the world; about AIDS; about language (I write that rebarbative rhetoric that angers you so because, when I read it in other writers, I *sometimes* find it beautiful; not because I *necessarily* find it intelligent; and though David tells me *The American Shore* has sold only some 158 copies, half a dozen of its readers have still written me that they've found it beautiful, luminous, or exciting; so I feel okay about it. And, like Poe with his *Eureka*, I'll always consider it among my best books, simply because it's among the best thought/written; and that virgule is not a mark separating style from content, but a mark of their ineluctable blesh[5]); about art. And no doubt because of what I care about, I pick friends who care deeply about the world, AIDS, language, and art too. I write what I can, and I bust my ass doing it. And part of the ass-busting means being as honest as I can bear to be with myself. And that's often painful. (Where you

---

[5] "Blesh," a verb coined by Theodore Sturgeon in his 1953 novel, *More Than Human*, means at once *to blend* and *to mesh*.

read "self-critical" in my various discussions of series stories, if you want, you can simply substitute "personal agony" and/or "angry friends.") I do the very little I can do—write the very little I can write—*because* I care (and because I couldn't stand not to); but because my friends also care so much, and because they would like to see it done their way (and often those would be *very* good ways), what I do has *always* been painful to them. Part of my own pain, if you will, is to listen to their angry and articulate criticisms and, the ones that I can understand down in my language pit (at the level of the you-know-what . . .), try to do something about them, even if it means forcing myself to grow into a different kind of person. (It was truly painful to Marilyn, at least back at the very beginning, that, after I'd won all sorts of awards, including a creative writing scholarship to NYU, I chose not to use it and chose to write SF at all—a pain exacerbated for her because she had won those same awards, more of them than I had, actually; and had used the scholarship; but her own first response to marriage was to find herself practically unable to write at all, after an incredibly prolific and talented adolescence, while mine was to turn from literature to SF.)

Personal friends have always turned virulently against my writing—intelligent and sensitive people, people close to me, people who cared for me, for writing, and for the world—with *every* book I've written. And for all the element of neurosis that may (or may not) have been present in the actual withdrawal of friendship, I still don't think *any* of their criticisms were necessarily wrong. So it's not new to me.

Writing of Camus, Susan Sontag once said that the most dangerous emotion a writer's texts can evoke from the reader is love. That's because, she went on, when we fall out of love with a writer, we feel betrayed; we feel that, indeed, we were fools ever to have been taken in by them in the first place. A writer is much more likely to endure if he (Sontag wrote "his" and "he") earns from us a distant, grudging, even uncomprehending respect. That's the writer who, years later, we take down again, read more carefully this time—suddenly to have our begrudging respect open up into a far deeper aesthetic appreciation. (That's another reason why "greatness" may be a *more* socially valuable "aura" in the end than the subjective experience of either "sophisticated" *or* "unsophisticated" enjoyment.) But once we are through with a writer whose work we once honestly and directly loved, we really *are* through. If we do go back to those texts, it's only to explore the more or less painful (or, indeed, sometimes charming; but always, ultimately, unsatisfactory) traces of our earlier vulnerability, naïveté, and immaturity. And that writer's new works, to the extent they have not grown as fast (or in the same direction) as we have, return us to all the torture of our own earlier failings and blindnesses.

In the first social circle around any artist working with any aesthetic energy at all, it's all love/betrayal. Nietzsche first played over the (then unperformed) music of *Tristan und Isolde* when he was fifteen, and fell in love with it; in his own words, it allowed the very unhappy adolescent "to go on living." At 23 (25?), he met Wagner, then in the final stages of the composition of the *Ring,* and the two became intimate friends for the next decade, through the *Ring's* premiere at Bayreuth in 1876. But when Wagner began to write first the poem, then the music, for *Parsifal,* Nietzsche broke off relations, painfully and woundingly for both men

and their families: For him, *Parsifal* was the vulgar pandering of a hugely successful artist to bourgeois religious prejudices. And what's more, Wagner didn't
realize, Nietzsche declared, that this was what he was doing! The self-deception,
for Nietzsche, made it even sicker. ("Wagner," he was soon to write, "is a disease!") And the flaw Nietzsche had seen went through all Wagner's work. It's
interesting, then, that once it was completed and performed, almost immediately
Parsifal joined that small group of religious works that atheists *particularly* have
turned to champion—while its first critics attacked it for being as intolerably sac-
rilegious as earlier critics had attacked *Walküre* and *Tristan* for being hopelessly
immoral. The religious superstructure of *Parsifal* was so clearly a metaphorical
construct to explore sexuality/asceticism, that by the end of the second act (merely a more horrendous rewrite of *Tannhauser* lost in the sensualities of the Venus-
berg, no?), the thing drips with as much smut as the rest of the Wagner canon.
Nietzsche never changed his position (indeed, he went mad); but to the extent we
can ferret out his notions from his strangely hysterical (yet often insightful) late
study, *The Case of Wagner,* published six years after the break, he seems to have felt
that because Wagner was playing both sides of the religous fence, rather than sub-
verting the very concept of the division (which I suspect was Wagner's intent
and, indeed, its effect on the late Victorian/Edwardian generation of Wagnerites),
it only made the work seem more dishonest, more duplicitous, more pandering,
and more inauthentic.

Still, *Parsifal* is the Wagner work that has gotten more than one atheist through
a bad night—not because it's religious, but because its religiosity is so transpar-
ently a metaphor for wholly secular philosophical concerns. Precisely what is perceived as its bad faith here is perceived as its strength there.

The thing that all these disapproving readings have in common is *not* that they
are wrong. That goes for a Nietzschean reading of *Parsifal.* That goes for Don's
reading of *The Towers.*

I listen to *Parsifal* and hear exactly what Nietzsche meant. That's why his critique is valuable.

I read over the galleys for a new edition of the *The Towers* and what elicited
Don's disappointment is all *too* clear.

In the same manner, I think Virginia Woolf's and Wyndham Lewis's criticisms
of *Ulysses* are dead-on.

And though I'm still a bit close for the clearest vision of it, I suspect Decarnin
on *Nevèrÿon* will prove to be just as right—especially if the perspicacity of S——
K——[6] is anything to go on. Yet *The Towers,* for better or for worse, was the only
direction I was *able* to grow in after *Jewels.* And the *Nevèrÿon* series was the only
direction I was able to grow after *Triton.* I didn't choose them. They chose me.
And for some readers that was valid.

The hard thing for any reader to accept is that none of the readings is privileged. That goes for Nietzsche's, Don's, yours, and, indeed, mine. None cut
through to fix beyond doubt a conscious *or* unconscious intention. (It's not that
my intentions are only expressible by my text. It's that intentions are *not* expressible. At best they're just another fiction, no matter how sincere one was about

---

[6] One of Decarnin's pseudonyms.

them, before or after the writing. And the text is only a more or less intricate shadow play. But the glassine puppets that throw their shapes and colors on the screen are *not* intentions.) About all these texts there's a lot *more* going on than the criticism (even our own to ourselves) can fix—even, I trow, about Delany's.

Still, I understand: If we are in the world with the writer (rather than simply being a reader with only the fiction of the author to deal with), we have to *act* as though our readings are privileged—if *only* with ourselves. I've done it many times. (Hell, I do it every time I do or don't choose to take a book off the shelf!) So I can't fault you for it.

Well, so much for my self-protection.

To practical matters: I'm still not sure how I'm to read your remark *anent* the dedication: "I wanted to ask you to take it out." If you meant: "Would you please take it out?" I'll certainly remove it. Just let me know by the 20th. If you meant, you wanted to ask but you've decided not to, I'll let it stay.

"In our case, the money question brings on this tremendous seesawing between feeling sorry for you and feeling great resentment at the idea of feeling sorry for you."

I've always questioned that kind of "feeling sorry for others" that leads to resentment. Certainly it's not a feeling that is good for anyone. (It does me no good, nor does it do you any.) And though I can't in good faith urge you to have or not have any particular feeling—your feelings are yours, for better or worse, and you have to negotiate them—I would certainly urge you to ask yourself what is really going on among their dark and painful coils.

About three days before I received your last letter (the one dated July 9th), I woke up in bed about two o'clock in the morning to find myself thinking about you—it was, in fact, about two days after I'd put *my* last letter to you into the corner mailbox. And for the next two hours, I lay awake, thinking—and feeling terribly sad.

You are one of the people I cherish deeply, Mog—certainly you're one of my closest friends. Back when I first knew you were coming to New York, on your way to Denmark, I was incredibly happy about it.

(Did I think, given what I knew of the situation with Jacob, you were out of your mind to go? Yes! Did I think you were probably going to be miserable when you got there? I feared it!)

But simply in terms of your visit, I've looked forward to few things with more ear-to-ear-grin excitement and anticipation. And, the next October, when you were coming back from Denmark, though I was burdened with the most hellish part of the tax hassle, I felt exactly the same way.

With wonderful ebullience and joy, I looked forward to entertaining you! I looked forward to your having a good time! I felt bad that we couldn't ask you to stay here as a house-guest, but that, alas, is part of our house rules; and the twice, years back, we broke them, it was disaster (in one case) and near-disaster (in the other); and most of that disaster is in terms of Frank's discomfort: That is why the rules are there. Still, I wanted you to like my home when you got here. In the past people have told Frank and me how warm and friendly they felt the place was when they visited us; and I hoped you'd be someone who, here, also felt that way. I wanted you to feel welcome and warm and comfortable.

I looked forward to talking with you, listening to you, sharing good feelings—and I wanted, if only for a few afternoons, to provide a place where you might ease some of the emotional tensions from the Jacob situation, either by talking about them, or by forgetting about them completely, whichever was best; and, what's more, my wanting all that was a rich and fine feeling (not a needy and desperate one), of a sort I just hadn't had much of in the past few years. And I loved being able to feel that for a friend.

Well, as I lay there that July night at two in the morning, I reviewed what had actually happened over the two visits at either end of your Denmark trip: I had cooked chicken wings and laid out fruit for you and your friend, Sue-Ray (?); I'd had you over for dinner with Greg Frux, a friend of mine I'd hoped you'd like, who shared your involvement in S/M; we'd gone to the Statue of Liberty together; we'd talked and walked and, four months later, when you came back to the States, we went to the opera, ran into Jacob, and so I'd had you and Jacob and his friend to dinner. Yes, suffering with standing-room through a bad production of *Tristan* was more of an imposition on you than not—still, I thought we had some pleasant and close times; I was sunk in the tax hassles, which I didn't yet feel I could share with you (and, yes, damn it, I didn't want you to worry); and I became aware soon they were putting a strain on me that certainly you felt and must have wondered at. Yet I hoped they hadn't put that much of a veil over the time with you; and during that time was as close as I came to forgetting them.

At any rate, what was the result of all this on you? On your first visit, you felt "uncomfortable," that there was a "weird feeling" in my apartment, that "unstated messages" were going back and forth over your head, and that, finally, during your second visit, you had been "set up" by either Frank or me and manipulated in a truly unpleasant way—none of which I'd known at the time, but all of which I found out from your letters months (!) after the fact!

For the first hour, I lay there unable to sleep, with a heaviness in my chest and throat and gut; I thought I was feeling sorry and guilty, because I'd wanted you to have a good time when, instead, you'd had such a wretched one, and, however inadvertently, I'd caused it. Then, at the end of that hour, after some tosses and turns, suddenly all my guilt overturned into a kind of anger.

Only the week before, I'd come back from visiting Joanna's for three days in Seattle. Now I've had all sorts of weird and strange friends. But if you wanted to do a sitcom episode about someone trying to make an unwanted house guest never, never come back again or even to *speak* to you any more, you could take Joanna's behavior while hosting me over those three days as the basis of your scenario and produce a riotous script that would only strain belief through its sheer extremity! And yet I know Joanna; I know that, whatever oddness she has, she really *does* like me, really *wants* me to enjoy the strict diet of yogurt and tofu and the leathery fried eggs she insists on cooking for me herself (and bought eggs especially *for* me; *she* uses low-cholesterol substitutes!) and the otherwise empty refrigerator and the endless complaints about her pains and her students which pass for her conversations these days; I know she really *wants* me not to be bothered by her exercises and the bizarre schedule of naps and arisings — and so, because her intentions were so patently, even childishly clear and good and fine, and because I recognized the utter and despairing social isolation in which, now, she largely lives and in which, still, she is able to maintain such intentions, I *did* have a good time! A real, honest, and sincere one—no matter *what* kind of sitcom her overt behavior might have made.

I enjoyed our trip to buy the single chocolate truffle; and I enjoyed our salmon lunch on the river; and I enjoyed being alone in my room, reading Brecht, while she napped or did exercises; and I enjoyed taking her shopping cart through the supermarket; and I enjoyed the call she got from her agent in New York while I was there; and I enjoyed reading all the reviews of her three new books. And I enjoyed talking with her and listening to her. And I enjoyed the disastrous food. And I was very moved by all the effort a woman who is, after all, only a step away from being physically crippled, put out to make the reception after my lecture so pleasant—at the same time as I smiled at its hopeless inefficiency and the scatter-brained selection of drinks and cheeses. And what I couldn't directly enjoy, I could still smile quietly over to myself. And the smile was quite sincere and with only the tiniest bit of self-protective derision—even though most of what I was smiling at was, in truth, pathetic, if not tragic, and comprised of just those things—food, shelter and severe personality disorder—that are the basis of all social discomfort.

As I lay there, it went through my mind: I've always given *my* friends the benefit of what I took to be their intentions in matters of hospitality. Why, I thought angrily, can't Mog do the same for me, in situations that *had* to be much more comfortable for her than mine, say, had been with Joanna? I began to think: Not only that, but Mog says she didn't even *begin* to have all these negative feelings (or to be bothered by them) until *after* she was *away* for a month! What kind of "bad time" is that? Just because, a month later, she's in a funk over something, she uses that as excuse to run down the last couple of times somebody who truly likes her worked his ass off to try and do something nice for her!

This is just a number she's putting me through for her own very bizarre reasons. Suppose, after having enjoyed my visit with Joanna the way I did, I suddenly turned around and decided a month later that she was a lousy hostess, that she had thoughtlessly put me into all sorts of discomforts of a kind I haven't come near experiencing when, say, I've stayed over for the night or the weekend at the homes of any number of other English professors who've invited me to their universities to lecture or to read; and suppose I wrote her all this in a letter, no matter how delicately I tried to put it, and what's more I went on to accuse her of exploiting me or manipulating me while I'd been there in a way that turned out to be either a patent fantasy or, at best, a patent misunderstanding? (The reason she asked me out, of course, was because she likes me and knew I truly needed the $300 honorarium!) What would that say about *me*? What would that say about our friendship? Well, I don't *like* what it would say about *me*. And I don't like what it says about Mog. Maybe Mog's just afraid of having close friends at all, I don't know. Maybe she just lashes out at people who like her. But why the hell should I lie here, ten months later, sleepless over it all . . . ?

Only the anger didn't dispel the heaviness in the chest, the constriction in the throat, the hole at the stomach's pit. And in somewhat under five minutes, the anger itself, which had lasted far shorter than the guilt, opened up into what it was:

Very simple, and very painful, my feeling was (and had been all along): "I like

Mog immensely; I wanted her to have a good time. And she didn't. So I failed. And that failure makes me feel worthless, lost, useless, and despairing, and generally terrible about myself — so much so that I cannot bear it." At that point I knew that what I was *really* feeling was neither sorry for you, nor angry at you. The only thing that made it "a number" was my response. If the situation between us had called up those feelings of worthlessness and despair, these feelings were very much mine and mine to deal with. They weren't something *you* had given to me. They had as much to do with my work, my life, my tax situation, my heaven-only-knows-what history with my family, and the-dear-knows-what-else. These were where my feelings came from. Certainly the letters you'd sent me had brought them up. But if the feelings *hadn't* been there all along, though I might indeed have been sorry you hadn't been able to enjoy yourself here, you can be sure I wouldn't have lost any sleep over it, if only because I *do* know that I sincerely like and admire you, however you feel about me. Or, indeed, my work.

And though you might want to point out this or that unpleasant or thoughtless thing I might, yes, have done, you no more wanted me to lie in bed with literally unbearable intimations of despair and terror and inadequacy and loneliness and powerlessness, any more than I would want you to. The one thing we all know: *No* human being deserves these feelings. Why else do we become so enraged at the people who, now and again, we are convinced are tearing us down till we have only those feelings to deal with?

And having had that revelation, did the feeling of worthlessness and despair go? No.

They had about another hour.

Still, once I knew what they were, they were a *little* easier, if only because I knew, like the weather, they would pass.

Then, three days later, your next letter came — which was so up and ebullient and cheerful. It made me feel wonderful — as good as I'd felt about you at any point in our friendship.

I don't know, Mog. The people who wish you well in the world are not the people you should feel guilty about or furious with. And I wish you only well, and would do anything I could to secure it for you. And I've only reason to believe you feel the same about me. But I know that when you start feeling badly about people who wish you well, it's a sign something's wrong.

In a really cruel way, it's only the people we're close to whom we *trust* enough to develop paranoid fantasies about—whom we *dare* let ourselves feel, either consciously or unconsciously, that they must be trying to do us in. But when we begin to believe our own defensive rationalizations, we hurt ourselves and the people who like us—all to cover up those dreadful feelings: "I'm not adequate to be anyone's friend. I am worthless and helpless. What could anyone see in me anyway? Who could possibly like me? Who could possibly like someone as weak and fault-filled as I? The demands of friendship—the demands to be a functioning person—are too much for me, and will soon kill me. I feel dead already. And anyone who claims to like or respect me must be lying or trying to use me, either for my help, or for some kind of emotional punching bag. And I am too empty and fragile and useless to take or give any more of anything, ever, ever again."

Those feelings are awful, Mog. I can't write down the words for them without crying. And when we can't bear them (or bare them to ourselves), we feel guilt or rage or terror instead, at whoever or whatever has called them up in us. Then we withdraw, hoping to escape.

Well, yesterday evening, walking up Broadway to the Baronet Stationery Shop to buy an envelope, I saw a bunch of people in front of the Discount Appliance Store, just above 82nd Street. Some kind of black velvet curtain had been hung from a frame in the street—maybe some kind of filming was being done inside. At any rate, I stepped up among the crowd to see what was happening, looking over the shoulders ahead of me. Inside were some TV sets showing the news, behind the store window's plate glass. But I couldn't tell just what was going on. About to leave, I stepped back, to feel my foot on someone's instep behind me. I threw my weight away from that foot, and staggered around—twisting my back (which has been on the verge of going out all month)—to see a homely blond man, about 28, in glasses, his hands down in his pocket, who, now, glanced at me.

"I'm terribly sorry!" I said.

But having finished his glance, his attention was back on the window.

"Really, I'm sorry!" I repeated. "Are you all right?"

Without looking, he gave the smallest nod and went on watching the window. But as I walked away, my back hurting, still confused at what the crowd had all been watching, suddenly I found myself furious! I wanted to stride back up to him and say: "Hey, you dumb twit, the fact is, I'm *not* sorry! What I really think is that you should watch where the fuck you put your goddamned dumb big feet!" And I walked the rest of the way up Broadway rehearsing this little dialogue to myself, varying my lines to him, varying his shocked or embarrassed response to me, for about five minutes.

Crossing the street from the stationery store, I walked right past it; and had to turn around and go back, I was so involved in my imaginary drama. (Has it happened before? The question is: Is it ever not happening?) But ten minutes later, I knew the mechanics were the same I'd gone through that night in July. What I'd wanted *him* to say, of course, was: "Oh, sure! It's okay. What about you? Are *you* all right?" And, indeed, it might have been nice if he'd said that or something like it. But chances are, since I'd thrown my weight, it probably hadn't hurt him nearly as much as it had hurt me. He couldn't have felt *my* back! But even if he *had* been particularly rude, or just preoccupied, the real question was: Why did the pain in my back, coupled with my bewilderment at not knowing what people were staring at, allow his absence of reaction to evoke this response in me that had moved, over moments, from guilty solicitousness to rage (neither of which had greatly shown, I suspect, in my overt behavior)? The answer is, again, because I don't feel very good about myself, and I haven't for some time. So what I'd read into his silence (or, better, what I'd written over his blank cheeks and tortoise-shell-rimmed lenses) was: "You clumsy oaf! You're not even careful enough to be allowed out on the street! And neither you nor your effort to spare me pain is worth a civil word! You're just a creep who can't write or support your lover and daughter!" And that, alas, was not his message to me; it was mine to myself, which, in the unguarded instant I had let myself write it out, I could not bear to read. And because I couldn't bear it, I masked it with guilt, then fled from the guilt into rage.

We all do this more or less, more or less all the time. It isn't something one escapes. It's something that one controls, and insight into its workings is *one* way to control *some* of it. But of such encounters, more or less intense, more or less painful, all communication is made — including these where what we write on our side of the glass happens to be, by skill, judgment, or intuition, more or less congruent to what the person on the other is trying, more or less hopefully, more or less helplessly, to scrawl on his or hers.

Probably Freud's most tragic revelation was one he made to this effect: Psychoanalysis cannot make you happy. All it can do is take irrational guilt, irrational terror, and irrational rage and turn them into ordinary sadness, fear, and anger before their proper object.

It goes for "getting in touch with your true feelings," too.

What such in-touchness gets us, I suppose, is that we're a little less likely to trouble with our fury, to confuse with our guilt, or to drive off by our terror people who don't deserve it or who even wish us well.

Okay. Moving right along . . .

Going over the section in your letter about you, me, and money, you must promise me, Mog (picture me laughing), you'll *never* write anything biographical about me! You have the most distorted picture of my life I could imagine! I mean, distorted just in terms of what things do or don't occur and when. I get this not just from the paragraph about my word processor, but also from various marginal comments to *The Tale of Plagues and Carnivals* about Jeff, or, indeed, about my taking care of Iva.

Where to start?

Perhaps three years ago, over a period of two or three months when I first met him, I paid Jeff for sex perhaps three times. (Maybe five?) The incidents that went into *P&C*, however, all occurred (save the stuff in the "documentation" section) after you first met him, on your way to Denmark! And I hadn't had anything to do with him sexually or monetarily for at least a year at that point — unless you count, as monetary, my very occasional "loaning" him a dollar or (after Dimension Convention in June) buying him a shirt and a bandage for his arm one day. I think the text implies strongly that at one point I was probably one of his johns. (The parallel between it and "The Mummer's Tale"—about first renting the hustler the room, which [that particular incident and the morning conversations; the argument, later in the story, was inspired by something else, years ago] was based on Jeff—should make that clear enough.) But writing it that way is what my "natural reticence" (Marianne Moore's words) is comfortable with. I'll stick with it. For the gay male reader, believe me, it's all there.

Next: I more or less raised Iva on my own during her first year while we were in England, despite Marilyn's three months of breastfeeding. During that year, M. was off at work, sometimes seven days a week, at her bookstall, and frequently off to Paris or the continent on buying trips, while I stayed home and took care of the flat and the kid, and wrote the last draft of *Triton* and "Shadows." Three weeks before Iva was one, we came back to the States; and, on January 12th, two days before Iva's first birthday, I went up to teach at SUNY Buffalo and M. took Iva back to England for four months, with a full-time baby-sitter (Louise White) looking after her while M. went to work again. Toward mid-April, M. came back to the States to do a reading at the YMHA, won the NBA two weeks after she was here (quite to her surprise), and went on a month-long reading tour while Iva stayed with me in my motel room up in Buffalo. Again M. took her back to England in mid-May. Then, in October, when Iva was nineteen months old, M. brought her back to the U.S. and left her to stay with me in the apartment I have now. A few months later, when she got settled into an apartment of her own, M. began to take Iva on weekends. When Iva was about three-and-a-half, M. began to take her half the time; that has been pretty much our arrangement ever since.

By the bye, M. pays for Iva's riding, summer camp, and dyslexia tutor. I pay her $4,000+ school tuition. (At least that's what it's gone up to this year.) This, at any rate, is the ideal plan. We've both deviated from it for greater or lesser periods many times. When I was doing well, I helped out M. quite a bit. Since M.'s mother died, four (?) years ago, M. has had a (very small) independent income—a useful thing for a poet—and a couple of times took over half a year's school fees. We never borrow money from one another and never will. But for all her oddnesses and eccentricity, money has never been one of M.'s crazy points. We've still never had a major argument about that—knock wood.

Oh, yes: You'll be happy to know, "Iva's attitude about women," is pretty much a thing of the past. And when all is said and done, her "attitude about women" was, finally, that they just weren't friendly, handsome men—whom she simply found every excuse possible to cuddle up to, climb all over and generally enjoy as physical objects, and to whom she talked enough to make acceptable an eight-year-old's basically sensual advances. Really, it was the rest of the world, male *and* female, that she ignored. But now that we're a mature ten, we've decided women are as interesting, if not more so, than men.

Onward: The way one gets an expensive word processor (or pays a half-year's installment on a child's private school tuition) when you're in my financial position is by saying to your accountant, when the next $7,000 check comes in: "Okay, $2,000 [if it's for the word processor and accessories; or $2,300, if it's a half-year school payment] has got to go out right now, Ed, before anyone—including the government — gets anything. After that, you can tell them whatever you like. Consider it a necessary business expense that will up my productivity—which is the only way I'll ever be able to pay back what I owe." Which, in the case of the word processor, purchased last July before things became acute in October, is true.

Your accountant then replies: "Is that an order, Chip? The money's yours, of course. But if you want my advice, there's just no way you can reasonably afford it. You're not expecting any more for another six or seven months. A third of it will have to go the government anyway. So you'll have to live off what's left for all that time . . ."

To which you answer, "Yeah, I know. But I'm afraid it is an order, Ed."

To which Ed says, "Okay. It's done." Then you live off what's left of that check for the next year — or, in my case, until the government comes and takes the remaining thousand or so away; which they had just done a few days before you arrived back in the country.

Onward (Mush, you huskies! Mush!): "I don't know how much beer and stuff cost these days, but in my imaginings it seems entirely possible that you spend my whole yearly rent on alcohol alone. (No—you'd have to spend about $7 a day to do that) . . ." It's just *barely* possible, Mog, that since last October, I've spent $45, all told, on alcohol, *including* the $6 for the magnum of zoave the night you, Jacob and his friend were here for dinner. Over the next few months I bought myself maybe half a dozen six packs, when, as someone who'd been a heavy drinker up till then, I was tapering off (No, not six. More likely three), and less than a dozen beers in bars—maybe a couple of dinner bottles of wine to friends (in fact, exactly three, because I've only been to three dinners with anyone other than my family since October); and that's the lot. It's funny, but only last week I was writing to John Mueller (*my* friend in jail), who's in an alcoholism program there, to tell him part of the fallout from my financial woes is that, for all practical purposes, I've given up drinking. As I wrote John, for a man in my financial straits to brag about not drinking is like a one-legged man bragging about never kicking his dog. Still, I was surprised how easy it was—which is to say, there were so many other things happening, I just didn't notice I'd stopped.

As far as confronting Lou about getting you galleys and MS, I confronted him *three* times, clearly, firmly and directly. Then, the next time I saw him, he volunteered to tell me that, indeed, they'd *been* sent to you! Obviously, someone from the mailroom had told *him* they'd already gone out. But when, two weeks later, an August 6th, your letter arrived which said you hadn't received them yet, I just did the most efficient-seeming thing possible. I got a copy and sent them myself.

Lou's sending you, Ron Drummond, or anyone else something from Bantam is not a matter of his wrapping it up and taking it to the post office. He phones the mailroom and tells them to get it out.

This is what happens when you don't get it.

This is what happens when you *do* get it.

I'm truly glad your letter to Lou got you the more readable set of galleys.

Still, at the point I got *your* letter, confronting Lou didn't seem particularly required to get it done. And getting it done, rather than scoring points, was what I was after. Though the variables are of immensely different sizes, my confronting Lou, strongly and pointedly, yet again, would be more or less the same (at least in form) as if you, on learning I'd never seen that *Riverside Quarterly,* instead of sending a copy to me, had sent Leland Sapiro a firm note!

And, yes, Bantam has *finally* gotten to Rowena for the cover (!).

I haven't seen her proposed sketch yet.

But I really don't feel I need to.

I know whatever she does will be fine.

Oh, yes, again: One other *good* thing! There's a seventeenth printing of *Dhalgren* scheduled for December, and unless something goes majorly wrong, the very last eighteen remaining corrections will be included in it. That, at least, has been smooth.

For all your dislike of the *P&C* tale, I've found (once again) most of your marginal comments both clear and useful. Yes, I'll try to make clearer in the non-fiction parts what's fact and what's fancy.

Thanks also for the lessons in animal anatomy. I'll make corrections where possible: the ox will become "he"; the donkey-killing, however, I envisioned a bit differently from the way you did. I saw the blow landing a little closer to the shoulder, cracking, or possibly smashing, a vertebra, but not severing the spine; then the blade was drawn down—by the woman's crouch—along the *side* of the neck, severing muscle and at least opening, if not cleaving, the carotid artery. It's clumsy, certainly; possibly it's anatomically unfeasible. But it has to stay.

I'm stuck with the "ceramic buckets." They were established back in *Neveryóna*. No doubt in a decade, if not less, they'll give way to wooden ones— going the route of the three-legged pot and the single-pronged yam-stick.

In the "microtype" version I sent you, there's a medical rider at the back of *P&C* which I'm glad you *didn't* comment on! It's been replaced by a *much* better one that's been looked over by both the GMHC and a gay doctor specializing in sexually transmitted diseases, including AIDS.

I wish you could send me, say, half a page (or a whole one) that talks about the female genitalia (and possibly some of what I [and many, many other writers, male and female] refer to as "vaginal symbols") using "vulva" in the proper way, just so I'd have a positive model to follow. I've seen men and women writers refer to the "external vagina," when they meant vulva; but I've never seen anyone refer to "vulval symbols." From your criticism (and your earlier letters), I can't tell if "vulva" is *already* accepted usage in some circles — in which case I'd like to explore that usage—or if it's a personal revision you're trying to institute. (Even if it is personal, I'd still like to explore it.)

But in either case, it *may* just be analogous to the "castration/piniotomy" problem in psychoanalytic jargon:

Technically, of course, castration refers to the testicles. Piniotomy refers to the penis. But Freud, knowing full well what he was doing, chose to generalize the meaning of castration. And to speak or write in a psychoanalytic context of "piniotomy" or "piniotomophobia" today would just be unnecessarily eccentric — unless, as I *have* written about in other places, one is writing specifically about the real and *current* confusions that stem *from* Freud's generalization—but those confusions have nothing to do with mistaking cocks for balls. Or even balls or cocks for clitorises. And "clitoral symbols" doesn't seem right for the same reason "glans symbols" doesn't.

At any rate, with an extended positive example, I can hold it up against my own language sense and — possibly — learn how to do it myself, if the gained accuracy and range of what can be said seems (to me) to outweigh the clumsiness. But it's not something I can learn just by your telling me that I and every other writer on the subject are simply wrong. After all, language *is* the way it's used, for better or worse.

There is no mention of "buboes" in the text; but I will try to make clearer that I am talking about swollen lymph nodes in both the ancient (fantasy) disease *and* the modern disease.

A last-ditch effort to rescue the *Plagues & Carnivals* enterprise in your eyes: ". . . maybe that's the point:" says Leslie to Kermit, "that we all close with that Masterly Discourse, from time to time, in pursuit of our 'liberation,' whether we like it or not." There, you underlined "close with" and wrote in the margin: "Means 'fight'—which is not what I *think* you mean to be saying!"

What I suspect, Mog, is that maybe somewhat more than half the readers will read "close with" as "join with." Perhaps another third will read "close with" as "end with." And the remaining sixth may recognize that "close with" means "fight." In each of these groups, however, a happy few (as Stendahl called them) will stop, at whichever reading, and wonder about one, or hopefully both, of the others. The multiple meanings for an instant, or a moment, or an hour, will battle in their minds. They'll ask themselves questions like: "Which one *should* Leslie mean?" Or: "Though it's obvious which one she *probably* means [though they may disagree among themselves about which meaning each finds obvious], do the others really lurk within it?" Or: "Is Leslie describing an inevitable human failing or an unavoidable moral imperative? And what is the difference? And do they depend an each other in any way?" Well, in terms of the rest of the book, I'd be *content* with *any* of those readings: join, end, or fight. But even if most readers totally loathe what the tale has to say of AIDS, art, or anything else, if *one* goes through that kind of thinking at that line, I'll feel the whole book was worth the effort of writing it: That reader will be giving at least that line, which is the center of that tale (if *not* the entire book), just the kind of reading Leslie requests and Kermit dismisses as impossible nonsense.

I'm writing for the happy few — though the happy few are often profoundly miserable people. Still, it's the process, rather than a particular conclusion to it, I feel is the Good Thing in the World I want my writing to encourage.

And, finally, yes: You, Eric, and Lyn are most welcome to use "Time Considered as a Helix of Semi-Precious Stones" for $100 in an anthology to be published by Alyson Publications. What would the title of the anthology be, by the bye? The most accurate version of the text is the one included in the *SF Hall of Fame, Vol. III,* edited by Clarke and Proctor, Avon Books: New York, 1982, pp. 593 through 632. I own the copyright, and the copyright notice should appear exactly as it appears in the Avon edition, i.e.:

> *Time Considered as a Helix of Semi-Precious Stones,* by Samuel R. Delany,
> Copyright © 1969 by Samuel R. Delany. Reprinted by permission of the
> author and his agents, Henry Morrison, Inc.

The check (and the contract for me to sign, whenever that comes around) should be made out to Henry Morrison, Inc., and sent to his Greenwich Village address.

Give my best to Lyn and Eric.

If I'm getting telegraphic here, it's just exhaustion.

(It's now Saturday, Sept 9th.)

In your letter, at one point you wrote about wanting to "call a moratorium" on our friendship for a while. If you still do, I understand. After all, whatever the emotional mechanics, how many sleepless nights can one take? That night in July I lay awake feeling so badly — well, I'd be lying if I said the idea of a respite hadn't crossed my mind as well. But just as honestly, it hasn't since.

Still, if you pull away from the friends who love you and want to see you happy, and limit yourself merely to the rages and miseries strangers in the street can cause you just by being preoccupied with something other than you, all you miss out on is that odd letter or conversation, three days or three hours later, that makes you feel good all ever again.

But you don't, in the end, avoid much pain — since, sadly and unfairly, so much of that pain is finally a defense, cruel to yourself, and painful to your friends (because, yes, it brings up all *their* own sense of [read 'my own sense of'] inadaquacy and worthlessness before the demands of friendship), against feelings one would rather be irrationally miserable or irrationally cruel than know.

Drop me a note about the dedication, and I'll remove it or leave it, as you wish. And as far as general communication, I'll take my cues from you. When you've got sore or irritated spots, you have to give them time and space to heal. And, yes, though it's not fun knowing that you've changed from a friend to a sore spot with someone you like a lot, I know how necessary healing is: I want you to have what you want, and what you need—even if that's an extended vacation from me.

People have wanted to be my friend because of things I've written since I was a teenager. And people who were good, and close, and dear friends have withdrawn from me because what I wrote troubled and angered them ever since I was 20. Such withdrawals are not fun; but they are not as shattering and bewildering now as they were when I was 20 or 25. And what angered and troubled this one made someone else, later, *want* to be friends; in both cases, the people involved were caring and concerned, not only about me and about themselves, but about the world.

Once again, thanks for all your time, your energy, and your sheer work on my behalf. And, more than all of these, thanks for just being you—for your posing your arguments and sending your letters and for writing your articles that sometimes I would just come across by accident in other places and for writing the pieces in *Coming to Power* and for all R—— J——'s[7] work (not to mention S—— K——'s!) and for sending me your disagreements and writing me about your frustrations and sharing your feelings and your criticisms and all your experiences and advice and concern.

If I've caused *you* the odd sleepless night—and, believe me, if I could take a dozen of yours from you by spending them myself, I'd agree in a second! — thanks for finding me important enough for that, too!

Thanks for being a good, good friend, over many times in these last years when it was terribly necessary for me to have one. That was what the dedication meant. And having said it to you, this way, here, I'll be content to leave what is, after all, a highly truncated version of it on the dedication page — an all-too-misunderstandable emblem, given the last tale—out of the book, if that's what you'd like.

All my love,

• 39 •

To Robert S. Bravard

September 15th, 1984

Dear Bob,

On the corner of 92nd Street and Amsterdam Avenue is Woman Books, a feminist book store. When Iva was a baby (stroller age), it was the only bookstore I felt comfortable browsing in for more then five minutes, because they had a crèche in the corner for toddlers, filled with toys and — usually — other children; so that

---

[7] Another of Decarnin's pseudonyms.

while you were there the kid had something to do, too. (They also had a very good selection. Today, Marilyn is part-owner — though she wasn't back then.) But further up the Avenue on the same block, a ribbed metal shutter was mostly down over another storefront. The sign above said: "Red Letter Books," and for many years, along with the Jefferson Bookstore down an 16th Street, it was the city's *other* Marxist bookstore. It had a very small space, dark, and narrow. In terms of populist pamphlets and books with exclamation points after the title, it was pretty well stocked. But if you wanted more intellectual Marxist works, you'd often do better at one of the Village bookstores or one of the shops closer to Columbia. I suppose I was in it not quite a dozen times in not quite a dozen years; and just about half those visits, the particular volume of Adorno, or Gramsci, or Althusser I was looking for was, sadly, not on their always somewhat bare shelves.

Nevertheless, as such things go, it was a New York institution.

Further up, over on Broadway, was Psalter's, the grungy but excellently stocked booksellers that took up two whole store spaces, entered by different doors, and that supplied most of the Columbia University area with books. Throughout the years of my patronage of Psalter's (where I went much more frequently than I did to the Red Letter), among the part-time university student clerks, I'd occasionally noticed a well-knit white man, perhaps a year or two older than I, with pink-plastic framed glasses, usually in shirtsleeves, and with the vaguely grayed hands of someone who spends much time moving many small old things. I was often in Psalter's three times a week, and perhaps every second or third visit, I'd see him coming up from the basement, delivering somebody some volume or other. Toward the back of the store there was an intercom which the clerks could use to call down to the basement for a title not on the shelves; and after a while I assumed it was probably he whom they were calling. About four years ago, someone reissued Alexander Trocchi's *Cain's Book* in a new $3.50 paperback edition (back when $3.50 was an expensive mass-market volume). I've always thought that 1960 novel one of the best books written in American English (by a Scottish writer) in the decade either side of it. I went to Psalter's to buy it, as my old copy of the trade paperback (one of the first printed in the country, by Grove) had vanished many moves back.

Behind the plain wooden plank, fixed between two green-painted metal bookshelves, that separated the clerk's area from the customer's browsing space, under the bare fluorescent lighting, Ed (I think I'd overheard his name by then) leaned the elbows of his rolled-up shirtsleeves on the wood while I told him what I wanted.

"We don't have the new edition," he said. "But wait a second." He turned and strode off into the back; then I heard his footsteps on the out-of-sight cellar stairs. Five minutes later he was up with the old Black Cat, rack-size, mass-market edition, second printing, from c. 1965. "I always liked this book," he said.

"You're selling it to me for the cover price?" I asked. It was 95 cents.

He leaned his elbows on the plank and folded his hands beneath his chin. "Um-hum."

"Thanks!" I said.

But from then on I knew he had that real book information at his fingertips that always makes me like someone, at least when I first find she or he has it; for it was now clear that he knew every book in the store's extensive collection, including the vast and hidden cellar stacks.

One day when Iva was still going to Manhattan Country School, on the corner of Park Avenue, I looked up to see this same man standing beside me, holding the hand of a little girl about Iva's age: We smiled, nodded (there in the autumnal urban afternoon, for moments I wasn't sure where I knew him from), crossed the street, and made our way to the school together: His daughter apparently went to Manhattan Country, too.

Perhaps a year later, I saw him delivering his little girl to the Claremont Stables, where Iva had just begun to ride. We spoke for a bit, and that time I placed him, though I don't remember whether or not I thought it a bit unusual for a bookstore clerk (for that's what I thought he was, then) to be able to afford a child in private school who was also taking horseback riding lessons.

But a year or so after that, the headlines carried the story of a piece of cornice falling from the apartments above Psalter's and killing a passing Barnard co-ed. (Shortly after that, a similar accident in Brooklyn killed my former student and friend, the young lawyer, Mayda Alcase.) The landlords covered the building front with scaffolding, put green wooden tunnels over the street for the pedestrians, repaired the building—and doubled the rents of all the stores along the block.

And Psalter's, along with several other shops along the building's base, closed.

About a month later—was it spring or fall, I don't remember—I stopped into the Red Letter, looking for a copy of Adorno's *Negative Dialectics,* to see Ed, still in shirtsleeves, sitting at the cash register behind the counter.

I said something like: "Oh, you're working here, now . . .?" And somehow, though we'd seen each other as customer and clerk for half a dozen years or more, and both had had daughters in the same school and riding at the same stable, we had our first conversation of more than four or five sentences. I found out he'd been the owner of Psalter's; and that he also owned the Red Letter! ("This store is really just a hobby, but I always felt it was needed.") He found out I was the SF writer Samuel Delany. It was a few months before the trade paperback of *Neveryóna* appeared; I remember he talked about ordering it for Red Letter.

And, no; he didn't have the Schocken NLB edition of Adorno.

But soon the metal cover was more and more frequently rolled down over the Red Letter's storefront. A couple of times I went there in ordinary business hours to find it unaccountably shut. Finally it fell off the usual bookstore rounds I make every few days for exercise and general book information.

And about six months ago I realized, as I wandered past it one afternoon, the store was permanently closed.

Well, three days ago, while I was walking up Amsterdam Avenue to bring some things to Iva at her mother's on 105th Street, I passed the corner plate glass window of Woman Books. Half a block on, the metal cover was still down over what had been the Red Letter. But there was a new sign up: "FUNNY BUSI-NESS!" ballooning (red) letters proclaimed. A colorful cut-out of Spider-Man in mid-swing hung at the left-hand edge of the store sign, and a stand-up plaque on the street showed Superman saying something like: "A Full Range of Comics!" The faintest wash of rust over the white enameled corners (perhaps from a bolt up under the gray-painted frame which some sprinkle of rain had washed down) suggested either that the sign had recently been transferred from some other outdoor location; or perhaps just that it now showed the first trace of the wear, erosion, and entropy—material and economic—that greets all new objects in the city; forces that would, how many months or years from now, cause "Funny Business" to give way to some other business, building, or what have you.

Smiling, swinging the plastic shopping bag with Iva's pink sweatshirt and black waistband in it against my leg (and wondering at the significance of such metamorphoses), I walked on up the avenue.

Many thanks for your last letter, and my apologies for taking so long to answer it. But most of the time between my own last letter and this has been taken up with production on *Flight from Nevèrÿon,* which followed hard on that of *Stars/Sand.* The latter now has its real and final cover—I truly hate the unnecessary hyperbole of the flap copy. But the black and silver starscape (with fairly simple, yellow/orange lettering) looks good—or at least respectable; and the copy hype, I suppose (or hope), finally vanishes into the conventions of advertising—or at least becomes more or less invisible against them. You're doubtless deep in the toils of opening classes and the beginning of the term. Our weather is decidedly cooler, even, now and again, uncomfortably cold.

A little earlier this afternoon, I was out on Broadway, crowded with strollers this chill and sprinkly Saturday, when I recognized a teddy-bear of a guy in a yellow slicker, a white knitted cap, and a full, reddish beard. He was looking in the wire trash-barrel, set by the phone stands on the corner in front of Shakespeare & Co., for discarded soda cans. Since the five-cent refund was instituted last year a whole new profession has bloomed in the city, one step higher than out-and-out bum, that, now and again, even I've fallen to for an hour or so: collecting discarded cans and taking them back to the stores; Mike, my aspiring SF-writer friend, who, when you first met him in my letters a couple of years ago, was hustling out of the Fiesta, and who is now rather successfully selling advertising for a slick fashion guide, lived that way for several months in the interim. At any rate, I called, "Paul . . .?"

The guy looked up.

"Hello," he said, without smiling. He almost never smiles when he talks to anyone else. "How are you doing—you know, I don't remember your name." I told him—for what? the third? the fifth time? In his late 20s or early 30s, he's rather intelligent, very well-spoken, and lives somewhere on 71st Street. We fool around when we meet in the movies. (Another indefatigable, three-orgasm-a-session guy—rather like Arly; though not so insistent about it.) The only thing really odd about him I've noticed so far is that, if you come upon him after he's been alone for more than fifteen minutes, he'll be talking and laughing to himself out loud to beat the band. Other than that, he seems normal enough.

We talked and walked for a block or so. Then, at the corner of 79th Street, he said: "'I'm going across the street here." And his closing salutation to me as he turned away in the thickening drizzle: "Now you stay warm and comfortable." But that's the kind of damp, chilly weather we've been having.

I was touched by your account of your and Cynthia's visit to your brother's. I looked back through some of your other letters where you'd mentioned him. I've only known two Mormons myself, and neither very well: One was Orson Scott Card, a practicing Mormon who struck me as one of the most moral—in the best sense—people I've ever met; and Theresa Neilson Heyden, an ex-Mormon who certainly has one of the best minds I've ever run into. Then, of course, there's the critic, Wayne Booth, whom I had a couple of interesting conversations with back at the Innovation/Renovation conference at Wing-spread, lo these many years ago. And he's no slouch either.

I will, as you advise, "stay tuned."

I was also touched by your concern that I not find myself "emotionally ripped off" by Mr. Mueller. Although, while touched, I also smiled, just a little.

Someday, Bob, I want to write an essay called "The Consolations of Promiscuity" — a phrase I know I've already used once in my essay on *The Dispossessed* in *The Jewel-Hinged Jaw*. Certainly one of these consolations is that, when one has both a promiscuous sex life *and* a solid central relation (with some- one who has his own more or less equally promiscuous outside life), you actually have a fair amount of material shored up against these disastrous infatuations which, yes, can wreak so much havoc in the lives of those of us between 35 and 55.

Despite our letters, I haven't seen John Mueller in the flesh for more than a year. And though I honestly like the young man and would be happy if he got his life together, I have no overwhelming desire to see him, either. And there are at least *three* other young men in the last six or eight months whom I am probably far closer to being emotionally vulnerable to than I am to John.

There's Arly (mentioned above), my 24-year-old, one-legged Colombian friend who lives in his 6th floor squatter's apartment on 97th Street. There's a red- headed, 31-year-old guy named J—— P——, who does shit-work for the Barry Roofing Company up on 126th Street, off Amsterdam Avenue, and who is married with two kids (eight and three) and lives in Brooklyn's Bay Ridge. And there's a 32-year-old Italian, somewhat mentally retarded, named R——, who just got on total-support from welfare, and who is busy burning what's left of his brain out by sniffing glue. (R——, sigh, is the only one who bites his nails. . .) They, all three more important to me than John, just haven't made it into my letters. More than once, Bob, while keeping you abreast of the Mueller correspondence, it's occurred to me to mention to you that, in neither its strengths nor its problems, is my friendship with John really characteristic of such relationships as I get into. Nor, so far, has it been notable for any particular extremities. It's simply the one that's left a written trace; therefore it's the easiest to share.

But you must neither think that (one) it's the unique such relationship in my life; nor, upon learning that there are several other such, progressing along with it and more important, I'd say, should you (two) generalize from it to them. Its epistolary side is precisely what makes it uncharacteristic — uncharacteristic in many, many ways.

Speaking of all this, an odd experience a few months ago, which I made a note to mention to you. In one letter or another describing some of my sexual "regu- lars," I mentioned a guy named Bob P——, who had a couple of kids, and a wife afflicted with lupus erythematosus. He came over here once, when Frank was in Europe last September, and was reading *The Brothers Karamazov* at the time, I believe. Well, after not seeing him for a couple of months, I ran into him in the

Capri, sometime in the midst of the summer. We fooled around for a while, the whole session having begun and terminated without words. But as he was buckling his pants in the theater chair, it was as if he suddenly remembered that, indeed, we had on several occasions actually talked to each other. He turned to me and said, softly, "Oh . . . by the way: My wife died."

I said, as softly: "Hey, I'm awfully sorry." Then I asked: "Your sister still taking care of the kids?"

He nodded.

And we parted. I've seen him once since, again in the Capri. But we didn't talk that time. A very strange level of communication.

Re communication in general: I've been debating muchly whether or not to send you a copy of the enclosed long letter to Mog Decarnin. But while wondering, I began rereading Clarence Brown's biography of Osip Mandelstam, where I came across the passage in which Professor Brown quotes from Marina Tsvetaeva's explication of a poem Mandelstam wrote to her during the brief period when he was infatuated with her. Tsvetaeva was a poet of equal rank with Mandelstam. Along with Pasternak and Akhmatova, the four are, of course, the great Russian modernists. When she wrote her essay, Mandelstam was already dead or missing. Tsvetaeva was to hang herself only a few years later. But at the time she wrote her piece, someone named Ivanov had published an explication of Mandelstam's untitled poem No. 90 (in the collected edition), "Not believing in the miracle of resurrection . . ." Ivanov's explanation involved a fancied romance with a woman doctor in the town of Kektebel. Incensed by the invention and speculation in Ivanov's essay (most of it presented as indisputable fact), herself a very private person (much more so than Akhmatova, who was something of a confessional poet before the term was coined), in her essay Tsvetaeva explained that the poem was written a year later about some incidents in Aleksandrovo, involving herself. Highly aware of Mandelstam's own much-professed dislike of biography, especially anything smacking of sensationalism, she also wrestles in her essay/explication ("The History of a Dedication") with the problem of what should be told and what should be withheld.

It's actually very moving. But at one point, she declares: "One way or the other, the biographer has a right to the official past (the *document*)" — and at that point, I decided I'd send a copy of the letter to you. At any rate, Bob, if you ever feel I am putting a strain on your discretion, please let me know.

There's a problem with a letter-writer of the sort that, for better or worse, I've turned out to be. I dwell on single incidents in such detail that sometimes it may be hard to see that the particular things I've written about are *not* necessarily those that give the contours of my life, at the time, or in the large. Indeed, if you were to get a general outline of what I've been doing in the last four years — or even year — you might have a hard time fitting some of these specific portraits and *feuilletons* into the overall picture.

By mutual agreement with Frank, for example (who is often appalled at the detail and specificity, if not just the length, I can run on about this or that), I mention nothing about his life, or friends, or doings — nor his very large part in mine. Nor, by extension, do I talk that much about Iva, except here and there, save this or that brief scene.

And although now and again I write you about some more or less interesting bit of editorial folderol at Bantam, I try very hard *not* to write about my actual work on my writing that I'm doing at the time—at least certainly not in anything like the proportions that it obsesses me hour by hour, day by day. It creeps in, of course, and I may mention that work on this or that is going well or badly (and, again, I may not) but my letters are, if anything, a way to escape that obsession for a while.

Once a week, on Thursday nights, for almost ten months now (another example), I've been going to meetings of *The Little Magazine;* we have published one issue, and are a handful of meetings away from sending a second issue to the printer. The meetings started in an apartment of one of the editors on the 46th floor of Manhattan Plaza, and early this summer moved to the apartment of another, on the second floor of a tenement on 48th and 9th Avenue, and, as of last week, are being held in my apartment here. In that time, we've lost three staff members and just gained (possibly) two new ones. And although I've become quite fond of some of the staff, and terribly committed to the magazine, I haven't described any of them in great detail, nor the entailed work (in or outside the meetings), nor the meetings themselves.

Yet the above three paragraphs are what an accurate overview for this past year, say, would have to concentrate on.

Possibly my tax problems would be next down on the list of major concerns—though they have taken their toll, sometimes in catastrophic amounts, on *all* the above.

Prowling through bookstores and prowling for sex, considered as a single block, probably come next, taking up about equal amounts of time.

The actual time encountering agent or editors takes up is, by far and away, the least I spend doing just about anything. I'm sure you could cram all I do for the year in that line easily within a single two-week—if not one-week—period of no more than six hours a day. This year, indeed, I'm sure I've spent more hours talking to my accountant, Ed Markum, than I have talking with my agent, Henry Morrison.

So you see, as I indulge it, garrulousness really is a form of privacy.

On the 15th, my mom took off on a cruise to Canada and Nova Scotia. The building she owns and rents out in Harlem (our old house) has had a few problems, so I've gone over there (to talk to one of the tenants behind in his rent, a Mr. Taylor). I've spoken to him on the phone several times and knew he had a grown son. But my visit (this morning, actually) was the first time I realized he was a year or so younger than I!

He's going into the hospital on Tuesday for an operation for blood clots in his legs; and even though he's between two and three months behind in his rent (well, actually, it's more complicated than that), and mother would like to get the apartment back, neither she nor I quite have what it takes to put a man out in the street the same month he goes in to have his legs operated on. So we're trying to work something out.

I took the bus up to 125th Street and Broadway, and walked the rest of the way with the rain (yes, past Barry Roofing on 126th and Amsterdam) pelting my umbrella.

Indeed, it was the first time I'd been upstairs in the living quarters since the night M. and I got back from our marriage trip to Detroit.

The stairway up to the first floor (European style, but for some reason that's the way we did it when I was a child) still had the same, delicate, vaguely plastery smell it used to have on wet days when I and my family lived there.

Though I've visited the building half a dozen times in the last 20 years or so, I've only been in the business section on the ground floor. This was the first time I've been upstairs.

The molding around the ceiling of the front room was the same. The fireplace with its yellow tile facing was still there, and the decorative panels around that, below the columned mantel. (There was a second fireplace in the big, back room, that used to be set up for gas: I can remember its rank of glowing blue nodes, like 75 matches all hissing in a row, during my second or third year. By the time I was five, though, the gas pipes had been, first, permanently sealed off and, finally, removed.) The big, sliding, double French doors were just as I remember. When I was younger than Iva, I took a shirt cardboard of my father's, made a scroll, decorated it and wrote a secret message on it, which I wanted "to be found in a hundred years." I slid it back into the housing of the door, and worked it back with the motion of the door itself, sliding it in and out. Half an hour later, of course, I decided that I wanted to get it out again. But it was impossible. I can only assume that it, or its crumbs, are still back there today. The big, walk-in closet in the brief hallway between the front rooms and the back one was the same. (It was always where I was *sure* the Christmas presents were hidden, somewhere up on the shelf behind my father's old Bell & Howell movie projector and my mother's ancient stenotype machine, above my father's old overcoat and my mother's old dark dresses. [The summer clothes were kept in the *other* walk-in closet, that, come the third week in December, I'd explore just as meticulously.] But they never were.) In the big kitchen, the cabinets that my father had had built above the sink, the stove, and the room-long counter were still there. The bits of stained glass among the little, irregular panes in the doors to the smaller cabinets inset directly over the sink were still intact. (When I was a child, the kitchen was always bright yellow; today it's a dingy beige, and in need of painting.) And when, at one point, Mr. Taylor opened the door to the bathroom to show me the toilet he'd recently had put in, I realized that the tiling on the walls and floor was the same that had been there when I was a child: those on the walls quite long and always somewhat yellowish; and the floor pattern, common in the '40s but rare today, white octagonal tiles, the size of a very big man's palm, set together, with blue squares in the spaces between.

I've written you about the time I was five when, terrified of dying from the corpse I'd been watching Freddy embalm down in the morgue, I'd run upstairs to my mother, who was cleaning the bathroom, to be comforted. (And you guys have recounted it in the introduction to your bibliography.) But it was strange to see the tiles on which she'd been kneeling as I threw myself into her arms, still there and freshly mopped, after more than 20 years—by Mr. Taylor—within the last day.

My two new culture heroes: Bruce Springsteen and Geraldine Ferraro. Am contemplating as a character for some future novel: a middle-aged black sociology professor at Howard University, from the upper black bourgeoisie, who finds himself, against his will, completely romanticizing poor white working class culture.

For him, the black middle class represents Real Culture; still, he finds himself deciding that these poor whites are the only *authentic* people there are in the country, that they are the people with real "heart" (which, as it gets non-defined, he realizes looks suspiciously like "soul") and that their music (despite the fact that *real* music is, of course, jazz; but who listens to jazz anymore...?), from Guthrie to Springsteen, is the true cultural heritage of America. Even while he sees himself falling into the same patterns as so many whites have, running to black culture, with every step he takes to avoid those clichés, he finds himself pushed, maneuvered, sucked into them even more deeply . . .

I hope it would be a funny tale.

Recent reading: Martin Jay's book on Adorno. It's obviously one of the fugitives from Frank Kermode's discontinued Modern Masters series. (George Steiner's book on Heidegger was another.) You can tell by the nature of the introduction and the general format. This one has found a home at last with Harvard University Press. It's incisive and has many of the same strengths as his history of the Frankfurt School—though I don't think it is as good as Susan Buck-Morss's *The Origin of Negative Dialectics.* ("If you must read only one book on Adorno this year, read . . .!") But, as he explains in the introduction, popularizing Adorno is just not possible.

The third chapter of Jay's book is a reading of a brief (twelve-page) essay by Adorno called "Subject-Object," that's included in *The Essential Frankfurt School Reader.* (A truly misguided title if there ever was one.) The essay is just about as long as Jay's reading of it.

I went back and read the essay itself. Jay calls it both minor and densely-reasoned. But there was an area, sometime in the '30s, '40s and '50s, where *belles-lettres* met traditional academic philosophy, in which you could almost be certain the results would be devoid of meaning, or at least devoid of communication potential. And it's precisely in that area where the essay lies.

Now I'm a reader who will wrestle happily and fruitfully through Lacan, or Foucault (or even Jeffrey Mehlman), or Charles Olson, or Derrida with no major adverse effects. This piece, however, defeats me. I haven't had the same problem with other bits of Adorno I've tackled. *Against Epistemology,* for example, goes down like good Viennese chocolate. *In Search of Wagner,* or *Philosophy of the New Music?* Mere child's play! *Prisms* and *Minima Moralia?* Now that's light, witty stuff . . .! But *this* essay . . .? It's not even that dense. Still, its intellectual pacing and sheer lack of rhetorical urgency derails me every time.

Yet Jay's reading of it makes it sound like a footnote to *Starboard Wine* on the priority of (or the tyranny of) the subject, not only in western literature but throughout western culture — whereas the Adorno essay itself seems insistently to repress just that aspect that Jay keeps pulling out of it.

For the rest, it's all Stephen Jay Gould (*Hen's Teeth & Horse's Toes,* a very reassuring book) and Jayne Anne Phillips (*Black Tickets,* a darkly pyrotechnical romp through the banality of the nightmare) and bits and pieces of Jody Scott (*I, Vampire,* stinging and astute).

Recent movies: *CHUD,* which, grade-C film that it was, had a couple of very good performances and *almost* had something to say; it was fun in much the same way as John Sayle's *Alligator* or *Q* (with the marvelous Michael Moriarity performance). Also, while she was here, I took Iva to see *Ghostbusters*—second time for me—which she loved. It's a marvelously "New York" film. It really captures something of the city. And the opening shot, by the bye, if you see it, is of the six late Bartlett statues on the pediment of the New York Public Library I once wrote you about at some length.

Also saw Jacques Tournier's *Out of the Past*, a delicate and beautifully shot bit of *film noir*, with Robert Mitchum, Kirk Douglas, and Rhonda Fleming, from the '40s. Tournier is the guy who directed those wonderful horror films for Val Lewton, *The Cat People, The Leopard Man*, and *I Walked with a Zombie* . . . This one is all about good-bad honorable gangsters and their bad-bad evil women (brunettes and red-heads all)—with one, pure-hearted, small-town girl (blonde, of course) named Anne; and a loyal deaf-mute adolescent boy who works at the local filling station run by the shady ex-private dick who's come to the little town to escape his dis-reputable past—till old gangster connections suddenly show up and drag him into violence, mayhem, and . . . death! In the same program (up at the Thalia) I caught *Nightmare Alley*, with Tyrone Power and Joan Blondel: mindless, moraliz-ing fun, with not enough about the Tarot. The Gresham novel had much more.

Oh, yes. *Two* bookstores here in the city are going to be having autograph ses-sions for me: the SF Bookshop down on 12th Street, and Shakespeare and Co. up in this neighborhood. And the last time I was in the rather prissy Endicott Booksellers (where the likes of Sontag and Eco and Alice Walker give monthly readings: Last time I was there, it was to hear a lecture by Joseph *[Hero with a Thousand Faces]* Campbell), Ely, of the sparse white hair and red beard, said something about my possibly giving a reading—though I won't hold my breath.

You know, Bob, thinking about the last ten months' work on *The Little Magazine*, it occurs to me: One way or another, in the vast majority of the poems we get, the language works as a metaphor for the impossibility of language's ever dealing with a more or less inexpressible subjective state associated with one or another experience more or less directly indicated in the poem—a subjective state which may, finally, not even exist save as a response to life mediated by art.

Was it Larochefoucauld who wrote in the 18th century: "If no one ever read about falling in love, no one would ever do it" — thus throwing the whole Romantic tradition into question almost before it began.

Well, today it's the whole aesthetic tradition that's under the same kind of questioning, and the fallout of that questioning has been everything from the "metafictionists" to Bloom's "anxiety of influence."

I guess the traditional modernist poetic enterprise (the ineffability of every-thing) is still valid, whether you take it back to the polite version in Arnold's *Dover Beach* or to the impolite version in Baudelaire's Parisian spleen: We publish our share of their descendants. But there are other ways to approach poetry, from the poetry of those committed to some political cause to the sound text poets or to experimentation in still other directions. And I'd like to see the magazine more involved on all those fronts.

And it's certainly the poems that avoid the traditional tack—the poems that focus our attention on one of the variety of new and unusual things that language *can* do, instead of on the (very real!) pathos of what it cannot, the poems that make us aware of whatever they're doing so intensely that, by the same gesture of awareness, we forget the type or category of poem they are (including the traditional type)—which evoke the most intense and interesting discussions in our editorial meetings.

The poet's traditional raid on the inarticulate can proceed in many untraditional directions.

And I *think*, Bob, I may just have written out a draft of the front-matter for our new issue![1]

My best to Cynthia and the boys. And

Much love to you,

• 40 •

To Robert S. Bravard

September 25th, 1984

Dear Bob,

Yours of the 19th September here, read, and re-read. Many thanks for the poems as well. I hear much of you—your voicing, as I get it from your letters—throughout them. Cynthia is a very lucky woman. And you are a fine friend; but though I could talk about how much I appreciate that friendship, I don't think I could convey the feeling it gives me, in a letter, no matter how long: friendship such as yours, laughter, the machineries of joy (as Bradbury calls them), these truly take whole novels.

Thank you for sharing the exchange with George Moran. (From his address, I see he's all but my next-door neighbor, here in New York.) And I'm very glad that it turned out for the better and that bygones are being allowed to be bygones.

The giving and the taking of offense is the most socially defining human situation there is. It's paradoxical: When we are stripped down to exactly who we are, to what we can bear, to what we cannot bear, to what leaves us only personal outrage and individual hurt, then we act in the most socially defined ways possible. But what better way to define the social than to specify what acts the individual people who comprise society find unbearable, unacceptable — along with the

---

[1] SRD's unsigned frontmatter from *The Little Magazine*, Vol. 14, No. 4, Pleasantville, NY, 1985:

> Was it Laochefoucauld who wrote in the 18th century: "If no one ever read about falling in love, no one would ever do it"—thus throwing the whole Romantic tradition into question almost before it began.
>
> Today it's the aesthetic tradition that's under the same sort of questioning, and the fallout of that questioning has been everything from the "metafictionists" to the "anxiety of influence."
>
> The traditional modernist theme from Eliot to Rilke (the silence and ineffability at the core of just about *every*thing) is certainly still valid. But it's the poems that avoid that traditional tack—the poems that focus our attention on one or another of the variety of new and unusual things language *can* do, instead of on the (very real!) pathos of what it cannot, the poems that make us aware of whatever they're doing so intensely that, with the same awareness, we momentarily forget the type or category of poem they are — that evoke the most intense and interesting discussions in our editorial meetings.
>
> How reassuring that the poet's age-old raid on the inarticulate can still proceed in so many untraditional directions!

ways they do find acceptable to communicate their outrage.

Not to mention the ways in which they make amends, heal the breach.

From *Pamela* on, the European novel is about nothing but what constitutes offense and about the psychological and ethical machineries surrounding it. I was re-reading *Mansfield Park* about a week back and, in the midst of the opening movement, found myself with a very odd readerly response. It was just after the witty account of Edward and Mary Crawford's sparkling conversation at their first dinner at Mansfield; afterwards, second son Edmund and poor-relation Fanny are dissecting the evening's pleasantry.

Both of them were most amused by the young Crawfords, but the first thing they home in on is Mary's speaking slightingly of her and her brother's guardian, the admiral. Both Edmund and Fanny noticed it; and their initial recognition of Mary's slight is presented as the sign that, indeed, whatever their differences in class, both are destined for one another (they speak, as it were, the same language; they recognize the same signs), and although Mary, in her previous visits to Mansfield, has already made Fanny miserable (by monopolizing Edmund's attention and Fanny's horse, in ways that any modern reader and, I suspect, any of Austen's contemporaries would certainly have found thoughtless), this is the first sign we are given in the novel that we are to take Mary's thoughtlessness as fallout from a true, inner, moral corruption.

The odd thing for me as reader was, however, that, while Edmund and Fanny spoke of Mary's slighting of her guardian as though it had been blazingly clear, I —who'd just read the scene—hadn't the vaguest memory of Mary's uttering the slightest criticism of the admiral. Indeed, I went back and re-read the scene twice. Edmund actually says, after one of Mary's mentions of the nuisances of improving property, that he was distressed to hear her speak "so freely" of her uncle. But the actual offense, I realized only after the third reading, was a single phrase: "The admiral," Mary says, "my honored uncle, bought a cottage in Twickenham for us all to spend our summers in . . ." But because the cottage turns out to be more trouble than it's worth, clearly we are to understand that "honored" was stressed to the point of sarcasm.

And that single sarcastic stress (terribly familiar today in British speech in general, but probably just becoming a part of English conversation patterns there toward the beginning of the 19th century [it's not really an 18th century attitude, you realize if you look over earlier British fictions]) constitutes the grounds for Edmund's and Fanny's taking their (very minor) opening offense. (Provocation will build up, of course, into a veritable orgy of . . . [gasp!] amateur theatricals!— at which point father will suddenly return, virtue will show its pristine face, and evil will stand revealed.) But it really takes the modern reader—or at least it took *me*—a few readings to locate the proper voicing for the single phrase that, finally, holds the novel's opening 50 pages together!

Saturday morning (the day before yesterday), I worked from about six. Conversation and coffee with Frank. Later, I walked down Broadway to 61st Street to catch the noon show of the Schaffer/Forman *Amadeus* at Loew's Paramount. A block away from the theater I saw John Douglas (formally David Hartwell's assistant at Pocket Books, now SF editor at Avon) and called to him. He turned around and greeted me: He was on his way to a noon squash date, he explained, and, as we were both 20 minutes early, we stood and talked about movies for a while. (The last time I'd spent any time with him, other than at David's various parties up in Pleasantville, was when I'd run into him and his wife at one of the opening performances of Friedkin's ill-fated and controversial *Cruising*.) The night before, he and Ginger (who left *The Little Magazine* staff just before I joined it), with another couple, had gone to see *Repo Man*. Ginger and he had liked it; the other couple had been divided. Then it was five to twelve; and in his blue T-shirt, glasses, and with his red-covered racquet, he strode off.

And at the end of a short line of desultory patrons, I went into the Paramount's round, squat tower, and descended the escalator to the underground auditorium.

For a first-run house, it's not a big auditorium. And considering this was the first show of the day, it was not very clean, either. I sat at about the 6th row. In a red T-shirt, two seats away, a blond kid about 20 looked over at me as I was writing in my notebook and asked, grinning, if I were going to be taking notes on the movie.

I laughed and told him, no, I was writing a letter. A few moments later, he went back to his Penguin *Moby Dick*, while, in the three-quarters-full house, we waited for the movie to start. When the piped in rock & roll (". . . this is WPIX, first on your dial for the Top of the Pops . . .") stopped, I asked him: "Now just suppose the music's stopping *didn't* mean the lights were going to go down and the picture was about to begin . . ."

It got another laugh.

The lights went down.

The picture began —

— with Salieri's amateurish, horrific, suicide attempt.

The film is stylish, filled with repeatedly, purposefully jarring and violent intercuts. (That cutting is, more than anything, what makes it an allegory of the contemporary.) There are certainly flaws: The women's costumes are largely unbelievable, mainly because of the quality of the sewing and the choice of materials. (Everything is rayon or polyester or some other anachronistically improbable fabric and, what's more, *looks* like it!) And the penultimate sequence (before Mozart's final burial in a communal pauper's grave), in which Salieri takes dictation from Mozart (on his deathbed) for the Requiem Mass, moving as it is, simply belongs to another film, to another story. The fact that the dictation scene is wholly ahistorical is not the point. But the assumption that Salieri's antipathy toward Mozart could melt, just like that, at the request for a favor, is simply unbelievable as Salieri's character has been set up all through the movie. It's just not dramatically prepared for.

Still, after the first 20 minutes, tears began to roll down my cheeks; and they continued drizzling and trickling until the closing credits were three-quarters over and I got up to leave the theater (the blond kid, once the credits started, jumped up and ran in the dark from his seat for the door), making my way by the crowds gathering for the next showing.

I'd be truly curious what you thought of it; and though I've since heard two TV critics pronounce it "boring," it's certainly worth a look.

Afterwards, I walked down Broadway toward the Lower East Side; went in to Variety Photoplays on Third Avenue. Stayed a few hours. Had an unexpected and pleasantly intense climax when, in his beard, red baseball cap and ancient thermal vest, the scrawny, 28-year-old Puerto Rican derelict masturbating two seats from where I was (he'd already shooed me away from him once), leaned forward and decided to pee on the back of the seat in front of him. Did a little more fooling around, with, among others, a regular of mine for some fifteen years now, but whom I've always thought of to myself as "Big John." I first used to run into Big John—back when he wasn't *quite* so big—in the larger and more active of the old 14th Street subway johns (remodeled out of existance a few years ago, when the station had its whole face lifted: The un-remodeled station is commemorated in the [fine, if flawed] film based on the Sol Yurok novel, *The Warriors*—though not, alas, the john; the one they *do* use in the film is *another* bathroom somewhere on the BMT line out in Brooklyn), back when I first lived at the Albert Hotel.

Every once in a while, the unusualness of my sexual situation vis-a-vis the standard bourgeois world does, I'm afraid, strike me. Save for the times I've been out of the country (or, indeed, the city), here is a man I've had some kind of sexual contact with between twice and ten times a year for fifteen years now. We've exchanged *perhaps* 500 words in the whole time. And most of those are monosyllabic grunts, "There," or, "Just a moment . . ." or, another time, after we've had three more encounters, and maybe "Okay . . ." two years and six encounters after that.

And I still don't know his name, nor he mine.

Yet these encounters are comfortable, comforting, often (as the years go on) more emotionally satisfying than they are physically rewarding, and, from time to time, deeply affectionate—without ever straying beyond the most tenuous rim of friendship or moving anywhere near what I or anyone else would call, by any catachresis, love.

(I suppose I should add: But not all of them are. Some, of course, are absolutely pedestrian — even disappointingly so. Though of course those partners who are repeatedly so don't remain regulars. And note: I almost never write of, say, those equally regular rejectors whom, year in and year out, you try to approach every few months, only to be turned away from, or walked away from, or sometimes simply told, "Un-un," yet again. Not to mention the few that you, for whatever reasons, regularly reject.)

About five-thirty I left the theater, took a leak against the brown wooden fence at the back of the parking lot off third and 10th Street, wandered around in the St. Mark's Bookstore awhile (I think, with my five-days-toward-a-winter-beard, they thought I was a bum. A new clerk, who didn't know me, kept asking if I wanted any help), then took the long, long stroll back up Broadway home.

Down and back, with various wanderings about, I walked ten miles that day.

Spent the next day working pretty much on *Splendor and Misery,* and listening to *La Nozze di Figaro* on my walkman: Lovely as it is, I'm afraid I'm still basically a Don Giovanni fan—with a leaning toward *Idomeneo* and *Zauberflöte.* Also read the first book of Rabelais; this in conjunction with reading Bakhtin's *Rabelais and His World,* a work about which I have heard much in the last three or four years and which I've actually read a few selections from: But now I am launched into the whole thing.

Small divagation, if I may: Last night (Thursday) was our *Little Magazine* meeting, and David Hartwell, after the women had left, thought he might stay over.

Frank was amenable. So David called John Douglas and Ginger (with whom he'd been planning to stay); then we went down to McAlier's for a couple of beers (Frank hates bars so, though he was invited, didn't come); half an hour later, we came back and David retired into Iva's room, which Frank (bless him) had neatened up at bit. (Iva comes back from her mom's on the first.) When he rose this morning at about 7:30, I'd already been up for an hour and was busy reading and making notes on the "Culture as Manipulation; Culture as Redemption" chapter in Martin Jay's book on Adorno, which I may have mentioned before.

Frank wasn't up yet; David came into the living room with his coffee, asked me what I was reading, and I showed him the book.

"Adorno? He's not someone I've ever heard of before," David said.

Now David is a highly cultured man; he has a Ph.D. in Medieval literature, has edited *The Little Magazine* for nearly 20 years, and is simply and unabashedly a wide-ranging mind.

So I launched in: "Well, Adorno was a kraut philosopher who worked primarily in the '30s, '40s and '50s, came here after World War II and ended up in California. He's the guy who helped Thomas Mann with the stuff on modern music in *Doctor Faustus.* In Europe, he was part of a group of thinkers known as the Frankfurt School, which finally moved to New York to escape Nazi persecution—and was probably the most intelligent, most original, and, until recently, one of the least known. The Frankfurt school included people like Hannah Arendt, Herbert Marcuse, Erich Fromm, Walter Benjamin, Fredrich Pollock, and, among the most important, Habermas and Horkheimer. Adorno wrote a great deal about modern music. He was a passionate advocate of Schönberg, a friend and pupil of Berg's during the composition and early success of *Wozzeck,* and he hated Stravinsky: He thought Igor was too pandering and popular. He loathed jazz, movies, and pop music in general—which didn't make his work sit too well with some of the other Marxist thinkers of his day who were busy trying to hail the work of the masses. His aesthetic is kind of the '50s view of culture raised to the highest brow. He coined the term 'culture industry' and used it instead of 'mass culture,' because he felt 'mass culture' suggested the idea of a folk-art welling up spontaneously from the people, whereas he felt 'popular culture' was entirely imposed upon the working class from above. I've read about five of his books, out of the 23 volumes of his collected works. There's one, *Minima Moralia,* which is full of aphorisms and essays between half a page and three pages long. You might try some of these, just to get the flavor of his thinking. Actually, as complex as he was, he was also a very fine writer. One thing that makes him particularly interesting today is that he always maintained the most important things about any work of art were the digressions, the eccentric parts, the things that didn't fit neatly into the work when considered as a system. What he valued most were the things that stuck out, that remained, and that defied the whole 'closing cadence' which we think of as the proper and resolved ending for a piece of music or writing.

"Also, he would have hated the kind of popularization this book represents. Or even more so what I'm telling you about him now. He was the kind of person who said: 'My work is difficult. It's meant to be difficult. Simplify it, and you distort it.'"

That got a laugh from David, who took another sip of coffee and said: "Chip, someday I'm going to commission you to write a book about who did what with whom and when. That's the kind of thing you're always full of, and it just fasci-nates me," which I took as a compliment.

However, I've been thinking—no doubt under the influence of Adorno himself (or, at any rate, more recently Jay *on* Adorno)—there's a great drive today to make philosophical thinking itself into a commodity: And after reading three or six books by this thinker or that, along with two or three more by their various com-mentators, you begin to have the feeling that you have now *consumed* Barthes's system, Focault's system, Derrida's system, Kristeva's system, Bakhtin's system, Adorno's system . . . even as each is busy explaining to you and proving beyond refute how illusory and impossible and contradictory the whole notion of system is. Yet you can't avoid it—another point that, indeed, the best of them all make.

I guess this moment of philosophico-critical despair (and, believe me, it grew quite deep and intense there for a while, after David left to go down to Tor Books) is the *haute* version of the same alienation I was feeling after Dimension Convention where I moderated the Lee/Ellison debate.

Oh, sigh . . .

Oh, angst . . .

(O Tempera! O Mores . . .!)

One can mount a perfectly rational attack on Adorno, by the bye, to the effect that he, along with the other contributors to the famous Frankfurt School study of fascism, *The Authoritarian Personality*, is probably more responsible than any-one else for promoting the uncritical idea that the Nazis were all sado-masochists, and that sado-masochists are, conversely, all Nazis. (Stravinsky's music is bad, according to Adorno, because it exploits the audience in a "sado-masochistic" way . . . Which is also his beef against popular culture: But for "exploits in a sado-masochistic way," you can simply read: "tries for *any* pre-meditated effect whatsoever.") Clearly Adorno's "sado-masochism" has absolutely nothing to do with the S/M I was discussing in my last letter to Mog, i.e., a real and human sexual impulse expressed in highly socialized behavior, highly conscious and conscientious, and woven round and through with a com-plex web of codes and communication modes and conventions, however mar-ginal that behavior seems to most.

In comparison, Adorno's "sado-masochism" is the fuzziest of metaphors for a kind of unfelt ur-urge that may not, when all is said and done, even exist. "Racine writes of a world," I remember reading someplace, "where politeness is one of the fundamental passions." Well, Adorno's world, where "sado-masochism" is a fun-damental passion, is just as much a fiction. And, indeed, the same kind of fiction. (It's the notion of fundamental passions, i.e., instincts, as they are usually con-ceived, that is the fiction.) And it's a dangerous fiction because so many people take it for the real and assume that that fiction has something truly revealing and fundamental to say about real leather bars and real women in studded black brassieres and men in black motorcycle jackets standing in the shadows on Christopher Street, e.g., Don DeLillo's *Running Dog* . . .

But this is only to go on with the negative version of the same *kind* of pseudo-critique I was giving David.

Still, how do you think about *anything*, then, without being reductive? And better reductive thought than idiocy, *n'est-ce pas?*

But back-tracking just a bit:

Last Monday, Marilyn very nicely took me for lunch up at Hanratty's an 92nd St. and Amsterdam. Something we've always tried to do: Every six weeks or two months, we get together and have a conversation where nothing controversial is discussed—usually just poetry and literature. (Or, if either one of us responds to anything as controversial [and I always do], we keep it to ourselves.) We decided this by mutual, more or less silent consent, after we separated, simply as a good way to help keep peace. Then, when we had the therapy session I wrote you about, when M. wanted to take Iva off to school for a year in France, the therapist suggested it all over (as it were) as a way to keep tensions down.

Somehow, though, we haven't gotten to it for a while. (The last time we saw each other to do anything more than exchange Iva and/or shopping bags full of Iva's clothes, M. was shouting after me in the street outside of the Planetarium Travel Agency because I wouldn't go down to get Iva a replacement passport for them to go to France. "You want to go to France," I'm afraid was my uncavalier attitude; "I happen to be *very* busy. Get it yourself.") Well, when M. suggested we get together, I kind of jumped at the chance to restore—or at any rate stabilize— the recent calm.

I told her I was too broke to go out to a restaurant, but she was welcome to come over and I'd whip something up at the house. To which she said: "Oh, good lord! You've taken *me* out to lunch enough times. I'll take you!" And so she did— she having only a bowl of fresh strawberries herself, while I had black bean soup, a club sandwich on a croissant, and a rich, thick, gooey piece of pecan pie with whipped cream.

And we both drank large glasses of club soda with lime.

While M. was in England (in June, with Iva), she told me, she developed a number of new poetic enthusiasms, including an Irish woman poet named Eavan Boland, as well as several others, male and female, whose names escape me this morning. Also, she and Tom Disch are in the midst of an interesting (?) poetic folderol. Tom published a long poem in the July *Poetry* called "Working on a Tan." In it, there's a reference to a female friend who's spent "the last three summers subsidized." ("How can she stand another day at McDowell?" the poem asks. Then goes on to say, "Do I smell sour grapes?") Nevertheless, M. took minor offense, and shot off a poem to Tom which, in my humble opinion, was mostly metered grumblings — sort of the modern equivalent of Robert Southey's moralistic homilies, only gone feminist—for the first seven (?) quatrains. The last few rise, however, to true wit. Tom answered with an equally witty letter.

And now he has found some editor who wants to publish the whole exchange; M. has been invited to have the last word.

My own advice to her was to cut the first few stanzas of her own poem and cover the same material in a letter, of whatever degree of seriousness, following Tom's. But she likes her poem and doesn't like my advice. So I let it ride.

At any rate, I don't know where it'll all go.

After lunch, M. walked me down a few blocks, then turned toward B'way. I stepped off back at the apartment here, picked up a copy of *Tides of Lust*, and brought it and a whole bunch of other books I'd been carrying with me down to Henry's office. (The Germans want to do my pornography now, and the French my non-fiction.) From there I called Bantam to find out, from Mary Lucas, that the page proofs on *Flight from Nevèrÿon,* due this past Friday, will be two to three weeks late. (Printer's overload.) Then — with an hour's stop-off in the Cameo above 42nd—back home.

The last installment for the day concerns one of the batch of letters I'm including along with all this.

The very nice letter from Umberto Eco to Lou had arrived (in Xerox) at my house in the mail that Friday — along with (another Xerox of) a very silly letter Lou had written in response, to the effect (I paraphrase wildly): "Dear Professor Eco, thanks for your letter, but I can't tell from it whether or not you mind if we quote you. We'd like to use the following lines . . . Please write back and let us know if it's okay."

If you look over Eco's letter, I think you'll find it obvious that he intended it to be used. At any rate, given how busy he is, it would have been far more considerate of Lou to say (in effect): "Thanks for your letter. We'd like to use thus and such a section. Write us back if you have an objection."

Anyway, it so happens that Eco is now in New York, teaching for a term as a visiting-professor at Columbia University, and that Monday evening he was scheduled to do a reading to open this season's program at the 92nd Street YMHA. "Look," I had said to Lou on the phone that very morning, before taking off to Hanratty's, "I'll go see Eco this evening at the Y." This was mostly at Frank's urging. "And I'll try to see him afterwards and get a verbal okay, so at least you can go ahead. You'll never have time to use the quote if you wait for him to answer your second letter, after he gets back to Italy, at the end of the term."

"Good idea," said Lou. "I just didn't want to — you know—ruffle his feathers."

(O Great Mother, protect this thy servant from timid, well-intentioned, overworked, 26-year-old editors.)

So I got $9 worth of dry cleaning out of the tailors, which I can ill afford (My Suit, and the Stuff That Goes With It); took $8 for the ticket, and two more bucks for transportation (all-in-all we're talkin' a $20 night here—for a man who can no longer *have* $20 nights; who, indeed, must save change for three days to afford a $2 porn movie, and for five days for a real $5 movie) and, in blue suit jacket, blue jeans, and blue-striped tie, totally exhausted, took off on the No. 17-M cross-town bus, through the leafy darkness of Central Park, for the Y.

I arrived an hour early on that dark, warm evening to find several hundred people already waiting — most of them with their tickets, reserved or purchased days ago. I joined a special line for those who wanted to buy tickets there and then. To make a long story short, I finally got in — at about five after eight — to the crammed Kaufman Auditorium. It holds about 800. Wonder of wonders, I got a seat at the very side, near the dark, wood-paneled wall, and sat (kind of having to pee, but not too badly) waiting another 20 minutes for the program to begin . . . half an hour late.

The last time I'd been in the Kaufman was to hear Grace Paley and Donald Barthelme read; and the time before that was when, in '75, I'd come down from Buffalo to the Y to hear M. and Margaret Atwood read together.

Tonight, however, Eco was reading alone.

At last the lights went down on the audience and up on the stage.

[Pause for announcement:

4:28, Friday afternoon, September 28th—that's about ten minutes ago—a tall black teenage messenger, who had me sign for it when I walked two landings down to meet him, delivered the first copy of *Stars in My Pocket like Grains of Sand* here to the apartment building with a small note from Lou: "Here's one of the first copies off press. Looks wonderful, doesn't it? Lou." Yes, Lou. It does! I got to play with it for about five minutes. Then Frank came out, and is looking at it inside now, while I'm back typing this.]

The director of the Y's Poetry Center, Shelley Mason, came out on the stage. (It used to be Grace Schulman.) She's a healthy-looking farm-girl, with short brown hair, no makeup, and a sensible gray dress. She announced that we were all invited "for a glass of champagne" in the gallery afterwards, during the reception for Mr. Eco. And I breathed a sigh of relief: The audience was so big I was afraid there'd be no way to get to him if he was on his way anywhere after the reading. Then she said that Richard Sennett would introduce Eco. (From somewhere I knew that the introducer had been supposed to be Eco's American translator, William Weaver. But from what newspaper squib or overheard bit of conversation, I truly don't remember.) Mason left the stage. And out came the thin and bespectacled Sennett, who took his place behind the podium, stuttered a few phrases (well chosen enough) about *The Name of the Rose* and the search for truth.

He left the podium; and as the side door opened to receive him, the black-bearded, medium-sized bear who is Eco came out in his red tie, gray suit, and black-framed glasses, with his papers, to take his place behind the podium to much applause.

Eco's informal English is very good. His accent is thick, but he manages to make some quite cutting jokes and conveys irony well; also, he can put across a friendly sarcasm when he needs to. Reading English out loud, however, is — I suspect — a trial for him. The long and short sounds of vowels become hopelessly and randomly interchanged. He consistently pronounced the word "none" as if it were some odd and awkward singular for the nine o'clock prayer. Yet all it meant was that we had to listen a bit more carefully — which made it more involving.

First he read a two-page section from *The Name of the Rose* in Italian—basically some euphonious and alliterative catalogue, so that the pure music was a delight. Then, in English, he read a philosophical colloquy between Adsell and William of Baskerville—the one where they talk about "animals with and without horns" which makes its little jibes at the current Parisian thinkers (of a decade ago, but who's counting?).

Next he read the section where, after screwing the peasant girl, Adsell, in the tower Library, looks at the books on the "sickness of love"; that was followed by a section from Adsell's dream, while he dozes off at the church service: full of sex, theology, and grue. (I suppose it would be impossible to write a book about a monastery full of medieval monks that *wasn't* sexist. Though, really, Eco didn't even try.) Finally, he closed with the finale: Adsell's return to the burned-out monastery ruins years later, to collect the fragment manuscripts.

After the reading, which I enjoyed about as much as any reading I've ever been to (it's a brand of social affair I don't really cotton to or approve of in general), Shelley Mason came out again to stand at a separate microphone to the side and help him field the audience's questions.

Those questions ranged from intelligent to idiotic. Ones that stick with me were:

"How long did it take for you to write the book?"

Two years of thinking—basically to build the world—but under three months of actual writing. (Ah, I thought: first novels!) I suspect what this means is: I thought about writing a book for almost two years—during which time I got and dropped all sorts of ideas. Finally, over three months, I sat down and did it.

"Could you tell us, exactly what is semiotics?"

"You may read with some profit," Eco responded with a raised beard, "my three books, *A Theory of Semiotics*, Bloomington, Indiana, 1976, *The Role of the Reader*, Bloomington, Indiana, 1979, and *Semiotics and the Philosophy of Language*, Bloomington, Indiana, 1984." That one got a laugh.

"Could you translate the Latin of the last line of the book?"

He answered this question quickly, even with (guarded) enthusiasm: "The pristine rose remains only as a name; we hold only its name."

He also mentioned a fragment of Abelard that had always intrigued him: "*Nulla rosa est,*" which could be translated two ways: "The rose is not there," and "There are no more roses."

In the course of the discussion it also came out that he'd always been fascinated by laughter. (Rabelais, quite coincidentally with my reading of the previous day, got mentioned a couple of times.) He said he had, as a younger man, wanted to write a treatise on laughter (*à la* Bakhtin?), but had never gotten round to it. (Doubtless that's the imaginary spur behind the Aristotle work "On Comedy" destroyed [in the novel] by Borges.) But it had occurred to him that man alone laughs. And that man alone knows he will die.

He was sure there was a connection between the two.

Afterwards, I made my way through the crowd, by the darkly paneled auditorium walls, through the side door into the white plaster of the gallery, where expressionistic portraits of Anne Frank and Einstein hung, along with pregnant quotes. ("I still think that people are good at heart. . ." "I cannot believe that God plays dice with the universe . . .") At the crowded bar, I got myself a long-stemmed plastic glass full of quite acceptable champagne, and, with notebook under my arm, took my place in the receiving line, at the far end of which Eco sat at a table, autographing books.

While I waited, a woman's voice cut through the crowd: "Chip. . .!"

I looked aside to see a wide bush of red hair, a waving hand; and Barbara Wise pushed up to me, kissed me, and declared, "No, that wasn't a *real* kiss," and kissed me again. "I knew I'd see you here," she said. "I told Fred—I'm here with Fred—this is just the kind of thing we'll run into Chip at. Fred's up front in the line, getting his book autographed. Fred's a friend of Bill Weaver's, you know. Only *he's* not here! Weaver, that is. He was supposed to be." And I nodded. Barbara was wearing yards and yards of something black and matte, belted tightly around her tiny waist. When I explained to her briefly why I was there, she said: "Look, don't stand back here. It'll take all night! Why don't you come up with Fred?" and dragged me from the line—only to find that Fred was no longer up front. So, laughing, I went back to the line's end. "Well, I'll get you a drink, then!" Barbara declared. Which, very sweetly, she did. More champagne. "I'm going to go up front where I can hear what the two of you *say* to one another, when you get there!" And she was off through the crowd toward the table again to linger at the front, where a photographer in glasses and a gray shirt was snapping flashes of Eco signing this book and that.

As such things go, the line really crawled. Everyone seemed to have something to discuss with Eco as well as a book to sign. I made my slow, slow way forward, running over what I was going to say. Which was (when I reached the table): "Professor Eco, I'm Samuel Delany —" and extended my hand.

There was a moment of non-recognition; then, a large smile, and Eco stood, leaned across the table, grasped both my shoulders, and exclaimed: "Chip! Chip! How are you!" He pulled back behind his beard a little. "Your publisher sent me your book? I was so sorry that I couldn't . . .? write an introduction to it . . ." I could see him searching through memory for what, indeed, had been the case with the MS; and I saw him remember: "But I have written him a letter! A little letter, that says what I think"—He joggled one hand— "you know . . ."

"Yes," I said. "It was a very nice letter, too! And I wanted to thank you for it. In fact, one reason I came is that my editor, Mr. Aronica, wanted to know if he could use a sentence from your letter in the advertising."

"But of course! Of course!" Umberto boomed. (Like Auden, he's another nail-biter: I shall always be fond of him.) "That's why I wrote it!"

"Thank you so much!" I said. "I know you're busy. So I won't take up too much time. But would you sign my program?"

He laughed. "Oh, you don't need an autograph . . ."

"But I would like one!"

Laughing again, he signed the gray program, *A Chip*. "Next time Teresa comes to town, we must all get together for lunch. I'm just uptown, teaching at Columbia this term. You must come to see me!"

"I'll certainly try. By the way," I told him, "I'm going to be doing an article on *'Lector in Fabula'* for the special *Substance* issue on your work." (Which, incidentally, I am.)

"Ah, yes. That . . ."

"And I just want to thank you again for your letter."

"Oh, by the way," he said, as I started to move off. "Afterwards, they are having for me a little . . ." He made a circular motion with his hand, that I assumed meant gathering. "I will tell them you will come too . . .?"

"Oh, thanks so much. But I've been working since five o'clock this morning. I'm exhausted. And I must get home. Your reading was wonderful, by the way. I truly enjoyed it!"

"Then we get together soon, another time . . .!"

But by now the next person was moving into place.

I stepped away, practically into Barbara, who took my arm and said: "Chip! Chip . . .!" and laughed, leading me away. "He's wonderful! You know I *told* that photographer, while you were talking to him, now *that's* whom you should be taking a picture of. You'll get *two* famous writers together! But of course he didn't.

And wouldn't you know, I didn't bring *my* camera." (For the last few years Barbara has been keeping a rather spectacular photographic diary, in which, now and again, I figure.) "I heard him say you could use it. That's wonderful. Let's find Fred."

Actually I'd been wondering who Fred was; but when I saw him, I realized he was someone I'd known years ago. He used to be the lover-*cum*-guardian of an old friend of Marilyn's and mine, P—— R——, and we'd actually been to Fred's house for dinner a couple of times (in an elegant tenement apartment on the site of what is now, I believe, the World Trade Center—but I may not have that right). That would have been in 1968, which is probably the last time I'd seen him. He's now in his late 50s or early 60s. (Fred said he'd just seen P—— that morning: P——'s long-time lover, R—— M——, was the guy I made my first film, *Tiresias*, with, back in San Francisco. P——, indeed, had a small part in it.) But he's still the same, gentle, soft-spoken southerner he always was.

Barbara and Fred were going on to a late opening at the Guggenheim Museum of some Australian painters, and wanted me to come along with them. But I really *was* tired. Barbara and I made a tentative Tuesday lunch date, and I walked them over to Fifth Avenue, and down beside the park to 89th Street, where a loose crowd milled before the beige-lit entrance to Frank Lloyd Wright's great concrete cupcake that is the Guggenheim.

I excused myself, left them there, and went on down to 86th, caught the crosstown back through the park, and got home at eleven-thirty.

Chatted with Frank a bit in the living room before going to bed. (Champagne is quite nice when you haven't had any for a good long while.) And the next day I phoned Lou to say, yes, Eco says we *can* use the quote.

Tuesday I did a TV show with Reverend Rose and Isaac Asimov: *For Our Times.* That's to be aired Sunday, Oct. 7th, at 10:30 in the morning on the CBS network. But check your local listings if (for God knows what reason!) you want to watch it—that's covered in some of the enclosures, anyway.

For the rest, it's just been eating and working, and grouching about the weather, which has turned *quite* cold since the warm Monday night of Eco's reading.

Ah, Bob: Something I haven't mentioned to you, because it's grown so slowly, but for almost two years now, I've had a permanent itch on my left shoulder blade. Sometimes it moves to the right shoulder. Indeed, for the last six months it's been more than an itch, most of the time; it's been a true pain. It never leaves. And three, sometimes five times a day, I have to back up against some sharp corner and rub/scratch it. And when it *does* move to the right, usually the whole right side of my body—thigh, hip, flank, and shoulder—soon begins to ache too, sometimes to the point where I have to lie down. Cold, damp weather aggravates it. It probably has something to do with my tendency to arthritis. But you can spread it, like a thin coating of oil, over my last couple of years' worth of letters. I try (usually) not to talk about it. Indeed, if the mumbled truth be known, I have so many little aches and pains and stiffnesses and headaches and small bladder and partially detached retina and what-have-you that the day age finally strikes me down with something serious, I won't be too surprised. Yet every time I go to the doctor's, I'm pronounced in perfect health. *I* think perfect health is a matter of having the right psychology to ignore all the pains most of us live with day in and day out. I don't think it's being without those pains, though.

I'm always fascinated by what sorts of things, as I look over my own varied "Presentation of the Self in Everyday Life," I find myself presenting — or, as it were, not presenting. Another interesting medical anomaly that never made it into my letters, yet has begun each of my days for how-long-now . . .

About eight months back, over a three day period, I found myself waking up with more and more sticky, almost gummy, if not rheumy, eyes each morning. This persisted, daily and without let-up, till some three weeks ago, when I suddenly decided (having nothing to do with my eyes) to start taking some vitamin pills, as I realized my food intake had gotten rather irregular. Once I started the vitamins, in 48 hours the eye condition cleared up. Which makes you wonder, no?

And did I ever mention to you that three months ago I went on a diet, lost twelve pounds, and have actually kept it off? Probably not.

But thus the vagaries of the epistolary form.

Well, I'm still rather up about receiving the first copy of *Stars/Sand*. Lou sent it by messenger with no warning—I guess he wanted it to be a surprise. And a nice one, in our cold, cold apartment, it was!

I'm having lunch with him on Monday.

I called him to say thank you.

And he tells me there are now bound galleys on *Flight,* so you will get a copy next week.

I've had a couple of comments on *Stars/Sand*. Marc Gawron, who's working in the computer department of NYU now, read the page proofs and liked it — though, like you, he objects to the first party scene. (I tried to shave it down, but finally had to content myself just with tooth-brushing; there was too much in it I couldn't see how to get in otherwise.) Baird Searles, who's reviewing it for *Asimov's*, called to say he'd just finished the bound galleys. While I made my excuses about the disordered pages, he said he'd liked it: He thought, perhaps, it was too dense for the ordinary reader. Then—one that surprised me—he said he found a kind of pornographic subtext, in that everyone wanted to go bed with everyone. (Well, I suppose. Do my letters suffer from the same thing?) He also said that he, personally, found bitten nails almost physically revolting and suggested I might lose a bit of my audience there. (Said it almost lost me him.) I suggested that desire and disgust ["abjection" is Kristeva's term for it: In her discussion, it represents the halfway point between desire and repression, and is thus particularly important to explore] are often sides of one response. He went, "Mmmm . . ." So I'm vaguely curious what his review will be like.

Again to your letter:

". . . Old mother hen Bob wrote: 'And my third thought is that you have indeed put yourself in a position where you can be ripped off, if no more than emotionally. And I think more of you for doing so.' And Chip writes: 'I was also touched by your concern that I not find myself "emotionally ripped off" by Mr. Mueller.' Perhaps there is no difference. And perhaps such is something that remains very much one of my problems in relationships — maintaining a decent relationship and yet not giving the other the tools to emotionally devastate me. And probably I was mistaken in that I thought you were investing quite a bit in John. The more

I go on the more tangled this gets, so in the end I guess you have me projecting a piece of me onto your situation, and I guess I shouldn't have, which is hardly where I started this paragraph."

Bob, there are times I just want to give you a big hug. You are a *very* good person. One of the things, alas, that was going on in my letter was simply:

I'd received yours, read it, then reread it, and actually started my letter to you, when I got a letter from Mog that occasioned my 80-page missive—which interrupted what I was writing you and occupied me on and off for about a week. Then, I went back to the letter I'd started:

But to finish it, I *didn't* re-read yours. And I just misremembered your phrase *anent* John when I got to that part: So what you've got in mine is *my* projections, *my* fears, and *my* failings, under the pressure of the Mog situation.

And you didn't think or write anything you shouldn't have!

I haven't heard from Mog since, by the bye, about the dedication or anything else. So, perhaps, another friend has just found the whole relationship too intense —or whatever. Alas, it might simply be that a relation basically epistolary sometimes can't stand up to a couple of live meetings; especially when the participants are under any kind of pressure. And when we met, here in New York, especially the second time when Mog was on her way back to San Francisco, she was under much pressure from her situation with Jacob and I had my taxes to deal with. And in the course of both of our tryings to keep it out of the other's hair, we probably left all sorts of room for damages and misreadings — or at least I did. Till two months after the fact, I'd thought she'd had a perfectly good time.

In a couple of Mog's letters, she said she felt I was a person who didn't like confrontations and went out of my way to avoid them. Odd: Q——, just before he (at first) ended our friendship, said my problem was that I tried to confront *everything* immediately, and didn't give things time to settle. I always wanted to find out what was wrong, discuss it, analyze it, and set it right, right away. I suspect that's closer to the truth. But if someone perceives you one way, your actions in the other direction are probably going to be quite confusing.

Sigh.

Interestingly, a poem that was just rejected at the penultimate *Little Magazine* meeting was one I liked very much; but nobody else could see it. The poem was in the form of a letter from a woman who taught writing in a prison for the criminally insane (observed accurately enough to make you suspect it was from experience) to a friend who had recently written her an angry letter, which the poet kept re-reading. Each time she would re-read the letter, she would hear different phrases differently, or realize she'd skipped over, or completely ignored, this phrase or that—with the letter becoming less and less angry on each re-reading. It's an experience I've had myself. (It's what "deconstruction" is all about—as well as the Barthes/Johnson quote on the last chapter of *Neveryóna*.[1]) But I guess none of the other editors had, so they just couldn't "hear" it; and I was the only one who voted for it.

Just got a call from my mom [it's now Sunday morning; brunch (bagels and

---

[1] "Those who fail to reread are obliged to read the same story everywhere." Barbara Johnson quotes this statement by Roland Barthes in her book *The Critical Difference* (Baltimore and London: Johns Hopkins, 1980).

bacon) with Frank just over], who went to her concert series at the Philharmonic last night with her downstairs neighbor, Anne Jackson (widow of Jesse[2]): They played a work by a black composer, Ulysses Kay, whose children had gone to school with my sister at Elizabeth Erwin. (Alma mater of Angela Davis, Kathy Bodene and Robert De Niro—all of them in the same high school classroom, with Anne's and Jesse's daughter, Judy (a year older than Peggy, a year younger than me;[3] and now an editor for the *Boston Globe*].) The rest of the program was Schubert and stuff. Zubin Mehta conducted. Mom said she had a small, free-floating anxiety attack in the middle but, other than that, the music was lovely. We talked some about 2250[4] and various problems with the building.

She really wants to sell it.

And though I understand perfectly why, I think if there were any way she could bring herself to hold on to it, she should.

Best regards to Cynthia and any of the boys who're there or with whom you're in communication in the next weeks; strokes and hugs to cats and other small creatures. And to you

Love, good thoughts, and good things,

• 41 •

To Bill Thompson

September 25th, 1984

Dear Mr. Thompson,

Enclosed is a batch of material that, while it isn't everything you requested, at least should get you started.

I called Bantam Books to ask for a publicity package. Sally Williams, my publicity person there, said, shyly, that they were just in the process of putting one together for my new book, *Stars in My Pocket like Grains of Sand*, which will be published in December. (Copies should begin turning up in bookstores by the second week in November.) When it is ready, I'll certainly send you one.

By the bye, one of Sally's specialties is getting Bantam Books practically anywhere in the country on about 72 hours notice, for Bantam writers who are speaking various places.

On the phone I mentioned a TV program I taped with Isaac Asimov and the Reverend Lois Rose this past Tuesday, on the unlikely topic of "Science Fiction and Religion." The program is called *For Our Time*, and will be aired on CBS, Sunday, October 7th, at 8:30 in the morning in the New York City area, and generally at 10:30 in the morning over most of the rest of the country. But, as they say, "check your local listings" to make sure. It's a half-hour informal discussion on a moderately intelligent level, and it should give you some idea of what (minuscule) "media personality" I possess.

---

[2] Not the politican, but a writer of children's books and an old friend of the Delany family.

[3] Peggy Delany, SRD's sister, the younger by two years; Judy Jackson, the daughter of Jesse and Ann, SRD's downstairs neighbors during his adolescence in Morningside Gardens.

[4] 2250 7th Ave., the building in which SRD lived for the first fourteen years of his life and which his mother now owned.

On the 5th, 6th, and 7th of October, I will be in Buffalo, NY, as a special guest at the "Anonacon Science Fiction Convention." I don't suppose there's time to find something between then and now in the Buffalo area for Monday, October 8th (which is about the only time I would be free to do something there) . . .? At any rate, after that I will be pretty permanently in New York City for the rest of the autumn and winter.

Thanks for your time and attention. And I hope things work out well for us both.

All good things and thoughts to you and yours,

LECTURE TOPICS
Comments and Considerations:

I lecture both at an introductory level and at an advanced level on MODERN SCIENCE FICTION, in terms of its history, its criticism, and it present developments:

Lecture titles:
"The Language of Science Fiction" • This is a lecture for an audience with an English Literature/Humanities orientation, interested in SF.

"Reading Science Fiction" • This is a lecture for an audience with a science [or social science] orientation. It covers much of the same material as the lecture above, but talks about specific experiments using volunteer readers unfamiliar with SF texts, and their particular reactions and problems.

"The Necessity of Tomorrow[s]" • This last is an introductory lecture for those who know nothing about SF and want to know why they might explore it further.

I am also widely acquainted with developments in structuralism, post-structuralism, semiotics, and contemporary literary theory — and enjoy discussing their implications for science fiction criticism. Currently this is indeed my favorite topic; but it of course requires a somewhat specialized audience, one at least at graduate-school level and with some previous interest in, if not exposure to, literary theory.

Lecture title:
"Deconstruction and Science Fiction" • I think of science fiction as a way of talking about the present—and not at all as a way of predicting the future. Thus I avoid taking part in programs with titles beginning with the phrase "The Future of . . ." Often the people who put together such programs think it would be interesting to hear what a science fiction writer has to say. But what they really need are experts in the particular topic. And since my own expertise is pretty well limited to science fiction itself and to literary subjects, there is little I can contribute to such programs.

At various times, for special occasions, I have delivered university lectures on topics as diverse as William Butler Yeats, Richard Wagner, Antonin Artaud, the problems of young black readers in our culture, and the problem of "male sexuality" from a feminist perspective, as well as the works of specific science fiction writers. Such presentations, of course, require special preparation.

I am happy to talk informally to young people (and, indeed, anyone else) on just about any topic concerning writing, reading, criticism, mythology or language,

from either a practical or theoretical standpoint. I enjoy students and like to inter-
act with them. But I avoid reading student papers and stories (in order, say, to give
individual critiques of student efforts). Nor am I terribly interested in (or good at)
converting audiences who start out hostile to the whole idea of science fiction. But
if there is general interest, honest curiosity and enthusiasm, I can add to them a
working science fiction writer's insight as well as the excitement that comes from a
sophisticated and specific knowledge of a fascinating practice of writing.

Fiction Readings:
I read from my own fantasy and science fiction novels (and take questions
from the audience afterwards) only if I am the sole reader on the program.
My fiction readings tend to be long (an hour-and-a-half, with a ten-minute
break in the middle) and dramatic. Thus an evening reading, with questions, is
usually a full two-hour program.
My fiction does not lend itself to short excerpts; and the standard university
reading program of two readers in an evening is one I avoid. In my experience,
when read out loud, SF does not blend well on the same program with either
poetry or other kinds of fiction: It requires a special mind-set from the audience.
I have found that people are happiest when they come expecting only science fiction (or fantasy) for the evening and get only science fiction (or fantasy). I have
no stories that can be read out loud in their entirety in half an hour or less, so that
for readings of such brief lengths I am stuck with excerpts. And even on a program with another SF writer, I still suffer the fate of the reader of *passages choisis*.
For this reason, I only read alone.
For higher fees, I am open to longer university visits of two or three days, with
a reading on the first night, a lecture the next, and visits to classes and as many
informal talks with student of faculty groups as can fit before and after, or
crammed into the time between.

• 42 •

ABOUT SAMUEL DELANY'S MOST RECENT SF NOVEL:
STARS IN MY POCKET LIKE GRAINS OF SAND
[PUBLISHED BY BANTAM BOOKS, DECEMBER, 1984]

Faren Miller's review in *Locus, the Newspaper of the Science Fiction Field* (Sept.,
1984):
"... *Stars in My Pocket Like Grains of Sand* reflects the development in [Delany's]
style from the early romanticism and adventure to the greater intellectual complexity of the *Nevèrÿon* books, while retaining the hallmark of all his work: a solid,
detailed, sensuous descriptive power surpassing that of anyone else in the field.
Turned upon a galaxy with 6,000-plus planets inhabited by human and alien soci-
eties, it is stunningly effective.
"The book begins with a long prologue telling the grim story of a man at the
opposite end of the spectrum from the usual SF hero. He's a slave, ignorant, without a spark of independence after the brain manipulation known as Radical

Anxiety Termination. When the world ends, swept away in flame, he proves to be the only survivor.

"Now the main narrator, the industrial diplomat, Marq Dyeth, takes over. The effect is like emerging from sensory deprivation, for Marc has all the freedom of movement, thought, and experience that the slave lacked. His mind bubbles with speculation, enlivening the book's considerable intellectual content so that it rarely seems pedantic. Readers will have to step lively, though, for Marq's language reflects an outlook so different from our own that it turns the world upside-down. Woman, mother, hunt, he—the most basic words have changed their meaning.

"After Marc hears a traveler's offhand comment about an obliterated planet, his eventual meeting with that planet's lone survivor rapidly changes from a statistical improbability to a carefully engineered destiny involving the two great factions of the human universe. The rescued slave's rehabilitation (in scenes recalling *Frankenstein*) transform him into a man capable of dealing with a new life and new worlds, even one as strange as Marq's.

"The narrator accepts it casually enough, but his home is an astonishing place, in a society . . . carried into a far more sophisticated future where our own High Tech would be stone-age primitivism. When the ex-slave, now called Rat Korga, comes here, Delany's intent is more than a 'gosh-wow' tour of wonders. The book carries the plot of political intrigue to a halfway point, and a tale of obsessive desire to the desolate point where the lovers—Marq and Rat—are parted. This theme of sexual obsession, familiar from Delany's other work, is the least accessible element of *Stars/Sand*; even the other characters have trouble understanding Marq's special needs and their effect on his life, though he finally offers a passionate explanation in the Epilogue. The formal dinner at Dyethsome is the book's triumph, a wonderful mingling of crossed purposes and wild surprises."

• 43 •

To Robert S. Bravard

October 1st, 1984

Dear Bob,

A rainy, rainy day: work from about five-thirty till nine; then, after coffee with Frank, I took off running around the city, looking for a needlepoint kit, so that Iva would have something for her (get this) "needlepoint mini-class" that she's taking, mid-day, at school. Our local Woolworths was out; so I had to subway down to a Lamston's on 34th Street, then back up to Fleming on 62nd Street to drop it off. For $4,000 bucks a year? Needlepoint?

Thence a long walk through mid-town in the rain, under a new umbrella, for a stop-off at the sprawling Dalton's Bookstore (sprawls through the ground floor of 666 Fifth Avenue) for half an hour. Then into the white, light lobby, and the elevator up to the 25th, where I met:

Mr. Aronica for a Bantam expense account lunch. We schlepped downstairs, out into the rain, and slogged through muddy streets a-roar with construction, to the George Ray; I began with pâté, Lou with the lobster bisque. Both of us went on to seafood crepes with a lightly browned mournier sauce. Then I had a

Napoleon, and he an apple tart. We both had knives, and so shared our deserts. Quite good. Chatted of John Crowley and David Brin and Rowena and sales strategies and the like.

Downright civilized it was.

Then home, where I found yours of the 27ᵗʰ waiting for me. Many thanks, Bob. I can only reiterate what I said last letter: You're a fine friend.

The simple truth, though, is that I don't offend very easily. And anything said with care is taken with care. It's of course true: I may run on *explaining* myself into the ground when I think someone doesn't understand me. But I really can't think of the last time somebody said something that actually offended me. The odd editor has, from time to time, *done* something that I've found wholly unacceptable. But myself I really have to intuit a strong intention to offend before I take offense — or at least *extreme* self-righteous thoughtlessness. But on some ideal plane, I've always felt that friendship precluded offense.

Rest assured. Anything you say with care or concern, even unto fatherly advice, I'm not very likely to fly off the handle at. (I may not take the advice; but that's something else again.)

Indeed, to the end of preventing offense on your part: something that I really should urge—

To give Mog her due: She's been doing volunteer work at the AIDS Society in San Francisco, and her landlord, Glen (who has a teenage daughter and lives upstairs from her in the two-family house where she rents out the ground floor apartment), is currently dying of Kaposi's sarcoma; indeed, she describes him as limping slowly about with large, purple bruises and lesions all over his face, and he's not expected to live till the end of October — whereas I have done very little directly for the cause, and actually know personally, right now, no one with the disease. So her objections to my third story are not wholly unfounded.

Not that she's told me what they are — only that she has them and has them strongly.

You should be receiving this a day or two after my last letter, mailed from Bantam this afternoon — included along with which should have been *at last* a set of bound galleys for *Flight from Nevèrÿon!*

Given the fact that the story (*The Tale of Plagues and Carnivals*) *is* as political as it is, and is also highly controversial (and, indeed, that the other stories more than touch on controversial topics), I urge you to read them over (especially *Plagues and Carnivals*) and decide if you *do* want your name in this particular book. Given the nature of the tale, it might well have been more sensitive of me to ask people first if they minded being included in the dedication.

Believe me, there's nothing that *you've* said that's making me reconsider. But I really think that Mog's reaction raises, however muzzily, some real considerations.

Greg Frux, who is a practicing bisexual, has read it, and is very pleased to be included. Same for Mike Elkins, who is, of course, gay. Robert Morales, however, who is straight, and whom I've had look over parts of it, had to hesitate a moment, actually, before he decided, Oh, hell, it was all right.

So without lessening any of my feelings of good will toward any and all of you, it might be a good idea if you and Pep looked over the tales. I'll assume, if you don't say anything to the contrary, that it's okay. But as I think on it, I guess in this case there really *are* extraordinary circumstances involved — and it might well have behooved me to have been more sensitive to them before I went and made my rather blanketing dedicatory gesture.

I still have about two (outside three) weeks during which time I can make changes. May I, indeed, charge you, Bob, when you finish with them, to pass on the bound galleys to Pep, apprise him of the situation, and let me know what he says?

And for what it's worth, Mog *hasn't* fired off a letter telling me to strike her name — only that she'd been considering it. So she's apparently, at least till now, still in.

I hope this all proves to be a tempest in a teapot. In the first enthusiasm of creation, I never thought there might be anything in my story anybody could *possibly* object to. I mean, it's just a little tale combining ancient fantasy and contemporary documentation on AIDS, drug addition, mass murder, promiscuous homosexuality, things like that . . .

So I think second thoughts, in this case, *are* called for.

And if, for *whatever* reason, you or Pep might hesitate to want your names on this particular work, believe me, I will understand totally — nor will *I* take the least offense.

A real letter will follow in a week or so, answering all the good and insightful things you say in yours.

But as, by now, you *do* (?) have a set of galleys, I just wanted to get this off.

Tonight I am *not* going with Richard Kostelanetz to the Kaypro User's Group Meeting at NYU. I was going to, but Iva objected: "Daddy, it's my first night here, for God's sakes!" True. Also it's pouring out! So I'm home.

Trials and tribulations of a ten-year-old: Iva lost her bus pass on the first day this month; and they will not give you a replacement till the next month. It's nearly $60 a month for transportation if you pay full fare; that means her $20 a month allowance now has to go for her bus fare from school — and Frank now has to drive her there every morning. But really, we just don't have an extra $60 this month. Not if we're to eat. The discovery that she was, virtually, without an allowance this month got some tears, a spoon dropped into her tomato soup — as she started to get up and storm out of the kitchen. But I blocked the way, and said, "No, kid! This is *not* acceptable behavior!" So then we went into her room and had a talk; and I explained we just couldn't do anything else.

Boy, has this kid grown up in the last year!

She really came around, took the responsibility for losing her bus pass (she'd dropped it in the Y when she was there for her Saturday morning swim), and I think has a real sense of the way her carelessness has inconvenienced not only herself but the rest of us as well. Finally, when we were sitting in her room talking, she said: "You know, I really don't care about the allowance. But sometimes it's so hard to admit you did something wrong." At ten, hey?

(Well, going on eleven.)

Finally she decided it was like *Little House on the Prairie* (!) [her — sigh — favorite TV show] and rallied. Finished her supper. She and Frank are in the other room, laughing very hard about something or other, right now. It's a rough lesson to have to learn at ten. But, in this case, it's the very harsh facts. And, I guess, it is just a bit like something on that otherwise atrocious TV horror.

> Best to Cynthia, and the kids.
> Love and stuff,

• 44 •

To Camilla Decarnin

October 12th, 1984

Dear Mog,

Back from Contradiction 4 in Niagara Falls. Rode through the fog and splatter at the base of the Horseshoe on the *Maid of the Mists* with an awful cold.

It was still awesome!

Just spent 24 hours putting your corrections from the galleys into the *Flight from Nevèrÿon* page proofs. All went into the office at nine-thirty this morning— not to be seen again till copies are available mid-April.

Once again, *many* thanks!

Typical of Bantam (or, should I say, typical of paperback publishers), said proofs didn't arrive until two weeks late. When, on the day they were due, they told me they'd be delayed, I made a note of it, and at four o'clock of the appointed afternoon, I gave Bantam a call and asked if they'd shown up yet: "Oh, hello, Chip. I just gave the proofs to Lou about five minutes ago. You must have telepathy." (No, just a notebook.) "But because we're late," the managing editor (slender, soft-spoken, black-haired Ms. Lucas) went on, "we need them back right away. They've got to go out Thursday morning."

It was late Tuesday afternoon.

"I was thinking," I said, "of picking them up tomorrow. But, on thinking again, I'll be down to get them in 40 minutes." And after speaking briefly to Lou, I hustled myself through the subway to pick them up at ten after five.

Soon as I got home, I went to work.

There'd been one big section I was particularly worried about—on the last pages, where I'd listed the corrections for the previous volumes. By galley time, that had expanded almost by a factor of three, and I wanted to see what they'd done with it. I turned to it immediately — to discover *none* of the corrections I'd indicated in galleys had been put in! *At all!*

Because the stuff was mostly on the last galley sheet, I could only assume the final page had come loose from the others and had been lost en route to the printer. Also, it seemed that about one out of five of the other corrections that *had* been made had been fumbled: The proper word had been inserted, but in the wrong place, or when a phrase had been re-written in galleys, the old version had been left in anyway after (or before) the new—stuff like that. I called up Ms. Lucas about nine-thirty on Wednesday to tell her this. "Now you understand," she told me, before I hung up, "we won't be able to put in any new corrections. We'll only be able to correct the things that the printer did incorrectly from the galleys." That's the sort of statement that would have given (and, several times, gave) me diarrhea when I was 20 or 25. But now I know you just ignore it and go on acting as if the world were sane anyway.

Nevertheless, I figured it would be a good idea to do some triage on the corrections, since there *were* so many "author's corrections" (which included yours —at least as far as the printer was concerned): You know that little configuration you always marked PDQ?[1] Well, is or is there not a space between the one-m dash

[1] Decarnin marked a close parenthesis, followed by a 1-m dash, followed by an open quotation mark [)– "] for PDQ.

and the open-quote? In the galleys, it had all been quite random — practically 50/50. The Chicago Style Sheet says "no space." But I've always felt that if a text uses a *lot* of them (and mine does), a space looks better. Apparently Thomas Pynchon (who also uses lots) feels the same way, because Bantam had used the space for *Gravity's Rainbow.*

So, back in galleys, I'd gone blithely through, opening up all the PD(open-)Qs.

Bantam's proofreader, however, had gone through closing up all the ones that the printer had initially left open.

And when the two sets of corrections had been correlated, the twit who did them never realized that they were both attempts to make the book consistent with itself — two attempts that, in this case, were mutually conflicting. As I checked pages against galleys, there they were: The whole book was just as inconsistent as it had been, only reversed — with the open PDQs all closed, and the closed PDQs all open! Well, technically, this is a production department error, and I could hold Bantam responsible. And, indeed, I found about 75 closed PDQs throughout the book. But I finally decided: If I *leave* the book stylistically inconsistent, then Bantam *owes* me, as it were, 75 "author's corrections." So—after noting where each one came (of course, so I could point them out to Mary and then magnanimously *not* claim them for my own)—that's what I did.

My immediate response to your comment about the sex of the ox was, of course, "Mog's right!" I'd really wanted the draft animal to be female; men with male animals in tow, if the animal is around for very many pages, form a kind of "buddy-relation" in most readers' minds, even when the writer doesn't encourage it. I just didn't want my smuggler to have such a relationship, even by such a ghostly implication. It would have made his encounter with Raven and her landswomen not quite as emotionally precarious.

The *ideal* way to deal with it all, of course, would have been to leave the animal female, but make her not an ox. (I'd been thinking of changing her to some kind of buffalo.) But that would have required real rewriting, of the sort one just couldn't do in 24 hours with all the other stuff. Also, when I looked it up in the *OED*, the first definition of "ox" it gives is: "a domestic bovine, sexually distinguished as bull and cow." Then, for the second definition, it goes on to say "commonly used for a castrated bull." Even though the second definition *felt* righter, I also remembered that "the oxen of the sun" were, certainly, mostly (if not all) cows. And I figured, after all, this is sword and sorcery, where words tend toward their more formal/archaic meanings. Besides, I like reviving sexually undifferentiated terms for species. And since the ox Rowena drew on her cover sketch is very much a fantasy species and not at all your common and garden American domestic bovine, I finally decided to let "she" and "ox" both stand. If anyone else questions it, I'll send them to the *OED*. Besides, it meant another fifteen-odd "author's corrections" I could use for something else.

I went the same route with the capitalization on implicit appositions of royal titles. Again, I *feel* you're right. Certainly I yearned to make them all upper case. Still, Chicago says: "I saw Empress Josephine dancing at the ball the other night," but, "I saw the empress Josephine riding through the Boise de Bologne Saturday morning." In this case, since that's the rule I (more or less) followed with *Neveryóna*, I let "empress" and "princess" stay lower-case—despite a gut urge to the contrary. And, again, it meant, finally, I could use my corrections for matters of wording, confusing punctuation, and the like.

Of which, as you know, there was much.

Some of your marginal comments (The Mummer: "What could I say?" Decarnin: "Try 'Sophistical snake!'") got me through some of the more exhausting hours over the text with quite a grin.

At any rate, all the rest I could manage went in—and at nine-thirty Thursday I took it into Bantam.

While I was waiting in the office for Lucas, F. X. Flinn came through the lobby where I was sitting, waiting for Mary to get back to her desk so I could go in to see her. He said hello; I told him some of the problems. "Ah," he said. "Now you see, if this were my department, you wouldn't have to worry about any of that. The trials and tribulations of 'mass-market'!" And, in his nicely seedy gray suit, he went off through the double-doors beyond the elevators, shaking his head in sympathy.

Once I got in to see Mary, there was only a *small* argument about the corrections. I presented all my ammunition, about the triage and trade-offs, pleaded with her for the sake of the cause; and Ms. Lucas, whose eyes were *very* red that morning, finally said: "All right, I'll make sure they all go in. But *next* time, Chip . . ."

A TV show aired last Sunday (while I was up at Niagara), with Isaac Asimov. (Taped two weeks back.)

And this morning (now Friday) an interview with one Greg Tate for *The Village Voice*.

Well, I've just been thinking of you, of Glen, of your work and finances, of your therapy (as one who gave up on therapy with a vengeance at 23, I'm always curious how other people find it today: I got lots of good out of it initially, but, once I'd been hospitalized, could get no more: The trade-off between gleaning honest insight on the one hand and learning how be a full-time mental patient [whether I wanted to or not] on the other just got too far into the red. There's great sense in Freud's observation that psychotherapy is really for people over 30. Unfortunately, I started at twelve), and generally wondering how all is going for you and around you—and hoping that San Francisco's annual "unseasonable October hot spell" is netting you a final burst of summer goodness; and, once again, just being very grateful for all your care and effort. Again, my deepest thanks; and

All my love,

• 45 •

To Greg Tate

October 14th, 1984

Dear Mr. Tate,

Only a quick note, first to say how much I enjoyed our talk on Friday morning, and second to add some thoughts to some of the things we talked about.

At one point, I said I was no longer interested in the closing cadence that ends so much narrative fiction—the fall from "seventh" to "dominant." Or some such. What I meant to say was, of course, "the fall from dominant to tonic." Even while we were talking, I intended to go back and correct the phrase. But we got off on something else.

Should you want to quote it (and *I* do, frequently)—you might put the proper terms in place. It's something I say often, but that time it slipped out wrong.

You'd also asked me about Sayles's *The Brother from Another Planet*, which I explained I hadn't yet had a chance to see. A point I had thought of making got lost, however, or put aside in the course of our talk:

In Sayles's film *Lianna*, practically the entire plot and the presentation of every relationship in the film—the life, times and progress of a young faculty wife in a small American college—hinges on the real existence of the women's movement. Practically everything we are asked to consider in the film is something the women's movement has particularly asked the world to consider and analyze. Yet neither the movement, nor women's liberation, nor any overt concern with the social rights of women is mentioned from one end of the film to the other. There is no women's center on the campus. There is no women's studies department (or classes) in the school. And no character ever refers to herself or anyone else as a member of a socially concerned group.

Considered as a portrayal of the lives of such women today, *Lianna*, then, is a fantasy—and a rather reactionary one at that: because women connected to colleges *do*, today, talk about their situation and their condition in term's of the women's movement, among themselves and with men, all the time. And such talk is very important.

A true brother from another planet, seeing *Lianna*, however, would have *no* way of knowing what had turned Sayles's gaze toward this particular topic nor what had articulated Lianna's choices, solutions, or failures, as male Sayles sees them.

Because of what struck me as a failure in *Lianna*, what I would be looking for in *The Brother from Another Planet* is any acknowledgment of blacks' talk among ourselves about our social conditions in the social terms which, day after day, hour after hour, we indulge. It's not the conclusions of these discussions that interest me artistically; just the acknowledgment that they exist; and I would also like to see some insight into the myriad ways such discussion relates to the rest of our lives. The artistic problem is, of course, how to do this without being propagandistic. As I said, I haven't seen the film. *Brother* may or may not be as good as or better than *Lianna* or *The Return of the Secaucus Seven*. But if I don't find in it some overt discussion of the racial situation in racial terms that I can recognize (not for the discussion's content, but to acknowledge that such discussion occurs and is powerfully important in black life), then Sayles will not have grown as a filmmaker in a direction that particularly interests *me* as a black viewer—or, indeed, as a black writer looking among the works of other artists, black or white, in my exploration of the aesthetic production around me—a black consumer, if you will, who must choose from among available films and books what I like or don't like.

To go to the film with Sayles's other work in mind means that's what I go looking for. Now, well before I get there, anybody, black or white, may come to me and say: "Hey, there's some really interesting stuff in that film"—referring to anything from the editing to the performances to the plot, quite aside from my own black critical expectations, contoured by Sayles's other movies. (I must note: Though I saw some *long* lines in front of the theater in the first weeks, so far nobody has said that to me. But then, enthusiastic intelligence among viewers is as rare as energetic smarts among artists.) Someone's saying that might certainly get me to the theater a little faster. And I might have any number of reactions to the film, above and beyond the fact that it did or did not meet my expectations after I saw it.

But, honestly, I don't expect it to meet them.

Very few films do.

Still, if the film is to satisfy me, somehow white director Sayles is going to have to answer the critical expectations of black filmgoer Delany. He may meet them directly, with invention, energy, insight, and discretion — or he may pander to them in propagandistic ways that are as wrong-headed as not meeting them at all. Conceivably, he may have made a film that is so fascinating, intricate, lively and beautiful that the movie itself makes me forget my expectations while I'm watching it. (Chances are, if he does that, he is sensitive to them on one level or another, and is rather answering them indirectly. Art always allows you that.) I point out, nevertheless, that such expectations are the kind I—or the black audience in general—don't forget *easily* . . .

All this is simply the political underside of Cocteau's exhortation to all artists: "*Etonnez moi!*"—Astonish me! And though the artistic problems are always political, invention, energy, insight and discretion (that is, artistic ingenuity in solving them) are always astonishing. What is rare astonishes.

Once again, I enjoyed our talk. The conversation was stimulating. Good luck with the article and, of course, with all your writing.

• 46 •

To Robert S. Bravard

October 16th, 1984

Dear Bob,

Many thanks for yours of October 8th. The kind and appreciative words on *The Tale of Plagues and Carnivals* were quite a lift.

Only the most passing of notes: The last scene is not laid in the Bronx, but in Riverside Park just above the 83rd St. playground (three long blocks to the west of where I live), where there is, indeed, an infamous wooded little hill that, every few years for the past 20, if not 40, has become quite sexually active among gays as a cruising ground. When it's not in use, bums, indeed, go there to sleep or, occasionally, to make their fires.

It's quiescent, now. But about four years ago, it was quite kicky; and when I was about 21, it also went through an active period.

It's had others from time to time.

I can't say most, but a good number of gay male New Yorkers would likely recognize it from my description. It might give them a smile. And as far as muggings are concerned, far more civilized-looking West End Avenue, only a block away, proves to be, by statistics, far more dangerous.

I spent a few hours with *Closing the Cycle*[1] when I first received it. And I

[1] A set of poems by Robert S. Bravard.

have, more recently, spent a few *more* hours with it. You convey moments and days of agrarian reality with intensity and insight—and without ever sounding like Robert Frost, which is an accomplishment. (Among my favorites are "Notes on a Grass Fire" and "Spring by Rain.") And if I had received the chapbook earlier, I would most likely have used some lines from "The Pennsylvania Archeologist in Turkey" ("All morning I've been turning over/ the wreckage of somebody else's city . . . / The distance now that matters most/ is not in years . . ."), much like I used the Jeremy Campbell quote, in *Plagues and Carnivals,* right after the Kermit/Leslie altercation.

I also have particularly good remembrances of "A Poet at His Beer" (the transition it ushers in is fascinating), "Iron and Copper," and "Lines for a Letter in Reply."

Also had some interesting thoughts about your postmodern *Manfred,* "The Hills Back of Home." (I liked it.) But I want to re-read it; so they must wait for the next letter.

It must be very nice to have them there between covers.

Thanks once again for sending them to me.

The problems of the library sound trying. Through my mother, I was trained to libraries so young[2] that the silence became second nature to me. But more than once, now on some college campus, now in some branch of the NYPL, I've suddenly winced—like a physical blow had been struck me—at some set of voices that are carrying on a discussion in normal tones.

I mean, it's like talking out loud in Church, or during the performance of a play.

When you called, back on Thursday the 4th (?), I was two days into a rotten cold and looking forward to flying (shuffling?) off to Buffalo the next noon, for Contradiction 4, where I had contracted (!) to be a "special guest," along with Donald ("*Courtship Rites*") Kingsberry, about a year and a half ago. Don is a mild-mannered, six-foot-four Scientologist who teaches math in Montreal.

I had dinner with him and Beth Meecham and David Hartwell together at some hotel restaurant last year (the Airport Hilton? Lunacon?), and found him bright and charming, as are all we brilliant and charming SF writers.

The first two days of Contradiction are largely a blur, thanks to my cold, which was in the same ballpark of awfulness as the one I had when I came down to see you folks at Lock Haven, years back. I did two panels, one on Alternate Governments, one on Alternate Families, both with Don.

At one point, an hour of my time was auctioned off to the highest bidder to raise money for the con. I went for sixty-five bucks to a very pleasant systems analyst from Canada, who basically took me for lunch the next day at the Wings 'n' Things in the local shopping mall. She was one of about six sisters, is all I remember, very thin, very blonde, with glasses. But what we talked about through the fog of fever and repeated "Excuse me"s while I blew my nose, I couldn't tell you.

At another, I was driven off to have breakfast at the home of Linda Michaels and Joe Margolis (married; and to each other), who are decorating some ancient 19th century upper New York state white elephant to the nines. Stained glass din-

---

[2] SRD's mother worked as a desk clerk in the New York Public Library system from c. 1951 on.

ing room window. A great stairway rising out of the living room. Joe is a college physics instructor turned carpenter (makes more money that way!) who has practically hand-carved new wainscoting for the entire mansion!

My old student Terry Nutter was there; she was a mathematical child prodigy, is on the heavy side, and is terribly smart, very sweet, has one Ph.D. in philosophy (the foundations of mathematics) and has recently gotten another in computer science—so she can earn a living. Terry, Lois Metzger, and Myada Alcase —along with Chuck Thomas—were my quartet of favorite students back when I taught at SUNY in '75. (Linda was also in the class.) Terry invited me to come down to New Orleans at Mardi Gras time and visit her. (She teaches in the Computer Science Department at Tulane.) I might well take her up on that . . .

Breakfast was fresh pineapple and coconut, waffles from an ancient waffle iron, coffee and orange juice, in a big, sunny, agreeably cluttered kitchen with yellow curtains, while Linda went from her painting clothes in which she served the first waffle to tailored slacks and a sequined top by the time she forked the last one down from the top of the iron—when Bill Bower, a thin, pleasant, aging fan, who was staying with them, finally got down from his morning ablutions (he has some medical problem that keeps him in the bathroom for an hour before he can emerge), to join us: Then we drove back to the Hotel Niagara where some to-do at the con was taking place—I have no memory of what.

I may not have even been involved in it.

For the most part, indeed, I stayed in my hotel room whenever I could get away with it and read Raymond Carver short story after short story. (I brought three volumes of them with me.) Carver is not a writer whom I like; but I respect him more and more. And his tales go down like chiclets — the point being, of course, that you are not supposed to swallow your chiclet; just chew it. Yet sometimes you do.

At one point, I realized that one young man who had been very friendly to me and whom I'd spent a lot of time talking to, and who was clearly very bright, was also absolutely stark raving bonkers. While we were in the bar, having a drink, he began to tell me about his work in economics, which led to the plot to keep him from receiving the Nobel Prize a few years back (he was perhaps 33) and on to the cosmic conspiracy that would end with his becoming the Messiah. All of it in dead earnest. I recommended a book to him called *Operators and Things*, but that was about all I could think of. He wrote the title down. Later he confessed he'd spent most of the year in a mental hospital. (He'd taught economics at the University of Virginia before he was hospitalized.) He had been the next highest bidder against the Canadian system's analyst for my 'hour,' and had, earlier, eagerly bought a copy of *Starboard Wine*, for which he paid me (sigh) by check. (I had him make it out to Marc Gawron, who has nicely volunteered to be a clearing-house for me.) But that was all before I realized he truly wasn't responsible. Thin, blond, stoop-shouldered, cheerful, and mercurial, with pale-framed glasses and white running shoes; his name was J—— P——.

I'm still waiting to see if his check bounces.

Sunday morning I was scheduled to read "The Mummer's Tale," and did, not badly, in a dramatic hour and a half.

A party in Don's suite on Sunday night.

At one point at the party I whispered to Terry: "There is someone in this room who is very nice, extraordinarily bright, but could be committed tomorrow without any difficulty at all. I wonder if you'll spot him."

Ten minutes later, Terry came up to me by the punch bowl and said: "I'm pretty sure I've found him, Chip—unless there're two. But that would be an awful lot for one small con." And she nodded across the room where, indeed, J—— P—— was earnestly going on to still someone else about the interstellar plot to elect him the Messiah.

Terry and I just looked at each other.

Monday morning the con was over; my plane wasn't till eight that evening. My cold had receded a bit. And I had been at Niagara falls for three days without seeing them. The town is *not* big; and the hotel is, I was told, only about a hundred yards away from them; so I decided to do some sightseeing. And then back for some more chicken wings at the mall.

Indulge me while I transcribe a few pages from my journal *anent* my Journey to Niagara:

Let's see what my Niagara Falls adventure (writing here at the Rainbow Center shopping mall) nets me. This afternoon, went on the "Maid of Mists," and tramped to the "Cave of the Winds"—but the cave itself hasn't been operative for some time, they tell us. The ceiling of the actual cave fell in during the '50s and killed nine people, so now you only go up to the foot of it, on a series of wooden stairs and railed platforms, awash from the splatter of Bridal Veil Falls.

The view up the streaming boulders and the misty cataract, roaring louder than you can scream, is awesome.

The boat trip into the white and mist-drenched pit of Horse Shoe Falls was chillingly fine. Do you remember the way old matte-shot special effects in pre-Kubrick/Lucas color films always had a greenish halo around them? Well, the entire rim of the falls, a wall of falling white rising 176 feet above us, stretching from one side of the sky to the other, was marked by the same, flickering green line.

The boat rose and bumped, and, in our black slickers, we squinted against a multi-directional, tiny rain. While the boat finally turned back, I loaned the wet wadded Kleenex with which I'd been occasionally wiping my glasses to an elderly Japanese tourist whose rimless lenses looked like a clutter of pearls.

After he finished carefully cleaning his bifocals, he looked out of his wet black rubber hood at his glasses, at me, at the linty lump of damp tissue, and said: "I keep," and put it in his pocket — while the loudspeaker told the story of seven-year-old Roger, who'd gone over the Canadian falls in only a bathing suit and a life-jacket, to be rescued by the tourist boat almost at the spot where we were now.

Later, on the tour ride around the park, from another loudspeaker I learned that Roger's seventeen-year-old sister had been rescued only yards away from the edge of the falls by two New Jersey policemen on vacation.

Roger's and his sister's uncle, who'd owned the unfortunate boat they'd all been in, died in the accident.

So I sit here, writing, in the shopping mall, stuffed up with cold, eating my chicken wings and drinking my beer.

* * *

[When I walked back into the hotel, waiting by the desk for me was Chuck Thomas, who'd driven over from Buffalo. The con committee turned me loose and said I was free. So Chuck spirited me off:]

Spent a truly pleasant evening with Chuck Thomas, who came down to the hotel, took me over, got me comfortably drunk (first time in *how* long—it only took three drinks for me; to his eight, nine or more) at the local bar he frequents across from the secondhand bookshop he owns, to the tune of $23 worth of liquor; then he drove me to the airport.

Chuck was one of my older students back when I taught at Buffalo, and my favorite person there. At that point, he was a carpenter, 28, and an aspiring poet. He was (and still is) a glorious nail-biter, which certainly didn't hurt our friendship. We styled ourselves drinking companions back then.

I think we're the kind of people who would become friends with each other anytime we met. It's not that we pick up where we left off. Every time we meet (last year, for instance, when I was up to do the reading at Hallwalls), we just become real friends, real fast, from scratch.

In ten years he's put on 50 pounds (and so have I). But he's an intensely good man. Ten years: from carpenter to Neighborhood Housing Services Administrator.

He drinks a lot (of highly watered drinks, let it be said), but that's okay. Somehow.

I would basically count this con a success.

(Am writing this on the plane as we taxi down the black runway between the blue lights, toward take-off; glimmering jewels on the horizon's velvet.)

Chuck remembered a despairing comment I once made to him while we knocked back Jack Daniels at Onetto's, ten years ago: "You said, 'If you get married, you'll never write again.' And you know," he told me, this evening in the bar, "you were right."

Only now, leaving Buffalo airport, do I actually recall making the comment; and the reason I made it to him had to do with my observations of Marilyn's drop in production at *her* marriage to me, though I worried about its sexist implications because I was saying it to a man—even as I said it to him back then. But there's something about his personality (an angularity and sharpness that, once you know him, you realize means absolutely nothing except a speech habit) that's rather like Marilyn's, though he has neither her I.Q., nor her creative commitment; only some of her insecurities.

Well, he's truly enthusiastic about his job ("I empower people to solve their own problems," is how he describes it), which—after his Peace Corps experience—is the kind of thing I would like to have expected from him; but didn't quite dare, given the kind of life he was living at 28. And the fact that, at 38, with a comfortable belly and a bald spot, he has gone on to it is, finally, wonderful.

And we are airborne, aloft from the night's jewel tray, run below with gold chains of highway lights and blotched with suburban clusters.

Remember your cold and the ear problems you have in landing—the near-deafness, the fullness in the forehead, in the cheeks, behind the eyes, the feeling that the mind is being crowded out of the skull, both coming and going, from Buffalo. The pins and needles in the hyper-occipital sinus.

* * *

Here, minutes away from landing (25 miles or less, announces the captain) the megalopolitan landscape is spread out in all its dull and dim silver (blue) and orange pin-pricks, to the vanished horizon closing on an all-but-starless night. (I can make out two night objects: Jupiter and Sirius, I'd bet.) And two more lights, distancing from one another as we turn away from them, no doubt other planes.

The dusty veil of our own winglight lies out over the alternation of water and city.

And the wheels (and the plane, a little) drop.

And bank again.

And bank more steeply; we slip inward on the dark currents toward touch-down, two or three minutes off, at LaGuardia.

Adults' ears do not 'pop.' At least not with colds like mine. Rather, they adjust in fits and starts, over the 20 minutes of landing, now the left, now the right. ('Popping' is for children.) To the extent it sounds like anything but itself, it's a cross between crunched styrofoam, and the bubbling of a leaky drain. Distressing to hear your own inner machinery, usually so silent, make such noise!

More thoughts about Chuck:

What makes a boy interesting is not what makes a man interesting. Yet the interesting boy has become an interesting man. That's an achievement.

* * *

[Jotted down on the all-but-empty M-104, as it made its way up Eighth Avenue from 42nd Street before turning onto Broadway, my suitcase behind my knees:]

Back in Buffalo, a Burger King has replaced Onetto's, and I see out the bus window that The Barking Fish has folded! It's sign is down from the aluminum poles that made up its awning. Wonder what Henry LaFarge will do now that his place has closed?

We ride up past the New York Institute of Technology, and the American Bible Society, through the B'way dark.

* * *

Well, Bob (back to the present), looking over these journal entries, I'm struck by something. I've been keeping a journal of one sort of another, without any particular plan or organization, since I was fourteen or fifteen years old. There's nothing systematic about it; it's not and never has been a diary—not an attempt to narrate what was happening in my life. Rather it was a case of telling what was happening, what I was doing or thinking, when I sat down to make the entry.

Writing presupposes a certain calmness, of course—which life (and, often, my life in particular) does not always provide. Thus the journals contour to the dramatic and even traumatic periods of my life by their absences, omissions, and lacunae—far more than by what they directly present. (But then, I think even Kid says something not far from this somewhere in his journal in *Dhalgren*.) To take those hundreds of notebooks, now up in Boston, and cull from them something with form and energy would require monumental editing; but it would be nice, someday, to put in the two or three years it would take and do it—if I had a publisher interested in such a project.

Well, Gide had to wait practically till he won the Nobel Prize to get to his.

Delany																																																																																																																																																																													1984

So I'll just go along filling them up, sending them up.

What follows is just a list of things, with the vaguest of amplificatory notes, I wanted to write you about. But pure exhaustion (and the cold, which still clutches with mucus-clotted fingers to the insides of my sinuses) constrains me to mere notation:

Tuesday morning down to traffic court with Frank, where I acted as witness for him, and got two of three rather annoying (and expensive) violations tossed out. Still, a $60 fine.

Went looking for Marc in his office at NYU but couldn't find him (his office had been changed that day). An hour after I got home, I decided to check on the page proofs of *Flight from Nevèrÿon*: See enclosed letter to Mog (#43) for details.

Next day Frank went upstate to see his mother; and Judith Merril arrived to spend a day (and night) from Canada. We had a nice talk in the kitchen while I made beef stew for Iva's and my dinner. Judy out for the evening; back for bed.

The next day, got Iva off to school in the morning.

Frank back; and the three of us, Judy, Frank, and me, all had a lovely beef-stew lunch, with yogurt, salad, sprouts, and I opened the bottle of Cordon Rouge the Contradiction con-committee had sent back with me as a gift when I left.

A very pleasant time.

Judy took off for Grand Central Station at four; Iva got home from her riding lesson at five thirty; fed and set up for her homework; and the *Little Magazine* editors arrived between 6:30 and 7:30 for our weekly meeting.

Friday night, Richard Kostelanetz and Aviva over for dinner with Iva and me. (Frank out for the evening, as is his wont for the last couple of years or more, whenever I have friends over.) Good conversation; good food. Broiled chicken. Spoonbread with yellow cornmeal. And spaghetti-squash (boiled, shredded, mixed with grated zucchini, cheddar cheese, garlic, and tomato sauce, then replaced in the squash skin and baked and browned under a sprinkling of parmesan — it was *quite* a success); and I made ice-cream balls for desert: lumps of Häagen-Dazs rolled in chocolate cookie crumbs and frozen. Served with strong coffee and almond flavored whip cream.

(Iva ate them for dessert for the next two days.)

Frank arrived in the last minutes to say hello; then to his room.

Saturday with Barbara Wise to see Sergio Leone's *Once Upon a Time in America*, all four-and-a-half hours of it, at Alice Tully Hall at Lincoln Center.

Along with Michael Cimino's *The Deer Hunter*, and Bernardo Bertolucci's *Nineteen Hundred*, *Once Upon a Time in America* is another marvelous and monstrous fascist fairy tale—and all of them (like Scorsese's *Taxi Driver*, really another one) hinge, of course, on Robert De Niro.

The film is meticulously researched, and yet this portrait of Jewish gangsters growing up on New York's Lower East Side has absolutely nothing to do with the real history of that area. It is entirely an America of the mind (as Bertolucci's film, populated by almost nothing but French [Gerard Depardieu, Dominique Sanda] and American [Robert De Niro, Burt Lancaster, Donald Sutherland, Barry Sullivan] movie actors, is entirely an Italy of the mind, as a number of Italians have pointed out, angrily and insistently). Yet the opium den scenes with which the film begins and ends are as poignant and powerful as the ones in Altman's

McCabe and Mrs. Miller. Though supposedly a film about America, and Jewish America at that, the sensibility is so Italian (specifically Italian gangster movie), that again and again the audience just giggles.

Things seem *that* off.

And yet, if you grant that this is a dark, dark fairy tale of murder, betrayal, mutilations, rapes, and suicide, it is unsettling and compelling.

The time span runs from 1908 to the mid- or late-1960s, and circles around an incident in 1932, when two Jewish youths, friends since childhood and criminals both, at the tail-end of the Depression commit a final job together, in which some of their childhood friends and accomplices lose their lives. De Niro thinks he is betraying his friend (for his own good, of course), but something goes disastrously wrong — and Noodles' (De Niro's) own life, already on the skids, from here on crumbles entirely, as he is forced to flee New York City and hide out for the next 35 years in Buffalo.

Thirty-five years later, he is called back, where, in the course of his explorations, seeing old friends, visiting old haunts, he slowly discovers that, indeed, it was he who was set up, betrayed, and destroyed by his friend, who has taken his money, his girl, and a son he did not even know he had.

The real-time action ends with a self-immolation that is so gruesome and yet so low-key (involving an old man who may, or may not, have thrown himself into the vicious screws of a garbage lacerating machine in the back of a refuse truck) that we cannot even be sure if it occurred. Was it, perhaps, another set-up, like the burned corpse we saw toward the film's beginning, just part of another fairy tale —and we are once again in an opium dream; and, indeed, back in the opium den where the story started.

But above and beyond the reality/illusion plot (an actress who does not age over 35 years, though her makeup becomes more and more smeared), the insistent clichés of the gangster film are all here, pushed to the gruesome limit and beyond, as though there were still some Hayes code in effect which the film-maker could take some inchoate and sensuous pleasure in violating with fast cutting, fake blood, explosive pellets, the occasional exposed breast (its nipple, of course, prodded with a loaded pistol) and, if the notice that tells us that a minute and a half was cut from the American version to get it an R-rating is true, probably, in the European version, some penises as well: It's pretty easy to figure out the scene where, three of them in a row, they must have been flaunted—all of them indulged with deadly, brutal, and meticulous seriousness, flying without compunction in the face of anything and everything we know as reality — following every social, every racial, every gangster-film stereotype, even when the Italian director, in an attempt to deal with New York Jews, just gets them wrong. It's a New York with neither blacks nor Hispanics, in a country which clearly never went through either World Wars One or Two: which is why one can do nothing, finally, but call it fascist. At the same time, the film is filled, loaded, almost sunk under the weight of a materialist critique, a pseudo-documentary recreation of background and sideplot (sympathetic presentations of socialist organizers in the '30s, the outdoor markets of Orchard Street, a reconstructed side-area of the long-ago demolished Penn Station, a '30s mattress factory explored lovingly by the camera [while a murder is, of course, occurring somewhere beyond the haze of stuffing puffed into the air by the ancient blowers] almost as if this were a training film on how to run it—among many, many others), a materialism that seems to fight that harsh, central fascist rod with an endless elaboration of intelligent and careful observation that finally unscrews the rod at both ends from its ideological bushings so that at last it just floats free to become the fantasy that the title, from the beginning, has told us it is:

"Once Upon a Time . . ."

The Week's Reading:

Terry Eagleton: *Criticism & Ideology*

William C. Dowling: *Introduction to the Political Unconscious*

Fredric Jameson: *The Political Unconscious*—this last a reread. Also dug out the *Diacritics* issue from two years back devoted to Jameson's book and reviewed the interview with Jameson, some of the articles, and my marginal notes.

Paul Fussell: *Class*, which was an often well-observed giggle.

Sunday, Gar, Iva, Frank and I drove up to Woodstock, where we bought a fifteen-pound pumpkin from a roadside stand. It was quite a monster, but with a handsome shape. While I mostly read in the back seat with Iva, we drove it home and eventually sat it on the kitchen table, to wait for Pumpkin Carving Night, a bit before Halloween proper.

Monday, I went to see Pasolini's *Medea*, with Maria Callas, up at the Metro. Miss Callas doesn't sing a note in the film, and indeed doesn't even say all that much. But it was still interesting.

I really feel Pasolini's last (?) four films—*The Decameron, The Arabian Nights, The Canterbury Tales,* and *120 Days of Sodom: Salo*—were incredible pieces of thinking, feeling, narration and filming. Wonderful, serious, sensuous, charming, they explored both the beauty (and, in *Salo*, the darkly obsessive side) of sex with the insight and awareness of someone who, you can tell, knew what he was talking about.

Medea is cold, intelligent, and one respects it—but it's a matter of watching a very smart man learn how to make a movie; which can only be but so interesting. There are sections of wit and dialogue where we are in some Giraudeaux philosophical farce—at the beginning, for example, with the scrawny centaurs (who turn out to be twins).

Then, we have a wordless documentary for 20 minutes on a ritual blood sacrifice in Medea's primitive Asian tribe.

We get an extraordinary portrait of Medea's distress when she comes to Jason's homeland of Greece, after murdering her brother and helping Jason steal the golden fleece: This dry, broken desert is yet a land of sensuality and freedom. Here, everything is not done according to ritual; here, everything is not fixed on the center, the origin, the ultimate reason, the artifice of logic—and Medea is absolutely at sea in her attempts to understand it, and reels in the barren 'spanse it represents for her.

The sex in *The Decameron* or *The Arabian Nights* is so warm and human, it's astonishing just how cold the love scenes in *Medea* are. But that is primarily the actors. For his other films, Pasolini simply picked up interesting-looking street hustlers and young prostitutes, in Rome, London, or Ankara (?), and got them to play his knights and princesses and kings and noble princes and fine ladies. It worked marvelously well, and produced a far more human-looking crop of fairy-tale aristocracy than he ever could have gotten with actors — especially in their attitude to sex and the body. It's instructive to realize just how similar the filming styles actually are (while one notes how different the effect) — even though the latter was finally loosened up by a morality which, at the end of the '60s in Europe, at least, would allow genitalia to be shown in the later films.

His "fine actors" don't do anywhere near as well.

Certainly the most sensual part of *Medea* is Callas bathing her young sons before (or, more accurately, while) murdering them.

For one section, in a filmic fantasia which rereads myth as psychological fantasy, we learn that Creon's daughter, Creusa, is not really destroyed by the fire in Medea's poisoned cloak, but by the fire of her own remorse at taking Jason away from his wife and sons.

Revenge is plotted by obsessive women, pacing in rank, back and forth across the ostracized queen's tower floor.

Following Robinson Jeffers's prototype, a morally and psychologically destroyed Jason and Medea shout at one another at the end, accusing and accusing and accusing:

On top of such abomination, Medea rages, almost through the surface of the overexposed film, "Nothing is possible anymore!"

And abruptly the film is, indeed, over.

It's an impressive intellectual exercise.

It is thoughtful, yes. But most of it is not "sensuous thought" — which is how Nabokov characterized art.

Earlier that day, after Frank and I had driven Iva's lunch to school (she'd forgotten it on the kitchen table that morning), as we were driving back across the park, I looked out the Rabbit's window to see we were moving beside a large, night-blue Chrysler, with Robert Ludlum at the wheel.

Later, at the Metro (I caught the last hour of *The Arabian Nights*, which I'd seen a couple of times before, so decided to skip it when it came 'round again), just before the lights went down for *Medea*, I realized that Eco was sitting directly across the theater from me, with a friend.[3] I don't believe he recognized me; I didn't speak, as there was the whole of the half-filled auditorium between us.

But what interesting things my city offers me.

Last night at the oil-cloth-covered kitchen table, working with a pencil and a sheet of scratch paper, Iva designed her pumpkin face; I took the knife, cut off the lid, and carved out eyes, eyeballs, eyebrows, nose, and mouth (with two gap teeth), while Lavada came over to return my third volume of *Clarissa* and Frank and Iva took pictures.

Iva tried on her Halloween costume; and we laughed ourselves silly over the idea of starting a "Pumpkin-gram" business — you know, New Yorkers will buy *any*thing!

After our Jack-o-Lantern was all scooped free of seeds and wet, stringy pith, we put a small, squat candle inside, lit it, and set Jack in the kitchen window, where, with gleaming brows and grin, he gazed across the kitchen until Iva went

---

[3] Sometime later, SRD checked with Eco whether or not he had been to see *Medea* at the Metro Theater that day. Apparently, it had just been someone who looked much like him.

to bed; then we turned him around to leer out onto Amsterdam Avenue, where the couples gathered across the street, waiting outside the Yellow Rose Cafe for a table, now and then looked up to point him out to one another.

And this morning a telegram from Chuck Thomas; a business trip is bringing him to New York late Thursday night (tonight); he'll be at the Milford Plaza; he suggests we get together for lunch on Friday.

Good thoughts to Cynthia and the boys; and to you, Bob,

All my love,

• 47 •

To Mrs. Joseph P. Marshall

November 3rd, 1984

Dear Mrs. Joseph P. Marshall,

I'm writing to tell you a little about Maya Amack-Ratner, an eight-year-old girl whose parents, Judith Ratner and Lee Amack, have asked me to write you about her.

I have been a long-time friend of both parents and am also their upstairs neighbor; and I have a ten-year-old daughter of my own, currently at the Fleming School, who has played with Maya for many years. I have known Maya since she was born. Seldom has a week gone by without my seeing her, and seldom a month without her coming up to play with my daughter, or my daughter's going downstairs to play with her.

Maya is an unusually intelligent and personable child. Her reading is substantially ahead of her age level; she is friendly, enthusiastic, and observant. Most often I have had a chance to watch her with children two years to three years older than she. Maya gets along very well with children of that age. She is a very verbal child and expresses herself accurately and creatively and is very relaxed about doing so. As a result (I suspect) she has simply bypassed a great deal of the whining stage common to so many children. And I believe she gets along equally well with children her own age.

She seems a very secure little girl; she is at once cooperative and spirited. In her friendship with my daughter, as she is the younger by two years, naturally she tends to be the follower rather than the leader. But if one game loses their interest, Maya is quick to suggest another. And in those quiet times, during an afternoon or a day together, when the two girls spend a half an hour or so playing separately, often Maya picks up a book from my daughter's bookshelf and reads to herself.

She is enthusiastic about doll and dollhouse play, and she also enjoys construction toys (Capsela, model space stations, trains, and the like). Their friendship has not led them yet into too many competitive games, which my daughter enjoys playing with me and some of her older friends (Othello, Dark Tower, Kensington); but that, I suspect, is simply age. And from time to time they will take out the Atari video-games system for a lively session of Frogger (the favorite) or Donkey Kong.

My daughter is in the fifth grade this year and her homework has, of course, become much heavier. About a month ago, after school, Maya phoned to ask if she could come up. My daughter told Maya she could come only if she brought her homework. The two of them, my daughter explained, would have to work silently together. I was dubious about this; but since it had already been arranged, I decided to give them ten minutes by the clock; at the first sign of giggling or distraction, Maya would have to go back downstairs. But the two girls sat together in my daughter's room and, in no more time than usual and without any unnecessary talk, both did their homework — thoroughly, quietly and efficiently. I was impressed by the maturity both showed; and I think it bodes well for Maya's work habits, as to those already established and those you may expect from her.

Maya has always enjoyed sleeping over at our house, and she has considered it quite a treat to stay over with her older friend. By her own wish, she first stayed over, I believe, when she was four or five — and I note that the anxiety and fear some children feel on a first overnight stay in a strange apartment was simply never present in Maya, from her very first sleep-over.

If strangers come to the house when the two girls are here, sometimes Maya exhibits a moderate amount of shyness; yet not enough ever to strike me as excessive. Indeed, if asked to choose four words to characterize her, I would pick: intelligent, friendly, secure, and observant.

I've read your booklet, *The Brearley School,* and I know the school, certainly, by reputation. Frankly, I cannot think of a child who would respond better to the rigorous, creative, and wide-ranging program Brearley offers. But I am, of course, simply and personally very fond of her. She is a wonderfully easy child to like.

I hope these observations will be useful to you. With them, I send you

All my best wishes,

• 48 •

To Robert S. Bravard

November 12ᵗʰ, 1984

Dear Bob,

Like yours of November 1ˢᵗ, I have much to say and not enough time to write it all.

Let me start with the warmest thanks for your letter — I was touched and intrigued by all in it you chose to share with me. As I said on the phone, it's important when discussing the "sexuality of a given period" not to lose sight of the vast variety of trees for concentrating on the forest's shadowy overshape. Indeed, also thanks for your phone call to tell me about the (rather glorious!) *Publishers Weekly* review of *Stars/Sand.*

It occurs to me, I'm not very good on the phone — at least at organizing what I want/need to say.

When you called, I'd just sat down to give Mr. Aronica a call at Bantam. Rowena had phoned me a few days before to say she'd finished the cover painting. She'd delivered it on Thursday. And I was all anxious to go in and *see* it.

Of course you would have been interested in that — but somehow, when we were talking I managed not to mention that was what I was about to do: though, indeed, 40 seconds after I hung up with you, I called Bantam. And Lou told me to scoot on down if I wanted and I could take a gander.

So about an hour after I spoke with you I was standing in the offices of the Bantam Art Department, gazing at the new painting.

In commercial terms, it's a stunner. Both Rowena and Lou are convinced it's the best of the three. The technical quality of the painting is certainly superb — she's actually become (if you can imagine it) even more technically adroit than she was. But the proof of the pudding, as they say, will be the three-inch by six-inch reproduction it makes.

But while I have no complaints at all, I still have a fondness for the atmosphere in the *Neveryóna* cover. This new one represents a basically white, overcast day — so that we have a generally light cover, rather than the dark ones of the first two volumes.

But we'll see.

Bantam's Jamie Warren showed me the type for the title. They got the umlaut over the wrong letter: put it over the O instead of the Y. But I assume, now that I've pointed it out to them and they have all jumped up and down and waved their hands in the air all about the art room, it will be taken care of . . .?

But then, with Bantam, you never know.

Again, I wanted to say (to reiterate our phone conversation) how much I liked "Species." It's a poem full of the light between the leaves that scatters the sky at the highway's edge. It's most finely observed. And the pick-up of the closing line is jolly smart and affecting. It's now in the pile of MS for the *Little Magazine.* I should be able to let you know in about four to six weeks.

I think I may have mentioned, in one letter or another, we're deep into the production of a new issue — indeed, last meeting, most of our time was spent negotiating a major production crisis: Our typesetter, one Michael Labrioli, who's *only* been doing the magazine for ten years now, has, despite the spec sheet that accompanies the manuscript, managed to set the whole thing in the wrong sized font.

It's a whole point too small and looks like microtype!

Were he a large business with many employees, we wouldn't think twice about asking him to redo it at the proper size. But he's a one-man operation, across the street from Grand Central Station, who charges us practically half-rates because he himself is something of a poetry-lover; and he makes no money at all, really, off the job. We were all prepared to have him say that, even though it *was* his mistake, he just couldn't afford to take the time to do the job twice at the price he was charging. So there was a lot of head-scratching and heart-rending, while we debated whether or not we could — just for an issue — "swallow," as it were, his error.

At the last minute, he saved us by volunteering himself to redo the job correctly. But he has to fit it in, here and there, which means another two- or three-week delay.

You haven't asked for, so perhaps I should not offer, any adverse criticism of "Species." But one line — more accurately, one phrase in one line — strikes me as less firm than it might be: I mean "It again stopped" that ends line five.

Perhaps I've just been brought up on a too-rigid diet of *Elements of Style:* But if the adverbial modifier "again" were moved from between subject and verb (a word to the right? a word to the left? But I wouldn't presume to suggest which), the first stanza would be nigh-on to perfect.

And though, through the whole, you negotiate them with an informal ease that coheres the whole most marvelously and magically, when the muse catches you up again you might keep on the lookout for concatenations of prepositional phrases. *If* you had only missed by *one* "the," the first line of your poem would have crumbled into ". . . *on* a side road *in* the middle *of* the summer . . ." It doesn't, of course, because of your wise omission of any final "the" before "summer." (As you have it, the strong accent on the first syllable of "summer" pulls the mind, the ear, and the eye across the "of," obliterating any possibility of a secondary accent on the preposition at all, so that we don't have time to consider its syntactical weakness.) Your lyricism, in the opening line, is achieved — and lovely in its lilt; but it skirts so *close* to a disaster, I am thrilled as when the circus aerialist catches the bar a moment after you've seen it joggle in its splotlit swing.

Thrilling, yes. And more than that, a lovely poem.

But I have to tear my sweating fingers from my seat arms in order to applaud.

The coming lunch with Chuck Thomas I mentioned to you at the end of my last letter indeed came off — and quite pleasantly: I was introduced to a small, busy, inexpensive Japanese restaurant down in the 42nd Street area that I hadn't known about before, and also to one of Chuck's friends who works with him at NHS, Terry Roberts. Between the sushi, tempura, and sukiyaki, we reminisced about the '60s, the three of us, like refugees from *The Big Chill.*

Since then, Truman Capote and Francois Truffaut have both died.

Two extraordinarily interesting celebrities.

Two extraordinarily interesting careers.

Two extraordinarily interesting talents.

Last weekend was a bit of hysterical socializing.

Mark Gawron and girlfriend Jenny came over to dinner, at Frank's suggestion: He cooked a resoundingly good spaghetti carbonara, and we realized it's the first time he's had people over to eat since the previous October — indeed, Mark and Jenny were the last people he had to the house to eat.

And in the same time I've only had perhaps two dinner parties myself, when Frank was out—Greg Frux one time, and Richard Kostelanetz and Aviva another.

The next day, however, was Mike Elkin's birthday, and I'd invited him for lunch. I put some candles in an Entenmann's "Louisiana Crunch Cake" and sang him happy birthday, after broiled chicken and salad.

And Sunday—well, that I'll recount somewhat at length:

A couple of weeks back I opened my mailbox to find a postcard picturing flowers from some early 19th century herbal compendium, printed in Italy—in 1966, I learned from the explanatory paragraph on the message side. In fact I realized, a day later, it was *two* postcards accidentally stuck together; but that doesn't come into my story. Written in fountain pen and not ballpoint, the blue, blue ink declared (I reproduce the capitalization as best the handwriting allows):

28 october . . .
can you come to a
lunch party for
Umberto Eco on
sunday November 4
at 1 P.M. at the
home of
        Barbara Jakobson

It was postmarked 29 October, and even the cancellation lines a-slant the 20-cent stamp had an archaic look — though today cancellation lines are straight, once upon a time they were (by tradition) parallel waves. Obviously machine rigid, these, somehow, seemed to maintain a ghostly sine curve within them.

Since I didn't know any Barbara Jakobson, I could only assume that, after I'd spoken to him briefly at the YMHA last month, Eco had asked I be invited.

A day or two later I phoned to say I would be coming. A friendly woman with only the tiniest drawl (clearly more class than region) answered. I introduced myself, thanked her for the invitation, and said I was happy to accept.

An excerpt from Eco's new book, *Postscript to the Name of the Rose,* had just appeared on the front page of that Sunday's *New York Times Book Review.* I asked her if the lunch were at all connected with the book.

"Not really," she said. "In fact, not at all. I've known Umberto for—well, many years; since he was in the country, teaching up at Columbia, I thought I'd have a few of my pals and a few of Umberto's pals here for lunch. Really, that's all."

"That's very nice of you," I said. "I'll see you on Sunday, then. I look forward to meeting you, and to seeing Umberto again."

At about seven each morning, from my fifth floor window, I often see the solid little proprietor of the Habana-San Juan Dry Cleaners open up his store across Amsterdam Avenue. (He used to have larger premises up the street, but—another Hispanic victim of the neighborhood "gentrification"—he had been forced to move into a smaller space a few years back.) Everything from the "k" in Jakobson and the eccentric capitalization to "lunch party" (rather than the more bourgeois "luncheon" or "brunch") to her drawl bespoke the upper classes; the postcard itself bespoke taste: And "pals" bespoke money. Later I brought my single three-piece brown suit and my Grand Canyon cowboy shirt down to the cleaner, and asked him, please, to patch the tiny rips that had begun to open up at the edge of both side pockets in the pants.

On Saturday, I dragged them, in their flimsy plastic envelopes, over the white formica counter and took them back across the street and upstairs. And on Sunday, after I got out of the bathtub and dried off, I put them on (with a dark blue tie, slanted through with thin maroon stripes) and, my omniscient notebook in hand, took off to the M-17 cross-town stop, and bussed by the Planetarium and through Central Park to the East Side.

I walked down Park Avenue to 74th Street and turned left. It's a block of trees and private houses. Saturday it had been in the low 40s; that Sunday morning had started out chill, so I'd worn Frank's stepfather's black cashmere overcoat, which is kind of our house dress coat—but the temperature had instantly gone up into the 60s, with minutes at a time of full sunlight, so that the coat swung open at my sides. I'd taped my postcard in my notebook, which I carried under my arm. But, as I hadn't checked the number, when I reached what I thought was the right place on the south-west corner, I found a new, gray, glass and concrete luxury apartment house, thrusting a dozen stories up into an aluminum sky. I'm afraid I smiled to myself and thought: Well, she loses points.

But the doorman ("All Vistors Must Be Announced" in white letters on a black, brass-framed plaque at the top of a thin brass stand) told me there was no Jakobson in the building. I flipped through my notebook, found the card and reviewed the number: I'd overshot the right address by a good handful of build-ings—even had the wrong side of the street. I wandered back and crossed over: It turned out to be a plain townhouse with a yellow brick facade and leaves scat-tered on the front steps. I climbed to the massively unornamented door and rang.

It was answered by a young woman of nineteen or so, in a white Alice-in-Wonderland dress, with long brown hair. Without make-up, she was awesomely pretty. I hesitate to use the word exquisite—it's overworked. But it was the word I first thought to characterize her to myself, as she smiled and offered to take my coat and cap; I just assumed she was a daughter or relative, helping out with the party. (Her dress was most definitely *not* a uniform.) But when she seemed unsure where to put it, I began to suspect that she was not that familiar with the house. (Later, I'd realize she was with the caterers.) Beyond the vestibule, painted a yel-low light enough to be taken for ivory, the front room was traditional, full of molding and crystal, with small tables and framed paintings. Beside me some particularly postmodern sculpture stood against the wall: Half a dozen or more maroon slats curved up from the floor to form a concave pyramid about as tall as I was. But I didn't really notice it so much as when I left.

Though I hadn't seen him outside, I'd apparently come in only moments after a tall gentleman in a dark suit, who, somewhat ahead of me, was approaching the top of a stairway. I followed him over the nondescript carpeting into what I'd thought was a living room, but it turned out to be a balcony, from which a stair, as modern as the front room had been traditional, led down to a room with rough brick walls painted rough white, whose far side was entirely glass: Beyond was a modest New York garden. As I started down, I realized among the many paint-ings, elegant and without frames, hanging at either side, one was the tell-tale black rectangles of an Ad Reinhardt while, across from it, hung a large beige and coral geometric construction by Frank Stella (?). Indeed, most of the paintings there were by recognizable artists.

On several pieces of free-form furniture, half a dozen men—one was Eco—and one woman sat. All of them stood as I came down behind the dark-suited man.

Such double entrances as we had made are the necessary nightmare of consci-entious hostesses — especially if neither incoming guest is known. I was about eight steps above the previous arrival, who turned out to be a German architect, here with some architectural commission.

At the bottom, I lingered a step behind, smiling, waiting my turn. Eco saw me and gave a kind of ebullient surge, with a big grin and both fists raised from his sides—just as the architect was presented to him; so that his greeting to me was somewhat sidetracked.

The woman turned to me, smiling.

"Barbara Jakobson?" I said, extending my hand.

She reached to take mine. "That's right."

"I'm Chip Delany."

"I'm so happy you could come." And a moment later she and Eco were intro-ducing me around the circle once more. Somehow, Barbara's introductions didn't stick; I was too busy smiling and shaking hands to remember names. But, min-utes later, Eco was re-introducing me to a tall, graying gentleman in his 50s with a navy blue blazer and gray slacks. "Chip, this is Bob Silver. He edits *The New York Review of Books*. I've just done a review for him of Teresa's new book."

"*Alice Doesn't?*" I said.

"Yes! A good long one, too."

"How nice!" I exclaimed, honestly surprised and pleased for Teresa. "I read it a couple of months ago. I thought she did a very good job."

"Now what's *that* about?" asked a third party, who'd joined our conversation group.

Eco made a dismissive, Italianate gesture. "Oh . . . semiotics, feminism, film. Everything, really."

"Semiotics? Ah, that must be very difficult."

"Oh, yes," said Eco. "Very dense, very academic . . ." As Teresa's book is a limpid introductory work, I assume he was just getting rid of the topic. He has the reputation of a man who does not suffer fools gladly—though in three meetings I have never seen him anything else but genial.

At that point, a waiter came by bringing mimosas and Bloody Maries and taking orders. I asked for a Bloody Mary, and thought, as Silver used the moment as an excuse to dart away: "*He* certainly hasn't read Teresa's book, even if he's publishing a review. How odd: There is probably no one in the world you can make more uncomfortable expressing an opinion about a book than an editor of a book review." My Bloody Mary and more mimosas arrived (and a single, very healthy martini on the rocks for Umberto) and a moment later I found myself in conversation with a middle-aged Italian gentleman, Carlo (?) Feruggi—a professor of Italian literature at Rutgers. "The only reason I'm here, I think, is because I wrote the review of *The Name of the Rose* that appeared in the *Times*." We talked for quite a bit: gentrification of the Upper West Side, the Village (where Feruggi lived, commuting from there to New Jersey), his three novels published in Italy—we played spot-the-artist with the paintings on Barbara's walls. To the back, under the balcony and behind the highly varnished wooden counter where the caterers were setting a row of chafing dishes, hung a Jackson Pollock. (We breathed a little.) Feruggi was pleasant, alert, and very sharp, but he really seemed to want me to stay and talk to him (waiters drifted up, were sent off after more mimosas, and returned several times; then began to appear with baked oysters and raw littlenecks in individual Chinese spoons, while we ate some and talked on). I realized that the luminous guests and surrounding artwork really made him feel a bit out of his depth. He'd just recently been asked to review the new Mandelbaum translation of the *Paradiso* that had come out from California. "How is it?" I asked. "I haven't read it yet. But I read the *Inferno* and the *Purgatorio* that he did."

"What did you think of them?" he asked back, without answering my question.

"Honestly? I didn't much like them. I still think the Ciardi translation is much better."

"Well, the one thing Mandelbaum is able to do is get the rhythm of the Dante," and he made a rhythmic gesture with his hand.

"I guess so," I said. "But the truth is, for the last 20 years or so, American English just hasn't been that intensely a rhythmic language—at least not in poetry. So that an *intensely* rhythmic translation is simply a sign of archaism in the diction." As I said it, I wondered if I wasn't being too pedantic. After all, I *hadn't* read the volume in question. "It's funny," I went on, "I liked his introductions *very* much."

"Well, that just convinces me," Feruggi said. "I probably should not be the one to review it. It really requires someone with English as a first language."

And I, I'm afraid, just felt confirmed in my doubt about my proclamation. "Well, now—" I back-tracked— "you really shouldn't take my word. I've compared perhaps 50 lines of the *Inferno* from the Italian with Mandelbaum's translation. But that's all. And, as I said, I haven't even *looked* at the *Paradiso* yet."

"You know, Mandelbaum is a poet too," Feruggi said.

I nodded.

"I've tried some of his poems. And they mean absolutely nothing to me. I can't understand them at all!"

I think I actually let myself say: "Well, from the Dante of his I've read, I'm not surprised." I hate the idea of people judging works they don't know; and I especially hate it when *I* do it, even in passing banter. "Now, you know, really: I thought his *Aeneid* was very hard and firm. But his Dante just seems rather, well, pompous and periphrastic."

"No," said Feruggi, "I probably shouldn't review it. And it's true, once I gave my class out at Rutgers the Ciardi to read—and they just loved it!"

For a while I talked to a young artist named David Salle and the blonde dancer he'd come with, Carol Armitage. Both of them had made gestures toward looking modishly punk. And by now some earnest young man about 30, in jeans, with a sport-shirt, navy blue tie, no jacket, and glasses, had arrived and was discoursing heatedly and enthusiastically among a more staid-looking bunch of suits and ties. I drifted up a couple of times, but it didn't seem the kind of conversation that allowed you to join.

So after a few friendly words with Umberto on this or that, I ended up with Carlo Feruggi again.

About then, Barbara came over and took me by the arm, just to say hello. She was as simply dressed as one could get away with at such a gathering: She wore a long-sleeved turtleneck of the quietest coral and a straight black skirt. Her hair, also black, was cut across level at her shoulders, and, as far as I could tell, she wore not a single piece of jewelry. "You know, Chip," she said, "when Umberto told me you were a writer and went on so about your books, naturally I wanted to read one. But when I went to my local book store, Books & Co. — " Having Books & Co. for your local bookstore, here in New York, is kind of like having Rizzoli's or the Gotham Bookmart— "and asked for some of the titles Umberto had given me, they said they didn't carry any science fiction. Nor did they want to order them for me! Why is that?"

A couple of other people had come up with her.

"Well," I said, "Just as you can't have the rich without the poor, you can't have literature without paraliterature — and science fiction, along with pornography and comic books, is a traditionally despised genre. At least by literature."

I watched Barbara decide whether or not she liked my comparison—although her actual decision on it I'll never know.

"'You mean Books & Co. actually won't *get* them for you?" said a tall, amiable looking man with a green turtleneck under his sports jacket. He struck me rather as a 49-year-old ex-football player who had worked very hard over the intervening years to keep himself in shape. "That's awful. Well, I'm not going to go there anymore!"

"You must meet my friends," Barbara said. "Carlo Feruggi, Chip Delany, this is Brooke Hayward and Peter Duchin. Brooke is a writer, too."

"You're good chums with Umberto," Brooke stated/asked.

"Well," I said (thinking "pals," "chums;" you want to hear it, I know, in the accents with which '30s and '40s movies burlesqued the New York 400; though the 400 has expanded, like everything else, to a good twelve if not sixteen; and though some of the mannerisms haven't changed, the accent has moved sharply down from Boston). "I've met him a few times."

"How?" asked Hayward, pleasantly and bluntly. Blonde and just the slightest bit horsey, she wore a white blouse with a white silk tie and a black velour mini-skirt and jacket.

"Back at the MLA a couple of years ago, I was on a panel devoted to his work in semiotics. He was there. We all had lunch together."

"So you're an expert in semiotics," said Mr. Duchin. "That's supposed to be very complicated stuff. I'm sure it's over all our heads." He put an inclusive arm around the diminutive Ms. Jakobson's shoulder. (She's about five feet two.)

"Now tell us what it is," said Ms. Hayward.

I glanced for a moment toward Feruggi, who was holding his tulip glass of orange juice and champagne in both hands, looking not quite pained. "Well, it's the study of signs," I said. "In a sentence, it deal with how things mean what they mean."

"Sighs?" asked Duchin, perplexed. "Or size . . .?"

"*Signs*," Barbara corrected. She shrugged out from beneath Duchin's hand. "You know, I *do* understand semiotics. It's a branch of linguistics." For a moment, she actually looked uncomfortable; and I gave her all points for it.

After debating whether I should ask or not, I decided that whatever the answer, it would simply help me orient myself, so when the conversation turned away from us, I asked Barbara if she knew Howard and Barbara Wise.

She knew *of* them, had met them—she characterized Howard as "the King of Kinetic Art," and reminisced fondly of Howard's gallery. But they were not, I gathered, in the same circle. (Though no husband was in evidence, she did mention a 21-year-old son who was a painter. Which Barbara Wise confirmed a couple of days later, when I saw her for lunch. She, apparently, didn't know Barbara Jakobson at all.)

Somehow Feruggi melted away from the conversation; minutes later, Barbara suggested we go to the counter in the back and start the ball rolling for lunch.

As I walked over with Peter and Brooke, I asked Brooke what she wrote. "Fiction?"

"No," she said. "Just non-fiction. I did a book about my family, called *Haywire*, which turned out to be almost ridiculously successful."

"I think I've heard of it," I said. "But I don't believe I've read it. And you," I asked Duchin. "What do you do?"

"I'm a musician," he said. "I have a small orchestra, that plays around."

"You're no relation to Eddy, are you?"

"I'm his son." He smiled.

And I smiled back, surprised. "Oh, I see!"

Wearing a white dress shirt with the sleeves rolled up, the chief caterer had set up several chafing burners on the blond wood counter, a small spotless aluminum pan over each.

Duchin apparently knew him; and as the slender, blond man arranged things for omelets, they talked of some mutual friend who was now "cooking for Mrs. Mellon." (I assumed that's Mrs. Mellon of AT&T.) Lunch was individually-prepared omelets with bacon, grated cheese, and herbs — the scrambled sort, which really do taste good but which, just on principal, I've never approved of in restaurants; further down the counter was a light green salad and a tray covered with toasted rounds of French bread spread with herb butter.

After we started things, people began to drift forward to be served. By now about 30 guests—perhaps 40—had come. I ended up (on one of the larger bits of freeform) sitting in a group that included Duchin, Hayward, Eco, the German Architect (to my left), a woman who'd been to University in Berlin, and Barbara.

Eco was energetically defending the new Proust movie (*Swann in Love*, with Jeremy Irons): "It's a very good film, an intelligent presentation of the *Belle Epoch*, and all that. As long as when you see it, you don't think of Proust, it's a good love story. And that's what it's supposed to be. It isn't Proust, but then how could it be? And you just mustn't expect Proust. That's all." From there he went on to talk of the age of the University of Bologna, where he teaches in Italy. It predates the founding of the Sorbonne by a couple of months. "Of course," he emphasized, "its age was only notable for Europe: One must make an exception for the University of Baghdad." And when I mentioned the University at Timbuktu, he launched into an appreciative disquisition on the great early universities of the Dahomey Empire.

For some minutes my attention went to the conversation on the other side of me, but came back when Umberto posed me some polite question about *Flight from Nevèrÿon,* which lead to his description of the carryings-on in the Village over Halloween night: "You see," he said, "I am staying in an apartment on Christopher Street, right below West 4th Street—so I am right in the middle of the Gay Movement. Absolutely in the middle. And I am all for it, certainly. Only they sing, all night long. And right under my window; I can get no sleep at all!" Somehow this led the conversation to another line that struck me: "When I am in the wilds," Umberto declared, "I desperately need a skyscraper. But it only takes a city around me to turn me into a savage." One moment he excused himself, either to get some more food or drink, and, as he was standing up, exclaimed, happily and loudly:

"I have written 20 books! I have a beautiful wife and two fine children. And I have achieved fame. If I die tomorrow, it will be all right." When he returned to sit with us again, he announced: "I love it here at Barbara's. She doesn't make her martinis with Martini. She uses Noilly Prat!" Indeed, he had been knocking back martinis on the rocks pretty steadily all afternoon.

The circle broke up before desert and coffee.

The artist I mentioned, David Salle, was a small, muscular young man in his early 30s with a punk haircut, a sports jacket over some legible T-shirt, big hands, and bitten nails: So, just beside the stairwell, I started a conversation. It seems, like Barbara, he was another long-time friend of Eco's. Turns out one of the paintings high on the eastern wall was his:

A warm gray field, up the left of which was a vague purplish cloud, the whole surface very smooth. Off center, painted thickly in acrylic impastos, eight or nine youngsters in blue shorts and white T-shirts mostly faced the right — one, I believe, was jumping a hurdle. Then, as if on a ghost layer, hung before the canvas or brushed over it, some yellowish strokes here, some purplish ones there first struck me as random—but, after moments, resolved into an extremely precise oil-sketch of a reclining female nude (the yellow), and a sketch of the head and bust of the same (?) figure (the purple). After looking at it a while, I told David it was a very satisfying painting. The combined sense of materials and draftsmanship was quite rich.

He seemed surprised to hear an intelligent comment in such a gathering; and went on to a kind of uncomfortable and obligatory request for some titles of my books. I become equally uncomfortable in such situations, and told him, really, SF was the kind of thing he mustn't feel obliged to read.

He answered: "Well, I've known Umberto for a long time, and I usually follow his recommendations. And he's recommended you very highly."

Dessert was little glass bowls of thinly sliced quince, poached in light syrup and served with a very spicy ribbon of whipped cream across them—and some innocuous heart-shaped cookies to the sides of the glass saucers.

The coffee was strong and good, available in demitasses or full cup. At different times, both Brook and Barbara fingered aside my vest to examine the brown piping on my ivory shirt and pronounced it: "Very good. That's very good."

Over the next hour, a few tulip glasses among the guests were refilled with straight champagne. I had an interesting conversation with the architect, who, it seems, had just designed a new electrical (!) transportation system for big cities, including New York, which sounded, I'm afraid, like bad SF from the late '20s. (Individual electrical cars, holding only one person apiece, equipped to run on magnetic tracks, overhead rails, or on several other conveyance means—that was their gimmick.) I reflected quietly that Frank R. Paul[1] would have loved them and that, indeed, they belonged in one of his '30s cover paintings; but certainly not in real cities. Talking to the man was fun nevertheless; and he was boyishly (Germanically?) enthusiastic in a way that only became frightening when you thought about some large city actually funding it all.

It was getting on toward five; the light was low and bronze through the glass wall. Many of the guests had left. I retrieved my notebook (it had moved from a chair, to the floor, to a desk in the corner), and said my good-byes — finally to Barbara and last to Eco.

"You know," Umberto said to me, with a hand on my shoulder, "before he left I was telling Bob Silver, you're the kind of writer, Chip, the *New York Review of Books* must start paying attention to. You're doing the kind of work that's really exciting. I told him that! I told him that directly!" I suspected there was an extra martini behind his intensity.

"Well," I said, "thank you very much, Umberto. But it won't work."

---

[1] Frank R. Paul (1884–1963), a popular science fiction cover artist from the '20s, '30s and '40s.

He exploded with laughter. "Yes, you're probably right!"

And we finished our good-byes.

He asked for a copy of my new book, and I told him I'd drop one off for him at the French department (where he's teaching) up at Columbia.

Upstairs (deserted) I located the closet where the black cashmere had been hung, then spent a few minutes looking for a bathroom. I found it at last and, while I stood, peeing listlessly but musically, realized the framed print I was staring at, among the many over the wall, was a Magritte (the tree with the crescent moon inside it), signed in pencil in the lower left hand corner with the signature familiar from how many art books, or from the Foucault study James Harkness had translated, *Ceci n'est pas une pipe.*

Then out the door and down the front steps, where, in the late afternoon, some leaves scraped along the pavement of 74th Street.

Back home, while I sat in the living room telling him about the party, Frank said to me: "Peter Duchin? Brooke Hayward — and *you* didn't know who they were? She's Jane Fonda's half-sister, Chip. Another one of the sisters committed suicide . . . I read her book, for God's sakes! And Duchin plays at all the society affairs. They're all society people that come up in the 'Suzy Says' column all the time. I bet you your party will be in the newspapers. If somebody introduced *me* to Peter Duchin, you know what *I* would have done? I'd have fainted!"

All of which was pretty much reiterated by my mother when I told her about it on the phone the next day. I guess there're some things a certain sort of ignorance just protects you from.

The day after the party, I called Barbara to tell her what a nice time I'd had. "It was a very pleasant bunch of people."

"Well," she said, after making an amusing comment about how many martinis Eco had put away, "I just thought some of my pals, some of Umberto's pals would make a nice group—and I really enjoyed meeting you. I hope we see each other again."

Alors, as they say in France (or *lipon,* as they say in Greece), we were talking of my hectic weekend.

Indeed it was so hectic it didn't really stop until Tuesday: up at four, to work by five, and at eight out to our local high school to vote. (The whole election passed almost as though nothing were actually happening.) Frank drove off that morning to see his mom in Albany. (Nick — Frank's stepfather, whose cashmere coat figured in the account of the party for Eco — has had to go into the hospital for some tests.) At one-thirty, Barbara Wise came over for lunch—it's actually the first time she's ever been to the apartment here. I think she quite enjoyed it.

Barbara's a (Pritikin) vegetarian — and our basic pattern, for some years, has been to eat out. But I put together a nice tofu, tomato and cucumber salad (with a little avocado to cheat), steamed some fresh asparagus, served with lemon on a bed of watercress, and hulled an autumnal punnet of strawberries; and, with a bottle of Muscadet — everything set out on the round dining room table beside our stained glass window—we had a very nice time of chat, food, and gossip.

An interesting suggestion in your letter: the fictive map of New York people have who don't live in it (and presumably have never visited it). For that's, of course, the "New York" in which much of what I write takes place—and it would probably be instructive to have a better grasp of its layout than I do. Not that I'm charging you, at all, with the responsibility of educating me to it!

I remember my own early fictive map of "Paris" and some of the violences it suffered in my first few days in that city. Most of my early picture came from Gide's *Counterfeiters* and *Journals,* and Barnes' *Nightwood,* along with various plunges into Proust—supplemented by the odd biography of Cocteau, or this or that bit about French theater.

Coming from New York, I suspect my first surprise was that so many of the landmarks I'd heard about were so close to one another—I remember discovering that the Fauxbourg St.-Germain (the elegant neighborhood where the Parisian aristocracy live) actually *was,* for all practical purposes, the Latin Quarter (the famous *cinqueme arrondissement*). It was rather as if the area New Yorkers refer to as Fifth Avenue and/or Park Avenue (which runs from the 70's to the 90's) turned out to lie along 8th Street or MacDougal Street in the Village. I remember I'd always assumed that the Luxembourg Gardens were a city park about the size of Washington Square that fronts NYU, i.e., about two full city blocks. It was quite a surprise to learn that it was a vast spread of city greenery (the old grounds of the Palais Luxembourg) that was almost a third the size of Central Park. Similarly, I had never realized that the Tuileries were just the palace grounds of the Louvre, now become a public park. I remember being astonished that the Odeon Theater was so small, and that the *Comedie Française* was so close—right across the Seine (which is just a stream running through town, compared to the Hudson or the East River, both of which are wide enough effectively to isolate Manhattan).

"Aye, and Gomorrah . . ." and *Nova* both contain the detritus of that shock of poligraphical revision.

Similarly, during my first hours in London in 1966, I remember learning that Hyde Park (as a child I'd been to the Hyde Park Museum up near Rhinebeck, which was the rather presumptuous name the Roosevelts gave their family home and the lawns and gardens around it) was actually the size of Central Park in New York City, i.e., miles long and a mile wide. And that Bayswater was, indeed, the street running along the park's edge — as Central Park West runs along Central Park in Manhattan.

Yet the most intriguing thing about our uncorrected fictive cities is how adequate they are as stages for Dickens and Queneau and Barnes and Proust and all the writers who, knowing the reality of their own cities with an intimacy verging on the obsessive, have set their novels, by accident, in ours.

For the intimacy is what comes across — even if it is only our own intimacy with these fictive towns, however distant from the real.

Two films taken in since I wrote you last: Hans Jurgen Syberberg's *Ludwig, the Mad King of Bavaria,* and Ken Russell's *Crimes of Passion.*

Robert Morales and I went to see the Syberberg at the Thalia some weeks back. I wanted to see it because I'd seen both his *Hitler* and his *Parsifal,* and since Ludwig is such an important character in Wagner's life (and Wagner is such an important one in Syberberg's personal image gallery), I thought it would be interesting, if not instructive.

Robert lent me the published scenario of Syberberg's *Hitler,* which I read; I'm afraid that reading it just confirmed a feeling that seeing all three films had given me: No matter how interesting a thinker he is (and no matter how interesting Sontag is when she writes about him), Syberberg's whole enterprise is simply and profoundly anti-filmic — the way piano works by certain composers (e.g. Scriabin) can be described as anti-pianistic.

Which is not the same thing, say, as the "anti-" feeling in the (Beckett style) anti-novel at all.

The sheer intelligence in which the scenario of *Hitler* is drenched, when you read it, just reinforces how little of that intelligence comes across in the film as film, when you see it. What one sees on the screen is a return to "the German studio style" of, say, Fritz Lang's *Niebelungenlied* of the early 1930s—a dead-on filming with no articulation into far-shot/close-up that makes film a language.

And when an image is clearly readable (e.g., Ludwig at his desk, distressed, rocks his head in his hands for perhaps five minutes, while, on the rear-projection cyclorama behind him, we see tourists gawking and gaping through the sumptuous halls of his "fairy-tale castle," *Neuschwanstein,* and the soundtrack plays Siegfried's "Funeral March" from the end of *Götterdämmerung,* Act II), it just seems obvious.

In *Hitler,* an actor playing Hitler's personal valet delivers a 45-minute monologue that recounts details about Hitler's shoes, underwear, and the minutiae of his personal toilet and dress: It ends — and we go on to another actor talking about the size of the universe, the distance of the stars and galaxies, outlining suggestions of infinity.

The change from the humanizing personal to the cosmic was, indeed, affecting in the film. And Sontag, in her consideration, compared it to the moment in *2001* when the tossed bone rising against the blue sky becomes a white spaceship sinking away into interplanetary night.

The difference Sontag does not acknowledge, however, is that the effect in *2001* is visual, while the transition in *Hitler* is entirely verbal (if not literary). Indeed, the visual transition simply between one actor and another, and both in the same claustrophobic studio-of-the-mind (in which all three of the Syberberg films I've seen take place), seems designed to *subvert* the change of scale—if anything.

There are images in all of the films that affect: the puppet of the Führer who is stripped of layer after layer of clothing, costume after costume, in *Hitler;* Kundry's entrance through the water in the leaf-strewn pond in *Parsifal;* the journey along the empty, snow-covered road to the second act duel from *Tristan* in *Ludwig.* What is lacking, however, is any *rhetoric* of images. Whatever dialogue they create with one another is so syntactically muted as to be all but unhearable, all but unseeable.

Adorno attacks Wagner's gigantism because, he declares, it abolishes the sense of historical time and places his works in a space without true history. For all its aim at the cosmic, the *Ring* only achieves it by the complete suppression of any sense of the flow and workings of material life through the ages. This is not a flaw of length in general—certainly one could not level such a criticism at, say, the five hours of Ganz's *Napoleon.*

One can, however, level it at Syberberg.

The isolated soundstage on which his progression of ideas and images (and the images are by far secondary) exfoliate is very much the protected temple of artifice Wagner desired Ludwig to isolate for him at Bayreuth: Like Wagner's, Syberberg's ideals are probably as democratic as they can be. But the reality of filmic discourse renders them one with the "idealism" Marxists are always decrying — an idealism so completely cut off from the reality of material life that the valet's banalities are actually the closest we get to the human — and that, in such a space, seems dubiously manipulative.

The view from too close, like the view from too far, is a way of repressing human misery. Not a way of exploring it: either the misery of Hitler *or* his victims.

I have no generic objection to being told, even for 45 minutes out of a seven-hour film, that Hitler was a human being like you, like me — that he preferred his old boots to spiffy new ones, that he preferred to wear his cap in an unfashionable way, that he liked underwear of one cut and disliked that of another. It is not the thrust of the entire film — indeed, it is a fragment of that larger message Hannah Arendt, years ago, writing on the trial of Adolf Eichmann in Jeruselem, characterized with the telling phrase, "the banality of evil." We need to be reminded, and reminded again and again, that evil, even to that which would indulge genocides, is a combination of big and little mistakes, inappropriate models for the human and the real, all of which create a self-maintaining system. And when this message, in whatever part, is used to destabilize some notion of an essentialist, unfightable, demonic evil against which there is no recourse, it is not only a good thing, it is an important thing.

But when such humanizing gestures are isolated so entirely from the world, both in visual terms and in intellectual terms, as they are in Syberberg's film, it is hard to read them as anything else save as an *excuse* for evil. And while that may be aesthetically interesting, it is not morally acceptable.

Well, I'm afraid that, save for a few sequences in *Parsifal*, after having seen nearly fifteen hours of Syberberg films and having read one rather immense scenario, that's my considered judgement on them: interesting, but not very filmic.

Now *Crimes of Passion* was intriguing if for no other reason than that I've *never* seen a movie with its particular plot before. Indeed, it's rather like a very bourgeois version of the *Rocky Horror Picture Show,* made to be palatable to the upper working classes of Queens (i.e., in Archie Bunker territory).

But because it *was* a new plot, and because (I assume) there are not hundreds of versions of it floating around in the filmmaker's head, there was almost *no* sense of psychological veracity to any of the characters — with the possible exception of the poor, unhappy wife the hero is in the process of dumping.

The film's main character (the heroine) is a sucessful sport-clothes designer by day who is able to maintain a white-towered mansion of fairy-tale proportions, but who works as a tenderloin prostitute all night, every night — at least it would seem so. (Or are we to believe that's just her Friday and Saturday evenings' diversion?) She is, of course, so schizo she can hardly see straight, unless she's involved in living out some man's fantasy, at which point she becomes *so* self-possessed you wonder about that too — a sexual superwoman with occasional attacks of the shakes.

At one point, our hero (an electronics repairman turned fashion spy) says to her: "Hey, when do you sleep?"

And I really think that *is* the burning question of the film.

Tony Perkins plays a twitchy derelict minister who also happens to be a sexual psychopath of the stab, rend, and (if you can remember to, after all that) rape variety.

Once Perkins breaks into our heroine's house and straps her to the drawing board, from then on in the film becomes, oddly, entirely about other movies, rather than about people—about Brian DePalma's filmic misogyny and the conventions of the "splatter" film, until even the final switcheroo in clothing (although you only have about three seconds to guess in, I saw it coming) is as much a comment on Perkin's portrayal of Norman Bates in *Psycho* as it is a comment on the confused ego identities of the characters in the film on the screen.

It's all supposed to end (more or less) happily ever after. You don't really believe it. But I give Russell a B+ for trying.

Would be curious what you thought, as it rather touches (however clumsily and obliquely) on some of what we've discussed in these last years.

This past Saturday (day before yesterday) the SF Shop, down on 12th Street and 8th Avenue, had a signing for me, from three to five. It was pleasant, low-key, and they sold about 30 copies of *Stars/Sand*, which is not bad. And beforehand, downstairs in the basement, I signed another 40-odd copies for mail orders that they were filling. Barbara Wise came by, with her daughter Julie and a number of her friends; and Monte Davis showed up, whom I haven't seen in over a year—which was also very nice. He said he was halfway through his second reading, and raised a couple of interesting points, one of which is directly helpful with the second volume where I am now.

Afterwards, I went back to Baird's and Martin's apartment for dinner. (Monte came for a while, but left before we ate.) Then their young friend Oliver joined us for a very tasty beef fondue—little cubes of meat on tiny forks, cooked in a pot of hot oil, bubbling merrily in the middle of the table: Then you dip them in one of a variety of sauces.

I found myself reminiscing that the first time I ever visited Baird and Martin for dinner, back when they lived in the apartment directly across the airshaft from the one I live in now, Sue Schweers, Neil Conan, and myself all came to dinner to celebrate the completion of *The Star-Pit* program for WBAI, and they served a meat fondue then.

It was quite nostalgic.

And after that, we watched a tape of Ingmar Bergman's *Wild Strawberries*, which, believe it or not, I'd somehow managed never to have seen before.

Well, there you more or less have it.

Work goes slowly but more or less steadily.

The next event in my life will be the publication of *Flight from Nevèrÿon* this coming May (i.e., copies available in April). And now (November 13th, this has run on to) off to a 12:30 lunch with Ellen Datlow of *Omni*, as sudden snowflakes, the first of the year, sweep across the back alley to tick my office window.

Once again, all best to Cynthia and the boys. And

all my love to you,

• 49 •

November 19th, 1984

Dear Marilyn & J. T.,

I'm just delighted to have been chosen for the staff of Clarion West '85. The Clarion Workshops have always been important to me—I taught my first, unofficially (as a kind of surprise guest teacher, along with Judith Merril), in 1967, and for the first time officially in 1968, back when Clarion was still held in Clarion, Pennsylvania. Since then I've ended up on the staff of various Clarions perhaps eight times now.

As such workshops go, Clarion has got quite a pedigree to it; there really *is* something special about the Clarion workshops. Where the graduates of other writing workshops tend to fade away into the reality of nine-to-five living, Clarion has produced a truly astonishing proportion of graduates who've gone on to publish widely in SF. But, then, at least two Clarion alumni will actually be on the staff this year. And Vonda, I gather, is around for advice. So I'm sure you both have more than enough sense of Clarion's history.

I don't want to be presumptuous. But I did want to talk for just a paragraph or two about some of the things that seem to have made Clarion work in the past— and, indeed, about a few of the things that have, from time to time, gotten in the way of one or another session's working as smoothly and richly as it might have.

If I rehearse material the two of you are familiar with, please put up with me —it's simply to make my own tale coherent to myself: I'm not really presuming about what you might or might not know.

Clarion differs from most writing workshops in that it's a high-pressure working session, where the students produce constantly throughout the six weeks. Although they are not set up to become so, many writing workshops very easily turn into places where students bring two or three old stories, written weeks to years before, have them critiqued by somebody "with a name" and then go home and put them away, satisfied that so-and-so "read my story and thought this or that part of it wasn't *too* bad." It doesn't have much to do with writing, but even so such workshops *can* be valuable to the participants as readers.

But Clarion really *is* something else.

The daily three-hour workshops where the students and the instructor critique the newly produced stories, the individual sessions the instructors have with each student, the weekly changeover of professional staff is all predicated on the fact that the students themselves are reading *and writing* constantly through the six weeks.

I've taught Clarions in any number of physical settings, from luxuriant to Spartan. But if I can cite a single, practical aspect that separates "good" Clarions from "not-so-good" Clarions, it would be the Xerox (or whatever duplicating) facilities. The students write; and what they write has to be duplicated *within hours* and distributed among them all—so they can read it that evening, while still doing their own writing, and be ready to critique it the next day.

At least twice I've taught at Clarions where duplicating was an overnight affair, which, from time to time, lapsed into two days. In both cases the general energy of the whole workshop seemed diminished by 30, even 40%. Figure:

Since the individual instructors are only there, really, for five workshop days, a delay of two days in duplicating manuscripts wastes almost *half* the instructor's time!

The duplicating costs for Clarion have always been high. I suspect that, in the kind of high-pressure situation Clarion has always been, they must be. There is always going to be *some* superfluous duplicating. And one must figure those costs in from the beginning. Somehow you have to devise a system that will allow students to hand in work (usually four to ten stories a day, figuring on a student enrollment of 25) at the beginning of the day's workshop session, which can be taken off, duplicated up to 25 or 30 copies (depending on the number of students), and distributed by lunchtime or just after *of the same day*.

This is a big order!

From time to time directors have tried to work it differently—because of very real economic and physical constraints. (Let me add, I know how hard the ideal is to achieve!) Nevertheless, it's been my unfailing experience that less-than-ideal duplicating services simply mean a less-than-ideal Clarion. So directly is the energy and efficiency of Clarion tied to the speed and efficiency of the MSS duplicating facilities, that I'd go so far as to say: To skimp on duplicating costs and efficiency is to skimp on Clarion itself.

Not having enough copies of the stories, and the debacle this makes of the workshop sessions, can be so serious a problem that most instructors would probably rather take less money than have their time eaten up by a situation which makes it impossible for students to discuss the stories accurately, from notes on their own copies, where they can point out page and paragraph and refer constantly to the text.

In most workshops, a criticism like, "The ending of your story is weak," is more or less acceptable.

At Clarion, we train students to say: "From the second paragraph on page seventeen to the end, your story loses all its energy. There's some pickup in the last two-paragraphs, but not enough to save it. And you really have to rethink the whole two and a half pages in-between."

But to teach students to give this kind of practical criticism everybody must have a copy of the story in hand, which they've already read and made their own notes on the manuscript.

Clarion can work with students sleeping in sleeping bags and bedrolls on the floor of rooms where the iron-frame bedsteads have not yet got their mattresses; it can work where the meals are endless bologna and mustard sandwiches from trips to the local supermarket because the staff at the school cafeteria has suddenly gone on strike—!

I have seen it rally spectacularly when faced with both.

It *can't* work—or can't work very well—with faulty, delayed, or underfunded duplicating services. I've seen it try—and fail.

And a Clarion with hellishly inadequate duplicating facilities is, itself, hell.

The other thing I wanted to mention is the "mix" of students. Again, I am sure this is something both of you have thought about in its various possibilities: race, sex, economic backgrounds. But of the many ways students can be "mixed" in a workshop situation, one of the most important for Clarion in my experience has been the mix of different *aged* students.

Of course you need talented, literate applicants for any good writing workshop: And I know that's what you'll be (or have been) looking for. Yet the following observation may be useful: The dullest Clarion I've ever taught at was one where the directors, that year, decided not to accept any students under twenty —and for some reason that same year few over twenty-five applied. Though we had people from all over the country, from various economic backgrounds and with some racial deployment (though never enough! never enough!), that year the ages ranged from 20 to 27. And, as I said, by comparison to other years, it was simply a very dull workshop.

Certainly one of the most spectacular workshops in terms of graduates who went on to publish SF novels was the 1969 workshop, which included Vonda McIntyre (20 [?] at the time), Marc Gawron (sixteen at the time), Octavia Butler (23 [?] at the time), Gerry Conway (seventeen [?] at the time), Glen Cook (23 at the time), George Alec Effinger (24 at the time), and Robert Thurston (34 [?] at the time). In that same year, we had students in their 40s and 50s, so that the age range went from fifteen to 57.

Myself, I think that's an ideal age-range. And the kinds of responses people bring at different ages is terribly helpful to the others. Goethe says somewhere, "One is not really any wiser at 50 than one is at 20. One simply knows different things." And that range of difference—indeed, a range even wider than 20 to 50 —has brought life and exciting critical perspectives to Clarion.

Clarion students work *very* hard. And every year three or four students tell you, quite directly, they have *never* worked harder at *anything* in their lives! (So, usually, do two or three instructors!) And I must note: It has been quite common for a student or two simply to find the pressure too much, who drop out after two or three weeks. (One year, so did a director!) For this reason, the directors have sometimes felt it would be better to limit enrollment to more "mature" students.

I certainly understand this.

Yet again and again students who have gone on to use the Clarion experience in ways leading to a professional career have come from the younger ones (i.e., under 20) or the older ones (Seattle's own F. M. Busby, a case in point). If the directors can make it very clear to the applicants at the beginning—especially to the younger ones—just how great the pressure at Clarion can get, then applicants can decide whether or not they want to spend that very pressured, but very rewarding, six weeks out of their summer at Clarion. And they will not come to the workshop unprepared.

Clarion has been a rich experience for most of its graduates—and a life-changing one for many of them. It can be a great deal of fun . . . but it has little to do with "fun and games." And it's better to stress (or even overstress) the work and the challenge to the incoming applicants than it is to let them stumble into it unprepared. Losing a student in the middle of a workshop as intense as Clarion is always rough—on everybody. And the best way to avoid that is to make it as clear as possible to the students at the beginning what they are getting into.

Well, there you have my thoughts from my last seventeen irregular years of Clarions: in a word, (first) good xerox facilities, and (second) a broad age range in students. These are not the only problems, but they are easy ones to let slip by. But

I'm sure you have your own thoughts on both subjects, along with all the real and practical organizational problems a workshop like Clarion always entails.

It's a *lot* of work: And just for taking it on, the two of you deserve congratulations!

I'm sending along an essay I wrote on the Clarion experience—Dear Lord— almost fifteen years ago now![1] Certainly recreating past pleasures is not what a present workshop should be about. And I've taught at enough writing work-shops since (Clarion-style and other) to know that the best of them—all of them —*are*, indeed, unique. Again, think of it as a sharing of experiences—containing some suggestions, yes. But *not* proscriptions.

I'd be very surprised if the various people around you who have dealt with Clarions before haven't gone over much of this with you—or, indeed, that you aren't aware of it simply from your own experiences in similar situations. Again, please don't take my sharing these thoughts with you as any attempt to "tell you how run your workshop." (Believe me, I have a very strong sense of the work-shop's being yours to run—and only mine to teach in for a week.) Rather, it's the result of my own enthusiasm for a continuing project that has meant a great deal, over the years, to me—and from which I've gotten quite as much, if not more, than I've given.

J. T., I really look forward to seeing you again; and Marilyn, I look forward to meeting you in person come July.

If, indeed, there's anything you want to ask me about further—or take excep-tion to, or do entirely differently because of whatever reasons . . . well, that's Clarion too. And in any case, I'm at your disposal in any way I can be.

Best of luck and all my good wishes,

Sincerely,

• 50 •

To Ron Drummond

December 4th, 1984

Dear Ron,

Thanks for your letter of November 26th—especially for your generous words about *The Tale of Plagues and Carnivals.*

Many thanks also for your errata on *Flight.* Alas, the long galleys were turned in months ago, and I delivered corrected page proofs to Bantam back at the begin-ning of October. So no further corrections can go into the book until there is a sec-ond printing.

This is kind of what I was talking about in my last letter to you, Ron. It seems a shame for you to have done all this work (fourteen pages of corrections!) and not have it be of any use.

I proofread *Flight* twice—but with my dyslexia, that's next to useless for the finer points of orthography; still, I was able to catch a goodly number of errors. Bantam's proofreader went over it; and I went over what the Bantam proofreader had done; and Mog Decarnin (thank God!) also got to go over the galleys—so I sus-

---

[1] "Teaching SF Writing," in *The Jewel-Hinged Jaw,* by SRD, (New York: Berkeley Windhover, 1977).

pect the printed book will be in at least as good shape as the trade paperback of *Neveryóna*. There were only about 45 or 50 errors there, and most of those were fixed in the mass market edition. Memory can't, of course, be perfect; but I suspect we got most of the errors you listed—though, I'm sure, a handful of them sneaked by.

At some point, when copies of *Flight* appear in late April/early May, 1985, I'll go over your list and see which of the errors that you found managed to creep by the rest of us—though I can't help thinking it would have been so much easier on us both if you'd only waited to list the errors directly from a reading of the printed book.

In general, bound galleys arrive at the publisher's office a few days to a week after page proofs have been returned to the printer. (And once page proofs are returned, nothing more can be done.) I have argued with editors for years now, since the practice of sending out bound galleys was instituted: "If you only held off two or three more *weeks*, you could send out Xeroxes of the pageproofs, rather than of the galleys — which would be infinitely freer of errors. And that really wouldn't hurt your lead time for reviewers at all." To which the general response is usually: "Yeah, you're right. I wonder why we *do* do it the way we do? It's pretty stupid, isn't it?"

But generally you can be sure that once you've been sent bound galleys on a book, it's a week to months beyond the correction stage.

I was sent bound galleys on Joanna's *Extra(Ordinary) People* for comment and noticed a dreadful typo in the first five minutes I was skimming through:

Joanna's epigraph to "Bodies" was attributed to one "Anna Tsetsayeva." There are, of course, two great Russian women poets of the 20th century: Anna Akhmatova 1889-1966) and Marina Tsvetaeva (1892-1942) (sometimes transliterated "Tsvetayeva," sometimes "Cvetaeva"). The quote is from a memoir by Tsvetaeva, and Joanna had, in a careless moment, grafted the first name of Akhmatova onto a somewhat mangled version of Tsvetaeva's last name.

With Joanna's feminist commitments, I knew this was just the last mistake she would want to make. ("That great American poet, Emily Millay . . ." You know: women poets are all interchangeable anyway . . .) I *phoned* the correction in to St. Martin's Press the morning I received the bound galleys in the mail. But it was still too late—and the glitch is there in the printed volume. But that's about how it works.

Printing and production schedules are just not sane things, Ron. *Flight*, for example, was originally scheduled to appear in February—that's even what it says on the bound galleys. (And I'm sure that's why Faren C. Miller's review appeared in *Locus* when it did, last week.) At least four months ago, however, the book was rescheduled for May, 1985. But for various and arcane reasons (i.e., so the typesetter didn't have an overload), the typesetting/correcting process all had to be carried out as if the book were, indeed, a February book; and I and Mog had to work our tails off to get our corrections done in time and spend money we didn't have on express mail—though, once it was done, believe me, the finished plates are still lying around on a shelf somewhere, untouched for three months, waiting to go on the presses in late-March/early-April.

At this point, of course, I just don't have a real errata sheet for *Flight*—at least not like yours. That will have to wait till I see the printed book in April/May.

Ideally what I wanted to do was re-read all three *Nevèrijon* volumes at a go and see if there were any things that could be brought in line for consistency's sake. (Most inconsistencies I'm willing to leave as they are, but any that were easily correctable — and whose correction would add something tangible to the overall effect of the series — I thought I might try to remedy.) Time prevented me from doing this when I wanted to, back at page-proof time. I'd planned to have page proofs for two weeks or so, but they arrived so late I had to pick them up from the Bantam offices on a Tuesday afternoon and deliver them that Thursday morning by ten. So I still haven't actually gotten a chance to do that full reading with an eye to corrections of the whole series yet.

It will have to wait till *Flight* appears; and the changes will have to wait for a future edition.

I will tell you that, between galleys and page proofs, the correction section (#20) in "Appendix B" was greatly expanded, so that a diligent reader will now be able to put together an almost letter-perfect copy of *Tales*, and do a bit of toothbrush work on the mass-market edition of *Neverÿóna*.

And while skimming, here and there, I've hit on a few further changes that I'd like to make in *Neverÿóna* and *Flight* both.

Neverÿóna (mass market edition):

194/2 should read in its entirety:

A leaf blew from the roof above, to spin and spiral at her, till a texture change in the earth underfoot made her look down—at the window, now before her, with its dark drapes.

194/3/4 should read:

drifted from the haloed moon. Light fell through the open roof into

195/2/5 should read:

one and looked, carefully, out. At the outbuilding men and women stood

Those more or less do it for the re-writings in *Neverÿóna* that aren't already covered in "Appendix B," #20, of *Flight*. In *Flight* itself, I want to make the following changes (see bound galleys):

"The Tale of Fog and Granite"

4/19/2:

your supporters. After today's victory, you are only a shadow away from becoming

4/20/2:

nothing in Kolhari, in Nevèrÿon. It was a precarious victory, and I would be the most unfortu-

Those changes in the two books would make it clear beyond doubt that the first scene in *Fog and Granite* takes place only moments before Gorgik's and Noyeed's encounter with Pryn inside the empty mansion, where Gorgik gives Pryn his astrolabe. That's what I intended when I wrote it—still, I realize now it takes a little adjusting to make it clearer than I'd given it.

And there are a couple more changes I'd like to make in *Flight:*

"The Mummer's Tale"

What is now 127/8 should be removed and replaced with the following:

— Well, I suppose you can come. But I made it clear to him there would be nothing monetary in it. He made it equally clear to me: He'd heard of the various

Kolhari festivals since before he'd come to the city, but he'd been afraid to go to any of them by himself. If he had a friend, like me, he wouldn't be scared. And he couldn't pass up the chance to go with someone actually part of the festivities.

As he fell in beside me, he called to a stranger standing only a little way down from us: another young man, I realized, working the bridge.

— Hey, give us a swig of your beer?

At which the youngster pulled his drinking skin from the wall, beat it against his thigh, and (to my surprise) stalked angrily off!

I raised an eyebrow to ask my friend what that was all about.

Grinning, he explained:

— Oh, I stole an old man of his this morning, who always comes around here looking for him. Only today, I was here first! When I came back, I told him all about it — about how much money he gave me. (He nudged my arm, his grin gone even broader.) I lied—about the price, I mean. *Nobody* gives that much. But I tell a good story. And now he thinks anyone who walks by and talks to me was really going to talk to him first.

I began to protest, but he went on:

— It doesn't matter. Last week, every time someone came near me, he was in my face, with his dumb smile and his stupid boasts about how much he can do and how long he can do it. I'm just getting him back.

He ended with a scalding insult to his rival's breeding, home land, and defecatory practices, which, in its country vulgarity, I actually found shocking here in the city—at any rate worrisome:

His rival just happened to have been—most visibly—of the same ethnic origins as the inhabitants of the neighborhood in which our festival was to occur.

A friend who has had much more experience in professional hustling than I have (one of the dedicatees of *Flight*), pointed out to me, after he read the book over, that I've rather romanticized the camaraderie among the "working men" on the Bridge of Lost Desire. While such camaraderie exists, it's shot through with endless jealousies, hostilities, and betrayals. As soon as he said this, I realized from my own experience he was right. There're hints and feints at that sort of thing through the book, but I think the insertion of the incident above will give their flavor directly (in New York, with almost equal numbers of white, black, and Hispanic hustlers up and down the strip, there's almost always some ethnic overtone involved in these hostilities, if only because the ethnic deployment is what it is); but having alerted the reader to that aspect of hustling life, I think this insertion will lend a clearer accent to those later traces of it now all but muted out of existence. Generally, it raises the verisimilitude factor of what is, after all, a highly stylized tale—as well as adds a nice formal touch (the use of the word "stranger") which, alas, you'll have to see the printed book to appreciate, since that represents more revision.

The Tale of Plagues and Carnivals

After 269/10, insert the following paragraph:

Soon he hobbled with me back through the dreary huts to point me toward my hosts' home at the other side of the village. We parted in a convivial glow of rum and late afternoon sun caught among leaves immobile in a breezeless spring. I walked through that little city, rehearsing the tale I would make of it for my friends when they arose from their afternoon naps: *You'll never guess who I . . .* or perhaps better, *While I was out walking this afternoon, of all people in the world I met . . .* But in this way I went on trying to tell myself what had just happened, for the whole of the 40-minute walk back. Yet as I came in sight of my hosts' garden wall, their two-story home showing above it, with its facing tiles and terra cotta cornices, any anecdotal account that contoured to the good feeling of the encounter so intimately and intricately worked through with its troubling revelations seemed more and more impossible — till, I confess, once I actually entered the gate, I could not bring myself to mention the meeting with Arly at all, for all my slightly tipsy rehearsals of it along the way: though, indeed, I feel sometimes I have been rehearsing it, now one way and now another, ever since — with this account only the most recent and by no means the final.

I'm glad you liked the Master's sub-tale of his attempted "flight from Nevèrÿon." It's certainly among my favorite parts, but how I managed to let it get by without the above section, I'm afraid I'll never know. Indeed, I suppose I can be just as seduced by the Discourse of the Master as anyone else. And there, I guess, I was taking part in the Master's own repression, rather than reporting on it with any artistic punctilio.

Of course, it's necessary to keep lucidly in mind, throughout that whole section, the desperate critique the mummer levels at the Master in §9.6 (courtesy of Karl Popper's *The Open Society and Its Enemies*); and every time the Master uses the exemplary "he" (e.g., for the Ulvayn genius who invented writing), or every time he misreads "Venn" or refuses to interview Pryn's great-aunt, if you've been properly "conditioned" by the rest of the tales, those spots should literally set your teeth on edge.

My worry is that he's *too* seductive.

Some of his observations are useful — and I want them to be: But I also want the reader to be constantly aware that, if only through his position in the social matrix, the Master is about as close to an evil man as you can get: And, as the "wisest man" in Nevèrÿon, he is the greatest danger to Nevèrÿon's true (and, indeed, real) history.

* * *

At any rate, getting these changes into the text of *Flight* (and *Neveryóna*) will have to wait for further printings.

Just a couple of things strike me as I look over your correction list:

"Incicurable" is a rare word meaning "untamable."

And there is an "art page" (a reproduction of the Hanged Man from the FitzGerald Tarot) that will appear in the printed book and that takes the lines at 315/9/1-2 as its caption. It appears facing that place on what is now page 314 of the bound galleys which says "art p. 575" (a reference to the page where the illustration occurred in my MS). But that was all taken care of in page proofs; and looks rather nice, I think.

I've also received an interesting letter and essay from a young engineer in Palo Alto, Bob Wentworth, on the mathematics of "Buffon's Needle," the method of calculating pi that Venn devises for Belham in "Chapter Eleven" of *Neveryóna*. It turns out that I have it slightly wrong. His correctionary comments are both amusing and instructive, and—as I did with Dr. Hoequist's letters, in *Neveryóna*—I'd love to use them as an appendix to *Flight* in some future edition.

As to the mistakes in *Dhalgren*, I just don't know how I managed not to get the ones you sent me, back in January '83, on the list that went to Bantam. But I put together that list *so* many times, while Bantam lost it, forgot to use it, misplaced it, found it again . . .! I have an article coming out in *Locus* in February (?) that natters on about how perfect the seventeenth printing now is. (I'll enclose a copy.) C. Brown said I'd have a chance to look over it before he printed it. Perhaps I can add the ones in your letter as a footnote—for I have just checked them out, and —you're right—they're there.

I'm leaving the last chapter of *Dhalgren* pretty much alone—as you say, it's an imperfectly typed notebook; still and nevertheless, I've selected the mistakes I *want* to leave there rather carefully.

The errors (all but one of which you mention) that *should* have been corrected are: 399/3/21, 389/7/1, 767/4/3, 795rubrics/1/2, 835rubrics/10/1, 863/2/2 — and though 838/6/1 (Mrs. Arthur Richards) *ought* to have been remedied, see my essay . . .

Once again, many thanks for your help.

Give my love to Don, Tatiana, and Deirdre. What is Don doing with *Inscape*? How is your novel coming? What do the clouds look like in the Seattle sky? Every time it rains, my sinuses fill with yellow gunk and my head hurts . . .

All best wishes,

• 51 •

TO ROBERT S. BRAVARD

November 28th, 1984

Dear Bob,

Good morning. It's moving on toward five-thirty, though outside my office window it's still dark. If I rise a bit in my seat and look down, over the back of my word processor and out the window, there are only the four lights beside the back-alley doors of the tenement buildings to the south; if I look up, I can see the beacon on top of what I assume is the Beresford, over on Central Park West, where Frank's brother, Tony, used to live until he gave up his rather elegant co-op apartment there a few years ago and moved permanently to the country. I've been up since four-twenty—the first time I've been up so early in almost a month!

The cold I mentioned to you that went with me up to Niagara Falls in October settled, by the beginning of November, in my sinuses. It kind of knocked me out; so, since Iva is with her mother this month, I've spent an indulgent few weeks getting up at seven, eight, and a couple of times even eight-thirty! It seemed to be a month of rest, rest, rest—I probably needed it. But a package of Sinutabs and a bottle of Vicks Vapo-Rub later, as of today, I'm somewhat back on schedule.

An hour ago, when I made coffee, we were out of milk, so I slung on my brown leather jacket, pulled on my knitted watch-cap, and tramped downstairs for a trip to the all-night bodega up on the northwest corner of 83rd Street.

Broad Amsterdam Avenue is almost trafficless at that hour. A mist hung before the streetlights converging down the Avenue, just dim enough to make me think — for a moment — that my glasses were dirty. Twenty years ago, when I was in Istanbul, the entire Old City (Kabatas, the European shore) had a kind of oily smell to it, as though some industrial pipeline had broken open a block or two away: walking over the Golden Horn and up from Galata Bridge along the leaf-clotted streets by Topkapi Palace I remember being surprised that the smell didn't dissipate at all: It was the first time I'd smelled that particular odor in a city. Months later, I remember smelling it again down by the Thames when I was staying near Putney Bridge in London, with Norman, that strange friend of John Witten-Doris's. The next time I smelled it wasn't till five or so years later, one night when I was walking on the levee in New Orleans with Joe Manfredini, back when I was teaching a Clarion workshop at Tulane.

From time to time I've smelled it since, now in Seattle, now in New York. But as I came down my stoop this morning, in the streetlight-shot mist, on my way to the bodega, I realized there'd been a hint of it ever since I'd woken up, and that here, crossing the misty Avenue, the odor, full out and slightly fetid, had permeated the entire neighborhood.

It was the first time I'd smelled it around here, so far (a third of a mile?) from a river (the Hudson, three long blocks, followed by Riverside Park, to the west). I passed maybe three people in the street.

The proprietor of the all-night bodega is a very nice man, but unbelievably *messy*. As of this morning, he seems to be a week or so into growing an unbelievably messy beard. And recently he's hired a new helper — large, Hispanic, and with glasses fixed to his head by a black elastic band that creases his rather abundant hair in the back: He is, if possible, even messier than his boss.

Ah, well.

Many thanks for your rich letter of November 16. Thanks also for the print-out on Ms. Jakobson. This really must be the modern world they all talk about, when I can go to a party in New York, then get the dope on my hostess from a computer in Pennsylvania!

A couple of weeks ago, I looked through the various copies of my letters I still retain to see what, if any, description I might have given of my very first meeting with Eco — our lunch, with the other panelists, back at the Modern Language Association gathering. Seems I covered it in a single sentence in a letter of 1/7/82:

"Did the MLA panel on Eco (see enclosed remarks)." — the enclosed remarks being a copy of "A Road for the (American) Reader."

Not much.

As I recall, *Il Nome della rosa* had just appeared, perhaps months before, in Italy, but, of course, had not yet been translated — though I believe it had already won a prestigious Italian literary prize. The people I knew who had read it — U——, and a young woman named K——, a student of Eco's in Bologna and, back then, a sometimes girlfriend of Marc's — tended to speak rather slightingly of it, as a piece of academic folderol. K——, as I recall, simply didn't like it, outright. And her description of it, one evening when she and U—— were here for dinner, didn't make it sound very promising.

The notion that it would become an international *cause d'estime* and the best-selling serious novel of the year in America, occasioning articles in *People* and with a million dollar paperback resale, was just not part of anyone's predictions back then.

Before our MLA panel, lunch, where I met Eco, was pleasant, if harried — as MLA shindigs tend to be. The lobby restaurant of the Hilton (or the Americana?) is separated from the lobby proper only by a set of steps and a bank of flowers — a design that presupposes neither lobby nor restaurant will ever be more than three-quarters full. All its pretensions to relaxation and informality break down, however, when the lobby is packed with several hundred English instructors and/or professors who don't quite know where they're supposed to be, and every seat in the restaurant is taken, with, at any moment, about 150 people who want to, and find they can't, pass from one to the other:

Which is what you have almost non-stop for three or four days at an MLA Convention.

Somehow our party got a seat, however. And we all shook each other's hands and made agreeable noises over the roar around us and between our rather rushed club sandwiches: I remember feeling some vague uneasiness because I wasn't sure if we were each paying for our own, or if Teresa, as the moderator and organizer of the panel, were treating us all. Several times Eco leaned toward one or another of us to hear what this or that one was saying. Several times he made expansive statements that were no doubt quite funny but which, because of his accent and the general hubbub, were impossible to catch. Finally Teresa did take the check, over various not terribly extreme protests, and we threaded our way through the crowd, went upstairs on a packed elevator, and (after the men made a stop off in the john) into some sprawling hotel ballroom where the panel — "Semiotics in Italy: A Conversation with Umberto Eco" — was to take place before the several hundreds who were already assembled.

As we were going down the aisle to the dais, off in the throng Leslie (in a bright red shirt) and Sally Fiedler grinned at me; I nodded back. And I believe the Hassans were sitting somewhere in the first five or six rows.

After Teresa introduced us to the audience, Eco gave an intelligent talk on the medieval image of the labyrinth vs. the classical image of the labyrinth.

As the first of the panelist/respondents, I presented "A Road for The (American) Reader."

The young woman on the panel, Mary Russo, did a rather amusing semiotic reading of an American advertisement for an Olivetti "Praxis" typewriter.

And finally Michael Silverman did a kind of survey (?) of where semiotics seemed to be going.

In the discussion period at the end of the panel, Eco took a polite exception to my characterizing *A Theory of Semiotics* as "humane positivism." He didn't feel it represented any sort of positivism at all. But after it was all over, and we were leaving the stage, Michael Silverman said to me, *sotto voce*, "He may not *like* the idea that his work is really another positivist system, but that's *precisely* what it is. And I think you were very generous to call it 'humane.'"

I believe after the briefest of good-byes I came directly home, stripped off my tie, got out of my suit, and put on some comfortable jeans.

But there you have pretty much all that remains in my memory, three years later, from that afternoon. But now you have at least a somewhat textured account of what is, after all, our three (and only three) meetings—Eco's and mine.

Sometime in the next month or two, I *must* put together my essay on *"Lector in Fabula"* for *Substance*. As it is, between a couple of 1982 notebooks, about half of it is already written. But not, of course, the difficult half.

While I was looking through my letters to see what I might have written you at the time, what struck me more than anything is the size the letter pile has grown to. And the pile for 1984 seems to be as thick as all the others (at least that I have copies of) put together!

The pile starts with a letter to you (January 9th, 1980), skips over to one to Joanna (May 9th, 1981), and thickens up, as it were, to about an inch that covers 1982. Then there are, by measurement, near six solid inches covering '83 and '84!

Shades of the three volumes of John Addington Symonds's epistles, sitting these four or five years on my upper bookshelf corner.

Like you, I also make notes from time to time on things I want to write you about. Sometimes they achieve full epistlehood. But, as frequently, they end up simply as some incomprehensible list of jottings in my journal that, a week or a month later I look over, trying to remember what in the world it was that I might have wanted to tell you about.

Indeed, turning to the most recent batch of notes, I find I have written:

"Delivering *Stars/Sand* to Eco's mailbox at Philosophy Hall, Columbia," "the Maison Française" "The Poetics of Gender": Scholes, "Le Guin and Derrida"; "Jane Gallop."

Well, that's still decipherable:

Before it turned cool, and while I was still heady with sinusitis, perhaps two weeks after the party at Ms. Jakobson's, one day when I realized I didn't feel like doing anything else and had not enough energy to get to work, I took a copy of *Stars/Sand*, signed it to Eco, put it in an envelope, and went outside (to discover it was much too warm for my winter down-filled anorak) and took the M-104 up to Columbia.

Eco had said he was in the French department. I figured he must have a mailbox somewhere on campus, and I would simply find it and leave the book off there for him.

I turned onto the campus beside the Journalism building at 116th Street, Ferris Booth Hall, with no idea where the French department was. Hurrying students everywhere—and the buildings and lawn were all just a little more grungy (you saw the view at the beginning of *Ghostbusters*) than you'd expect of an Ivy League campus; but that's New York.

I asked a couple of students at random if they knew where the French department was, and one very helpful black kid directed me to the Maison Française, which is an old house standing just to the east of the Seth Lowe Library—the one with the big green/black alma mater crouching on the steps before it.

Here and there on various plaques about were taped or stapled printed signs for the symposium going on that weekend: *The Poetics of Gender*.

Among the names of the participants I recognized were Jane (*The Daughter's Seduction, Intersections*) Gallop; and Robert Scholes was presenting a paper called

"LeGuin and Derrida;" I actually felt a tiny thrill of jealousy: "Why," I wondered, "isn't that paper about Derrida and me?" I walked on, consoling myself: "Well, I'm probably mentioned in it somewhere."

In the Maison, one of the sessions was going on, and, in a dark hall crowded with young women mostly (several in wheelchairs by the door), a slide presentation was in progress, and I caught the woman lecturer saying, ". . . on the *second* page of the *Vita Nuova* . . ." which was apparently the punch-line to a joke, because everyone laughed.

I slipped out again and went across the lobby to the glass reception window behind which a young woman sat reading a book, and asked in tones dulcet as all hell: "Excuse me. Could you tell me where I can find the offices of the French department?"

Nobody must have spoken to her in 20 minutes: She jumped nearly two inches, then looked embarrassed. "Over in Philosophy Hall," she said. "Turn to the right, just as you go out the door."

There are, today, several ramps around Philosophy Hall, so that finding its working front entrance was a bit difficult; but, after going in the wrong way twice, I did.

By the right-hand wall of the vestibule were a whole rank of wooden mailboxes, each with a slit just large enough for my book (in its envelope) to slide through. They bore various names, and one, indeed, said "Eco." I actually started to slip the book through; then I thought: These are probably for student papers and, unless he's assigned one recently, he might very well not look in here. And the box was set up so that once a book went in, you really couldn't tell that anything was in there unless you opened the key-locked wooden door.

So I slid it back out and decided: Let me find the French department proper, and see if there isn't a way of getting it to him there that's a little less risky.

Wandering into the Language Lab on my right, I was told the French department was on the sixth floor. I took a drab little self-service elevator up. When I stepped out, the dull hallways, the big windows with their tan shades, and the wide wooden doorjambs made it all feel like an institution from 25 or 30 years ago. Through broad double doors, I walked into the French department office and asked a young woman with very short hair, sitting at an immense old-fashioned desk, where the mailboxes were. She pointed to the wall, where a rank of green metal pigeon holes stood to the back of a worn, wooden table.

I found "Eco," but there already *was* a book there, in a brown book mailer: and there wasn't room for another.

"Just leave a note in the box, then put your package on top. He'll get it," she said. "Don't worry."

So that's what I did.

Then I rode down in the elevator, and walked out on the balmy campus—and a day or two later, the weather dropped to where it actually would be cold enough for the coat I'd had on.

Let's see. Other things I have down on my list? "D&D, with Julie, Carla, John, and Roddy (the D-Master), at Barbara's."

That's just a reference to my first official, real, and actual game of Dungeons &

Dragons, a couple of Wednesday nights back: Barbara Wise's 20-year-old daughter, Juliet, has been holding a regular weekly game down at their house on West 13th Street. The Dungeon Master is a 21-year-old dancer, who studies at the Joffrey, named Roddy. Probably because I was there, Barbara joined the game too. Frank was quite poo-pooing about the whole thing. ("You're really going to go down there and play some game all evening long with a bunch of children?") But I'd decided that, since Iva was growing out of our own private version (and has played the real game a couple of times now and enjoyed it), I might as well learn something about the real thing. And I rather enjoyed it, too.

"Interesting how a second language turns a subtle writer and sophisticated thinker into a charming primitive."

That's just a last thought on Eco, conjoined with the memory of some of the interviews I gave in French last year when I was at the Metz Festival. Really do wish they'd sent me the promised cassettes of the radio program I did in French. I think I was pretty intelligent in that agrammatical and creative way one can occasionally hit when one is foundering in a language one can't really speak. But it would be nice to have the evidence.

"Marc's office at NYU."

Well, let's see: Just recently Henry Morrison, my agent, moved his whole offices and operation out of New York City up into Westchester. This means that my major check-cashing channel had to be suddenly switched. But fortunately, Marc Gawron, a few weeks before, moved back to the city. He's working for a year on the research staff in the Computer Science department at NYU, just below Washington Square in the Village, and he has very kindly consented to act as my check casher for as long as I need him.

Marc is tall, swarthy, and almost scrawny, with a mop of bronzish hair. He's quite brilliant, and also has one of the sweetest personalities of anyone I've ever met. He lived here in the apartment with me for about eighteen months, during which I basically gave him spending money and in general supported him. (No, we were *not* lovers. He's straight. Though, some years earlier, when he was about eighteen, I went through a couple of weeks where I was rather infatuated with him — but, after a bit of experimenting on his part, I returned to sanity. *Moth* is the detritus of that period.) He published his first novel when he was nineteen (*An Apology for Rain,* by Jean Mark Gawron [New York: Doubleday, 1974]) and his second when he was 24 (*Algorithm,* [New York: Berkley, 1978]), then went off and got a Ph.D. in linguistics, and worked for a while at Hewlett Packard out in Silicon Valley. (He's now 30.) Most of last year he had a fellowship at a university in Edinburgh; and, at one point, he was a guest at the University of Bologna; he gave a presentation on Artificial Intelligence to Eco's class — indeed, he has his own store of humorous Eco anecdotes: My favorite involves the paperback cover for *The Name of the Rose.* Eco had just been sent a color proof when Marc went to lecture at his class. The original cover showed pretty much the same monk who is there now, under all the gold, holding a rose. Only before it was a rose, it was a sword, and he was standing above the prone body of a naked woman stretched out on a primitive stone altar with the flames of hell in the background. Eco took

Marc to lunch, where he showed him the original proof, and a copy of a letter he had sent the publisher to the effect that, while he thought the painting would make a good wall mural for the vestibule of a brothel, he did not think it was in the least appropriate for his book. Apparently his publishers concurred. The sword was repainted as a rose. The monk was enlarged and moved up closer so that the naked woman (literally) dropped out of the bottom of the picture. And gold foil was slathered over the upper part of the flames and a reproduction of the medieval scene that had graced the cover of the hardcover was put over the lower half.

Interestingly, if you look inside the current paperback bestseller on what might be called, for want of a term, the "frontispiece," you get a shadowy notion of the "original," wholly tasteless and unrevised cover.

Another of Marc's stories (not concerning Eco) has become something of a modern touchstone for me. When Marc was in the graduate linguistics department at Berkeley, he did some work with an obscure branch of language/mathematics study called "Montague Grammar." Montague Grammar is a mathematical approach to language which grows out of the work of a young linguist/mathematician named Richard Montague. His papers on the subject (I have read them, and they are daunting!) were collected (posthumously) in a volume from Yale University Press called *Formal Philosophy*. Montague, besides being brilliant, happened to be gay, something of an alcoholic, and was murdered in a knife fight in a Tenderloin gay bar in San Francisco at a ripe old 28.[1]

For a while, shortly after his death, people really thought Montague Grammar was going to lead to something revolutionary in linguistics. But after about three years, interest in the dense and occasionally rather sophomoric collection of papers fizzled.

At any rate, we now switch to Marc, working away diligently on a vocal computer for Hewlett Packard, several years later. The particular part of the particular program he and a number of other bright young computer scientists were working on in order to get the machine to speak required two memory bins that had to be kept separate, in which (in Marc's words) the information that went into them had to be played around with rather violently. "And from time to time," he went on, "all the information in one or the other would have to be killed—wiped out, that is — and in rather dubious circumstances." The two bins needed to be referred to in the program a lot, and it fell to Marc to name them; so in a whimsical moment, he named one of the bins *Montague* and the other *Pasolini*. "To give you some idea of the kind of people I was working with out there," Marc told me, "though most of them realized it was supposed to be kind of a joke, for the next three weeks, one after the other of them would come up to me and ask, on the QT, 'Hey, by the way; I know who Montague is. But who's this Pasolini . . .?'"

"Barbara: lunch at Harvey's Olde Chelsea."

On and off for some years now, Barbara Wise and I have been going out to lunch together — perhaps once a month to once every six weeks — and we rather enjoy our little gossip sessions. When I was much younger and poorer, Barbara was very

---

[1] This is incorrect. Montague was 42 and the bar was in Los Angeles. In 1994 the story would, however, become one of the sources of SRD's novel, *The Mad Man* (New York: Rhinoceros, 1995).

generous in always taking the bill. But about five years ago, when I was doing very well, we began to switch off: I would pay one time, she would pay the next.

Once she understood my recent monetary catastrophe, however, she very easily and generously slipped back to our old pattern. But I still felt I ought to do something: So I have recently been suggesting that she come by the house for lunch, where I fix something here—which is both more affordable for me (especially as she is a vegetarian) and fun (since I enjoy cooking, and find anyone's special diet something of a challenge).

She has been over here twice for lunch now.

But somehow the new arrangement has freed Barbara to be much more adventurous in her choice of restaurant on the alternate months when we go out. I suspect that, *knowing* she's going to be paying the bill, she doesn't feel obliged to choose some place inexpensive on the possibility that I *might* be able to offer something toward the tab. At any rate, about three weeks ago, we tried a brand new place (for me) called Harvey's Olde Chelsea Restaurant at about 20th Street, just west of Sixth Avenue.

Someone had taken her there the previous week. And she wanted to show it off to me.

It's a restaurant that really has been there for almost 50 years in one guise or another—it's the sort of thing that can only happen in a huge city such as New York, where even the natives can take years to discover the existence of local treasures.

You enter a set of wooden doors inset with glass, to find yourself before a bar with the darkest of dark wood paneling. (Around on Columbus Avenue, numerous places have tried to achieve this look with pine, stains, and varnishes. But the polishing here is all clearly by hand and/or time.) Behind a half-wall, topped with a brass rail that looks to be of the same ilk as that on the top of the marble balustrades in Grand Central Station (only kept in much better repair), there are various small tables.

The place is full of efficient middle-aged waiters and caters to the businessmen who work on lower Fifth Avenue.

The food is insistently American.

I had a truly superb chicken pot-pie, where all the vegetables, not to mention the chicken and the crust, were as fresh as it's possible for food to be.

And Barbara had a steamed vegetable plate, for which ditto.

"Bill's window full of *Stars/Sand* at Shakespeare & Co."

On the corner of 81st and Broadway there is a large bookstore, Shakespeare & Co. It appeared in several of my letters in the '70s under the name Bloomsday, when it was rather oddly run by a man named Enrico, who tried out an endless string of grandiose ideas there, some of which, such as holding annual 24-hour readings of *Ulysses* on June 16th, in which I took part for three (?) years, came to pass; but many of which did not. He managed to hold various autographing parties for various writers, including Isaac Bashevis Singer (our neighborhood Nobel laureate) and Alberto Moravia. But he was simply incapable of focusing on the day-to-day work needed to manage a successful bookstore.

And so, finally, he lost it.

The location was an ideal bookstore space, roomy, with an upper floor for storage (one of Enrico's more quixotic projects had been to turn that into a café, where you could take your newly purchased book and sit and read over ice-cream or espresso—it lasted about three months), beautifully placed on a busy Broadway corner, in the midst of a very heavy book-reading neighborhood; people used to wonder how anyone could fail to make a success of it. Yet Enrico managed to go out of business, and quite spectacularly so, about four years back, whereupon the store was taken over by a young man in his mid-30s, named Bill, who remodeled it from top to bottom and has turned it into the solid, well-run and successful bookstore it should have been.

With his good-looking face, just a bit pixyish, and a bush of well-salted black hair, Bill is friendly, relaxed, and indefatigable. He's also a science fiction reader, who's always enjoyed my books; and we often talk about this, that, or the other novel. (Like everyone else, he was terribly impressed by the Gene Wolf tetralogy, *The Book of the New Sun*.) But about two weeks ago, as I was walking down Broadway toward the IRT subway at 79th Street, I passed Shakespeare & Co.— only to see, to my surprise, that Bill had filled one whole window with copies of *Stars in My Pocket like Grains of Sand*.

He'd gotten a big blow-up of the front cover, which was the center of the display, and, on pedestals all around it, under three, large, white globes, he'd arranged a dozen other copies, with a copy of *Starboard Wine* flanking the sign at each side. Down along the front were a row of my Bantam paperbacks.

I was really quite surprised—and moved.

As soon as I saw it, I called Frank from the pay phone in front of the store to tell him that I finally had my first bookstore window full of books, just like a real writer. I was on my way downtown somewhere—probably to meet Marc and get a check cashed—and I asked Frank if he'd take Iva's camera, in which there was still some film, and take a picture of the window.

He got a couple of snapshots.

But we still haven't gotten them developed.

The window was up for a solid week, if not eight days. Usually, of course, and for the last 25 years of my life, the physical appearance of a new book has meant an "on publication" payment so that the actual showing up of copies in bookstores has heralded, by a week or six, the arrival of new money. But thanks to Uncle Sam [and, yes, my own earlier borrowings against future Bantam payments to partially pay him off, two or three years ago], there's no publication payment at all on this book. And, on the second or third time I passed the window and realized it was all glory, but no money, for a moment it gave a funny cast to the whole business. But that only now and again added an odd cadence to what was still basically harmonious and pleasing.

But here we come to the second installment of the story.

Marc's girlfriend, Jenny (I think I told you), turns out to be the niece of a girl I was friendly with—indeed, whom I thought I was passionately in love with—when I was in elementary school:

Wendy Osserman.

Wendy as a child was very interested in dance. Her older sister, Carol (today Jenny's mother), was a professional dancer, who knew personally people like

Bambi Lynn and Rod Alexander, the regular dancers on Channel Two's weekly *Show of Shows.* I remember going to the Osserman's Park Avenue apartment and coming in on Carol and two young men rehearsing in the living room, while, in my scarf and snowsuit, I stood beside the glass-paneled doors, watching, fascinated. During the second and third grades, Wendy would teach me what she was learning in her ballet class, and I picked up a good many ballet terms and movements—the terms well, the movements badly. We practiced back-bends and splits together. Finally I got to where I could do the latter, without ever quite mastering the former. I became concerned with my "turn out," and learned that my odd, bobbing walk, about which I was often teased by my classmates and still have today, was called "dancers' bounce." I heard from Wendy about great dancers, Fontayne and Tallchief and Martha Graham; sometime amidst it all, my parents went to see what was then still called the Sadler Wells Ballet, come from England to perform at the old Metropolitan Opera House; for weeks afterwards I listened to my father rave about Michael Soames's performance of the "Bluebird Variations," while I pored over the program book they had brought home and its full-page black and white photographs of the solo dancers. Wendy made me go see the film *The Red Shoes,* with Moira Shirer; and only months later, Robert Helpman brought his Old Vic production of *A Midsummer Night's Dream* to the Met with himself as Oberon, Moira Shirer as Titania, and Stanley Holloway as Bottom. In my suit and tie, I was taken by my parents one Friday or Saturday evening, and we sat just before the thick, carved and gold-leafed rail of one of the narrow, ornate balconies: In that performance Puck was a near-naked young actor in a leafy, cut-away g-string, and his relation with Oberon was presented as about as openly homoerotic as it was then legal to put on a European or American stage; and all of it was shot through with stretches of Mr. Helpman's rather chintzy, formally balletic choreography — a sop to the culture vultures, but which I thought was the pinnacle of all elegance. I went home and spent hours with glue and glitter and wire, trying to make a pair of wings and antennae such as Helpman had worn, slinking about in his black, glitter-dashed tights, over the broad but shallow stage of the old Metropolitan, crowded with its lavish and gaudy scenery. Channel Five, at some point in all this, ran the opera film of *The Tales of Hoffman,* which I watched, stretched out on our living room rug, on our ancient Zenith console black and white TV, again with Helpman's choreography; and in my own mind, at least for a while, my destiny was fixed: I *must* become a dancer when I grew up!

Today, Wendy is the director and choreographer of the Osserman Dance Company, which has had an on-again/off-again existence for more than ten years now.

My own further dance experience was limited to a month of East Indian dancing lessons, which, for some reason, my mother decided I should take when I was nine, some modern dance classes at Camp Woodland (where I heard about more dancers, José Lamon and Daniel Negrin, whose company, when I was eighteen, I had the gall to audition for! No, I didn't make it), a summer at the American Ballet Theater School when I was seventeen (in calm but vigorous defiance of my father), and my participation in a half-dozen dance concerts of the late Charles Stanley's dance company, back in '71/'72, where — basically — I was one of two on-stage stage hands, who, through the course of the performances, would lift, carry, and place both abstract bits of scenery and, now and again, a dancer: in the Stanley concerts I wore black tights, gratifyingly like Mr. Helpman's, though without antennae, wings, or glitter. But the rest of that childhood fascination has all been sublimated into a love for the art in any form, from the Grand Union Construction Company and Twyla Tharp to the kids around the city, moon-walking and shoulder-spinning and breakin' on cardboard sheets or linoleum swatches before their portable "ghetto blasters," and even *Dance Fever*, which I still watch weekly with Iva. And sometimes I think: Now, if I could only get her to watch "Great Performances in Dance" on PBS with *me* . . . but that hasn't come yet.

But back in the seventh and eighth grades, my passion for Wendy eventually shifted to a small, ebullient girl named Priscilla Meyer, who happened to be Wendy's best friend. Nightly we would call each other and ask, "What's the price of eggs in Afghanistan?" — our ritual preface to a half hour's to an hour-and-a-half's conversation and gossip and/or the exchange of the day's math problems, because one of us, usually me, had forgotten the math textbook *(Working With Numbers)* back at school. (In the sixth grade, with great excitement, Priscilla had loaned me my first *Mad* comic book, for which, as I read over Harvey Kurtzman's lampoon of "The Raven," behind the black door and between the marble sides above the cool tiles floor of a john stall in the sixth-floor boys' bathroom, with my jeans around my calves, I developed an abiding enthusiasm that would continue for a decade.) ". . . the price of eggs in Afghanistan?" The phrase was fallout from our math teacher, H. M. Newby (who occasionally joked that H. M. stood for "Hepzibah Mehitabel" — or, sometimes, "Her Majesty." Actually it was Hannah Maud), a small, thick-set woman with white hair tightly pinned to her head and silver-rimmed round spectacles, who wore black dresses with white lace collars and who, when she would grow frustrated with one of the slower students' confused attempts to explain some point back to her, would exclaim: "Now what does *that* have to do with the price of eggs in Afghanistan?"

Priscilla had the first "compatible" color television set I ever saw in someone's house—a great dark console whose shelves and speakers took up half of one wall of her family's extensive living room. Even my best male friend, Geoff Cowan, whose father, Lewis G., produced most of the color television shows at CBS, didn't actually *own* one back then.

Like Wendy (like Geoff), Priscilla vanished from my life on my eighth grade graduation. I didn't see her again till I trained across country from San Francisco one November (1970?), to be a guest for two weeks at Wesleyan University's Center for the Humanities, where she turned up, looking as if she had not aged a whit since '56, the chairman of Wesleyan's Russian Department. There she introduced me to Michael Holquist, then teaching a course at Yale called "Literature X," i.e., contemporary pornography. Mike had delivered a very sensible paper on American SF at the seminar the Center was sponsoring (no, he's no relation to Charles Hoequist, Jr., also late of Yale), and he spent an afternoon translating Stanislaw Lem on Samuel R. Delany from the Polish for me. While I was at Wesleyan, the three of us went together to hear Roman Jakobson lecture on linguistics at Yale (where I sat in on a Contemporary Russian Literature class Priscilla was also teaching there) and we had a couple of pleasant evenings with one another, talking and drinking wine at Priscilla's comfortably informal house in Middletown. (Mike has since ridden on to academic prominence for his work as translator of, and—just a month or so ago—biographer to, M. M. Bakhtin.) Though, from time to time over the previous ten years, I'd seen posters for the Osserman company stuck up with masking tape on various lamp-posts around the Village, I hadn't seen Wendy herself (as I said) since we'd parted at my eighth grade graduation. But I also learned that November that Priscilla had kept up her friendship with Wendy—they still saw each other four or five times a year, she told me. Also I learned that Wendy had kept up her interest in dance; that she was, as I'd suspected but had not known for sure, the Osserman of the Osserman Dancers.

The same day I saw the window full of *Stars/Sand* at Shakespeare & Co., I learned later that afternoon from Marc, down at NYU, that the Osserman Company would be performing in a couple of weeks at St. Mark's Church in the Bowery; Wendy, Mark told me, remembered me and would be very happy if I could come. Mark also told me that Priscilla would be in town that day and would be there—though he was not exactly sure which of the three performances she would be at. Perhaps we could all get together, nevertheless. It sounded quite pleasant. And a day or two later, I received a flyer in the mail for the performance, with a note from Wendy scrawled engagingly across it (first I'd heard from her in 30 years!) that she'd love to see me and that, indeed, Priscilla would too.

A day after that, Frank phoned me to say that Bill's was not the only bookstore in the city with a window display of *Stars/Sand*. He'd just walked past the Classic Bookstore, down on 48th and 6th Avenue, and had seen a baker's dozen copies set up along the window. And so I decided, as I occasionally do, to spend an afternoon checking out the various bookstores in the city, to see how my book was doing—and, indeed, to look at my displays.

It was a bit before our current cold snap, but it was still winter-coat weather; and the day was on the gray side. I thought I'd start just by taking one more gander at Bill's window (I figured they'd be pulling it down soon). I strolled down Amsterdam and turned along 81st, to approach it from across Broadway.

As I was coming from the island in the middle of the avenue, toward the striped awning above the outdoor stands of books before the large corner display windows, I saw a tall woman with short dark hair and a brown jacket, striding across 81st Street. My immediate thought was that I knew her. Was it Judy Sherwin (you'll remember, another Daltonite she, though some years ahead of me)? No, but the association was definitely Dalton—probably she only reminded me of someone I knew then, come to ghost the back of my mind because of the coming reunion with Wendy and Priscilla. But the woman was out of my line of sight, now, as I walked up to the window and tried to look at it without appearing *too* much like a writer gazing in tickled awe at the multiplied objects of his own production: the black and silver cover, the orange letters . . .

Suddenly, the same women I'd seen moments back stepped practically in front of me and asked, "Excuse me? Are you Sam Delany?" in a strangely familiar voice.

"Yes." I smiled. "That's right."

"I'm sure you don't remember me," she said with slightly breathless excitement. "But I'm Hyla Newman—well, now I'm Hyla Feil. But I was in your class at Dalton . . ." and I was struck by the memory of a tall, gawky girl with the identical voice, while the girlish face in my mind, with one blink and another, adjusted into that of the woman before me.

"Hyla!" I declared. "Of course I remember you!"

We grasped each other's shoulders and exchanged kisses on the cheek.

"It's so funny," she said. "I didn't think I would have recognized you, because a few days ago I was in the store, here, and I looked at your picture on the fly-leaf of your book. I'd heard you lived around here — I'm on 80th, myself. But then, just now, I looked at you . . . and I recognized your walk! This seems to be my week for Dalton run-ins," she went on. "On Saturday, I'm going to be seeing Priscilla Meyer."

"So am I!" I declared. "You must be going to Wendy's dance concert."

"That's right!" She seemed quite surprised. "There's a party of us, me, Priscilla, and Lynn Salinger . . ." whom I had not thought of either in 30 years, but who was a tiny, shy girl with dark hair, who was part of the Gimbels family (the people whom R. H. Macy does not tell . . .). "You're going too?" she exclaimed. "How wonderful! We were all going to go out somewhere for dinner before the concert. Perhaps you could join us. Really," she laughed again, "we should have *one* male to dilute all those Dalton ladies."

"I'd love to come," I told her (noticing at that point that she had a small tattoo on the fork of her right hand between thumb and forefinger—an "M" or an "I W" —not what one expects of most Dalton ladies; but definitely intriguing). "But actually I'm going with some other people—Marc Gawron and Jenny Walker . . . that's Wendy's niece. We'd probably just be too many people."

"Oh, I see. Well, still, it's wonderful to see you again. And we'll see each other at the concert, of course. I've got to run and meet my husband—" and she nodded across Broadway. "Oh, by the way. You have a very enthusiastic fan. Tom Pynchon is great admirer of your work. Really, every other time I see him, your name comes up, and he asks me: 'You mean, you *really* know Chip Delany?' That's your nickname now, isn't it?"

"Yes, it is." I laughed. "How nice of you to tell me. You know, about a dozen years ago, he wrote a letter to a mutual acquaintance, J. Kirk Sale, in which he got very enthusiastic about one of my books; and eventually it got back to me. But it's kind of good to know he still enjoys them. And this is my first confirmation of it in over ten years!"

"Well, we'll see each other on Saturday," she said, glancing across the street again.

"Yes," I said. "Now you've got to run, and I have to get downtown. It was so good to run into you again. And it's nice to know you're in the neighborhood!"

And, with another exchange of kisses, we were off in our various directions; and down on 48th Street, around the corner from 6th Avenue, I found the Classic Bookshop window, with its row of black and silver copies, while dark-hatted Hasidim from Diamond Row (47th St.) hurried by, and the young Hispanic men who form the area's cheap labor hustled onto the Avenue of the Americas to join the secretaries and junior executives of midtown, making their way to bus stops and subways.

The actual concert, two Saturdays hence (my first time actually inside St. Mark's Church proper since its reconstruction after the terrible fire of some years back), the reunion with Priscilla and Hyla and Lynn and Wendy herself (someone has characterized her as the "Carol Burnette of Modern Dance," and it's not a bad description of her solo work) and the party afterwards at Wendy's and Ken's loft on 27th Street was quite as richly pleasant as all this prologue might lead you to believe—if not, indeed, more so. And since I saw her at Wesleyan a dozen years ago, Priscilla has developed her own nine-year-old daughter, Rachel, who came to the concert that night.

But I suppose I want to get on with my list.

"Saturday at the Variety" is what it says next.

I think I mentioned in a former letter that the most dramatic occurrences in my life are those which present the greatest difficulty in writing. And I tend to stay away from them in letters, if only because the epistle is a relaxed and easy form — something that flows out, that, indeed, with the help of a word-processor, might sustain some revisions now and then. But not something one ponders and works on and over in great internal turmoil.

Well, what happened to me on the second or third Saturday in November I'd class as one of the most important things in my life: It rates with that incident I told you about that occurred when I was sixteen or seventeen, that morning in Central Park, when, sitting on the bench in that somewhat overcast dawn, I had that revelation of my multiply marginal/ambiguous status as to race, sex, and social position: a black man, a gay man, a writer . . .

During the time you guys were writing the biblio "Introduction," Pep, I recall, wrote back rather fliply (and accurately): "That one's really too good to be true, Chip," and henceforth dropped it from the account. But that drama, too, like the one on a November Saturday, was largely internal.

And the failure was mine then (as it might well be here) to recount it with the accuracy which would recreate its import.

I'm not, as you know, a very "mystical" person. Yet the density and feel of it all (in both cases) was as close as I, personally, will probably get to a mystical experience — which is to say, the feelings, the conclusions, the grounding and process of it all were immensely and solidly *real.* And the difficulty of writing that solid reality has, more than anything, else, kept this letter so long from the mail-box, so long in my word-processor.

How do I write about this . . . ?

What "happened" was simple:

On Saturday at about noon, in my grungy beige winter coat and my tan watch-cap, I took the subway down to 14th Street and Union Square, came up the steps to walk past the large hole in the ground that was once Klein's-on-the-Square Department Store, walked by the dark green shell of the old Luchow's Restaurant, passed the boarded-up Palladium (once the New York Academy of Music) and Julius's Billiard (a still-thriving, upstairs pool hall, which has been there for 50 years or more), and over to Third Avenue and turned down to go to Variety Photoplays. I brought my $2.25 ticket from the elderly suited-and-tied Puerto Rican cashier, who has been mumbling and arguing in that glass booth of his for going on 20 years now. (Six months ago the price went up from $2.00, and for a week there was an apologetic sign taped to the glass: "We're sorry about raising our price. But at $2.25 we're still a bargain," which, of course, was true. Three years before they'd upped the price from $1.50.) The usual clutch of four or five young Puerto Ricans (between 25 and 40) who have managed the theater for at least ten years now were talking as usual just behind the door. I gave my yellow ticket to the one in the black shirt on the stool, who tore it and handed me back the stub, and wandered across the worn maroon floor of the small lobby, and into the vestibule of the theater proper (a water fountain, a soda machine, a door at each side) and strolled into the darkness down the right-hand aisle.

From the back, I recognized one of my regulars of the last eight months or so. He's a physically immense man. He's Puerto Rican, with a white speckled beard, and wears glasses—from his huge and rough hands (a nail-biter, yes), I know he does some kind of physical labor. He arrives at the Variety at 11:30, practically by the clock, every Saturday morning. From time to time we've talked some, and I know he's married, though he has no kids. He lives somewhere in the Bronx. But I still don't know even his first name—nor he mine. He's terribly good-natured and not particularly bright—indeed, I suspect any group of normal men would find him notably slow. His particular thing is to spend ten minutes or so "talkin' dirty" about the porn movie in progress in front of us, which apparently turns him on as much, or more, than the movie itself. This gives way to a blow job. I really enjoy him a lot. He's both enthusiastic and affectionate.

He always sits one in from the aisle in about the same seat, each week. And he was in his usual position.

I sat down beside him. He glanced at me, recognized me, put his arm around my shoulder, and said: "How you doin'?" and went on to make some comment about what one of the actresses on the screen *really* needed.

When we finished, I noticed that sitting in the row just behind us well forward in his seat was a slight, effeminate Hispanic in a beret and glasses, the collar of his pea-jacket turned up around his neck and some kind of tote-bag slung over his shoulder. He'd been very intently watching us. I don't mind this kind of thing; if you really don't like to be watched, you don't come to such a place. Indeed, if you want to sit a seat away and masturbate, it's fine by me and can even lend something to the atmosphere of the whole encounter. But just to sit, lean over, and *stare* throughout a whole encounter has always struck me as bad form. It often bespeaks someone who really is looking for an opening to move in and take over — which is a no-no. And sometimes it tends to add the dampening of the deprived and the despairing to it all.

Indeed, when, a few minutes later, I got up, this guy immediately scooted forward into the seat I'd vacated; and I heard my big Spanish friend say, rather gruffly: "Hey, no! I don't want no more. Didn't you see? I just done it already!" and a moment later, the thin little guy, looking about through his glasses and nursing his bag below his forearm, got up and hurried down the aisle toward the men's room, which, illegally, still has a dime pay-box on the door, under a yellow light, in its recessed alcove to the left of the screen.

As I walked down the aisle, toward the front of the center section I recognized a young guy in his mid-20s towards whom I always have felt rather friendly. He's thin, Irish (I can bet you that if I found out his name, it would be either Billy, Joe, or Mike), almost scrawny, with many attributes of a junky—save that he dresses a little too well: He usually wears some kind of sweater over a white dress shirt and black slacks or jeans, with only his incredibly worn basketball sneakers and his always grubby hands and dirty fingernails (not a nail-biter at all, this one) setting him apart from the somewhat preppy look he aspires too. My initial journal note on him says "a lost-wax face," which refers to the casting method for metal sculpture. But there's a quality to his features as if all of them had once been molded sharply from some white wax that had eventually been drained and blunted by an inner heat, then had set that way from an internal chill that has, more recently, seized his body. He's almost as much of a Saturday morning regular as my big Puerto Rican friend. He always brings in one or two quart bottles of Bud in a paper bag, and sometimes a knapsack. He sits in the first six rows of the orchestra, opens his pants — fly, belt, and upper button all — tucks his shirt and sweater halfway up his pallid belly, slouches down with his knees wide against the back of the theater seat before him, and masturbates furiously, usually two or three times over a three- or four-hour visit, drinking his beer between bouts. He starts off very shy of other people, pulling his pants closed quickly if anyone comes near him or looks. But once he gets into his thing (and halfway through his beer?), he becomes both friendly and uninhibited — even something of an exhibitionist to the older men who, slowly but inevitably, are drawn to sit around him, a couple of seats or rows away, to watch. The first time I saw him, sometime last spring, we got into quite a conversation. I was sitting two seats away from him, also masturbating, when the projector broke down for about five minutes, and, along with the rest of the audience, we complained volubly, now shouting out to the whole house, now wisecracking to each other — without a pause in stroke. Indeed, I wondered then, if that was part of his trip—but I suspect, rather, it's just part of mine. His particular kink, which bewildered me the first few times I saw it, but which I finally read right is: Just before he comes, he quickly pulls his shirt down over his erect penis, gives a few quick rubs through his clothes — and, almost immediately, falls asleep for up to a half an hour, head to the side, lank hair straggling his bony forehead, small mouth open . . . all heightening the junky-like impression. Apparently he likes to come inside his clothes.

I guess he likes the feel.

I've seen him there perhaps six times; I've blown him once: He asked me if I could give him any money, and I told him I didn't have any. He let me do it anyway. He was salty and took a good 20 minutes to come; afterwards he said I was very good. Only once have I ever seen him accept a blow job from someone else (though he probably gets an offer every half hour), and that time there was a minor argument about payment afterwards. More recently, he tends to wave away anyone who tries to sit directly beside him or come on to him for anything more than visuals; so I don't bother him now.

I went out in the lobby and up the narrow stairs to the balcony, past the posters to the various porn films to come over the next months, that no one ever looks at, but which the management shifts around religiously, week to week. ("Next Tuesday!" "Next Wednesday!" say the permanent letters over the blue painted poster frames.) On Sundays and Mondays the Variety's double feature always includes one non-porn film (a decade or more ago, I actually went there once to see Peckinpah's *The Ballad of Cable Hogue* and not for sex, which probably made me unique in that day's audience); those posters are there too—though now I'm almost strictly a Saturday visitor. The non-porn relief was actually very nice when, years back, I lived in the neighborhood, but it's a drag if you only come down there to cruise.

The balcony of the Variety is where most of the action is, anyway. It's about a quarter of the size of the orchestra, and deserves an essay to itself, but I'm not going to write it here—other than to say that, in the open area behind the seats on the left-hand side of the projection booth, sometimes referred to as "the lounge," is where I first met Frank, on a torrential July 12th, back in 1977, when the rain battered and chattered on the filthy skylight you can just, here and there, see through for the dirt that's collected on it over the ages.

Sitting in the front row, down in what no doubt was once the loge, off to the side, was a tall guy in his late-20s/early-30s whom I'd already seen wandering about the theater two or three times when I'd been downstairs. He wore a black leather jacket and a black plastic cap. But it wasn't your standard motorcycle drag that signals S/M interests; rather, he seemed some East Village local who was simply into the "punk" look you see all up and down the streets of the neighborhood outside.

He was playing with himself.

I slipped in beside him, thinking for a moment as I did so that I was sure he'd been wearing black pants before, but now he was in white ones—no, I realized a second later: His pants *were* black, but he'd pushed them all the way down around his ankles, so you could see his pale legs.

There was a can of beer in a paper bag on the flat rim of the balcony in front of him, which he occasionally picked up and drank from. He had a very broad forehead, large eyes set quite far apart, and a full mouth. Indeed, the distance between his eyes verged on deformity: His face was vaguely like that of some dwarf's—though, as I said, he was quite tall: six foot two or more. The pants down around his ankles suggested he was open for just about anything. So I reached over and touched his leg. He didn't stop me or move away. So I moved to sit beside him.

He was very well hung.

Two things I found quickly. First, from the way he squirmed whenever I got near them, his testicles seemed to be very ticklish, so that I finally left them alone. Second, he had two warts, or polyps, on his penis: one right under the glans, and one further down the shaft. I blew him anyway, and the one on the shaft felt a little funny, sliding in and out the corner of my mouth. I wondered if this made for problems with other people. I remember I eventually got a finger up his ass, which he also seemed to like—as long as I stayed free of his nuts. After a few moments —I guess when he decided I knew what I was doing—he really got into it.

When I finished, I sat up and gave him a pat on the thigh; he took another swig from his beer can—but didn't pull his pants up; and I left without either of us saying anything, to wander around the balcony a little more and see what was going on.

There were eighteen or nineteen men, in their late 30s to early 70s, standing around under the skylight in "the lounge." (Twenty-five, and the dark, dirty space —where invariably someone has broken down and peed against the back wall—

is *very* crowded.) A couple of blow jobs were going on in a couple of the corners. A couple of guys were watching and masturbating. But the feeling was — as it often is here—that not much was happening. To one side of the space is an old ice-cream freezer—white enamel sides and a shiny steel upper surface with rounded corners, then square, black lids set along the top—of the sort that used to be in certain drugstores in the '40s. Among the dustier images I carry about from the Variety, I remember the freezer used to be down in the lobby, right where the guy now sits on his stool, taking tickets, and ice-cream cones were once available in the theater . . . for about three or four months—till it was acknowledged that ice-cream just wasn't what people were coming there for, and the freezer (more than fifteen years ago now), disconnected, had been moved up here.

(I first went to the Variety when I was 20, and I'd swear some of the men walking around it today were there when I made my first visit.)

Standing behind it, a slightly pudgy black guy with pink-framed glasses leaned forward with his elbows on the top, watching the men ambling quietly, intently, and slowly. (Some bald guy in glasses was smoking the inevitable cigar.) Like the guy out in the balcony, he had on a zipped-up jacket, but his pants were either way down, or completely off, so that his buttocks were available to anyone who wanted to wedge in behind him. Maybe once an hour, there'll be a taker. In my mind, the archetypal servicer of these guys is some stubble-cheeked, thick-set Puerto Rican gorilla of 35, with fraying thermal underwear showing at his neck, a soiled blue sweatshirt over that, and a tattered denim jacket on top of it all (maybe a baseball cap and his hair held back in a black rabbit's tail by a three times rolled-up red rubber band), his belt buckle flapping and clinking at his hips as he humps for all he's worth, panting, grunting, now and again, "*Hay de mios . . .!*"

Though certainly I've seen enough whites and blacks, too, pitching and catching, on that freezer in the last decade. Till I was 30, I used to enjoy sitting out in the orchestra, letting two or three different guys blow me, then coming back here to finish up and off in whoever was bent over and waiting. Since then, though, my pleasures have moved toward the oral. So now usually—back here I just watch.

A guy very much like the archetypal pitcher I just described sat on the freezer's end, staring around the shoulders of the men in front of him, down over the half-wall at the edge, where, on the screen, you could still see the movie. I found myself watching him pretty intently; but everytime I moved up, he definitely turned away. So finally I thought: Things are going much too well today for me to court such overt rejection. So I shouldered to the narrow gateway in the forward wall to walk down the steps between the seats, busy with the coming and going traffic.

Before I went downstairs, I looked over again toward the front of the balcony, to the side where the guy in the cap and no pants I'd blown before was sitting. I could see the tan jacket of another man, hunkered down over his lap: He was already working out again.

I went back down through the lobby and into the orchestra. Strolling down the aisle, I noticed Billy/Joe/Mike was heavily into his thing; he must have just started, because the crowds hadn't gathered yet. I went on down to the front row, walked across in front of the screen, came up the other aisle, and slid in to sit a seat away from him, opened my coat, my pants, and masturbated along with him.

He glanced at me a couple of times, but whether he recognized me or not, I don't know. I came about three minutes before he did, then watched till he reached his nervous, quickly covered finish — and sank into sleep, seconds beyond it, one sneakered foot now up over the seatback in front of him.

As I glanced around, something going on a row behind, which I'd noticed out of the corner of my eye, cleared now: The small Hispanic with the beret and bag was just moving over beside a blond guy with a full, lumberjack-style beard; the little guy bent down, and, as his head disappeared, the white guy put his hand up on the seat back beside me: His fingers were small, clean, neat, and hairless, a hand that, as a hand fetishist, I find somewhere between uninteresting and repulsive—though otherwise he was quite attractive.

I looked around a few moments more, then left my seat to prowl further. I went to the john to see what was going on, rattling the door and waiting for someone already inside to let me in—though with all the action in the theater proper, people tend only to look at each other in that narrow space (painted maroon, with a sink at one end, two urinals, and a commode at the other). I walked up and down the aisles a few more times, noting the irregular pattern in which some of the lights were on and some were out in their holders on the night blue walls. When I went upstairs again, the guy in the cap and jacket was still in the front row, alone. On a whim I moved in a seat away from him: His pants were still down. He was still jerking off.

So I moved directly next to him, put my notebook on the floor to kneel on, got down and blew him again. He seemed even more into it than before. After he came, I sat up on the seat. "You're really workin' out today," I told him. "How many times did you get off, anyway?"

He looked over at me, a little surprised that I was talking, I suppose. "A few," he said. "Yeah, I got off a few times today." Then he reached down and pulled his jeans over his knees, lifted his buttocks from the seat, and slid his pants up under them.

I said, "See you around," and left.

There's a woman (or a transsexual) who works the Variety regularly, asking $20 for a blow job and often taking $10. She's blonde, somewhere around 30; she wears jeans, boots, and a blouse, which she leaves spectacularly unbuttoned over generous breasts. I would think, by now, she would recognize me, but perhaps every third time I visit, she accosts me with a smile and "You wanna go out?" which means going off with her to the side of the theater for a quick suck. As I was coming down the stairs, she turned to me with her line. I smiled. "Sorry, not today," I said. "By the way," I said, "you know I see you here almost every time I come. What's your name?"

She smiled back, quite pleased, leaned forward and touched my shoulder with red-nailed fingers. In the yellowish light, I could see her knuckles were puffy and mottled from the cold outside—or drugs. "My name is Linda," she said with the inflection of someone giving me a friendly business tip.

"I'm Chip," I said. "Nice to meet you. I'll probably see you around."

Downstairs once more, as I was coming down the aisle, I saw the blond bearded guy with the small hands was by himself again, but he was joggling the crotch of his pants while he watched the movie. I sat down beside him; he didn't stop. But when I put my hand on the leg of his jeans, he shook his head a little, and pushed my hand away. So I got up again—consoling myself with the fact that I'd really disliked his hands so much it would have been largely charity on my part anyway. I'd been in the theater by this time not quite two hours. Why didn't I leave, I thought, and see what was new on the shelves of the St. Mark's Bookstore?

So I got up, walked up the aisle again, out into the bright lobby—squinting a little—and onto loud Third Avenue. Down at the parking lot, I turned in to take a leak against the back wall (this has become something of a ritual with me on my last dozen visits); as I was coming out, I saw the tall guy in the leather cap and jacket from the balcony crossing over, but we didn't speak. And 40 minutes later, after I had spent half an hour browsing in St. Mark's, when I was stepping out of Gem's Spa, drinking an extravagant egg cream, the same guy came barreling around the corner just as I stepped out, so that for a moment we stood, quite astonished, no more than eight inches from each other, face to face: He blinked his large, wide-set eyes (he may have been Puerto Rican, I realized that moment, or possibly even a light black of about my complexion), then ducked away, and I walked back down the street, drinking my egg cream with a straw through the plastic top, till the foam chattered at the bottom of the waxed cardboard container and I tossed it into one of the green gondolas at the curb.

That, physically, was the incident—no, not an average day of cruising: For me, at 42, I'd put it in the top 20% both for activity and pleasure.

But the inner drama, which I've omitted so far from my account, and which must be re-inscribed over it all—what makes it so important—was simply (and most complexly) this: I entered the Variety, no doubt like half the men there, terrified of AIDS. When I left, I no longer had any fear of the disease.

Concern? Yes. Of course I retain that. All the feelings that impelled *The Tale of Plagues and Carnivals* in a three-month burst of energy last winter are still intact. But I spent the whole time that afternoon, as I roamed the theater doing all the things I've recounted to you, thinking with a violence and an intensity it will be very hard to convey. And the result was that the fear—the dull, so reasonable, yet so crippling terror that has been a part of my life and the life of so many gay men for several years now—has vanished.

How has AIDS affected the cruising scene? As far as I can tell, there are less people out—by about ten or fifteen percent. But those who are seem more serious in their sexual pursuits. It's the ones who tended just to stand around, thinking about doing something (and, maybe, if something excited them enough, got down; but otherwise just drifted around taking up space) who've ceased to come out because the epidemic has scared them off.

As I've written you before, even someone of my age and very ordinary attractiveness (I'm 42, overweight, and I wear glasses) need only spend two sessions a week of the sort I've just outlined to log over 300 partners a year; younger and better looking men can spend half that time and log much greater numbers, making use of what is easily more than a hundred locations in the city, including theaters, public restrooms, peepshows, park areas, bars, and baths: And this does not include the "sexual binge weekend," where you can have contact with a dozen to three dozen partners in a couple of days—a common practice for younger guys—which can net you a hundred partners a month; and I'm still not talking about anyone who indulges in the sexual panoply to the point where the time he puts into cruising endangers his five-day-a-week eight-hour-a-day office job. I am much less sexually active in my 40s than I was in my 20s and 30s. And though I've talked to many gay men—some of them working with AIDS—who claim their own sex lives are and always have been far more limited (half-a-dozen partners a year, many say, is a *lot* for them), I still suspect, simply from what I've observed over the years in terms of what is available, that I'm pretty average.

But the psychological problem for those of us who do cruise is complex—and though I've put in real effort into curtailing and modifying my cruising habits in the light of AIDS, I've never, for more than a month at a time, been able to cut out OMR (Outside Main Relation) sex entirely; at best I've reduced 300-plus contacts a year to about a hundred, and even that may be due to my age more than my effort: Because of the 6-to-36-month incubation period for AIDS, those of us who have traditionally lived our lives at the 300-and-above sexual partners a year level move through our lives not afraid that we might *catch* AIDS: Rather, we moved through life dully and continually oppressed by the suspicion we must already *have* it. When sex *is* so available and plays such a large part, sexual activity fulfills many psychological functions, as chosen recreations often do: It helps you deal with any number of tensions and becomes a stabilizing and balancing force in one's life—and it provides an object for as much or as little intellectual analysis as anyone, by temperament, might require. (Sex and Death, William Butler Yeats wrote somewhere, are the only subjects truly complex enough to engage the serious mind.) Indeed, both Frank and I have noted that the pressures of OMR sex have left their most positive marks on the regular sex between us. With the kind of lives we both lead, outside sex has always bolstered and nurtured the regular sexual relations between us. So when general life-tensions get high, it is almost impossible to avoid the logic: Well, I probably have it anyway. I might as well go out and do at least *some* of what I was doing. The argument is there at one level or another of consciousness in us all, believe me, who do. But what this effects is turning something that, for years, has been considered an active pleasure into a mortal and self-destructive pursuit.

Yet one of the strongest realizations I had, while I was walking up one or another aisle of the Variety, was that this was precisely what the situation had been for me—indeed for many gays—who came out in the '50s, for homosexuality in the first place. Psychologically, we were all back in the same situation we were in 1958 when the only official information we took with us out into the world to cruise was that gleaned from the appendix of some 1950s psychology book, where we'd learned that to indulge homosexual urges at all was to foredoom oneself to an unavoidable career of alcoholism, devoid of any "rewarding" or "mature" relationships (whether sexual or just friendly), with an almost certain probability of suicide sooner or later. It was a no-win situation, in which to be concerned about it at all was, in itself, to be doomed; so that one went into the world carrying a mantle of death and resignation as heavy as Childe Harold's, relieved only by years of asking yourself: Could all these people around me—many of whom seemed very nice, many of whom seemed as happy as any one else—be both crazy and damned? . . . till, at last, because one was dealing with the satisfaction of an appetite, you just relegated the psychology books *et alia* to the place where one stores those abstractions that don't relate to the real world around you.

I had ceased, somehow, to be terrified then.

And somehow, moving around in the Variety, I ceased to be terrified now.

The medical aspect of the logic, is, of course, very different between the two situations (though the etiology of AIDS is astonishingly similar to the etiology of homosexuality itself in the conservative view that sees it as a disease, i.e., a sickness that can be carried about asymptomatically for years, till it eventually appears as a sudden, deadly weakening of the system that leaves one a victim of every possible evil contractable): What preceded my vanquishing of terror last month ran, *in precis,* something like this: Given the statistics both of the disease and my own sexual history, the chances are high that I have been exposed to it. More and more, it looks like a two-population situation, with one population, most probably the larger, largely immune, or at least highly resistant, to the disease—though there is no way to tell *which* population you belong to.

I know I'm resistant to hepatitis-B.

I seem to have a strong resistance to herpes.

If low-grade exposure to the disease over a period of time *can* produce an immunity, chances are I've acquired it.

I've never used poppers (other than half a dozen times in my youth when I experimented with them and found out I didn't like them); I don't smoke. Today I drink only occasionally but not at all heavily, and my yearly checkups regularly pronounce me healthy — including the couple where I went specifically worried about AIDS. My own precautions include limiting myself as best I can to a circle of regulars. And I've only taken it up the ass once in the last ten years. (Anecdotal evidence has it that passive buggery [or "Greek Passive" as they say in the Personal Ads] is, indeed, the major form of contagion.) I don't swallow any more—at least not often. I don't cruise when I've got a cold or am feeling physically run down. And (this last my own little quirk which may be pure superstition) I don't suck within three hours of brushing my teeth in the morning; and I don't brush my teeth within eighteen hours of sucking, as the minuscule sores connected with bleeding gums are a regular point of circulatory system infections, so that, in this case, that just seems to be asking for it.

The thing that I am terribly aware of is that, until much more is known, there is no earthly way I can, with any degree of responsibility, recommend this logic or these precautions to *any*one else with any sort of suggestion of even probable safety. They are *all* entirely a blind gamble. Still, until much more is known, any course of action is more or less a gamble—even unto cutting out all sex entirely. And in such a situation, *every one* of us must put up our own stakes and know that the outcome can be death—that, indeed, 43% of the over 7,000 men and women to come down with AIDS to date are already dead; and that, yes, for those of us living in New York, a couple thousand of those cases have occurred in our own incredibly sexually busy backyard.

And yet it is the realization that one *is* gambling, and gambling on one's own —rather than seeking some possible certain knowledge, some knowable belief in how intelligent or in how idiotic the chances are—that obliterates the terror.

For better or worse, I've chosen my course: It's a possible course *for me,* and in a year or ten years or twenty, its results can be judged and, in such a statistical context where it is compared with many other courses, as well as the results of research, it can become part of what may then be reasonably called knowledge by others . . . but it very possibly may never be "knowledge" for me. But what I must live with is a certain sense of its reasonableness, a certain sense of its risk—knowing those "senses" are *absolutely* without experimental foundation; and, somehow because of it (is this what existentialism was about?), I can now live without any *basic* terror or *basic* hope.

Intellectually, needless to say, I hope for (and would, indeed, work for in any way I could) a cure, an alleviation, a scientific certainty as soon as a reasonable path toward one were pointed out to me. Of course.

Still, within the realm of one's own chosen gamble, the obliteration of terror allows you to act as sensibly as you can given those limits. In the six weeks since this revelation occurred, I probably have gone out less than I did before—and have enjoyed myself more when I did. Yes, there is a New Feeling of Power and Strength; and one of the odder fallouts of *that* is that in the next three weeks I had three, completely unrelated to cruising, arguments/fights with Frank . . . but they, I suspect, analyzed and fictionalized, will form a significant part of my next novel. They have to do with the abuse of power on my part—and, let me add, I think they were satisfactorily resolved by us both.

Still, I feel like a stronger person.

We shall see if I'm a stronger writer.

At any rate, the experience itself in the Variety felt, through the course of an hour or so, as though my whole brain were untying itself, neuron by neuron, thought fragment by thought fragment, if not synapse by synapse—then reweaving itself into a new pattern, in which the heavy, nervous and interminably obsessive, wheedling fear of AIDS, with and without that name, that has been part of my life for three or more years now was simply no longer there—the way an ugly, nonfunctional, and depressing room, with its shredding wall paper, broken light fixtures, and cracked molding vanishes when the house that contained it is at last pulled down.

I don't know if you can follow this. I really sometimes wonder what all this has got to look like to somebody so outside this particular life as yourself. But it all feels very sane and good. Or, at least, as sane as I can be, right here, right now, at this moment in medical history.

Well, there are other things on my list:

Before the cold spell broke on this stretch of mild weather, Frank and I, coming back one night from an evening of *nouveaux beaujoulais* at Larry Gaunchman's (the temperature was in the 20s), found a black epileptic having a seizure in the street and carried him around to the police precinct. That may also go into the novel.

I delivered 20 copies of *Stars/Sand* to my mom, who is giving them away as Christmas presents to the family.

We had a nice Thanksgiving at Anne Jackson's. Frank went (most unusual for him) and Mother cooked the turkey up in her apartment, and Anne and her daughter Judy (feature editor for the *Boston Globe*) did all the rest. The homemade pumpkin pies were truly spectacular.

A party at Richard Kostelanetz's and Aviva's. Then (just yesterday on the 12th of December, which tells you how long this has run on to) Richard taped an interview with me for a series of ten one-hour-long radio programs he's putting together on "The Sixties." He was only going to interview me for an hour—but he ended up taking two hours of tape, and mouthed the word "brilliant" a lot, all through it, at me. So perhaps it was pretty good. He'll be editing the various interviews into a set of collages. More about that anon.

The Saturday morning a week after the revelation at the Variety, just as I was about to leave the house, the doorbell rang and, when I answered it and stepped out on the landing to see who was coming up, who should peer over the banister up the stairwell, calling, "Is Chip there . . . ?" but John Mueller, whom we last saw in jail in Florida. With his blond mane and beard, he looks more like a lion than ever. He'd acquired a green down-filled jacket and orange construction boots from somewhere. I walked him down to 42nd Street, listening to his adventures of the past three months in Miami, in Atlanta, and, at last, in New York, since his release on September 16th. I gave him all sorts of big brotherly (or young fatherly) advice and treated him to a two-dollar ticket to the Cameo, where I left him a bit later, to continue on downtown.

I've seen him once, briefly, since, for a little more talk and ego support. He really needs it. One of the things I was struck with, over the course of our walk down town, was how accurate my off-the-cuff diagnosis of "anxiety neurosis" seems to be. The simplest prescription for a regular tranquilizer could probably turn that kid's life around. He's sleeping at the Men's Shelter, here in the city, working on "shape-up" jobs during the day, drinking some but, so far, not heavily, and supplementing his income by intermittent evenings hustling on the strip—which is to say pretty much what he was doing before. He really should be into something better. John was 22 when I met him; he's now 25. In those three years (nearly two of which, now, he's spent in jail) there's a real closing-off of options, which is sad. He's still a good guy. But it strikes me, if every action you perform terrifies you (and John functions hugely out of fear), even if it *is* because your old man beat on you endlessly and unmercifully when you were between the ages of three and fourteen (when you first started running away from home), you *still* build up an incredible amount of rage at the world—if only because it is constantly scaring you so badly. And if you can't get it out in some constructive way, maybe it has to explode in intermittent self-destructive drunken binges that end you up in the hoose-gow.

Another party, at Barbara Wise's, for her son David (many years ago the camera man on *The Orchid*) briefly back from L.A. Much fun and a fine pre-Christmas dinner to boot, as well as a chance to speak with one of my all-time heroes, Maria Irene Fornes. She's conducting a playwriting workshop and, after half an hour's conversation at Barbara's, invited me to sit in on it! Also, I talked with Norman McAfee, who translated the Pasolini poems for Vintage Books with Luciano Martinengo. His current project is a video production of Helen Adam's wonderful verse/musical play, *San Francisco's Burning*. Some day I've got to write you about its initial New York production (several years after its San Francisco debut) at the Judson Poet's Theater, in 1966 ('67?), as well as the "scandal" of Michael Smith's *Village Voice* review. The play was certainly one of the great influences on *Dhalgren*, and, even more so, one of the most delightful theater experiences of my life — all of which I told young Mr. McAfee, which he said gave him renewed enthusiasm for his project.

I hope it comes off.

I couldn't be happier for Helen.

Saw Chuck Thomas again, for dinner at the Lion's Head, with some ten of his friends: an ebullient, lively group of out-of-towners, too loud and too boisterous, but all good-hearted and well-meaning men and women.

We are deep into Christmas preparations for Iva. Things are, of course, a bit tight this year, but I think it will all work out. And she, herself, is in great form — though, right now, she's got a cold; so will be skipping her gymnastics class this afternoon (Friday, December 14th).

We have two new members on *The Little Magazine* staff; we met here last night and had a productive meeting, though all our energies went into wrapping up the physical layout and production of the new issue. We won't be reading again until our meeting on the 3rd of January, next year. By three weeks after that, we should have word on "Species," which I shall be arguing heatedly for in the discussion.

Lou just sent up a color proof for the cover of *Flight* by messenger. I was out when it arrived. But Frank was here to receive it. It's truly lovely — though they've gone with red type, which jars a bit to me. But it's certainly eye-catching. Next letter there will be more on the Bantam newsfront: In brief, along with the proof, Lou sent me a letter saying that Bantam is going to go the way of Timescape/Daw/Quantum/Del Rey in its SF program, i.e., a separate Bantam SF imprint, to be called "Spectra Books," with Lou at the head.

Do I think it's a good idea?

Well, actually I don't. And my evidence is that two of those special imprint lines are dead, and the two who've survived have managed to do it by publishing nothing but pabulum. But later for that. I'll enclose his "Press Release." Stay tuned . . .

I've been meaning to ask you, for some letters now: Have you taken a look at a novel called *Saul's Book* by one Paul T. Rogers? It deals, vividly, if romantically, with 42nd Street and the hustling life. I mention it because, about three or four months ago, Rogers was found dead, in his closet, where his body had been stuffed five days before by the young (one-legged!) hustler he'd dedicated the book to and had also officially adopted a few years before: It seems the young man and one of his hustler friends had devised some preposterous scheme to murder Rogers and steal the royalties from the book, which had done moderately well as such things go.

Oh, well . . .

Tomorrow, Iva, Mike Elkins (who's bringing a friend — I hope not *too* disreputable), and myself are going to see *Dune* at noon at the Loew's "Quad," around the corner on Broadway. (They're currently in the midst of vast construction to build an extension onto it that adds three more screens to the complex. Years back, what's there now used to be one large multi-balconied movie house; now it's four small ones.) I'm not expecting much — yet I'm also strangely intrigued. The particular flavor of the bad press it's been receiving suggests it *might* just be an interesting movie.

Well, this letter has, by now, run on in the writing over several weeks: it's the evening of December 15th. Frank is up in Albany for the night; and I'm in the middle of cooking Iva's and my dinner. So I'll wind this up.

This may be my last letter before Christmas. If so, all good thoughts and things to you, Cynthia, and the boys, on the coming return of the light. Hugs and strokes to all small creatures, and

Best of the season,

• 52 •

To Camilla Decarnin

December 5th, 1984

Dear Mog,

Many thanks for the Masson article — though it gives me a strange sense of *dejá vu.*

For about ten years of our correspondence, Joanna and I used to fall into a pattern that must have repeated itself at least ten times.

We'd get into some discussion/argument, in the course of which I'd recommend she read this, that, or the other — which, like most such suggestions, in either direction, would go by the board.

Anywhere from six months to three years later, she would write me back an impassioned letter that I *must* read precisely the piece I'd recommended to her a year before, speaking of it as if I'd never heard of it.

The first three times it happened, I just smiled and let it go. The next three I simply mentioned that it had occurred. (She would write back: *Oh, dear. So it did . . .*) And once or twice among the last couple of times it happened, I actually tried to analyze what it meant—and we had a good laugh.

Is it eight full months ago now I suggested that you read Masson's book, *Assault on Truth,* and (very important!) Janet Malcolm's *In the Freud Archives . . .*? I read both of them over about three days last winter, and I *know* I wrote you about them.

Since I suspect you'd like what Masson has to say, I'll just send you *my* copies. (His article is kind of a rehash of some of the less interesting parts of his book.) You can have fun with my marginal notes—I hope they don't make you feel like I'm hanging over your shoulder. (Frank says he just can't read a book any more that I've already annotated.) Something I suspect you'll have already noticed about Masson is that his villain is *always* a woman: first Anna Freud and, more recently, Ms. Malcolm . . .

I'm just curious if you will come away from the first-hand evidence with the same conclusions I have.

I don't want to prejudice you, but I followed the controversy fairly closely over several years even before the books were published. No one that I've seen (and I've read some pretty scathing attacks on Masson) has seriously claimed that the information he's dug up is either false or unimportant.

People have merely questioned, first, his construction of the information and, second, the rather sensationalistic and self-serving way he has, from time to time, gone about using it. And as far as any "feminist sensibility," I suspect you'll agree, after reading Malcolm, that Masson has about as much of *that* as a male Doberman Pinscher in rut!

Masson, all through his own work, constructs a theory that alternates between being bizarrely psychoanalytical (a theory about as clumsy as the one he outlines in the article about the intelligent, cultured woman and the dumb analyst) and taking an "it's a mystery we can never know" point of view to account for Freud's "reversal" (the seduction theory "abandoned," and the fantasy theory "taken up")—when the real explanation would seem (dare one say?) blatantly social.

It seems to me that, chances are, were Freud confronted with Masson's information about the vast amounts of real and documentable incest Freud was familiar with, concerned with, and had studied, and then asked about this "reversal," Freud would most likely say: "My long-time exposure to — and study of — the real and bodily horrors of sexual abuse of children, especially girl children, is precisely the authority by which I feel I can adequately distinguish between fact and fantasy in my largely upper-middle-class 19th century female patients."

Now: *I* don't feel this is the best answer, by any means. But it's a reasonable one. And the theoretical point that is totally "repressed" from Masson's analysis (can I call it anything else? Suppressed, perhaps?) is that what came along *with* the "reversal" was Freud's insistence of the primacy of "unconscious fantasy" in psychic life: i.e., if you unconsciously *believe* you were raped, then it doesn't *matter* whether you were or not. The "reversal" was not used, by Freud, to invalidate the experience of his female patients; that, again, falls to his disciples to do. It was used by Freud rather to *validate* their psychological reality. This is the same period that produced the Freudian notion, for example, of *Nächtraglichkeit* — I quote from Jonathan Culler [*On Deconstruction*, p. 162&ff]:

> *Nächtraglichkeit* names a paradoxical situation that Freud frequently encounters in his case histories, in which the determining event in a neurosis never occurs as such, is never present as an event, but is constructed afterwards by what can only be described as a textual mechanism of the unconscious. In the case of the Wolfman, the analysis of key dreams leads Freud to the conclusion that the child had witnessed his parents copulating at age one-and-a-half. This "primal scene" had no meaning or impact at the time; it was inscribed in the unconscious like a text in an unknown language. When he was four, however, a dream linked to this scene by a chain of associations transformed it into a trauma . . . The case of "Emma" is another classic illustration of the textual, differential functioning of the unconscious [through *Nächtraglichkeit*]. Emma traces her fear of shops to an incident at age twelve when she entered a store, saw two shop assistants laughing, and fled it in fright. Freud traces it to a scene at age eight when a shopkeeper had fondled her genitals through her clothes. [Emma presumably entered many shops between the ages of eight and twelve without a phobic reaction. But . . .–SRD] "Between the two scenes," writes Jean Laplace, "an entirely new element has appeared—the possibility of sexual reaction" [*Life and Death in Psychoanalysis*, p. 40]. The sexual content is neither in the first scene when she was aware of no sexual implications, nor in the second scene. "Here," Freud writes, "we have an instance of a memory exciting an affect which it did not excite as an experience, because in the meantime changes produced by puberty had made

possible a different understanding of what was remembered . . . the memory which has only become a trauma *by deferred action* ["Project for a Scientific Psychology," vol. 1, p. 356].

Now, you may well ask me, do I believe in this *Nächtraglichkeit*, this deferred action, this unconscious reality constructed of a collection of different experience fragments rejoined in the unconscious to produce the same unconscious effects that a real event might have occasioned, the way a kidnapper might assemble words cut from a newspaper to produce a ransom note?

Well, like most things, I suspect it's more complicated than that. But I think it's worth noting that in this, Freud's theory is far closer to current feminist theories of what *I* would have to call "a more conservative bent," which privilege women's subjectivity over "objective" events.

The following is *perfectly* consistent with Freud's "fantasy" theory and his "abandonment" of the "seduction" theory, what Masson calls his "reversal":

Real sexual abuse to real young women causes real conscious, and real unconscious, scars. The conscious ones can presumably be dealt with consciously and rationally. The unconscious ones cause problems that the woman herself will experience *as* problems because they promote real behavior that is overtly at odds with what *she* consciously feels *she* would like to do, or they promote conscious feelings overtly at odds with what *she* feels should be her appropriate feelings. (That is what defines them as problems. If she feels her behavior and feelings *are* appropriate to what she would like to do and what the situation is, then there is no *psychic* problem. There may well, however, be social ones.)

The "fantasy" theory simply says that a woman who has *not* been sexually abused has, nevertheless, in a society saturated with the abuse of women at all levels, more than enough real material from which to put together the *identical* unconscious scars that will cause the same behavioral and emotional problems (i.e., that she experiences as the same problems) as a woman who *has* actually been abused.

One possible *symptom* of the unconscious scars may be a conscious belief that an incident of sexual abuse that would, indeed, have produced such scars directly did occur when, indeed, it didn't.

Once more, the thrust of Freud's "reversal" was not to dismiss his patients' protestations of sexual abuse *because* they hadn't "really" occurred. Its thrust was rather that we *must* deal with all such protests as psychic reality *even if* they did not occur—because the *unconscious* damage was identical. (*Not* similar; *identical!*) And only one step away from his articulated theory was the overpowering suggestion that the reason for this was that society was so saturated with the real and bodily abuse of real women, any woman can put together such an unconscious text for herself all too easily from the reality of her own life—that, indeed, most women *must* put it together by the time they reach adolescence.

(The "male" version of this theory was, of course, the one put forward in *Civilization and its Discontents*, where it is argued that modern life is so full of Oedipal conflicts that anyone can put together for "himself" the real unconscious scars of an unresolved Oedipal trauma even if "he" has come from a family where the specific Oedipal stage was gotten through with all the necessary support and love from both parents.)

I say once more, Mog, remember: Freud *was* the translator of John Stuart Mill.[1]

Freud *was* the student of Charcot on child abuse, the autopsier of their mutilated bodies, and the stunned observer of the overwhelming percentage of girls in their number.

Freud *was* the man who took for his motto, "Poor child, what have they done to you?"

Freud *was* the man who actively encouraged women, again and again, to take part in his "new science."

Does this mean Freud *is* some kind of male, proto-, modern-day feminist? Absolutely not! But it also means that you can't really criticize Freud's theory as theory if you mistake what, in his theory, *was* a response to what was there in Freud's world.

It also means that such historical insensitivity is no place from which to criticize responsibly modern psychoanalytic practices that grow out of that theory. And it goes without saying (rather, it *must* be said!): Such practices are deeply and radically in need of criticism today.

Masson has revealed very important information and (five to 50 years after a number of women analysts raised them) raised some very important questions.

But it is Masson's answers to those questions that are under attack. Masson's question — Why did Freud change from the "seduction" theory to the "fantasy" theory?— is a reasonable one. But his characterizing of this change as a "reversal" is already an answer. And most people who have examined the material don't find a "reversal" there. Rather, they find a moving-over, a more accurate homing-in on the problem. To strain an analogy perhaps: It's as if in the case of treating bruises, doctors had been spending all their time burning the sticks that caused them, when another doctor decided that perhaps it would be better to treat the pain and damage of the bruise itself—and, in the course of it, noticed that not all bruises were caused by sticks: that some were caused by rocks and some, indeed, by leukemia; and that, occasionally, when the cause of the bruise was found to be internal, people fancied that at some point they'd nevertheless been hit.

In the light of what Freud was, it is simply easier to read what Masson takes for a "reversal" to be, rather, the development of such a man as the 19th century could allow it—indeed, a man who certainly did not achieve absolute answers, but a man who got us further along the track toward reasonable provisional answers than anyone has a right or a reason to expect who looks at the European scene before Freud got there.

The Eckstein/Fliess case was appalling.[2]

It's the center of Masson's book and it's a Good Thing he uncovered it.

---

[1] Freud translated and approved of Mill's 1869 essay "The Subjection of Women," among the more radical calls for equality between the sexes yet penned.

[2] Emma Eckstein (1865-1924) was a patient of Freud's. She entered analysis at the age of 27. Freud recommended her to his colleague Wilhelm Fliess (1858-1928), who performed an operation on her nasal cavity, in accordance to what we today would consider a totally lunatic theory, in order to end her masturbation. After the operation, a three-foot length of gauze was accidentally left in her nose, which caused a major hemorrhage. The gauze was finally removed, her life was saved, and she went on to become the second psychoanalyst in history. But the operation represents an appallingly embarrassing moment in Freud's history.

And no one I've read has said anything else.

Most of us have some notion that such things happened with frightening frequency in the moneyed classes (blessedly small!) during the early days of "modern medicine." But what a modern reader is likely to be *most* appalled by is Freud's continued support, all through the incident, of Fliess — "You are not to blame," Freud repeats, over and over, to a man who was clearly a charlatan (however self-deceived) and a pathological medical twit.

If you read it, however, in the light of, say, Lewis Thomas's *The Youngest Science*, and you get some notion of what medicine in general and surgery in particular was before World War I, not to mention in 1895 (when the Eckstein incident occurred), you begin to realize that what, for the time, was remarkable was the accuracy with which Freud kept confronting Fliess, in his letters about the operation, with the medical reality of the atrocity! And I don't care what you say, Freud never recommended another patient to Fliess's care. And that tells me, however much Freud tried to soothe his friend's feelings, Freud was not an idiot or a monster.

It seems to me that the best explanation of the "suppression" of the scandals Masson unearthed is this: The 19th century had sharply drawn lines between what could and what couldn't be talked of in public — lines that were almost unchangeably in place as late as 1955. This was social and, today, we consider it wrong. (And "we" includes me.) But these "suppressions" run entirely along those 19th century lines. And the fact that the evidence *was* preserved is more to Freud's (and Fliess's!) moral credit than not — Fliess could just as well have destroyed such letters himself; or Freud could just have not written them! But Masson's project, looked at in the larger light, seems to be to question why things in 1895 (or in 1954, when the substantially doctored *Sigmund Freud: The Origins of Psychoanalysis: Letters to Wilhelm Fliess* were originally published by Basic Books) were not done as things *occasionally* have been done since 1980. And, to the extent that he tries to construct an intra-personal psychoanalytic explanation located wholly in Freud's personality for that historical difference, it's simply the same mystification that he very rightly decries in other places.

What one really wants to see, of course, are the vanished letters between Eckstein and Freud: After all, after the appalling incident in which she nearly lost her life, she went on to become the first psychoanalyst after Freud — the first woman analyst, and the second in history — and remained a believer in Freud's theories (if not Fliess's!), however little splash she made doing it.

The "Eckstein affair" is, of course, precisely the kind of *scandale* an institution like the Freudian establishment would want to cover up. Who wouldn't? But does it reflect on psychoanalysis as a theory?

Well, you read the books and see what *you* think . . .

If these interest you, do hunt up in your library *Psychoanalyzing Psychoanalysis: Freud and the Hidden Fault of the Father,* by Marie Balmary (translated by Ned Lukacher), Johns Hopkins University Press: Baltimore and London, 1976. (And does it just seem like I'm trying to intimidate by saying the women who are writing most intelligently on Freud [and/or Lacan]—Felman, Spivak, Balmary, Kristeva, Irigaray, Gallop, Mitchell, Turkle, Clement . . . to name some of the ones I've read with more than passing attention—are all very serious feminists . . .?)

I read the Balmary a year or two before I read either Masson or Malcolm. (And, yes, Malcolm's previous book, *Psychoanalysis: The Impossible Profession* is a much better book than her book on Masson, *et alia*.) It simply struck me as more responsible use made of the same information (taken from some of Masson's earlier papers, re-recounted for the book).

Oh, well. If we keep *this* up, Mog, you'll end up some kind of Lacanian analyst in three years!

You say 'no'; but Mark My Words: Historically speaking, Freud has seduced a *lot* more brilliant women than Jacob Holdt has . . .

As more than one feminist commentator on Freud has noted: We have to go beyond Freud. We really do. But any quick dismissal of Freud's theories is doomed to failure. Freud's theories were all mounted to explain the repeated behavior of real men and women, behavior observed repeatedly, again and again, among many individuals, over many years. The quick dismissal is almost always in the form of, "Oh, people don't act like that." But that's precisely the argument that *must* fail, because people *do*. If you say, "Penis-envy doesn't exist," then you *must* come up with a theory that explains the real action of two- to five-year-old girls in every family that has any!

I think I did *just* this, by the bye, in *The Tale of Old Venn*; but I did it not by dismissing Freud, but by rereading his *Three Essays on the Theory of Sex*, where he poses the penis-envy theory (as speculation!), and by observing my own daughter and her fellow playschool attendees, female and male, in their many sessions of naked play in the 82nd Street playground fountain (in three-year-old peeing contests [which the girls frequently won] and God knows what else), as well as at home, over several months: And, believe me, for the first two weeks of that observation, I came *very* close to coming out on Freud's side!

Though, at this point, I believe *I'm* right and Freud's wrong.

But people act *just* the way Freud said they did — even, or especially, when they act unpleasantly; and that's precisely *why* the endlessly dovetailed explanations that constitute his theory remain so powerful.

Oh, yes. One more thing.

There are one-and-a-half typos, it turns out, in the copy of "Time Considered as a Helix of Semi-Precious Stones" I sent you!

Page 559, paragraph 10, line 6:

After the word "wounds" insert ")," (i.e., a closed parenthesis and a comma).

The half-typo comes on page 598, paragraph 9, line 2: A wood-chip in the cheap paper Avon uses makes it look, in Xerox, as if there were a comma after the word "know". There isn't.

Perhaps you could white it out . . . ?

Again, once more: Thanks for the article.

Hope you enjoy the books. They're yours till the next time I visit San Francisco.

All my love,

• 53 •

To David Samuelson

December 21st, 1984

Dear David Samuelson,

My indefatigable bibliographers down in Lock Haven, Pennsylvania, Bob Bravard and Mike Peplow, sent me a Xerox of the article you did for *Survey of Modern Fantasy Literature* on *Tales of Nevèrÿon*—otherwise, alas, I probably wouldn't have seen it.

I'm writing to tell you how much I enjoyed it. A clear and simple account of what others have occasionally found hopelessly complex often bespeaks a sharper critical faculty than the intricate untangling of only vaguely apprehended complexities. And you are the first person to mention in print Venn's critique of Freud's "penis-envy" theory! I was beginning to think that it was all-but-unseeable by most readers, since even the sympathetic ones, in writing about the book, passed right over it.

If what one reads generally is true, most writers, I gather, disdain the criticism written about them — if not criticism in general. But I am a criticism-lover, and often read it for pleasure. And when it is done well, and is about me to boot, I like to encourage it! Indeed, at this point, the secondary Delany bibliography is getting rather long, but I can still think of only a handful (and a small handful at that) of pieces that seemed to have both energy and precision. And yours is one.

Thank you very much.

I pass on a couple of comments on your piece just as they strike me: I feel I can say them to you so easily simply because, even as they struck me in reading, they did not obliterate my general pleasure at the piece — so that if they dampen any good feelings you have at my praise of your work, know that you are over-reading them!

"*Tales of Nevèrÿon* is an excellent illustration of the hybrid term, 'speculative fiction,'" you write, and it may well be. One could even argue that they could not have been written without their forerunners in *New Worlds* of the late '60s, where much of the significant "speculative fiction" appeared. Nevertheless, myself, I've gone back to the more conservative terms, "science fiction," "fantasy," and "sword and sorcery." The demotic distinctions implicit in the terms are the distinctions which, as a writer, I'm interested in working with, wrestling with, possibly even changing — but unless the reader/critic keeps some sense of those distinctions in mind (preferably with the help of the common terms), I suspect it will be hard or impossible to hear the dialogue I try to engage in, most heatedly (in the *Nevèrÿon* stories), with a tradition that runs, fueled by whatever amounts of pulp, from Robert E. Howard through Karl Edward Wagner and, presumably, beyond.

Hopefully I bring a lot *to* that dialogue—Freud, Derrida, Foucault, Lacan . . . But the site of the argument (which is, of course, as much with Freud and Lacan as it is with Howard: the Freud and Lacan *in* Howard . . .) is still sword and sorcery. And to shift the site in the critical account of it is to risk missing some of the polemical subtleties.

At any rate, within the community of SF writers, I don't know of anyone who's seriously talked about "speculative fiction" since 1972—which is more than twelve years, now. Myself, I gave it up in 1970. Today, I think the term functions reasonably and accurately as a historical reference to a type of writing done largely between (approx.) '69 and '70. In that period there are clear aesthetic programs that you can cite; various writers were clearly and conscientiously concerned with those programs; and there were publishing outlets that sought work (or rejected it) that was recognized as expressing (whether intentionally or not) those concerns. No, none of these were necessarily hard-edged and absolute situations; nor did they have absolute ends or beginnings. Still, they were real and are historically verifiable.

But as the term strays outside those historical limits, it becomes more and more metaphorical—and finally mystificational, in that it obscures and distracts precise attention from a real historical moment in the development of SF, a moment of great worth in its own right and great influence on what came after it (both in terms of acceptance and reaction), a moment with many roots entangled in what came before it—a moment in which real texts were written by real men and women in response to the real world around them, and in which readers and writers both had real responses to those texts that left them and the practice of SF changed.

My only other comment, really, is just a passing mention: On page 1879, you write: "Noel Stock (*Reading the Cantos*) comments on the reality of fiction (Ezra Pound's in this case) regardless of the falsity of its premises." The particular section of *Reading the Cantos* from which the headnote to "The Tale of Small Sarg" comes was not a direct discussion of some part of the *Cantos* themselves, but rather a side discussion of St. John-Perse's *Anabase;* thus it compliments the headnote to "The Tale of Potters and Dragons" from T. S. Eliot's introduction to his translation of the same poem. And both headnotes should be reread, I suspect (if not *Anabase* itself), in the light of the opening motto of *Neveryóna*, from Sontag's wonderful essay, "Approaching Artaud."

Well . . . !

The third and final volume of the *Nevèrijon* series is due out from Bantam in May.

I am sure a writer should never say this to a critic. Yet I say it quite bluntly and honestly: I hope you write more about the *Nevèrijon* series. The reason is a highly selfish one: I've so much enjoyed what you've written already.

Good luck in all your projects and undertakings, and my best wishes of the season to you.

• 54 •
IN THE ONCE UPON A TIME CITY[1]

In December 1984, with *Stars in My Pocket like Grains of Sand*, Bantam Books will release a seventeenth printing of my 1975 novel, *Dhalgren*. *Dhalgren* was "published" on January 1st, 1975, but copies were in bookstores and supermarkets and airports by the second week of December 1974. The seventeenth printing, which should be dated December 1984 (it's not; but that's getting ahead of my tale), will show up in November 1984. It's only a month off, then, from a tenth anniversary edition.

---

[1] Written November/December, 1984. Published in *Locus*, Feb. 1985.

In the first few months of *Dhalgren's* life, ten years ago, the book went through five printings. And thanks to an imaginative interpretation of a phone conversation with a Bantam editor, one reviewer printed a story that Bantam was allowing the writer, even encouraging him, to rewrite sections of the book from printing to printing, changing characters, action, and outcome, almost as, in the novel itself, the city of Bellona, from time to time, changes.

Needless to say no one at Bantam ever told *me* about this.

A column or two later, the reviewer retracted his story—a preposterous one for anyone who knows the commercial exigencies of mass-market publishing. Putting out a book with three different covers is one thing; publishing a book with three different plots is, however, something else. But in one form or another the tale has been repeated for nearly ten years, now in fanzines, now in literary periodicals, now in the odd letter from the curious reader who simply wants to know if it's true.

I'd like, then, to tell, here, what has (and has not) happened to the text of *Dhalgren* in the last decade.

As the book's near-million readers know, *Dhalgren* is a long novel (just under 900 pages), and is occasionally of great typographical complexity. But during the book's production, I was living in London, and I did not have the customary chance to check over the copy-edited manuscript before it went to the printer. Also there was some mix-up in the mailing of galleys, so that, when I received them in England along with a note on the production schedule, with five days for first-class air-mail, I had only four days to correct them. *Dhalgren's* diction is heavily stylized, and its punctuation is correspondingly informal; pointing is used to make the unspeakable comprehensible, rather than to conform to ordinary grammar. Appositional commas do not always come in pairs. And semi-colons and colons are used to establish an artificial breath line, rather than to attend the logic.

I cringed, thinking of what Bantam's proofreaders would do to it; and their corrections, I knew, would be superimposed, willy-nilly, on mine, without me there to arbitrate.

But I finished that long pale sheaf of nightmares—in four days. And sent them off. I still don't know if they arrived on time or not.

Two days before Christmas 1974, with my family, I flew back from London to New York; and saw my first copies of *Dhalgren* in three ranks across a book rack, Christmas Eve, at a Kennedy airport newsstand.

I bought one (for $1.95; sigh . . .) and, over the next few days at my mother's, read it. I felt then, and still feel, that, given the circumstances, Bantam's printers and production department did a commendable job on a daunting project. Nevertheless, by my informal estimate, a fifth of the corrections I had made in galleys had just been ignored or bungled. And in a less pressured reading, other errors (many self-evident, and many practically unspottable by anyone but me) emerged.

I made a list of some 85 corrections and, a day or two after New Year's, went into Bantam's offices and asked if they could be inserted at a new printing—as the galley and copy-editing process had been so rushed.

Certainly, they said.

Indeed, they told me that afternoon, the book had already gone into a third printing before publication day; and a fourth was on order. (That's when I first learned I had a surprisingly successful SF novel on my hands.) The corrections, they told me, would be included when and if there was a fifth — which at that point looked likely.

You need a three-month leeway to insert corrections in a new printing. Though in theory it's possible to strip a single line of type onto an old plate, in practical terms for mass-market paperbacks, it's easier to cut in a new page; thus, with any correction, even if only a comma, it's customary to reset the entire page. A hundred corrections in a paperback book means resetting a hundred pages — unless several show up together.

I left my correction list with Bantam. I also left Xeroxed copies at the Science Fiction Bookshop down on 12th Street, which hosted a friendly and successful book signing for *Dhalgren,* in the midst of which Ted Sturgeon called to tell me how much he liked the book (the first time I'd spoken to him in person), providing me with the most euphoric moments of my life, before or since. In various bookstores around the city, over the next week, I left copies folded inside the front covers—much to the annoyance of the clerks at Ed Wolenz's 8th Street Bookshop, who finally left me a nasty note: "Will whoever is stuffing our books with their shit stop it!" is what they typed out on an index card taped to the shelf edge.

The fifth printing of *Dhalgren* is dated April 1975. I first found a copy in a bookstore up in Buffalo, New York, where I was teaching that term. Clutching it in its flimsy white bag, I stomped through the Buffalo snow back to the motel where I was living, climbed up the outside stairs to the balcony along the second floor rooms, shouldered inside, shrugged off my parka, threw myself down on the bed and opened the book.

There were no corrections.

The explanation was simple, though the next day when it came from Bantam, it still pained: The order for the fifth printing had come too quickly, and my correction list, by only a few days, had missed that all-important three-month leeway. Over the phone Bantam assured me that corrections *would* be made in the next printing. By now my list had grown to 98. I sent my revised list in, posthaste. And, in the sixth printing, dated June 1975, a rather arbitrary 65 of those corrections from that list were incorporated into the text. Whether my list was subjected to printerly triage, or whether some of my notes were confusing, or whether pages from the list were lost, I've never learned.

But the 65 corrections that were actually made involved changing things like "fisherman" to "fishermen," "lip" to "lap" and "admit" to "admiss," as well as spelling errors, transposed letters or words, and punctuation. The biggest corrections in terms of meaning — the reinsertion of two dropped lines of dialogue on page 414, a single dropped line on page 342, and the change of two words in Earnest Newboy's dialogue, one on page 178 and the other on page 180, to bring his speech into line with one of the more ineradicable dialectal variants of someone raised in an English public school—were among those not included.

Until 1982, through the next ten printings, those 65 were the only changes in the text of the Bantam *Dhalgren.*

In 1976 Boston's Gregg Press decided to publish a hardcover edition, as part of David Hartwell's series of SF library editions. A friend of mine in San Francisco, Camilla Decarnin, re-proofread the book thoroughly and made an exhaustive list of errors which she sent me. As she had read the novel a number of times before, written on it, and had a sense of its style and intent, her list was, of necessity, both more sensitive and more exhaustive than the one Bantam's proofreader had been able to come up with under the pressure of imminent publication; and Douglas (*Worlds out of Words: The SF Novels of Samuel R. Delany*) Barbour, of Alberta, Canada, sent a dozen from his own reading, three or four of which had actually escaped Decarnin. Here and there, one or another reader had pointed out one or two others to me, which I'd jotted down—again, I'm not talking of content, but of proofreading glitches. Correlating all these corrections with those from a careful rereading on my own, I put together a list of about 108 errors. Working photo-offset from Bantam's ninth printing (the paper was of a particularly good quality, making the print appear bold and clear; and the 65 corrections were in all the subsequent printings) Gregg Press stripped the corrections into its hardcover edition.

A Bantam editor who'd once done some scholarly editing pointed out, while I was working on the Gregg edition, that an error-free text simply presupposes several editions over a number of years with new corrections in each one. It's a standard scholarly process and not unusual when accuracy is the goal. More mistakes *would* turn up, she assured me. The only thing unusual was my aspiring to such accuracy for a science fiction novel. She had seen the initial galley mix-up. And she very generously felt that *Dhalgren* deserved an accurate text—and made me a generous offer. Every fifth printing, she told me, I could insert whatever corrections had surfaced — starting with the tenth printing, which, when it appeared, would be the same as the forthcoming corrected library edition from Gregg.

I was very touched.

Three days later, in July of 1976, I gave Bantam the list I had prepared for Gregg Press.

The tenth printing of *Dhalgren* is dated October 1976 and contains no corrections. Again, only by days, I and my editor had misjudged that three-month leeway.

Over the next year, half a dozen more errors turned up.

The Gregg hardcover of *Dhalgren* appeared in December 1977, with a note from me on the textual changes. In the Gregg edition, where the corrections are stripped in by line, not by page, the corrected lines are just different enough in their type so that you can spot them by running your eye down the page—should you want to compare them with the Bantam printings.

In 1980, just before the fifteenth printing, I reminded Bantam of their promise; editors had, indeed, changed; but Mary Lucas, Bantam's current managing editor, knew of it—and also remembered their failure to implement it. And, as my late editor had told me it would, my list had indeed grown by a solid 20 errors (which included the new half-dozen). I handed in the revised list well in time for the printing.

The fifteenth printing, dated December 1980, contains no corrections. But a very contrite Mary Lucas explained that it had been an oversight. And, no, because Bantam had failed to put in corrections when promised at two points now, I would not have to wait till the 20th printing. The corrections would be included in the sixteenth.

The sixteenth printing of *Dhalgren*—December 1982—incorporates about 130 new corrections, most of them included in the Gregg Press library edition, along with about 20 new ones. Looking over the book, however, as I checked the errors against my list, I saw that again a few corrections had just not been made—for whatever reason or oversight.

The two dropped lines of dialogue on page 414, for example, had still not been inserted, though clearly in this printing the type had been moved back on the previous page to accommodate them—so that now there was a three line paragraph on the bottom of page 412 repeated verbatim on the top of page 412, instead of the insertion toward the page's bottom third.

I have mentioned that even the smallest correction involves resetting the page. On a number of pages where corrections *had* been made, new (and terribly minor) errors had been introduced at other spots on the page—though none greater than a single letter or punctuation mark. Still, Bantam's production department had taken a science fiction novel that, in its first printing, had had over 200 errors and turned it into a book that now had less than two dozen. I was as pleased as an SF writer could be.

And, when I mentioned the remaining (and new) errors to Mary, she said: "And *they'll* be corrected too! It just means somebody didn't proofread the new pages. And that's silly. We'll take care of them."

"In the 20th or the 21st printing?" I asked.

"In the next one," she said. "The seventeenth."

Writing to some of my trustworthy error-spotters over the next months produced a flurry of reexamination; and turned up a small handful of new typos that had slipped by. And so a list of eighteen corrections, old and new, was submitted to Bantam in the middle of last year. And I would like to add the names of Robert Morales, Ron Drummond, and Victor Gonzales to those already mentioned, who have helped with that list.

The second week of October 1984, I received a carton of copies of *Dhalgren's* seventeenth printing. After a couple of days checking it against the various correction lists (going over the entire page), here are my findings:

In the body of the text I can find only *two* errors:

Page 414 finally contains all the dialogue it's supposed to; but higher on the page a phrase that, for the last sixteen printings, has unquestionably been "the whole city," has inadvertently been reset as "the while city." And the very last correction on my list has not been made: On page 838 what should be "Mrs. Arthur Richards" remains "Mrs. Arthor Richards." I sigh, only noting that this particular correction was on my first list to Bantam ten years back, as it was on my last one, and all in between; once more it has simply been left out.

There is a third error, which I referred to parenthetically in my first paragraph. On the copyright page, it is particularly interesting: The list of printings *still* ends with "Sixteenth printing—December 1982," even though it is the seventeenth. The seventeenth printing has a mention of *Stars in My Pocket like Grains of Sand* on the cover, a new price ($4.50) and seventeen of the last eighteen corrections have been made; along with one new error. But since the printing notice can't be changed until the next, or eighteenth, printing, the omission of the "Seventeenth printing—December 1984" notice remains intriguingly uncorrectable. (Collectors please note.) Yet the fact that what is, for all practical purposes, the definitive edition has not been (and cannot be) properly named (at best bibliographers must describe it) seems right for a novel whose hero suffers from a similar problem.

When I called Bantam's Lou Aronica and Mary Lucas this morning to thank them and tell them the outcome, Lou said: "Well, drop me a note about the first two, and we'll just get to them in the *next* printing. At this point I have a kind of obsession to get it right!" And Mary reiterated the offer spontaneously the moment I mentioned them to her.

But I'm going to leave them as they are. The single 'o' for 'u' in "Arthur" is practically undetectable. And those who spot it might take it as a reminder that there are a number of other hard-to-spot things in the book that, unlike this one, may be worth looking for. And "the while city"? Well, it's so obviously a printer's mistake, so obviously not a phrase the character speaking it might say, I'm sure readers will correct it on the run as, for ten years, they have done with all the others.

". . . the while city . . ."

In the old sense of "whilom," perhaps? The *OED* gives its meaning as "at times," "at times past," and, "once upon a time."

The "once-upon-a-time city" — certainly that should be somewhere in *Dhalgren's* portrait of Bellona, if only by a third finger's slip from a printer's right hand.

Also I'd *like* the text to retain a couple of fighting scars—one old, one new— as battle memorabilia.

I am ten years older; so is *Dhalgren*. We are content.

Epilogue
1985

• 55 •

To John P. Mueller

January 14th, 1985

Dear John,

Hope your holidays were good. Christmas this year was the tightest Christmas I think I've ever had in my life! But there was lots of good spirit. My daughter was with us, and she said it was the nicest Christmas she remembers — which proves, once again, that it's not money; it's love. We all had Christmas dinner with my mom. Everybody had a wonderful time.

And two days afterwards, we had our first snow!

New Year's Eve a couple of Frank's friends came over: And, at midnight, we all went up on the roof to watch the fireworks over in Central Park. (Iva, who was wearing some Christmas "bunny rabbit slippers," got her feet soaked through, and had to run down quickly to change!) They came from two locations this year. The flares lit up the whole cold, foggy winter night, horizon to horizon, above the West Side's ragged tenement roofs, and as we watched the colored sparks bloom off in the dimming mist, I kept thinking: If the city is ever actually bombed, this is probably what it will look like.

Then downstairs and to bed.

The biggest news of January is that, on the 3rd, Frank and I decided, after seven and a half years, to split up. I asked him to leave — and after three pretty hysterical days, he agreed. When I see you, I can list the reasons why the split had to come. But you can probably figure some of them out for yourself. He'll be moving out of the house by the end of the month, January 31st. The result is, of course, that it's been a kind of trying few weeks here. I'll tell you more about it next time I see you.

Got your letter of January 9th, for which many thanks! I know you've called three different weekends, now. Once I was out taking my daughter to see *Dune*. And last night (Sunday), I'd gone to bed ridiculously early — at about four in the afternoon! But I'd had some kind of virus the day before: diarrhea, sneezing; and that night I'd gone to a birthday party that didn't put me home until one in the morning, pretty much *soaked* in champagne! Iva (my daughter) had been over to see us for a few hours, so that Frank and I could talk to her about our breaking up. (He's been with me since she was three-and-a-half and she really doesn't even remember a time when he wasn't here.) After we'd all talked, separately and together, and I'd walked her up to take her horseback riding lesson at two-thirty, when I got back home I just completely fell out. I probably needed the rest.

So that's why I missed your call.

Among other things, Frank's leaving means no more standing around in the hallway (for you and various other people) when you drop over to see me. Although Frank is basically a good guy, and I still like him and hope we'll be some kind of friends, there's a lot of shit that I don't know how I put up with.

I suppose, after seven and a half years, I've just decided that I'm the type of person who really *has* to live alone. Except for my daughter, I intend to remain that way. And that's a New Year's resolution I'm sticking to!

I'm awfully glad to hear you're working. I know you were working for a florist in New Jersey just before you went off to Florida. Is this the same guy?

Grandfather Chip says: Try to stay cool and stick it out.

The rent doesn't sound too high.

And don't let the extraneous bastards (of either sex) bug you.

On February 9th or 10th (Saturday or Sunday), when and if you come into New York, why don't you drop over one of those afternoons for some dinner with me and Iva? (Straight dinner, maybe a couple of beers, and no fooling around.) You can tell me how things are going, and I can give you lots of advice you don't need.

Write me and let me know which day you can come. Or give me a call and we'll set up times and the whole bit.

Until February, when Frank leaves, however, visiting would be a bit rough — on everybody!

Still, it's very good to hear from you. I'm trying to do a lot of work — and succeeding about halfway. I hope things keep going well for you. Best of luck for '85. I really look forward to seeing you and hearing from you; and send you,

All best wishes,

• 56 •

To Robert S. Bravard

January 19th, 1985

Dear Bob,

I'm rather exhausted. So this will be very brief. A warm thank you for your last two letters, which, I hope, in a couple of weeks, I'll be able to answer more at length.

On January 3rd, after seven and a half years, Frank and I have broken up. I've asked him to move out, and he has promised to by the end of the month. So it's been a rather strange time.

Details, I'm sure, will come out eventually. But I'm too bushed by it all to talk about it too much now. Briefly, there are certain things, in the ballpark of alcoholism or severe mental disturbance, which it is just very hard or impossible for a relationship to survive. And Frank suffers chronically from three. So, finally, as a self-protective measure, I've had to call a halt to what has become an impossible situation. Basically, I still like the man; and I hope, after some settling-down period, we'll remain friends. But the living situation is impossible.

Last week we had Iva down to let her know about the break-up. She was mature beyond all expectations and set a good example for us both. I picked her up at her mother's and walked her down to my place to see Frank, who of course wanted to talk to her and tell her about his leaving. While we were walking along slushy Broadway, I'd told her briefly what had happened. She came out with two observations that—in the manner of children's perceptions—kind of awed me. First she said, "You've known this was going to happen for a long time, didn't you?"

To which I had to admit, yes, I'd realized as long ago as the summer that I was going to have to end things.

Then she said, "I don't think Frank's been very happy with us. I think he wants to leave—but he's just very scared."

That last, of course, I wish were entirely a case of stunning juvenile insight, but

I'm afraid she's simply overheard too many of Frank's multiple-hour tirades to the effect that the relationship is terrible for him, he's miserable in it, he wants desperately to get out of it, that it's stifling him, and that I am some kind of monster for keeping him in it. I've never argued with him about any of that; I've always told him that if he wants to leave, I wouldn't think of stopping him — though when, most usually, he decides he's going to take the car, drive into the country somewhere, and put a hose in the tail pipe and gas himself, I've suggested he wait until he feels a little more together about things before doing anything rash. But I think it was a shock to him that, now, I suddenly said I wanted him to go, and, indeed, insisted on it.

He really must be gone before Iva comes back to me in February.

For the first three days, after I told him on the Thursday morning after New Years, he sat in the living room naked and screamed and cried. A couple of times he took a swing at me — once, catching his arm along a pen that was in my shirt pocket, when I ducked back, opening up an eight-inch gash along his forearm. From then on, when things approach argument, I simply leave the house.

"You must realize," he said on the second day, "suicide is a real option for me." (He has eight actual suicide attempts in his past, and has been hospitalized several times — though none of them have been in the past seven and a half years. Somewhat due to me? But that's a rather futile effort to make myself feel better about something that, basically, is just not good at all — only dully, survivally necessary.) But this has been an uncountably repeated refrain over the last seven and a half years. On the third night, after I'd left for a few hours when our voices had again begun to rise, I came back to the apartment to find him and the car keys and much of his stuff gone. There was an Ace of Spades stuck neatly by the corner under the table lamp.

The next afternoon, however, he came wandering back in, looking quite shattered. First he told me that he'd spent the night with Lou Christie, a mutual friend. He explained that he'd destroyed all my letters to him, all pictures of me, as well as all presents I'd ever given him. (I didn't tell him that I thought the last was rather silly, as mostly they consisted of several thousand dollars' worth of camera equipment and movie projectors, which, since he will need money, he might want to sell.) And the Ace of Spades? Well, while he was cleaning out his stuff, he'd just run across it.

It scared him to death, he said, and he decided it was some terrible omen.

So he threw it down on the table, where it *happened* to land with the corner wedged under the lamp . . .

And there are five or six irregular scars on the inside of his other arm now — though not very deep. He says he has no idea how they got there.

Two days later he explained he hadn't stayed at Lou's; he'd gone to spend the night with his brother; and though letters and pictures had all been destroyed or were thrown away, the camera equipment had not been smashed after all: It was safe at someone's house.

And he's made some kind of desultory plans to stay with various friends in February . . . though they are punctuated with rather unrealistic flights about going off to Paris for a photo project he wants to do on the Père Lachaise cemetery. Well, whatever he does, I wish him luck.

347

But he must leave here at the end of the month.

Ah, well.

I owe you and Michael both huge apologies. When I read in your letter that you'd given Mike a copy of *Stars/Sand*, with the implication that you had to go out and *buy* it, I felt just dreadful! Yes, I'd given Bantam both your addresses and asked them to send you copies. But I hadn't given them to them in triplicate, checked on the request five times, and done all the arcane and magic rigmarole that, as this point, we both know seems to be required to get anything out to you through their troglodytic mail room. Apologies. Though, really, at this point, I feel like I owe the whole world an apology.

This must be the longest month of my life.

Yet I'm working.

Having made the break with Frank, it seems to have released some dammed-up waters, however cluttered and drab and generally shattered the banks on either side are.

Have received a letter from someone in PA who first met me at Lock Haven, and who's asked me to be a guest at NovaCon. If I can find either of the two letters they've sent me to answer, in all this confusion, I'll accept.

So far your poems (both) have received four favorable readings from various *LM* editors. Things have slowed a bit for the winter. (There was no meeting last Thursday because of the snow.) We should get around to discussing them in two/three weeks at most.

Enclosures should all be self-explanatory.

Forgive the brevity, if not outright incoherence of all this.

Love to Cynthia and the kids.

It's snowing again. Hug a cat for me.

And all my love to you,

• 57 •

To Robert S. Bravard

January 25th, 1985

Dear Bob,

Many thanks for your heartening and caring letter of January 22nd. Once again, this is not a real reply. (That must wait till after the first of February.) This is just an early morning note, really, to answer some of the specific questions in your last couple of letters.

And an excuse to read them over again.

They do buck me up.

Starting with yours of November 16th:

My memory is that I read *Naked Lunch* when I was still in high school—within days or weeks of its publication. (Copyright says 1959, so that would have been possible.) I had heard of it, of course, through the note in Ginsberg's *Howl* ('56), and a section of it, I believe, had been published in *Big Table*, which I know I read anywhere from six months to a year before the book appeared from Grove.

During my senior year at [the Bronx High School of] Science, I spent a lot of time hanging out at an apartment on 74th Street, occupied by some young men in their early 20s (Lloyd Maclow, Stewart, Steve and Paul Israel [cousins], an NYU graduate student who went by the nickname of "Granny" [and was only there three or four months] and Victor Arwas [a young Englishman, also at NYU, then 21, I believe, to whom M. had the dubious distinction of losing her virginity when she was fifteen, and who was later very friendly to us when, in '73, I came to stay with M. in London]). At any rate, Lloyd bought the book almost as soon as it was published, and I laid around on their living room couch (where occasionally I would sleep) and read it.

Yes, as you say: Burroughs is an acquired taste. But it was a taste I acquired early.

There is much more I'd like to comment on in your letter — especially the "Drug Epidemic." But I'll leave that to another day.

On to yours of January 3rd:

First, the McEvoy book from Ungar.[1] About every two months, I give Seth a call, and he tells me more or less the following: The book has not been scrapped, only delayed—Ungar moved its offices last year, almost completely changed over its editorial staff, and, for a while, held a more or less total hiatus on all new printing. But recently they have started releasing books again.

Seth corrected galleys on the book almost a year ago, now. (I still haven't seen the "final" version, where he got a chance to respond, however he might, to all the notes that I sent copies of to you . . .) The first release date for the book was April '84. Since then, there have been several revised, "definite" release dates, the most recent of which was "November, 1984." Seth says that, on his last call (about two weeks ago, now), they told him that the book would actually appear "any week."

I asked if he had any information on the printing schedule and told him it might not be a bad idea to get some when next he called.

I said as gently as I could that, generally speaking, once a book is sent to the printers (as opposed to the typesetters), the printers immediately give the editorial office a "delivery date" (or "shipping date") for copies. This is usually set at minimum six weeks after the finished type gets to them — and is usually more in the neighborhood of three months. What you do is, I told him, next time you phone them, ask all innocent-like: "Have the printers given you a delivery date yet?" If they tell you, "No," then you *know* that the book is minimum six weeks to three months away from appearing—because the type hasn't gone to the printers yet. (If it had, they'd have a date.) And you can save yourself a *bit* of anxiety over it all.

At any rate, the book has *not* been officially scrapped yet. Or, if it has, Ungar hasn't told Seth—who has been inquiring after it regularly. But as to when it will actually appear, your guess is as good as mine.

Yes, of course, I guessed the writer of "A Poet's Journal" that appeared in *Alive!* (Was it my dyslexia? The first three times I looked at the magazine cover, I read it as *Olive!*, and thought: "What an interesting title for a magazine . . .") What does it feel like to be a fictional character? you ask. Oddly, I don't think any particular *feeling* per se got evoked!

Certainly I was complimented by the existence of the piece. And *do* inform "P. W. Michaels" how pleased I was — and I say this most sincerely — to receive

---

[1] *Samuel R. Delany,* by Seth McEvoy, Ungar, New York, 1985.

such a compliment! But I don't think that's what you're asking about . . . unless I mistake you.

This, out of context and fragmentary, from my journal of the morning of January 5th, back when I thought Frank might, at last, have gone off and killed himself:

> It's not that the unexamined life isn't worth living; rather the non-narrat-ed life (with the self as audience) is often too painful to bear. Lord have pity on those who, too young, learn only the awfulest of stories—from awful lives —which they are doomed to retell themselves forever, wondering in stunned disbelief that anyone might have a better tale to tell than theirs.

I suppose I have simply been telling myself the "story" of my life, more or less as it happens, for so long now (indeed, since I was a child) that, when someone else takes over the narration for a moment, all I *feel* is—at most—the slightest bemused interest. But it doesn't produce any sense of disorientation or displacement. The fact of its happening seems, if anything, more familiar than anything else.

(And on to your most recent letter of January 22nd.)

Yes, there was a "mysterious letter" from Dr. Gotlieb up at the Mugar Memorial Library a month or so back to the effect that they had received the *Neveryóna* drafts. But I pretty much figured out myself what had happened, smiled briefly over it, and let it slip from mind—until you mentioned it in your letter.

And I have now written to Eric Browning, have talked to him on the phone; and I will be the GOH at NovaCon '85.

Oh, yes. I handed in the first hundred-odd pages (93, actually) of *The Splendor and Misery of Bodies, of Cities* to Bantam a few weeks ago, in hopes of prying some money out of them. There is, by contract, a payment of $40,000 due when they accept "half" the completed manuscript. And then another $40,000 when the completed manuscript is accepted. I'm going to suggest (later this afternoon, on the phone, to Lou) that they revise it as follows:

Since the book is planned at 150,000 words, I'm going to suggest that they pay me $10,000 with the acceptance of each 28,000 words. (That's what I've just deliv-ered.) In the long run, it's cheaper for them (in terms of interest). Though the first payment of $10,000 will go mostly for debts:

$1,500 for Henry's commission
$2,550 for Iva's school tuition
$365 for Blue Cross/Blue Shield
$3/4,000 to the government, who will try to take more

But that's what I think I'll be able to get away with, if I work quickly . . .!

Then, I live on the remaining $1,000 or $1,500 for another two or three months . . .

Well, right now my rent is actually paid up through March, thanks to various arcane manipulations that may work their way into another letter.

Only real problem is a surge of arthritis in *both* hands now, as well as the usual shoulder and hip — the thumb of the left, the middle two fingers of the right. (Now try to type that way, even on a very *easy* word processor keyboard.) I assume it's aggravated by stress . . . With that to contemplate, I must go peel a turnip for lunch.

And so bring this letter to a close.

It's Monday. Frank leaves finally and for good (first, to stay with his friend

Gar, then Paul, then . . .) on Friday. Actually, we've been pretty okay with each other, once the initial week of craziness got over with. (I've typed up some material for him on his "Père Lachaise" project; and just this morning, in the bathroom, I helped him trim his beard, after which we actually hugged. Which was nice — though a sad side lingers.) Iva comes back next Monday.

I will print this up and get it off to you.

All my love,

PS—Can you get me a copy (xerox) of Mog's recent *Advocate* article? I seemed to have missed it. But only if it's easy . . .

Note for Readers

ROBERT DRAKE, a 37-year-old author, literary agent and prominent figure in the Philadelphia gay community, was the victim of a life-threatening, hate-motivated assault at his home in Sligo, Ireland on January 30, 1999. Since that time, Drake has battled many severe complications resulting from this vicious attack. In October of 1999, he was discharged from hospital to a Philadelphia apartment he shares with his lover, Ciaran Slevin. The pair are receiving support from a core group of volunteers and the local Quaker community in their efforts to generate the personnel and finances required to fund Drake's lengthy, ongoing recovery.

Robert Drake is currently receiving outpatient therapy at one of the nation's finest rehabilitation centers—Moss Rehab—where he is slowly relearning the basic skills required for independent living through intensive physical, occupational, and speech therapies. Nearly a year after the asssault, Drake's attackers were convicted of recklessly and intentionally causing bodily harm and are currently serving eight years of imprisonment in Ireland. It is believed that Drake's recovery will take far longer than eight years.

Robert Drake is a close friend of the publisher and was an instrumental figure in the launch of VOYANT PUBLISHING. A portion of the sales of this book will be donated to the ROBERT DRAKE HEALTH FUND. To find out how you can make a direct donation to the fund, write to:

ROBERT DRAKE HEALTH FUND
c/o Arch St. Meeting
320 Arch St.
Philadelphia, PA 19106
tel: 215.629.0257

or visit www.voyantpub.com for more information.

WHAT IS
VOYANT PUBLISHING?

VOYANT PUBLISHING'S name derives from the term Arthur Rimbaud coined in his famous *Lettre du Voyant* (*voyeur*: one who sees + *savant*: one who knows), in which he describes the self-inflicted tortures that await writers who wish to be among the great poets of the age. VOYANT was founded in the interest of literature that values the sentence in its own right rather than as a simple tool for moving a story along. While plain prose meant to be accessible to the most ordinary of readers certainly has a place in the world, it has none here. We do *not*, however, wish to exclude anyone from reading a book published by VOYANT. Nonetheless, we do not think it necessary for writers to rein themselves in, to downgrade their prose for some chimerical "common reader." Rather, we'd like to encourage readers to step up to the plate and take a few swings at pitches from non-conventional writers—no matter how the ball might curve or snake beyond the bounds of readerly expectation.